THE NEW NATURALIST LIBRARY

BIRD
POPULATIONS

IAN NEWTON

WILLIAM
COLLINS

This edition published in 2013 by William Collins,
an imprint of HarperCollins Publishers

HarperCollins Publishers
77–85 Fulham Palace Road
London W6 8JB
www.williamcollinsbooks.com

First published 2013

A CIP catalogue record for this book is available
from the British Library.

Set in FF Nexus

Edited and designed by
D & N Publishing
Baydon, Wiltshire

Printed in Hong Kong by Printing Express

Hardback
ISBN 978-0-00-742953-0

Paperback
ISBN 978-0-00-752798-4

Contents

Editors' Preface

FOR THIS, HIS THIRD NEW NATURALIST volume after *Finches* (NN55) in 1972 and *Bird Migration* (NN113) of 2010, Ian Newton has again elected to review a major component of the biology of birds in general rather than dealing, as has been the norm in this series, with all aspects of the life of a group of related species.

Bird populations are moderated from year to year by the balance (or indeed the imbalance) between recruitment during the breeding season and mortality, mostly but by no means exclusively during the winter months. Beneath this superficial simplicity lies the substance of this volume. In 20 chapters, Professor Newton explores and reveals the vast array of varied and often interacting factors that can influence bird populations. The first part of the text is devoted to the range of natural factors influencing bird numbers, from food and nest site availability to predators and parasites, and on the impact of interspecific competition. The section closes with three chapters on the often intriguing interactions between these various natural limiting factors.

Although the chapter entitled Weather relates to natural influences, in Climate Change a human impact becomes evident, and human influences are more obviously apparent in the remaining chapters devoted to hunting and to the often seemingly disastrous problems caused by pesticides and other pollutants. Sobering, even alarming, as this must appear to today's reader, in his closing chapter Reflections, Ian Newton emphasises that despite the 'modern' problems caused by man and his rapidly developing technologies, most birds today are limited by 'natural' factors, whereas a century ago 'many (perhaps most) bird species in Britain and Ireland were limited by human killing'.

Professor Newton's credentials for addressing the comprehensive analysis entailed in this volume are impeccable. A Fellow of the Royal Society, his working career was spent in governmental research, starting with the old Nature Conservancy, which through a series of (taxonomic) changes became the Institute for Terrestrial Ecology at Monks Wood, sadly now no more. His international standing in avian ecology has been recognised by service as President of the British Ecological Society and of the British Ornithologists' Union, by an Honorary Fellowship of the American Ornithologists' Union and as Chairman of the Royal Society for the Protection of Birds and of the British Trust for Ornithology, and to his appointment as OBE.

We are fortunate in Britain and Ireland, as Ian Newton notes, that modern ornithology benefits from a range of comprehensive censuses and surveys that draw on the wealth of records available from skilled amateur ornithologist volunteers. These offer to ornithological researchers interested in understanding the mechanisms and implications of population changes opportunities not available to zoologists in other disciplines. The New Naturalist is doubly fortunate that Ian Newton is admirably placed to review, as an active and life-long participant in many of them, the results of these researches and to distil them thoroughly and lucidly to an appreciative readership. This volume is a noteworthy and most welcome addition to The New Naturalist Library.

Author's Foreword and Acknowledgements

THIS BOOK IS ABOUT BIRD NUMBERS, and about why these numbers vary in the way they do, from year to year or from place to place. It is therefore concerned with the various factors that limit bird numbers: with the role of food supplies and other resources, of competitors, predators, parasites and pathogens, and of various human impacts.

Earlier naturalists, with less information at their disposal, formed the impression that, despite annual fluctuations, bird numbers remained more or less stable through time. Species that were common remained common, while species that were rare remained rare. In his influential book on *The Natural Regulation of Animal Numbers*, published in 1954, David Lack – the then doyen of British ornithology – put it this way:

> *The impression of the naturalist is that, in areas where conditions have not changed, the number of breeding birds is nearly the same each year. Moreover, of the species which are familiar to us in England today, most were familiar to our Victorian great-grandparents and many to our medieval ancestors; and the known changes in numbers are largely attributable to man.*

These statements, strictly interpreted, would hold true today, but in the years since they were written, unprecedented changes have occurred in the landscapes of the British Isles and in the seas around our coasts. The combination of a rapidly expanding human population, a predominantly utilitarian attitude to land, central government policy on land use, and increasing mechanisation have combined to promote more massive changes in land use – and hence in bird habitats – in recent decades than at any comparable period previously. The intensification of agriculture and the introduction of pesticides brought huge changes to farmland; a new national forestry policy saw extensive conifer plantations spring up over previously open upland; widespread drainage schemes destroyed much marshland and meadowland; so-called 'reclamation' work brought former coastal marsh and mudflat under the plough; and the construction of reservoirs and digging of gravel-pits provided more open waters than existed formerly. At the same time, in the seas around our coasts a more intensive fishing industry developed, increasing amounts of fish waste were thrown overboard, and gradually fish stocks became depleted. These developments have in turn brought huge changes in bird populations, as some species dependent on the old landscapes declined, and others benefiting from the changes increased. Over the same period, changing public attitudes to wildlife, protective legislation and a growing network of nature reserves allowed previously scarce bird species to recover from past onslaughts, while climate warming has promoted further changes.

It was perhaps fortuitous that over this period of rapid environmental change, interest in bird-watching and conservation grew. Bird-watchers became better equipped and more informed, and in the age of the motor car became increasingly mobile. By the combined and coordinated efforts of volunteer bird-watchers, increasing numbers of bird populations became regularly monitored on a national scale. The result is that we now have better and more extensive data on the year-to-year and long-term changes in British bird populations than at any time previously, than in any other country in the world, and for any other groups of animals and plants. Information on the population sizes of different bird species in Britain and their trends over recent decades can be found on the website and in the publications of the British Trust for Ornithology (BTO), the organisation which has coordinated much of the information gathering by volunteer birders, together with its analysis and publication. My aim in this book is not to repeat these data, but to try and explain why different bird species are distributed in the numbers that they are, and have changed over the years in the way that they have. It is the factors that influence bird numbers, rather than the numbers themselves, that provide my emphasis.

On these aspects, much of our understanding comes from a mass of detailed and localised studies conducted over several decades by ornithologists working in universities and research stations, whose findings are widely scattered through the scientific literature. The major organisations involved in this work, besides the BTO, include the Royal Society for the Protection of Birds (RSPB), the Wildfowl and Wetlands Trust (WWT), the Game & Wildlife Conservation Trust (GWCT) and various statutory bodies, such as the Centre for Ecology and Hydrology (CEH), whose names have changed with bewildering frequency during the 60 years or so of their existence. This book is an attempt to bring this information together into a coherent whole; but it also provides around 1,400 references to the original sources for those who want to delve more deeply.

Understanding the factors that influence bird numbers is not merely of academic interest. It is necessary if we are to successfully manage bird populations, whether for conservation reasons, for sustainable hunting or for crop protection. The continued monitoring of bird numbers can also alert us to impending environmental problems. In addition, the regular watching and study of birds now provides a source of recreation and pleasure for very large numbers of people, who would find a world with fewer birds a poorer place. In recent years, more than 40,000 volunteers have helped to collect field data on birds for the BTO, putting in an estimated 1.82 million hours in 2010. At the same time, more than a million people were members of the RSPB. These figures give some idea of the degree of interest in birds shown by the people of the United Kingdom.

This is not the first book I have written about bird populations. Some of the information presented here is taken from an earlier work, *Population Limitation in Birds* (Newton 1998), which was aimed primarily at professionals, including research students, and which dealt with most aspects of the subject, drawing on studies worldwide. The present book provides a briefer account, updated with many new findings, nearly two-thirds of the references cited having been published since the previous volume. Although the present book concentrates on birds that occur in Britain and Ireland, I have also drawn on studies of these same species elsewhere, including their various wintering areas. Throughout, I have tried to write simply, avoiding jargon as much as possible, in the hope that the book will be of value to anyone with an interest in natural history, amateur or professional. For bird names I have used the British vernacular names throughout, as listed by the British Ornithologists' Union, while the scientific names of birds and other organisms are given in the tables, figures and index.

The following pages will reveal how much I owe to the generosity of some bird photographers who have allowed me to use some of their best work as illustrations. The many images that enliven the text were provided by Peter Beasley, Daniel Bergmann, Roy Blewitt, David Boyle, Kurt Burnham, Laurie Campbell, Richard Chandler, John Coulson, Tony Cross, David Culley, Edmund Fellowes, Sean Gray, Alan Hale, Keith Kirk, Chris Knights, Becky Lawson, Alan Martin, Alan McFadyen, Jill Pakenham, RSPB Images, Harry Scott, Bobby Smith, Frank Snijkers, Jack Stevens and Andy Thompson.

During the writing process, I have benefited greatly from comments by Peter Evans (most of the seabird sections), Robert Kenward (Chapters 6, 7 and 16), Will Cresswell (Chapter 12), Rob Newton (Chapter 13), Rhys Green (Chapter 15),

Jim Flegg (in his role as editor), and also from David Jenkins, who commented thoughtfully and helpfully on the whole book. The penultimate draft was read by Tim Birkhead, who made many helpful suggestions on presentation. To all of these I am most grateful. Finally, I thank my wife, Halina, for encouragement and support throughout.

CHAPTER 1

Preview

THIS BOOK IS ABOUT BIRD NUMBERS. It discusses why particular species are as numerous as they are, and not more or less numerous, and why some species are increasing while others are decreasing. It is concerned with the various things that influence bird abundance, such as food and other resources, competitors, predators, parasites and pathogens, and also various human impacts. These matters are of interest to anyone with a concern for birds, whether naturalists or researchers, or people involved in managing bird populations for reasons of conservation, crop protection or hunting. This initial chapter introduces some of the main ideas in bird population ecology, and outlines some of the aspects developed in detail in later chapters.

Much of what we know about the population processes of animals comes from studies on birds. The reasons are not hard to find, for compared to many other animals, birds are relatively easy to study. Most species are active by day; they are conspicuous and can be recognised by their appearance, songs or calls, which makes them easy to detect and count. In addition, most birds can be trapped and marked with leg rings or other tags. They then become identifiable as individuals, enabling their movements and life histories to be followed, and their survival rates to be calculated. Many species, too, are large enough to carry radio-transmitters or other electronic devices, so that their day-to-day activities and movements can be recorded. When tracked using satellites or geolocator tags, individuals can also be followed on their migrations, wherever on earth they travel. Hardly any other kinds of animals show such an obliging combination of characteristics.

In addition, most bird species rear their young in nests which can be found by watching the adults or searching likely places. Their individual breeding rates can then be measured in ways that are not possible for most other creatures, which show no parental care and in which the young from different parents soon intermingle. The highly developed social structure of birds has also enabled the role of territorial and other aggressive behaviour to be studied in greater detail than for most other animals, revealing its role in population regulation.

All these features combine to make birds popular with their human observers, and ideal subjects for study, whether by professional ornithologists based in universities and research institutes or by others for personal interest. Organisations such as the British Trust for Ornithology (BTO) rely on the combined voluntary efforts of bird-watchers to monitor changes in the numbers and distributions of birds, both countrywide and long-term. Not surprisingly, then, the population ecology of birds has been studied in greater depth, and by more participants, than that of any other group of organisms, and the general principles that have emerged have wider relevance.

BIRD NUMBERS

About 260 bird species occur regularly in Britain and Ireland at the present time, and a similar number occur as rare visitors or vagrants. Among the regulars, some species (144) occur here throughout the year, others as summer visitors (54) and yet others as winter visitors (142), or as passage migrants (122) which travel through the country twice each year on their migrations. Many species occur in more than one category, and for part of each year, two or more different populations of the same species are represented in the British Isles (Newton 2010).

The species that breed here vary from widespread and abundant, numbering several millions, to extremely local and rare, with fewer than 100 individuals. Among land-birds, the most numerous breeding species include the Blackbird and Wren, both of which number more than ten million individuals in the breeding season, and are now more plentiful than the House Sparrow, which over most of the country has suffered a marked decline in recent decades. Some species give the impression of huge numbers because they gather in great concentrations. The Starling is no longer one of the commonest breeding birds in Britain, but can still be seen in big numbers at its winter roosts, comprising tens of thousands of individuals. Formerly roosts were even larger, frequently containing over 100,000 individuals and occasionally more than a million. Seabirds gather in large breeding colonies, yet spread out to forage over wide areas of open sea, where their average densities can be quite low. At the other extreme, the rarest regular breeding birds in the British Isles, such as the Red-backed Shrike and Purple Sandpiper, probably number no more than a few pairs in any one year.

FIG 1. The Blackbird *Turdus merula* is one of the commonest bird species in Britain and Ireland, occurring anywhere with trees and bushes, from countryside to city centres. (Keith Kirk)

In general, Britain and Ireland have fewer breeding land-bird species than other comparable areas at similar latitude in continental Europe, and Ireland has notably fewer than Britain, but both islands have more seabirds. These differences can be attributed to the position of our islands, off the main continental landmass but surrounded by highly productive seas. For wintering birds, however, Britain and Ireland hold a relatively large number of species, present in much greater numbers of individuals than comparable parts of continental Europe. This can be attributed to the mild climate, making our islands attractive as a wintering area for birds drawn from a large span of the Arctic, from eastern Canada through Greenland, Iceland and northern Europe to central Siberia. Not all birds from these northern areas winter in Britain and Ireland, but these islands draw wintering birds from a wider swathe of the Arctic than any other equivalent area at comparable latitude.

FIG 2. Pre-roost gathering of Starlings *Sturnus vulgaris*. These birds tend to roost in the same places year after year, whether conifer woods, reedbeds, cliffs or city buildings, gathering each evening from the surrounding countryside up to 20 km away. (Keith Kirk)

FIG 3. The Canada Goose *Branta canadensis* was introduced from North America in the seventeenth century, but is now one of the most widespread non-native bird species in Britain, estimated at more than 60,000 pairs. (Richard Chandler)

To the various species native to Britain and Ireland we can add more than a dozen introduced (or escaped) alien species, which now have self-sustaining resident breeding populations (Holling *et al.* 2012). The most widespread of these aliens include the Pheasant, Red-legged Partridge, Little Owl and Canada Goose, but other aliens currently have more restricted distributions, while new ones are continually being added as they escape from bird collections. These non-native species must be separated from other naturally occurring ones, such as the Capercaillie and White-tailed Eagle, which were reintroduced after their earlier elimination.

COUNTING BIRDS

The first step in any study of bird populations is to count the birds reliably. Except for highly localised species, it is seldom possible to study the whole population of any bird. Instead the researcher has usually to work within a defined area, whose avian occupants may form a tiny part of a much wider population. Individuals may move freely in and out of the study area, and the birds which breed there may occupy a wider area, or even a different part of the world, outside the breeding season. Hence, most population studies of birds have been concerned with the numbers found in defined areas at specific times. The general applicability of the conclusions from such localised studies depends partly on how typical is the study area of the bird's range as a whole, and on whether the area is big enough compared with the scale over which the factors influencing overall population levels operate.

In recent decades, however, more widespread data on bird populations have become increasingly available. Most of our information on the population trends immatures may make up a large part of the non-breeding contingent. But in many bird populations, some mature individuals may also be found among the non-breeders. This situation mainly arises when more adults are present than the available nesting habitat can hold. Once this habitat is fully occupied, any additional birds must live non-territorially and usually cannot breed. In some such species, such as Carrion Crows or Mute Swans, non-breeders usually occur in flocks, which can be readily seen and counted. Flocks of non-breeding crows sometimes occur on rubbish dumps, while flocks of non-breeding swans often occur on extensive shallow lakes or on rivers near town centres. In other species, including many songbirds and raptors, non-breeders live secretive solitary lives in and around the territories of breeders, or in areas unsuitable for nesting. Such non-breeders are therefore not much in evidence, and in many species they are practically impossible to count.[1] However, two lines of evidence have repeatedly confirmed their existence. Firstly, if territorial birds are removed from their territories, they are often replaced within a few days by other individuals that then proceed to nest (reviews in Newton 1992, 1998). Secondly, in species that are limited by nest-sites, such as many cavity-nesters, the provision of artificial sites (such as nest-boxes) often leads to an immediate rise in breeding density (Chapter 5). The implication is that these incoming birds were previously present in the vicinity but unseen or unrecognised, and would not have nested if opportunities had not been created. In both types of experiment, care is needed to ensure that incoming birds derive from a non-breeding sector, and have not simply moved in from other territories or nesting sites nearby. For a worthwhile experiment, therefore, knowledge is needed of all the breeding pairs of that species present in the surrounding area before any removals of individuals or additions of nest-sites are made.

Despite the advantages of knowing the numbers of breeders, some bird species are most easily counted in winter. This is the case for many waterfowl and shorebirds which nest in remote or inaccessible places, such as the Arctic, but which migrate to winter at lower latitudes, including Britain and Ireland. The fact that such species often gather in large numbers at traditional sites makes the job of counting that much easier. In some species, adults can be distinguished in the field from young of the year, so that winter counts can

---

1 For some species, special efforts were made in some studies to count the non-territorial non-breeders. These were estimated to form, as a percentage of the total spring population in the area at the time, some 10% of Skylarks, 14% of Blackbirds, at least 19% of female Sparrowhawks (Newton & Rothery 2001), 40% of Magpies, 20–31% of Shelducks, 46% of Oystercatchers and 64% and 70% of Mute Swans in two areas (Delius 1965, Ribaut 1964, Birkhead *et al.* 1986, Jenkins *et al.* 1975, Ens *et al.* 1995, Meek 1993, Spray 1991). Clearly, in some species at some times and in some places, non-territorial non-breeders can form substantial proportions of the overall numbers.

reflect both numbers and recent breeding success. In other species, separation of age-groups is not possible except in the hand, so field counts reveal only total numbers. In Britain and Ireland regular counts are made to monitor the numbers of these wintering waterfowl and shorebirds, published in the annual reports of the Wetland Bird Survey (WeBS).

Other bird species can be readily counted on migration. This is true of some raptors and other soaring birds which migrate by day and in which huge numbers from large areas pass specific concentration points each spring or autumn. There are no established watch-points in the British Isles for raptors, but well-known sites elsewhere include Falsterbo in southern Sweden and Tarifa in southern Spain. Around the British Isles, specific coastal headlands offer good opportunities for counting migratory seabirds. Variations in weather may affect the proportions of migrants that pass specific sites from year to year, so localised counts do not necessarily reflect year-to-year changes in numbers; but when repeated over many years they can reflect long-term trends. Various other constant-effort or observational schemes have been used to detect year-to-year changes in bird numbers, and sometimes it has been possible to compare the results from different monitoring methods on the same populations (Furness & Greenwood 1993).

POPULATION TRENDS AND FLUCTUATIONS

If we examine counts of breeding birds in the same area year by year, almost any pattern of fluctuation can be found (Fig. 5). In some species, breeding numbers remain fairly constant through time. Examples of such stability are provided by some birds of prey, such as the Golden Eagle, in which the density of territorial pairs in some large areas of stable land use may vary by no more than 15% on either side of the mean level over several decades (Watson 2010). Most small-bird populations fluctuate somewhat more, perhaps halving or doubling in size from one year to the next, or declining sharply after hard winters, and increasing again in subsequent years. In species which exploit sporadic food suppies, such as finches that rely on tree-seeds or owls that rely on fluctuating rodent populations, the numbers at particular localities can vary by more than 20-fold from year to year, as many pairs settle in years with abundant food, and move elsewhere in poor years. But even these fluctuations are small compared with those in other animals such as certain insects, in which annual changes of 100-fold or more are not uncommon.

In most bird species, the year-to-year fluctuations in numbers are irregular. But some owls and raptors that depend on cyclically fluctuating rodent populations undergo regular fluctuations of abundance in step with their prey,

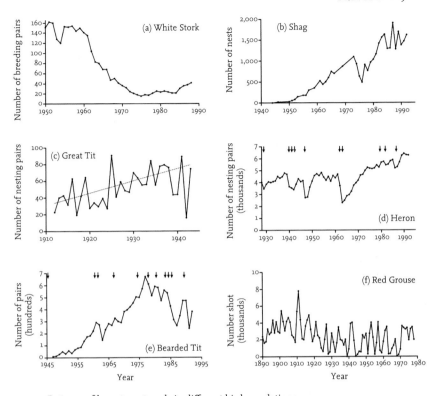

FIG 5. Patterns of long-term trends in different bird populations.

(a) Long-term decline in the numbers of White Storks *Ciconia ciconia* in Baden-Württemberg, Germany. Based on annual counts of occupied nests, 1950–88. (Redrawn from Bairlein 1996)

(b) Long-term increase in the numbers of Shags *Phalacrocorax aristotelis* on the Isle of May, Scotland, showing how numbers increased and then levelled off, but with large annual fluctuations. Based on annual counts of occupied nests, 1944–92. (Redrawn from Harris *et al.* 1994)

(c) Irregular annual fluctuations superimposed on a long-term increase in the numbers of Great Tit *Parus major* pairs in gradually maturing woodland on Texel Island, Netherlands. Based on annual counts of occupied nest-boxes, 1912–43. (From Kluijver 1951)

(d) Numbers of nesting Grey Herons *Ardea cinerea* in Britain, showing declines after hard winters (shown by arrows), followed by recoveries. Based on annual nest counts, 1928–92. (Redrawn from Greenwood *et al.* 1994)

(e) Weather-driven fluctuations in the numbers of Bearded Tits *Panurus biarmicus* in southern England. Trends were influenced mainly by the frequency of cold winters (shown by arrows). Based on annual counts of breeding pairs, 1947–92. (Redrawn from Campbell *et al.* 1996)

(f) Cyclic fluctuations in the numbers of Red Grouse *Lagopus l. scotica*, Scotland. Based on numbers shot, 1890–1978. (Redrawn from Hudson 1992) usually with peaks every 3–4 years. Similarly, some northern gallinaceous birds, such as grouse and ptarmigan, undergo regular cycles of abundance, with a periodicity varying between regions (Chapters 4, 7, 9). The cycle periodicity (length) refers to the regular intervals between peaks, but the size of the peaks often varies greatly from one cycle to the next in the same area (Fig. 5f). The cycle period is not species-specific, and individual species, such as the Red Grouse, have shown cycles of 4–5 years, 6–7 years, 7–8 years and 10 years on different Scottish moors or over different time periods (Watson & Moss 2008). However, different grouse species that live side by side in the same region tend to fluctuate together, so the patterns of fluctuation seem to depend more on local circumstances than on species. Moreover, in some European regions these cycles in gamebird numbers are matched by similar fluctuations in some of their predators, such as the Goshawk and Gyr Falcon, whose numbers typically go up and down in step with their prey (Chapter 4). Yet within suitable habitats, the mean level of abundance of these cyclic species does not necessarily change much over periods of several decades, providing that their habitats remain essentially unchanged. In modern Britain, cyclic fluctuations are evident mainly in extensive stretches of habitat, and much less so in fragmented habitat, such as grouse moors surrounded by grassland or forestry plantations. Perhaps for reasons of habitat fragmentation, cycles are no longer apparent in Black Grouse and Capercaillie in Britain. Also, predator control by gamekeepers is so rife in Britain that it is usually impossible to tell whether specific predator species would fluctuate in parallel with grouse, as they do in the rest of northern Eurasia and in North America.

Although many bird populations, while fluctuating from year to year, do not normally change much in the long term, such constancy would be expected only in stable environments. Many bird species prefer particular stages in the development of forest or other vegetation. Some species prefer newly planted

FIG 6. A Golden Eagle *Aquila chrysaetos* at winter carrion. In areas of stable land use, where they are not persecuted, Golden Eagles have shown stable nesting densities over long periods of years. (Laurie Campbell)

forest, others thicket stage, and yet others more mature stages. Species of such temporary habitats typically reach high densities in particular localities only for the few years in which their habitat is suitable there, and then decline again as the habitat develops and becomes better suited to other species. But while they decline in one area, they may increase in another, wherever the habitat is reaching a favourable stage. These changes, depending on vegetation succession, can be regarded as natural, although for forest and other habitats, areas at early growth stages have probably become more widespread as a result of human activities. In particular, heather moors, as managed for Red Grouse, represent the first stage in forest succession after a fire, and are artificially maintained in this state by deliberately burning different patches every 10–15 years.

For birds of wetlands, the amount of habitat available in some parts of the world varies greatly from year to year, or over longer periods of time, according to rainfall (Chapter 14). This is true for much of Africa, where many of our summer visitors spend their non-breeding season. Usually such populations expand during wetter periods, only to contract again during drier ones, following the trends in their habitats.

Whatever the type of fluctuation, the degree of variability in any population tends to increase with the span of years over which counts are made. This is partly because the chances of including an unusual year increase with the length of study, and also because short-term fluctuations may be superimposed on a long-term upward or downward trend. In fact, whenever bird species have been studied over periods of several decades, their abundance and distribution patterns are often found to have changed greatly. Some such changes would be expected to occur naturally, perhaps in response to climate or habitat changes, but many can be attributed to human action. In recent decades, many farmland bird species have declined greatly in association with changes in farming practices, as discussed in Chapters 4 and 18.

Other birds have greatly extended their ranges, becoming common breeders in areas where they were formerly absent. Among land-birds, the most striking example of the twentieth century was the Collared Dove, which until 1930 extended no further west than the Balkans, but then spread rapidly across Europe, reaching Britain about 1955. For many years in newly colonised regions, its numbers increased exponentially (by a constant percentage each year) until habitats became filled and numbers levelled off (Hudson 1972, Hengeveld 1988). The present population of Britain is estimated at around a million pairs.

Most species that have spread in this way clearly benefit from human activities. Among seabirds, the most spectacular example of range expansion is the Fulmar, which prior to the mid-eighteenth century bred in Europe only

FIG 7. The Collared Dove *Streptopelia decaocto* spread westward across Europe in the twentieth century, reaching Britain around 1955, and subsequently increasing to become a common bird of towns, villages and farmsteads. (Frank Snijkers)

in 1–2 colonies in Iceland and on St Kilda off northwest Scotland. A spread started around Iceland at this time, and the Faeroes were colonised in the mid-nineteenth century. The spread continued, and in 1878 Fulmars began to nest on Foula in Shetland. From then on, new colonies appeared successively further south around Britain and Ireland, and the species now also breeds in France, Denmark and Germany. This expansion was linked with the growth of the whaling and fishing industries, which led to much offal and waste being thrown overboard, providing a new food source for Fulmars and other seabirds (Fisher 1966). Initially, overall Fulmar numbers in Britain grew at 13–19% per annum, decreasing to 8% per annum in the mid-twentieth century and to less than 4% towards the end, as they came to exceed 500,000 pairs.

Other conspicuous species have begun to breed here only in recent decades, including the Little Egret and Mediterranean Gull. These are among various bird species that have apparently benefited from climate warming, enabling them to spread northward. As climate continues to warm, we can expect that more bird species will colonise from the south and spread northwards, and perhaps that some other species will retreat and disappear altogether from our islands (Chapter 15). No doubt extreme range changes occurred in other bird species in the past, long before there were ornithologists to record them.

Within a human lifetime, such spectacular expansions in range and numbers are exceptional, as are precipitous declines to extinction. Yet every species when unchecked has an intrinsic rate of natural increase (r) until it reaches a level (K) at which its numbers become limited by the habitat and resources available locally. If the local environment remains essentially unchanged, the species then tends to remain fairly stable in numbers over the years, fluctuating between limits much narrower than those that would be theoretically possible (Lack 1954).

The patterns that emerge from studies of bird populations thus depend partly on the timescale over which the studies are made, and partly on the changes in landscapes and food sources that occur in that time. They also depend on the spatial scale. Wide-scale studies of bird populations, involving large numbers of observers, have increasingly enabled the question of spatial synchrony in bird population changes to be addressed. In general, if the factors that influence bird abundance themselves operate over wide areas, such as aspects of weather or human land use, fluctuations on particular study plots can be expected to parallel those occurring over a wider scale. But if the factors are localised, such as some disease outbreaks, then the patterns of fluctuation in bird numbers are likely to vary from place to place across a region.

ENVIRONMENTAL LIMITING FACTORS

Bird habitats

Some bird species are associated with woodland, others with open land of one type or another, and yet others with wetland or sea-coast. In fact, most species are even more specific, being found, for example, in particular stages of forest growth, or in coniferous as opposed to broadleaved woodland, in grassland as opposed to heathland, or in marshland as opposed to open water, and so on. However, some species make use of more than one type of habitat at the same time of year, nesting mainly in one and foraging mainly in another. Species such as the Rook and Woodpigeon nest in trees but feed chiefly on open land, while some upland species, such as the Twite and Golden Plover, nest mainly on moorland but get much of their food from nearby pastures. The requirements of such species are perhaps best described in terms of landscapes or habitat mosaics rather than specific vegetation types, with individuals using different habitat components for different purposes. Seabirds nest on land, mainly on coastal cliffs and offshore islands, but forage widely over the sea, at distances that vary widely between species. Some bird species also use different types of habitat at different times of year, with many waders, for example, nesting inland and wintering on the coast.

In asking what limits the distributions and numbers of particular bird species, the most obvious answer is that it depends on the amount and quality of habitat available. Recent declines in the distributions and numbers of many bird species in Britain and Ireland can be attributed to the destruction and degradation of their habitats, and consequent reduction of living space. They include, for example, many species of marshland and wet meadows, which now have far fewer places to live than in the past. Conversely, other species have

FIG 8. The Siskin *Carduelis spinus* is a small seed-eater which nests in conifer forests. It increased and spread widely in Britain and Ireland following widespread afforestation. (Laurie Campbell)

expanded as new habitat has been created. They include birds of conifer forest, such as the Common Crossbill and Siskin, which spread greatly during the last century following the widespread afforestation of former open land, and various waterfowl which expanded in association with the construction of reservoirs and gravel-pits. Other species have increased through targeted conservation actions, the Bittern for example benefiting in recent years from a concerted programme of reedbed creation (Brown *et al.* 2012).

Although the habitat tells us where to find particular species, it gives no indication of the densities at which those species are likely to occur, or even whether they will be present at all. These densities may be influenced by the resources (such as food and nest-sites) or natural enemies (such as competitors and predators) that occur there. It is with these *limiting factors* – which determine the abundance of species within the habitats they use – that this book is largely concerned. As a result of the effects of different limiting factors, areas of essentially the same habitat can hold markedly different densities of birds. The richest conifer forests in Britain can support more than 1,000 songbird pairs per km², but the poorest ones hold fewer than 100. Similarly, although farmland in Britain and Ireland looks on a casual glance the same today as it did in 1960, it now supports far fewer birds, chiefly as a result of changes in management.

Limiting factors

To understand how bird populations are limited within the habitats they occupy, it is helpful to distinguish between the external (environmental) factors that influence populations and the intrinsic (demographic) features that these factors affect. External limiting factors include resources (notably food) and natural enemies, including competing species, predators and parasites (some of which cause obvious disease). Any one of these factors can be considered limiting if it prevents a population from increasing or causes it to decline. Particular populations may be affected by more than one, perhaps all, of these different factors, but often one factor emerges as overriding at a given time. These different biotic factors also interact with one another, and with non-biotic factors such as weather. Intrinsic (demographic) limiting factors include the rates of births, deaths and movements, the net effects of which determine local population trends. Both extrinsic and intrinsic factors can be considered as 'causing' population changes, the former as ultimate environmental factors and the latter as proximate mechanisms. Thus, within suitable habitat, a population might be said to decline because of food shortage (the ultimate cause) or because of the resulting mortality (the proximate cause).

It is not just a matter of finical semantics to distinguish between these two types of explanation for population changes. If we are to understand what determines the average level of populations, and why this level varies from year to year or from place to place, we must study the external factors. In our attempts to manage bird populations, it is these external factors that must be altered before any desired change in population level can be achieved. All the external limiting factors mentioned above can have immediate direct effects on bird breeding, mortality or movements, and hence on local numbers.

Food and other resources

To be limited by food, a species need not be up against the food limit all the time. Shortages may occur only occasionally, under specific weather conditions, or every few years. Some resident bird species are limited by winter conditions, and may be cut back so severely by lack of food in hard winters that several years of recovery are necessary until numbers reach their former level (for Grey Heron see Fig. 5d). Similarly, many species of arid regions, including British breeding birds that winter in the Sahel zone of Africa, tend to decline from food shortage during periods of drought, only to increase again as food becomes more available during the intervening wet periods. The season when limitation occurs can also change over time as feeding conditions alter, with shortages falling in winter in some years (affecting mortality) and in the breeding season (affecting reproduction) in other years, as in some seabirds (Chapter 4).

The evidence that certain bird species can be limited by food is mostly circumstantial: (1) long-term or sudden changes in bird numbers often accompany long-term or sudden changes in food supplies; (2) numbers are higher in years when food is abundant than when it is scarce; or (3) numbers are higher in areas where food is abundant than where it is scarce. Additionally, in a few species, experimental manipulations of food supplies have been followed

FIG 9. Grey Heron *Ardea cinerea*, whose nests have been regularly counted in Britain since 1928. The species suffers marked declines in hard winters when fresh waters are frozen, denying the birds access to fish. (Frank Snijkers)

by appropriate changes in numbers, giving firmer evidence for the role of food, as explained in Chapter 4.

The relationship between birds and their food is not always straightforward. With certain types of food (such as tree-seeds), the amount eaten in one year may have little or no influence on the amount available the next. But with other types of food (such as many invertebrates), the amount eaten in one year can greatly influence the amount available the next. In this way, prey and predator can interact in various ways, with both short-term and long-term consequences to the population levels of both. Secondly, it is not only the quantity and availability of food that are important, but also its quality, especially for herbivores, whose food can vary greatly through the year in digestibility and nutrient content (Chapter 3).

Some birds can store large amounts of food as reserves within their bodies, so that (at least in larger species) the food acquired at one time of year can affect their breeding or survival at another (Chapter 3). Other species store substantial amounts of food externally in caches, and can thus survive periods when food would otherwise be difficult to obtain. Examples include those species of tits that store beechmast and other seeds for later use (Chapter 3). While food is the main resource limiting bird numbers, some species can at times be limited by other resources, including water and other components of habitat, such as safe nest-sites and roost-sites (Chapters 5 and 11).

Interspecific competition

Most bird species overlap in their resource needs with other species, both closely related and more distant, including other kinds of animals. The seeds eaten by finches, for example, are also consumed by many other creatures, including other birds, mammals and insects. Such food sharing creates the potential for competition, because some of the food removed by one species might otherwise have been available for a second. If either of such species is limited by food, then it follows that the numbers of the one could influence the numbers of the other. Similarly, many species require special nest-sites, such as tree-cavities. If such cavities are in short supply, their use by one species can exclude another, restricting the number that can breed. In any pair of competing species, one species is usually more successful than the other, but the winner in one type of situation may be the loser in another (Chapter 10).

Predators and parasites

With or without competitors, food and other resources can provide a ceiling on bird numbers. In some species, however, breeding numbers may be held well below that potential resource-ceiling by natural enemies (Chapters 8 and 10). In some areas, for example, the numbers of Grey Partridges are held at a low level by predators, and when predators are removed, Partridges can increase to achieve much higher breeding densities (Chapter 8; Potts 2012). Similarly, the numbers of some ducks and gamebirds are sometimes greatly reduced by parasites or pathogens, so that in some years their numbers sink well below the level that might otherwise be expected. Because of spatial variations in impact, a predator or parasite can have devastating effects in a small area for a short time, but averaged over a larger area the impact might be small.

Relationships between resources and natural enemies

It is often hard to tell whether bird breeding numbers are limited primarily by resources or by natural enemies, without a field experiment in which one or other is manipulated against an appropriate control. Studying the causes of mortality will not necessarily help to identify the limiting factor. Imagine that the density of a territorial bird species is limited by habitat quality or food supply, so that some individuals, unable to obtain a territory, are forced into unsuitable habitat, where they were eaten by predators (the 'doomed surplus' idea of Errington 1946). From a study of mortality, one would conclude that predators limited numbers, because virtually all the deaths occurred through predation; however, the underlying limiting factor was habitat quality or food supply, which influenced the density of territories in which survival was possible. To change density in the long term would entail a change of habitat, not of predators. The key point is that the factors that cause most mortality in bird populations are not necessarily those that ultimately determine their population levels. Experiments are often needed to reveal the true limiting factor.

In any case, assessing the causes of mortality in a bird population is not always straightforward. A bird weakened by food shortage may succumb to disease, but just before death it may fall victim to a predator. For this bird, food shortage is the underlying cause of its death, disease appears irrelevant but potentially fatal, while predation is the actual immediate cause of death. In reality, no single causal factor is likely to account wholly for a given population level. Reproduction and survival are seldom influenced by one factor alone, but by several, which may act independently or in combination. In situations such as these, the main limiting factor can be considered as the one that, when removed, will permit the biggest rise in numbers. Again, this factor can best be revealed by appropriate field experiments.

Different limiting factors can interact in complex ways. For example, if food were abundant, a bird with many gut parasites might be able to keep itself just as well-nourished as one without parasites, simply by eating more. But if food were scarce, a parasitised bird – through having part of its daily intake absorbed by the parasites – might die of starvation, while one without parasites might survive. In such cases, parasites accentuate the effects of food shortage. Similarly, if food were plentiful, a bird might be able to obtain its needs in only a small part of each day, keeping a constant watch for predators and foraging only in safe sites, thereby reducing its risk of being caught and killed. But if food were scarce, the same bird might have to expose itself for longer each day, reduce its vigilance, and feed in less safe places, thereby increasing its risk of predation. In cases like these, alterations in either food supplies or predator or parasite numbers could have marked effects on bird numbers. Our understanding of the interactions between different limiting factors is advancing year by year, and is discussed in Chapters 11, 12 and 13.

Weather impacts

Extremes of weather clearly affect the numbers of birds and other animals. At high latitudes, where life is governed primarily by temperature, the numbers of many resident bird species become lower than average after unusually cold winters, and higher after mild ones. At lower latitudes, where life in arid regions may be limited by water, the numbers of many birds decline during extreme drought years, and recover again in more normal ones. For the most part, weather patterns influence birds indirectly, by affecting their habitats and food supplies. Some such weather effects can be delayed, as when rain stimulates plant growth which only later will provide food for birds, while other weather effects can be immediate, as when a snowfall suddenly makes food on the ground unavailable. Sometimes, however, extreme weather can reduce bird numbers directly, as when individuals die of hypothermia or heat stress or, in some parts of the world, are battered by hailstorms or hurricanes (Chapter 14). Such extremes can sometimes cause sudden catastrophic declines in bird numbers, after which several years are needed before their numbers fully recover.

Human impacts

In addition to various natural limiting factors, human activities can impose great losses on bird populations, sufficient to cause widespread population declines. The most obvious impact is through habitat destruction, as forests are felled and marshes drained and converted to farmland or other human use. At the same time, modern agricultural practices are continually reducing the habitats and foods available to birds on farmland. Because the overall numbers of any species depend on the amount of habitat available, destruction of habitat results in reductions in both local and overall population levels. It is not only the overall loss of habitat that is important, but also its fragmentation, as a result of which the distributions of species become increasingly patchy. With only small numbers in each patch, and little or no immigration from elsewhere, it is easy for populations to die out in habitat fragments, reducing their overall numbers below the level expected in the amount of habitat remaining (Newton 1998).

Other losses imposed by human activity are more direct. Examples include the heavy mortalities inflicted on certain species by excessive hunting or unlawful killing, wind-turbines, overhead wires, fences and fishing gear (Chapter 17), and on other species by various pesticides and pollutants (Chapters 18 and 19). Some pollutants have affected birds and other animal populations over wide areas by influencing the physical or chemical nature of their habitats, the acidification of some lakes and rivers by atmospheric pollutants being an obvious example. Of all these various human impacts on the natural world, ongoing climate change is the one likely to affect the greatest range of species, and to have the biggest long-term influence on plant and animal distribution patterns (Chapter 15).

DEMOGRAPHIC FACTORS

Measuring breeding and mortality rates

Counts of bird numbers, accumulated over many years, are important because they tell us about the fluctuations and trend of a population, which can then be related to changes in environmental variables such as weather. But to understand the internal workings of bird populations, the reproductive and mortality rates must also be studied. Reproductive rates can be assessed either by finding the nests and recording the numbers of young produced by individual pairs, or by measuring the overall ratio of young to adults at the end of the breeding season. Annual survival rates are usually measured from ringing, which enables individuals to be identified in subsequent years. From survival rates, mortality rates can be readily calculated, for when expressed on a percentage scale, both together add to 100% (for example, 60% survival means 40% mortality).

Some studies in particular areas involve checking to find what proportion of birds present in one year are still there the next. This method does not tell us where or when particular individuals die, nor does it separate deaths from permanent emigration, but it does give a measure of year-to-year persistence in an area. This measure can be close to annual survival in species in which individuals normally use the same nesting places in successive years, and rarely change sites.

An alternative method of estimating mortality depends on comparing the numbers of individuals ringed as chicks that are subsequently found at different ages by members of the public. From the ratios of birds reported in their first to second year, second to third year, third to fourth year and so on, the mortality in different age classes can be estimated. This method requires that many young birds have been ringed, but does not usually suffer from the emigration problem because it does not depend on recoveries from a single researcher operating in a limited study area. It provides some information on the seasons of death, although there are potential biases in estimates. It also depends on people reporting a sufficient number of the ringed birds that they find, whether dead or alive. Such data have indicated that for most species the main period of natural mortality of full-grown birds is in winter, while for others it is during the breeding season when the birds are most active. Examples of species in which ring recoveries indicate that adults die mainly in winter include Grey Heron and Oystercatcher, and in the breeding season Blackbird and Marsh Tit.

Ringing has also shown another important point: namely, free-living birds are not like captive birds, or like people in modern societies, where most individuals can expect to reach old age. In wild birds, deaths are frequent across all age-groups, and very few individuals achieve what would be old age for their species. Most do not even survive to halfway through their potential lifespan. Hence, for wild birds, knowledge of maximum longevity is much less meaningful than knowledge of the annual mortality rate, the average age at death, or the average expectation of further life, all of which can be calculated from ring recoveries. Some early estimates from bird-ringing, which revealed annual mortality rates in small birds well in excess of 50%, were met with scepticism, because people knew that in captivity the same species could live for many years. However, the estimates from wild birds turned out to be correct.

Once estimates of reproductive and mortality rates are available for a population, they can be used to calculate the trend of the population: whether it is likely to increase or decrease, and at what rate. It is unwise to predict far into the future, however, because reproductive and mortality rates often change as a population grows or contracts, so constant re-assessment of demographic rates is necessary. Demographic data gathered nationwide by the BTO have proved useful for studying population processes at regional or national scales where the effects of dispersal can be safely ignored, but less so at local scales where changes in population levels can be greatly influenced by immigration/emigration rates, as well as by reproduction and mortality.

Movements

Despite national monitoring programmes, most detailed studies of bird populations have been concerned with the local processes that affect local numbers. Yet almost all species have geographical ranges larger than an observer's study plot, and individual birds continually move in and out, on local or longer journeys. Such movements can produce much more rapid and pronounced rises in local density than any increase in fecundity or survival. They can also cause rapid abandonment of areas if conditions suddenly become unsuitable. Moreover, as natural habitats become ever more fragmented by human activities, movements are likely to play an increasingly crucial role in maintaining local populations and the genetic interchange between them.

Movements are important, therefore, because they facilitate rapid changes in local densities in response to changes in local conditions. They enable birds to leave areas where survival or reproductive prospects are poor and to find other areas where conditions are better. In any widespread species, we can expect that in some areas (called *source* areas) production of young is more than enough to offset mortality (net exports), whereas in other areas (called *sink* areas) the reverse could hold, so that densities there can be maintained only by continued immigration (net imports). In such sink areas, movements thus become crucial in the maintenance of local densities. Among many bird species, dispersal occurs chiefly in late summer, in the period just after the young become independent of their parents, but in some species also at other times in the non-breeding season.

Migration is the most spectacular of bird movements, occurring in response to seasonal changes in food supplies, themselves governed by seasonality in climate. Typically, many birds travel over hundreds or thousands of kilometres each autumn to lower latitudes where food suppies remain more available in winter. They then move back to their higher-latitude breeding areas in spring to reproduce on the summer flush of food that occurs there. The species that leave Britain and Ireland completely for the winter include aerial insectivores, such as swifts and swallows, and warblers that eat mainly aphids and other insects from fresh leaves. Birds that come from higher latitudes to winter in Britain and Ireland include species whose food supplies in their breeding areas become inaccessible under snow or ice, such as waterfowl and waders, and passerines that eat seeds and berries, such as some finches and thrushes. These large-scale seasonal movements of birds illustrate how food supplies influence bird densities and distributions through long-distance movement patterns.

While most migratory bird species move for the winter to lower latitudes in the same hemisphere, some travel longer distances to the opposite hemisphere. Because the seasons are reversed between the northern and southern hemispheres, with the northern winter coinciding with the southern summer, such species gain the advantage of summer conditions year round. They include such impressive migrants as the Swallow and Arctic Tern which breed in the northern hemisphere and winter in the southern, and the Sooty and Great Shearwaters which breed in the southern hemisphere and winter in the northern. As a result of migration, some tropical areas, already rich in resident birds, may receive migrants from the northern hemisphere for half the year (the northern winter) and from the southern hemisphere for the other half (the southern winter). Migration formed the subject of an earlier New Naturalist volume (Newton 2010), so I shall not discuss it further here.

Use of information on demographic rates

While knowledge of the external limiting factors is required to understand what determines the level and trend of any bird population, studies of reproductive and mortality rates allow us to understand the mechanics of population change. Remember, though, that two populations may have identical rates of births, deaths and movements, and yet persist indefinitely at quite different densities, if the resource levels on which they depend differ between areas (see below). Conversely, populations at the same density may have different rates of births, deaths and movements. Providing that in each population the inputs (from births and immigration) equal the losses (from deaths and emigration), numbers will remain constant through time, regardless of density. For continuing stability, a change in one parameter must be offset by a corresponding change in another. For example, each year Blue Tits reared up to three times as many young per pair in an area in southern France as they did in another area in Corsica. However, the breeding populations in both areas remained approximately stable, evidently because after leaving the nest the juveniles survived better in Corsica than in France and began breeding, on average, at an earlier age (Blondel et al. 1992). Similarly, Blackbirds in southern England had better breeding success in suburban London than in rural areas (2.0 versus 1.7 young per year), but this difference was offset by differential mortality, so that both populations were balanced in the longer term (Batten 1973).

FIG 10. The Lapwing *Vanellus vanellus* has declined greatly in Britain over the past 50 years, associated with a decline in breeding success. (Alan Martin)

Where reproductive and survival rates have been studied in the same population during periods of increase (or stability) and decline, the comparison has pointed to where the cause of the decline might lie. If reproduction declined while survival stayed the same, the problem would probably lie in the breeding areas, but if survival had decreased the problem could lie in the breeding or wintering areas, depending on when the extra deaths occurred. Long-term decline in the numbers of Lapwings in Britain was associated with a decline in reproduction but no change in survival (Peach *et al.* 1994), while changes in a Puffin population were attributed to changes in survival rather than reproduction (Harris & Wanless 1991).

In many other bird populations that have been studied in recent decades, long-term change in breeding numbers has been associated with change in annual survival, while in other populations it has been associated with change in reproductive success (Newton 1998, Saether *et al.* 2004, Saether & Engen 2010). The latter include several ground-nesting waders and gamebirds which in recent decades have experienced poor breeding, caused mainly by predation (Roodbergen *et al.* 2012). In other species, long-term population decline was associated with reduction in both breeding and survival. For example, the White Stork has suffered from poor reproduction in its European breeding areas, caused by food shortage resulting from land drainage and pesticide use, and also from poor survival in its African wintering areas, caused by food shortage resulting from drought and pesticide use (Dallinga & Schoenmakers 1989, Kanyamibwa *et al.* 1993, Bairlein 1996).

It is not only the long-term trends, but also the year-to-year fluctuations that can often be explained in terms of either breeding or mortality. In some bird populations, breeding numbers increased in years that followed good breeding and decreased in years that followed poor breeding. This was true of Pied

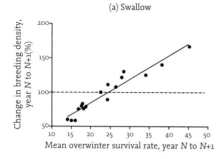
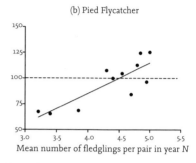

FIG 11. Demography and population change. (a) Relationship between the annual survival of adult Swallows *Hirundo rustica* and annual change in breeding density (from Møller 1989). (b) Relationship between the annual breeding output of Pied Flycatchers *Ficedula hypoleuca* and annual change in breeding density (from Virolainen 1984). Significance of relationships: Swallow, $b = 3.44$, $r^2 = 0.93$, $p < 0.001$; Pied Flycatcher, $b = 0.15$, $r^2 = 0.74$, $p < 0.001$.

Flycatchers, for example, and also of Capercaillie and Black Grouse in different areas (Fig. 11; Virolainen 1984, Summers *et al.* 2010). It seemed that, in these populations, spring/summer conditions in breeding areas had most influence on subsequent year-to-year changes in breeding numbers, and that such populations were therefore below the level that winter habitat would support. In other bird populations, such as the Great Tit and Swallow, breeding numbers varied from year to year according to previous winter conditions, implying that such populations were close to the level that winter habitat would support (Box 1). However, over several years, the same population could change from one state to another, as its status with respect to available resources and other limiting factors changed. In yet other bird populations, changes in breeding numbers from year to year were associated with changes in both breeding and mortality, which together caused an increase or decrease in numbers. They included species that ate the same type of food year-round in the same area (such as some owls dependent on voles, Chapter 4) and other species in which changes in breeding numbers were affected by conditions in both breeding and wintering areas (such as the White Stork, mentioned above).

Sometimes a long-term upward or downward trend in a bird population can be caused by different factors to those that affect the year-to-year fluctuations about the trend. For example, over the latter half of the twentieth century, the Dark-bellied Brent Geese wintering in western Europe (including Britain) increased in numbers by more than tenfold, in recovery from over-hunting in the past. Nevertheless, winter numbers still fluctuated substantially from year to year, as a result of annual variations in breeding success in the Siberian nesting areas, caused mainly by fluctuating levels of predation on the eggs and chicks (Chapter 7). Hence, in this population the long-term trend could be attributed to conditions in wintering areas, and the short-term fluctuations to conditions in breeding areas.

Without information on trends in breeding numbers, one cannot judge the effect on a population of a decline in either reproduction alone or survival alone. Decline in the production of young does not necessarily lead to population decline, because it may be offset by improved survival. Decline in survival does not necessarily lead to population decline, because it may be offset by improved reproduction. One species that increased during a period of declining adult survival was the Kittiwake (Coulson 2011), and some that increased during periods of declining reproduction were the Wigeon (Mitchell *et al.* 2008) and the wild geese discussed in Chapter 2.

Studies of population limitation are especially difficult in migrants that divide each year between breeding and wintering areas far apart, because conditions in either or both areas can affect their breeding numbers, as in the Brent Geese just discussed. In recent years, many species of migratory birds that breed in Britain and Ireland have declined. These declines seem to have been both more prevalent and more marked among species that winter in Africa than in those that winter in Europe (Sanderson *et al.* 2006). Europe-wide trends in breeding numbers between 1970 and 1990 were analysed in 30 pairs of closely related species. In each pair, one species wintered in Africa and the other in Europe (as in Tree Pipit and Meadow Pipit, Whinchat and Stonechat). Significantly more negative trends emerged in the African-wintering species, regardless of breeding habitat. This is perhaps not surprising, considering the rate at which habitat in Africa is degrading under human influence, but more study is needed to understand the details. European breeding birds that winter in the Sahel zone of Africa declined to low levels during the period 1969–76, when rainfall there was low, increasing afterwards. However, from about 1987 to the present, as these species recovered, other species that winter in more humid habitats further south in Africa began to decline, with the causes yet to be established (Thaxter *et al.* 2010). Nevertheless, it seems that both groups were at the time limited primarily by conditions in their wintering areas.

LIFE-HISTORY FEATURES

Birds span a wide range of life-history types, from short-lived, mostly small-bodied species to long-lived, mostly large-bodied ones. Those species native to the British Isles range in weight from less than 6 g (Goldcrest) to 18 kg (large male Great Bustard), so that the biggest species is more than 3,000 times

Box 1. Winter-limited and summer-limited populations

Seasonally breeding birds tend to reach their peak numbers each year just after the nesting season when young are produced. Their numbers then decline through mortality over winter to reach their lowest level at the start of the next breeding season. It is usual to find that nesting habitats can support only a limited number of pairs, influenced by the available territory space, nest-sites or food supplies. After winter mortality has occurred, and the remaining birds re-assemble in their breeding areas to compete for territories or nest-sites, we can envisage two scenarios:

(1) Too few birds are left at the end of winter to occupy all available nesting habitat, so that, given an appropriate sex ratio, practically all individuals of appropriate age and condition can find a place and breed (curve A in Fig. 12). Such populations could be described as *winter-limited*, because to increase breeding numbers in the long term would entail some favourable change in winter conditions, such as an increase in the extent or carrying capacity of winter habitats.

(2) More birds are left at the end of winter than the available nesting habitat will support, producing a surplus of non-territorial non-breeders, unable to find a place (curve B in Fig. 12). Such populations could be said to be *summer-limited*, because to raise breeding numbers in the long term would require an increase in the extent or carrying capacity of the nesting habitat. The same holds for populations in which birds remain on their nesting territories year-round, but at the start of breeding

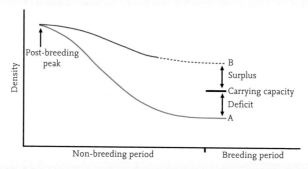

FIG 12. Model showing seasonal changes in the total numbers of a species in relation to the carrying capacity of the breeding area (thick line). In the lower curve (A), numbers left at the end of the non-breeding season are fewer than the nesting habitat could support, and in the upper curve (B) numbers are greater than the nesting habitat could support, leading to a surplus of non-territorial, non-breeders. In (A) breeding numbers are limited by conditions in the areas occupied in the non-breeding season, and in (B) by conditions in the areas occupied in the breeding season. (From Newton 1998)

still show a surplus of non-territorial mature adults, as exemplified by Carrion Crows and Mute Swans in some areas.

Another form of summer limitation occurs where breeding success falls below the level at which adult numbers can be maintained on the normal adult mortality rate (as in the Lapwing and others), or where annual variations in breeding success are reflected in subsequent fluctuations in breeding densities, as in the Pied Flycatcher and others (Fig. 11).

In this book, examples are given of some species in which breeding density appeared, in the study concerned, to be winter-limited (such as the Grey Heron, Great Tit and Sedge Warbler) and of others in which it appeared to be summer-limited (such as the Pied Flycatcher, Lapwing and other waders). However, because the extent and carrying capacities of habitats vary from year to year, and from area to area, we can expect that the same species might be winter-limited in some years or areas and summer-limited in other years or areas.

heavier than the smallest. Worldwide, the heaviest living bird species is the Ostrich, which weighs up to 150 kg, some 75,000 times heavier than the smallest bird species, the 2 g Bee Hummingbird. This huge range of variation has big repercussions on bird life histories and population dynamics.

Among birds as a whole, body size correlates to some extent with life-history features. The larger the species: (1) the longer it tends to live; (2) the later the age at which it begins breeding; (3) the longer the annual breeding cycle; and (4) the fewer the young produced at each attempt. Near one extreme among British birds, the small Blue Tit, with an annual survival of less than 30%, can live up to about eight years and begins breeding in its first year. It lays 10–12 eggs in a clutch, with one-day intervals between each egg, and has incubation, nestling and post-fledging periods lasting about 14, 16 and 10 days, respectively, bringing the total breeding period from the first egg to about 50 days. Moreover, two broods may be reared by a pair in a single year. At the end of the breeding season there would therefore be 12–14 birds for every pair at the start, assuming that both parents survive, giving a 6–7-fold increase, and an even greater increase if a second brood was reared. In practice, while some individuals might reproduce at the maximum possible rate, the average for the population as a whole is much lower, but the potential rate of increase in the absence of mortality is still high. The term *r-selected* is sometimes applied to such fast-breeding species, from the technical notation for the intrinsic rate of increase, r (as mentioned above).

At the other extreme, the Fulmar has an annual survival of around 97%, and some individuals live for more than 40 years. It does not begin breeding

FIG 13. The Blue Tit *Cyanistes caeruleus* is short-lived and has a high reproductive rate, laying an average of around ten eggs per clutch. (Keith Kirk)

until around nine years of age (range 6–19), lays only one egg at a time, and has incubation and nestling periods lasting about 52 and 46 days respectively, bringing the total breeding cycle from egg-laying to 98 days. Because each pair produces at most one young per year, the maximum possible annual increase in numbers is 1.5 times the breeding population, less than one-fourth as great as the maximum rate in the Blue Tit. In practice, the maximum rate in the Fulmar is lower still, not only because some birds fail in their breeding but also because individuals wait so long before they start to nest, which would slow the rate of increase even further, at least in the initial years. The term *K-selected* is sometimes applied to such slow-breeding species, from the technical notation for carrying capacity, *K* (mentioned earlier). The idea is that, since the population normally fluctuates less, both within and between years, it remains for most of the time close to the level that the contemporary environment could support.

These two contrasting species lie near opposite ends of a spectrum, between which other bird species show a continuum of variation in life-history traits. Although, in general, life-history features relate to body size, exceptions are numerous, and the type of bird has an important influence. Thus swifts as a group are fairly small, but are long-lived with small clutches, while ducks and grouse-like birds are medium-sized but short-lived with large clutches. Also, the smallest of all birds (hummingbirds) lay only two eggs, while the largest (Ostriches) lay up to ten. Overall, however, the main life-history features among birds are correlated, so that long life, low annual mortality, delayed maturity, long breeding cycles and small broods usually go together, as do short life, high annual mortality, early maturity, short breeding cycles and large broods. In particular species, mortality rates are considerably higher in first-year than in older individuals, and to judge from those species for which sufficient detail is available, annual mortality rates tend to decrease progressively during the first few years of life, and then increase again in old age. Senescence has proved hard to study in wild birds, largely because most individuals die well before they reach old age, as mentioned above. Similar patterns occur in mammals, where they also broadly relate to body size.

Although the basis of these trends in breeding and mortality rates is far from understood, it is clear that the particular life-history features shown by different bird species greatly affect their population dynamics. In short-lived species, population turnover is rapid, with relatively little overlap between generations, a relatively unstable age structure, and a high production of young, all of which facilitate short-term fluctuations in numbers. Most individuals that survive a winter are capable of breeding in spring, so that the non-breeding sector usually remains small. Such species are highly sensitive to reductions in breeding rates, but because these rates are normally high, these species can recover rapidly from a population reduction. For the same reason, they are better able to withstand heavy predation or human killing.

In long-lived species, by contrast, population turnover is generally slow, with relatively more overlap between generations and a more stable age structure, both of which tend to dampen short-term fluctuations in numbers. Such species are sensitive to changes in adult mortality, but relatively insensitive to changes in reproduction and recruitment to the breeding sector. Even if no recruitment occurred for a period of years, breeding numbers would decline only at the rate of the annual mortality (3% in Fulmar, 5–15% in most other long-lived species). Hence, even complete breeding failures in occasional years can have relatively small effects on subsequent breeding numbers, without a simultaneous increase

FIG 14. The Fulmar *Fulmarus glacialis* is long-lived, with long-deferred first breeding and a low reproductive rate, laying only one egg per year. In the past 130 years, the species has increased and spread around the British and Irish coasts to give a population now exceeding 500,000 pairs, benefiting from the huge amounts of offal produced by the fishing industry. (Laurie Campbell)

in adult mortality. Moreover, in such long-lived species, there also tends to be a large non-breeding sector, consisting mainly of birds in the younger age-groups. The existence of these birds can to some extent buffer the breeding population against decline, because after large mortality events vacant breeding sites can be rapidly taken over by young birds, which then start to breed at an earlier age than they otherwise could. Counts of breeders would then remain relatively stable.

SOCIAL INTERACTIONS

Because birds are easier to watch than most other animals, it has proved possible to study the role that behaviour plays in the regulation of local densities. Whenever individual birds come into contact with one another, they usually reveal some form of dominance hierarchy or 'peck-order'. Anyone who watches birds as they feed together – for example at a garden feeder – can easily discern that some individuals dominate others. The dominants may drive subordinates from food sources, but are seldom challenged themselves. In competitive situations, social interactions of this kind can lead to an uneven sharing of resources, and when supplies are limited they can help to regulate density, through influencing how many individuals survive and reproduce and how many do not. As the total numbers of competitors rise, or as resources dwindle, increasing proportions of individuals fail to obtain their needs, so leave or die. Such social interactions can thus provide a means by which numbers are continually adjusted to the resources available, whether living space, food, nest-sites, roost-sites, mates or any other requirement that is in short supply or of variable quality.

Aggressive interactions between individuals, whether momentary over food-items or long-term over territory defence, provide a form of contest, in which each individual attempts to commandeer from a limited supply the resources it needs to survive and breed. Territorial behaviour is an extreme example, because, with each pair in its own defended area, it leads to the spacing out of birds through the available habitat, and to the exclusion of other individuals once all potential territories are occupied and the habitat is saturated. Territorialism may also correspond with resources, such as food supplies, because in many species pairs defend smaller areas where food is plentiful than where it is scarce (Newton 1998). In such cases, food supply can be viewed as the main environmental factor influencing density, and territorialism as the behavioural mechanism through which this correspondence is achieved. Although the experimental removal of territory holders often reveals the presence of surplus birds able to occupy any newly vacated sites, this does not mean that territorial behaviour evolved in order

FIG 15. Goldfinches *Carduelis carduelis* fighting for a position on a hanging feeder. (Laurie Campbell)

to limit population density. Ownership of a territory confers advantages on the individuals concerned, including the ability to breed, and natural selection acts on individuals not on populations. Hence, the limitation of density by territorialism is best regarded as an incidental consequence of behaviour evolved to benefit the individual. Nevertheless, such behaviour can play a major role in the regulation of local bird densities, adjusting them to the resources available.

Even in species that are not markedly territorial, aggressive behaviour can still mediate the effects of competition, concentrating the shortages on particular individuals, and resulting in continual re-adjustment of numbers (or breeding) to resource levels. An early study involved Woodpigeons that were individually tagged and watched as they fed in fields on spilled grain or clover leaves (Murton 1968). Within the flocks, dominant birds fed at a consistently high rate, but the subordinates – which spent much of their time avoiding the dominants – fed only two-thirds as fast, on average, as judged by the numbers of pecks per minute. Accordingly, the subordinates more often starved over winter. So whether birds live in territories, social groups or large flocks, dominance behaviour can result in changes in the amounts of food or other resources being translated into changes in demography and population density. The whole sequence of events between changes in resources and population level may be depicted as follows:

change in resource level → change in proportion of birds affected by the dominance behaviour of others → change in rates of birth or death or movement → change in local population density

Among birds, older individuals of a species tend to be dominant over younger ones, and in most species, males (being larger) over females of similar age. Although dominance may give greater access to resources, it is a status that not all individuals can achieve. So for the time being, subordinate individuals must remain submissive in social interactions and suffer the consequences of their low status. There would be no advantage in subordinates starting a fight if they had no chance of winning.

If they survive without fighting to the death, their status may improve in later life, as they gain in body size and experience, and the opposition weakens.

Not all territorial behaviour may result from the need to protect food or other resources. Similar spacing behaviour may result from the need to avoid predation, especially on nests, where wider spacing reduces predation rates, as in ground-nesting species such as Grey Partridges (Chapter 6). Many ground-nesting waterfowl, which in areas with mammalian predators space their nests widely, often nest 'colonially' at high densities on islands lacking such predators. The implication is that nest spacing can be adjusted not only to resources but also to prevailing threats, although this aspect has been little studied.

CONCLUDING REMARKS

In this introductory chapter, I have tried to give some idea of the general content of this book, of the main ideas that underlie it, and of the way in which bird populations 'function'. All bird species are restricted to the habitats that suit them, and in broad terms the amount of habitat available to them can influence their overall population levels. Among the various factors that affect bird numbers within these habitats, it is useful to distinguish between the extrinsic factors (such as food supply, predation and disease) and the intrinsic demographic factors (such as birth rates, death rates and movements). Extrinsic factors affect intrinsic ones, causing changes in population levels. In some bird populations studied in recent decades, changes in breeding numbers – either year-to-year or long-term – have been attributed primarily to conditions that affect reproductive rates, and in others primarily to conditions that affect mortality rates. In general among birds, with some exceptions, large species have lower inherent reproductive and mortality rates than small ones, and also start breeding at a later age. Large species tend to show less annual variation in abundance than small ones, have larger proportions of non-breeding immatures, and slower potential rates of increase. In competition for resources, whether food, territories, nest-sites or roost-sites, dominance behaviour provides a mechanism through which the effects of shortages are translated into changes in bird numbers.

In the following chapters, different aspects are developed in more detail, beginning with the mechanisms of population regulation, then the main limiting factors of resources, competition, predation and parasitism. Other chapters discuss how different limiting factors can interact in their effects on bird numbers, and these are followed by chapters on hunting and other forms of human impact. The book ends with some reflections on the main conclusions.

CHAPTER 2

Population Regulation

W HERE HABITATS ARE NOT DISTURBED, most bird species remain relatively stable in abundance over long periods. Their breeding numbers may fluctuate from year to year, but within narrow limits compared to what their reproductive and mortality rates would allow (Lack 1954). This implies that their breeding numbers are regulated in some way, by factors that act to curb the rate of increase as numbers rise, and to curb the rate of decrease as numbers fall. Without the operation of stabilising density-dependent mechanisms, populations could increase without bounds or collapse to zero.

Potential regulating processes include competition for resources, such as food, nest-sites or territories, as well as predation and parasitic diseases, all of which can affect an increasing proportion of individuals as their overall numbers rise. Immigration/emigration can have an additional influence. Such factors contrast with density-independent factors, such as extreme weather or pesticide poisoning, which can affect a large proportion of a population regardless of its size. While density-dependent factors tend to stabilise populations around an equilibrium, density-independent factors tend to destabilise them, causing large, unpredictable fluctuations. The size and fluctuations of any bird population are determined by all the factors that impinge on it, whether or not they are influenced by density. And while some factors, such as predation and disease, have the potential to act in a density-dependent manner, they do not always do so, as described later.

Some years ago, arguments raged on whether bird numbers were limited primarily by density-dependent or by density-independent factors, some people being impressed by the stability of populations and others by their instability. It now seems more sensible to ask, for any one species, what is the relative importance of the two types of factors in causing the changes observed? In general, the more dominant the influence of density-dependent regulating mechanisms, the more stable the population through time, but even in populations that fluctuate widely, some aspect of breeding or mortality must be density-dependent, otherwise such populations could increase indefinitely or die out. Density-dependence is thus one of the central concepts of population ecology. It underlies many important aspects of animal populations, including the dynamics of predation and disease, hunting and other human impacts (Chapters 7, 9 and 16).

The fact that many of the bird species that have been monitored over several decades have changed greatly in abundance does not argue against regulation. It highlights the fact that environmental conditions change, so as to alter the population level around which regulation occurs. To use an analogy, populations behave like the temperatures in a room in which the controlling thermostat is periodically set at different levels. In the case of birds, food supplies might change from year to year or gradually over a period of years, causing change in the equilibrium level around which numbers fluctuate. However, populations sometimes decline because other factors (such as human hunting) act so severely as to override any density-dependent compensation possible. If the factor causing decline continues unabated, extinction is inevitable. But if this limiting factor relaxes, and other conditions have remained unchanged, numbers will rise again until they reach the previous level. Examples are given later in the book.

FIG 16. The Gannet *Morus bassanus* is one of the most striking of all the North Atlantic seabirds. It is a pelagic feeder, and the 232,000 pairs found around Britain and Ireland are distributed in more than 20 colonies. Throughout the twentieth century, the species increased at about 3% per year. (David Boyle)

Throughout this book, I have used the term *limiting* for any factor that can restrict bird numbers or densities, whether or not it acts in a density-dependent manner. Following the usual convention, I use the term *regulating* for factors that operate in a direct density-dependent manner, acting to prevent both indefinite increase and decline to extinction. In some species, densities remain more stable (and hence more regulated) in main habitats, and are more fluctuating (less regulated) in subsidiary habitats (Newton 1998).

DETECTION OF DENSITY-DEPENDENCE

Given the central importance of density-dependent changes in birth and death rates in the regulation of animal numbers, much effort has been devoted to measuring these rates. In order to detect density-dependence, we have to examine whether changes in numbers, birth or death rates, immigration or emigration correlate appropriately with changes in population density. This is harder than it seems, and usually requires a long series of records obtained over many years. One common problem is that density-independent factors may cause such big changes in numbers that they mask the effects of density-dependent factors. Another problem is that the resources over which birds can compete often change greatly in abundance from year to year. The density at which competition sets in is then likely also to vary from year to year, so that density-dependence operates against a continually changing resource base. Hence, unless densities can be expressed as numbers per unit of relevant resource rather than as numbers per unit of area (as is usual), any density-dependence can be easily overlooked (Newton 1998, Lindström *et al.* 2005). A third problem is that density-dependent processes may begin to operate only when the population exceeds a certain size, so that there is no chance of detecting it below this critical (but unknown) level. However, the widespread operation of density-dependent mechanisms in bird populations has become evident in various ways, as explained below.

Increasing populations
When a species establishes itself in a new area, following introduction or natural colonisation, its numbers usually grow rapidly for several years and then level off. The initial growth phase confirms the capacity for rapid increase, while the levelling off implies that the capacity for increase has been checked by factors that act most strongly at high density. In nature, many populations appear to follow this general pattern, but often with fluctuations, because numbers are also

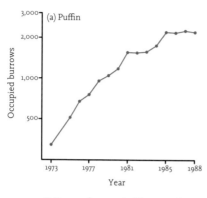

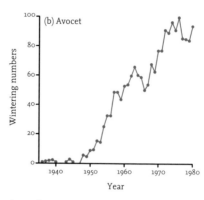

FIG 17. Patterns of numerical increase in two bird populations following colonisation of a new area. (a) Avocets *Recurvirostra avosetta* at a wintering area in southwest England (redrawn from Prater 1981). (b) Puffins *Fratercula arctica* on part of the Isle of May, eastern Scotland (redrawn from Harris & Wanless 1991). In both species, numbers increased for several years and then levelled off.

influenced by density-independent factors. The examples in Figure 17 refer to both a breeding and a wintering population.

In the absence of immigration, the rate of population growth that can be achieved by a species depends on its intrinsic rate of increase (*r*), which, as explained in Chapter 1, is higher in small fast-breeding bird species (such as Blue Tit and Wren) than in large slow-breeding species (such as Golden Eagle and Fulmar). In practice, immigration often contributes to increases in local populations to give much faster rates of growth than are achievable on reproduction alone. For example, over many decades the global population of Northern Gannets grew consistently at about 3% per annum, a rate that matched the known reproductive and mortality rates. Some long-established colonies grew at rates less than this, but some newly formed ones grew for a time at rates up to eight times faster than this through immigration (Nelson 1978, Murray & Wanless 1997). Similarly, among Kittiwakes, small colonies in Britain

FIG 18. Avocet *Recurvirostra avosetta*, whose breeding numbers on Havergate Island increased and eventually stabilised, with their overwinter losses being density-dependent. (Frank Snijkers)

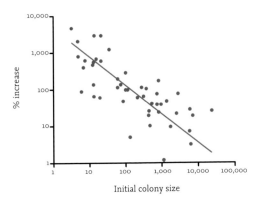

FIG 19. The relationship in the Kittiwake *Rissa tridactyla* between colony size and proportional increase between 1959 and 1969. The smallest colonies showed the greatest rates of increase, implying density-dependent growth. (From Coulson 1983)

showed higher growth rates during 1959–69 than larger ones (Fig. 19), implying that as colonies grew, their rates of increase progressively slowed (Coulson 1983). The same held for Herring Gulls during 1976–94, and for Guillemots during 1985–2002 (Raven & Coulson 1997, Mitchell *et al.* 2004). The interpretation was that smaller colonies provided less competitive conditions, so attracted more recruits, a process which continued until resources, such as nest-sites or food, were fully exploited and no longer surplus to needs. In all these species, therefore, growth rates varied between colonies, depending on how close the colonies were at the time to their ultimate level. The initial stages of rapid growth were fuelled mainly by immigration of young raised elsewhere, but as the colony continued to grow, home-produced young became increasingly available to contribute to further growth. However, whatever the rates of local or overall population growth, these rates can eventually be expected to decline to nil, as numbers stabilise at a level set by environmental conditions, or the supply of potential recruits runs out.

Another indication of density-dependence comes from natural events, such as hard winters, which suddenly reduce bird numbers well below the usual level. In most such examples, numbers recovered within a few years, but the pattern of recovery, in which the rate of increase slowed progressively as numbers returned to normal, was consistent with the operation of regulating factors that acted more strongly at higher densities. Such patterns were evident in the annual numbers of Grey Heron nests counted in Britain, which showed not only rapid recoveries after hard winters, but also relative stability at other times (Fig. 5d). Similar patterns were apparent in Wrens and other species recovering after hard winters or other catastrophes, as well as in species exposed to a sudden increase in food or habitat.

For some bird populations that were seen to increase to a plateau, attempts were made to identify the demographic variables involved in slowing population growth, whether changes in reproduction or mortality, immigration or

(a) Greylag Goose

(b) Barnacle Goose

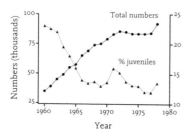

FIG 20. Reduced production of young by Greylag Geese *Anser anser* and Barnacle Geese *Branta leucopsis*, as their numbers grew. The populations concerned breed in Iceland (Greylag) and Svalbard (Barnacle) and winter in Britain, where the counts were made. The graphs show five-year moving mean values. (Mainly from Owen *et al.* 1986)

FIG 21. Barnacle Geese *Branta leucopsis* in winter. (Frank Snijkers)

emigration. Among wild geese that winter in western Europe, several species increased greatly over periods of several decades, apparently mainly in response to reduced shooting pressure (Owen *et al.* 1986, Madsen *et al.* 1999). As their numbers grew, some populations showed reductions in the proportion of young present in wintering flocks, consistent with a density-dependent reduction in breeding rate. This occurred partly because fewer birds of breeding age produced young, and partly because broods were smaller. The pattern was most apparent among the Svalbard Barnacle Geese and Icelandic Greylag Geese that winter in Britain (Fig. 20). In the Barnacles, natural adult mortality rates also increased over the years, from 2% per year at a population level of 5,000 birds to 8–10% per year at a level of 10,000 birds. This increase in mortality rate occurred naturally (rather than through increased shooting), and was attributed to competition for food in breeding areas. Among other effects, this food shortage resulted in insufficient fat deposition for autumn migration, so that increasing proportions of birds died on the journey (Owen & Black 1991). Other expanding goose populations showed no such demographic changes and continued to increase in the period during which they were studied, so they had presumably not then reached a level at which competition was important (Owen *et al.* 1986, Fox *et al.* 1989, Summers & Underhill 1991, Madsen *et al.* 1999). Similar density-dependent changes in demographic measures emerged from studies on other expanding bird populations, affecting, for example, the reproductive rates of Herring Gulls in the Netherlands (Spaans *et al.* 1987) and of Wigeon wintering in Britain (Mitchell *et al.* 2004), and the overall mortality rates of Oystercatchers wintering on the Exe estuary (Durell *et al.* 2000). In some species, it has been noted that density has a much stronger effect on the survival of juvenile birds than adults in the same population, a consequence perhaps of juveniles being less competitive or efficient at foraging than older birds (Arcese *et al.* 1992, te Marvelde *et al.* 2009, Doxa *et al.* 2010).

Gradual changes in demographic variables were also noted in some birds of prey whose numbers were reduced by organochlorine pesticide poisoning in the 1950s, and then recovered after organochlorine use was stopped. A recovering Sparrowhawk population showed a similar reproductive rate to a stable one in another area, but higher adult survival, more immigration than emigration and a lower mean age of first breeding (Wyllie & Newton 1991). Moreover, as the recovering population grew, all these demographic measures progressively converged to match those in the stable population. Similar changes in demographic variables over time were also noted in various seabird species during periods of colony growth or decline. These variables included various aspects of reproduction (Potts *et al.* 1980, Coulson *et al.* 1982), age of recruitment to colonies (Duncan 1978, Klomp & Furness 1992), immigration/emigration (Duncan 1978, Potts *et al.*1980, Phillips *et al.* 1999a) and adult survival (Coulson & Wooller 1976, Harris & Wanless 1991, Frederiksen & Bregnballe 2000). The fact that it was mainly breeding performance that changed in some species and mainly survival and movements in others may have reflected whether competition occurred mainly during the breeding season or mainly in winter.

Fluctuating populations
From counts of breeding birds of various species undertaken year after year, it has become apparent that years of low numbers are usually followed by the greatest proportionate increases, and years of high numbers by the greatest declines. There thus emerges a correlation between numbers in one year and percentage upward or downward change to the next year. Such a correlation was apparent, for example, among five songbird species studied over a 22-year period at Bookham Common in Surrey (Newton *et al.* 1998), in Sparrowhawks in Eskdale in southern Scotland (Newton 1986), and in Goshawks in several areas of Europe (Rutz *et al.* 2006). In none of these studies was the cause of mortality or non-breeding known,

but whatever the factors involved, they acted in a density-dependent manner, and were thus regulatory in their effects on breeding numbers. Similar year-to-year patterns were also evident in Redshanks and Dunlins wintering on the Forth estuary in eastern Scotland, where they were killed by Sparrowhawks (Whitfield 2003a, 2003b). Predation on both waders was density-dependent, with greater proportions of individuals taken in years when numbers were high.

Other studies have examined not only the year-to-year changes in numbers, but also the annual survival and reproductive rates. They have shown that the mortality of juveniles and adults can vary from year to year in a density-dependent manner, as can most aspects of reproduction, whether the proportion of pairs that attempted to breed, the clutch size, chick survival, or overall nest success (Newton 1998). Some of these relationships were caused by competition for food, territories or nest-sites, and others by predation or parasitism.

The timing of the major density-dependent events in the annual cycle can influence our perception of the degree of stability in a population. For convenience, the degree of stability is usually judged from the year-to-year fluctuations in breeding numbers, as mentioned earlier, and if counts of breeders usually follow a period of strong density-dependent adjustment (such as overwinter mortality), the counts at that time would vary less than they might otherwise do. In contrast, if the counts of breeders followed a period of variable density-independent loss, they could show great year-to-year fluctuation. For example, in the Avocet, the population at two sites in southern England increased and then levelled off. In the level phase, overwinter loss was almost perfectly compensatory, with the numbers lost overwinter matching the numbers previously gained from breeding (Hill 1988). In this species, overwinter loss, whether from mortality or emigration, was clearly responsible for stabilising the local breeding population. In contrast, in a study of Woodpigeons, egg predation was strongly density-dependent, but was incapable of stabilising breeding numbers, because it was quickly offset by replacement egg-laying and followed by large density-independent winter mortality (Murton & Westwood 1977). In general, populations that are strongly regulated in the period before breeding will show greater stability in breeding numbers than those in which losses at this time are density-independent.

In species in which a stable breeding density is regulated by territorial behaviour, the number of new breeders recruited in any one year depends largely on the number of vacancies created by the loss of previous breeders. In years of high adult mortality, many new breeders are recruited in spring to make up the losses, while in years of low adult mortality few new breeders are recruited because most territories are already occupied. This was apparent

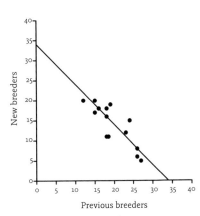

FIG 22. Density-dependent recruitment to a breeding population of the Sparrowhawk *Accipiter nisus*, south Scotland, 1975–89. The breeding population remained fairly stable during this period, and the numbers of new breeders recruited each year (y) were inversely related to the numbers of established breeders remaining from the previous year (x) (regression relationship: $y = 31.7 - 0.90\,x$, $r = 0.69$, $N = 14$, $p < 0.003$.) Population stability was itself a consequence of a fairly stable territorial system, in which the landscape was apparently occupied to a similar level each year. (From Newton 1991)

in a Sparrowhawk population in which breeding numbers fluctuated by no more than 15% of the mean over a 15-year period (Fig. 22). One consequence of limited recruitment to the breeding sector is that surplus birds die or emigrate or accumulate locally as non-breeders, in many species occupying areas not used for breeding. Such a system of regulated recruitment from a non-breeding sector might be expected in any territorial species, and has been demonstrated experimentally in various songbirds, grouse, waders and others (Watson & Jenkins 1968, Harris 1970, Nilsson 1987). It would also be expected in species limited by availability of nest-sites (Chapter 5).

Population reductions

As every pest controller knows, when Feral Pigeons, gulls or other nuisance birds are removed from an area, newcomers soon begin to move in, and in a short time numbers may return to normal. It is not the fact that birds move into newly emptied habitat that is surprising, or that this can sometimes occur within days or weeks. What is interesting is that numbers often return to about the same level as before. This in itself provides a compelling indication that densities are regulated in relation to some feature of the local habitat. There are many such instances among birds of prey, which have long been persecuted in Britain and Ireland. For example, one observer reported how four pairs of Merlins were shot from the same area of moorland each year for more than 20 years. During this time no adult survived there and no young was reared, yet every year four new pairs settled on the same sites (Rowan 1921–22).

Recovery of breeding numbers after any cull could result from increased reproduction or survival in the remaining birds, from an increase in immigration over emigration, or from a lowering in the age of first breeding. In one species or another, changes in response to a culling programme have been noted in all these demographic measures. For example, a cull of Feral Pigeons resulted in improved reproduction and survival among remaining birds, and increased immigration, while a cull of Herring Gulls similarly resulted in improved reproduction among remaining birds, and increased immigration, but also reduced age of first breeding (Kautz & Malecki 1990, Coulson *et al.* 1982). Likewise, the experimental removal in autumn of full-grown Willow Tits from an area resulted in an improved survival of remaining adults and juveniles and an increase in immigration (Ekman *et al.* 1981).

In many bird populations, as mentioned already, breeding density may be limited by the numbers of territories or nest-sites available in the area, and surplus adults simply accumulate as a non-breeding component, living in or near the area but not breeding. While the breeders may be easy to count, the non-breeders may not. The breeding performance of those pairs that breed may be fairly stable from year to year, giving a fairly consistent ratio of young per breeding adult. If breeding success is examined in relation to breeding adults alone, it does not then emerge as density-dependent. But if breeding success is examined in relation to the total adults in the area (breeders plus non-breeders), it inevitably appears as density-dependent. This is because above a certain level breeding numbers and productivity are capped, while the non-breeders can continue to increase (within limits), thereby lowering the production of young per individual adult. Thus some attempts to check for density-dependence in bird populations may have failed to find such evidence because they failed to account for non-breeders.

Experimental evidence for density-dependence

Observational studies, such as those described above, can at best only indicate likely density-dependent relationships. It is always possible that, over a period of years, density-independent losses by chance conform to a pattern expected of density-dependent losses. The risk of such chance effects is of course lessened the longer the study can be continued, but the evidence for density-dependence can never be as strong from observational studies as from experiments in which densities are deliberately altered, and the ensuing demographic response of the population is monitored.

A particularly telling experiment was conducted on Great Tits nesting on the Dutch island of Vleiland (Kluijver 1966). Over a period of years on this island, Great Tit pairs produced an average of 11 young per year, but only about 27% of adults survived from one year to the next, and only about 6% of young were later found breeding locally. Then, in each of four experimental years, more than 60%

of the young were removed from the nest, so that each pair raised an average of only four young. In these years, the annual survival of adults rose to about 56% and as many as 22% of the remaining young subsequently bred locally. This was sufficient to compensate for the experimental removal of young, and breeding numbers were restored within a year, thereafter continuing to fluctuate around the same level as before. This experiment thus gave a clear indication that the survival or emigration rates of both adult and juvenile Great Tits varied at this location in a density-dependent manner, serving to regulate the local population broadly around a consistent level.

In another experiment with Great Tits, breeding density was manipulated by providing nest-boxes in uniform habitat to give densities about eight times higher in one plot than in another. During the 11 years of the experiment, clutch size, nestling mass and the proportion of females starting a second brood were all significantly lower in the high-density plot. In five years with equal breeding densities in both plots, clutch size did not differ between them (Both 1998). In other words, breeding output was again affected by density.

OTHER DENSITY-DEPENDENT RESPONSES

The emphasis above was on processes that operate in a direct density-dependent manner and act to stabilise densities. However, not all factors that act in a manner correlated with density necessarily promote population stability. They might, for example, be *inversely density-dependent*, affecting a smaller proportion of individuals as their numbers rise (Fig. 24). This situation would occur, for

FIG 23. Guillemots *Uria aalge* benefit from nesting in dense colonies in which they are better able to protect their chicks from predatory gulls. (Edmund Fellowes)

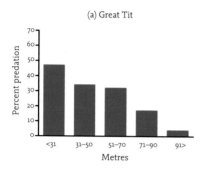
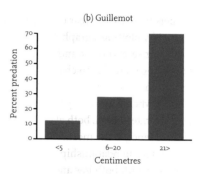

Nearest neighbour distance between nests

FIG 24. Density-dependence in nest predation.
(a) Direct density dependence. The closer together were Great Tit *Parus major* nests, the more likely they were to be preyed upon by Weasels *Mustela nivalis*. (From Krebs 1971)
(b) Inverse density dependence. The closer together were colonial Guillemots *Uria aalge*, the better able they were to defend their eggs and chicks from predatory gulls. (From Birkhead 1977)

example, if predators removed a constant number of prey individuals each year from a varying prey population. They would thus remove a smaller, rather than a larger, proportion at high prey densities, tending to accentuate the year-to-year fluctuations rather than dampen them. In colonial birds that show communal nest defence, birds are better able to defend their nests against predators when they nest at high densities or in larger colonies, so that predation becomes inversely density-dependent within the colonies (Kruuk 1964, Birkhead 1977, Andersson & Wiklund 1978). This was found among Guillemots subjected to egg predation by gulls, and it thus had no regulatory role. Similarly, Lapwings often join together to defend their nesting areas against crows and other predators, so several pairs nesting close together can mount a more effective defence than single pairs nesting away from others. Not surprisingly, then, it has emerged that Lapwing clutches and broods are much more likely to be preyed upon at low than high densities, giving another inverse density-dependent relationship (Seymour *et al.* 2003, Eglington *et al.* 2009). Poor breeding or juvenile survival at very low densities, improving as numbers rose, has also been recorded among Mediterranean Gulls, Dalmatian Pelicans and others, but the mechanisms were less obvious (te Marvelde *et al.* 2009, Doxa *et al.* 2010).

Other regulating mechanisms involve a time lag, causing a delayed density-dependent response, which in some circumstances can cause populations to fluctuate in regular cycles (Chapter 7). The term *delayed density-dependence* is used when the changes in a population correlate, not with present numbers, but with numbers in an earlier year or generation. Such a system can most readily be detected by plotting a graph. Suppose that the numbers of a bird species first rise steadily for several years, and then fall steadily for several years, and suppose that these changes are due to changes in the death rate. Throughout each period of population increase the death rate is low, both at the start when numbers are low and later when they are high. Likewise, during each period of population decrease the death rate is high, both at the start when numbers are high and later when they are low. Hence, if the mortality at each stage is plotted against the initial numbers at that stage, no relationship between the two is at first apparent, because low death rates occur with both low and high numbers, as do high death rates. However, if the data points for the mortality in successive years are joined, a regular pattern is found in which the points, running anticlockwise, form a rough circle (Fig. 26c).

This type of pattern is characteristic of predator–prey (or parasite–host) oscillations, in which the numbers of the prey (or hosts) rise steadily for several generations and then fall, while those of the predator (or parasite) do the same but lagging behind. When the prey is abundant the predator increases, which eventually leads the prey to decrease, which in turn leads the predator to decrease, after which the prey can increase again and the cycle is repeated. Under these circumstances, the death rate of the prey does not vary directly with its own numbers at the time, but depends on the relative numbers of the predator. The latter have been determined by the numbers of the prey in a previous year, hence the term *delayed density-dependence*.

On a European scale, some rodent and grouse species show fairly constant year-to-year densities in the south of their range, but increasingly marked and regular fluctuations towards the north, with gaps of several years between the peaks. This geographical change is associated with a switch from predominantly direct density-dependence in the south to delayed density-dependence in the north, possibly associated with a change in the type of predation and the

FIG 25. Shelduck *Tadorna tadorna*, in which chick survival has been found to be lower in years of high density (see Fig. 26b). (Edmund Fellowes)

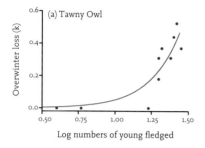

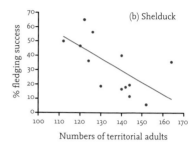

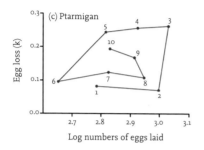

FIG 26. Some examples of density-dependent relationships in bird demography. In each example, each point refers to the value from a particular year. (a) Relationship between overwinter loss and fledgling production in the Tawny Owl *Strix aluco*, expressed as *k* values. The *k* values are calculated as log numbers at the end of breeding minus log numbers at the start of breeding in the next year. Overwinter losses become density-dependent only above a certain density, probably through competition for territories. (Calculated from Southern 1970)
(b) Relationship between duckling survival and territorial density in the Shelduck *Tadorna tadorna*. The linear pattern indicates that losses (mainly through predation) were density-dependent over all densities encountered, increasing to affect an increasing proportion of birds as density rose. (Calculated from Patterson *et al.* 1983)
(c) Relationship between egg loss (through predation by Stoats *Mustela erminea*) and breeding density in the Ptarmigan *Lagopus muta*, showing the typical circular pattern of a delayed density-dependent process, formed by joining the loss values from successive years over a ten-year period (see text). Plotted on logarithmic scale. (From Weeden & Theberge 1972)

range of predators available (Chapter 7; Hanski *et al.* 1991). Most examples of delayed density-dependence in birds come from cyclically fluctuating grouse populations; they include predation on Hazel Grouse by Goshawks (Lindén & Wikman 1983), and parasitism of Red Grouse by strongyle worms (Chapter 7 and 9). Again, however, when a population fluctuation involves mortality or reproductive changes of the type shown in Figure 26c, these changes could be caused by any process acting with a time lag and not just predation and parasitism. Over short periods, they could also result from variable density-independent losses which by chance follow a cyclic pattern. There are still many things we do not know about population cycles in birds and mammals.

SPATIAL DENSITY-DEPENDENCE

Most attempts to detect density-dependence in birds have involved the analysis of year-to-year demographic changes within the populations of single small study areas. But we should also expect that density-dependent processes would operate in a spatial context, with high reproduction, low mortality and net immigration in areas where numbers are low, and the opposite conditions in areas where numbers are high. Such processes would tend each year to even out densities between areas, but only providing the areas were similar in other respects. The fact that many birds can make local movements at almost any time of year makes for a swift response, and could lead to reduced fluctuations in local numbers and in the overall wider population.

Some clear examples of spatial density-dependence have emerged among bird studies. Two examples showing overwinter loss in different areas are shown for ducks and grouse in Figure 27. In both studies, those areas that started with the highest densities of birds in September or October lost the greatest proportion of individuals overwinter. The role of movements was shown by the

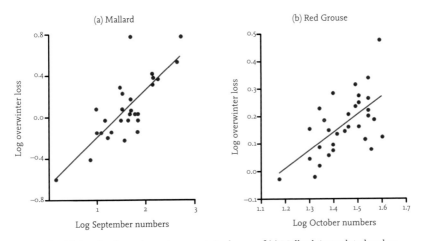

FIG 27. Spatial density-dependence in overwinter losses of (a) Mallard *Anas platyrhynchos* and (b) Red Grouse *Lagopus l. scotica* in different areas. The greater the density in September or October, the greater the proportionate losses by the following March. Mallard numbers on different waters and Red Grouse numbers on different 0.5 km² sectors of heather moor. Negative values indicate immigration. Significance of relationships: Mallard, $b = 0.46$, $r^2 = 0.62$, $N = 28$, $p < 0.001$; Red Grouse, $b = 0.66$, $r^2 = 0.38$, $N = 31$, $p < 0.001$. (Calculated from Hill 1983 and Redpath & Thirgood 1997)

fact that areas that started with the lowest densities gained birds overwinter, rather than losing them. Similar changes were recorded among Grey Partridges in different parts of a large study area (Jenkins 1961).

Further indications of spatial density-dependence have come from studies on seabirds. In some species, colony sizes were related to the numbers of birds of the same species at neighbouring colonies, and colonies were larger in places where no other colonies occurred nearby (through shortage of nesting habitat). Inverse relationships between colony size and numbers in other colonies within specified distances were revealed among data for Gannets, Puffins, Shags and Kittiwakes (Fig. 130; Furness & Birkhead 1984). All these species bred in larger numbers at colonies that were distant from other colonies but whose members could have competed for the same local food supplies. In other words, within species, colonies of different size seemed to be distributed so as to avoid excessive local densities of birds at sea during the breeding season. In addition, studies on several seabird species around Britain revealed that the lengths of feeding trips increased with colony size. This was apparent from comparing birds from colonies of different size in the same year, and from within colonies as they grew in size over a period of years (Lewis *et al.* 2001). These findings implied that food became scarcer near the colonies as they grew, as more birds exploited the local supplies. Moreover, in other studies, chick fledging weights were found to decline with increasing colony size among nine colonies of Brünnich's Guillemots and six colonies of Puffins in various locations (Gaston 1985), as did various aspects of breeding performance in Brünnich's Guillemots, Common Guillemots and Kittiwakes elsewhere (Hunt *et al.* 1986). These various correlations indicate spatial density-dependence in reproductive rates arising from competition for food supplies near colonies, but none has been tested by any kind of experiment or measurement of food supply.

HABITAT QUALITY AND POPULATION REGULATION

In Chapter 1, we saw how social interactions between individuals, notably territorial and other dominance behaviour, can act to adjust the numbers of birds in particular areas to the resources available there. Such interactions can limit the numbers of individuals present at one time, but they can also regulate numbers in the longer term, both in individual habitat patches and over the wider landscape. This statement is based on two findings, both supported by observational evidence from a wide range of species (Newton 1998). Firstly, for any bird species, habitat varies in quality from place to place; that is, in the benefits in terms of survival and reproduction that it confers upon its occupants. Secondly, as bird numbers rise, good habitat is occupied first and in preference to poorer habitat. Such a pattern depends on individuals distinguishing and preferring good habitat, and, beyond a certain level of occupation, deterring settlement by further individuals, which then move into poorer habitat. If these conditions hold, as observations on many bird species confirm, it follows that, as total numbers rise, an increasing proportion of individuals is pushed down the habitat gradient, where (on the definition above) their survival or breeding success is reduced. Some individuals may be excluded from nesting habitat altogether, accumulating locally as a non-breeding contingent.

As a result of these processes, the average per capita performance (survival or reproduction) of individuals in the population as a whole declines progressively as their overall numbers rise, and increasing proportions are relegated to poorer habitats (as indicated above). Birds in the best habitats may continue to reproduce as well as ever, and it is the increasing proportion in poorer habitat that brings about the overall decline in reproductive rate. In the absence of other constraints, the total numbers (of breeders plus non-breeders) will then stabilise when the mean mortality rate of the entire population exactly balances the mean reproductive rate (including non-breeders). In this way, variation in habitat quality could function in regulating the overall population level, breeders and non-breeders. Food resources and other limiting factors are involved in this regulation because they influence the quality and carrying capacity of habitats.

Variation in habitat quality can of course occur on different spatial scales, from different territories or nest-sites in the same patch of habitat, to different types of habitat in the same general area, to different parts of a geographical range. On the smaller scale, it is often found that, over a period of years, certain territories are occupied more frequently than others nearby and that, on average, birds in favoured territories produce more young per nesting attempt. The poorer territories are occupied mainly in years of high population, resulting in a decline in the average nest success. This process has been described in a wide range of species, from Wheatear to White-tailed Eagle.[2] The second

---

2 For Sparrowhawk *Accipiter nisus* see Newton 1991, Kruger *et al.* 2012; for Wheatear *Oenanthe oenanthe* see Brooke 1979; for Magpie *Pica pica* see Møller 1982; for Nuthatch *Sitta europaea* see Nilsson 1987, Matthysen 1990; for Tengmalm's Owl *Aegolius funereus* see Korpimäki 1988; for Jay *Garrulus glandarius* see Andrén 1990; for Imperial Eagle *Aquila adalberti* see Ferrer & Donazar (1996); for Partridge *Perdix perdix* see Panek 1997; for Goshawk *Accipiter gentilis* see Kruger & Lindström 2001; for Black Kite *Milvus migrans* see Sergio & Newton (2003); for Buzzard *Buteo buteo* see Kruger *et al.* (2012); for White-tailed Eagle *Haliaeetus albicilla* see Kruger *et al.* (2012).

situation, with differences in bird performance between habitat patches, is also well described, and encapsulated in the concept of *source* and *sink* areas mentioned in Chapter 1. It is evident in comparisons of the performance of Great Tits, Chaffinches and Pied Flycatchers in different types of forest (Kluijver & Tinbergen 1953, Glas 1960, Lundberg *et al.* 1981), and of Dotterels on different mountaintops (Thompson & Whitfield 1993). In each case, change in overall numbers is accompanied by greater change in the numbers present in poor areas than good ones. Habitat-related trends in bird performance across a geographical range are harder to demonstrate, because reproductive and mortality rates vary across large distances for reasons other than habitat variation. However, they are apparent at range boundaries, where species can grade from abundant to absent over distances of a few tens of kilometres. This is evident in the northern range boundaries of many species that cut through the British Isles.

All these gradients in habitat quality, coupled with appropriate habitat preferences, result in greater proportions of birds appearing in poorer areas in years of high overall numbers, bringing about a decline in overall survival or reproductive success. During a population decline, birds in the best places may breed at the same high rate throughout, and most of the change is brought about by decline in the proportions of birds present in poor habitat breeding with poor success (Ferrer & Donazar 1996). In other words, performance is density-dependent at the level of the overall population.

CONCLUDING REMARKS

The fact that wild bird populations normally fluctuate within restricted limits implies that their numbers are regulated in some way. For without regulation, their numbers could decrease to zero or increase without bounds. Density-dependent factors act to curb the rate of increase as numbers grow, and to curb the rate of decrease as numbers fall. Competition for food and other resources can act in such a density-dependent manner, as can predation and disease, all affecting greater proportions of individuals as their numbers rise.

Almost all aspects of bird demography, including reproduction, mortality and movements, have been found to vary from year to year in a density-dependent manner in one or more bird populations. This is despite there being two main problems in detecting density-dependence. The first is that food and other resources often change, so the level around which regulation occurs can change through time. This can make it difficult to detect density-dependence unless resources are also measured, enabling numbers to be expressed as per unit of resource, rather than per unit of area. The other difficulty arises from being able to count only the territorial birds in an area, and not the non-breeding non-territorial ones. The problem here is that, while aspects of demography may not appear as density-dependent when expressed in terms of number of breeders, they would do so if expressed in terms of total numbers, including non-breeders. While most attempts to detect density-dependence have been made using year-to-year demographic comparisons of the same population in the same area, others have used comparisons of several populations in different areas of similar habitat in the same year.

In many bird species, habitat quality and territorial behaviour can interact to influence overall numbers in a density-dependent manner. The habitat of any species can vary in quality from place to place, and as numbers rise, increasing proportions of individuals are relegated to poorer habitat where their probability of survival or breeding success is reduced. In this way, the mean per capita performance of individuals declines as their overall numbers rise. Early researchers used the term *density-dependent* because they assumed that a change in density was required to bring about a change in the proportion of individuals affected by whatever was limiting their numbers. But the relationship with habitat just described does not necessarily involve an increase in density, only an increase in numbers, which then leads individuals to settle in previously vacant (but poorer) areas. It involves increase in the area occupied, rather than in the number of individuals per unit area. For this reason, the term *density-dependent* would be better replaced by the term *number-dependent*, but I am not advocating change in the use of a well-used traditional term.

Not all limiting processes act in a direct density-dependent manner. Some act in a delayed density-dependent manner, which can lead to fairly regular fluctuations in numbers. Others may act in an inverse density-dependent manner, affecting smaller proportions of individuals as their numbers grow, while yet others may act in a density-independent manner, affecting variable proportions of individuals regardless of density. These last two types of response tend to destabilise numbers rather than stabilise them, causing enhanced fluctuations. Probably all bird populations are influenced by both density-dependent and density-independent factors, the relative timing and strength of which influence the extent to which breeding numbers fluctuate. The way in which different limiting factors act in relation to existing numbers clearly has a major impact on subsequent variations in numbers. In the following chapters, examples from the field are given of these different types of relationships.

CHAPTER 3

Food Supplies: General Principles and Individual Impacts

EW ORNITHOLOGISTS WOULD QUESTION the importance of food supply in influencing bird numbers. It is one essential resource on which all species depend, and large populations can only be sustained by large amounts of food. Changes in food supplies, through their effects on survival and reproduction, can bring about changes in population levels. This chapter is concerned with the effects of food supply on individual birds, paving the way for the next chapter on the impacts of food on population levels.

The most obvious sign of food shortage in individuals is starvation, when loss of body condition leads to death. In bird populations, periods of starvation tend to occur infrequently, falling in particular seasons or years, and they sometimes last for no more than a few days or weeks at a time. During hard winters or other extremes, numbers may be reduced so much that a species may then experience several years of progressive recovery until the next major shortage. Food shortage can also reduce population size through lowering breeding rates, affecting the proportion of pairs that lay eggs, or their clutch and brood sizes, and survival of chicks, but without necessarily affecting full-grown birds. In some long-lived bird species, such as many seabirds, individuals do not normally start breeding until they are several years old, so it may take some years before the effects of poor breeding in one or a few years show in lowered breeding numbers. Decline occurs when too few young are produced to offset the usual adult mortality. More commonly, however, food supplies act less directly on birds, by influencing the densities at which they settle in particular areas and their movements from one area to another.

Studies of birds in relation to their food supplies require measures of both. This is especially difficult when the birds eat a range of different items, most of which need separate assessment. However, some birds are sufficiently specialised that their foods can be measured, including finches that depend on specific seed crops, raptors and owls that specialise on small rodents, and seabirds that exploit specific kinds of fish. Some of the most telling studies have therefore been conducted on these species, as described later in this and the next chapter.

Even though food-items may be plentiful in the environment, they are not necessarily always available to birds. Many intertidal invertebrates retreat deeper in the mud during cold weather, putting them beyond the reach of some shorebirds, while many soil-dwelling invertebrates move deeper during drought. These examples illustrate the general points that only a proportion of potential food-items may be available to birds at any one time, and that this proportion may change in response to other conditions. In addition, if food is plentiful but of low nutrient content or digestibility, a bird may be unable to process enough each day to maintain its body weight. This is particularly true of herbivores eating fibrous vegetation, and shortage may arise partly from crop or stomach capacity (which limits the amount that can be stored for overnight digestion), or from gut morphology (which limits the processing rate). The nutritive value of winter food is sometimes so low that grouse can lose weight over difficult periods (Seiskari 1962). Nutritional shortages can therefore arise in birds from food being inadequate in quantity, quality or availability.

Some birds appear to be surrounded by food, and it is hard to imagine that they would ever be short of it, but this is not necessarily so. Take the Red Grouse, whose food-plant – heather – forms its habitat. The bird would seem to have limitless easily available food. However, the grouse eat mainly the fresh green heather tips, and in some winters with little insulating snow these tips are killed by frost, so are no longer suitable food for grouse. In years of such extensive 'heather browning', grouse are in poor condition, and many become moribund and die, with deaths continuing into spring (Watson & Moss 2008).

Many bird species prepare for predictable periods of food shortage by accumulating extra body-fat. In small birds, fat reserves are accumulated during the course of a feeding day mainly for use overnight, and few species can survive more than a day or two without eating. Larger birds, with their relatively lower metabolic rates, can store more energy per unit body weight. As a result, larger birds can rely on internal reserves for longer than small ones, more than two weeks in some large waterfowl. Most migratory birds also accumulate extra body-fat to fuel their journeys, the amount depending on the duration of the non-stop flights they have to make (Berthold 2001, Newton 2008); and some species store extra body-fat and protein in preparation for breeding, extreme examples being Arctic-nesting geese in which the females in some populations produce and incubate their eggs almost entirely on reserves accumulated in wintering or migration areas (see later).

Other bird species store food-items for use at a later time. Some meat-eaters cache prey for short-term storage, while some resident seed-eaters may store food in autumn to last through the winter, or even year-round. Long-term storage is frequent among various tits, nuthatches and woodpeckers, reaching its extreme in certain jays and nutcrackers. In some such species, stored food can provide more than 80% of the winter diet, and can also feed the adults into the next breeding season and influence the numbers of young produced (Källander & Smith 1990). In years with good seed crops, huge amounts can be stored. Individual nutcrackers, for example, can cache 20,000–100,000 pine seeds each autumn, some 2–5 times their total winter energy needs (Lanner 1996). Successful food-hoarding requires that individuals should either guard or hide their stores to reduce pilfering. Some species store items individually, each in a separate place, and show incredible feats of memory in retrieving them (Krebs *et al.* 1996). This caching behaviour enables birds to use their foods more effectively, taking advantage of temporary gluts to lessen later shortages, but it

does not protect them from shortages in years of poor seed crops.

Yet other birds can cushion themselves against temporary food shortages by becoming torpid, achieving an inactive state in which body temperature and heart, respiratory and metabolic rates are depressed, thereby conserving energy. Some species, such as the Swift, can remain torpid for several days at a time when cold weather renders their insect prey inactive (Koskimies 1950), and at least one species, the Common Poorwill in North America, can remain torpid for several weeks, in a state akin to mammalian hibernation (Bartholomew *et al.* 1957). These adaptations help the species concerned to last through difficult periods, whether hours, days or weeks, but again they cannot eliminate the risk of starvation.

FIG 28. The Nuthatch *Sitta europaea* is a regular food-hoarding species which stores seeds in autumn for later use. (Frank Snijkers)

EFFECTS OF FOOD SUPPLY ON INDIVIDUALS

That food shortage can affect individuals directly, through causing breeding failure or starvation, is beyond question. But we can expect to see an effect of food supply on bird survival or breeding only over a restricted range of food levels. Imagine a landscape devoid of food for a particular species, in which, over a period of years, a food supply develops and increases. In the early stages, any immigrants dependent on that food may survive in that landscape for short periods, but may soon die or leave, as food is insufficient to sustain them long-term. At slightly higher food levels immigrants might survive there, and might even establish nesting territories in the better places, but food is still insufficient to allow them to produce eggs. At somewhat higher food levels, birds may manage to produce eggs, but not to incubate them or feed any resulting chicks, so reproduction is still not possible. At even higher food levels, however, they may manage to raise young, and in increasing numbers as the food supply continues to rise. At higher food levels still, no further increase in reproduction is possible because other factors, such as daylength and work capacity, limit the ability of the parents to collect the food, or the young to digest it. Regardless of any further increase in food levels, therefore, other factors intervene to cap the maximum rate of individual reproduction or survival. This is not just a theoretical scenario. Populations at various stages in this process can be seen among many birds, especially those that exploit highly variable food supplies which alternate repeatedly between scarce and abundant.

FOOD AND BREEDING

Raptors and owls
Most information on the effects of food on bird breeding comes from correlations between productivity (young raised per pair) and food supply, either year to year or place to place. Bird species that experience pronounced annual variations in food supply, such as some rodent-eating raptors, show marked annual variations in breeding success (Newton 1979). The abundance of small voles or lemmings on which such species depend can be readily assessed by a regular trapping programme, measuring the numbers of animals live-trapped per day in a fixed number of traps. In one ten-year study of Rough-legged Buzzards in Norway, mean production varied from nil in poor rodent years to four young per pair in the best rodent year (Hagen 1969). In other raptor species, dependent on similar prey, annual production of young varied threefold in Hen Harriers, up to fourfold in Kestrels, up to fivefold in Buzzards, all in association

FIG 29. Kestrel *Falco tinnunculus* male hovering in search of prey. In many regions, breeding densities and success vary according to vole densities. (Frank Snijkers)

with measured year-to-year variations in prey densities (Newton 1979). Some of these annual variations may seem extreme, but they came from detailed studies in which many territorial pairs made no attempt to breed in poor food years. Studies which record only the number of pairs with active nests, and disregard non-breeding pairs, could therefore miss the main cause of reproductive failure, and the main source of annual variation in productivity.

The ten species of European owls that depend on fluctuating rodent populations have been studied in greater detail than diurnal raptors, enabling different aspects of breeding to be examined in relation to the food supply available in different years. These studies give rise to a number of generalisations, though not all aspects have yet been convincingly shown in every species. In good food years compared to poor ones: (1) greater proportions of new breeders are recruited into the breeding population; (2) greater proportions of territorial pairs attempt to breed (annual variation from less than 5% to more than 95% in some populations); (3) among birds that lay, mean laying dates are earlier (the mean dates of clutch initiation between good and poor years can differ by more than four weeks in some populations); (4) egg clutches are larger (annual variation more than threefold in some populations); and (5) more fledglings are produced (annual variation in number of young raised per pair more than tenfold in some populations), with starvation as the most obvious cause of chick deaths; (6) annual survival of full-grown birds is higher (annual variation up to twofold or more in some populations); (7) natal and breeding dispersal distances are shorter (but hard to quantify accurately); and (8) in irruptive species, smaller proportions of birds migrate away from the breeding range (again hard to quantify). In addition to these major aspects of performance, other aspects studied in only a small number of species include: (9) egg size, which is larger or less variable between individuals in good food years than in poor ones; (10) repeat laying after nest failure, which is more frequent in good food years; (11) female body mass, which is greater in good food years; and (12) nest defence against potential predators, which tends to be more vigorous in good food years. There is presumably more point in defending the nest in years when the chance of raising young is high. With so many aspects of performance affected, it is little wonder that food has such a major impact on the ecology of owls and other vole-eaters.

At least three species of European owls have been found to raise two broods in a season when food permits, namely the Barn, Long-eared and Short-eared Owls. In a study in France, 34% of 146 Barn Owl pairs raised two broods in a good vole year (Baudvin 1975). In addition, in good years, occasional males have been found to have two mates, as recorded in Barn Owl, Tawny Owl, Tengmalm's Owl, Great Grey Owl, Hawk Owl and Snowy Owl. With variation in both breeding density and breeding output related to food, the number of young owls produced per unit area of habitat, even in resident species, can vary enormously from year to year: for example from 27 to 246 young Barn Owls per year in the same area of southern Scotland over a 13-year period; from 7 to 142 young Tawny Owls in an area of Kielder Forest in Northumbria over a seven-year period; from 12 to 336 young Ural Owls per year in the same area of Finland over a 25-year period; and from 8 to 163 young Long-eared Owls in an area of Germany over a 24-year period (Taylor 1994, Petty 1989, Saurola 1992, Block 2009).

Similar year-to-year fluctuations in breeding success have been recorded in other raptor species which depend on other fluctuating prey, such as hares or grouse, whose abundance can also be readily assessed. For example, the breeding success of Gyr Falcons has been found to fluctuate up to threefold between years (Nyström et al. 2005), and Goshawks up to sixfold, in parallel with fluctuations in these larger prey species. In yet other raptors, massive reductions in breeding success have followed catastrophic declines in food supplies. This happened in Buzzards in Britain in the 1950s, following the collapse of Rabbit populations caused by the newly introduced viral disease myxomatosis. It also happened in various other raptor species (Golden Eagle, Imperial Eagle, Eagle Owl) in Spain in the 1990s, following a collapse in Rabbit numbers caused by viral haemorrhagic disease (Dare 1961, González et al. 2006). In contrast to all these species, raptors that have more varied diets tend to have more stable breeding rates, because they are then less affected by shortage of any one prey type, the Sparrowhawk and Merlin being examples.

Seabirds
The seabirds that breed around Britain and Ireland depend largely on three main food sources: (1) the waste discarded from fishing boats, (2) small and medium-

FIG 30. The Puffin *Fratercula arctica* is one of several seabirds found around Britain and Ireland which feeds its young primarily on Lesser Sandeels *Ammodytes marinus* and other small fish. As shown, it can carry several at a time in the bill. (Laurie Campbell)

sized fish (up to the size of Mackerel), and, in the case of some gulls, (3) waste from rubbish dumps and sewage outfalls. All three main food sources have declined since the 1980s, with effects on the breeding, survival and population levels of seabirds. In recent decades, in parts of Britain, (a) reductions in the breeding success of Kittiwakes, Shags, Guillemots, Razorbills, Puffins, Arctic Terns and Arctic Skuas have coincided with reduced availability of sandeels; (b) reductions in the breeding success of Lesser Black-backed Gulls and Great Skuas have been associated with the reduced availability of fishery waste; and (c) reductions in the breeding success of Herring Gulls have been associated with the reduced amount of food available from rubbish dumps and sewage outfalls.[3] These events have been repeated at different times in different places, depending on local circumstances. The same responses have been recorded each time, involving reduced clutch sizes (except in one-egg species), and reduced chick growth and survival, as many young starve to death. They clearly show the effects of reduced food supplies on seabird breeding.

In years of extreme food shortage, some seabirds can fail to raise young, producing not a single chick from sizeable colonies. For example, during 1984–90, changes in currents, perhaps coupled with overfishing, created a scarcity of sandeels around Shetland, which resulted in almost total breeding failure of some surface-feeding seabirds, such as Arctic Tern and Kittiwake, owing to nest abandonment and chick starvation. In contrast, most colonies of diving species dependent on the same prey, such as Guillemots, Razorbills, Black Guillemots and Puffins, were much less affected as they could search over a wider range of depths (Heubeck 1989, Monaghan 1992). In the latter two species, whose

---

3 (a) Aebischer 1986, Heubeck 1989, 2000, Monaghan *et al.* 1989a, Hamer *et al.* 1993, Phillips *et al.* 1996, Caldow & Furness 2000, Rindorf *et al.* 2000, Wernham & Bryant 2002, Frederiksen *et al.* 2004b; (b) Hamer *et al.* 1991, Perrins & Smith 2000, Votier *et al.* 2008; (c) Pons 1992, Raven & Coulson 2001.

chicks were secure within burrows and crevices, both parents could be safely away foraging at the same time, whereas when both Kittiwake parents were simultaneously absent from their open cliff nests, the chicks were left exposed to predation by large gulls or Great Skuas (Chapter 7). In general, then, sandeel abundance has influenced the breeding success of several seabird species in northeastern Britain, both directly and indirectly, but to different degrees. The surface and shallow-water feeders were for various reasons more vulnerable than the deeper-diving species, especially those that nest in hidden sites. Inherent features, such as surface feeding, specialised and inflexible feeding habits, limited foraging ranges, and energetically expensive foraging techniques all made species less able to resist reductions in their food supplies. The diving species had an advantage over surface-feeders in that they could forage at a greater range of depths, and exploit alternative demersal fish such as Whiting and Saithe. However, some of these less-preferred fish had lower calorie contents, so provided a less nutritious diet for fast-growing chicks.

FIG 31. The Guillemot *Uria aalge* is one of our commonest seabirds, but in contrast to the Puffin it carries only one item at a time to the young. In recent decades, in the northern North Sea, Guillemots have suffered from decline in the size, as well as the numbers, of their sandeel prey. (Alan Martin)

Although surface-feeding seabirds, such as the Kittiwake and various terns, seem the most sensitive to changes in sandeel availability, diving species such as the Guillemot, which bring back single items of food for their young, have also shown poor breeding years. This may be linked with reductions in the size of prey, for on the Isle of May the average length of sandeel prey in the early 2000s was only 60% of that 30 years earlier (Wanless *et al.* 2004). The situation became extreme in 2004 when mean sandeel length was the lowest recorded over a 30-year period, resulting in the energy value of individual meals being greatly reduced. In the main alternative prey, Sprats, the energy contents were also lower than expected, and so chicks were fed on low-fat rather than on high-fat food. It seemed that the main prey species of seabirds, sandeels and Sprats, were also suffering from food shortage in those years. In an earlier event, Puffins on St Kilda suffered from a dearth of Sprats and sandeels in July 1959, when at least 8,000 well-grown chicks of 4–6 weeks old died (Boddington 1960).

Among Kittiwakes at a colony in northeast England, clutch size and hatching success declined during the 1960s and 1970s, in association with a marked reduction in North Sea Herring stocks (Coulson & Thomas 1985). Then during the 1970s and 1980s, the smaller sandeels and Sprats apparently increased in numbers, possibly due to reduced predation from Herring and from Mackerel, which had also declined. This change then led to Kittiwakes and Guillemots breeding well again and increasing in numbers.

Elsewhere in Europe, poor breeding in Common Terns was associated with declines in the availability of small fish in the German Wadden Sea (Szostek & Becker 2012), in Puffins and Guillemots with collapse of fish stocks in Norway (Lid 1981, Anker-Nilssen 1987, Vader et al. 1990, Anker-Nilssen & Aarvak 2003), in Audouin's and Yellow-legged Gulls with discard reductions in Spain (Oro et al. 1995), and in Herring Gulls with changed garbage management in Brittany, where closure of a rubbish dump was followed by smaller clutches and a halving in the production of young (Pons & Migot 1995). In addition, relationships between food supply and breeding success of Common and Roseate Terns emerged from studies in eastern North America (Safina et al. 1988). Overall, then, food supplies clearly affect the breeding success of seabirds, and extreme food shortages can lead to total (or almost total) breeding failure in whole colonies, sometimes occurring over several successive years.

Other birds

Similar correlations between annual food supply and breeding success have been documented in a wide range of other bird species, including seed-eating finches, insectivorous warblers and hirundines, gallinaceous birds (insectivorous as chicks), and many others (e.g. Bryant 1975, Rands 1985, Martin 1987, Baines 1996, Newton 1998). Depending on the stage at which they occur, food shortages can have effects manifest through non-laying, small clutches, egg desertion, poor chick growth and survival, and (in multi-brooded species) in reduced numbers of nesting attempts per season, as well as in loss of weight and reduced survival prospects in adults. In some multi-brooded species, much of the variation in annual productivity is caused by variations in the mean number of broods raised per year, a figure partly influenced by the period over which breeding is possible each year. At times of exceptionally abundant food, species which normally raise only one brood per year, like the owls mentioned above, can occasionally raise two. Conversely, species that normally raise 2–3 broods per year rear only one in years when food is plentiful over a shorter period than usual. The recent declines in Turtle Doves and Corn Buntings in Britain were associated with reduced seasonal reproductive output resulting from a curtailment of nesting seasons. These species have shown no decline in individual nest success, but no longer continue breeding as late into summer as they formerly did (Brickle & Harper 2002, Browne & Aebischer 2003).

When food supplies change, either year-to-year or long-term, the effects on bird breeding are readily apparent, but effects of food are much harder to detect where supplies vary little from year to year. However, the effect of spatial variation in food supplies is sometimes apparent in comparing the breeding performance of birds in different localities. This applies at various spatial scales, from birds nesting in different territories in the same general area to large-scale regional differences.

Experiments on the effects of food on breeding rates

In addition to the observational studies described above, three types of field experiments have served to confirm that food supply can influence the breeding output of birds. One type has involved the manipulation of food supplies, most often by providing extra food. In most such experiments, feeding was stopped before hatching but was sufficient to advance the egg-laying dates and increase the clutch sizes compared to birds that were not given supplementary food. In nine out of ten species in which extra food was also provided during the nestling period, survival and production of young improved. In various parts of Europe, these species included Crested Tit and Willow Tit (Bromsson & Jansson 1980), Starling (Crossner 1977), Jackdaw (Soler & Soler 1996), Carrion Crow (Yom-Tov 1974, Richner 1992), Magpie (Högstedt 1981), Coot (Brinkhof & Cavé 1997), Kestrel (Wiehn & Korpimäki 1997) and Imperial Eagle (González et al. 2006). Increases in production were most marked in experiments that were done in years when natural food supplies were low or when breeding densities (and competition for food) were high (Smith et al. 1980, Newton & Marquiss 1981, Dijkstra et al. 1982, Wiehn & Korpimäki 1997). In these circumstances, food provision usually raised productivity to the levels seen in the best natural food conditions. Among fed birds, increases in mean production up to fourfold or fivefold were recorded, compared with control birds that received no extra food (Hansen 1987, Arcese & Smith 1988). In these and other species, food provision also altered other aspects of performance in a way likely to improve post-fledging survival: for example by resulting in earlier egg-laying or heavier fledglings. In some species, extra food acted partly to reduce rates of predation, because when food was provided, fed birds could spend more time at the nest to better protect their eggs and young

(Yom-Tov 1974, Högstedt 1981). The young were also less hungry, so called less, and attracted less attention from predators.

The failure of supplementary food to influence reproduction, as observed in some experiments, could be variously attributed to: (1) reproduction being limited by factors other than food; (2) natural food supply being so abundant, or population density so low, that additional food had no extra benefit; (3) the food provided being inadequate in some way; or (4) food being given at an inappropriate stage of breeding (say at the chick stage when the main limitation occurred at the egg stage). For example, in Tengmalm's Owl in Finland, fed pairs produced more fledglings even though feeding was stopped after egg-laying. This was because fed pairs produced more eggs, implying that productivity was limited at that stage rather than later in the cycle (Korpimäki 1989). Feeding oats to Black Grouse in winter had no obvious effects on laying dates, clutch sizes, overall breeding success or survival, compared with unfed birds, so – assuming that oats provided an adequate supplement – food supply was presumably not limiting in any way to Black Grouse in this Finnish area (Marjakangas & Puhto 1999).

In other experiments, attempts were made to reduce bird food supplies and measure the effect on bird breeding. Some such experiments in North America were conducted in conjunction with forest spraying programmes aimed to reduce defoliating caterpillars. Following spraying, production of young by caterpillar-eating Black-throated Blue Warblers was reduced in a year of moderate caterpillar abundance, but not in two years of low caterpillar abundance, when warbler breeding was poor anyway (Rodenhouse & Holmes 1992). In Britain, reduction of insect abundance through insecticide use in various experiments was associated with reduced breeding output of Grey Partridges, Yellowhammers and Corn Buntings (Boatman et al. 2004).

The second type of experiment, involving adding extra chicks to nests in order to find whether parents could raise larger-than-normal broods, gave variable results. In all cases the adults accepted the extra chicks and fed them as their own. In 11 out of 40 brood-enlargement experiments reviewed by Dijkstra et al. (1990), enlarged broods suffered greater mortality and yielded fewer fledglings than normal-sized broods. These findings implied that the parents were already operating close to a limit, and were unable (or unwilling) to collect even more food per day. In the remaining 29 experiments, however, enlarged broods produced more fledglings, on average, than control broods. These results implied that, for these birds, food at the nestling stage was not limiting (although in some of the studies the young were underweight). Such experiments did not exclude the possibilities that food might have been limiting at a different stage of the breeding cycle (laying or post-fledging stages), or that adults that raised extra young might themselves have suffered reduced future survival or reproduction (as shown in eight out of twelve species investigated: Dijkstra *et al.* 1990).

The third type of experiment involved the removal (or natural loss) of the male after hatching from species in which both sexes normally help to raise the young. These broods were then raised by the female alone, which – if food were limiting – should have resulted in poorer chick survival. From experiments on 14 such species reviewed by Martin (1987), 13 recorded increased chick starvation and reduced overall production of young. The implications were that food was not sufficiently plentiful to enable the female alone to raise as many young as the pair together, and that they were operating close to the food limit.

These various types of experiments confirm that food supply can be important in limiting breeding output in at least some types of bird, drawn from a wide range of species. This limitation arises because adult birds are constrained by their food-gathering abilities in the numbers of eggs they can produce or in the numbers of young they can feed. Even with food available in the environment, individual adults may be unwilling to increase their daily work above a certain level if this would harm their future survival and reproductive success. In precocial species such as ducks and gamebirds, the chicks seek their own food under parental guidance, but cannot obtain enough when food is scarce.

FOOD AND ADULT MORTALITY

Most direct information on the causes of mortality in full-grown birds comes from autopsies of birds found dead, among which starved individuals can be recognised by their low weights, absence of body-fat, and emaciated pectoral and other muscles. Because autopsy samples usually depend on carcasses found by chance, they almost certainly give an unrepresentative cross-section of mortality causes. Particular problems are that birds consumed by predators cannot be examined, and many starving birds are almost certainly caught and eaten before they can die from weight loss, so that victims of both predation and starvation are under-recorded in carcass samples. Nevertheless, in some species, starvation accounted for a substantial proportion of recorded deaths – some 29% of 616 Kestrels, 26% of 1,101 Barn Owls, 18% of 172 Tawny Owls, and 18% of 123 Long-eared Owls found dead in Britain (Hirons *et al.* 1979, Newton *et al.* 1982, 1997a, Wyllie *et al.* 1996). In other species, starvation appeared rare or non-existent, accounting, for example, for none of 407 Mute Swans found dead in Britain (Birkhead 1982, Sears 1988, Spray & Milne 1988), although heavy losses of Mute

FIG 32. Barn Owl *Tyto alba*, a rodent-dependent species in which individuals frequently die of food shortage in snowy winters. (Chris Knights)

Swans to starvation occurred elsewhere during unusually hard winters (Bacon & Andersen-Harild 1989, Meek 1993).

Other information on causes of mortality has come from samples of radio-tagged birds, in which each individual was followed until its death. This method is assumed to give unbiased information on the causes of death. For example, 37% of 67 Goshawks that died in Sweden had starved, against none of 207 Red Grouse that died in southern Scotland (Kenward *et al.* 1993, Redpath & Thirgood 1997). Other information on the causes of death in birds has come from reports of ringed birds, but here one is further restricted to forms of death easily recognised by the finder, without the benefit of autopsies. In summary, all these sources of information, biased as some may be, confirm that full-grown birds of various species frequently starve to death, but suggest that the proportion relative to other deaths varies greatly between species.

Deaths of adult birds from starvation are usually restricted to the non-breeding season, when food is scarcest. In many species, it is only at times of massive food shortage, such as during intense cold or drought, that starving birds are much in evidence (Chapter 14). Most examples of weather-induced starvation involve small songbirds, waders and waterfowl, birds of prey and occasionally seabirds. Among large concentrations of birds, the death toll can be spectacular. Examples include the 18,000 water-birds (including 14,000 diving ducks) that died on the Dutch Wadden Sea in March 1986, or the 14,000 Eiders that starved off Denmark in the winter of 1981–82, and the estimated 21,000 Eiders that died on the Wadden Sea mainly in the mild winter of 1999–2000 out of a total wintering population of around 120,000 individuals (Wrånes 1988, Suter & van Eerden 1992, Camphuysen *et al.* 2002). In the last case, starvation was judged as the primary cause of death, caused by human overfishing of Cockles, Mussels and Trough Shells, which were the main foods of Eiders in this area. Nevertheless, about 94% of the birds examined were also infested with

FIG 33. Oystercatcher *Haematopus ostralegus*, in which mass mortality events in winter have been associated with shortage of its main foods (cockles and mussels), caused by human overfishing. (Edmund Fellowes)

an intestinal parasite, a thorny-headed worm, *Profilicollis botulus* (see Chapter 9). Although such high infection rates were considered 'normal' in this species, they may have exacerbated the effects of food shortage.

Shortage of Cockles through overfishing and poor recruitment has also caused increased mortalities among Oystercatchers and Knots in the Dutch Wadden Sea (Ens *et al*. 2004, Kraan *et al*. 2009), and of Oystercatchers on the Wash in eastern England and at Traeth Lathan in north Wales (Atkinson *et al*. 2003, 2005). On the Wash, in the 1990s, Oystercatcher numbers declined from 44,000 to 11,000 birds. As shellfish reached record lows from overfishing, the mortality rates of Oystercatchers rose in three winters to 5–13 times higher than in previous years. Thousands of dead birds were found in late winter, apparently starved. Shellfish decline was confined to these sites, and Oystercatcher numbers across the rest of Britain were stable or increasing.

Mass mortality among Oystercatchers in the Wadden Sea occurred only when both Mussel and Cockle stocks were low. At these times Oystercatchers took small Cockles, Baltic Tellins, Soft-shelled Clams and Lugworms, but their intake rates were low. Normally, these organisms are of low value to Oystercatchers, and not a major component of the diet. During cold weather they also tend to become less available as they burrow deeper in the mud, beyond the reach of Oystercatchers. Prevailing daylengths and the number of hours that tidal mudflats remain exposed also influence the situation. Feeding inland can be regarded as a 'top-up' strategy, practised by a proportion of Oystercatchers, normally at high tide when the main feeding areas are flooded and marine prey are unavailable. During the three mass-mortality events on the Wash, many more birds than usual fed inland on grass fields and amenity grasslands, even on roundabouts in busy roads, but there was little evidence of mass movements to other estuaries, which may in any case have been full to capacity.

Staying with mollusc-eaters, Knots also declined by 44% on the Dutch Wadden Sea (from 60,200 to 34,000) between 1996 and 2005, owing to a decline in Cockle settlement (Kraan *et al.* 2009). Annual mortality of Knots increased from 11% to 18% over the same period, but this accounted for only part of the decline, the remaining birds having moved elsewhere. As on the Wash, the Cockles were fished by hydraulic suction-dredging, a method which not only removes full-size Cockles but also reduces settlement in future years through disrupting sediments. The practice was subsequently banned in the Dutch part of the Wadden Sea.

Among seabirds, food shortage usually affects breeding, but under exceptional shortage adults can also die at greater rates than normal, with recent examples of increased annual mortality in British populations of Guillemots (Reynolds *et al.* 2011), Puffins (Harris & Wanless 2011), Kittiwakes (Oro & Furness 2002, Frederiksen *et al.* 2004b), Arctic Skuas (Davis *et al.* 2005) and Great Skuas (Ratcliffe *et al.* 2002). Elsewhere in Europe, reduced survival in relation to dwindling food supplies has occurred among Guillemots in Norway (Vader *et al.* 1990) and among subadult Common Terns in the German Wadden Sea (Szostek & Becker 2012). During bad weather, which is assumed to make feeding difficult, mass mortalities of some seabirds occasionally occur through 'wrecks', when thousands of poor-condition birds are washed up dead (Chapter 14).

Further evidence for the influence of food supply on the survival of full-grown birds has come from correlations, over several years, between mean annual (or overwinter) survival and measures of food supply. In various species, mean survival rates were higher in years of plenty than in years of scarcity, with juveniles usually affected more than adults. Such relationships have been found in a wide range of species, from Great Tit and Nuthatch to Barn Owl, Turtle Dove and Oystercatcher (Perrins 1979, van Balen 1980, Nilsson 1982, Taylor 1994, Atkinson *et al.* 2003, Verhulst *et al.* 2004, Eraud *et al.* 2009).

Experiments on the effects of food on adult survival

Other evidence has come from experiments in which extra winter food was provided by the researcher. The survival rates of local birds receiving extra food were then compared with those of other birds nearby, which had only natural foods to eat. In such experiments, improved survival (especially of juveniles) was evident in all six species in which survival was measured, being up to twice as high among fed birds as unfed ones. Such species included the Great Tit, Crested Tit, Willow Tit in European studies, and three other species in North American studies. All the species involved were short-lived, with relatively low annual survival rates, and in some cases part of the improvement in survival was attributed to reduced predation, with well-fed birds being less vulnerable (Jansson *et al.* 1981).

CARRY-OVER EFFECTS

Sometimes, food conditions at one time of year can affect the performance of the birds at a later time, through their effects on body condition. Winter conditions can influence subsequent breeding success, and summer conditions can influence subsequent survival, as found in some of the experiments mentioned above. These carry-over effects can be felt at the level of the individual bird or at the level of the entire population. At the level of the individual, birds that are well-fed in winter and spring can accumulate substantial body reserves, which support subsequent reproduction. For example, among wintering Brent Geese, marked females that were seen with offspring in autumn had been heavier at the time of spring departure from their staging areas in the Netherlands than females that returned without young. This difference between the two groups was statistically significant, even after correcting for variation in body size (Ebbinge & Spaans 1995). Males generally accumulated smaller reserves than females, and showed no relationship between body condition and subsequent breeding success. As in all geese, males have a less demanding role in breeding than females, so do not need such large body reserves.

At the level of the population, where all individuals are exposed to similar winter weather, this weather would be expected to affect the average fecundity of the population in the following breeding season. Accordingly, among Whooper Swans wintering in Sweden, the proportion of young in winter flocks was found to be correlated with the mean temperature over the preceding winter (see Chapter 14, Fig. 150c). The interpretation was that in mild winters, the adult swans achieved better body condition, enabling them to produce more young the following breeding season, as evident on their return to wintering areas. In some species of migratory geese, in years when feeding conditions in wintering or spring staging areas were poor, smaller proportions of females laid eggs, and clutches were smaller, than in years when conditions in these areas were good. This was shown, for example, among Barnacle Geese wintering in Britain and Ireland and Lesser Snow Geese in Canada (Cabot & West 1973, Davies & Cooke 1983, Trinder *et al.* 2009). These various studies implied that breeding success of some migratory waterfowl depended partly on feeding conditions experienced in wintering and spring staging areas, which influenced the body reserves accumulated.

Following food-induced mortality of Eiders in the Wadden Sea in the winter/ spring of 1999/2000, the numbers of local breeding pairs had fallen by 38%, and females began laying 2–3 weeks later than in the three previous years. Clutch sizes did not differ between years, but hatching success declined from 41% in 1999 to 18% in 2000. In this latter year many of the females deserted their eggs

FIG 34. Pair of Whooper Swans *Cygnus cygnus* with five young. The annual production of young depends partly on weather during the preceding winter, affecting body condition of the adults. (Edmund Fellowes)

before hatch, often within two weeks after incubation began. Only a quarter as many chicks hatched in 2000 as in 1999. Like some Arctic-nesting geese, Eiders accumulate body reserves in late winter, and do not feed during egg-laying and incubation, so food shortage in the preceding winter may have caused poor body condition and breeding failure in many of these birds (Oosterhuis & van Dijk 2002). In addition, on the Farne Islands, female Eiders that bred in poor years (with much non-breeding and low clutch sizes) suffered higher subsequent mortality (Coulson 1984). In other words, among female Eiders, poor food supply in one winter may result in poor breeding the following spring, and among birds that attempt to breed, poorer survival through the next winter.

Other carry-over effects are apparent in smaller birds in which breeding depends less heavily on prior body reserves. Among colour-ringed Black-tailed Godwits, individuals that occupied the best wintering habitat (offering higher feeding and survival rates) were able to depart earlier on spring migration, and were then first to arrive in their Icelandic breeding areas. They thereby acquired the best nesting habitat (offering higher prey densities and breeding success), and subsequently produced more young, on average, than later-arriving individuals that had occupied poorer winter territories. In this way, the effects of winter habitat carried through the whole annual cycle, from the British Isles to Iceland (Gill *et al.* 2001, Gunnarsson *et al.* 2005).

Individual Swallows were affected by conditions in African wintering areas, as judged from the annual state of the vegetation there,[4] which depends on rainfall. Years with good vegetation growth (and presumably insect activity) in African wintering areas were followed by earlier arrival and egg-laying in Italian breeding areas, more second broods and an increase in the total seasonal production of

---

4 Recorded as the 'normalised difference vegetation index' (NDVI), high values of which reflect higher photosynthetic activity and hence greater plant growth than in years with low values. These indices may be recorded from images taken from satellites.

young, compared with other years (Saino *et al.* 2004a, 2004b). This relationship was apparent at the level of the population, and also in individual adults that were studied in consecutive breeding seasons. Similar carry-over effects from winter to summer, affecting migration dates and breeding, were described in another population of Swallows nesting in Denmark (Møller & Hobson 2004), and in various New World songbirds (Bearhop *et al.* 2004, Norris *et al.* 2004).

In addition, events in breeding areas can apparently affect subsequent survival in migration or wintering areas. This was evident among Sand Martins, in which heavy summer rain in breeding areas in central England was associated with reduced subsequent survival of adults (Cowley & Siriwardena 2005). A more detailed example concerns female Barnacle Geese, in which non-breeders (that had made no nesting attempt) survived significantly better than failed breeders, which in turn survived slightly better than successful breeders. The annual survival rates in the three groups were 95%, 86% and 82% respectively (Prop *et al.* 2004). In other words, reproduction in these geese had a cost which was reflected in reduced subsequent survival. In male geese, which played no part in incubation and were free to feed throughout, survival did not differ significantly according to breeding status.

Experimental evidence that reproduction could affect subsequent survival emerged when artificially increased brood sizes resulted in reduced body condition and subsequent survival of parents. This was demonstrated in field trials on Kestrels (Dijkstra *et al.* 1990), Pied Flycatchers (Askenmo 1979), Collared Flycatchers (Cichón *et al.* 1998), Blue Tits (Nur 1988) and Great Tits (Visser & Lessells 2001). The implication was that parents worked so hard to feed their enlarged broods that they lost body condition, with effects on their subsequent survival. Although poor body condition was experimentally induced, it confirmed that events acting at the time of breeding could influence the later survival of individuals. In some experiments, effects of hard work and reduced body condition in one breeding season were also carried over to reduced breeding success in the following year, as found, for example, in Blue Tits and Rooks (Nur 1988, Roskaft 1985).

In yet other experiments, researchers provided additional food to parents who were raising young in conditions of poor natural food supply. They found not only that parents reared more chicks, but also that subsequent parental survival was increased over that of unfed pairs. Among Arctic Skuas in Shetland, pairs that were given supplementary food in the chick-rearing period showed significantly higher nest attendance, improved breeding success and higher return rates than unfed pairs nesting nearby (Davis *et al.* 2005). The return rates of fed birds were around 90%, similar to previous measures from this population during a period of abundant food, but they compared with a 73% return rate among unfed birds during the prevailing period of food shortage.

Similarly, among Kittiwakes in Shetland, availability of food (sandeels) influenced the body condition of adults at the end of the breeding season, and their subsequent survival, as again assessed from return rates (Oro & Furness 2002). The act of rearing chicks in years of food shortage caused a reduction in the body condition and fat level of parent Kittiwakes, and led to reduced subsequent survival rates compared with other Kittiwakes whose chicks were removed, relieving them of parental duties and thereby improving their body condition (Jacobsen *et al.* 1995, Golet *et al.* 1998, Golet & Irons 1999). In addition, a study of Puffins showed that, following reduced reproductive effort in one year (through supplementary feeding), individual adults showed not only improved survival the following year but also improved breeding success, compared to other birds which had received no supplementary food in the previous year (Wernham & Bryant 2002). All these studies, both observational and experimental, across a range of species from songbirds to raptors and seabirds, imply that there can be costs to raising young, which can affect adult body condition and subsequent survival, but that these costs are greater in years of poor food supply.

There is another way in which carry-over effects at the population level are felt, namely through density-dependent effects. In years when birds produce large numbers of young so that post-breeding numbers are high, average mortality during the ensuing winter is often greater than usual. Similarly, in years when winter mortality is higher than usual and breeding populations are low, mean breeding success is often greater than usual (Newton 1998). These tendencies would be expected in any species in which individuals competed for some limited resource, or in which predation or disease effects varied from year to year in a direct density-dependent manner (Chapter 2). Mortality and breeding rates have

FIG 35. The most numerous species of gull in the world, the Kittiwake *Rissa tridactyla*, is also the most pelagic, and the best adapted for nesting on the tiny ledges of vertical sea cliffs. Around Britain and Ireland it feeds mainly on sandeels and other small fish. (Laurie Campbell)

been shown to vary in this way in a number of different bird species,[5] implying that numbers at one time of year can influence the average performance of individuals subsequently. Among migrants, the crucial conditions may be experienced in one region, while the effects are manifest later in another region far away.

CONCLUDING REMARKS

One might expect that food supply would influence the breeding and survival of individual birds. But demonstrating this effect depends on measurements not only on the birds themselves but also on their natural food supply, or on experiments in which the food supply can be manipulated artificially. These requirements reduce the range of species on which such studies can be made, because many birds exploit too wide a variety of food types for them all to be measured, or they eat foods that cannot be provided artificially. Without experiments, we have to rely on measurements of the performance of birds in relation to naturally occurring changes in food supplies, either year-to-year or place-to-place, from which correlations can be derived and tested. In experimental studies, we have to monitor the survival and breeding of fed birds, to compare with those of other, unfed control birds nearby. But whether from observational or experimental studies, in many species food emerges as a major factor influencing breeding output, and occasionally also survival, overriding any additional influence of other potential limiting factors.

The fact that some birds die of starvation, or that survival and reproductive rates can be influenced by food supply, does not on its own mean that food supply affects subsequent breeding densities. Indeed, in some winter feeding experiments, improved overwinter survival did not lead to higher local breeding density (which was evidently limited by some other factor), but merely to greater emigration before nesting began (Brittingham & Temple 1988, Desrochers *et al.* 1988). In other situations, reduced losses from food shortage might be compensated by greater losses from some other cause, such as predation, giving no apparent effects on population levels. Nevertheless, there is no question that food supply can in some circumstances have a major influence on bird breeding densities, an aspect discussed in the next chapter.

---

5 Mortality has been shown to vary from year to year in a density-dependent manner in many species, including Sedge Warbler, Blackcap, Whitethroat, Willow Warbler, Pied Flycatcher, Redstart, Redshank, Mallard, Shoveler and Barnacle Goose. Breeding success has been shown to vary in this way in Great Tit, Nuthatch, Pied Flycatcher, Grey Partridge, Shelduck, Barnacle Goose, Avocet, and Oystercatcher, among others (original references in Newton 1998: 104–5).

CHAPTER 4

Food Supplies: Population Impacts

IRCUMSTANTIAL EVIDENCE FOR THE INFLUENCE of food supplies on
bird populations comes primarily from correlations between changes
in bird numbers and changes in food supplies – either from time to
time or from place to place. Such correlations are evident at various spatial scales,
from particular localities to large geographical regions, and at temporal scales
from a few minutes (as in seabirds attracted by surface fish) to periods of years.
Examples derive from various songbirds, raptors, shorebirds, seabirds and others,
in all of which individuals occur at greatest density when or where their food is
most plentiful. For present purposes, such correlations can be divided into three
main types:

(1) Progressive changes in bird numbers, continuing over periods of years, and
associated with long-term changes in food supplies. Some such changes occur
naturally, for example as a marsh dries or a forest grows, but many in the
modern world result from human activities, especially in land use and fisheries.

(2) Annual or other short-term fluctuations in bird numbers which match
similar fluctuations in food supplies. Such associations are most apparent in
species that exploit variable food sources, such as tree-seed crops or rodent
plagues, which provide abundant food in some years but not in others.

(3) Consistent spatial variations in bird numbers which are associated with
spatial variations in food supplies. Some such variations are associated
with regional differences in underlying rock or soil type, which influence
biological productivity, including bird food supplies. In marine areas, they
are associated with geographical variations in currents and the nutrient
content of sea water.

The sections below illustrate these various relationships in particular kinds of birds, which have been well studied but differ markedly in the types of foods they eat. Later in the chapter, we will turn to some experimental evidence showing the influence of food supplies on bird numbers.

Birds react to changes in their food supplies in two main ways (Newton 2002). One is by their movement and settlement patterns, as individuals concentrate in places where food is plentiful and leave areas where food is scarce. By moving around in this way, birds can respond to changes in food supplies more or less immediately, so that their local densities match food supplies at the time. On a longer timescale, they can also respond to food supplies through changes in local survival or reproductive success. Response by reproduction produces a lag – the time taken to breed – so that high breeding densities typically follow good food supplies and low densities follow poor supplies. The two responses (simultaneous and delayed) are not mutually exclusive, as many bird species respond to a local increase in food supply both by immigration and by enhanced survival and breeding success. However, on the same local food supply, different species may respond in different ways, as exemplified below.

RAPTORS AND OTHER PREDATORY BIRDS

Those species that depend on cyclically fluctuating prey provide examples of both types of responses to changes in food supplies (Newton 2002). In many parts of the world, including Britain and Ireland, small rodents in grassland typically fluctuate on a 3–5-year cycle of abundance; but in North America hares fluctuate on an approximately ten-year cycle in boreal forest and grassland (Elton 1942, Lack 1954, Keith 1963, Sundell et al. 2004). The numbers of certain grouse species also fluctuate cyclically, in some regions in parallel with the rodent cycle, in others with the longer hare cycle, and in yet others apparently independently of both rodents and hares (Chapter 7). Within each of these prey species, numbers do not reach a peak simultaneously over their whole range, but the peak may be synchronised over thousands of square kilometres. In Fennoscandia, the periodicity of vole cycles tends to increase northwards from about three years between peaks at 60° N to about five years between peaks at 70° N. The amplitude of the cycles also increases northwards from barely discernible cycles south of 60° N to marked fluctuations at 70° N, where peak vole densities typically exceed troughs by more than 100-fold (Hanski et al. 1991). Where more than one rodent species is involved, the synchrony between their cycles also tends to increase northwards, which further accentuates the

FIG 36. The Short-eared Owl *Asio flammeus* concentrates to breed each year in areas with abundant voles, raising large broods when conditions are favourable. (Chris Knights)

fluctuations. While it is uncertain what role food plays in the cycles of these mammalian prey species, there is little doubt about their avian predators, all of which tend to breed most densely and prolifically in conditions of peak prey numbers.[6]

In Britain, Kestrels, Short-eared Owls and Long-eared Owls respond to peaks in vole numbers mainly by immigration, and in Europe other species show similar mobility. In the farmlands of southern Europe, they include the Montagu's Harrier, in the northern boreal forest zone, the Hawk Owl and Tengmalm's Owl, and in the tundra zone, the Snowy Owl, Short-eared Owl and Rough-legged Buzzard. Most of these species also move south to some extent for the winter, especially in years when rodents are scarce in the breeding range, but the Montagu's Harrier moves out totally each autumn to winter on the African grasslands. Long-eared and Short-eared Owls from northern Europe regularly visit Britain in winter, while Rough-legged Buzzards and Snowy Owls occur more rarely.

Among the more mobile species of vole-eaters, in which individuals may change their breeding areas from year to year, annual fluctuations in local densities can be substantial (Fig. 37). In an area of western Finland, for example, over an 11-year period, numbers of Short-eared Owls varied between 0 and 49 pairs, numbers of Long-eared Owls between 0 and 19 pairs, and Kestrels between 2 and 46 pairs, all in accordance with prevailing spring densities of *Microtus* voles (Korpimäki & Norrdahl 1989, 1991). All these birds were entirely or mainly summer visitors to the area concerned, and settled according to vole densities at the time. In Britain, similar fluctuations in annual breeding densities have been noted in Kestrels, Short-eared Owls and Long-eared Owls in upland areas where they were mainly exploiting cyclically fluctuating Field Voles (Village 1990).

Other vole predators, such as the Ural Owl and Tawny Owl, are residents which turn to other prey when voles are scarce (Saurola 1989, Petty 1992). Because they remain in the same territories year-round, they respond to a vole peak mainly by

6 Study of these cycles has provided great insight into the factors involved, including the role of food supply in predators, but the situation is now changing apparently under the action of climate warming. In many regions cycles have become much less marked since the 1980s, so that predators can no longer take such great advantage of food peaks (Chapter 15).

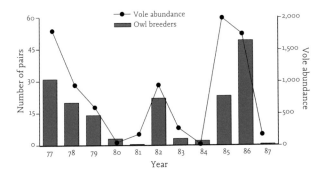

FIG 37. Numbers of Short-eared Owls *Asio flammeus* breeding in an area in Finland each year in relation to the abundance of *Microtus* voles. (From Korpimäki & Norrdahl 1989, 1991)

improved reproduction and survival, reaching peak numbers one or more years after the peak in food supply. The same is partially true for the Barn Owl in Britain (Fig. 39), which remains in the same areas year-round, but whose numbers usually decline most markedly a year after vole numbers have collapsed. However, the Long-tailed Skua, which is a summer visitor to the tundra of northern Europe, returns to the same territories year after year, but breeds only in years when voles or lemmings are sufficiently plentiful.

FIG 38. The Tawny Owl *Strix aluco* retains the same territories from year to year, nesting mainly in tree-cavities, but produces most young in years with abundant rodents. (Peter Beasley)

Year-to-year fluctuations in numbers and breeding success, in response to prey fluctuations, are also apparent in Goshawks and Gyr Falcons in regions where they specialise on grouse or ptarmigan. This seems to be a lagged response, with peaks in raptor breeding populations following peaks in prey numbers. In Iceland, the Ptarmigan fluctuates in long cycles, with peaks averaging 11 years apart, and Gyr Falcons show a similar cycle, but lagging about three years behind (Nielsen 1999, 2011). This would be expected, because Gyr Falcons breed for the first time at about three years of age, so the many young falcons produced in peak Ptarmigan years are recruited to the nesting population about three years later.

Widening the comparison to include other raptorial birds and other prey types,

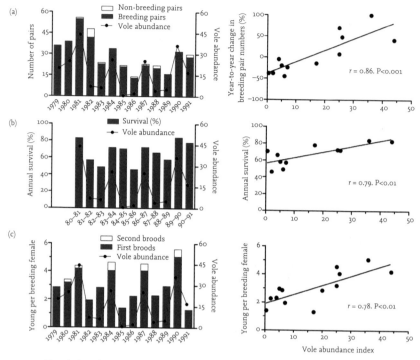

FIG 39. Population change, survival and breeding success of Barn Owls *Tyto alba* in relation to the abundance of Field Voles *Microtus agrestis* in an area of south Scotland. In this population, immigration/emigration was slight and year-to-year changes in numbers were due mainly to local changes in survival and breeding success. (From Taylor 1994)
(a) Numbers of breeding pairs in different years in relation to an index of vole abundance. Owl numbers were higher in the peak vole years, but were also high in the years after the peaks. Changes in the numbers of owls followed changes in the winter/spring vole population (variation 14–54 pairs between years).
(b) Overwinter survival of adults in relation to an index of vole abundance. Survival was highest in the good vole years (variation 20–56% between years).
(c) Number of young produced per breeding female in relation to an index of vole abundance. Production was highest in the good vole years (variation 1.3–5.6 young per pair between years).

three levels of response to annual prey numbers can be recognised (Newton 1979). Those populations that are subject to the most marked prey cycles show big local fluctuations in densities and breeding rates (e.g. Barn Owls in Britain, Kestrels in boreal regions); those subject to less marked prey cycles show fairly stable densities, but big fluctuations in breeding rates (e.g. Buzzards and Tawny Owls in

FIG 40. Gyr Falcon *Falco rusticolus* pair at a breeding site in Iceland (female left). This species fluctuates in numbers and breeding success, according to the cyclically fluctuating numbers of Ptarmigan *Lagopus muta*, the main prey. (Daniel Bergmann)

Britain); while those with fairly stable prey populations show stable densities and fairly stable breeding rates (e.g. Peregrines and Sparrowhawks in Britain). Much depends on how varied the diet is, and whether alternative prey are available

FIG 41. The Ptarmigan *Lapopus muta* is the main prey species of the Gyr Falcon *Falco rusticolus* in Iceland and elsewhere. Its numbers undergo regular cyclic fluctuations, and in Iceland the peaks in numbers come at roughly ten-year intervals. (Edmund Fellowes)

when favoured prey are scarce. The more diverse is the diet, the less the chance of all prey species being scarce at the same time. Raptors that have fairly stable food supplies show some of the most extreme stability in breeding populations recorded in birds, with breeding numbers often varying by no more than 15% of the mean over several decades (Newton 1979). This level of stability has been recorded in a wide range of species, from Sparrowhawks and Peregrines to Golden Eagles, but only in areas where land use remains stable, and where they are not heavily persecuted by gamekeepers (Ratcliffe 1980, Newton 1986, Watson 2010). Moreover, the same species may fluctuate numerically in one region, but not in another, depending on the stability of the local prey supply, as indicated above for the Kestrel and Goshawk in different parts of Europe.

The above relationships provide strong circumstantial evidence that raptor numbers can be influenced by food supplies. Other changes have occurred in recent years which point to the same conclusion. For example, in some species, long-term declines have occurred in association with change in land use which has led to reduction in food supplies. Affected species include vole-eaters, such as the Kestrel and Barn Owl, which have declined in association with reduction in the areas of rough grassland, the main habitat of Field Voles *Microtis agrestis*. In Orkney, the Hen Harrier has also been affected. Here it feeds largely on the Common Vole *Microtus arvalis*, and in the 1970s occurred at some of the highest densities recorded anywhere, with many males mated to more than one female. Over the period 1980–2000, as vole habitat declined under agricultural development, Hen Harrier nest numbers declined by about 70% and overall production of young by about 60%. At the start of this period, about 75% of males bred polygynously, but by 2000 this figure had declined to 15% (Amar & Redpath 2005).

Another example of a sudden decline involved Buzzards in Britain in the early 1950s, following the collapse of Rabbit populations that followed the introduction of the disease myxomatosis. In one area numbers fell from 21 to 14 pairs between one breeding season and the next, and to 12 pairs by the following season (Dare 1961). The opposite situation, where a new food supply led to a rise in breeding density, was illustrated by Red Kites, following the establishment of regular feeding stations, mainly for the benefit of bird-watching tourists. At one such site in central Wales, more than 100 Kites could be seen in the air together, and from the start of feeding in the early 1990s the numbers of pairs nesting within 10 km of the food source increased steadily, at rates becoming more than four times greater than in areas chosen randomly within the breeding range (Cross 2010). This showed how local concentrations of food, consistently available, could promote increased local breeding densities. Overall, then, substantial circumstantial evidence indicates that food supplies influence the population levels of birds of prey, at least in areas where they occur at natural densities.

SEABIRDS

For much of the twentieth century, some seabird species around Britain and Ireland showed unbridled population growth, attributed at least partly to increased food supplies. For some gull species, as mentioned in the previous chapter, the new food sources were largely land-based, provided by sewage outfalls and rubbish dumps. In affluent post-war Britain, rubbish dumps grew in number and size, and people threw out much uneaten food. The clean-air acts of the 1950s increased the waste further, by banning the burning of rubbish in open fires. The main seabird species to take advantage of garbage dumps were the Herring Gull and Lesser Black-backed Gull, and to a smaller extent the Common Gull and Black-headed Gull. All these species increased greatly between the 1950s and 1980s. Some rubbish dumps support huge numbers of birds: the site at Pitsea in Essex is one of the largest in the country, supporting up to 40,000 gulls in winter, along with many corvids and other species.

For most seabird species, however, food supplies were largely or entirely marine-based. One component was the offal and other discards thrown overboard from fishing vessels and factory ships. The spectacular expansion of the Fulmar, which in Britain (excluding St Kilda) increased from 24 pairs in 1878 to nearly 600,000 pairs in 1990 (Mitchell *et al.* 2004), paralleled the growth of the fishing industry and the huge supplies of offal food that followed, first

LEFT: **FIG 42.** The Herring Gull *Larus argentatus* has benefited from food provided at rubbish dumps and sewage outfalls, and from fish processing, but is now declining, as these food sources are diminishing. (Alan Martin)

BELOW LEFT & BELOW: **FIG 43.** The Black-headed Gull *Chroicocephalus ridibundus* is the most widespread gull nesting in Britain and Ireland, with similar numbers breeding inland as on the coast. It often follows the plough, seizing any invertebrates turned to the soil surface. (Alan Martin and Richard Chandler)

from whaling and then from fish trawling. In the 1980s, fishing boats in the waters around Britain were discharging an estimated 95,000 tonnes of offal and 135,000 tonnes of whitefish discards every year, enough to feed a calculated two million scavenging seabirds (Furness *et al.* 1992). Although Fulmars took much of this material, other beneficiaries included Gannet, Great Skua, Great Black-backed Gull, and (in smaller numbers) Lesser Black-backed Gull, Herring Gull and Kittiwake. Among these species, Fulmars tended to dominate in competition for offal, and Gannets and Great Skuas for discards (Furness *et al.* 1992). All these seabirds showed huge increases in numbers during the twentieth century, at least up to the 1980s (Mitchell *et al.* 2004).

Other seabirds benefited from the increased abundance of sandeels and other small fish which supposedly occurred in response to the removal of larger predatory fish (Cod, Herring and Mackerel) for human consumption (Furness 2003). Sandeels form an important part of the chick diet of many seabird species, including terns, auks, Kittiwakes, Shags and others, some of which also eat Sprats and small gadoid fishes. Although all these birds feed largely on sandeels in the breeding season, different species take fish of different sizes, from different depths and from different distances offshore, reducing the potential for competition between them. Not all seabird species fall neatly into one or other of these three dietary categories, however, and the Herring Gull, in particular, exploits all three food sources (garbage, fish waste and live fish).

It is hard to say how much of the increase in seabird numbers over much of the twentieth century was due to increased food supply, and how much to a recovery from past human persecution, but protection was clearly needed before these species could take advantage of burgeoning food supplies. Evidence for the role of food is reinforced by the subsequent declines in the numbers of many species seen from the 1980s on. These declines accompanied changes in the management of land-based waste, making it less available to gulls and other birds; and further declines in fish stocks, including smaller fish, associated with changes in oceanographic conditions and human fishing, with reductions in overall fishing effort, increased mesh sizes and retention rather than dumping of offal (Reeves & Furness 2002, Furness 2003). In particular, during the 1980s and 1990s there was heavy sandeel mortality from industrial fishing, both in the North Sea and around Orkney and Shetland, which contributed to declines in sandeel abundance.

In association with these various changes, overall seabird numbers around Britain and Ireland increased from about 4.5 million pairs around 1969–70 (the years of the first national survey) to 7.5 million pairs around 1985–88 (second national survey), declining back to 4.5 million pairs by 1998–2002 (third survey). The effects of these different changes fell unevenly across species, depending on

FIG 44. Four seabird species which have declined in recent years around northeast Britain, in association with decline in their main summer prey species, the Lesser Sandeel *Ammodytes marinus*. Upper left: Kittiwake *Rissa tridactyla* (Alan Martin). Upper right: Arctic Tern *Sterna paradisaea* (Laurie Campbell). Lower left: Guillemot *Uria aalge* (Kurt Burnham). Lower right: Razorbill *Alca torda* (David Boyle).

their foraging behaviour and dietary ranges. The most marked declines in the overall British and Irish populations between 1985–88 and 1999–2002 occurred in the Arctic Skua (–37%), Roseate Tern (–83%), Arctic Tern (–31%), Little Tern (–23%), Shag (–27%) and Kittiwake (–23%), all largely dependent on sandeels, but most seabird species were affected. In subsequent years the downward trends continued.

The recent declines have been better studied than the earlier increases, and have involved a huge research effort. Effects of food shortages became apparent locally in some species from the mid 1980s, but spread to other species and regions in the ensuing years. The general pattern was of decline in breeding success, with some years of almost total reproductive failure, as seen in Arctic Terns, Arctic Skuas, Kittiwakes, Guillemots and others (Chapter 3). Breeding failures led eventually to reduced recruitment of new breeders, which together with increased mortality of established adults in some species (notably Kittiwakes) led to rapid population declines (e.g. Frederiksen *et al.* 2004b). In addition, under shortage of their main fish diet, Great Skuas began to prey more heavily on other seabirds, especially chicks and adults of Kittiwakes, further hastening their declines (Heubeck *et al.* 1999, Oro & Furness 2002, Votier *et al.* 2004a; Chapter 7).

Arctic Terns have been studied in detail in Orkney and Shetland, where they depend almost entirely on sandeels during the breeding season, their annual productivity being strongly affected by the size of the prevailing stock (Monaghan *et al.* 1989a, 1989b, 1992, Suddaby & Ratcliffe 1997). Ideally, they need juvenile (class 0) fish for small chicks, and older (class 1) fish for older chicks and adults. A rise in local sandeel stocks, which occurred through the 1970s and early 1980s, was accompanied by an increase in breeding numbers of Arctic Terns (Monaghan 1992). Sandeel stocks then declined rapidly during 1983–90, due to poor recruitment of juvenile fish and subsequent decline in the older spawning stock. From 1984, Arctic Terns throughout Shetland experienced almost complete breeding failures for six consecutive years. Clutch sizes were atypically small, eggs were abandoned during incubation, and chicks starved within days of hatching, all symptomatic of severe food shortage (Monaghan *et al.* 1989a, 1989b, 1992). In addition, adult weights were depressed during the period of severe food shortage, and this may have resulted in increased mortality or intermittent breeding which in turn caused the population to decline more rapidly than expected from reproductive failure alone, especially in the early years (Avery *et al.* 1992). Between 1981 and 1992, Arctic Terns on Shetland declined by 55% (Phillips *et al.* 1996). Compared to some other species which eat sandeels, terns suffer from being able to take fish only from near the water surface, from within restricted range of the nesting colonies, and through having no alternative prey abundantly available locally.

In 1990 the Shetland sandeel fishery was closed, and in 1991 the stock recovered owing to large numbers of juvenile fish being swept northward in currents from Orkney. Recruitment of these fish into the Shetland stock resulted in an abundance of adult (class 1) fish in 1992, which bred, producing a carry-over in subsequent years enabling the productivity of Arctic Terns on Shetland to improve (Suddaby & Ratcliffe 1997), as did that of other sandeel-feeders, such as Kittiwakes and Arctic Skuas (Hamer *et al.* 1993, Phillips *et al.* 1996). Tern numbers in Shetland changed little between 1989 and 1994, whilst those on Orkney declined by 47% (Brindley *et al.* 1999). The most plausible explanation for these divergent patterns was that about 10,000 Arctic Terns shifted from Orkney to Shetland to take advantage of improved food availability there, effectively following the sandeels northward. Improvements in productivity on Shetland in response to increased sandeel availability in the 1990s probably allowed the population of the Northern Isles as a whole to recover slightly between 1994 and 2000, but the effects of poor recruitment were felt for further years. Over the period 1987–94, variations in sandeel abundance (classes 0 and 1 together) accounted for 96% of the variation in chicks raised per pair. In

FIG 45. The Black Guillemot *Cepphus grylle* occurs around rocky coasts. It has declined less markedly than other auks in recent years, probably because it takes a wider range of prey species, including the Butterfish *Golis gunellus* shown here. (Jack Stevens)

subsequent years, as sandeels declined again, so did the breeding success of the main sandeel-feeders – Arctic Terns, Arctic Skuas, Kittiwakes and Guillemots. In contrast, Common Terns avoided these effects, owing to their more catholic diet, as they turned instead to small gadoid fish, such as Saithe (Uttley *et al.* 1989). Similarly, the Black Guillemot declined much less markedly than other auks, possibly because it feeds not only on sandeels, but on a variety of other inshore fish, including Butterfish, so it has an alternative food source.

The cause of the massive decline in Lesser Sandeels in the seas of northeastern Britain in the 1990s has still not been fully resolved, partly because it coincided with two major events, namely an increase of large-scale industrial

FIG 46. The Common Tern *Sterna hirundo* is the most familiar of the terns nesting in Britain and Ireland, occurring around most of the coastline, and inland on lakes, reservoirs and gravel-pits. With its more varied habitat and diet, it has suffered much less than the Arctic Tern from the decline in Lesser Sandeels *Ammodytes marinus*. (Alan Martin)

fishing for sandeels, and profound oceanographic changes, including a gradual warming of the North Sea. Throughout this period, the Kittiwake was studied in detail on the Isle of May, in the Firth of Forth off eastern Scotland (Frederiksen *et al.* 2004b). In these birds, annual survival and breeding success were low when the sandeel fishery was active (1991–98), and also after winters with relatively high sea-surface temperatures (when sandeel recruitment was reduced). The observed changes in annual survival and reproduction of Kittiwakes could explain the changes in population trend from +8% per year in the late 1980s to –11% per year in the late 1990s. Modelling showed that Kittiwake numbers were unlikely to recover if the fishery remained active or if sea temperatures increased further, and that numbers were almost certain to decline if both occurred. Following a 50% decline in the Kittiwake population in the northern North Sea during the 1990s, the fishery in the western part was closed in 2000 as a precautionary measure. For a time Kittiwakes bred well, but under a continuing rise in sea temperatures, sandeels continued to decline, along with Kittiwakes and other seabird species that depended on them.

The remote islands of the St Kilda group hold the biggest concentrations of seabirds around Britain. Since the first count in 1969, many species have declined steadily there, including Puffin, Kittiwake and three *Larus* gull species. The reasons may be various, but there is no evidence that these birds have suffered from overfishing of sandeels (the west of Scotland fishery has always been inshore and negligible) or any other fish, but sandeels and Sprats have probably declined in response to oceanographic changes or to the known increase in Herring stocks, leading to greater predation.

Other changes in seabird populations, related to changes in food supplies, have been described in continental Europe. For example, a decline in Common Terns since 1980 was associated with a reduced availability of small fish in the German Wadden Sea (Szostek & Becker 2012); declines in Guillemots and others paralleled the collapse of Capelin stocks in 1985–86 in the southern Barents Sea (Vader *et al.* 1990); while a marked decline in Lesser Black-backed Gulls in Norway since 1970 coincided with a decline of spring-spawning Herring, itself associated with warming sea and air temperatures (Bustnes *et al.* 2010). Meanwhile, the numbers of Lesser Black-backed Gulls, Guillemots and Razorbills nesting on a Swedish island changed over a 50-year period in parallel with one another, and in parallel with the changing biomass of Sprats in the Baltic Sea (Hjernquist & Hjernquist 2010). Similar marked changes have occurred periodically in seabirds elsewhere in the world, linked either with fishing activities (Chapter 11) or with natural events, such as changes in sea currents, which have affected local fish stocks (Chapter 15).

For some seabird species, as indicated already, attempts have been made to find which demographic variables were associated with the declines. In certain species, after the collapse of fish stocks, declines in breeding numbers were attributed primarily to low recruitment after several years of poor breeding (for Puffin in Norway, see Anker-Nilssen 1987; for Arctic Tern in Shetland, see Monaghan et al. 1989b). In other species, declines were attributed to increased overwinter mortality of adults (for Guillemot in the Barents Sea, see Vader et al. 1990; for Guillemot and Shag in Shetland, see Furness & Barrett 1991). In yet other species, declines were attributed to a combination of poor breeding and increased mortality (for Great Skuas in Shetland, see Ratcliffe et al. 2002; for Kittiwakes on the Isle of May, see Frederiksen et al. 2004b). The differences between species in the importance of poor breeding or enhanced mortality depended largely on the extent to which alternative foods were available in summer or winter, and, as expected, declines in breeding numbers were most rapid when they involved increased adult mortality.

Like other birds, seabirds can offset declines in food supply to some extent by working harder to get it, perhaps foraging for longer each day and at greater distances, by taking alternative (but usually less nutritious) foods, or by reducing nest attendance to release more time for foraging. However, all these behaviours have costs in reduced body condition and survival of adults, or in increased exposure of chicks to predation (Hamer et al. 1993, Phillips et al. 1996). They are not sufficient to offset big reductions in food availability. In a good food year, adult radio-tagged Kittiwakes foraged within 5 km of the colony, but in a poor year they foraged more than 40 km from the colony and stayed away for three times as long (up to 44 hours) before relieving a mate at the nest (Hamer et al. 1993). In the poor year, both adults were sometimes away at the same time during the nestling period, leaving their chicks exposed to predation. Adults examined during incubation had lower body weights, so were less able to resist shortages. As alternative foods, Kittiwakes are known to take Whiting and Saithe, which are of much lower calorific value than sandeels, and in some years also Snake Pipefish, which contain little of nutritional value, and are almost impossible for chicks to swallow (Chapter 19).

Unlike many other seabird species around Britain and Ireland, the Gannet and Cormorant increased continuously over recent decades. Gannets feed not only on fish discards, but also on mid-sized fish such as Herring and Mackerel, which they obtain by plunge diving. After past overexploitation, these fish are now abundant around our coasts, and there has been little recent demand for Herring. Cormorants have increased in recent decades partly through a rapid growth of inland breeding in England, coinciding with a rising food supplies from inland waters stocked with fish, the low levels of competition enabling inland-nesting Cormorants to breed more successfully than coastal pairs (Newson 2000, Carss & Elkins 2002). Around the year 2000, more than 1,300 pairs nested at inland sites, forming about 10% of the entire British and Irish populations. Many of these inland birds were of the continental race *P. c. sinensis*.

These various data indicate that, at least in recent decades, the numbers of many species of seabirds around Britain and Ireland have changed repeatedly, upwards or downwards, in relation to changes in food supplies. In other words, they are apparently food-limited. The fact that different bird species depending on the same prey species fluctuate in parallel with one another adds strength to the argument.

Changes in sewage disposal and fishing pressures also affected shellfish-eating species, such as the Oystercatcher and Eider. These species increased through much of the twentieth century, in association with reduction in the commercial exploitation of shellfish, itself the result in some areas of growing pollution, especially from sewage outfalls from coastal towns and cities. However, as sewage treatments improved from the 1970s, nutrient input to the sea decreased, mussels and cockles then declined or became fit for human consumption, which led to a resumption of commercial fishing, and to collapse in the numbers of mussel-eating birds. Such changes occurred around the North Sea and Baltic coasts (Camphuysen *et al.* 2002, Christensen 2008).

Some species declined rapidly, in response to a sudden drop in food supply. Near Edinburgh in southeast Scotland, every year some 17,000 sea-ducks wintered offshore. They fed on the rich invertebrate life that was in turn fed by raw sewage from the large human population of the region. The sewage was discharged at eight main outfalls distributed along 15 km of shoreline. After the construction of a new sewage processing plant in 1978, and the consequent reduction in organic input, the marine invertebrates declined, and in two years the total duck population had fallen to about 3,000, about 18% of the original number (Campbell 1984). Between the winters of 1975/76 and 1979/80, Scaup numbers fell to only 7% of their original 10,000, Goldeneye to 26% of their original 2,000, Common Scoters to 11% of their original 400, and Eiders to 41% of their original 3,800, while Long-tailed Ducks remained at around 220–250 throughout. The remaining ducks concentrated around outfalls that continued to discharge some raw sewage. Other studies, elsewhere in Britain, documented similar sudden declines in the numbers of waterfowl, gulls and shorebirds, following the installation of sewage treatment plants during the 1960s–1980s (Furness *et al.* 1986, Raven & Coulson 2001). Some of the species involved, notably gulls, ate the solid matter itself, while others benefited from the invertebrates that thrived on the added nutrient. Mussel-feeding Eiders were apparently affected by this

FIG 47. Goldeneye *Bucephala clangula* (left) and Scaup *Aythya marila* (right), two duck species which benefited from the rich invertebrate life found around sewage outfalls. (Richard Chandler)

reduction in food supply in many northern coastal areas of Britain, including those nesting on islands off the Northumbrian coast (Coulson 2010).

Years of serious fishing pressure, mainly using suction dredging, led to big declines of shellfish resources in several major estuaries, and corresponding declines in shellfish-eating birds. In the Wadden Sea, Oystercatchers, most of which breed in the Netherlands, showed a steep decline, incurring the greatest losses at times when high food demands coincided with restricted access to partially ice-covered mudflats during severe winters (Camphuysen *et al.* 1996, 1999). Eider ducks, consisting of local breeders and a much larger contingent of wintering birds from the Baltic, also showed mass starvation and movements out of the Wadden Sea (Camphuysen *et al.* 2002). Similar large-scale reductions also occurred among Oystercatchers on the Wash during the same period, again through shortage of Cockles and other shellfish (Atkinson *et al.* 2003). Oystercatchers and Eiders are large birds, and their deaths are easily recorded, autopsies confirming the role of starvation (Chapter 3).

Over the ten years 1996–2005, Cockles were progressively reduced in abundance in the Dutch Wadden Sea, so that by the end of this period, they remained sufficiently plentiful for birds in only 45% of their former area (Kraan *et al.* 2009). Being dependent on cockles, wintering Knots declined over the same period to about 56% of their former level. Survival, as assessed from colour-ringed birds, fell from 89% in the first part of the study to 82% in the latter part, accounting for almost half the decline in numbers; the remaining birds that went missing having moved elsewhere to winter (Chapter 3). Throughout the ten years, densities of Knots in suitable foraging areas remained roughly constant, which suggests that throughout this period they used the available area to maximum capacity, as set by the food supply. This constant density averaged about 10 birds per hectare, allowing for the fact that the Knots fed in large and dense flocks which occupied only part of the mudflats at any one time.

In recent decades, as mentioned above, enormous volumes of waste food have been discarded at rubbish dumps, providing abundant feeding opportunities for gulls and other scavenging birds. Refuse tips are known to affect the numbers and breeding success of birds that use them, as shown by studies on Herring Gulls (Pons 1992, Pons & Migot 1995, Kilpi & Öst 1998), Black-headed Gulls (Lebreton & Isenmann 1976), White Storks (Massemin-Challet *et al.* 2006) and others. The trend away from refuse tips for waste disposal, and changed management of existing tips which includes the use of smaller active work areas, rapid covering of dumped material and bird control practices, means that there are now fewer scavenging opportunities for gulls and other birds (Pons & Migot 1995, Kilpi & Öst 1998). One of the main beneficiaries of rubbish tips in Britain and Ireland – the Herring Gull – has halved in numbers since 1970, and effects on specific colonies have been documented. The dependence of Herring Gulls on refuse tips was confirmed by diet studies. For instance, in the Bristol Channel, 70% of the food taken during the breeding season was from tips (Mudge 1978), and in Brittany some 61–85% was derived from this source (Pons 1992). The breeding success of Herring Gulls nesting close to tips was better than those nesting further away, and when the amount of refuse dumped at one site was reduced by 80%, the breeding numbers of Herring Gulls nesting 12 km away were reduced by 12% between 1988 and 1989, and breeding success from 1.3 to 0.5 young per pair (Pons 1992).

While the general trend of the Herring Gull population in Britain since the 1970s has been downward, in some situations numbers have increased, and over the years some colonies seemed to grow and then decline, as local food supplies waxed and waned. In recent years colonies have grown in the west of Scotland in association with the construction of Salmon farms, and elsewhere numbers have increased following the proliferation of fast-food outlets in towns and cities, resulting in more food being discarded in open-topped bins or onto roads and pavements where it is taken by gulls and other scavengers (Rock 2003). Many gulls in seaside towns also obtain food directly from tourists, and these urban food sources may have encouraged the recent rapid growth of inner-city gull populations (Chapter 5), in the face of more general declines elsewhere.

It is not only gulls that have been affected by changes in the management of garbage. One study examined the effects of rubbish dumps on Rooks in Spain (Olea & Baglioni 2008). The entire Spanish population of around 2,000 pairs was distributed in 15–20 colonies in a relatively small area in the northeast, isolated from other populations. Over a 28-year period from 1976, birds in colonies that were within 10 km of tips fed largely on refuse, especially during periods of low natural food availability. The influence of this food source on breeding numbers was shown by the facts that: (1) the two populations with access to tips increased

2.1 and 3.7 times more than the one without a tip nearby, and (2) the number of breeding pairs in refuse-feeding colonies declined rapidly after the closure of two local tips in 1996 and 2000, and recovered only when a supply of refuse was restored. Similarly, in Finland, the decline of Eagle Owl numbers since the 1990s has been associated with the closure of more than 90% of local rubbish dumps, which had previously offered a stable and abundant food supply in the form of rats (Saurola 2009). An EU directive encouraging the closure of open tips across Europe is likely to have major effects on other scavenging species. In addition to the gulls and corvids found at dumps in Britain, refuse-feeding species in southern Europe include White Storks, Red and Black Kites, Egyptian Vultures, Yellow-legged and Audouin's Gulls.

SEED-EATING BIRDS

The seeds of most herbaceous and woody plants develop during spring and summer, and reach peak abundance in late summer and autumn, from which time they are gradually shed. Plant species differ in the exact dates at which they form, ripen and shed their seeds. But once on the ground, seeds gradually disappear through soil movements, weathering, germination and the feeding activities of animals. The result is that seed stocks decline over winter. This seasonal pattern, from a late-summer peak to extreme scarcity a few months later, enables some seed-eaters to continue breeding later in the year than most other birds, but means that they are shortest of food in late winter and early spring.

Forest seed-eaters

Some finches, such as the Common Crossbill and Siskin, fluctuate in breeding density from year to year, in parallel with the tree-seed crops on which they depend (Newton 1972, 2008). These crops vary in size from year to year, depending partly on the natural rhythm of the trees themselves and partly on the weather. Trees of some species require more than one year to accumulate the nutrient reserves necessary to produce a seed crop; and for a good crop the weather must ideally be fine and warm in the preceding late summer, when the flower buds form, and again in the spring when the flowers set. Otherwise the crop is delayed for another year. In any one area, most of the trees of the same species fruit in phase with one another, and often trees of different species also fruit in phase, partly because they are influenced by the same weather. This pattern gives an enormous profusion of tree-fruits in certain years and practically none in others, for big crops are nearly always followed by small ones. However,

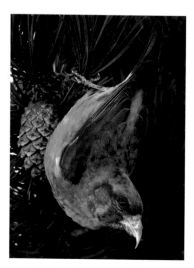

FIG 48. The Common Crossbill *Loxia curvirostra* feeds mainly from the seeds in conifer cones, and concentrates in different areas in different years, wherever the crops are good. (Sean Gray)

the trees in widely separated areas may be on different cropping regimes, partly because of regional variations in weather, so that good crops in some regions may coincide with poor crops in others. Usually, each productive area extends over thousands or millions of square kilometres. In some years, the productive patches are plentiful and widespread, and in others few and far between, so that the total production of seeds over Europe varies greatly from year to year.

Besides their total production, the timings of ripening and release of seeds also influence seed-eating birds. Some tree species release most of their seeds within a short period in autumn, others more slowly over winter, and yet others in spring, or more gradually over two or more years. Prolonged release occurs in some pine and larch species, which can thereby provide food for seed-eaters even in non-cropping years. For most finches, the seeds are readily available while they remain on the tree, but some species can obtain conifer seeds only when the cones open; once seeds fall to the ground they may be rapidly removed by other animals or covered by snow. Among the European finches that depend largely on tree-seeds, only the Brambling and Chaffinch feed mainly from the ground in winter, although others may do so occasionally.

The birds that depend most heavily on tree-seeds generally concentrate wherever their food is plentiful at the time, and ringing has confirmed that individuals may breed or winter in widely separated areas in different years (Newton 1972, 2008). In this way, their numbers in particular localities fluctuate greatly from year to year in parallel with local seed crops, and may range between total absence in years when appropriate tree-seeds are lacking, to thousands of birds per km^2 in years when such seeds are plentiful. Some of the earliest data from a single area were collected by Reinikainen (1937) in mid-Finland. He travelled the same route by ski each Sunday in March for 11 years, counted the Crossbills met on his journeys, and estimated the cone crops of spruce and pine. The numbers of breeding Crossbills seen each year were strongly correlated with the size of the spruce crop (though not with the pine crop), the highest number of

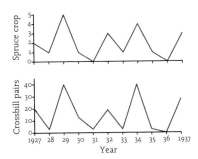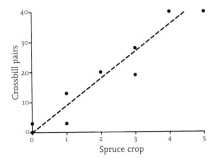

FIG 49. Relationship between the population density of the Common Crossbill *Loxia curvirostra* and the cone crop of Norway Spruce *Picea abies*. Crossbills shown in numbers of pairs per 120 km transect; spruce crops classified in five categories. (From Reinikainen 1937)

birds being 20 times the lowest, with an increase of this order occurring from one year to the next (Fig. 49). Similar relationships between local numbers and local food supplies have been found for Siskins, redpolls and other boreal seed-eaters elsewhere (Haapanen 1965, Newton 1972, Petty *et al.* 1995, Newton 2008).

Such species adjust to changes in their food supplies largely by movements, but they can also produce more young in years of good seed crops. So far as I know, no information is available on year-to-year survival rates of tree-seed-eating finches, but it would not be surprising if their survival rates were also higher in good seed years. Some tree-seed-eaters, notably Crossbills, remain in the boreal forest through most years, moving from area to area in line with seed crops, and leaving southward only in years of widespread crop failure. Other species, such as Siskin and the redpolls, seem to move to lower latitudes each autumn, stopping when they find areas rich in food (Svärdson 1957). In consequence, the distance travelled by the bulk of the migrants varies from year to year, according to where the crops are good, and only when the migrants are exceptionally numerous, or their food is generally scarce, do they reach the furthest parts of their wintering range, as an irruption.

In the various forest seed-eaters, year-to-year correlations between local densities and seed stocks have been described mainly within the northern 'regular' range (Newton 2008). They would not necessarily be expected in the most southerly wintering areas, which the birds reach only in occasional years of food shortage further north. In some years, as observations confirm, seeds are plentiful in southern areas, but no wintering finches arrive to exploit them. In other years, many birds arrive, but local seed crops are poor. This happened in 1983 when huge numbers of Jays arrived in Britain, but there were hardly any acorns on which they could feed (John & Roskell 1985). Other species, such as crossbills and nutcrackers, sometimes migrate beyond the geographical range of their main food-plants, feeding instead on whatever seeds they can find. Mortality is almost certainly heavy in such years.

Some seed-eaters, notably crossbills and some other cardueline finches, can if necessary rear their young on seeds alone, free of the need for insects (Newton 1972). These species can thereby take advantage of abundant seeds, and breed over a longer period in years when seed crops are good. Some seed-eaters, such as redpolls, may even raise successive broods in the same breeding season in localities up to several hundred kilometres apart, as they exploit temporary seed crops in different places at different times (Peiponen 1962, Newton 2008). All these finches fluctuate in numbers in relation to food supplies, which clearly influence their movement patterns, local population levels and breeding output. In the marked fluctuations of their local breeding and wintering populations, boreal tree-seed specialists contrast with some other seed-eaters which feed from many kinds of herbaceous plants, and have more stable food supplies from year to year (Newton 1972).

Farmland seed-eaters

The importance of the seed supply in influencing the numbers of farmland finches is shown by recent trends in their foods and numbers. Many species have declined in recent decades, in association with the loss of their food-plants. Among the finches, the Linnet, Twite and Bullfinch have been most affected, while other seed-eaters that have declined include four buntings (Yellowhammer, Reed, Corn and Cirl), two sparrows (House and Tree), Skylark and Turtle Dove, some 11 species in all.

In all these species, the main causal factor identified in detailed studies was decline in food supply, but some species have also suffered from reduction in habitat (Bullfinch and Turtle Dove through loss of tall hedgerows, Twite through loss of saltmarsh wintering habitat, and Reed Bunting through drainage of wet areas). Declines in food supply were attributed mainly to: (1) herbicide use, which reduces current-year weed-seed production, and leads to long-term depletion of the seed bank in the soil, and (2) loss of winter stubble fields, with their associated weed-seeds and spilled grain, resulting from the switch by farmers mainly in the 1980s from spring-sown to autumn-sown cereals (Newton 2004). The relative importance of these seed sources varies between species, depending on their dietary needs, and the House Sparrow has probably also suffered from the increased bird-proofing of farm-stores for grain and other animal feed. Herbicide use has also reduced the abundance of weed-dependent insects that some seed-eaters feed to their young.

FIG 50. Four species of seed-eating birds which declined greatly in recent decades (1970–2010), in association with the loss of their foods from farmland. Upper left: Tree Sparrow *Passer montanus* declined by more than 90% (Harry Scott). Upper right: Linnet *Carduelis cannabina* declined by more than 50% (Richard Chandler). Lower left: Yellowhammer *Emberiza citrinella* declined by more than 50% (Alan Martin). Lower right: Reed Bunting *Emberiza schoeniclus* declined by more than 30% (Edmund Fellowes).

While living primarily on seeds, these species vary in the extent to which they need insects to feed their young. So for some, shortage of insects (leading to poor chick production), as well as shortage of seeds (leading to poor adult survival), may have contributed to their demise. However, at least six seed-eating species experienced a decline in survival rate during the period of population decline; and in at least four of these, the measured decline in survival was sufficient to account for the observed rate of population decline, without any concurrent change in reproductive rate (Peach *et al.* 1999, Siriwardena *et al.* 1999, Newton 2004). These findings implied that their population declines could be explained by seed declines alone without the need to invoke insect shortages. At least three species did show a decline in seasonal reproductive rate, and in one

(Turtle Dove) this change was judged to be sufficient on its own to account for the observed rate of population decline (Browne & Aebischer 2001). However, this species rears its young on seeds and green leaves, so is again independent of insects. It is mainly the buntings and sparrows in which insect shortages may have contributed to population declines. Changes in the success of individual nesting attempts were recorded in seven seed-eating species (in five increases, in two decreases), but as explained in Chapter 3, in multi-brooded species these measures need not necessarily translate into changes in seasonal production (Siriwardena *et al.* 2000). So the role of insect shortages remains unresolved for some of these seed-eaters.

Even in arable areas, few seeds remain available on the ground from January on, leaving a dearth of food for the rest of the winter. In the past, this late-winter shortage was compensated by the start of spring cultivations from February, which continually brought fresh seeds to the soil surface, making them available to birds. Unlike invertebrate-feeders, such as corvids and gulls, seed-eaters do not have to 'follow the plough', because seeds do not re-bury themselves but can remain available on the surface for weeks afterwards, with more exposed by rainfall. In the past, ploughing, harrowing and sowing continued into April or beyond, as did threshing operations which released seeds stored in cereal ricks, while hay fed each day to stock was another constant source of grass and other seeds. It is this late-winter dearth of food that now provides the bottleneck for some species of seed-eaters and which must be addressed if they are to recover their former numbers, although other seed-eaters now find alternative foods at garden feeders (see below).

In modern farmland, seed-eaters tend to concentrate at any one time in the very few fields that provide food, such as game-cover crops, where seed-eating birds have been found in winter at densities more than 100 times greater than in more conventional crops (Parish & Sotherton 2008). Besides gamebirds, the main beneficiaries of game crops include the Chaffinch, Greenfinch, Linnet and Reed Bunting. Such game crops usually consist of a mixture of cultivated plant species which produce seeds that birds like, such as kale and rape (both brassicas), quinoa (a polygonum), triticale and millet (both cereals) (Stoate *et al.* 2003). These plants are favoured by different bird species; but differ in their dates of seed shedding, and therefore in the amount of food they provide through the winter. Use of nitrogen fertiliser increases the seed yield. Game crops have found favour among farmers because they can usefully be grown in small areas (patches of only a hectare can support hundreds of small birds in winter). But they do not remove the main problem, which is that most of the seed is shed and unavailable after late January, so such crops support fewer birds through the pinch period in late winter and early spring (Siriwardena *et al.* 2008).

The importance of food supplies for farmland seed-eaters has also emerged from comparisons of densities or breeding success: (a) between localities with different food supplies; (b) between organic and conventional farms; (c) between first-year set-aside and cropped fields, (d) between localities with and without pesticide use; or (e) between seed-bearing 'game crops' and conventional crops.[7] In addition, the provision of winter seed sources has promoted increases in the wintering and breeding densities of seed-eating birds, at least at the farm scale (Siriwardena *et al.* 2007, Hinsley *et al.* 2010, RSPB 2012). However, note that temporary concentrations of birds in winter, as occur on weedy fields, do not necessarily lead to increased local breeding densities, as the birds can disperse before the nesting season.

Considering the massive changes that occurred in recent decades under the drive for greater crop production, it is perhaps surprising that some farmland seed-eaters increased in numbers. For those species, a plausible food-related reason for their expansion is apparent. For example, Woodpigeons eat green leaves as well as seeds, and do not require animal matter for their young. In southern Britain, Woodpigeons were once largely dependent in winter on the clover sown into cereal stubbles. As this crop lost favour in the 1960s, Woodpigeons began to decline, but soon increased again when a substitute winter food supply, namely the young leaves of oilseed rape, became widely available (Inglis *et al.* 1990, Isaacson *et al.* 2002). This crop occupied less than 1% of arable land in the 1950s but spread to more than 8% by 2000. This expansion may also have partly supported the increase in Stock Dove numbers since the 1960s. During the period 1970–2002, both these pigeons increased by about 87%, according to BTO surveys (Gregory *et al.* 2004). The seeds of rape also provide food for Linnets and other seed-eaters, but chiefly in the summer, as the fields are usually ploughed after harvest. Unlike the pigeons, these finches cannot survive on a diet of winter rape leaves, so it is doubtful whether their numbers have benefited.

Three species of finches did not decline during the period of agricultural change, namely the Chaffinch (29% increase during 1970–2002), Greenfinch (22% increase) and Goldfinch (35% increase). However, Chaffinches benefit from Pheasant feed sites, which are maintained into the winter, now providing more than an estimated 200,000 tonnes of cereal grains per year nationwide (according to estimates by the GWCT). In addition, Chaffinches and Greenfinches have fed increasingly in gardens since the 1960s, following the

---

7 (a) Donald & Evans 1994, Wilson *et al.* 1996, Robinson & Sutherland 1999, Brickle *et al.* 2000, Moorcroft *et al.* 2002, Hancock & Wilson 2003; (b) Boatman *et al.* 2004, Christensen *et al.* 1996, Wilson *et al.* 1997, Chamberlain *et al.* 1999, Chamberlain & Wilson 2000; (c) Watson & Rae 1997, Henderson *et al.* 2000; (d) Boatman *et al.* 2004; (e) Stoate *et al.* 2003.

FIG 51. The Woodpigeon *Columba palumbus* has increased greatly in recent decades, in association with the growing of oilseed rape, the leaves of which form an important winter food. (Edmund Fellowes)

provision of peanuts and other suitable seeds. The same is true for Goldfinches since the early 1990s, but in any case a large proportion of Goldfinches that breed in Britain winter further south, including Spain, where some favoured food-plants grow and seed throughout the winter (Newton 1972). Changes in the numbers of Goldfinches during 1962–93, both ups and downs, were correlated with measured changes in annual survival rates (Siriwardena *et al.* 2000).

Garden bird feeding

Several seed-eaters have benefited from the growth of garden bird feeding in recent years, and the provision of an ever-widening variety of seeds has gradually expanded the range of species involved. Following the introduction of peanuts for this purpose in the 1960s, Greenfinches and Siskins became regulars, as well as various tits, Nuthatches and Great Spotted Woodpeckers, and following the introduction of nyger seed in the 1990s Goldfinches and then Lesser Redpolls were added, with Siskins gaining additional benefit.[8] Bullfinches were attracted by sunflower seeds, but did not become frequent at garden feeders in Britain until after 2005, and then only in a localised manner.

An estimated 12.6 million (48%) households in Britain frequently provide supplementary food for birds, 7.4 million of which use special seed-holding feeders (Davies *et al.* 2009). A typical feeder holds 350 g of seed, so if each was filled only once, they would together hold a total of 2,590 tonnes. If each bird took only 5 g of food per day, this amount would be equivalent to 518,000,000 'bird-days', or

---

8 Nyger *Guizotia abyssinica* is a tall herb in the family Asteraceae, originally from the Ethiopean Highlands, but now grown widely to provide seeds for aviary birds and garden birds.

FIG 52. The Goldfinch *Carduelis carduelis* has benefited greatly in recent years from the provision of Nyger *Guizotia abyssinica* seed in hanging bird feeders. (Keith Kirk)

enough to feed about 2,830,000 birds every day for six months. Since many people fill their feeders many times each winter, the total amount of food provided is clearly much greater than this. Little wonder that the species which make the greatest use of garden feeders have increased substantially over the past few decades.

In recent years, the numbers of seed-eating birds visiting gardens has been correlated with the crops of wild seeds, with Woodpigeons, Jays, Great Spotted Woodpeckers, Chaffinches, Great Tits and Nuthatches coming to gardens in greatest numbers in years with poor Beech crops (Chamberlain *et al.* 2007), and in northern Britain Siskins and Coal Tits in years with poor Sitka Spruce crops (McKenzie *et al.* 2007). Near forestry plantations, the numbers of Siskins present in gardens varies greatly from day to day, according to weather, as spruce cones open in warm periods and close in wet ones, affecting the availability of their seeds. To judge from winter feeding experiments described later, the presence of this garden food source probably enables these birds to maintain good numbers through poor natural seed years or hard winters, and has contributed to the overall increase shown in the numbers of some of these species in recent decades, notably Great and Blue Tits, Siskins and Goldfinches. The finch species that make use of garden feeders provide a striking contrast in their recent population trends with those that still depend primarily on farmland weeds, such as the Linnet and Twite, which have shown marked declines.

In conclusion, the local densities of tree-seed specialists generally fluctuate in parallel with annual tree-seed crops, while many farmland seed-eaters have declined over recent decades, in line with declines in the availability of weed seeds and winter grain. Species have responded positively where alternative foods have been provided, as in agri-environment measures or garden bird feeding. All these correlations imply that the population levels of seed-eating birds in Britain and Ireland have been greatly influenced by their food supplies. This is not to say that their numbers have not also been influenced in lesser degree by other factors.

INSECT-EATING BIRDS

Some bird species eat insects or other arthropods year-round, and others only in summer, turning to plant material in winter. Like seed-eaters, some insect-eaters may more rapidly respond to a food peak by moving into areas where their food-species are temporarily plentiful. In northern Fennoscandia, the geometric moth *Epirrita autumnata* feeds on the fresh leaves of birch trees, and reaches extreme abundance about every ten years. In these years, Bramblings settle at very high densities, and produce larger clutches and broods than usual (Hogstad 2005, Lindström *et al.* 2005). Other species also benefit, with Reed Buntings, Common Redpolls, Willow Warblers and Bluethroats all showing improved breeding success. The last two species also show higher return rates the following year. To my knowledge, the Brambling is the only European species to respond to insect plagues mainly by immigration, but the Wood Warbler may also do so to some extent. However, in North America many small insectivorous birds respond in this way to Spruce Budworm outbreaks. Through increased immigration, numbers in outbreak areas can show spectacular increases from the previous year; breeding success also improves, and recruitment to next year's breeding population can lead to further increase. Caterpillar outbreaks are sometimes so severe that whole areas become defoliated.

In some other insectivorous bird populations, too, year-to-year fluctuations in breeding numbers have been linked to food-related fluctuations in previous breeding success, themselves associated with insect food supplies. A year of good breeding is followed by increased breeding density the next spring in a lagged response, as noted in Pied Flycatchers (Fig. 11b). Similarly, among various duck species at Lake Myvatn in Iceland, production of young was correlated with the abundance of chironomid midges and other insects which formed the food of ducklings. The mean number of fledglings produced per female in any one year influenced the subsequent change in spring population density, with increases following good breeding years. Over a 20-year study, this relationship was apparent in Wigeon, Tufted Duck, Scaup, Common Scoter and Harlequin Duck (Gardarsson & Einarsson 1994, 1997). In only one species, Barrow's Goldeneye, did the relationship not hold, but this species nests in cavities, so may have been limited by shortage of nest-sites. In at least the Wigeon, greater proportions of adults from the previous year returned to the lake each spring after good chironomid years than after poor ones. This could have resulted from greater homing after a good year or greater winter survival brought about as a carry-over effect through body condition from summer to winter (Gardarsson & Einarsson 1997). Whatever the mechanisms, breeding densities were largely related to food supplies in the breeding area the previous year, with winter conditions being much less important.

On farmland, species which feed on insects and other invertebrates have declined in recent decades, just like seed-eaters. Invertebrate-feeders are affected by insecticide use (and resulting reduction in arthropod populations), by herbicide use (and resulting loss of insect food-plants), by the conversion of pasture to arable (and associated reduction in earthworm and other soil invertebrate populations) and by land drainage (which dries the top soil, making surface-dwelling invertebrates less active, and soil-dwelling ones less available, especially in late summer). The quality of evidence on the role of food supply in these population declines varies between species: in some, it is mainly correlative, but in others, such as the Grey Partridge, the conclusions from field observations have been confirmed by experiments (Potts & Aebischer 1991; Chapter 18). Other studies have linked the changes in regional or local agricultural practices with the timing of declines in invertebrate and bird densities (Benton *et al.* 2002).

Many other examples of long-term or sudden changes in bird populations and their food can be found in ornithological journals. They suggest that food limited numbers at different levels in different periods, and that sudden declines in numbers were often associated with sudden declines in food; in some cases, other factors, such as disease and predation, were excluded as being important. Such events form 'natural experiments' demonstrating the effects of food supplies on birds, but they usually lack controls, and often one cannot exclude the possibility that some unknown limiting factor changed at the same time.

AREAS OF DIFFERENT PRODUCTIVITY

For geological or other reasons, some areas of land and sea are more productive than others, and support more life, including birds. In some studies, variations in bird densities have been related, not to food directly, but to some supposed index of food, such as soil productivity. Data of this type were collected long ago for forest birds in Finland, where there are three main forest trees, namely birch, spruce and pine (Palmgren 1930, von Haartman 1971). On similar soils in mature forest, breeding songbirds were most numerous in birch, less numerous in spruce, and scarcest in pine, while in mixed spruce/birch woods they were most numerous of all. Most of the birds concerned were insectivores, whose densities were paralleled by similar variations in insect abundance. For any one forest-type, however, songbirds were more numerous in forests on good fertile

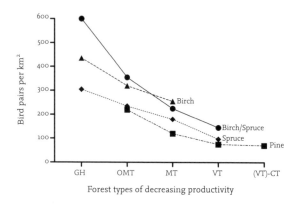

FIG 53. Densities of breeding birds in Finnish forests in relation to forest type and dominant tree-species. GH, grass–herb; OMT, *Oxalis–Myrtillus*; MT, *Myrtillus*; VT, *Vaccinium*; CT, *Calluna*. (Modified from von Haartman 1971)

soil than in forests on poor acid soil (Fig. 53). This was again attributed to food supply, for several aspects of productivity were better on good ground, such as the growth and fruiting of trees, insects on the foliage, and earthworms in the soil below. Many of the birds concerned were summer visitors to Finland, and of those that stayed the winter, some moved outside the woods. Hence, the variations in bird breeding numbers were due, not to birds surviving better overwinter in some woods than in others, but to their settling patterns in spring. Similar patterns were noted in songbirds elsewhere in Europe, including Britain, whether or not they wintered locally (Moss 1978).

The studies above were concerned with the entire songbird fauna, all species together. But correlations between bird density and soil fertility have been noted within species, comparing the densities in different areas. Among gamebirds, Red Grouse were more numerous and more productive on moors overlying

FIG 54. Sparrowhawk *Accipiter nisus* breeding densities in suitable woodland correlate with songbird prey densities, in turn influenced by soil productivity and elevation (see Fig. 55). (Chris Knights)

basic than acidic rocks, associated with greater nitrogen and phosphorus content in their food-plant (heather) growing on soil derived from basic rock (Miller *et al.* 1966, Moss 1969). Among raptors, Sparrowhawk densities in 12 regions of Britain were strongly correlated with soil productivity and elevation, and, in areas where counts were made, with the abundance of small bird prey (Fig. 55). Within woodland, different hawk pairs nested only 0.5 km apart in areas where prey species were most abundant and more than 2.0 km apart in areas where prey were scarce. Similar relationships were found for Peregrines, which spaced themselves at 2.6–10.3 km apart in different regions of Britain, according to soil productivity and associated prey densities (though prey were not measured directly) (Ratcliffe 1969). Higher Peregrine densities than any in Britain were found on the Queen Charlotte Islands, off western Canada, where the mean distance between about 20 pairs was 1.6 km, in this case linked with myriads of small seabirds taken as prey (Beebe 1960). Following a collapse in seabird numbers through food shortage, the Peregrine population dropped to about six pairs (Nelson & Myres 1975).

Similar relationships hold in water-birds, comparing nutrient-rich (eutrophic) lakes with nutrient-poor (oligotrophic and dystrophic) ones. In Finnish studies, the greater productivity of eutrophic lakes was reflected in greater densities of invertebrates and fish, and in turn of birds (von Haartman 1971). Other factors were involved, however, for the vegetation was better developed in and around eutrophic lakes and offered more nest-sites; also bird densities varied partly with the lake depth, with the length of shore in relation to water surface, and with the presence or absence of islands. In this case, as for the woodland birds discussed above, the density differences resulted from the settling patterns of breeding birds, not from their survival outside the breeding season. The lakes in question supported no birdlife in winter when they were frozen. The species of birds involved also differed between the different types of

FIG 55. Mean nearest-neighbour distances of Sparrowhawk *Accipiter nisus* nesting territories in continuous woodland shown in relation to altitude above sea-level, land productivity and food supply in different parts of Britain. Nearest-neighbour distances widen with rise in altitude or fall in land productivity and food supply. (From Newton *et al.* 1986)

lake, with plant-feeders commonest on eutrophic ones. On Swedish lakes, bird densities were linked specifically with phosphorus content, the main limiting nutrient, as well as with edge vegetation (Nilsson & Nilsson 1978). Similar conclusions could be drawn in Britain and Ireland, comparing the rich eutrophic waters of the lowlands with the sterile acidic waters of the uplands, except that here, in the absence of winter ice, the differences in bird populations hold year round. If the upland waters hold big numbers of birds, these are usually roosting gulls and waterfowl which obtain their food elsewhere.

One species examined in detail is the Dipper, whose territories along streams were longer, and densities lower, in more acidic waters (with low pH) than in more neutral ones (Fig. 56). This was in turn associated with decreases in suitable prey-items, such as mayfly nymphs and caddis larvae (Ormerod *et al.* 1985, Vickery 1991). By contrast, other stream-nesting birds, the Grey Wagtail and Common Sandpiper, showed no link with stream acidity, but these species fed mainly on terrestrial insects unaffected by stream pH (Vickery 1991). Similarly, in the Outer Hebrides, lakes of varying nutrient status occur almost side-by-side, with little difference in elevation, yet the abundant Mute Swans of those islands are found only on eutrophic, mesotrophic and saline waters which offer food, and are absent from the more abundant oligotrophic (acid) waters (Jenkins *et al.* 1976).

Among shorebirds wintering on coastal flats, densities were related to the types of sediments present, with fewest birds on sand and most on mud which held the greatest densities of invertebrate prey (Yates *et al.* 1993). On the Wash in eastern England, spatial variations in the densities of each of eight shorebird species were related to the densities of their prey species, which were in turn related to substrate type (mainly particle size) and to inundation time (Fig. 58).

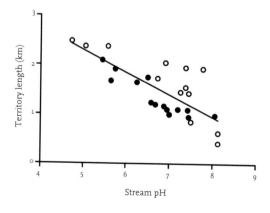

FIG 56. Territory length of Dippers *Cinclus cinclus* in relation to mean stream pH in Wales (open symbols) and Scotland (filled symbols). The birds nested at greater density on rich alkaline than on poor acidic waters, with fewer food organisms. (Redrawn from Vickery & Ormerod 1991)

FIG 57. The Knot
Calidris canutus
assembles in large
dense flocks to feed
on small molluscs
found in estuarine
mud sediments.
(Frank Snijkers)

On a world scale, large concentrations of seabirds are usually associated with oceanographic features, such as upwellings and convergences of currents, which promote water mixing and nutrient cycles. These in turn promote the growth of plankton and other marine life on which seabirds depend. Some of the largest seabird concentrations in tropical seas, which are generally poor in birds, occur at upwellings (as off the coasts of northwest and southwest Africa, where some of our breeding seabirds spend the winter) or where cold nutrient-rich currents penetrate warm nutrient-poor seas (as off the Peruvian coast and the Galapagos Islands). On a somewhat smaller scale, seabirds associate with other features that promote concentrations of food, such as ice edges, coral reefs and algal rafts, and at even smaller scales they associate with moving fish shoals, fishing boats or other local food sources. Hence, partly through the influence of external physical features, correlations between seabird numbers and food supplies are evident at a range of different spatial scales.

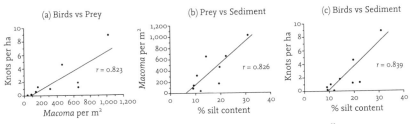

FIG 58. Relationship between the density of Knots *Calidris canutus*, the molluscan prey *Macoma balthica* and the sediment type on the Wash, eastern England. (From Yates *et al.* 1993)

In the absence of human intervention, such geophysical and chemical attributes of the environment promote consistent regional differences in biological productivity, affecting almost the entire biota. Within limits, they give a rough indication of what would be expected in particular areas, in the absence of detailed counts and surveys. They underlie general trends in overall bird densities across Britain, from the rich productive lowlands of the southeast to the barren acidic uplands in the north and west. They also indicate the changes in bird and other wildlife populations that are likely to occur under certain types of human impact, such as eutrophication and acidification (Chapter 19). Indirectly, they provide further evidence for the influence of food supplies on bird densities.

EXPERIMENTAL MANIPULATIONS OF FOOD SUPPLIES

Only certain species are suitable for food manipulations, in that they eat nutritionally adequate foods that can be easily provided (or removed), live at high densities and remain in the same locality year-round, so that the effects of food manipulation on subsequent numbers can be readily assessed. On these criteria most bird species are excluded as easy subjects for experiment, but for some species suitable food could be provided in winter, and its effect on subsequent breeding numbers assessed. Most such experiments have concerned tits (Paridae), which were given sunflower or other seeds in winter as a supplement to the natural diet. Breeding numbers in the same area were then measured from the numbers of pairs using nest-boxes, which were supplied in excess.

Experimental design

The simplest type of experiment involves a single area in which bird numbers are monitored for some years, then food is added continually and bird numbers are monitored again for several further years, giving a before-and-after comparison. The weakness of this procedure is that, without a control, one cannot be certain that a change in bird numbers was due to food provision and not to some other unknown factor which changed at the same time. The second type of experiment involves two similar areas studied simultaneously, with food supplied in one area but not in the other. If bird numbers increase more (or decrease less) in the treatment area than in the control area, this is taken as evidence that food supply influenced numbers. Ideally, the two areas should be far enough apart that food addition in one area could not benefit birds in the other. The third type of experiment involves some replication: either by reversing the treatments, so that after a time the experimental area becomes the control area and vice versa,

FIG 59. Great Tit *Parus major* numbers are greatly influenced by the winter food supply (see Fig. 60). (Keith Kirk)

or by the simultaneous use of several experimental and several control areas, ideally chosen at random. Such replication strengthens the findings because it increases the likelihood that any response observed in the study species resulted from the treatment and not from some other feature peculiar to a particular area or time period. Among 26 food-provision experiments conducted on birds, five involved simple before-and after-comparisons in the same area, eleven involved a simultaneous control area, while ten involved reversal of treatments or replication, with several experimental and control areas (Newton 1998). We can now examine some of these experiments in more detail.

Experimental findings

The most substantial feeding experiment yet undertaken, covering several successive winters, involved Great Tits in the Netherlands (van Balen 1980). This experiment was based in two areas of similar woodland 7 km apart, in one of which extra food was provided while the other acted as a control. Before winter feeding began, Great Tit breeding numbers in the two areas were similar, and fluctuated more or less in parallel from year to year (Fig. 60). But after feeding started, breeding densities in the two areas diverged and no longer fluctuated in parallel. Over several years, nest numbers in the experimental area averaged 40% higher than those in the control area. The impact of artificial feeding varied between years depending on the Beech crop, which was the most variable major component in the natural food supply. Comparing numbers in the experimental area in the years before and after food provision, it seemed that extra feeding doubled the population in poor Beech years, but made little difference in good Beech years (Fig. 60). This contrast provided further evidence that winter food

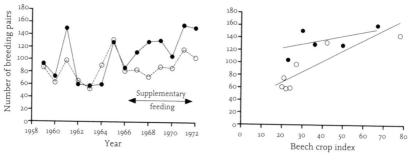

FIG 60. Numbers of Great Tits *Parus major* breeding in two areas in the Netherlands of similar size and habitat, in one of which extra winter food (hemp and sunflower seeds) was provided from 1967. From this year the two populations diverged and no longer fluctuated in parallel. Filled symbols, experimental plot; open symbols, control plot. This experiment showed the role of winter food supply in influencing local breeding density. (From van Balen 1980)

supplies influenced local breeding densities, with shortages most marked in years of poor Beech crops.

Further north in Europe, Great Tit breeding densities were greatly influenced by winter severity, with the lowest densities following the coldest winters. When food was provided artificially in three winters, the same relationship held with weather but breeding densities were correspondingly higher (von Haartman 1973). Other experiments on tits, covering 1–2 winters, gave variable results. In some studies, two tit species had access to the supplementary food, and if each of these is counted as a separate experiment, then eight out of 15 winter feeding experiments led to obvious increases in subsequent breeding densities (1.3–2.4-fold), compared with control areas. The same species responded to food provision in one area but not in another, or in one year but not in another; and in the same area and year sometimes one species responded while another did not (e.g. Krebs 1971, Källander 1981). In some of these experiments the birds were ringed, showing that increases in breeding density resulted from some combination of increased local survival and increased immigration, both affecting mainly first-year birds (Krebs 1971, van Balen 1980, Jansson *et al.* 1981, Enoksson 1990). In experiments in which food provision did not raise subsequent breeding density, this density may have been capped by some other factor, such as shortage of nest-sites (Chapter 5). Similar feeding experiments on different species in North America produced similar results.

In Red Grouse, fertilising areas of heather (the food-plant) promoted an increase in breeding density one year later over the previous year, as well as over that in control areas nearby (Miller *et al.* 1970). This occurred when experiments were started in years with low or moderate grouse densities, but in a later trial, fertilising an area at high grouse density failed to halt a big decline (Watson & Moss 1979). The Red Grouse in the area concerned underwent marked fluctuations, and these experiments suggested that the birds could respond to improved nutrition during a period of increase but not during a period of decrease (Watson et al. 1984). Some other factor was involved here. In another area, however, where Red Grouse did not fluctuate in a cyclic manner, fertilising an area of moorland led to a 20% increase in breeding density, compared with an unfertilised control area (Watson & O'Hare 1979).

Artificial feeding of Black Grouse in winter started in Finland as a widespread management procedure, in an attempt to stop their numbers declining. The birds were provided with oats at lek (display) sites throughout the winter. Although the birds took the food, the long-term population decline continued, as did shorter-term cycles in numbers (Marjakangas 1987). The same procedure was evaluated in Sweden, where Black Grouse were fed at two leks for four years, while those at three other leks in the same area were left as controls. No differences in body weights or survival were noted between birds at the two types of lek (Willebrand 1988). This last experiment was in an area of abundant natural winter food (birch), but the conclusion from both studies was that Black Grouse numbers were not limited by winter food. This was in line with other studies which pointed to deterioration in habitat and summer insect supplies as causing long-term decline, through poor chick production (Baines 1996), with predation also accounting for heavy losses in some years (Angelstam et al. 1984, Marcström et al. 1988).

Summer food supplies have also proved important in some species, mainly in influencing breeding output. In particular, through collapse in food supply, some species have produced too few young to offset normal adult mortality, so populations have declined. For example, in the Grey Partridge on farmland, widespread declines in numbers were attributed to poor chick survival, in turn resulting from pesticide-induced reductions in insect numbers (Potts 1986). Experiments on farmland, omitting pesticide use, resulted in more insects, better chick production, and greater subsequent breeding density (Rands 1985). Similar improvements in chick survival also occurred in the Red-legged Partridge and Pheasant (Green 1984, Hill 1985), as well as in various passerines, as discussed in Chapter 18.

In summary, winter food supplementation has often led to an increase of local breeding density in birds, and had most effect in years when the natural food supply was poor. However, such experiments have so far involved only a limited number of species. Where mechanisms were examined, extra winter food altered the rates of survival and immigration/emigration. Increases in subsequent breeding density up to 2.4-fold were recorded, and these were evident after only one winter of experimental feeding. Failure to achieve an increase could be attributed to other factors limiting breeding numbers (including natural food being superabundant at the time), or to limitations in density imposed by local nesting habitats, so that any rise in winter density was not reflected in subsequent breeding densities. Summer food supplementation, brought about by curtailing pesticide use, has resulted in improved breeding success and subsequent breeding numbers of Grey Partridges and other farmland species (Newton 2004).

In addition to the experiments described above, other manipulations of bird food supplies, brought about by agri-environment schemes, allowed some local bird populations to increase. At least five seed-eating species showed increased breeding densities after the local introduction of schemes designed to provide more food (Newton 2004), and similar results emerged from winter feeding experiments (Siriwardena *et al.* 2007); but these local increases were insufficient to reverse the overall downward national trends. The most striking example of population increase was provided by the Cirl Bunting, which was once widespread across southern Britain, but by the 1990s had become confined to a part of Devon. In this area its numbers increased about fourfold over ten years in response to increased food supplies provided by a targeted agri-environment scheme to produce seed-rich winter stubbles, insect-rich meadows and tall thick hedges (Wotton *et al.* 2000). The species was subsequently reintroduced to a second area (in Cornwall) where appropriate land management was also provided. Without this manipulation of its food supplies, and the willing collaboration of farmers, the Cirl Bunting may well have disappeared altogether from the British Isles.

OTHER MEASUREMENTS ON BIRDS AND THEIR FOOD SUPPLIES

Apart from measures of survival and reproductive rates, at least four other types of data from the birds themselves have been used as evidence indicating food shortage: (1) low weights and poor body condition; (2) low daily food intakes and feeding rates; (3) large proportion of available time spent feeding; (4) fighting over food (Newton 1998). When based on large samples of individuals, all these various measures have proved helpful in indicating the times of year when feeding was difficult, and in certain studies the proportions and types of individuals that were worst affected. All are more useful for certain species than for others, but in any case must be interpreted with care and along with other data, ideally on seasonal changes in numbers. They do not on their own constitute firm evidence of food shortage.

Much the same could be said about measurements of bird food supplies, which have also been used to indicate times of shortage. Many birds of high latitudes (including the British Isles) have a more or less fixed amount of food to last them through the winter, with little or no replenishment of stocks until the spring. For some species, the standing crop of food was measured, together with its decline over winter. If the birds removed a large proportion, the argument goes, they were more likely to be up against a food limit than if they removed only a small proportion. The problems are that, even if the initial food can be measured accurately, it is normally not known what proportion is available to the birds, nor what proportion they could remove before suffering a lethal decline in their intake rates. Further information is needed, and measurements of food stocks can usually do no more than define the periods and localities of likely food scarcity.

For several species studied in this way, food stocks were depleted by more than 50% during winter, and in extreme cases by more than 90% (Lack 1954, 1966). For Bullfinches in Wytham Wood near Oxford, practically all the seeds from favoured food-plants disappeared during winter in years of poor seed production, but only a small proportion in years of good production (Newton 1972). It was therefore in the poor years that numbers were most likely to have been limited by food.

Results from winter studies often contrast strikingly with those from summer, when plants are growing and animal prey-species are more abundant and reproducing. In most such studies, birds took less than 10% of potential food in the breeding season, but occasionally up to 50% (for examples, see Lack 1954, 1966). However, herbivores were sometimes affected by shortage in summer, as shown for Barnacle Geese in Svalbard (Prop et al. 1984), and for Snow Geese in parts of northern Canada, in both of which depletion of vegetation limited breeding output.

Herbivores often feed selectively on the most nutritious or palatable items (Watson & Moss 1979). Preferred plants often show obvious overgrazing, while other plants nearby remain untouched. If only these preferred plants provide food adequate for survival, then overgrazing of these could often occur. Plants might respond to heavy grazing by reducing their nutrient content or by increasing the chemicals that make the plant unpalatable or indigestible, thus reducing their food value even further (Schultz 1964, Haukioja & Hakala 1975). Capercaillie feed heavily on Scots Pine foliage, which contains various monoterpines, but they avoid trees whose foliage contains high levels of some types, notably alpha-pinene (Iason et al. 2011). So as far as Capercaillies are concerned, not all pine trees are good to eat.

FIG 61. Bullfinch *Pyrrhula pyrrhula*, whose numbers are limited by winter food supply, especially in years of poor tree-seed crops. The species feeds upon seeds until buds become available in late winter and spring. (Richard Chandler)

Measures of the proportion of food removed may sometimes be useful in showing how close birds are to the food limit. If it is found, for instance, that birds already remove more than 90% of their food, and that no obvious alternatives are available, then a big increase in bird numbers locally is clearly not possible. In many cases, however, the proportion of food removed may be less than 20%, in which case other information is needed in order to predict whether a further rise in numbers would be possible. It would also be useful to know whether any decline in food stocks was due to the birds themselves, or to something else, such as other animals or weather. If it was due to the birds, then larger numbers would lower food density further, increase competition, and cause more losses. But if it were due to something else, bird numbers may have relatively little influence on trends in food supply.

The consumption of living prey animals by birds does not necessarily lead to their long-term depletion, because their biomass can be replenished by the growth and reproduction of remaining prey individuals. Replenishment is more likely to happen during spring and summer, whereas in winter most prey species do not reproduce. There are cases, too, where bird feeding can enhance a food supply. This is true of some herbivorous birds, which by grazing grass or young cereals stimulate further plant growth, and provide a continual supply of fresh protein-rich tissue. In one study, the grazing activity of Wigeon resulted in a 52% increase in leaf production over winter, and at the end of winter 5% higher protein levels, compared with ungrazed areas (Mayhew & Houston 1999). Similarly, among raptorial birds, continual predation on small mammals may stimulate further reproduction in populations in which breeding is density-dependent.

In conclusion, then, measurements of food supplies can normally do no more than measurements on the birds themselves, and indicate likely periods of difficulty. Again, they are of more use on some species than on others, and special care is needed with species that feed selectively on vegetation. Some examples of population studies, accompanied by measures of bird food supplies, are given in Table 1. The studies on Oystercatchers provided some of the best non-experimental evidence for the role of food supply in limiting bird numbers because they linked measured declines in numbers with measured declines in food supplies, and the many dead birds that were found had clearly starved without the complication of huge parasite loads.

Longer-term effects of birds on food supplies

Most measurements of the effects of birds on their food supplies have involved assessments in particular years, as described above, but there can also be longer-term effects if the amount of food removed in one year affects the amount available in the next. Herbivores in particular can gradually destroy their food supply over a period of years so that their habitat becomes less able to support them. Such effects are well known in deer and sheep, but have also been documented for geese nesting in the Arctic, as indicated above. A colony of Snow Geese at La Perouse Bay in Manitoba built up from 2,000 to 8,000 pairs over a 15-year period (Kerbes *et al.* 1990). As the colony grew, the geese gradually removed their favoured food-plants (sedges), allowing mosses and other less

FIG 62. Over a period of years, Barnacle Geese *Branta leucopsis* at high densities can overgraze the vegetation in their breeding areas, reducing breeding output. (Edmund Fellowes)

TABLE 1. Evidence for population limitation by food shortage in various bird species.

Species	Evidence
Great Tit *Parus major* in southern England and the Netherlands (Perrins 1979, van Balen 1980)	Increase in breeding density after winters of good beechmast crops and known high overwinter survival; decreases after winters with poor crops and known low overwinter survival. Increases in breeding density after winters of experimental food provision.
Coal Tit *Periparus ater* in southeast England (Gibb 1960)	Over five years, a close correlation between winter bird density and winter food stocks (arthropods on foliage): survival from October to March varied greatly from year to year in relation to measured food stocks. During this period, the birds ate around 50% of several main prey species, and in midwinter spent more than 90% of the day feeding.
Rook *Corvus frugilegus* in northeast Scotland (Dunnet & Patterson 1968, Feare 1972, Feare et al. 1974)	Population at lowest density, and spread over largest area, in mid-summer. At this time food stocks were minimal, because of a reduction in the numbers of fields in which birds could feed, an absence of grain, and the disappearance of large invertebrates (earthworms and tipulid larvae) from near the soil surface of dry short-grass fields. Mid-summer population decline associated with high mortality (especially of juveniles) and low weights, and with lower feeding rates (150 kcal per day) and longer feeding periods (90% of daylight, or 15 hours) than at any other season. Another potential food shortage occurred during periods of deep snow in winter, when birds competed for space at localised feeding sites; however, birds then spent only 30% (3 hours) of the daylight period feeding, and obtained an average of 240 kcal per day.
Woodpigeon *Columba palumbus* in southeast England (Murton et al. 1964, 1966, Inglis et al. 1990, Isaacson et al. 2002)	(1) Period of population decline in winter coincided with depletion of grain, then clover stocks. The lowest bird densities, low weights, low feeding rates, and most starving birds occurred in late winter, when clover stocks were minimal. Temporary food shortages occurred during periods of deep snow, when the birds were concentrated on localised brassica crops. (2) Winter numbers declined steeply from the late 1960s, following the change from spring-sown to autumn-sown cereals and ploughing of clover leys and pasture, which reduced the winter food supply, but increased from the late 1970s following the expansion of an alternative winter food-crop, oilseed rape.
Oystercatcher *Haematopus ostralegus* (Ens et al. 2004, Atkinson et al. 2003, 2005)	Period of population decline in winter, independently on the English Wash and Dutch Wadden Sea, followed collapse of cockle and other shellfish stocks caused by suction dredging, mainly during the 1980s on the Wash, and the 1990s on the Wadden Sea. Through the 1980s, the Wash winter population fell from 40,000 to 11,000 individuals.

Species	Evidence
Oystercatcher *continued*	Increased mortality rates, poor body condition and starvation coincided with the period of food shortage in winter. Other shellfish-feeding species, such as Eider and Knot, also declined on the Wadden Sea over the same period (Camphuysen *et al.* 2002, Kraan *et al.* 2009)
Kittiwake *Rissa tridactyla* on Isle of May, eastern Scotland (Frederiksen *et al.* 2004b)	Known marked decline in sandeel food supply, accompanied by increased annual mortality, decreased breeding success and population, continued over several years. Obvious starvation of chicks. Similar events recorded in other sandeel-eating seabirds in the same area, and further north, around Orkney and Shetland.

palatable plant species to spread, and in some areas reducing the ground to bare mud. As this happened, the geese had to walk progressively further from the nesting colony to find suitable food, and the growth and survival rates of young geese declined. The same has been documented among Snow and Barnacle Geese elsewhere, so perhaps this is a common process, with goose colonies periodically becoming established in new areas, building up over two or more decades until the vegetation is degraded, and then declining.

Geese can also damage the vegetation in their marshland wintering areas to their own short-term detriment. This is familiar in Snow Geese on some east-coast refuges in North America, where the destruction of dense saltmarsh vegetation gives rise to areas of bare mud known as 'eat outs'. Because the geese have alternative feeding areas, their numbers are as yet unaffected (Hindman & Ferrigno 1990). In these areas, however, the geese are in effect pushing back vegetation succession, so they may actually help to maintain the habitat in a marshy state for longer.

CONCLUDING REMARKS

Food supplies can affect bird breeding densities by influencing settlement patterns, immigration and emigration, the survival of full-grown birds or their production of young. For any given population, food may be limiting only at certain times of year or in certain years. It may sometimes involve deaths from starvation, but not always. Lack of starvation is especially evident: (1) if territorial or other aggressive behaviour regulates local density in relation to food supplies, and if excluded birds succumb to other mortality, such as predation; and

(2) if food shortage lowers breeding and recruitment rates, and thus population density, without increasing starvation rates in full-grown birds (Chapter 3).

Circumstantial evidence that food supply can influence bird numbers comes from: (1) sudden or long-term changes in bird numbers that accompany sudden or long-term changes in food supplies; (2) year-to-year changes in local densities that correlate with year-to-year changes in local food supplies; and (3) spatial variations in bird densities that correlate with spatial variations in food supplies. A parallel response by several species which share the same food source, as found in all the main groups discussed, provides further weight to the correlative evidence for the role of food. Effects of food supplies on bird populations have become particularly apparent in recent years because human activities in agriculture, fisheries and waste management have greatly reduced bird food supplies, causing massive declines in populations, sometimes involving obvious starvation of adults and young.

The above account was based on certain kinds of birds that happen to have been well studied, but we can assume that other species are affected by food in similar ways. In all the examples given, drawn from different types of birds, temporal correlations between bird numbers and food supply in particular localities were sometimes impressive, with changes in numbers keeping strict parallel with changes in food, or keeping in step but a year or more behind. Such correlations were consistent with the idea of food affecting numbers, but on their own they do not prove a causal link because of the possibility that other influential factors may have changed along with food. Nor do they tell us if populations were as high as they might have been if food alone were limiting, so one cannot exclude an influence of other limiting factors.

However, observational evidence from a wide range of species that food supply influences numbers has been confirmed by experimental evidence from a narrower range. Experiments that are carefully designed to test ideas represent an improvement over observing natural changes, because in experiments it is the observer who brings about the change. Such experiments need careful forethought, however, based on knowledge of the birds' annual cycle of numbers and behaviour, so that any manipulation of food supply can be made at an appropriate time. Field experiments have shown clearly that winter food supplies can influence the subsequent breeding numbers of some species, and that summer food supplies, through their effects on breeding success, can influence the subsequent breeding numbers of other species. However, even where a clear-cut result is obtained, allowing the conclusion that change in food changed numbers, it is not of course safe to assume that all changes in numbers are due to changes in food. Food may be sufficient for some changes, but not necessary to explain them all.

CHAPTER 5

Nest-sites

W HILE FOOD SUPPLY COULD POTENTIALLY limit the numbers of all
wild bird species, the breeding densities of some are often held
at a level lower than food would permit by shortage of some
other resource, such as nest-sites. Limitation by nest-sites is evident mainly in
species that use relatively scarce places, such as tree-cavities or cliff-ledges. The
evidence is partly correlative, in that variations in breeding density, from year
to year or place to place, often parallel similar variations in nest-site availability;
and breeding pairs are generally absent from areas that lack nest-sites but which
seem suitable in other respects (non-breeders may live there). More convincingly,
however, the experimental provision of extra nest-sites has often led to increases
in local breeding densities.

Much of the evidence comes from tree-hole nesters, because of their
willingness to accept nest-boxes, but also includes species that use underground
boxes (burrow-substitutes), buildings (cliff-substitutes), pylons (tree-substitutes)
and rafts (island-substitutes). In each case, in assessing the effect of site
provision, one has to check that the acceptance of new sites has allowed extra
pairs to breed, and has not merely encouraged existing pairs to move from
natural sites nearby. Experimental demonstrations of nest-site shortages provide
some of the clearest examples of resource limitation in birds. They also show
the action of successive limiting factors, for once the shortage of nest-sites has
been rectified, numbers usually increase to a new higher level, at which they
may be assumed to be limited by some other factor. In addition, appropriate
manipulations of limited nest-sites have shown clearly the effects of interspecific
competition – of how one species, by taking most of the available sites, can affect
the numbers of another (an aspect left for Chapter 10).

Where nest-sites are scarce, the process of density limitation depends on defence of the nest-site, or of the territory containing it, by the pair in occupation, so that other pairs are excluded. In species that defend little more than the nest-site itself, such as the Starling or Pied Flycatcher, maximum breeding density can be set by the number of nest-sites, regardless of the numbers and interrelationships of contenders. In other species, such as tits, each pair defends a large feeding territory containing up to several potential sites. In these species, then, it is not necessarily shortage of sites as such that limits density, but shortage of sites outside the territories of existing pairs. In such species, territories are often compressible or otherwise adjustable to some extent, giving a more flexible ceiling to density, sensitive to the numbers of contenders (Newton 1998). In addition, in some species polygyny can increase nest numbers above one per territory. But whatever the social system, nest-sites can clearly constrain breeding numbers and nestling production in a density-dependent manner. As the numbers of potential breeders increasingly exceed the number of sites available, the greater the proportion of birds that fail to obtain a nest-site and so are unable to breed. Moreover, where shortage of nest-sites limits breeding density, it must eventually also limit the total population size, for where the output of young is limited, no population can increase beyond a certain level (Chapter 2).

SPECIES THAT NEST IN TREE-CAVITIES

About 5% of all European land-bird species are obligate hole-nesters, while another 9% use holes but can also use other sites. Obligate hole-nesters include species of woodpeckers, swifts, rollers, and some types of songbirds, owls, doves and waterfowl. Certain species, notably woodpeckers, can excavate their own holes, but most other species (the 'secondary cavity-nesters') cannot, so they have to rely on existing holes produced earlier by woodpeckers (which usually make new holes each year), by insects or by fungal decay. Among British species, obligate secondary cavity-nesters in trees, buildings or other sites include the Chough, Starling, Great Tit, Blue Tit, Nuthatch, Pied Flycatcher, Redstart, Wryneck, Swift, Barn Owl, Little Owl, Rock Dove, Stock Dove, Goosander and the introduced Mandarin Duck. Other species prefer cavities, but also use more open sites, including the Jackdaw, House Sparrow, Tree Sparrow, Tawny Owl and Kestrel, while Marsh Tit, Willow Tit, Coal Tit and Crested Tit can excavate or enlarge existing holes in rotten wood. Yet others, such as the Spotted Flycatcher and Treecreeper, nest in more open niches, such as behind loose tree-bark, and some cavity-nesters, such as the two sparrows, can also build domed nests in

FIG 63. The Redstart *Phoenicurus phoenicurus* is one of about 15 cavity-nesting species in Britain that can benefit from the provision of nest-boxes. (Keith Kirk)

dense bushes. Nuthatches use holes, but can plaster the entrance with mud to reduce its size and exclude larger species. It is the non-excavators that are most often short of sites, and with which this section is mainly concerned.

Formation and density of tree-cavities

In any tract of woodland, once the trees reach about 30 years of age, the numbers of usable cavities generally increase as the trees continue to grow, giving rise to more dead wood in which most holes are formed. By providing foraging sites, dead wood also favours woodpeckers, which further increase the numbers of holes available for other species. In undisturbed forest, therefore, the abundance and diversity of hole-nesting birds generally increase with forest age (Haapanen 1965, Mannan *et al.* 1980). Eventually, the number of cavities is likely to stabilise, as the rate of annual cavity gain (through decay, woodpecker or insect activities) roughly matches the rate of loss (through deterioration, natural sealing and tree-fall).

In the absence of human intervention, any long-established woodland can be expected to contain some large dead trees (or *snags*), each of which may stand for up to several decades, gradually losing limbs and softening as it decays and finally falls. In natural woodland, large standing dead trees are an important source of nest-sites for cavity-nesting birds. In general, the bigger the tree when it dies, the longer it will remain standing, the bigger the range of cavity sizes it can eventually provide, and the greater the range of bird species that can make use of it. Ancient pine forest in the Scottish Highlands contained large dead trees at densities of 15–102 per hectare (Summers 2004).

Other cavities develop in the trunks of living trees where branches become detached. Such holes also increase in numbers as the forest ages. Broadleaved trees provide more holes of this type than do conifers. This is because when a limb detaches from a hardwood tree, protective gum-filled cells form only in the living sapwood around the edges of the wound, for a time leaving the heartwood exposed to fungal and insect attack. But when the same process occurs in a conifer, resin released from the living tissue impregnates the heartwood, protecting it also against decay. Hence, many hole-nesting birds in conifer forests have to rely on occasional broadleaved trees (Haapanen 1965), although small numbers of cavities also develop in living conifers by the action of lightning, frost cracks and other trunk wounds, or by the breakage of tops.

In Britain and Ireland, most forest and woodland has traditionally been managed for timber and other wood products, processes that typically involve the shortening of rotation lengths (= tree lifespans), the suppression of fires and the routine removal of snags and other dead wood. The result is that cavities become scarce, restricting the diversity and densities of cavity-nesting bird species. If you are familiar only with the birds of young managed woods in western Europe, you may be surprised at the abundance and diversity of hole-nesting birds found in older, more natural hardwood forests, such as Białoweiza in Poland, where dead and dying trees are left in place. In such forests woodpeckers can form a substantial part of the local avifauna, and hole-nesters in general can be very abundant. It is mainly the larger woodpeckers that excavate holes in living wood, the smaller ones preferring dead wood. Among broadleaved woods in southern England, for example, about 14% of Green Woodpecker holes were in dead wood, compared with 48% of Great Spotted Woodpecker holes, and 94% of Lesser Spotted Woodpecker holes (Smith 2007). The soft rotting wood of birch was particularly favoured.

In managed forest, with no dead trees, cavities resulting from branch scars typically reach only 6–7 (occasionally up to 15) per hectare in mature broadleaved areas, and less than one per hectare in conifers (van Balen et al. 1982, Waters et al. 1990). These figures refer to all cavities, and large ones suitable for owls and ducks may be far fewer, usually less than one per hectare, but occasionally up to five (Bellrose et al. 1964, Souliere 1988). Moreover, not all holes of appropriate size for a given species are necessarily suitable. Some might be damp, infested with parasites or stuffed with nest material from previous years, while others might lie within the territory of another pair of the same species. In managed woods under 50 years of age, or with trunks less than 60 cm in diameter, tree-cavities of any kind can be almost non-existent, unless old trees remain from earlier times.

Species differences

It is obvious that larger species need bigger cavities, and that in most woods bigger cavities are likely to be scarcer than small ones. But beyond these gross trends, species differ in other ways – in the preferred sizes of cavity and entrance hole, in whether the cavity is high or low within the tree, on the trunk or side branches, and in whether it is exposed or secluded, and near or far from feeding areas (Edington & Edington 1972, van Balen *et al.* 1982). In a study in the Netherlands, Great Tits nested mainly less than 4 m above ground, in fairly deep cavities with small (< 35 mm) entrance holes; Blue Tits nested either low or very high, mainly in small and shallow cavities with narrow entrances; Coal Tits nested in low cavities with a small bottom area and slit-like entrance; Marsh Tits used extremely narrow holes, also with small entrances; Redstarts nested in low cavities with fairly large and variable entrances; and Nuthatches nested at greater heights than most of the tits, preferring fairly large cavities whose entrances they reduced with mud to a fairly constant 27–30 mm. These differences may have resulted partly from inherent preferences and partly from prevailing competition with other species (Chapter 10). Some excavating species, such as certain woodpeckers, can cope with hard wood, while others, such as some nuthatches and tits, need softer, more decayed wood. Overlap is considerable, however, because species are often constrained by the types of site available, or by the presence of competitors which exclude them from some of the sites they might otherwise use (Chapter 10). Starlings can exclude most species of small passerines, Great Tits can exclude Blue Tits, and all three

FIG 64. Nuthatch *Sitta europaea* at nest site. To exclude predators, this species often reduces the size of the entrance hole by plastering mud round it. (Bobby Smith)

species can exclude Pied Flycatchers. The smaller species are thus found mainly in holes small enough to exclude the larger species. In Sweden four hole-nesting species all chose higher over lower holes when they had a choice, the lower having greater predation rates. On average, however, they occupied decreasing nest heights, in order of the decreasing dominance status of each species, with the Starling taking the highest holes, followed by the Nuthatch and Blue Tit, and the Marsh Tit the lowest (Nilsson 1984). Particular species generally show considerable year-to-year consistency in the types of site they use (van Balen *et al.* 1982). Competition for nest-sites occurs not just with other birds, but also with other animals. In some areas, it is not

FIG 65. Great Spotted Woodpecker *Dendrocopos major* juvenile. By excavating cavities in dead wood, this species provides nest-sites for itself and other species (notably Starlings *Sturnus vulgaris*), but it is also a major predator on the chicks of other hole-nesting birds, if necessary by digging through to the nest chamber. (Keith Kirk)

unusual to find smaller boxes taken over by wasps or hornets, and larger ones by Grey Squirrels.

Even though Great Spotted Woodpeckers dig their own nest-holes, they can suffer from Starlings, which take over new cavities, as well as old ones (Smith 2005). Until the 1980s, Starlings were so abundant in much of Britain that they may have affected the numbers and distribution of Great Spotted Woodpeckers. The subsequent decline in Starling numbers was followed by increased nest success in Great Spotted Woodpeckers and an expansion of breeding distribution into less wooded habitats. Through competition for nest-sites, therefore, Starlings may have limited Great Spotted Woodpecker numbers, in the same way that, following their introduction, they limited several cavity-nesting species in North America. While providing nest-sites, Great Spotted Woodpeckers are also significant predators on the young of smaller hole-nesting birds. It is perhaps for this reason that some species avoid woodpecker holes, including Collared Flycatchers in the Białoweiza Forest in Poland, in which up to 40% of nest-failures in deciduous areas were attributed to woodpeckers (Mitrus *et al.* 2007).

Differences between species in preferred natural sites are reflected in their preferences for boxes of different sizes, hole diameters and positions in the tree, and surrounding habitat. Nevertheless, overlap occurs, and over a period of years the same box may be used by different species (Löhrl 1970, 1977, Nilsson 1984). In both natural and artificial sites, therefore, the potential for competition is great. The size of the entrance hole is important because it influences whether competitors and predators can get in. Each species is safest with the smallest hole through which it can squeeze to reach the cavity beyond. For any one species, moreover, the size of the cavity itself has been found to influence the clutch size and the number of young raised, smaller cavities leading to smaller broods, as found in Great Tits, Willow Tits, Marsh Tits, Pied Flycatchers, Tengmalm's Owls, Kestrels and others (Ludescher 1973, Korpimäki 1985, van Balen *et al.* 1982, Snow 2008, Lambrechts *et al.* 2012). The fact that predation rates are often higher in natural holes than in better-protected nest-boxes provides further indication that hole-nesters must often make do with what is available rather than with what is optimal.

Observations on the role of tree-cavities in limiting bird breeding densities
Several studies, in various places, showed that the numbers and diversity of cavity-nesting birds increased with the density of dead trees available (Haapanen 1965, Mannan *et al.* 1980). However, beyond a density of about seven dead trees per hectare, bird density levelled off. Presumably, at such high snag densities other limiting factors, such as food supply, came into play. Yet other studies showed that the densities of hole-nesting birds declined following the removal of dead trees (Scott 1979, Raphael & White 1984). Whereas some species used snags only for nest-sites, others used them also for roost-sites, and yet others (notably woodpeckers) as foraging sites.

Other arguments proposed to support the view that cavity-sites might often be limiting include: (1) the occurrence of fighting for holes, and of evictions, both between and within species; (2) successive use of the same hole by different birds in the same season; and (3) shifts in territory boundaries to incorporate nest-holes in territories otherwise lacking them (recorded in Great Tit: van Balen *et al.* 1982, East & Perrins 1988). However, all these events are open to other explanations, and only experimental manipulations can prove conclusively that nest-sites limit breeding densities.

Experiments on the role of tree-cavities in limiting bird breeding densities
In the managed woods of western Europe, studies of birds in nest-boxes have become popular with ornithologists, because boxes can be designed to attract the desired species and, once in place, they can provide large samples of easily found nests in accessible and standardised sites. Moreover, where natural sites are scarce or lacking, it is possible to get the entire local population of a target species into boxes, and as some species also roost in boxes, individuals can be easily caught and examined both inside and outside the breeding season. Not surprisingly, then, nest-boxes have formed the basis of many long-term studies of bird populations, and some box-nesting species, such as the Great Tit and Pied Flycatcher, are now among the best-known birds in the world. But despite the popularity of nest-box studies, relatively few observers have monitored the

FIG 66. Pied Flycatcher *Ficedula hypoleuca* numbers often increase greatly following the provision of nest-boxes in woodland. (Edmund Fellowes)

effect of nest-site provision on breeding density, by before-and-after comparisons. Fewer still have monitored density changes in the treatment plot against those in a similar control plot with no boxes, and even fewer have replicated the experiment on several plots. Overall, however, more than 30 experimental studies in Europe have involved the provision of nest-boxes for breeding birds, whether songbirds, ducks, owls or raptors. Almost all of these studies recorded an increase in breeding density over former levels or over densities in control areas where no boxes were provided (Newton 1998). In most, breeding density of the target species more than doubled after box provision, and in some it increased more than 20-fold. Sometimes the presence of boxes enabled species to breed in abundance in areas previously closed to them. Common findings following the addition of nest-boxes were that: (1) some species increased much more than others, (2) species increased more in plots with few natural sites than in plots with many natural sites, (3) numbers often increased in the first year of box provision, and further in successive years, and (4) nest success was often better in purpose-built boxes than in natural sites.

Care is needed in interpreting the findings of nest-box studies. Many species of birds, not limited by shortage of nest-sites, will readily accept well-designed artificial sites in preference to inferior natural sites. For example, Tawny Owls in conifer plantations at Kielder in northern England used a range of natural nest-sites, including cavities in old broadleaved trees, crags and ground sites, man-made structures and stick nests of other species (Petty 1992, Petty *et al.* 1994). But after nest-boxes were erected, 83% of the population of more than 40 pairs switched to using boxes from the first year that boxes were available and all pairs had switched by the fourth year. Thereafter, for the remaining 12 years of study, no nests were recorded in natural sites, so complete had been the adoption of boxes. Yet no obvious increase in Tawny Owl breeding numbers had occurred in response to box provision. So in any such experiment with nest-boxes, one must check to what extent increased box use is due to (1) an increase in the density of territorial pairs, (2) existing territorial pairs lacking sites being provided with an

FIG 67. Tawny Owl
Strix aluco and chick in
nest-box. (Harry Scott)

opportunity to nest, or (3) existing territorial pairs shifting from natural sites. Only in situation 1 would shortage of nest-sites limit pair density, whereas in 2 it limits the proportion of pairs that nest, and in 3 it limits neither pair numbers nor the proportion that nest. Insofar as could be judged from the information provided, all the experiments mentioned above in which a response occurred involved an increase in the density of pairs (situation 1). In other experiments, the numbers of hole-nesters fell after nest-boxes were removed. Not all species responded similarly, however, and in one experiment in an English wood, the removal of nest-boxes caused a decline in the numbers of Great Tits, but not of Blue Tits; the latter simply moved to natural sites, which were evidently available in sufficient numbers (East & Perrins 1988).

In young woodland in Europe, where natural sites are scarce, nest-box provision has repeatedly led to massive increases in the breeding densities of Pied Flycatchers, Collared Flycatchers, Redstarts and various tit species, and in some localities also Tree Sparrows and Starlings. The two flycatchers showed some of the strongest responses. These migrant species arrive after resident hole-nesters have started to breed, and are unable to displace existing occupants from holes. They can therefore normally breed only in woods with many natural sites, and since they are not strongly territorial (defending only the nest-hole), they have often increased spectacularly in numbers after nest-boxes were installed. For example, in Finland Pied Flycatcher densities equivalent to 2,000 pairs per km^2 were achieved, greater than all other forest birds together (von Haartman 1971). Without the boxes, few if any flycatchers could have bred.

Many birds that seem restricted to deciduous woods in Britain could probably occupy conifers too, if suitable nest cavities were made available. In a study in Estonia, Great Tits nested at much higher densities in deciduous than coniferous woods, but when nest-boxes were provided in both types of woodland, Great Tit densities increased by a similar number of pairs in both types, but with deciduous areas maintaining their lead (Mänd *et al.* 2009). Unlike Great and Blue Tits, the numbers of Coal and Crested Tits do not usually increase following the provision of nest-boxes. This is because these smaller species nest in a wider range of sites, including holes in the ground, and can also enlarge sites in rotten wood, so they are less often limited by shortage of cavities.

Among non-passerine species, box provision has been followed by large increases in the numbers of various hole-nesting ducks (Sirén 1951, Fredga & Dow 1984). In parts of northern Europe, nest-boxes for Goldeneyes have been provided for several hundred years, initially to obtain eggs for human consumption. In the 1970s, there were an estimated 75,000 such boxes in Sweden alone. Typically, when boxes were first erected in a new area, Goldeneye numbers increased slowly over a period of years, and then levelled out, often at 0.3–0.5 pairs per km of shoreline. This was another indication that, once the shortage of nest-sites had been rectified, other factors limited numbers at a higher level (Eriksson 1982, Fredga & Dow 1984).

The colonisation of northeast Scotland by Goldeneyes followed the provision of wooden nest-boxes near to suitable forest-lake habitats. During the 1960s, Goldeneyes wintering in northeast Scotland began to stay in increasing numbers until late May, so boxes were provided in the Spey valley in the hope that some would nest. The first evidence of breeding came in 1970, since when boxes have been provided in growing numbers, and Goldeneyes have increased and spread as breeding birds, with more than 150 pairs estimated by the year 2005 (Buxton 2007). A few nests have been found in natural tree-cavities, but almost certainly the species could not have become established in such numbers in northern Scotland without the provision of boxes.

While the erection of boxes can allow more pairs to nest, it does not always lead to more young being produced. In southern Finland, Goldeneye nesting densities increased over a period of years on lakes where boxes were provided, but not on lakes left free of boxes (Pöysä & Pöysä 2002). However, neither the average number of broods per lake nor the total number of flying young produced per lake increased significantly on the experimental lakes following box provision. Using all the data from all lakes combined, overall reproductive output emerged as density-dependent, with the average success per pair declining with increasing nesting density. In this study, therefore, reduced breeding success negated the effect of increased nesting density on the overall production of young. Although this result was unusual among cavity-nesting

FIG 68. Female Goldeneye *Bucephala clangula* exiting a nest-box. In Britain this species nests almost entirely in such boxes. (Harry Scott)

birds, Goldeneyes and other cavity-nesting ducks are often seen to fight over nest-holes, and sometimes more than one female may lay in the same nest, which can in turn reduce breeding success.

Among raptors, Kestrels have often responded to the provision of nest-sites, both in Britain and in other parts of Europe (Cavé 1968, Village 1990, Fargallo *et al.* 2001). For example, at Eskdalemuir in southern Scotland, in 1976 and 1977, some large areas of hill ground had no useable nest-sites and no breeding Kestrels (Village 1990). Some Kestrels hunted in these areas, but they were either birds breeding in the valleys or unpaired non-breeders. In January–February 1978, 17 nest-boxes and artificial stick nests were erected in these areas, and in the ensuing breeding season about half the newly provided sites were used in each area. In contrast, no Kestrels bred in similar areas nearby where no artificial sites were provided. Lack of nest-sites was thus limiting Kestrel breeding density in these large open areas. The provision of boxes in two areas of English farmland led to no obvious increase in Kestrel breeding densities over the next three years (Village 1990). Apparently in these areas sufficient natural sites were available, although some birds shifted from natural sites to boxes.

Various species of owls also readily accept boxes, and in many areas densities of Little Owl and Barn Owl increased substantially after box provision (Exo 1992, Petty *et al.* 1994). Several organisations have provided nest-sites for Barn Owls either in farm buildings or on poles in open farmland; in general these new nest-sites have been well taken up, leading to increases in nesting densities. By the mid-1990s, some 25,000 boxes had been provided for Barn Owls in Britain, enabling the colonisation of many areas (such as the Fens) previously almost devoid of potential nest-sites. Elsewhere in Europe, other owl species have also benefited from the provision of nest-boxes in areas deficient in natural sites (Saurola 1997).

Experimental demonstration of the presence of non-breeders
To test whether shortage of nest-sites prevents some birds from breeding altogether in certain years, leading to a non-breeding surplus, two types of experiment have been done. In one type, nest-sites were installed late in the season, after other pairs had settled and started to nest. In normal circumstances, any birds that had not started by then were unlikely to nest anywhere that year, so occupation of late boxes could be taken as evidence of a non-breeding surplus. In one experiment, 10 out of 19 artificial nest-sites made available to Kestrels late in the season in south Scotland were soon occupied by new pairs (Village 1990). By implication, these birds would not have bred that year if sites had not been provided. In this study, the increase in breeding pairs depended on the provision of extra nest-sites, yet similar vacant sites were already present within the territories of some established pairs, whose defence behaviour was seen to prevent access by other individuals. Hence, to be occupied, new nest-sites had to be placed outside the areas already defended by existing pairs. Again this effect was not duplicated when extra nests were provided in two farmland areas, evidently because sufficient nest-sites were already naturally available in every potential territory.

    In the second type of experiment, occupants of nest-boxes were removed well after nesting began. Some were then promptly replaced by other individuals which proceeded to nest. This again showed, not only that nest-sites were limiting, but also that other birds previously excluded from sites were available locally to take up the vacancies (Newton 1992). Such replacements have been documented following removals in resident Starlings (Heusmann & Bellville 1978) and House Sparrows (Anderson 1990). Where removals were continued, several individuals sometimes occupied the same box in quick succession, as shown in House Sparrows and Pied Flycatchers (Nelson 1907, von Haartman 1957). In all these species, in which individuals locate a hole and then defend it against other contenders, the nest-site is the crucial resource and defence the behavioural mechanism securing ownership. In some other hole-nesting species, such as tits, which defend large feeding territories containing one or more potential nest-sites, replacements have also occurred following removals (Chapter 1); but in these species it is not always certain whether territories or nest-sites are limiting.

Conclusions on tree-cavity nesters

These various studies, together with those in other parts of the world, show that, in some areas, the breeding densities of many cavity-nesting birds that cannot excavate their own holes are limited by shortage of nest-sites. This is not always the case in mature unmanaged woods, where natural holes are plentiful, but it is almost invariably the case in younger managed woods, as in much of Britain and Ireland. Provision of nest-boxes has almost always increased the local breeding densities of one or more species of hole-nesting birds.

In several studies (notably on Pied Flycatcher), numbers increased abruptly from the year that boxes were installed, implying that large numbers of potential occupants were available locally. Without the boxes these birds would presumably not have bred locally, but moved on to search elsewhere or remained as part of a non-breeding contingent. Other studies indicated that, following box provision, numbers increased slowly over several years (up to 20 years in Goldeneye), implying that no more than a small surplus was present in any one year, and that reproduction or continued immigration contributed to the longer-term increase. But whatever the species and its rate of increase, numbers eventually levelled off, however many extra boxes were provided. The implication was that, once the shortage of nest-sites was rectified, another factor took over to limit numbers at a higher level. Evidence from various tits, owls and raptors showed that this second factor was food supply (Chapter 4). In such species, therefore, densities in different areas were limited by either nest-sites or food, whichever was in shortest supply (see also Newton 1979 for raptors). The finding that some small birds can be limited by shortage of tree-cavities has found practical application, for in some woods and orchards nest-boxes have been provided for small insectivorous birds in an attempt to reduce caterpillar damage to trees (Mols & Visser 2002).

SPECIES THAT NEST ON CLIFFS

Swallows and others

Some bird species that normally nest on cliffs will also accept buildings, allowing increases in both numbers and distributions. Striking examples are provided by swallows and other hirundines, which throughout much of the world have occupied buildings of one form or another, spreading with human settlement. Some such species, which formerly used cliffs or caves, have now become so widespread that it is hard to imagine how scarce and localised they must once have been. They have switched so completely to using man-made structures that it is now hard to find them in natural sites anywhere. This is true of the Swallow, which throughout its extensive range has taken to nesting in barns and sheds, or under bridges and house porches, and is still expanding into new areas following human settlement. However, in a few places, it can still be found nesting in caves, the presumed original sites. Similarly, although House Martins now nest mainly under the eaves of buildings or under bridges, they still occupy natural cliff sites in a few localities around the British Isles.

The Sand Martin nests naturally in holes which it excavates in the earth banks of rivers, but has spread with sand and gravel workings, and road cuttings. It also uses artificial 'banks' which have been purpose-built at a number of wetland reserves, including Minsmere, Rutland Water, Frampton Marsh and the London Wetland Centre, where nesting could not otherwise occur.

Like hirundines, some species of swifts that formerly nested in rock crevices or tree-holes have also taken to niches in buildings, extending their range in consequence. The most obvious European example is the Common Swift, which has been found nesting naturally in niches in the dead tops of large trees protruding above the forest canopy, but is now almost entirely restricted to niches in walls and under roof tiles of old buildings. In Britain and Ireland, the species has declined in recent years, at least partly because roof renovations have increasingly blocked previously available nest-holes.

Raptors and others

Buildings have also enabled some cliff-nesting falcons to nest in areas otherwise closed to them. The German name *Turmfalke* ('tower falcon') for the Kestrel is testimony to this habit in central Europe. Nesting on buildings is one of the factors that has enabled the Kestrel to penetrate towns so successfully. In 1967,

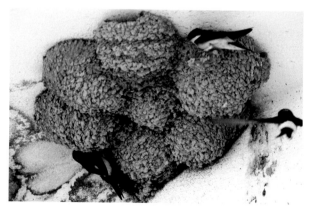

FIG 69. Mud nests of House Martins *Delichon urbicum* in an open building. (Edmund Fellowes)

FIG 70. Sand Martins
Riparia riparia at nest
burrows on a riverbank.
(Chris Knights)

FIG 71. Artificial bank constructed for Sand Martins
Riparia riparia to nest in at the RSPB reserve at Frampton in
Lincolnshire. (Ian Newton)

FIG 72. Swift *Apus apus*
leaving nest hole under
roof tile. (Chris Knights)

142 pairs were found within about 30 km of St Paul's Cathedral in London, a
density of one pair per 23 km² (Montier 1968). Even greater numbers were found
in Berlin, with 200–250 pairs, but most using nest-boxes rather than ledges on
buildings (Kübler *et al.* 2005).

In southern Europe, the Lesser Kestrel now nests colonially almost entirely
on old buildings, in holes and crevices in walls or under roof tiles. It was once
one of the most numerous birds of prey within its range, but suffered a 95%
decline in the latter half of the twentieth century (mainly 1970–90). This was due
mainly to reductions in food supplies caused by agricultural intensification, but
in parts of the range also to declines in nest-sites, resulting from the collapse
or renovation of old rural buildings (Catry *et al.* 2011). Following a major

programme of nest-site provision, the Portuguese population increased more than threefold, from 155–158 pairs in 1996 to 527–552 pairs in 2007, with 52% using artificial nests. Over the same period, colony numbers increased from 10 to 53. Predation rates were also lower in nest-boxes, which were less accessible to cats and other predators than natural sites.

Turning to larger falcons, the Peregrine nests mainly on cliffs, but also uses buildings to some extent, either isolated or in towns and cities. Until 1970, the cities involved showed a curiously scattered distribution in many different countries, implying that the habit arose independently each time, and in most cases persisted for no longer than a few years (Newton 1979). However, since the 1980s, Peregrines have nested increasingly in British cities, usually choosing some of the highest sites, as on cathedrals and disused chimney stacks, although in many such sites a box or platform was provided for them. It seems that most large towns in Britain now hold one or more pairs of nesting Peregrines, with at least seven pairs in inner London (with the first nesting on Battersea Power Station in 2001) and at least 18 pairs in the wider area of 'Greater London' by 2010. The fact that most cities contain tall buildings, as well as plentiful Feral Pigeons as prey, may have helped the habit to spread. The result is that the Peregrine, which until the 1970s was restricted to about one-third of the surface area of Britain where suitable cliffs were available, now nests in every county, using quarries and buildings. Similarly, in Hungary, the Saker Falcon expanded from eight known pairs in 1980 to 113–145 pairs in 2002, owing mainly to provision of nest platforms (on power poles or trees), with 95% of pairs using these artificial sites (Bagyura *et al.* 2004).

FIG 73. Peregrine *Falco peregrinus* on Norwich Cathedral. In recent years, Peregrines have increasingly roosted and nested on tall buildings in cities and towns. (Andy Thompson)

Among other raptors, Ospreys have long used artificial structures, including tree-substitutes such as pylons, and in recent decades special platforms, especially in North America. Some of the nests recorded in Scotland in the late nineteenth century were on old castles and other deserted buildings, but as the population expanded during the twentieth century, almost all recorded nests were in trees, in some of which secure platforms were provided. By using man-made structures, all these raptor species could increase their nesting densities and distributions in places where natural sites were scarce or lacking. In some instances birds accepted new structures immediately, but in others only after many years or only in particular areas. In continental Europe, the White Stork has for centuries used buildings more than natural nest-sites, gaining safety from human presence. Again, old cartwheels or other platforms were provided for the birds to build on.

Colonial seabirds

Seabirds nest in dense colonies chiefly in places which are inaccessible to most predatory mammals, such as cliffs or offshore islands, the locations of which largely determine seabird distributions. Around the coasts of Britain and Ireland, safe nesting places within range of foraging areas are widely available for many seabird species, but the lack of cliffs and rocky offshore islands in much of southeast England and elsewhere excludes many cliff-nesting species from those coasts. In the presence of mammalian predators, the Kittiwake and Guillemot prefer vertical cliffs for nesting, so the largest gaps in their distributions occur along the low coastlines of southeast England, northwest England, and southwest Scotland. The Shag and Razorbill can make do with lower rocky coasts and islets, so are more widely distributed, but they are still absent as breeders from the soft coasts of southeast England. Shortage of suitable coastline could also limit the overall population sizes of such species, for if suitable nesting places were more widely available, additional colonies could become established and additional feeding areas brought within range. This is already evident in soft-coast areas, where normally cliff-nesting gulls have taken to nesting on buildings.

While some bird species accepted buildings as soon as they were built, others have only recently begun to do so, usually as their populations expanded and natural sites became saturated. Various gull species have in some areas established colonies on the roofs of town buildings, enabling further expansions in local distribution and breeding numbers (Raven & Coulson 1997). Roof-nesting colonies of Herring Gulls and Lesser Black-backed Gulls are now widespread in Britain, but are mainly confined to eastern coasts in Ireland. In most regions, it is coastal towns that have been colonised by Herring Gulls and inland sites mainly by Lesser Black-backed Gulls. In both species, the habit developed with the general increase in their populations during the mid-twentieth century.

In the *Seabird 2000* survey of 1999–2002, over 7% of all British and Irish Herring Gulls were found to be nesting on roofs, more than 20,000 pairs distributed in 225 localities (Mitchell *et al.* 2004). Six sites each supported more than 500 pairs, and the biggest (in Aberdeen) held more than 3,000 pairs, forming the largest urban-nesting concentration of gulls in the world. Since an earlier survey in 1976, roof-nesting Herring Gulls had increased at average rates of 10% per year in nest numbers and 5% per year in localities occupied. The reason for the continuing upward trend in roof-nesters, while the overall population was declining, was uncertain. However, food available in towns, particularly discarded material from fast-food outlets and garbage from restaurants, was increasing. This contrasted with other Herring Gull food sources in the wider countryside, which were in general decline (Chapter 4). Herring Gulls nesting in urban areas appeared to have better breeding success than their conspecifics elsewhere, partly because on rooftops they have fewer predators to contend with than in many natural sites. In South Shields, Herring Gulls on rooftops reared 1.2–1.6 chicks per pair in the 1970s, compared with 0.6–1.2 chicks per pair in natural coastal colonies elsewhere (Monaghan 1979). While these gulls do well in urban areas, their human neighbours are less enamoured, with noise and fouling being the main complaints.

Roof-nesting by Lesser Black-backed Gulls was first recorded in Britain in 1945, and during *Seabird 2000* some 10,900 nests were found at 127 sites in Britain and Ireland, comprising nearly 10% of the overall population. Most colonies were on industrial buildings, with at least five exceeding 500 pairs, and one of 250 pairs on the HarperCollins Building at Bishopriggs in Glasgow. Since the survey of 1976, roof-nesting Lesser Black-backed Gulls continued to increase at around 17% per year in nest numbers and 13% per year in localities occupied.

Strangely, few Great Black-backed Gulls have so far taken to nesting on roofs, with totals of 83 pairs in 26 sites recorded during *Seabird 2000*, but the species itself is much less common than the others. Since the 1960s, Common Gulls have also nested on roofs in Aberdeen and neighbouring towns, with 621 pairs in 14 colonies discovered during *Seabird 2000*, all in Scotland.

As Kittiwakes increased in numbers during the twentieth century, they accepted lower cliffs and eventually also buildings. The first documented example for Britain was on the harbour wall at Granton, Midlothian, in 1931–33, but the birds then moved to the window sills of a building at Dunbar, East Lothian, before shifting to a nearby ruined castle (1,100 pairs in 2000), later spreading also to nearby cliffs (*Seabird 2000*). They also started nesting on the window sills of a warehouse at North Shields on the River Tyne in 1949, where

FIG 74. Kittiwakes *Rissa tridactyla* nesting on a building in Tyneside. (John Coulson)

they thrived until they were displaced in 1991 by netting hung over the sills. The displaced birds moved to other colonies, mainly nearby, but one ringed female was later found nesting 400 km to the south in Lowestoft. Kittiwakes have now nested at several sites on the Tyne, up to 20 km from the sea, mainly on the riverside (Coulson 2011). Other nests on tall man-made structures were recorded elsewhere, including drilling platforms in the North and Irish Seas and other structures at Lowestoft and Sizewell in Suffolk, where Kittiwakes could not otherwise nest because of lack of cliffs.

Some unexpected roof-nesters

Some other birds have taken to nesting on the roofs of buildings, changing their nest-sites in unexpected ways. One of the most curious examples is provided by Oystercatchers in the city of Aberdeen. Normally these birds nest on shingle and feed on the seashore or in nearby fields, but in Aberdeen they have started to nest in safety on the flat gravelled roofs of buildings, and feed on the larger lawns and playing fields. The same is true for some other plovers elsewhere, including the Killdeer in some eastern North American cities, the Little Ringed Plover in parts of Europe and the Senegal Thick-knee in Egypt. In parts of North America, the Common Nighthawk, a relative of the European Nightjar, nests on flat roofs, and hunts the moths that gather around street lamps. For all these species, roofs provide secure and safe nesting substrates near to profitable feeding areas. With changes as striking as these, it is hard to predict which species might colonise towns in future.

SPECIES THAT REQUIRE SAFE GROUND SITES

In contrast to cliff-nesting seabirds, most tern species nest mainly on stretches of coasts where sand or shingle substrates free of mammalian predators occur within reach of extensive shallow water. This means they are more widespread on the eastern than on the western coasts of Britain and Ireland, but continual changes in suitable areas result in periodic shifts in colonies. Some sandbanks get eroded altogether, while others form elsewhere. The preferred open, well-drained substrates with scattered low vegetation are found naturally only where plant succession is prevented by periodic flooding, erosion or accretion during winter storms or floods. In addition, human activities often create open sparsely vegetated substrates that terns can be quick to exploit. Examples include open industrial land (including gas terminals in northeast Scotland), flat roofs (in Angus), factory lagoons, and islets on gravel-pits and reservoirs. Breeding success is often high at these artificial sites owing to low disturbance and low predation. Common Terns in particular have benefited from habitat creation in the form of islets in gravel-pits and industrial lagoons, and tern rafts in reservoirs, and from the maintenance of bare substrate on nature reserves by control of vegetation. On the other hand, many natural sites have been lost in recent decades to human activities, including sandbars in rivers that have been dredged and canalised, sandy beaches used for recreation, and former bare sandy areas which, through tidal control measures, overgrew with dense vegetation.

In some places, additional measures have been taken to protect terns from displacement and predation by gulls. Since the mid-1970s, numbers of Roseate Terns nesting on Coquet Island off the Northumberland coast had declined by two-thirds. In 2000, an artificial gravel terrace was built, on which nest-boxes were placed to provide shelter for tern eggs and chicks (Booth & Morrison 2010). From 2003 all the Roseate Terns nesting on Coquet used boxes, and the numbers of pairs rose from 34 in 2000 to 94 in 2006. Productivity also increased well above the levels found in neighbouring Common and Arctic Terns which nested in the open. Attempts were also made to deter large gulls from nesting on Coquet, so that predation declined, and adverse weather and food supplies came to have most influence on the breeding output of all three tern species.

At several sites in Scotland, fences around coastal industrial and military sites have excluded mammalian predators from potential nesting areas, enabling large numbers of terns to breed safely in areas previously shunned. In other areas, terns have taken to nesting on rafts built specially for them, but whether these events led to increases in regional numbers (rather than to shifts from nearby areas) often remains unclear (Dunlop et al. 1991). However, little doubt remains over the importance of nesting rafts to Black Terns in continental Europe. The sizeable population of the Netherlands declined by more than 95% between the 1950s and 1980s, owing to reduced production of young attributed to loss of natural nest substrates, reduction of food supplies, and human disturbance (van der Winden &

van Horssen 2008). The decline would almost certainly have continued if not for the provision of anchored nesting rafts on slow-flowing rivers and canals, enabling the population to rise from 110 pairs in 1985 to 400 in 1999. In the later years, more than 80% of all nests were on rafts. In a neighbouring part of Germany, increase in the number of rafts from 10 to 60 over a five-year period was accompanied by an increase in the numbers of nesting Black Terns from 12 to 41 pairs.

SPECIES THAT NEST IN BURROWS

Among land-birds, Sand Martins and Kingfishers nest in burrows they dig for themselves in the earth-banks of rivers, and expansions of Sand Martin numbers into similar sites provided by human activity was mentioned above. However, some seabird species also nest in burrows in sloping or flat ground which they dig for themselves or take over from other seabirds and Rabbits. Puffins and Manx Shearwaters habitually nest in holes in friable soil, while Razorbills and Black Guillemots nest in cavities among rocks, and Storm and Leach's Petrels in both types of sites. In dense colonies, burrows can crisscross in all directions, so that the whole area can become honeycombed and unstable. Over long periods of years, continual digging can lead to gradual soil erosion, especially if gulls or other species nest on the ground surface and tear out the protective vegetation. Gradually some species can thus destroy their own nesting habitat, especially in shallow soil. This happened with Puffins on Grassholm Island off southwest Wales, and on part of Dun, St Kilda, where a nesting area containing some 5,000 burrows disappeared between 1974 and 2000, apparently due to severe soil erosion (Mitchell *et al.* 2004). Collapse of burrows can also occur if people or livestock continually walk over the area. On the island of Auskerry in Orkney, Storm Petrels nested mainly in old rabbit burrows, but declined greatly between 1995 and 2001, because 65% of the rabbit burrows were destroyed by increased sheep numbers (Mitchell & Newton, in Mitchell *et al.* 2004). On an islet off the Brittany coast, trampling and manuring by ground-nesting seabirds (mainly Cormorants) over an 18-year period led to erosion and collapse of many Rabbit burrows previously used by Storm Petrels, causing a big reduction in breeding numbers, the remaining pairs occurring mainly in rock fissures (Cadiou *et al.* 2010). Reduction of breeding habitat for some species may also result from takeovers by other burrow-nesting species, as when an expansion of Puffins resulted in a decline in Storm Petrels, as seen on Sule Skerry and Skokholm (Chapter 10). Some biologists have attempted to make good the loss of natural sites by providing plastic pipes for burrowing species, or boxes with a plastic

FIG 75. The Puffin
Fratercula arctica is a burrow
nester found on offshore
islands. It sometimes nests
at such high densities
that its constant digging
leads to soil erosion and
destruction of nesting
habitat. (Alan Martin)

pipe attached, with the length and diameter of pipe adjusted to the target species. In some places they have met with considerable success (Bolton 1996).

Some seabirds are now excluded from islands they previously occupied because introduced mammalian predators, especially rats, have rendered them untenable (Chapter 7). Otherwise, among most seabird species, limitation by nest-sites appears to be exceptional rather than widespread around Britain and Ireland. But wherever birds occupy newly provided or newly discovered sites at long distances from others, they can gain access to new feeding areas, leading to further growth in numbers. The expansion of Cormorants throughout inland Britain was facilitated not only by the construction of reservoirs and their stocking with fish, but the leaving of tree-covered islands within these artificial lakes to provide attractive nest-sites.

OTHER SPECIES AND OTHER NEST-SITES

Shortage of trees for tree-nesting species is most apparent in open landscapes, where the planting of even single trees can bring in Carrion Crows, Magpies or other tree-nesting birds. In one experiment, the placement of 12 small trees in an open area allowed eight pairs of Carrion Crows to settle where breeding was not previously possible, all the birds concerned coming from a known non-breeding flock (Charles 1972). Other species which do not build nests of their own depend on old stick nests of other species. Various owls and raptors are in this category, but the Hobby is the only species in Britain which nests entirely in such sites.

FIG 76. The Hobby *Falco subbuteo* depends entirely on old stick nests built in trees by other species, especially Carrion Crows *Corvus corone*. (Peter Beasley)

Herons have also benefited from nest-site provision in some parts of the world. A remarkable experiment with Snowy Egrets and related species was conducted on Avery Island, Louisiana, by McIlhenny (1934). In 1892, when he began, such species had been greatly reduced in numbers by commercial plume hunters. His management measures included: (1) providing large nesting platforms about 2 m above the surface of an artificial lake, each platform large enough to hold many nests; (2) fencing the lake against human disturbance; (3) providing the birds with sticks for nest-building; and (4) introducing alligators 'to deter children' and to control nest predators such as Raccoons. By 1912 the overall numbers of several egret and heron species on the platforms had reached 22,204 nests. In this instance, it was the provision of safe nest-sites that was crucial, rather than shortage of potential (unsafe) sites in the surrounding area. In this extensive coastal area, feeding places were unlimited.

Some 63 rafts were provided for Black-throated Divers in Scotland, each placed in the territory of a known pair, with preference to pairs that had failed in their breeding from flooding or other reasons. These served mainly to increase breeding success, rather than territory numbers (Hancock 2000). Otherwise, these various examples indicate that limitation of breeding density by nest-site shortages is widespread among many types of birds that use special sites, whether cliffs, caves, burrows, islets free of mammalian predators, or scarce trees in open land.

CONCLUDING REMARKS

We can conclude that the breeding densities of many bird species are in some areas limited by shortage of acceptable nest-sites. This is apparent from circumstantial evidence in which the numbers of breeding pairs in different areas correlate with the numbers of local nest-sites, or where changes in the numbers of nest-sites are followed by corresponding changes in the numbers of breeding pairs. It is confirmed in areas where artificial nest-sites have been deliberately provided, leading to substantial increases in subsequent breeding densities. Although most experiments have been done with cavity-nesting species (by providing nest-boxes), a wide range of other species has benefited from the provision of other sites, whether buildings, islets and rafts on lakes, or other flat substrates secure from mammalian predators. In bird species which use more commonly available nest-sites, as among ground vegetation or the canopies of trees and shrubs, shortages are seldom manifest.

While experiments confirm the importance of nest-site limitation in some species, it is hard to be sure over what proportion of the breeding range such limitation might occur. Researchers may be discouraged from publishing negative results from studies where extra nest-sites caused no change in breeding density. Against this, nest-site provision has now been practised over wide areas in special schemes, as for Barn Owls in Britain, all reporting substantial rises in breeding numbers in at least parts of the areas covered. When nest-sites were provided for a species, they were often occupied in the same year, leading to an immediate rise in breeding density. This implied that surplus birds were available in the vicinity and immediately able to take them up. In future years, pair numbers often increased further but eventually they levelled off. This implied that, at this higher level, other limiting factors came into play. Evidently, different factors acted successively to limit bird breeding densities at different levels.

Because for some bird species shortage of safe nest-sites can limit the numbers of pairs that can breed, the question arises as to what constrains the types of site used. If species accepted a wider range of nest-sites, they would be less likely to be limited by shortages. Interspecific competition is one factor involved (Chapter 10). From the examples given earlier, particular species may use only part of the potential range of nest-sites available to them, because they are kept out of other sites by dominant competitors. In addition, predation pressure can influence the range of sites that particular species use, and the types of site that are acceptable can change if predation pressure alters, either from place to place (with or without mammalian predators) or from one time to another (as mammalian predators are added or removed). Acceptance of less safe sites, where mammalian predators are absent, enables pairs to occupy nest-sites otherwise unacceptable, and thereby expand their numbers and distributions. In other words, the types of nest-site used by a given species are not fixed, and minimum requirements (in terms of security) can alter in response to changes in disturbance and predation pressures. This aspect is taken up in Chapter 12.

CHAPTER 6

Predation: General Principles and Individual Impacts

W HILE THE SUPPLIES OF FOOD and other resources provide an ultimate ceiling on bird numbers, some populations may be held by predators below the level that resources would permit (Lack 1954, Newton 1993). Although nearly all bird species experience predation, at least at the egg and chick stages, it is not easy to assess its effects on population levels. Even where predators kill a large proportion of their prey each year, they do not necessarily affect subsequent breeding numbers. The numbers of many bird species can more than double each year through breeding so that, if breeding numbers are to remain stable in the long term, more than half the individuals present at the end of one breeding season must die before the next, if not from predation then from some other cause. When prey individuals are killed, the resources that they would have used – such as food or nest-sites – become available for others that might otherwise have died or been unable to breed. For predators to reduce breeding numbers below the level that would otherwise occur, at least part of the mortality they inflict must be *additive* to other mortality, and not simply *compensatory*, replacing other forms of death.

Losses from predation can be compensated only if the other factors affecting survival or reproduction vary in a density-dependent manner. Such a situation would be expected in populations that are close to their resource limit, and experiencing strong intraspecific competition, whether for territories, food or nest-sites. It is in these circumstances that predation is most likely to be compensated by reduced losses from other causes, and so to have least effect on breeding numbers. Conversely, populations that are well below their resource limit, and relatively free of intraspecific competition, are those most likely to suffer reduction from any predation (or parasitism) that they experience. In this chapter, I shall be concerned with some basic concepts concerning predation, with the predators themselves, and with their effects on prey breeding and mortality rates. Effects of predation on population levels are left for the next chapter.

THE PREDATORS

Birds fall victim to a wide range of predators, avian, mammalian or reptilian. In the British Isles, the commonest mammalian predators include Red Foxes, mustelids (such as Stoats, Weasels, Pine Martens and Badgers), Hedgehogs and various rodents. Added to these are the introduced species, mainly domestic and feral Cats, American Mink, Brown Rats and Grey Squirrels. These various species hunt mainly on the ground and vary in their ability to reach tree-nests, but some mustelids (notably Pine Martens) and squirrels are adept climbers. The commonest avian predators include corvids, gulls, skuas and raptors. Corvids take mainly eggs and small chicks, raptors take chicks, juveniles or adults, while gulls and skuas eat eggs and birds at all stages. Snakes and other reptiles take mainly eggs and chicks. Typically, any particular prey species may have a small number of important predator species, but suffer occasional attacks from a much larger number. For example, most predation on Pheasants in Britain is from Foxes and in some areas also from Goshawks, but more than a dozen other species of birds and mammals have been reported as eating Pheasant eggs, chicks or adults from time to time. The eggs of ground-nesting birds are also occasionally taken by some unexpected species, such as deer, as confirmed by cameras placed at nests.

Most predators are generalists and take a wide variety of prey, switching from one prey species to another as opportunities and needs arise. Because the population levels of such predators can be influenced by the sum total of their prey, they are not often greatly affected by shortage of any one type. Generalist predators do not usually take their various prey species in strict relation to their numbers, but kill some (vulnerable) species more than expected from their numbers, and others less so. For example, House Sparrows are especially vulnerable to Sparrowhawks, whereas Swallows and Wrens are not, with Swallows gaining protection from their flying skills and Wrens from their skulking cover-dwelling behaviour. Certain prey species may experience heavy predation not because of their own numbers, but because other prey species are sufficiently plentiful to attract many predators to the area, or because alternative prey suddenly become scarce (Tinbergen 1946, Kenward 1985, Keith & Rusch 1988). It is common experience that, when a predatory species is short of its main prey, it

FIG 77. The Carrion Crow *Corvus corone* (shown at Rabbit *Oryctolagus cuniculus* carcass) and the related Hooded Crow *Corvus cornix* are probably the most significant predators on the eggs of ground-nesting birds in Britain and Ireland. (Edmund Fellowes)

will switch to other prey, which then suffer greater losses than normal, sometimes with effects on subsequent breeding numbers. For example, an outbreak of haemorrhagic viral disease reduced Rabbit numbers in Spain, which led to eagles and other predators switching more heavily to Red-legged Partridges, causing a decline in Partridge numbers (Moleon *et al.* 2008). In this type of situation, if the predators themselves then decline, the affected prey species may rise again.

Other predators are specialists, concentrating on one or a few main prey species, although this may often result through lack of alternative prey. The dependence of Gyr Falcons on Willow Ptarmigan and Rock Ptarmigan over much of the inland Arctic provides an example. Understandably, specialists are highly susceptible to shortage of their main prey, so that the numbers of predator and prey are often closely interdependent. It would be unexpected for a specialist predator to eliminate its prey, for its own numbers fall before the prey is extinguished. Moreover, because of delays in response, with the predator taking time to increase in response to a rise in the prey population, closely coupled predator–prey populations tend to oscillate, with the two fluctuating in parallel but out of synchrony (see below).

It is not usually sensible to classify predators as generalists or specialists, because the same predator can fall in either category, depending on the range of prey species available locally. In addition, different individuals of the same predator species in the same area can concentrate on different prey. This is often apparent among large gulls, of which a few individuals might specialise in eating birds, while the majority take mainly fish or other foods. For example, among 27 pairs of Great Black-backed Gulls nesting on the Isle of May, three pairs specialised on Puffins, killing more than half of the 191 taken that year (Harris & Wanless 2011).

Whether generalists or specialists, predators seldom operate evenly through a prey population. They may concentrate in particular localities, perhaps near where they themselves are breeding or where prey are unusually plentiful or vulnerable (Geer 1978, Erikstad *et al.* 1982). They may also concentrate on particular age-groups, such as the young and inexperienced (Newton 1986, Bijlsma 1990), on particular social classes, such as the non-territorial in a territorial species (Jenkins *et al.* 1964), or on one sex more than the other. In many ground-nesting birds, the female is often killed when the nest is found by a Fox or other mammalian predator. Because in most waterfowl and gamebirds the males do not incubate, they avoid this type of predation, accounting in part for the usual predominance of males among adult ducks and gamebirds. In such species that have been studied, the sex ratio at hatching was about equal, but among increasing age-groups of adults, the ratio became progressively weighted towards males, giving overall ratios in some duck species as distorted as three males to every female (Lack 1954, Bellrose *et al.* 1961). This distortion – resulting at least partly from predation – has population consequences, for with a more equal sex ratio there could be many more potential nesting pairs. In effect, the breeding population becomes limited by the number of females available. Predators take disproportionately more females also at other times, especially in polygynous gamebirds, such as Capercaillie, Black Grouse and Pheasant, in which males are much bigger than females, and thus more difficult for some predators to tackle (Kenward 1977). Although the females of these species are more camouflaged than the highly coloured males, these benefits are negated during snow cover when females become as conspicuous as males (Kenward *et al.* 1981a). In addition, in parts of the breeding season, females are more active in food collection than males and thus are rendered more vulnerable to Goshawk predation (Widén 1987). Among the males, the breeders are more active and hence more susceptible than younger, non-breeding ones. In one study of radio-tagged Black Grouse, some 31% of adult cocks displaying at leks were taken by predators in spring and summer, whereas no non-breeding cocks that did not visit leks were taken in that time (Angelstam 1984). Hence, the behaviour of the different sex- and age-groups at different times of year can influence their susceptibility to predation.

IDENTIFICATION OF PREDATORS

When the remains of a killed bird are found, it is usually possible to tell whether it was taken by a mammalian or avian predator, but often not possible to identify the predator to species, unless some other clue is available at the scene, such

FIG 78. The Jay *Garrulus glandarius* is a woodland omnivore which eats the eggs and chicks of other birds, and in winter feeds heavily on acorns which it collects and stores in the ground. (Frank Snijkers)

as a dropped feather. In recent years, however, much has been done to identify predators of eggs and chicks by placing cameras at nests. As expected, the types of predators varied with the habitat and situation of the nest, and with the size of the eggs and chicks. One of the biggest studies of this type was in the Czech Republic, where 22 species of predators were filmed at 171 woodland songbird nests during a five-year period (Weidinger 2009). About two-thirds of these predation events occurred by day and the rest at night. Mammalian predators were responsible for 22% of diurnal and 95% of nocturnal events. Some nests suffered from more than one predation event, and Jays sometimes visited the same nest on successive days, each time removing an egg or chick. A Long-eared

FIG 79. Male Merlin *Falco columbarius* recorded unexpectedly on camera taking young from a Ring Ouzel *Turdus torquatus* nest. (Edmund Fellowes)

Owl was seen to remove an incubating adult Chaffinch at night. Another camera-based study was of Blackcaps nesting along wood edges near Lake Constance in Germany over a three-year period, when eleven different predator species were identified (Schaefer 2004). The main culprit was the Jay, which accounted for 21% of all nests and 46% of all failures, all by day, but other predators included Tawny Owl, Stone Marten, Weasel, Red Fox and Wild Boar, most of which hunted at night. The cameras themselves had no effect on nest success, judged by comparison with other Blackcap nests that were not filmed.

In a study in Britain, 20 predation events were recorded by cameras placed at Spotted Flycatcher nests (Stevens *et al.* 2008). All these events occurred in daytime. The main predator was again the Jay (12 nests), but others included the Great Spotted Woodpecker, Buzzard, Sparrowhawk and Jackdaw. The only mammalian predator recorded was the domestic Cat, which accounted for three nests, and no evidence was obtained against Grey Squirrels, which have often been suspected of destroying the contents of tree-nests. Another study recorded predation at some Slavonian Grebe nests, where three predation events involved Otters which took two clutches and one adult grebe and its chicks from a nest, a fourth involved a Stoat, and a fifth involved an unidentified predator (Perkins *et al.* 2005). As an extreme example of nest predation, a single Polar Bear can destroy hundreds of nests in a day if it enters a colony of geese or seabirds, while its disturbance also allows access by Arctic Skuas and other predators, as described for Brent Geese on Svalbard (Madsen *et al.* 1989). Similar mass predation events have involved Arctic Foxes which gained access to seabird islands, although the Foxes carried away and buried many of the eggs, rather than eating them all on the spot (Bailey 1993, Birkhead & Nettleship 1995).

Across ten areas in the Netherlands, egg predators were identified by using temperature loggers and continuous video recording of 792 clutches, and chick predators by radio-tagging 662 chicks of Black-tailed Godwits and Lapwings (Teunissen *et al.* 2008). Some 56% of all clutches were lost to predators, and 38% of all chicks. Eggs were taken chiefly by mammals operating at night and chicks chiefly by birds operating by day. In total, 22 species were identified as predators, of which the Red Fox and Stoat were the main consumers of eggs, and the Buzzard and Grey Heron of chicks. Overall levels of egg predation differed greatly between sites and years, as did the species of egg-predators involved, but there was less variation in chick-predators. In consequence, no correlation was apparent between levels of egg predation and levels of chick predation within the same sites. These various studies served to confirm that a wide range of birds and mammals eat the eggs and chicks of birds, and that predation rates can be high, depending on the habitat and species present.

ANTI-PREDATOR BEHAVIOUR

Birds are characterised by flight, well-developed cognitive abilities, and the laying of eggs that require incubating to give chicks that require feeding. These various features shape the anti-predation behaviour of birds, and therefore their survival and reproductive chances. Anti-predation behaviour involves the avoidance of dangerous places, continual vigilance, fleeing or 'freezing', flocking, alarm calls, mobbing, distraction displays, and so on. The advantages of flocking are that each individual benefits from the watchful behaviour of others as well as itself, while at the same time reducing its own chance of being caught during an attack. Alarm calls warn others of an approaching predator, and alert the predator to the fact that it has been detected, while distraction displays are aimed to draw a predator away from eggs or young. Many birds utter different calls for mammalian and avian predators, triggering behaviour appropriate to the occasion. Some calls lead birds to crouch and freeze, while others lead them to flee. Reaction to these calls appears instinctive, but individuals can also hone their responses through learning.

It is in the breeding season that birds are at their most vulnerable, whether as eggs, young or parents. Some species rely on the security of the site to protect their nests, others on dense cover in which to conceal their nests. Some sit tight on the approach of a predator, relying on their camouflage, while others sneak away unseen, or mob and dive at the predator to distract and drive it away. In most colonial species, individuals may join together to mob a predator, in a form of communal defence. Shearwaters and small petrels nest underground, hidden from view in burrows or in rock fissures, and only come and go at night, when their main avian predators are at roost. In this way they can minimise predation risk, but cannot avoid it altogether, as large gulls or skuas still catch some individuals, especially at times of full moon. The particular suite of anti-predator behaviours that any species shows depends on its size and flying skills, its habitat, nest protection and escape strategies, and its ability to change its behaviour through learning.

Following a successful nesting, many birds return to the same site next year, but following a nest failure they tend to move to a different site (Newton 2008). In areas where nesting places are plentiful, terns and small gulls often move en masse between different colonies following large-scale nesting failure, whether caused by predation, parasite infestation or tidal flooding. Individuals may move up to several hundred kilometres at such times. Similar mass dispersal has also occurred among colonial land-birds, such as Lesser Kestrels, following total breeding failures (Serrano *et al.* 2004). By moving away from places where they have experienced nesting failure from whatever cause, birds seek to reduce future nest losses.

Avoidance of predation is often viewed as an arms race between predator and prey, in which each evolved protective measure is offset by some counter-measure in the predator. However, selection pressure seems stronger on the prey than on the predator, for the cost of a mistake is clearly greater for the prey (death as opposed to a missed meal). Admittedly a predator that never caught any prey would starve to death, but nevertheless natural selection is likely to have acted more strongly to improve the ability of prey to escape than the ability of predators to make successful captures. We may then ask why prey species have not become so efficient at escaping as to drive their predators extinct. One hypothesis is that, as predators become rare, they exert little selection pressure on their prey for further improvement. Another possibility is that the more efficient the prey become, the less scope there is for further improvement. Thirdly, the prey may be compromised, and able to improve their escape ability, or apply that ability, only at the cost of some other aspect important to their survival (see Chapter 12).

IMPORTANT CONCEPTS

In terms of its effect on a population, predation can be either regulatory (density-dependent) or non-regulatory (density-independent). In density-dependent predation, the proportion of prey which is killed increases with rising prey density, so that eventually prey numbers stop increasing (or conversely, stop decreasing before they reach extinction). This provides one mechanism by which a prey population could be held near an equilibrium level below what resources would permit. Two responses of predators to changing prey populations can act in a density-dependent manner: (1) the so-called *functional response*, in which individual predators include greater proportions of a given prey species in their diets as the numbers of that prey increase; and (2) the *numerical response*, in which predators increase in density (through greater immigration, reproduction or survival) as the prey itself increases. Either or both of these responses could result in relatively greater kill rates in conditions of high prey densities than low. In practice, the exact forms of numerical and functional responses are hard to measure for predators of birds, because fluctuations in the abundance of alternative prey often distort the relationships.

Sometimes predators remove approximately the same number of prey individuals each year regardless of the numbers of prey present. This leads to a situation in which a relatively greater proportion of the prey population is removed when prey numbers are low, impeding population growth. The

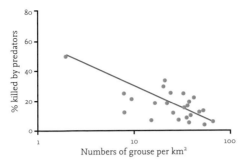

FIG 80. Density-independent predation on female Red Grouse *Lagopus l. scotica*, mainly by Peregrines *Falco peregrinus*. The points refer to overwinter losses in different areas and years, and are shown in relation to autumn grouse densities. The greater the density of grouse, the smaller the percentage taken. This situation arose partly because Peregrine densities remained roughly constant (being determined by other factors), regardless of the densities of grouse. (Modified from Hudson 1992)

relationship is then *inversely density-dependent* (Chapter 2). This could happen, for example, if the numbers of the predators were limited by some other factor, such as nest-site availability (precluding a numerical response), and if the functional response was also weak. An example of inverse density-dependence in predation on Red Grouse is shown in Fig. 80. In such a situation, the numbers of prey removed each year by predators bear no consistent relationship to the numbers of prey present. Inverse density-dependence can also occur when predation on a given prey species depends not on its own numbers but on the abundance of alternative prey. In one of seven case studies, predation by Goshawks on Pheasants was much greater than expected, apparently because Goshawks were maintained at high numbers by a local abundance of Rabbits (Kenward 1985). In these circumstances, Goshawks removed more than 50% of hen Pheasants over one winter, a proportion that Pheasant populations could not sustain in the long term.

Density-independent predation can also occur when predators, whose numbers were determined elsewhere, suddenly move into an area (as during migration) causing a marked decline in prey numbers, before the predators themselves move on or die. In theory, predation that was either inversely density-dependent or density-independent could lead to decline and eventual local extinction of a prey species. There are also situations in which a predator can regulate a prey species when prey numbers are low, but not when the prey can break free of this regulation and reach much higher numbers (Box 2). This might happen, for example, in years that are particularly good for prey breeding, or if there is massive immigration of prey from elsewhere.

Box 2. The predation trap

Some prey species may be regulated by predation when they are at low numbers, but not when they can break free of this regulation to reach higher numbers. Under conditions of rising prey numbers, a point may come when predators can increase their kill rate no further. This happens because of limits both to the amounts that individual predators can eat and to the numbers of predators that can live in a given area. The numbers of prey that are killed then level off so that, if prey numbers but not predator numbers continue to rise, progressively smaller proportions of prey are taken. In this process, predation switches from density-dependent (regulatory) to inversely density-dependent (non-regulatory). One consequence of this switch is that prey populations could have two fairly stable levels, a lower level at which they were regulated by predation, and an upper level at which they were limited by a number of factors, including predation. A prey population might break free of regulation by predators if, for example, predation pressure lapsed temporarily, or if a sudden change in environment led to increased reproduction or immigration of prey. Once the higher level has been reached, if prey numbers then remain at that level we can be sure that the prey, by increase alone, has escaped the regulating influence of predators (the so-called 'predation trap'). On the other hand, if numbers fall to near their original level, this might be because predators have re-asserted their regulatory influence, or because other factors (such as food shortage or disease) have intervened to reduce prey numbers. Escape from regulation by predation can explain occasional outbreaks of some insect and other pests, which persist at high densities until other factors reduce their numbers again.

The role of predation in influencing prey numbers thus depends on the way in which predators operate. Only if the combination of functional and numerical responses provides an appropriate total response to changes in prey density can predators regulate prey numbers. Moreover, because predation is only one of several factors affecting prey populations, any regulatory effect it has may be supported or counteracted by other factors.

EFFECTS OF PREDATION ON INDIVIDUALS

Predation on eggs and chicks

In many bird species, predation is by far the biggest cause of egg and chick losses, commonly accounting for more than half of all nesting attempts (Lack 1954, Ricklefs 1969). But because many species can re-lay after a nest failure, such losses may have less effect on the annual production of young than these striking figures suggest. At the population level, the loss of say 50% of nests to predators often translates to a much smaller loss in eventual production, even though late (repeat) broods may do less well than early ones. Moreover, the staggering of breeding attempts resulting from re-lays means that, in species that raise only one brood each year, the young appear over a longer period than otherwise and are thus not all equally vulnerable to infrequent destructive weather events, such as storms.

To protect against predators, some bird species put their nests in relatively inaccessible sites, such as cliffs or trees, others hide their nests in shrubs or ground vegetation, while yet others nest on bare ground, relying on camouflage of the eggs or incubating female for protection. Rates of predation on nest contents vary greatly between species, depending partly on the position of the nest (Lack 1954, Thiollay 1988). Losses tend to be lightest among birds that use relatively protected sites, such as tree-cavities or cliff-ledges, somewhat heavier among species that build open nests in shrubs and trees, and heavier still among species that nest on the ground (in which the sitting hen is sometimes also taken). In addition, in any situation, species which have open nests suffer more predation than those which build domed nests. All these findings would be expected from knowledge of the behaviour of predators. They are only tendencies, however, and in some areas different patterns may occur, depending on local circumstances.

Moreover, for any particular nesting situation, some sites seem to offer more protection than others. In species that hide their nests in ground vegetation, predation rates tend to be higher in sparse than in dense cover, as shown by many studies. In the Mallard, for example, the proportion of clutches that hatched in one area varied from nil in the most open types of vegetation to more than 50% in the densest (Cowardin *et al.* 1995). Marked differences were found in some shrub-nesting species, in some of which nest success also increased through the season as cover thickened (Newton 1972, Tuomenpuro 1991, Hatchwell *et al.* 1996). Such findings imply that nesting places vary in quality, and there may therefore be strong competition for good ones. In some species, nest predation is also influenced by the nutritional state of the female, which may affect the amount of time she spends off the nest or the vigour of her defence against predators (Newton 1986). It is because predation rates are so heavily influenced by features of the habitat, and of the birds themselves, as well as by the numbers and behaviour of predators present, that they vary greatly in the same species between different areas and years.

Hundreds of assessments have been made of nest predation rates, but studies of radio-tagged birds provide some of the most accurate because they are not biased towards the most easily found nests. The fates of approximately 450 nests of radio-tagged hen Pheasants studied in six English farmland sites between 1990 and 2003 were examined in relation to habitat, predator numbers and other variables. Some 34% of nests hatched successfully, while 43% failed from predation, and 23% from other causes, including predation of the hen away from the nest (Draycott *et al.* 2008). Nest predation rates were significantly lower in two areas where intensive predator control was undertaken than on four areas with only low levels of predator control. Red Foxes accounted for at least 23% of all nest predation events, other mammals for 20%, corvids for 24%, while for 33% the predator was unidentified. Foxes also accounted for all 31 hens that were killed away from their nests.

In the study referred to earlier in 15 areas of the Netherlands, some 662 chicks of Lapwings and Black-tailed Godwits were radio-tagged and their survival assessed. In the different areas, 0–24% of chicks survived to fledging. Most losses were traced to predation (70–85% in different areas) or to grass-cutting operations (10–15%), and the remaining 10–20% to various other causes (Schekkerman *et al.* 2009). Numerous predators were involved, including crows and gulls, storks and herons, birds of prey and mustelids. Godwits suffered less predation in long grass than in recently cut or grazed areas, while Lapwings suffered less predation in grazed than mowed fields. In godwits, predation was predisposed by poor body condition, but whether the radio-tags themselves influenced predation rates remains an open question.

Several other studies examined predation rates on nests of passerines, waders or other species in areas with different densities of predators, or in the same areas in periods with and without predator control (Parr 1993, Donald *et al.* 2002, Stoate & Szczur 2001, 2006). They showed that predation on nest contents was

FIG 81. Over parts of Britain and Ireland, the Curlew *Numenius arquata* suffers heavy predation on its eggs and chicks, and in some areas it has greatly declined. (Richard Chandler)

lower in conditions of low densities of predators, but again most did not examine whether enhanced nest success led to increased subsequent breeding numbers.

While assessments of predation rates are usually not on their own sufficient to show that predation is limiting breeding numbers, rates can sometimes be so high that this conclusion is inescapable. For example, Curlews in Northern Ireland declined by 58% over the period 1987–99. A study showed that 82–85% of all breeding attempts failed before hatching, with predation accounting for about 90% of the losses (Grant et al. 1999). Foxes appeared to be the main culprits in one area (in Co. Antrim), with Hooded Crows and Lesser Black-backed Gulls in another where Foxes were largely absent (Lough Erne islands). Annual breeding success of Curlews averaged 0.19 young per pair in Antrim and 0.38 young per pair on the Lough Erne islands. Calculations showed that, if the breeding success in Antrim was typical of most of Northern Ireland, it was sufficient to account for the rate of population decline across the whole region (Grant et al. 1999).

Predation on full-grown birds

Far fewer studies have been made of predation on full-grown birds. Individuals killed by predation are mostly consumed before they can be found by human observers, leaving only remains. Although these remains can often be attributed to avian or mammalian predators, they seldom reveal the importance of predation in relation to other mortality causes. In addition, predation victims are greatly under-represented among carcasses received for autopsy studies (Chapter 3). Radio-tracking studies are of more value, and have implicated predation in the recorded deaths of many species. In a study of radio-tagged Black Grouse in Sweden, predators accounted for almost all deaths recorded over three years, removing some 48–72% of all males in different years and 48–52% of all females (Willebrand 1988). In another study in France, some 257 hand-reared Pheasants were radio-tagged and released when full-grown, along with 72 wild birds. In the course of the study, 203 of the hand-reared and 30 of the wild birds were found dead and the causes identified. Predation was the most common cause of death, accounting for 89% and 87% of recorded deaths in the two groups. About 70% of the predation events involved Red Foxes, and 10–20% raptors, probably Goshawks (Mayot et al. 1993). Among Grey Partridges in Poland, 48% of radio-tagged birds were lost to predation in the breeding season, mainly from Red Foxes, with about half of all victims killed away from the nest (Panek 2002). The validity of such findings depends, of course, on whether radio-tagged birds were representative of their population and whether tagging itself influenced predation risk; moreover, they cannot usually reveal to what extent predation is predisposed by other factors, such as starvation. At the other extreme, in some large species, such as swans or eagles, the adults appear to be practically immune to predation, except from humans.

Other studies have involved estimating the numbers of birds killed by predators in a given time, and expressing these numbers as a proportion of birds in the area. For example, at Tyninghame in southeast Scotland, the overwinter losses of various shorebird species to raptors were estimated at 0–57% of the autumn populations (Cresswell & Whitfield 1994). In general, smaller species suffered greater predation than large ones, but Turnstone, Snipe and Redshank were especially vulnerable, partly because they fed nearer the shore. Large species, such as Bar-tailed Godwit, Oystercatcher and Curlew were virtually never taken. The main predators at this site were Sparrowhawks, Merlins and Peregrines. Within species, juveniles were taken disproportionately more often than adults. In other studies, in summertime, Sparrowhawks removed an estimated 3–14% of the breeding adults of all prey species together in different areas, and 0–47% of the adults of individual species in particular study plots (Tinbergen 1946, Opdam 1978, Solonen 1997).

Studies of prey remains have repeatedly been used to estimate the numbers of gamebirds taken by Goshawks. At a number of sites across northern Finland,

these hawks were estimated to take in the breeding season alone an average of 16% of Hazel Grouse, 22% of Willow Ptarmigan, 14% of Black Grouse hens, and 9% of Black Grouse cocks (Tornberg 2001). These species together formed more than two-fifths of the breeding season diet of Goshawks. The data were averaged from a number of sites over 11 years, and applied only to the deaths attributed to one predator species, but they nevertheless represented appreciable proportions of the adult prey populations. In Sweden, Goshawks were estimated to take 12% of adult Hazel Grouse during the breeding season, and up to 36% over the whole year (Lindén & Wikman 1983), and to kill in the breeding season 4–14% of Black Grouse males and 6–25% of females, turning mainly to Red Squirrels in winter (Widén 1987). In southern Sweden, radio-tagged

FIG 82. The Goshawk *Accipiter gentilis* is a major predator of gamebirds, pigeons and corvids. This one has killed a Grey Squirrel *Sciurus carolinensis*. (Peter Beasley)

Goshawks took approximately 19% of 4,300 released captive-reared Pheasants during the autumn and winter (Kenward 1977), and at another site were responsible for 56% overwinter mortality of wild hen Pheasants, and for 17% of wild male Pheasants (Kenward *et al.* 1981a). Clearly, Goshawk predation of these various gamebirds can be a significant mortality factor. Other studies, involving radio-tracking individual grouse and recording how they die, have confirmed the importance of both avian and mammalian predation in the overall losses, but in all such studies it is hard to judge how much the radios may have affected predation rates (Park *et al.* 2008).

PREDATION IN THE ANNUAL CYCLE

Deaths from predation must reduce prey numbers at least temporarily, and could reduce their average level over the year as a whole. The question of most interest is whether the predation to which many species are subject throughout the year reduces their breeding numbers. In any seasonally reproducing species, numbers are at their lowest point in the early stages of breeding, after most overwinter mortality of adults has occurred but before any young are produced. If predation does not reduce breeding numbers, it has no effect on the numbers of eggs laid to start the next generation, and is not limiting in the long term. It is thus irrelevant to the long-term persistence of the population at that level. In many species during the breeding season, more adults are present than the nesting habitat can hold, leaving a surplus of non-breeders (Chapter 1). In these species, then, even after year-round predation, predators cannot be said to limit breeding numbers, which are instead influenced by the amount or carrying capacity of nesting habitat.

Game managers have a different perspective, because they aim to produce birds for shooting. They are thus concerned both with maintaining breeding stocks from year to year and with producing lots of young birds for hunters to kill.[9] Any natural predation or other mortality that lowers the production of young might reduce the numbers available for shooting in autumn, even though it may have no effect on subsequent breeding numbers. It is not paradoxical therefore that predation might reduce numbers at one time of year but not at a later one. Similarly, predation might lower breeding numbers, but the reduction might be compensated by improved nesting success, so that big numbers still

---

9 Maintenance of breeding stock is important only in traditional game management based on wild-bred birds, and not in modern game management based on captive-reared Pheasants or Red-legged Partridges, which can be bought in and released. In these situations, maintenance of wild breeding stock is often irrelevant (Chapter 16).

occur in autumn. In general, we can envisage three scenarios involving predation effects in the annual cycle of any seasonally breeding bird species:

(1) Predation reduces post-breeding numbers below what would otherwise occur, but not the subsequent breeding numbers. This scenario requires total compensation of predation through density-dependent overwinter survival.
(2) Predation reduces breeding numbers below what would otherwise occur, but not subsequent post-breeding numbers. This scenario requires total compensation of predation through density-dependent reproductive output.
(3) Predation reduces both breeding and post-breeding numbers below what would otherwise occur. In this scenario, compensation is insufficient to offset the full effects of predation, and throughout the year numbers remain below the level they might otherwise achieve.

As a general point, predation on eggs and chicks is much less likely to affect subsequent breeding numbers than is predation on the adults themselves. This is because, the earlier in life that losses are imposed, the greater the opportunity for these losses to be made good before the next breeding season, by re-layings, by improved survival of remaining young and adults, or by immigration from elsewhere. Similarly, losses of adults at the start of winter are less likely to reduce breeding numbers than are similar losses at the end, just before nesting begins.

PREDATION BY HOUSE CATS

Two predation issues in particular have generated heated discussion in recent years, but for neither of them have effects on population levels been established. The first concerns the numbers of house cats in Britain, and their potential effects on garden bird populations. Even though they are fed daily by their owners, free-ranging pet cats kill many wild birds. Given their high densities in towns and cities (typically more than 200 individuals per km^2), cats could have a substantial influence on urban bird populations. A questionnaire survey in various cities, covering the six-month period April–August 1997, showed that a total of 986 cats, living in 618 households, brought in 14,370 prey items, consisting of 69% small mammals, 24% birds, 4% amphibia and 1% reptiles (Woods *et al.* 2003). At least 44 bird species were represented. In households that provided food for birds, fewer birds were brought in, but of a greater range of species. The number of items brought home declined with increasing age of the cat. On the basis of these figures, the total British cat population, then estimated at 8 million house cats and one million feral cats,[10] was calculated to bring home about 92 million (range 85–100 million) prey items in this six-month period, including 57 million small mammals (including bats), 27 million birds and five million amphibia and reptiles.

In a second study, questionnaire surveys in ten areas within the city of Bristol enabled average cat densities to be estimated at 348 cats per km². In five of these areas, cat owners were asked to record all prey items brought home, from which the numbers of birds killed annually could be estimated (Baker et al. 2008). These figures were then compared with the breeding density and productivity of local birds to estimate the potential impact of cat predation on the bird population. Considering the eight species most commonly taken by cats, only 1.17 adult birds were found, and only 3.07 juveniles were produced, for every cat present, giving a very low ratio of birds per cat in these high-density urban areas. Approximately 60% of the cats studied for up to a year never returned home prey items of any kind. Despite this, for at least three prey species (House Sparrow, Dunnock and Robin) the estimated predation rates were so high that cats may have created a sink habitat in which bird numbers were maintained by continued immigration from more productive areas elsewhere. Predation on birds was greatest in spring and summer, reflecting the vulnerability of juveniles. Across species, birds killed by cats were of significantly lower weight than those killed following collisions, suggesting that some birds killed by cats might soon have died anyway. Their loss would thus have represented a compensatory rather than additive form of mortality. Overall, the predation rates estimated in this Bristol study suggested that cats were probably a major cause of mortality for some species of small birds, but the study could not show whether cats were limiting bird breeding densities.

Another study, this time in a rural area, looked at the items brought home by approximately 70 cats in the Bedfordshire village of Felmersham over a one-year period (Churcher & Lawton 1987). A total of 1,090 prey items was recorded, including 535 mammals, 297 birds and 258 unidentified items, an average of about 14 items per cat per year. Twenty-two species of birds and 15 species of mammals were identified, the most important being Woodmice (17%), House Sparrows (16%) and Bank Voles (14%). Old cats of both sexes caught fewer prey over the year than young cats. Female cats on the edge of the village also caught more prey than female cats in intermediate or central areas of the village; but male cats showed no such effect. The type of prey caught also varied with position in the village, with 'core' cats catching proportionately more birds than 'edge' cats. Weather apparently influenced hunting success, with fewer prey caught in winter; and on wet or windy days. Estimates of the number of House

---

10 The numbers of house cats in Britain has since been estimated at 10.5 million individuals.

Sparrows in the village at the start of the breeding season, and the number of Sparrows known to have been caught by the cats, suggested that at least 30% of the Sparrow deaths in the village were due to cats. The impact of domestic cats on local birdlife clearly warrants more study.

PREDATION ON RACING PIGEONS

Pigeon fanciers often complain about Sparrowhawks and Peregrines killing their pigeons. Sparrowhawks take homing pigeons mainly at the lofts, whereas Peregrines take them mainly away from lofts on training flights or races. Towards the end of the twentieth century, there were an estimated 69,000 pigeon fanciers in the UK, operating some 52,000 lofts, from which 3.8 million pigeons were trained and raced each year (Shawyer *et al.* 2003). It was calculated that, on average, each loft fielded 73 racing pigeons of which 38 (52%) were lost during a year. Peregrines and Sparrowhawks were estimated to account for 3.5% and 3.7% respectively of the lost birds. Overall predation was therefore not great, but it

FIG 83. The Peregrine *Falco peregrinus* is a major predator of feral and domestic pigeons. (Peter Beasley)

varied substantially between regions, and was unevenly spread among pigeon fanciers, some suffering disproportionately high losses.

Despite the small proportion taken, feral and homing pigeons form a large part of the diet of Peregrines in many parts of Britain and Ireland. In some regions, such as south-central Wales, variations in Peregrine breeding densities were found to be related to variations in the availability of racing pigeons, which were taken in greatest numbers during the racing season, April–September. In these months pigeons formed more than half the total prey items taken, and three-quarters of the food by weight (Dixon *et al.* 2003). Peregrines thus showed both a numerical and functional response to this major prey.

Predation rates are relatively high in southern Scotland. In one investigation, the numbers of Scottish racing pigeons taken by Peregrines were assessed from the recovery of pigeon rings from Peregrine eyries and measures of the daily food intake of Peregrines (Parrott *et al.* 2008). It was estimated that 7–23% of Scottish pigeons died in this way, representing 13–40% of the total losses to all causes. Conversely, 60–87% of losses could not be attributed to Peregrines. Many of the killed pigeons were probably strays, already lost to their owners. In fact, more than half of all domestic pigeons are estimated to become strays, many adding to the Feral Pigeon populations of towns and cities, although this figure is disputed by some pigeon fanciers. The number of pigeons available to raptors has declined in recent years, partly because fewer people are keeping pigeons, but mainly because some major race routes have been deliberately shifted away from the hill districts where most Peregrines breed. A recent decline of Peregrines in the Lake District has been attributed to such a shift in race routes.

FIG 84. Female Sparrowhawk *Accipiter nisus* feeding on a Woodpigeon *Columba palumbus*. (David Culley)

The future of Peregrines over much of Britain and Ireland will probably depend largely on trends in pigeon racing, the seasonal timing and the routes used.

Individual Sparrowhawks kill far fewer racing pigeons than Peregrines do, and are much less dependent on them, but because Sparrowhawks are more numerous and widely spread, their overall impact is similar according to the figures given above. Goshawks also take racing pigeons, and this predation is likely to increase if Goshawk numbers in Britain continue to rise. There are some interesting Dutch data from rings on racing pigeons based on systematic searching of Goshawk nesting areas with metal detectors. In one study near the coast, the tracing of ownership from rings showed that 81% of 465 pigeons had overflown their destination and could have been permanently lost. For the most part, they were not birds that would have been of great value to their owners. Other data showed that only 0.1% of the pigeons taken had been trained in local villages, so that most would have been passing birds from further afield (Vlugt 2002). The majority of pigeons were killed in their first year of life, which enabled another researcher to estimate, from the rings found, the years of occupancy of 22 Goshawk nests for the previous 15 breeding seasons. The results of this exercise agreed with observational data on occupancy (van Haaff 2001). In earlier centuries, many other conflicts concerned predation of chickens and other domestic livestock, but now that poultry are mostly kept in sheds or other enclosures, these problems have shrunk to insignificance.

CONCLUDING REMARKS

Predation is a natural everyday phenomenon, and has presumably occurred throughout the history of life on earth. But many people find it hard to look at it dispassionately. All the bird species now found in the British Isles suffer predation at some stage of their lives, and most at every stage from egg to adult. Many different predators are involved, whether other birds, mammals or reptiles, although, in any given situation, a small number of predator species account for most deaths. Occasionally, predation rates on eggs, chicks or adults are found to be so high that they are clearly unsustainable, and will inevitably cause population declines. But most predation rates are well below this level, and can seldom tell us much about the role of predation in limiting bird numbers, because much natural predation can be offset by reduced losses from other causes, such as food shortage. To assess the impact of predation on the levels of breeding populations, other types of study are needed, which takes us on to the next chapter.

CHAPTER 7

Predation: Population Impacts

B IRDS FALL VICTIM TO A WIDE RANGE of predators, whether as eggs, young or adults, but what impact does this predation have on subsequent breeding numbers and general population densities? From field studies, situations have been described where predators: (1) have no obvious effect on the breeding numbers of their avian prey; (2) limit prey breeding numbers below what the habitat would otherwise support; (3) cause oscillations in prey numbers; and (4) exterminate their prey locally. These are all direct effects of predators on bird populations, but predators also have indirect effects by restricting the number and types of places where birds can feed, nest and sleep safely, an aspect discussed in Chapter 12.

In the British Isles many predators of birds have increased in recent decades (Tapper 1999, Gibbons *et al.* 2007). Most were recovering from the impacts of past human persecution or organochlorine pesticide use, while others may have benefited from recent land-use practices, including the large-scale captive-rearing and release of gamebirds. Over the same period, many wild prey species, including songbirds and waders, have declined, again in association with land-use changes. Inevitably, this has raised questions about whether the increases in predators have caused declines in their prey, or whether the two sets of trends are independent of one another, correlated but not causally related. The main voice of concern has come from game management interests, and much recent research has been aimed at addressing these issues. But whatever the relationships between predators and prey, predation is a natural phenomenon to which all bird species are exposed, and predators have lived alongside their current prey species for millennia without eliminating them. If anything has altered these long-standing relationships, it is likely to be the landscape and other environmental changes wrought by humanity.

NO EFFECTS ON PREY BREEDING NUMBERS

In some bird species, predation might remove so few individuals that it has no discernible effects on breeding numbers. In other species, which are subject to substantial predation, the losses involved are compensated by reductions in other losses, so population levels are maintained in the longer term. This happens when total mortality is density-dependent and 'predetermined' by the extent to which numbers exceed the available territories or other resources.

This latter situation underlies the notion of a 'doomed surplus' from which predators take only the number that would die anyway. This idea was first proposed by an American gamebird biologist, Paul Errington (1946). He found that coveys of Bobwhite Quail in winter territories with poor cover suffered more predation than those in areas with better cover. He therefore concluded that lack of cover was the ultimate cause of death. He suggested that each habitat had a limited carrying capacity and that it was only when the numbers rose above this level that predation became limiting (Errington 1946). You cannot study the effects of predation, he argued, by counting the numbers of prey killed. You have to determine the factors that predispose predation and make some individuals vulnerable and others not. His idea was that numbers were trimmed each year to a level that the habitat could sustain, and that the excess succumbed to whatever mortality agents were available locally, whether predation, disease or starvation. This was an interesting point because it meant that, even though predation could be substantial, it might have no effect on breeding density.

Support for the notion of a doomed surplus came from a later study on Red Grouse in eastern Scotland (Jenkins et al. 1963, 1964). These birds took territories in autumn, but their density on the heather moor habitat was limited, leading to exclusion of a proportion of birds, called the 'non-territorial surplus', which could not breed. By tagging both territorial and non-territorial individuals, it was found that mortality was largely restricted to the non-territorial birds, the remains of many of which were found in the area. If a territorial bird died, its place was rapidly taken by a non-territorial individual, so that territorial (breeding) density was maintained through to the following spring, but by that time most of the non-territorial birds had disappeared. It thus seemed that predators and other mortality agents were merely removing the non-territorial surplus, and causing no reduction in breeding density. In this area, however, the various predators of eggs and chicks were controlled by gamekeepers, so that the post-breeding grouse population may have been higher as a result. One can imagine that, if the post-breeding population were lower, the surplus might have been small or non-existent. In these circumstances, predators could well have removed some territorial birds, and reduced the breeding density, a situation subsequently described for Red Grouse in other areas where predators were commoner, and discussed later in this chapter (Hudson 1992, Redpath & Thirgood 1997).

Another situation in which predation might be compensatory, rather than additive, is if sick or starving prey are taken by predators in numbers greater than expected from their proportion in the population. Selection of weaker individuals is most evident in species that are normally difficult for the predator to catch, or among individuals caught after a tiring chase rather than quickly by surprise (Kenward 1978, Temple 1987). In one study, many of the Woodpigeons caught by Goshawks were thin, with 28% of victims already starved beyond the point of recovery (Kenward 1978). In such cases, the impact of predation on the population is clearly less than expected from the numbers taken. Also, by taking diseased individuals, predators might limit the spread of the disease, and hence have positive effects on breeding numbers (see Chapter 9).

A case study: Sparrowhawk predation on songbirds

The Sparrowhawk is one of our commonest raptors, nesting in woodland and hunting small birds, in both woods and open country. It can remove a large proportion of prey individuals each year, but in most prey species it seems to cause no obvious depression of breeding density, as concluded from many detailed studies (Tinbergen 1946, Perrins & Geer 1980, Newton 1986, McCleery & Perrins 1991, Newton *et al.* 1997a, Thomson *et al.* 1998, Dhondt *et al.* 1998, Newson *et al.* 2010).

Lack of obvious impact was shown incidentally over much of Europe around 1960, when Sparrowhawks were eliminated from large areas through the use of organochlorine pesticides, recovering and re-colonising years later when

FIG 85. Male Sparrowhawk *Accipiter nisus*, a major predator of small birds, on a frequently used plucking post. (Edmund Fellowes)

organochlorine use was reduced (Chapter 18; Newton 1986). When Sparrowhawks declined, no great upsurge in songbird populations occurred. This was apparent, for example, in a single 16 ha oakwood on Bookham Common in southeast England, where all breeding birds were counted every year from 1949 to 1979 (Newton *et al.* 1997a). These counts covered both the decline and the recovery periods of Sparrowhawks, which bred in the wood and in the surrounding area up to 1959 and again from 1973. This gave three periods for comparison: 1949–59 (hawks present), 1960–72 (hawks absent) and 1973–79 (hawks present). If Sparrowhawks affected these songbirds, their numbers should have increased as Sparrowhawks disappeared, and then decreased when Sparrowhawks re-colonised. Thirteen songbird species were sufficiently numerous for analysis, and nine showed significant variations between the mean counts for the three periods. Seven species showed a sustained increase over the whole 31-year period and two a sustained decrease. These trends coincided with changes in the internal structure of the wood, which made it more suitable for some species and less suitable for others. No species was present in significantly greater numbers when Sparrowhawks were absent from the wood and at their lowest numbers in the surrounding area. These data therefore gave no indication that Sparrowhawks had any negative impact on the breeding densities of these 13 woodland songbird species. No other predator in Britain could take on the role of the Sparrowhawk during its period of absence, so other mortality agents among small birds must have achieved greater importance in the years when these hawks were absent.

This finding was paralleled by a more detailed study of Sparrowhawk predation on tits nesting in the 320 ha Wytham Wood near Oxford (Perrins & Geer 1980). Most tits bred in nest-boxes, and had been studied for many years, with adults and young ringed each year. As in much of southeast England, Sparrowhawks were effectively absent from Wytham during the period 1959–73, again giving three successive periods for comparison. Both Blue and Great Tit breeding numbers fluctuated greatly from year to year, but in general the numbers of nest-boxes occupied each year were not conspicuously higher in the period when hawks were absent than when they were present (Fig. 86). A surplus of boxes was available throughout.

After Sparrowhawks returned, some 6–8 pairs nested in the wood each year, and during 1976–79 nine hawk nests were studied intensively, recording all the prey that the adults brought for their young. Within 60 m of each successful hawk nest, both the occupancy and the success of nest-boxes were reduced, compared with boxes further away. This was attributed to the hawks removing more of the breeding tits near their own nests than elsewhere. No such effects were noted around hawk nests that failed soon after eggs had been laid, nor around one

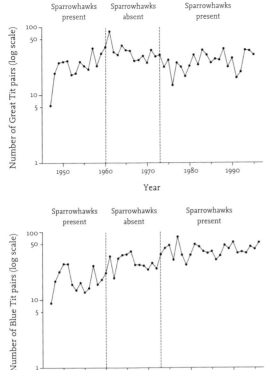

FIG 86. Numbers of Great Tits *Parus major* and Blue Tits *Cyanistes caeruleus* nesting in Marley Wood, Wytham, Oxford, during a 50-year period. Excluding the first year of study (when nest-boxes were first provided), nesting numbers were not conspicuously higher in years when Sparrowhawks were absent than in years when they were present. (Based on data provided by C. M. Perrins: see Newton & Perrins 1997)

successful hawk nest on the edge of the wood whose owners hunted chiefly in farmland. The results were consistent between years, even though the locations of the hawk nests changed. The effect of this local predation of breeding tits on the subsequent tit population of the whole wood was immeasurably small.

The hawks whose nests were watched ate many fledgling tits. Extrapolating these findings to all successful hawk nests in the wood each year, Sparrowhawks would have removed an estimated 18–34% of young Great Tits in the different years, and 18–27% of young Blue Tits. Nevertheless, an average of more than six young tits per tit pair (including failed pairs) was raised in these years. Only about one chick per pair was needed to replace the annual losses of adults in order to maintain the nesting population at a constant level, so many young tits must have died anyway from predation or from other mortality causes at other times of year.

These findings thus gave no convincing evidence that Sparrowhawks, despite their heavy predation, depressed Great and Blue Tit breeding densities (see also McCleery & Perrins 1991). Indeed, Blue Tits showed a long-term increase over the whole study period, both in Wytham and more widely in southern England. These various findings could probably be generalised to many other Sparrowhawk prey species, in that the main direct effects of predation were to: (1) change the seasonal pattern of mortality; (2) reduce the size of the post-breeding peak in the population; and (3) change the main agents of death; all without causing any noticeable decline in annual breeding numbers (Newton 1986). In practice, this meant that, instead of dying mainly in winter from food shortage, for example, potential prey birds died at all seasons largely from predation.

In a further study, this time in Belgium, the annual survival of Blue Tits (as assessed from ringing) averaged about 49% during 11 years when Sparrowhawks were absent, but fell to 38% in three years after a pair had started to nest in the study plot (Dhondt *et al.* 1998). This decline in survival was attributed to Sparrowhawk predation, mainly in spring. Again, however, the size of the Blue Tit breeding population did not decline, but there were fewer non-breeders than before, because, owing to the generally lower population, birds that would previously have not have bred until their second year of life were able to obtain territories and reproduce in their first year.

The effects of high predation on young Great Tits were simulated experimentally on the Dutch island of Vleiland, where natural predation was negligible (Kluijver 1966). Over four years, the production of young was deliberately reduced by about 60% of normal, yet no decline in subsequent breeding numbers occurred. Immigration did not increase, but survival rates in the remaining birds (especially adults) improved to almost twice their previous values. The implications were that individual survival was influenced by the numbers of conspecific competitors and that breeding numbers were limited by factors other than predation, at least up to a 60% loss of young. Compensatory changes in subsequent survival rates more or less offset the effect of removing young. This could well mimic the situation of high predation on young tits by Sparrowhawks, as studied at Wytham. None of these various studies was replicated, so some might argue that they were not typical of a wider area or a wider range of species.

Let us then examine the situation further. Many people who feed birds in their gardens witness frequent attacks by Sparrowhawks. They find it hard to believe that such predation causes no long-term decline in bird breeding numbers. In addition, a marked decline in the songbird populations of farmland occurred during the last quarter of the twentieth century, coinciding with the recovery of Sparrowhawks from past organochlorine impacts. Not surprisingly, then, some people have asked whether songbird declines were due to increasing predator populations, either of Sparrowhawks, Magpies or others. Further studies were therefore undertaken, using the nationwide databases of the BTO. From the early 1960s, the BTO organised annual surveys in which volunteer bird-watchers counted the birds nesting on particular study plots. Because the surveys recorded avian predators as well as songbirds, it was possible to test whether the presence or absence of Sparrowhawks and Magpies was related to changes in songbird numbers at those sites. If these predators were affecting songbird breeding numbers, we might expect these numbers to decrease more (or increase less) where predators were present. One study analysed songbird population changes over 30 years on nearly 300 lowland farmland and woodland sites (Thomson *et al.* 1998). It included 23 songbird species that are eaten by Sparrowhawks, or whose eggs and chicks are eaten by Magpies. In only two out of the 46 comparisons made (23 prey species and two predators) did a songbird species decline more when a predator was present than when it was absent, a number fewer than expected by chance alone. So again there were no strong grounds for thinking that Sparrowhawks or Magpies could have caused the long-term declines in songbird breeding numbers. Furthermore, other studies indicated that declines in many songbird species seen in recent decades resulted primarily from agricultural changes which reduced bird food supplies (discussed in Chapters 4 and 18).

A more recent study on possible predation impacts used nearly 40 years of BTO data on predator and prey numbers, and looked at a wider range of predators, using an improved method of analysis (Newson *et al.* 2010). The conclusion was essentially the same as in earlier studies, but again a small number of negative relationships emerged. The study asked whether English populations of 29 bird species, mostly songbirds, could have been depressed by increases in two groups of predators. One group included predators of both juvenile and adult birds, namely the Sparrowhawk, Kestrel and Buzzard; while the second group included five predators of nest contents, namely the Carrion Crow, Magpie, Jay, Great Spotted Woodpecker and Grey Squirrel. For 22 of the 29 potential prey species (76%), there was no link between the increase of predator and decline of prey numbers. Hence, for the majority of prey species this additional study provided no evidence of predator effects. Among the remaining seven species, in which there were significant negative correlations with particular predators, some seemed unlikely to be causal (for example, Goldfinches declined at a time when Common Buzzards increased), but others were more plausibly attributed to predation, such as links between increasing Sparrowhawks and decreasing Bullfinches, Tree Sparrows and Reed Buntings. Such correlations did not necessarily indicate causal relationships, however, for the species may have changed in the way they did for different independent reasons, nothing to do with predation (for example, the last three species also experienced massive reductions in their food supplies during their periods of decline: Chapter 4). Interestingly, this study also uncovered a large number of positive relationships in which prey and predators had increased or decreased in tandem.

These findings again lent no support to the view that predation has had major across-the-board negative effects on songbird breeding numbers, but left open the possibility that Sparrowhawks may somehow have affected Bullfinches, Tree Sparrows and Reed Buntings, all of which reached temporally high numbers when Sparrowhawks were reduced (Newton 1967, Marchant *et al.* 1990, Summers-Smith 1996; for further discussion of Bullfinches, see Chapter 12). Sparrowhawks may also have reduced Blackbird numbers on Bardsey Island off the Welsh coast, but this island offered somewhat unusual habitat for Blackbirds, with little cover (Loxton & Silcocks 1997). In addition, several studies have suggested that Sparrowhawks could have influenced House Sparrow populations, especially in urban areas (Sanderson 2001, Bell *et al.* 2010). The argument is based on the observation that, as Sparrowhawks moved into cities from the 1980s, following their recovery in the surrounding countryside, House Sparrows in many cities began to decline. Bell *et al.* (2010) argued that these two events were so closely correlated in space and time that they were almost certainly causally related. However, other changes occurred in cities over the same period, including a big reduction in potential foraging areas, as 'brownfield' sites were developed and garden areas reduced. These changes would have greatly lessened the food supplies available for city-dwelling sparrows, whether seeds for adults or insects for chicks. Similarly, in the countryside, House Sparrows had to contend with the 'bird-proofing' of barns and grain-stores, as well as the agricultural changes that reduced the foods of all seed-eating birds. The role of predation in House Sparrow declines therefore remains unresolved, and we cannot yet class it as significant or insignificant.

Any generalist predator, such as the Sparrowhawk, might eliminate a rare species from a particular locality, either by chance or because that species is highly vulnerable compared to other prey available locally. During the first detailed study of Sparrowhawk predation, made in the Netherlands, Sparrowhawks were thought to have eliminated Tree Pipits from the study area (Tinbergen 1946). Compared to

FIG 87. The House Sparrow *Passer domesticus* is a favourite prey of the Sparrowhawk *Accipiter nisus* that has declined in recent decades. (Alan Martin)

other prey species, Tree Pipits were relatively scarce, and their behaviour – singing from exposed twigs and parachuting slowly down from their song-perches – made them obvious and available to predators. But Sparrowhawks have clearly not eliminated Tree Pipits from the whole of their wide breeding range.

LOWERING OF PREY BREEDING NUMBERS

In other situations, some predators have been shown convincingly to reduce the breeding densities of their prey. The prey species concerned were mostly ground-nesting species, which for obvious reasons are vulnerable to a wider range of predators than are birds that nest off the ground in safer sites. Moreover, it is not only the eggs and chicks of ground-nesting species that are vulnerable, but the incubating adults as well.

The ability of predators to hold prey breeding density well below the level that could occur in the absence of predation was shown by research on Grey Partridges on English farmland (Potts 1980, 1986). The nests of this species are often located along hedgerows or other field margins which predators can easily search. The eggs are favoured by Crows and Magpies, while the tight-sitting females are often killed by Foxes, Stoats and Cats.

Field studies and mathematical models indicated how Partridge breeding densities could be regulated under different levels of predation (Potts 1980, 1986, 2012, Potts & Aebischer 1991). In areas where predators were present at near-normal densities, predation on Partridge nests was strongly density-dependent: the greater the density of nests, the greater the proportion of eggs and females

FIG 88. Grey Partridges *Perdix perdix* were once common over much of lowland Britain, but are now scarce, as a result of the pesticide-induced shortage of insects on arable land. Densities can be lowered further by heavy predation on adults, eggs and chicks. (Frank Snijkers)

that were destroyed, and the lower the breeding success. However, the form of this relationship varied between areas, depending on the amount of nesting cover present. Where cover was plentiful (around 8 km of hedgerow per km² of farmland), the predation rate increased only slowly with a rise in nest density, but where cover was sparse (say less than 4 km of hedgerow per km²) the predation rate rose steeply, perhaps because, with so little cover, the predators had less to search. At levels of hedgerow cover greater than 8 km per km², Partridges gained no additional protection and there was no further change in the relationship between predation rate and nest density. Simulated population trends, based on field data, indicated that density-dependent nest predation was capable on its own of stabilising Partridge breeding densities at relatively low levels. The equilibrium level increased with the amount of nesting cover available (see also Chapter 12). As in the Bobwhite Quail studied by Errington (1946), the habitat influenced the level of the breeding population through predation. Other examples of density-dependent nest predation are mentioned in Box 3.

Over the years, the experience of gamekeepers was that in any given habitat a considerable increase in Partridge post-breeding and breeding numbers could be achieved by reducing the numbers of relevant predators. In areas where this occurred, the density-dependence in nest failures was almost removed, and nest success remained consistently high. This led to a big improvement in post-breeding density, and also in spring breeding density. Under such reduced predation, breeding densities were generally higher than under normal predation, but were again related to habitat quality, as reflected in the amount of ground cover.

When spring numbers exceeded the carrying capacity of the habitat, the surplus was removed by emigration, and when spring numbers were deficient they could be made good by immigration (Jenkins 1961). Partridges thus

---

Box 3. Density-dependent nest predation

Because of the potential importance of density-dependent predation in regulating bird breeding densities, much effort has been devoted to checking for such relationships. As in the Grey Partridge, nest predation has been found to increase disproportionately with nest-density in some other ground-nesting game birds, including the Red-legged Partridge and Pheasant (Potts 1980). Hence, in these species too, both post-breeding and breeding densities might be reduced by predation below what would otherwise occur, an inference supported by comparisons of Red-legged Partridges in areas with and without predator control. But these relationships did not exclude the possibility that predation was also affected by habitat, especially by the amount of nesting cover, which could influence the equilibrium population level in the presence or absence of predators. Moreover, where additional species nest in the same type of site in the same habitat, predators may respond to their combined density, so that they all suffer greater predation than when nesting alone (Blancher & Robertson 1985).

Density-dependence in nest success has also been detected in species other than gamebirds. In the Great Tit, predation on nestlings was found to be density-dependent, as greater proportions of broods were taken by Weasels and Great Spotted Woodpeckers in years of highest breeding densities (Krebs 1970, Dunn 1977). Density-dependence in predation rates is often evident on spatial, as well as temporal scales, as found by observation on the natural nests of songbirds, ducks and others (Fretwell 1972, Dunn 1977, Fleskes & Klaas 1991). It has also been shown by experiments which involved laying out artificial nests (with quail or chicken eggs) at different densities in similar cover, and finding what proportion had their eggs removed by predators (Tinbergen et al. 1967, Göransson et al. 1975, Esler & Grand 1993). Predation on artificial nests may not be the same as on natural nests, but in all such experiments, predation again emerged as density-dependent, being disproportionately higher in the high-density situations. The main observed predators were various crow species which, after finding an egg, increased their search in the immediate vicinity, enhancing the risk for other eggs nearby. Although predation on eggs and nestlings can often be density-dependent, it does not necessarily stabilise the breeding population, either because it is not sufficiently strong, or because subsequent events act to nullify its effects (Chapter 2).

For nests within colonies, the situation can be more complicated. On the one hand, nesting in colonies often confers some protection against predators of eggs and chicks because the colony members can join together to attack marauders (Kruuk 1964). Where communal defence is the main factor operating, it can lead to inverse density-dependence within the colonies, with better breeding success at higher densities or in larger colonies (Kruuk 1964, Birkhead 1977, Andersson & Wiklund 1978, Péron et al. 2010). This was found among Guillemots subjected to egg predation by gulls (Fig. 24b), and, as indicated above, it has no regulatory role. In some colonial gull species, however, the gulls themselves prey upon the eggs and chicks of neighbours. Such cannibalism is often the main cause of individual breeding failure, and tends to be greatest in the densest parts of colonies, so may help to regulate their populations (Spaans et al. 1987). Among roof-nesting Herring Gulls, pairs nesting in groups produced fewer young than pairs nesting singly on isolated sites (Monaghan 1979). Within a single ground-nesting Herring Gull colony, however, the greatest success occurred among pairs nesting at the most common density, with success declining at both lower and higher densities (Parsons 1976). This was taken to illustrate the compromise in a colonial species between the conflicting advantages of clustering and spacing out.

redistributed themselves each spring, so that breeding densities were matched to habitat quality. The spring population, prior to the redistribution, had usually been influenced by winter shooting, leaving a surplus (relative to habitat) in some areas and a deficit in others. There were thus two natural density-dependent processes in the annual cycle of Grey Partridges that could regulate their numbers: (1) predation on nest contents, which in the presence of predators gave a breeding density lower than the habitat could otherwise support, and (2) pre-breeding redistribution, which was the main regulating influence where predators were controlled. Such spring movements could to some extent mitigate the effects of high nest predation where predators were not controlled.

These conclusions were based on comparative field studies in different areas, coupled with simulation modelling. They were later supported by a predator-removal experiment conducted over six years in two areas of similar habitat on Salisbury Plain in southern England (Tapper *et al.* 1996). Predator killing was undertaken in one area for three years, leaving the second area as a control, and then switched to the second area, leaving the first as the control. Predator removal was done mainly in spring and involved chiefly Foxes, Carrion Crows and Magpies, whose spring densities were thereby much reduced. These operations led to significantly improved nest success and brood sizes among Partridges. Allowing for effects of site and year, August numbers increased by an average of 75% following predator removal, and breeding numbers the following year increased by 36%. At the end of the three-year period in each area, autumn populations had increased by 3–5-fold and breeding numbers by 2.6-fold relative to numbers in the control area. Legally protected predators, such as birds of prey, were left unharmed throughout, and each year after the Partridge nesting season, other predators re-colonised the area from which they had been removed. This experiment confirmed that removal of these key predators in spring could increase the post-breeding and subsequent breeding densities of Partridges. Similar results were obtained in a later nine-year study in Hertfordshire (Aebischer & Ewald 2010). In other words, Partridge numbers were limited by predation.

Because the above experiments involved the removal only of legally controllable predators, leaving raptors untouched, other work was needed to assess the impacts of raptors, which have increased in recent decades. It is in spring (February–April), when cover is sparse and coveys break up as pairs are formed, that Partridges are most at risk from raptor predation. Isolated pairs lose the collective vigilance of the covey, and become preoccupied with other things, such as searching for potential nest-sites. On British farmland, with Goshawks currently absent from most areas, the main raptorial predators on Partridges are female Sparrowhawks, and to a lesser extent Buzzards. Using data on Partridge survival rates and estimates of raptor densities from 20 study sites in England, it was calculated that Partridge populations above five pairs per km^2 would be little affected by raptor predation (Watson *et al.* 2007a, 2007b). This is partly because Sparrowhawks do not increase in response to Partridge numbers, but remain spaced out in relation to their woodland nest-sites. Their predation was therefore inversely density-dependent, and the more numerous the Partridges the lower the proportion killed. Raptor predation could accelerate the decline of Partridge populations already reduced to densities below about five pairs per km^2 by, for example, farming practices or over-shooting.

Another three-year study in France highlighted the importance of predation on Partridges studied in the breeding season at ten different sites (Bro *et al.* 2001). Among more than a thousand radio-tagged females, survival through spring–summer varied between 25% and 65% between areas. Overall the main cause of mortality was predation, with mammalian predators causing 64% of these losses and raptors 29%. These proportions varied between sites, mainly according to the combined densities of Hen and Marsh Harriers, which were common on some of the French farmland. A doubling of predation on female Partridges was associated with a fourfold rise in the densities of harriers. No evidence was found that captured Partridges were suffering from starvation or high parasitism, and predation seemed additive to other losses. Within sites, Partridges were at least risk from harrier predation when they were near woods, trees or buildings, or near crops that provided good cover. With different raptors, such as Sparrowhawks and Goshawks, this situation may have differed, as these raptors tend to hunt from the cover of woodland.

Predators and grouse

The study mentioned earlier, in which predators concentrated on the non-territorial sector of a high-density Red Grouse population and had no effect on breeding numbers, was conducted in 1957–62, a period when Fox and raptor densities were generally low in northeast Scotland (Watson 1985). A later study of a low-density grouse population was conducted during 1985–90, a time when predators were generally more numerous (Hudson 1992). In this study, overwinter survival rates of territorial and non-territorial grouse were similar, and at least part of the winter predation was additive to other mortality, reducing the density of breeding grouse in spring. By this time, some parts of the moor had fallen vacant.

Two other studies investigated whether Red Grouse densities were higher where generalist predator numbers were lower. The first looked only at the numbers of grouse shot, as a measure of post-breeding densities, and showed

FIG 89. The Red Grouse *Lagopus l. scotica*, endemic to Britain and Ireland, and the subject of many studies on predation impacts. (Laurie Campbell)

that bags were largest on moors with the greatest densities of gamekeepers, supposedly because these moors had the most effective Fox and crow control (Hudson 1992). The second found that breeding densities of Red Grouse were twice as high on moors managed for grouse shooting as on other moors (Tharme *et al.* 2001). This difference in grouse densities again reflected the presence or absence of predator control, but was somewhat less pronounced after taking account of habitat and other differences between the two types of moor. Taken together, these studies suggested that predation could reduce Red Grouse breeding densities. Killing of some predators, such as Foxes and Carrion Crows, is still legal, whereas killing of raptors is not, although it is still routinely practised on many moors (Chapter 17). Turning to Black Grouse, the findings differed, in that a replicated study at five sites in northern England and Scotland revealed that densities and breeding success were no higher on moors with a gamekeeper (and associated predator control) than on moors without (Baines 1996).

The Langholm study

A study during the 1990s was aimed specifically to find the effect of raptor predation on Red Grouse numbers (Redpath & Thirgood 1997). It was based at Langholm in southwest Scotland, but was also extended in part to five other moors elsewhere in Scotland. On all these moors raptors were protected, but the numbers of Foxes and Carrion Crows were reduced by gamekeepers. Each year during 1992–97, the researchers estimated on each moor the abundance of grouse, songbirds (mainly Meadow Pipits) and small mammals (mainly Field Voles), and monitored the numbers, breeding success and diet of Hen Harriers and Peregrines, the main avian predators of grouse. They also studied grouse mortality, and raptor numbers and behaviour in winter, in addition to measuring a number of habitat features. Aerial photographs revealed that nearly half the heather cover had been lost from Langholm moor between 1948 and 1988, mostly at lower altitudes, and had been replaced by grasses. This vegetation change was attributed to heavy grazing by sheep. Grouse bags on the same moor showed a steady downward trend since 1913, superimposed on which were six-year fluctuations, with the last peak in 1990. Given that raptor breeding densities on and around the moor were very low before 1990, it was extremely unlikely that raptors were responsible for either the long-term decline or the fluctuations in grouse bags. The fluctuations paralleled those recorded in northern England, where strongyle parasites were implicated as the causal factor, so these parasites may also have been important at Langholm (Chapter 9).

Under strict protection during 1992–97, Hen Harrier numbers at Langholm increased from two to more than 20 breeding females, and Peregrine numbers increased from three to six pairs. In winter, the numbers of harriers seen per unit time in standard watches fluctuated in line with grouse densities (more harriers with more grouse), while the numbers of Peregrines seen remained similar from year to year.

In each year, raptor predation between April and July removed on average 30% of the potential breeding grouse, and was density-dependent, and in the summers of 1995 and 1996 harrier predation also removed on average 37% of grouse chicks (from a total loss of 45%). Most of these adult and chick losses were probably additive to other forms of mortality, and together reduced the post-breeding numbers of grouse by an estimated 50% within a single breeding season. In each year raptors also killed an average of 30% of the grouse between October and March, but this mortality varied from area to area and year to year in a density-dependent manner, and it was not possible to judge what proportion of these grouse would have survived in the absence of raptors. In addition to the grouse killed by raptors, another 3% of the birds present in October were lost over winter from other causes, including predation by Foxes. A mathematical model of the grouse population at Langholm, combining the estimated reduction in breeding productivity with observed density-dependence in winter loss, predicted that over two years, in the absence of breeding raptors, grouse breeding numbers would have increased by 1.9 times and post-breeding numbers by 3.9 times (Redpath et al. 2000). The conclusion was that raptors, at the densities prevailing, were holding the grouse population down.

Red Grouse breeding numbers did not change significantly during 1992–96, averaging 66 birds per km^2, but they declined subsequently. Grouse bags did not peak in 1996 or 1997 as expected from previous cyclic fluctuations. In contrast, grouse bags on two other nearby moors, which had previously fluctuated in synchrony with those at Langholm, increased to high levels in 1997. These moors held only low levels of raptors. Predation by the much larger numbers of raptors at Langholm was considered the most likely explanation for the continued low grouse density and low grouse bags on this moor during the study. The impact of raptor predation was sufficient to dampen the usual cyclical changes in grouse populations, and prevented these increases from occurring. At the same time, grouse numbers did recover from cyclical lows on nearby moors where raptors were not protected (Redpath & Thirgood 1997). Bags on five other moors where raptors were protected did not show the same patterns as observed at Langholm. On four of these moors driven shooting was already not viable by the time raptor protection occurred, and on the fifth raptors remained at low density.

The main conclusion of this study was that raptors (mainly Hen Harriers), at the densities at which they occurred, removed so many grouse that the grouse population remained low, and produced insufficient young to support driven grouse shooting. The post-breeding grouse population did not reach a high peak similar to those reached in the past in about every sixth year. Raptor predation seemed the most likely process to have set this new level and, as such, could be considered limiting.

This study raised other interesting questions. For example, why did Hen Harriers reach such high densities on this moor? The main factor influencing the densities of breeding harriers was the abundance of small prey, such as voles and pipits, eaten by the males in spring, at which season the males provided food for their larger mates. Where Meadow Pipits were abundant, so were harriers, and where small mammals fluctuated in abundance from year to year, harriers fluctuated in parallel (Redpath & Thirgood 1999). These prey species prefer grass or a mixture of grass and heather, so their numbers are likely to have increased as a result of heavy sheep grazing in the past. Harriers were not found to reach anywhere near these densities on moors consisting almost entirely of heather, where such small prey were less plentiful. It seemed, therefore, that the 'harrier problem' at Langholm was partly the result of past land-use practices (intensive sheep grazing) which permitted a high ratio of harriers per grouse. In none of the moors studied were the breeding densities of Hen Harriers or Peregrines related to the densities of grouse themselves (Peregrines being influenced mainly by the availability of nest-sites). Limitation of grouse numbers by raptors is also likely to occur on moors where grouse are at low densities for some other reason, such as low points in population cycles, or poor moor management over a long period (Thirgood et al. 2000).

After the end of this project, when grouse had reached low levels, attempts at grouse management ceased, and all predator control and heather burning stopped, but bird populations continued to be monitored for several further years (Baines *et al.* 2008). In this second phase, Red Grouse, Golden Plover, Lapwing and Curlew declined further, whilst Carrion Crow and Snipe increased. Hen Harriers, which had increased from two to more than 20 breeding females, declined back to two. Increased Crow and Fox numbers in the later years probably contributed to the observed declines in grouse, waders and Hen Harriers, as most of the observed harrier nests failed to produce young in these years. The implication was that high densities of Hen Harriers were themselves dependent on control of larger predators, such as Foxes.

The Northumbrian study

Another experiment during 2000–08 in Northumberland examined the effects of predator removal on grouse, waders and other birds (Fletcher *et al.* 2010). In this area, Carrion Crows, Foxes and mustelids were removed, while birds of prey were left alone, but no harriers bred there, and the overall numbers of raptors were generally lower than at Langholm. In the event, control of mustelids was ineffective, as there were few Stoats on the plot, and Weasel numbers were not noticeably reduced by control measures. In effect, then, the experiment tested the effects of Fox and Crow removal, and it was estimated that, on average, control operations reduced spring Fox numbers by 43% and Crow numbers by 78%.

The study covered four moorland plots, each of about 12 km², and lasted eight years. On one plot no predator control was undertaken; on the second, predator control was undertaken every year; on the third plot predator control was undertaken only in the first four years; and on the fourth plot only in the second four. In other words, two plots received the same treatment throughout, while on two other plots treatments were reversed half way through the study. On all four plots the numbers of territorial grouse, waders, Meadow Pipits and Skylarks were recorded every year, and their breeding success assessed.

Over the years of the study, predator removal increased the breeding success of Red Grouse, waders and Meadow Pipits, on average by about threefold. In addition, Golden Plovers, Lapwings and Curlews increased in abundance with predator removal (mean annual change +37% across species), but decreased where predators were not removed (mean annual change −28% across species). These changes were statistically significant for Curlews (with a three-year lag because Curlews do not breed until their third year) and Lapwings, but not for Golden Plovers. In addition, Red Grouse showed significant increases where predators were removed, and significant declines where they were not, but no such differences were detected for Meadow Pipits or Skylarks. This study therefore showed that the breeding densities of several species of ground-nesting birds could be increased by control of generalist predators, despite the continued presence of low numbers of raptors. In other words, the numbers of some ground-nesting birds were limited by predation.

These findings were also interesting in light of an earlier study which had shown that densities of Golden Plovers, Lapwings and Curlews (but not Snipe) were markedly higher on grouse moors (with predator control) than on other moors that were not managed for grouse (Tharme *et al.* 2001). In this study, densities of Golden Plovers and Lapwings averaged about five times higher on managed grouse moors, while those of Curlews and Red Grouse averaged twice as high. By contrast, in this same study three small songbird species (Meadow Pipit, Skylark, Whinchat) were less abundant on grouse moors, as were Carrion Crows (which were controlled by gamekeepers).

Capercaillie and Black Grouse in Abernethy Forest

Capercaillie had been in general decline and had shown poor breeding success for several years when a study began in Abernethy Forest in the Spey valley of Scotland (Summers *et al.* 2004). Production of young was studied there over 11 years, 1988–99, while crow numbers were reduced by culling from ten pairs to one during the middle five years, 1992–96. Attempts were also made to reduce Fox numbers, but few were killed, and regular scat and den counts indicated that no significant reduction was achieved. Because Capercaillie nests were hard to

FIG 90. Male Capercaillie *Tetrao urogallus* displaying. This declining species of pine forests in northeast Scotland has been subject to studies of predation impacts. (Laurie Campbell)

find, predation rates were measured instead on artificial nests of chicken eggs set out in the forest each spring, and the productivity of Capercaillie was measured by the number of chicks seen per female in late summer. Predation on chicken eggs was lower, and Capercaillie productivity was higher, during the period of crow control than before or after. But productivity was also higher in years when the small chicks experienced dry weather in June. In effect, Capercaillie produced most young in years when low June rainfall coincided with low predation rates by crows on artificial nests. In addition, over the study period, Pine Martens unexpectedly increased in numbers, and took increasing numbers of eggs.

Productivity of Black Grouse in Abernethy Forest was higher than that of Capercaillie, but showed a similar temporal pattern, so was also probably influenced by crow numbers and June rainfall. In both species, breeding success influenced subsequent breeding numbers: years of high productivity were followed by an increase in breeding numbers, and years of low productivity by a decrease in breeding numbers (Summers *et al.* 2010). To maintain breeding numbers from one year to the next in Abernethy, it was calculated that Capercaillies had to produce 0.9 chicks per female each year and Black Grouse 1.3 chicks per female. Despite confounding variables, a general conclusion was that egg predation by crows could reduce the breeding success and breeding numbers of both species.

Lapwings and other waders

Numbers of waders, such as Lapwing, Redshank, Snipe and Curlew, breeding in lowland wet grassland in Britain and Ireland have declined greatly in recent decades. The main causal factor seems to be increased predation on eggs and chicks, itself resulting partly through changes in agricultural procedures, and perhaps also from a general increase in Foxes and other generalist predators. For the Lapwing, an analysis of British ringing results revealed no rise in the annual mortality rate of full-grown birds over the period 1930–90 (rather a slight increase since 1960). On that level of mortality, Lapwings would need to produce an estimated 0.83–0.97 young per pair per year to maintain their numbers.[11] This level of productivity was found in only eight out of 24 studies in different areas, those least subjected to agricultural changes (Peach *et al.* 1994). The most detrimental change was the draining and re-seeding of former wet pastures, which reduced feeding opportunities and lowered nest success. Eggs and chicks were much more conspicuous to predators on the uniform green of re-seeded areas than against the more varied background of rough undrained ones, and reduced food supplies made chicks more active and vulnerable to predators (Baines 1990).

---

11 Subsequent estimates suggested a lower figure, around 0.6–0.8 young per pair.

Later experimental studies examined the effects of Fox and Crow control on Lapwings nesting on 11 lowland wet grassland nature reserves, where nest success was often low. These studies continued for eight years, on each site comparing four years with predator control against four years without (Bolton *et al.* 2007). In some areas, predator removal led to increased nest success and breeding numbers, and in others not. Positive results were more often found in areas where predator densities were naturally high, and where the biggest reductions in their numbers could be achieved. For example, on Berney marshes in Norfolk, Lapwing breeding success improved over the first period of predator control, deteriorated dramatically when control stopped, and improved again when control was reinstated after the study. The numbers of breeding pairs followed a similar trajectory. By contrast, at other sites, such as Pulborough Brooks in Sussex, Fox and Crow control had no clear effect on Lapwing breeding success or adult numbers. Temperature loggers deployed in nests in seven areas revealed that most egg predation occurred at night, thus implicating nocturnally active mammals as the main culprits. Overall, the best predictor of predation was nest density, with losses declining with increase in nest density, probably because at high densities communal defence against predators was most effective. In addition, nests closest to field boundaries were more likely to be destroyed than those in the middle (MacDonald & Bolton 2008). Again, it seemed that in some areas nest success and breeding numbers of Lapwings were limited by predation, mainly on eggs, but perhaps also on chicks. Similar conclusions were also drawn from a later study on the South Sheppey marshes in Kent, comparing areas with different levels of predator control (Merricks 2010).

FIG 91. The Golden Plover *Pluvialis apricaria* is usually found at higher densities on grouse moors (with predator control) than on other moors. (Edmund Fellowes)

Similar results have been found in upland habitats. One example was mentioned above, in connection with a grouse study, but in addition a before-and-after study at a site in east Scotland during 1981–89 found that nesting success for three out of six wader species was significantly lower in 1981–86 with no predator control than in 1987–89 when avian predators alone were killed (Parr

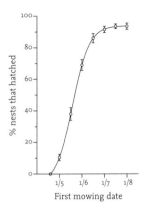

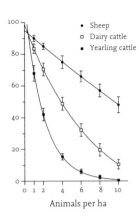

First mowing date

Animals per ha

Sheep
Dairy cattle
Yearling cattle

FIG 92. Proportion of Lapwing *Vanellus vanellus* clutches that hatched successfully, in relation to stocking densities and mowing dates in Dutch meadowland. Nest success declined with increasing densities of farm stock and earlier grass cutting. (From Beintema & Muskens 1987)

1993). Carrion Crows and Common Gulls were controlled using chicken eggs laced with alpha-chloralose, but no mammalian predators were affected. Under predator control, success improved significantly in Curlew (26% of 50 nests rising to 82% of 50 nests), Redshank (0% of 14 nests rising to 75% of 20 nests) and Lapwing (29% of 54 nests rising to 75% of 49 nests), but not in Golden Plover (17% of 56 nests vs. 0% of 8), Snipe (32% of 11 nests vs. 57% of 32) or Oystercatcher (0% of 22 nests vs. 29% of 16). No effect of predator control was apparent on the subsequent breeding numbers of any of these wader species.

In some farmland areas, the crushing of nests of ground-nesting birds by farm animals or machinery is frequent, and equivalent in its effects to predation. In a study of Lapwings and other waders in Dutch meadows, the proportion of nests that hatched varied according to stocking density (lower success with more animals) and to mowing date (lower success with early mowing) (Fig. 92). As in Britain and Ireland, breeding success and population sizes of several species declined in recent decades in the Netherlands because of improved land drainage, which reduced feeding opportunities for waders and encouraged earlier grass growth. It also gave farmers earlier access with tractors, allowing grass rolling and fertiliser applications, which in turn led to earlier grass cutting (especially for silage) or to higher stocking densities, both of which increased egg and chick mortality (Beintema & Muskens 1987, Schekkerman *et al.* 2009). The importance of nest crushing is that, for the most part, it is density-independent: every nest is destroyed in rolled or cut areas, so nest failures cannot decline in proportion at low bird densities. It is therefore a very effective means of eliminating species from wide areas, as happened with the Stone-curlew over large swathes of arable land in southern England (Green 1988a).

Goshawks and corvids

Several researchers have noticed that Goshawks can affect corvid populations. These birds tend to place their nests away from nesting Goshawks, and those nesting within 500 m usually fail. In a study near Saarbrücken in Germany, Carrion Crow nests were never successful within 500 m of Goshawk nests, and nor were Magpie nests within 1 km. From prey remains, it was estimated that Goshawks ate more Magpies and Jays than were produced annually in an extensive study area, in addition to 43–62% of the Carrion Crows, Woodpigeons and Pheasants. They also had a substantial impact on Grey Partridges, Mistle Thrushes, Hobbies and Sparrowhawks (Ellenberg et al. 1984). Goshawks could therefore be said to limit the population densities of these species, at least by deterring them from nesting in parts of the area otherwise suitable. Over most of the study area, breeding numbers of these prey species were maintained from year to year by immigration. However, Goshawks themselves avoided nesting near Ravens, which thereby provided secure areas for smaller species (Ellenberg & Dreifke 1993). In Britain, Goshawks have also been found to limit the numbers of other raptors, including Sparrowhawks, Kestrels and Short-eared Owls, in areas around their own nests (Chapter 11).

OSCILLATIONS IN PREY NUMBERS

Modelling suggests that simple two-part predator–prey cycles are most likely to arise when the predator is a specialist on that prey. The idea is that, as the prey increases in abundance, the predator follows the upward trend, eventually reaching a level at which it can tip the prey into decline, following the downward trend as its prey crashes. The predator eventually reaches such low numbers that it cannot prevent the prey from increasing again, and the cycle begins anew, but all the time changes in predator numbers lag behind changes in prey numbers. One example of a cycle involving a single main prey species and a largely specialist predator concerns the Ptarmigan as preyed upon by the Gyr Falcon in Iceland (Nielsen 1999, 2011). Study through the whole of a ten-year cycle showed that Ptarmigan densities were 4.3 times higher at the peak than in the trough. Gyr Falcon breeding densities increased and decreased in line with Ptarmigan numbers, but showed a three-year lag (as Gyr Falcons do not breed until they are 2–4 years of age). Because of this lag in the numerical response of breeding Gyr Falcons, their predation was greatest during the decline and low phase of the Ptarmigan cycle, which depressed Ptarmigan numbers yet further and delayed the recovery. Only when Gyr Falcon numbers had themselves declined were the Ptarmigan able to rise again, starting the next cycle. Falcons showed both numerical and functional responses to their prey, but also used alternative prey, including waterfowl, waders and seabirds. It was not shown that the number of Ptarmigan killed was in itself sufficient to bring about the decline.

Similar lagged responses, with delayed density-dependence, have been shown for Goshawks in relation to various forest grouse species in western Finland, a region where few alternative prey are present in winter. This numerical response was measured by the number of occupied Goshawk nests found each year, but because Goshawks normally start breeding in their second year, the peak in Goshawk nest numbers occurred two years after the peak in grouse numbers (Tornberg 2001, Tornberg et al. 2005, 2006). By responding in this way to changes in grouse numbers, Goshawks could have contributed to the cyclic fluctuations in grouse, even though they may not have been the main drivers. There is some question about how well Goshawk or Gyr Falcon nest numbers give a reliable index of total numbers of these species, because they cannot reveal the numbers of non-breeders in the population (Selås & Kålås 2007). But any Goshawks or Gyr Falcons that do not breed will surely kill far fewer grouse than those that do, because of the numbers of prey required to raise a brood.

In Britain, Red Grouse are preyed upon by various generalist predators, so a simple two-species predator–prey relationship of the type described above seems less relevant here. However, an alternative system involving another type of cyclic prey, such as voles, could impart some cyclicity to populations of grouse and other species. Thus, the main known feature that invariably links different species on the same cycle in the same area is that they share the same predators (in some areas they may share some of the same foods, but in other areas they do not). In seeking causes of the cycles, however, it is important to separate the primary prey species (voles or hares) from the secondary (scarcer) ones (grouse). The evidence for predators causing the cycle is much stronger for the secondary prey species than for the primary (mammalian) ones. The supposed mechanism is as follows: as the numbers of herbivorous mammals rise over a period of years, so do the numbers of the predators that depend on them. Then, when mammal numbers crash, the abundant predators switch their emphasis to grouse (eggs, chicks or adults), reducing their numbers, and eventually themselves decline through starvation, emigration and non-breeding (Lack 1954, Hagen 1969). This could then enable both mammal and grouse numbers to rise again to start another cycle, and the remaining predators to shift their emphasis back to mammals. In these circumstances, grouse breeding numbers could be said to be limited by predation, at least in the decline phase of the cycle. Another likely effect of avian predators is in helping to synchronise the fluctuations in their prey over wide areas, as their movements lead them to concentrate at any one time in localities with the highest prey densities. What causes the cycles in mammal numbers is a more controversial question, but it is not necessarily predation.

Some evidence favours this 'alternative prey hypothesis', as applied to some grouse populations. In northern Europe different species of grouse fluctuate in synchrony, and in parallel with rodent numbers (Hörnfeldt *et al.* 1986, Small *et al.* 1993, Ranta *et al.* 1995). Moreover, predation on the different grouse species clearly varies with the stage of the vole cycle. Among Willow Ptarmigan in Norway, annual nest losses varied between 10% and 63% (Myrberget 1984), among Capercaillie and Black Grouse in Norway between 11% and 78% (Storaas *et al.* 1982), and among Black Grouse in Sweden between 7% and 78% (Angelstam 1983). In all three species, the lowest nest predation occurred in years of peak rodent numbers and the highest when rodents declined. This was consistent with the view that generalist predators, such as Red Foxes, switched to eating grouse when rodents became scarce and back to rodents when their numbers recovered (Lack 1954, Angelstam *et al.* 1984). Appropriate changes in diet were recorded in the relevant predators, which took relatively fewer voles and more grouse in years when voles were scarce. Moreover, when extra food was provided for predators during a vole crash, a higher autumn ratio of young to old grouse was found in an experimental than in a control area (Lindström *et al.* (1987). This helped to confirm that predation on grouse was reduced when alternative food was available for the predators.

One of the best experimental studies of the effects of predators on grouse was conducted on two forested islands off northern Sweden (Marcström *et al.* 1988). These islands were large enough to sustain populations of several mammalian predators, but were also joined to the mainland in winter by sea ice, enabling such predators to move on and off. On one island, mammalian predators (mainly Red Foxes and Pine Martens) were removed, while on the other island they were left. After five years, the treatments were reversed for four further years, so that the experimental island then became the control and vice versa, giving nine years of study in all. The effects of predator removal were measured on four species of grouse, mainly Capercaillie and Black Grouse. Where predators were removed, more young grouse were produced, and subsequent breeding numbers were higher than where predators were left. The conclusion was that mammalian predation limited both breeding success and breeding density in the grouse species concerned.

On these islands, as on the mainland, the predators fed chiefly on rodents, and only secondarily on game birds. Where predators were left undisturbed, grouse breeding success was correlated with vole abundance, as most young grouse were produced in the peak vole years; but where predators were removed, no such relationship held. This finding was consistent with the view that predators turned more to grouse when voles were scarce, and confirmed that predation was mainly responsible for synchronising grouse productivity with vole abundance, as described above. However, the removal of Foxes and Pine Martens had no significant effect on vole abundance itself during two four-year cycles, suggesting that these predators did not drive the vole cycle.

The view that predators are responsible for cycles in grouse numbers in northern Europe thus has considerable support from both observational and experimental evidence. However, Red Grouse in parts of Britain show cycles of abundance even though predators are kept at low density by gamekeepers, parasitic disease being one contributing agent (Chapter 9; Hudson 1992). Thus, while predation might contribute to the cyclic fluctuations of grouse populations in some regions, it cannot explain them in other regions.

In addition to experiments, occasional natural events have affected predator numbers, thereby revealing impacts on prey. For example, an outbreak of the disease sarcoptic mange was prevalent among Red Foxes in Sweden for about ten years from the late 1970s, substantially reducing their numbers. Breeding and post-breeding densities of several prey species increased then, including Capercaillie, Black Grouse, Hazel Grouse, Brown Hare and Mountain Hare, only to decline again when the disease subsided and Fox numbers recovered. During this period, fluctuations in these species also became de-coupled from those of voles. These events provided further evidence that Foxes can limit the numbers of gallinaceous birds, and that in Sweden they are important in transferring the 3–5-year cyclic fluctuation in voles to other species (Lindström *et al.* 1994).

The link between mammal and grouse cycles is not confined to the Eurasian landmass, but also occurs across North America, where regular cycles in hare and grouse numbers are linked by common predators, mainly Red Fox and Canadian Lynx, but also Goshawk and Great Horned Owl (Keith 1963). Moreover, just as the same grouse species, such as Willow Ptarmigan, may show ten-year cycles in North America and four-year cycles in northern Europe, the same predator species may show different cycles on different continents, depending on the role it plays. The Goshawk, which eats both hares and grouse, can help to drive the ten-year grouse cycle in North America but, because it does not eat voles, it can only follow (or contribute to) the shorter grouse cycles in Europe, which are driven mainly by mammalian predators.

There is yet another twist to the story. Because many species of birds produce most young in years with rodent peaks, predators that feed on these young may also benefit. In northern Sweden, the brood sizes of different Gyr Falcon pairs were correlated with the number of ptarmigan (mainly Rock Ptarmigan) in the surrounding areas where the falcons hunted (Nystrom *et al.* 2005). Ptarmigan were most plentiful in the peak years for rodents. Other predators concentrated on the rodents, enabling Ptarmigan to breed more successfully, and in turn providing more prey for the falcons.

Other birds affected by rodent cycles

Other birds are also affected by the rodent cycle. Correlations between nest success and rodent densities have been described for various hole-nesting and open-nesting songbirds in woodland (Fig. 93), in some species affecting subsequent breeding densities. These relationships have been found from

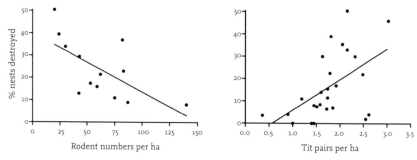

FIG 93. Predation by Weasels *Mustela nivalis* on the nest contents of tits (Paridae). (a) Relationship over 13 years between percentage of nests preyed upon and the density of rodents, which formed the main prey of Weasels. Nest losses were greater in years with lowest rodent densities. (b) Relationship over 26 years between the percentage of nests preyed upon and the density of nests. In addition to the relationship with rodent density, predation was density-dependent with respect to tit density. (Modified from Dunn 1977)

FIG 94. Brent Geese *Branta bernicla*, whose annual productivity is linked, though predation, to the lemming cycle in the Arctic tundra (see Fig. 95). (Chris Knights)

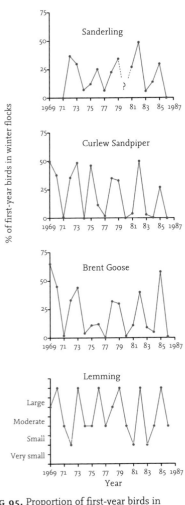

FIG 95. Proportion of first-year birds in wintering populations of various bird species that breed in the Arctic, in relation to numbers of lemmings in the breeding areas in different years. High production of young in Sanderling *Calidris alba*, Curlew Sandpiper *Calidris ferruginea* and Brent Goose *Branta bernicla* occurred about every three years when lemming numbers were also high, providing alternative food for predators. (From Summers & Underhill 1987)

study sites in Britain, as well as in continental Europe (Dunn 1977, Järvinen 1985, 1990, Orell 1989, Hogstad 1993, McCleery *et al.* 1996). They have also been described for some waterfowl and waders on northern tundra (Pehrson 1976, Roselaar 1979, Summers & Underhill 1987, Underhill *et al.* 1989). For example, among Brent Geese and two shorebird species which nest on the Taimyr peninsula of Siberia and winter in western Europe (geese) or southern Africa (waders), the proportion of young in wintering flocks has tended to fluctuate on a three-year cycle (Fig. 95). Years of high production, which occurred in all species together, coincided with peaks in Taimyr lemming numbers, while years of low production coincided with lows in lemming numbers or with late cold springs, which also reduced breeding success (Summers & Underhill 1987). The same pattern was later shown among Grey Plovers and Long-tailed Ducks from the Taimyr Peninsula (Hario *et al.* 2009) and among White-fronted Geese from the Barents Sea coast (van Impe 1996). These last three species all winter in western Europe, where the counts were made. The data for these various tundra-nesting birds thus seem to support the notion that predators, such as Arctic Foxes and Arctic Skuas, switch to eggs and young of birds when their primary prey (lemmings) are scarce, causing large variations in wintering bird numbers from year to year, and probably also in subsequent breeding numbers. However, declines in the nest success and numbers of these various bird species may also occur for climatic or other reasons in years when rodents do not decline, which sometimes masks an otherwise cyclic pattern (Angelstam *et al.* 1985).

Cycles in the numbers of small rodents are most marked on the northern tundra, and become progressively less marked in forested areas to the south, especially where continuous forest is replaced by a mixture of forest and farmland. In southern Sweden, for example, rodent numbers stay fairly stable from year to year (Erlinge *et al.* 1984). This non-cyclic pattern is ascribed to the continuous high predation rate from generalist predators, such as Red Foxes and Buzzards, which subsist mainly on other prey but change their diet to concentrate on whatever is plentiful at the time. These predators are thus always numerous enough to prevent outbreaks of voles, a situation that depends on the presence of a wide range of alternative prey. In this way, they supposedly keep vole densities relatively low and relatively stable, and hence prevent both voles and grouse from achieving the periodically very high densities found further north. The same idea, of continued pressure from generalist predators, may explain why cycles often disappear in fragmented habitats, supporting a range of prey and predators species, while they remain marked in more extensive areas of uniform habitat, whether forest or moorland.

These various studies illustrate the importance of vole cycles to other species, and the various interactions that can occur between predators and prey. That these cyclic phenomena are less obvious in Britain than elsewhere is probably due to the extreme fragmentation of landscapes in Britain, and the depletion of predator populations in many areas by gamekeepers. In recent years, moreover, over much of northern Europe, cyclic fluctuations in small rodents have dampened or stopped altogether, apparently under the influence of climate change, and this is also reflected in reduced cycles in predators, grouse and other connected species, as discussed in Chapter 15.

Other interactions involving alternative prey species
Although not concerned with cyclic species, there are many other examples of predators switching to alternative prey when their main food becomes scarce, with effects on populations. One example concerns Great Skuas, which feed mainly on fish but are also formidable predators of birds. They are capable of killing all the seabird species that breed around Britain and Ireland, including full-grown Gannets, but favour smaller species, such as petrels, Puffins and

FIG 96. Under reduced waste from fishing vessels, the Great Skua *Stercorarius skua* switched to preying heavily upon birds, especially Kittiwakes *Rissa tridactyla*. (Richard Chandler)

Kittiwakes. As supplies of fish and discards have declined in recent years, the proportion of Great Skuas feeding on seabirds has increased, leading to substantial numbers of seabirds killed each year. At Hermaness on Unst, Shetland, around 726 Great Skuas were calculated to consume 13,000 seabirds per year out of a total seabird population of around 150,000 (Votier *et al.* 2004a). The main prey species at this locality were auks (7,500 adults and 1,500 chicks killed per year) and Fulmars (3,000 killed per year). For some species, the estimated rate of predation was probably unsustainable without some compensating immigration, and Great Skuas have been held partly responsible for the marked declines in the numbers of Kittiwakes and other species that have occurred on Shetland since the 1980s (Hamer *et al.* 1991, Heubeck *et al.* 1997, Heubeck 2000, Oro & Furness 2002, Votier *et al.* 2004a).

From the first nesting in 1963, Great Skuas have also increased dramatically on St Kilda, rising to 233 pairs in 1997 (Phillips *et al.* 1999a). Throughout this period, growth was sustained largely by immigration, perhaps stimulated by food shortage at other colonies, but on St Kilda the skuas fed mainly on other seabirds. Breeders and non-breeders were calculated to take around 7,450 Storm Petrels and around 14,850 Leach's Petrels each year (Phillips *et al.* 1999b). It is not known whether the killed birds were mainly breeders or non-breeders, or whether they were taken on land or sea, but Leach's Petrels seem to have declined (Mitchell *et al.* 2004). In another prey species, the Kittiwake, breeding numbers declined by about half in less than 20 years (Murray 2002).

ANNIHILATION OF PREY: INTRODUCED
PREDATORS AND ISLAND BIRDS

Predatory mammals have been introduced to many offshore and oceanic islands around the world, often with devastating effects on the local birdlife. Such case histories provide some of the most spectacular examples of predators eliminating their prey. In addition to seabirds, they have sometimes affected land-birds, which on oceanic islands have usually evolved in the absence of mammalian predators, and often lack defensive behaviour of any kind.

On a world scale, rats are the most widespread of introduced predators, and have had the most serious impacts, especially on burrow-nesting seabirds, such as the smaller petrels. On some islands, cats were released to control rats, which then extended the predation problem to larger birds as well. Where cats occur along with potential mammalian prey, such as rats or rabbits, their predation on seabirds can be greater than where they occur alone. This is because, with alternative mammalian prey, the cats can maintain bigger numbers through the winter, when seabirds are largely absent. They are therefore present in larger numbers when the seabirds return to nest. Under pressure from introduced predators, some bird species have been eliminated altogether from many islands, while others have been reduced to a new lower level, confined to nesting in places inaccessible to the predators, such as steep cliffs or offshore stacks (Newton 1998).

Rats and seabirds

On many of the islands around the British and Irish coasts, Brown or Black Rats have been accidentally introduced, and on some islands feral Cats or American Mink have become established. Brown Rats are the most widespread, and have clearly had massive influence on the numbers and distributions of some seabird species. Most of these effects occurred before ornithologists could record them, but some are still ongoing. The evidence is of three types: (1) some seabird species are now found only on rat-free islands, yet historically occurred on other islands which now hold rats; (2) on some islands with rats, seabird breeding success is too low to sustain numbers, which are therefore declining; and (3) on islands that have been cleared of rats (by use of poison), formerly eliminated or reduced seabird species have re-colonised or increased, and breeding success has improved.

Petrels are especially vulnerable to rat predation owing to their small body size, lack of appropriate defence behaviour, and their habit of nesting in burrows or crevices accessible to rats (Jones *et al.* 2008). Leach's Petrels are now wholly restricted to remote islands lacking any mammalian predators, and Storm Petrels largely so. In Orkney and Shetland, Storm Petrels were found breeding on

FIG 97. The Storm Petrel *Hydrobates pelagicus* is vulnerable to predation by rats, and has been eliminated from many islands colonised by these predators. (David Boyle)

42 out of 142 islands surveyed, Brown Rats were present on 29, while on only a single island were both species found. Overall, Storm Petrels nested only on 8% of the total island area – the part which was still free of rats (De Leon *et al.* 2006). Similar findings emerged from a survey on the Isles of Scilly where, out of 28 islands visited, Storm Petrels were absent from all those supporting rats (Heaney *et al.* 2002). Where rats were present, caves accessible only from the sea offered the only safe sites for this species.

Manx Shearwaters and rats still occur together on some islands, but predation of eggs and chicks is rife, and numbers of birds are declining. Shearwaters virtually disappeared from the Calf of Man apparently because of rats, and also from Canna apparently through the combined actions of rats and cats, while once-thriving colonies on Foula and Fetlar have also almost gone. Compared to other seabirds, shearwaters and small petrels now have very localised distributions around the British Isles, a pattern almost certainly created by the presence of rats on other potential (and some formerly used) nesting islands (Ratcliffe *et al.* 2009). On Canna, Razorbills and Guillemots went from boulder sites, accessible to rats, while Shags shifted from boulders to safer cliff-ledges (Swann 2003).

Puffins have also suffered declines on many rat-infested islands, including Ailsa Craig (Firth of Clyde), Handa (Sutherland), Lundy (Devon), St Tudwal's Islands (Gwynedd) and Puffin Island (Angelsey). Where Puffins and Brown Rats occur on the same island, numbers of Puffins are either small and declining, or restricted to places beyond the reach of rats. However, Puffins can apparently co-exist with the smaller Black Rat, and on the Shiant Islands their numbers have remained more or less stable for 30 years, despite some loss of eggs and chicks (Brooke *et al.* 2002, Harris & Wanless 2011).

Another interesting example concerns Kittiwakes, which usually nest on steep cliff faces. On one island off Denmark, lacking cliffs, Kittiwakes began to nest on large boulders on a beach, mainly where one boulder met another to form a ledge. As the colony expanded, birds spread to nearby dunes, nesting on flattish ground. But then, when rats became established on the island, the Kittiwakes totally abandoned it (Coulson 2011).

Since the 1950s, more than a dozen rat eradication projects have been implemented on islands around Britain, treating a total area of 2,617 ha (Ratcliffe 2004, Ratcliffe *et al.* 2009). Initial responses have been encouraging. Numbers of Puffins on Ailsa Craig, which numbered tens of thousands of pairs, declined dramatically in the late 1800s, following the arrival of rats, and by the 1930s Puffins were virtually extinct there as breeders. After rats were eliminated in 1990–91, Puffins began to appear ashore and in 2002 started to nest again, increasing to more than 100 pairs by 2008. Increases also occurred in Black Guillemots, Shags, Shelducks, Ringed Plovers and Wheatears (Zonfrillo 2002, Zonfrillo & Nogales 2002). Similarly, on Lundy Island in about 60 years from 1940, seabirds had declined from more than 40,000 to less than 6,000 pairs, and at least the burrow-nesting species were heavily preyed upon by rats. Manx Shearwaters probably declined by around 90%, and Puffins almost to the point of extinction, but following a rat control programme in 2003–04, remaining pairs began to produce young for the first time in decades, and the numbers of both species began to increase, with Shearwaters reaching more than 1,000 pairs by 2008 (Brown *et al.* 2011). Similarly, following rat removal from Ramsey Island (Pembrokeshire) in 1999, Manx Shearwaters increased from about 850 to 3,835 pairs by 2012, and Storm Petrels re-colonised (Morgan 2012). Shearwaters also re-colonised Canna, while Puffins began to increase on Canna and Handa. On other islands from which rats have been removed in recent years, it is too early to assess the effects on seabirds. Rats have apparently re-invaded some of the islands from which they were removed, but all these islands lay within 300 m of the mainland or some other island with rats. It seems that rat removal is likely to be effective only on islands separated by greater distances from source areas.

These various findings emphasise the role that this one alien predator has played in limiting the distributions and numbers of burrow-nesting seabirds on the islands around our coasts. Almost certainly, the removal of Brown Rats from more offshore islands could greatly extend the distributions of such species around Britain and Ireland, giving them access to more foraging areas and leading to greater overall numbers.

FIG 98. Black-headed Gulls *Chroicocephalus ridibundus* have declined in recent decades in some areas in association with heavy predation by introduced American Minks *Neovison vison*. (Richard Chandler)

Mink and seabirds

Another major problem has resulted from the escape and release of American Minks from fur farms established in Britain in the 1950s and 1960s. These semi-aquatic animals are associated with sea-coasts and inland waters, and prey upon the eggs, chicks and adults of ground-nesting birds, especially gulls, terns, waterfowl and divers. They often kill far more individuals than they can eat at one time, and such 'surplus killing' can cause the breeding failure of entire colonies, much adult mortality, and ultimately site abandonment. In western Scotland, years of Mink predation have resulted in a redistribution of small colonial seabirds to offshore islands free of Mink, and an overall decline in the numbers of several species, including Common and Arctic Terns, Common and Black-headed Gulls, Black Guillemots and Razorbills (Craik 1995, 1997, 1998, 1999).

Mink became established on the Argyll coast during the 1960s to 1980s. On one stretch between 1987 and 1998, Arctic Terns declined by 58%, Common Terns by 48%, Black-headed Gulls by 49%, Common Gulls by 39%, and Herring Gulls by 37%. This was equivalent in all species to a net annual decline of 5–7%. Some of the displaced birds moved to Mink-free islands elsewhere, but the overall regional trend was downward. During 1996–98, when Mink were experimentally removed from certain islands each spring, breeding productivity was restored and colonies grew as birds moved in from elsewhere. In contrast, colonies on islands not subjected to Mink control continued to suffer breeding failure and were ultimately abandoned (Craik 1997).

Attempts are now being made to remove Mink from several other offshore islands, including the Outer Hebrides. It is too early to assess the full effects of these efforts, but Arctic Terns are already beginning to re-colonise areas previously abandoned, reversing the trend to nest in fewer and larger colonies, and in several sites their nesting success has much improved.

It seems that only islands more than 2 km offshore can exclude Mink, as these animals are easily capable of swimming shorter distances. Because most islands around Britain are much closer to the mainland than this, they are within range. Mink are present on more remote island groups, such as Lewis and Harris in the Outer Hebrides, only because permits were issued for fur farms there. In the same places, native Otters also prey upon seabirds and waterfowl, but they occur at lower densities and do not indulge in surplus killing, so have much less devastating impacts. They also reduce Mink numbers.

Mink are also affecting the birds of inland wetlands. Comparison of successive Atlas surveys shows that in recent decades the Black-headed Gull population of Britain and Ireland has declined in numbers, and become concentrated in a diminishing number of larger colonies. A huge decline of Black-headed Gulls in Ireland since the 1990s has been attributed to Mink predation, and, seemingly in response, many colonies re-locate almost every year (Dunn, in Mitchell *et al.* 2004).

Cats and other predators

Cats have become established on many islands inhabited by people now or in the recent past, affecting seabird populations. In recent decades, they have been involved in declines of Storm Petrel numbers on Foula, Noss and Fetlar in Shetland, and on Canna in the Inner Hebrides. On Foula, the once sizeable colony of Storm Petrels is now reduced to just a few pairs nesting on remote inaccessible ledges alongside a few Leach's Petrels. Cats also eat tern chicks at some colonies on the Scottish mainland, but so far effects have been localised.

FIG 99. Sandwich Terns *Sterna sandvicensis* sometimes abandon their colony sites completely after a major predation event, as by Red Foxes *Vulpes vulpes*. (Richard Chandler)

Red Foxes have increased and expanded their range in many parts of Britain, reaching some remote beaches, sand spits and inshore islets where terns nest, and often causing complete breeding failures, as recorded in some years for Common and Sandwich Terns at Sands of Forvie, Scolt Head, Hodbarrow, Foulness, Havergate, Foulney and Dungeness. Once a colony had been discovered, it was usually attacked annually until several years of breeding failure led to its decline and abandonment (Ratcliffe *et al.* 2000). For example, Gunn's Island (Co. Down) is connected to the mainland at low tide when Foxes gained access, reducing a colony of 2,000 pairs in 1990 to 55 by 1997, and none subsequently (Maddon & Newton, in Mitchell *et al* 2004). At some sites wardens attempt to protect terns by use of electric fencing, nocturnal patrols or shooting. This has been only partly successful, because even a single incursion by a Fox can result in large-scale losses of eggs and chicks (Ratcliffe *et al.* 2000). Mass predation events were sufficient to explain a large proportion of the national population decline in Sandwich Tern numbers during the 1980s and 1990s (Ratcliffe *et al.* 2000).

Hedgehogs and waders on the Outer Hebrides
Hedgehogs occur through much of mainland Britain, but are not native to the Outer Hebrides, where they were introduced in unauthorised manner to South Uist in 1974. Since that time, the species has spread to two other islands linked by causeways, and wader numbers have declined markedly, including Dunlin, Ringed Plover, Lapwing, Redshank, Snipe and Oystercatcher. Predation on eggs became sufficiently high to account for these declines (Jackson & Green 2000,

FIG 100. Hedgehogs *Erinaceus europaeus* are serious predators on the eggs and chicks of ground-nesting birds. Introduced to the Outer Hebrides in the 1970s, these animals have caused marked declines in breeding wader populations, especially Dunlin *Calidris alpina* and Ringed Plover *Charadrius hiaticula* (right). (Ian Newton and Richard Chandler)

Jackson *et al.* 2004). Other introduced mammalian predators are also present on these islands, but have not had serious effects on waders.

These islands were known for exceptionally high densities of waders nesting on the machair land near the west coasts, with Dunlin and Ringed Plover densities the highest recorded anywhere in the world. Experiments at two sites in 1998 measured the effect of removing Hedgehogs from two fenced plots (Jackson 2001). Avian predators could not be excluded, but the subsequent hatching success of waders (Dunlins and Lapwings) inside the plots was roughly 2.4 times higher than in adjacent areas where Hedgehog densities remained high. These findings led to a programme aimed at removing Hedgehogs totally from these islands. Only time will tell whether the programme will succeed, and allow a recovery in wader numbers. Hedgehogs have created similar problems on islands off Germany and in New Zealand where they have also been introduced.

Most of the evidence for the effects of introduced predators on island-nesting seabirds is based on circumstantial evidence: decline of seabirds follows the establishment of an alien mammalian predator. But the facts that this sequence has been repeated again and again at different times on different island groups, and that recovery of bird numbers has followed predator removal, make a compelling case for causal relationships. Such case histories from islands show what can happen when birds that have lived in the absence of mammalian predation are suddenly exposed to it. They include the only certain cases of bird species being eliminated from parts of the British Isles entirely by non-human predation.

MANIPULATION OF PREDATION

Predator-removal studies

Any supposed effect of predators on their prey can be shown most convincingly by experiment. If predators are limiting their prey, their removal from an area should be followed by an increase in prey numbers. Some predator-removal studies were described above, but many others have been undertaken elsewhere, and these add to the story. As in food manipulations, several experimental designs have been used. Among 30 experiments discussed by Newton (1998), nine involved before-and-after comparisons in the same area, 12 involved a simultaneous control area where predators were left, and nine involved reversal of treatments or replication using several experimental and control areas (Chapter 7).

Of the 30 predator-removal studies, 13 involved gallinaceous birds (such as grouse and pheasants), 11 involved ducks (including two with simulated nests) and six involved other species (Newton 1998). The parameters that were most commonly measured included nest success, post-breeding numbers (or ratio of large young to adults) and subsequent breeding numbers. In 27 studies in which nest success was measured, 23 showed an increase in success under predator removal; in 17 studies in which post-breeding numbers were measured, 12 showed an increase under predator removal; and of 17 studies in which subsequent breeding numbers were measured, ten showed an increase. Improved nest success was not always reflected in increased post-breeding numbers, and similarly, an increase in post-breeding numbers was not always reflected in increased subsequent breeding numbers. However, in more than half the studies with relevant measures, breeding density was apparently limited by predation.

Increases in breeding densities achieved under predator removal varied from nil to 2.6-fold, compared with unmanipulated control areas. The degree of increase depended partly on the number of years that predator removal was continued on the same area. In some studies, effects on breeding numbers were cumulative, at least up to three years (for example, 1.4× after one year and 2.6× after three years in Grey Partridge: Tapper *et al.* 1996). These effects were similar in magnitude to those found in food-provision experiments (Chapter 4). In all the experiments, however, the effects of predator removal were short-lived, and when control stopped, predators soon moved back, and predation rates and populations reverted to former levels.

There are various reasons why removal of predators may not always have led to an increase in the breeding density of the prey. First, predation may not have been limiting the population concerned; second, control efforts may not have removed all predators from the study area or others may have moved in; and third, many prey birds may disperse from the study area, so that their better survival is not reflected in local breeding density.

Almost all the species studied in these experiments were ground-nesters, which as a group may have been more vulnerable to predation than birds that nest in safer sites. In addition, the predators were all generalists and fed chiefly on other prey (such as voles or rabbits), which mainly sustained their numbers. It is these circumstances in which marked effects on vulnerable subsidiary prey species might be expected, because the predators are buffered against the effects of decline in their subsidiary prey by the presence of their main prey. Experiments that involved removal of only one predator species (whether crow or mammal) showed no significant effects, mainly because many nests were still found and robbed by other predators (Parker 1984, Parr 1993, Clark *et al.* 1995). In some studies, predation was influenced not only by the numbers and types of predators present, but also by the availability of alternative prey and by habitat features such as nesting cover. None of these experiments involved the removal of raptors.

Increased breeding density was usually assumed to follow from the improvement in nest success and chick survival the previous year. However, in some experiments involving various duck species, breeding densities increased in the experimental area from the first year of predator removal, before any improvement in nest success could have occurred (Duebbert & Kantrud 1974, Duebbert & Lokemoen 1980). This implied that predator removal had influenced the settling patterns of ducks, with substantial immigration to the newly created predator-free areas. It provided a parallel with local variations in spring food supply influencing settling patterns (Chapter 4). It thus seems that spatial correlations between high nest success and high breeding densities in birds can be brought about by two mechanisms: either by good production and site fidelity leading to high breeding numbers, or by many birds being attracted to a safe site where they stay and then enjoy good nest success. Attraction is certainly involved where safe new islands or nesting rafts are placed on lakes and reservoirs, and are immediately occupied by large numbers of terns or gulls.

In a later review, involving 83 predator-removal studies (including those mentioned above), similar conclusions held whether the predators were native or introduced; and whether the prey were declining or not, migratory or resident, or game or non-game species. This study also confirmed that, in general, removing all predator species achieved a significantly larger effect on prey than removing only a subset of predators (R. K. Smith *et al.* 2010).

Predator-exclusion studies

Instead of predator removal, other experiments have involved the provision of safer nest-sites. The breeding success of various tit species in Wytham Wood near Oxford increased significantly after wooden boxes nailed to treetrunks, which were accessible to Weasels and Great Spotted Woodpeckers, were replaced by concrete hanging boxes (Dunn 1977). Prior to 1976, annual nest predation by Weasels averaged 30%, but after predator-proof nest-boxes were provided in 1976, it fell to less than 5%. However, the resulting increase in production of young had at most a small effect on subsequent breeding densities (McCleery & Perrins 1991).

In other experiments, fences placed around individual nests or around large areas of nesting habitat to exclude predatory mammals resulted in improved nest success (Lokemoen *et al.* 1982, Jackson 2001, Malpas *et al.* 2012). In Britain, fences have been used mainly to exclude dogs and other mammals from tern colonies on mainland beaches. However, even a single intrusion by a Fox can cause severe losses of eggs and chicks (Patterson 1977, Smart 2004), and a Fox pacing round a fenced area at night can result in disturbance of parent birds and chilling of their eggs or chicks. Around ten areas of wet grassland, electric fences resulted in improved nest success and productivity of Lapwings and Redshanks, and in some localities also in increased breeding density in subsequent years (Malpas *et al.* 2012). It was uncertain whether the increased breeding densities resulted from previous productivity or from immigration, but one Sandwich Tern colony in northeast Scotland expanded the year after fencing (from 80 to 450 pairs), evidently from immediate immigration to this newly secured site (Forster 1975). Fences cannot keep out avian predators, however, and in some fenced areas their predation can be locally significant, as exemplified by the almost total loss of Little Tern chicks to Kestrels in some years in colonies at Great Yarmouth, Chesil Beach and Langstone Harbour.

Protective cages over individual nests have been used mainly on waders, so as to allow walk-in access to the parent bird yet exclude larger predators. At Welney in Norfolk, Little Ringed Plovers suffered high nest predation, mainly from Coots and Moorhens. Wire mesh cages placed over their nests caused no desertions, but increased the annual productivity from 0.6 young per pair for unprotected nests to 1.6 young per pair for protected nests (Gulickx & Kemp 2007). Using this procedure, together with some extension of nesting habitat, breeding numbers increased from 1–3 pairs in the early years of study to 8–12 pairs in later years. In a similar study in Sweden, protected Lapwing and Redshank nests had higher hatching success than unprotected nests, but incubating Redshanks were sometimes killed by the predator (Isaksson *et al.* 2007). This was probably because, unlike Lapwings, Redshanks tended to sit tight, and only flew when the predator was close. They tended to fly first to the top of the cage, and may have been unable to escape the predator fast enough. The effectiveness of the cages thus seemed to vary with the behaviour of the species. Protective cages also improved the hatching success of Dunlins in Sweden, but comparing years with and without the use of cages, no effects on the number of fledglings produced per adult or on the subsequent recruitment of breeders were found (Pauliny *et al.* 2008).

Other attempts to reduce predation have involved other forms of habitat manipulation, diversionary feeding, sonic deterrents to keep cats from gardens, conditioned taste aversion and methods that warn prey of approaching predators (such as fixing bells to house cats). In diversionary feeding, predators are provided with alternative food in the hope that they will kill fewer prey individuals. This is applied only as a short-term measure, at times when prey are most vulnerable, for if it were maintained long-term, predators numbers might themselves increase. It has been used on Hen Harriers at the nestling stage in an attempt to reduce predation on grouse chicks. At individual trial nests, diversionary feeding led to an 86% reduction in the numbers of grouse killed, compared with control harrier nests in another part of the moor (Redpath *et al.*

FIG 101. Supplementary feeding of Hen Harriers *Circus cyaneus* in the nestling period (with rats and day-old cockerel chicks) to reduce predation on Red Grouse *Lagopus l. scotica*. (Laurie Campbell)

2001). However, grouse chick mortality remained high, possibly because other predators took many of them. Other studies have provided supplementary food to the prey rather than the predator, which reduced the amount of time the prey spent foraging in dangerous places. Another potential method to reduce predation is to provide individual predators with a bait that resembles their prey but which is dosed with a noxious chemical (such as methiocarb) to make them sick. Over time, the predator will learn to stop taking the real prey, believing that they too have unpleasant consequences. This method of *conditioned taste aversion* has been found to reduce predation on birds' eggs by corvids and mammals (Avery *et al.* 1995). Other chemicals, such as creosote, deter predators simply by their smell – an innate aversion rather than a learnt one. None of the experiments mentioned above gave any assessment of the treatment on subsequent breeding numbers, but the methods used might prove useful in game management or conservation.

CONCLUDING REMARKS

Many bird species suffer heavy predation at the egg and chick stages, and some also at the fledgling and adult stages. The effects of predation on any population depend on the extent to which losses from predation are offset by compensatory reductions in other losses or by improved reproduction. To reduce breeding or post-breeding numbers, at least part of the predation experienced by a population must be additive to other losses. Many species face a food bottleneck in late winter, and the fact that some individuals may have died from predation before they reach the bottleneck may have no influence on the number that get through it, for the food available at this difficult time may support only a limited number. Many bird populations withstand heavy predation year after year and yet maintain their breeding numbers. This is apparent in some species whose breeding densities are clearly limited by other factors, such as territories or nest-sites, often leading to a surplus of non-breeding adults. Reduction of predation would not change this situation.

Among the birds that breed in Britain and Ireland, four types of situations have been described: (1) predation is light or heavy, but has no obvious impact on subsequent breeding numbers, as exemplified by Sparrowhawk predation on tits and other songbird species; (2) predation is sufficient to hold breeding numbers below the level they could otherwise achieve, as exemplified by predation on various ground-nesting birds, such as some gamebirds and waders; (3) predation can cause cyclic fluctuations in the breeding numbers of some grouse species and in the breeding success of some other birds, as predators dependent primarily on cyclically fluctuating voles switch their attention to birds in years when vole numbers decline; and (4) predation can eliminate a population completely, as exemplified by the effects of rats and other introduced predators on some island-nesting seabirds. It also seems likely that the ongoing declines in Lapwings and other waders in Britain are being caused primarily by heavy predation on eggs and chicks, itself partly the result of land-use changes. A wide range of predators is involved, but mainly Fox and Carrion/Hooded Crows.

Ground-nesting birds may be more susceptible to predation than other species because their eggs and chicks are accessible to a wider range of predators, including Foxes which can also kill the incubating female. This predation may partly explain the distortion of adult sex ratios seen in many ducks and gamebirds. Experiments have shown that predator removal can increase the breeding productivity of many species, and the subsequent breeding numbers of a smaller number. Many wild birds can sustain poor breeding success, without it affecting subsequent breeding numbers, but this is not true of all species (Chapter 1), and good production of young is especially important in gamebirds, in order to sustain a subsequent harvest.

The introduction of rats and other mammalian predators to offshore islands has probably had a huge influence on the distributions and numbers of burrow-nesting seabirds around Britain and Ireland. Some species are now almost entirely confined to islands lacking rats, but on islands where rats and other predators have been removed, some previously lost species have returned, thereby gaining access to additional nesting and feeding areas. More recent problems concern introduced American Mink which are now widely distributed through the British Isles and affecting a wide range of seabirds and water-birds, and Hedgehogs introduced to the Outer Hebrides, which are now affecting previously high-density wader populations.

CHAPTER 8

Parasitic Diseases: General Principles and Individual Impacts

WHEREAS PREDATORS KILL AND CONSUME their prey, parasites and pathogens usually live on or within the bodies of their live hosts. They occur there either as individuals or as populations. They gain nourishment and protection from their hosts, but cause tissue damage, with effects ranging from negligible to fatal. As with predation, there are conflicting views on the effects of parasitism. On one view, parasites tend to evolve in such a way as to become less harmful to their hosts with time, because they have a better chance of long-term survival if they do not destroy their habitat (unless transmission depends on the host's death). Likewise, host species tend to evolve resistance to their parasites and to any toxins they might produce. Such co-evolution would in time result in parasites having minimal effect on their hosts. In practice, however, parasites often harm their hosts and in certain conditions kill them. These two extremes probably represent opposite ends of a continuum of situations found in nature, and it is unlikely that any parasite would not disadvantage its host in some way.

The costs of parasitism become important to individual hosts when they are sufficient to lower their reproduction or survival chances. They become important at the population level when they cause sufficient reproductive failure or mortality to reduce the breeding numbers of their hosts below what could otherwise occur. This chapter is concerned with these individual effects, while population impacts are left for Chapter 9.

Hundreds of parasite species of great diversity have been identified from wild birds, and it is unlikely that any individual can live its entire life free from parasites living on it or in it. Each species of bird (or other animal) that has been studied in detail has been found to have one or more species of parasites that are host-specific, together with other 'generalist' parasites that can also live on other host species. The implication is that there must be many more species of parasites on earth than there are hosts, especially when allowing for the fact that some parasites can host their own parasites. Another implication is that, while some parasites can be acquired only from members of the same species, others can be obtained from other species. As an indication of the number of parasites that some birds can support, the Grey Partridge has been found to host at least 24 species of trematodes, 21 tapeworms, 37 nematodes, four acanthocephalans, and at least 21 arthropods living among the feathers (Potts 2012); and the Swallow hosts at least 16 species of helminths, eight species of mites, three species of louseflies, seven species of fleas, one species of feather louse and 11 species of protozoan blood parasites (Møller 1994). There is no reason to suppose that these lists are complete, or that the Grey Partridge and Swallow are unusual in these respects.

Most parasites identified from free-ranging wild birds produce no clinical signs that would be diagnosed as disease, while others cause varying levels of sickness. The ability of different species of parasites to cause disease – their *pathogenicity* – varies with: (1) the type and numbers of parasite involved; (2) the species of host invaded; and (3) intrinsic features of the host, such as the level of immunity (Box 4). When birds are in poor nutritional state, are already infected with other pathogens, or are subject to other types of stress, some parasites that do not normally cause disease can do so. Throughout this chapter, I shall use the term *disease* only to cover a clinically abnormal state resulting from parasite infection, and not to encompass the effects of other degenerative and metabolic disorders, nutrient deficiencies and toxic chemical effects that in medicine may go under the name of *non-communicable disease*.

The important point about parasitic diseases is that they are *communicable* (infectious), passing from one individual to another (by direct contact or by vectors such as blood-sucking insects). As with predators, it is useful to distinguish specialist (host-species-specific) parasites from generalists, which can have more than one definitive host species. In general, host-specific parasites are transmitted most readily at relatively high host population densities, so they can act on host populations in a density-dependent or delayed density-dependent manner, affecting greater proportions of individuals at high host densities. They can thus contribute importantly to host population regulation, even if they cause only a small proportion of host deaths. Because host and parasite are coupled in a closed system, the host must usually attain a certain density (contact rate) before the parasite can persist and spread, and a disease tends to become self-limiting before it can annihilate a host population.

For generalist parasites, which can live in several different host species, the situation differs. The numbers of such a parasite are influenced by all the host species together, so that a particularly vulnerable host may be kept at low numbers because a *reservoir of infection* persists in alternative, less susceptible hosts living in the same area (the disease louping ill which grouse get via ticks mainly from sheep is an example described in the next chapter). The level of infection in the vulnerable host is not then density-dependent with respect to its own numbers, but could be density-independent or inversely density-dependent. The latter situation arises because the ratio of reservoir hosts to susceptible hosts increases as individuals of the susceptible host species die. Whereas it is difficult for a specialist parasite to drive its host species to extinction (because the parasite population itself declines as host densities fall), a generalist parasite could in theory extinguish one or more host species locally (or globally) so long as the population density of the parasite is maintained by other, more robust, hosts.

There is no doubt that many generalist parasites can affect some host species more severely than others, either because some species are infected more easily or because they are more susceptible to the effects of the parasite once acquired. For example, different duck species, studied in North America, varied in their susceptibility to the bacterial disease avian cholera. Smaller species suffered more than larger ones, Teal for example being 22 times more susceptible than Mallard, judging from the proportion that died (Petrides & Bryant 1951). In extreme cases, the same pathogen may seem innocuous to one species but fatal to a closely related one, especially if that species comes from another part of the world where it has not previously been exposed to that type of pathogen.

Birds differ from most other animals in that they are more mobile, and can occupy different habitats or different parts of the world at different seasons. This means that they can be exposed to a wider range of parasites and pathogens than most other animals, and can also transport diseases or disease vectors over long distances, as exemplified by the H5N1 version of avian flu, which causes concern to the poultry industry. But pathogens do not necessarily persist in all regions to which they are transported. For example, the protozoan blood parasite *Haemoproteus payevskyi* was found in Great Reed Warblers nesting in southern Sweden (Hasselquist *et al.* 2007). Its abundance declined during the course of the warbler nesting season, and it was not recorded in young of the year. This implied that infection occurred elsewhere, in migration or wintering areas, but petered out in the breeding area. The parasite may have required a specific insect vector which was found in migration or wintering areas but not in Swedish breeding areas.

THE PARASITES

The wealth of parasites that affects birds and other animals fall naturally into two groups, often called microparasites (viruses, bacteria, fungi, protozoa), which are invisible to the naked eye, and macroparasites (helminth worms, arthropods), most of which are larger (Anderson & May 1979). The former are characterised by their small size, short life cycles, and high rates of reproduction within their hosts (Table 2). With few exceptions, the duration of infection is short relative to the lifespan of the host. Some are transmitted by direct contact between host individuals, and others through vectors such as blood-sucking ticks or mosquitoes. Either way, the rate of spread of infection depends partly on the contact rate, which in turn is dependent on the host density (for directly transmitted pathogens) or on both vector and host density (for

TABLE 2. Comparison of characteristics and usual mode of action of microparasites and internal macroparasites.

	Microparasites	Macroparasites
	Viruses, bacteria, protozoa, fungi	Helminths: platyhelminths (trematodes, tapeworms, flukes), acanthocephalans (thorny-headed worms), nematodes (roundworms, hookworms)
CHARACTERISTICS		
Size	Invisible to naked eye	Usually visible to naked eye
Life cycle relative to host's	Short	Long
Population growth within host	Through reproduction	Through continuing uptake of infective stages
Immune response	Usually strong and long-lasting	Usually weak and short-lasting, or non-existent
Transmission	Through direct uptake or vector, dependent mainly on density of hosts	Through food, body fluids or intermediate hosts, dependent on density of hosts and parasites
MODE OF ACTION		
Effect depends on	Initial infection	Total cumulative burden
Cause deaths	Often	Seldom
Outbreaks	Frequent	Occasional

vector-transmitted pathogens). In those hosts that survive the initial onslaught, microparasites can promote some immunity to re-infection, and recovered hosts can be recognised by the presence of appropriate antibodies in the blood.[12] For microparasites, then, the host population can be subdivided at any one time into distinct classes: susceptible, latent-infected, infectious, recovered-and-immune. Microparasite diseases have caused many dramatic effects on animal and plant populations, including myxomatosis (viral) in Rabbits, bubonic plague (bacterial) in humans and Dutch elm disease (fungal) in elm trees. Some of the best known microparasitic diseases of birds include Newcastle disease (viral), salmonellosis (bacterial), malaria (protozoal) and aspergillosis (fungal), but in recent years avian influenza (H5N1 strain, viral), trichomonosis (protozoal) and West Nile virus disease have also achieved some notoriety.

In contrast to microparasites, most macroparasites are visible to the naked eye (Table 2). Some, such as lice and ticks, are found on the outside of the body (*ectoparasites*), while others are found inside (*endoparasites*). The internal ones (parasitic worms or *helminths*) do not multiply directly within a host, but produce eggs or other infective stages which usually pass out of the host before transmission to another host. The adults are relatively long-lived, and usually elicit only a limited and short-lived immune response, so that macroparasite infections tend to be persistent, with hosts accumulating parasites through life or continually being re-infected. Nevertheless, some helminth worms can induce recurrent epidemics that spread through a host population with devastating effects similar to those observed for microparasites (May & Anderson 1978, Hudson & Dobson 1991). This happens especially if the free-living infective stages are long-lived. Acanthocephalan (thorny-headed) worms in Eiders provide an example (Chapter 9).

The variety of parasitic worms found in different bird species depends on the bird's diet (which influences infection risk), lifespan (which affects the time for accumulation), social and nesting behaviour (which influences transmission), migratory habits (which affects the number of parasite species to which the bird is exposed), body size (larger having more) and habitat (aquatic species having more) (Gregory *et al.* 1991). Most water-birds support a diverse community of parasitic worms, mainly in the digestive tract, sometimes with large numbers of individuals per host. Some helminth species may be present in almost every individual of a population, while others are present in only a small proportion. They lack a digestive tract and absorb nutrients through their skin (tapeworms, roundworms and acanthocephalans). As larvae, many nematodes migrate

---

12 An *antibody* is a defensive substance produced within the body in response to an *antigen*, the latter defined as any foreign material (including parasites) within the body which induces an immune response.

FIG 102. Pied Flycatcher *Ficedula hypoleuca* (female), subject of studies of nest-dwelling parasites. (Frank Snijkers)

through their host's body tissues until they reach the site where they can mature and reproduce. Tissue damage can sometimes be serious.

Transmission of macroparasites depends not only on the density of host individuals, but also on parasite density and other factors. Some parasite species require higher host densities than others before they can become established, so that the number of parasite species, as well as of individuals, can increase with a rise in host density (Dobson & May 1991). Within their hosts, parasitic worms almost always have clumped distributions, being found in small numbers in most host individuals and in large numbers in a few. This is important, because the effects of such parasites on individual hosts typically depend on the total burden of worms, and not simply on whether or not the host is infected (Anderson & May 1978, May & Anderson 1978). The death of only a few hosts (those with heavy burdens) can lead in turn to the loss of a large number of worms. This process tends to reduce the impact of macroparasites on host populations. Why certain individuals in a bird population acquire heavy parasite loads, while others do not, may depend on behaviour, diet, body condition, age and genetic predisposition, as well as on chance. Some helminth species tend to be concentrated in particular age-groups of birds, perhaps the young or the very old, but the individual variation in total burdens is still substantial.

Life cycles differ greatly between major types of parasites, but they are divisible into two main categories, called *direct* and *indirect*. Direct life cycles do not require an intermediate host species, and the parasite undergoes most or all of its development within one host. Indirect life cycles may involve one or two intermediate hosts in which the parasite undergoes part of its development before passing to a definitive host of a different species to complete its development and reproduce. Once within the intermediate host, the parasite may be actively transported to a definitive host (e.g. a mosquito transporting malarial pathogens), or the intermediate host may be eaten by a bird which thereby becomes infected (e.g. a shorebird eating a mussel and thereby acquiring a helminth). Wild birds serve as the sole or definitive hosts for all the parasites discussed in this chapter.

In contrast to macroparasitic worms which live within the bodies of their hosts, parasitic arthropods mostly live on the outside. Such ectoparasites include various lice (Mallophaga), mites and ticks (Acarina), flies (Diptera), fleas (Siphonaptera) and bugs (Hemiptera). The majority feed on blood, causing tissue damage and anaemia, as well as allergic responses and bacterial infections. In large numbers, they can weaken and sometimes kill their hosts. Importantly, however, they can also act as vectors of microparasitic diseases. This is especially true of some ticks, which can attach themselves to several hosts in succession, infecting one after another. Some ectoparasites are transmitted from host to host at times of physical contact, but most can move from environment to host. As with internal macroparasites, therefore, transmission of ectoparasites depends on both parasite and host density and behaviour, as well as on other factors. Ectoparasites themselves do not usually cause heavy mortality, except among the chicks of some species (see below).

Because birds may be more vulnerable to parasite infections when they are in poor body condition or stressed in some other way, the independent effects of parasites on host populations are best assessed by experiment. In recent decades, attempts have been made to remove parasites from wild birds, enabling their effects to be more reliably assessed. This has been done by use of pesticides which destroy the vectors of the parasites, by pesticides or drugs which destroy the parasites themselves, or by vaccination which reduces the impacts of the parasites on individual hosts. Most such manipulations have been concerned primarily with the effects of parasites on individual breeding and survival, but some have examined effects on population levels, as described in the next chapter. Moreover, natural experiments, involving the accidental introduction of a disease or disease vector to a new area, have occurred from time to time, sometimes with devastating effects on the local fauna. Examples are again discussed in the next chapter.

ANTI-PARASITE MEASURES

Considering the variety of parasites that most birds have to contend with, it is not surprising that they have evolved defence mechanisms to reduce the risks or costs of infection. Perhaps the most important is the immune system, which comprises a coordinated system of tissues, cells and soluble molecules that together constitute the body's defence against invasion by foreign entities. The system is aimed primarily at internal microparasites, such as bacteria and protozoa, but also protects against other parasites, inert foreign matter and tumour cells. It acts by reducing the viability and fecundity of the parasites.

Box 4. The measurement of immune responses

The immune system is the most important physiological means by which animals can control parasite infections. Although aimed primarily at internal microparasites (viruses, bacteria and protozoa), it also gives protection against other parasites, inert foreign matter and tumour cells. It seems to have almost limitless ability to produce antibodies against a wide range of parasite antigens. An *antigen* can be defined as a foreign body which induces an immune response, while an *antibody* is a defensive substance produced to combat it. It is assumed that parasite infections are the main factors which, through natural selection, promote the maintenance of an immune system in vertebrate animals. In the hypothetical extreme case of a parasite-free environment, any immune system may be pointless. In contrast, individuals living in high pathogenic environments should invest heavily in immune responses (Piersma 1997). In view of the costs involved, investments in immune defence seem to be adjusted not only according to the risk of parasitism, but also according to the availability of necessary resources. Individuals in good physical condition are more likely to resist infections than those in poor condition. In light of these facts, it becomes important to measure the immune responses of individuals to parasite infections.

In live birds, immune capability has been measured from blood samples by assessing either (1) leucocyte concentrations as general measures of immune function, or (2) antibodies (immunoglobulins, especially gamma-globulin), T-cell and B-cell lymphocytes as more specific measures. The monitoring in blood samples of the immune status of the host gives some idea of past exposure to pathogens, and can also indicate how exposure changes through time, in response to specific challenges or stresses, including changes in body condition. In addition, specific tests have been developed that allow us to measure the current strength of immune responses in birds (and other animals). To assess the T-cell lymphocyte-mediated response, a non-pathogenic lectin *phyto-haemagglutinin* (PHA) is usually injected just below the skin on the web of the wing (a haemagglutinin is a product that causes red blood cells to agglutinate, usually stimulating an immune response). The method was first developed for use on poultry. The thickness of the wing webs at pre-marked sites are measured before and after injection with 0.2 mg PHA in 0.5 ml of phosphate-buffered saline. The other wing, used as a control, is injected with saline alone. The thickness of the web on each wing is then measured a set time (say 24 hours) later, and the difference in the thickness of the two webs is used as a measure of the T-cell response. Alternatively, response to immunisation with sheep red blood cells (SRBC) gives a measure of both B-cell and T-cell activity following a single intraperitoneal injection. One blood sample is taken before the injection and a second about seven days later, allowing comparison of immunoglobulin levels between both samples. The degree of difference is taken as a measure of the strength of the immune response.

Part of the immune system is innate and non-specific, giving immediate front-line defence against any foreign invader. This part includes phagocytic leucocytes in the bloodstream which are able to attack and absorb any foreign cells. A robust defence from this part of the immune system may reduce the need for the second, more expensive and specific part, which develops in response to a particular infection (or parasite strain), and acts with a 'memory', which after the first infection gives lifelong protection against the same specific pathogen. This part of the immune system provides the mechanism which underlies immunisation. The first encounter with a particular microparasite may cause severe sickness, but if the animal recovers, subsequent infections with the same microparasite may have little or no impact, thanks to the acquired immunity. Components of this adaptive system include two kinds of lymphocytes, called T-cells (in the *cell-mediated* system) and B-cells (in the *humoral* system), whose concentrations in the bloodstream rise as an immune response is mounted (Box 4). The functioning of the immune system, like most other bodily processes, is dependent on adequate nutrition. Severe malnutrition leads to immunodeficiency, which allows parasitic diseases to take hold.

In addition to the immune system, birds have more direct ways of avoiding parasites. Infestations of ectoparasites are reduced partly by their direct removal from the plumage and nest, and by routine preening, scratching, sunning, bathing and dust-bathing, or by anting, in which the plumage is treated with formic acid (Clayton & Wolfe 1993). In this last act, the bird crushes an ant in its bill-tip and wipes it frenetically through the plumage. Routine nest sanitation includes removal of faecal sacs and dead chicks, ejection of faeces over the nest rim and frequent renovation of nest material (Bucher 1988). The nest material used by some birds may reduce parasite loads, as several favoured plant materials emit volatile chemicals that have repellent or pesticidal properties (Clark & Mason 1985, Gwinner & Berger 2005). Species that use the same nest-sites in successive years, such as cavity-nesters and large stick-nesting raptors, are especially likely to suffer from carry-over of parasites from the previous year, and these are the species that most often incorporate aromatic green material into their nests, continually refreshing it throughout the season.

Observers operating nest-box schemes have often noticed that birds prefer new boxes to old ones, and parasite avoidance may be one reason for this preference. This was shown by experiments in which cavity-nesting birds given a choice of boxes avoided the heavily infested ones for both roosting and nesting (Christe *et al.* 1994, Oppliger *et al.* 1994, Merilä & Allander 1995, Rytkönen *et al.* 1998). While many cavity-nesters have no choice but to re-use nest-sites, other

FIG 103. The Starling *Sturnus vulgaris* incorporates aromatic green material into its nest structure, supposedly to give protection against nest parasites. (Frank Snijkers)

open-nesting birds generally build themselves a new nest in a different site for each attempt. This may be yet another anti-parasite strategy.

Birds that ingest parasites from their food are sometimes able to recognise parasitised prey individuals and reject them, so as to avoid infection. This was apparent in Oystercatchers feeding on the Baltic Tellin (a bivalve mollusc) which was sometimes infected with a trematode parasite. This parasite would normally complete its life cycle in a bird (Hulscher 1982). Oystercatchers made their choice after the bivalve had been dug out of the mud and smashed open with the bill, allowing the soft parts to be inspected visually. Parasitised ones were rejected. This study revealed selection of individual prey, but the extent to which whole species are shunned to avoid the risk of parasitism remains uninvestigated.

Contagious parasites that can be transmitted directly include all ectoparasites passed over during body contact, and venereal ones transmitted during copulation. Foregut parasites, such as *Trichomonas*, can also be transmitted directly by infected males which feed their partners by regurgitation, or by adults which feed their young by regurgitation, such as pigeons and some finches. The problem for a bird is recognising an infected individual in order to avoid it, and one proposal is that the state of the plumage reflects the bird's health with respect to parasites, females preferring males with the most immaculate plumage (sexual selection). By whatever means, individuals of some bird species clearly prefer to mate with unparasitised partners, as found, for example, in wild female Swallows and captive female pigeons when given the choice of louse-free males (Clayton 1990). Evidently, there are many and various ways in which birds might reduce their exposure to parasites, or the effects of parasites once acquired.

EFFECTS OF PARASITES ON BREEDING SUCCESS

Parasites can reduce the breeding success of birds, either by lowering the body condition of the adults or by lowering the body condition and survival of the chicks. In certain bird species, deaths from parasitism are a major cause of reduced breeding output. Most studies have concerned ectoparasites (such as blood-sucking ticks, bugs and fly larvae), which can reach high infestations in species that use the same nest-sites year after year, such as many cavity-nesters, cliff-nesters and colonial seabirds (Rothschild & Clay 1952). This is because some ectoparasites can survive for months or even years in sheltered nest-sites, reproducing each time the sites are occupied, and building up substantial populations over a period of years. In most other bird species, however, despite occasional heavy infestations, chick deaths from parasitism seem few or non-existent, and assume nowhere near the importance of deaths from predation.

In one survey, nests of Stock Doves built year after year in the same cavities were found to support no fewer than 58 species of nest parasites at a mean density of 6,573 individuals per decimetre of nest material. In contrast, the flimsy nests of Woodpigeons built on the open branches of bushes, and used for one brood only, supported only one parasite species at 20 individuals per decimetre of nest material (Nordberg 1936). By nesting in holes or in colonies, birds gain some protection from predators but suffer more from parasites.

While bird species that use the same sites year after year are often victims of wingless ticks and bugs, other species, which nest solitarily in different sites each time, are most often attacked by flying insects (flies) or by parasites that travel easily on their hosts' bodies. The most damaging are the blowflies and muscid

FIG 104. The Stock Dove *Columba oenas* often nests in the same cavities in successive years, and supports many more nest parasites than the open-nesting Woodpigeon *Columba palumbus*. (Keith Kirk)

botflies whose maggots feed from live nestlings. Blood-feeders may reduce both haematocrit (% red cell volume) and haemoglobin, making the host anaemic, as well as stimulating an immune response via white blood cell production. Nestlings may be killed outright or fledge anaemic and underweight, reducing their subsequent survival prospects. The effects of parasites on breeding success have been assessed in both observational and experimental studies, comparing breeding between lightly and heavily infested nests. From studies available at the time, Møller & Erritzøe (2002) summarised the overall nestling mortality attributable to parasite infections in 18 European species with adequate samples as follows: Magpie (0%), Bearded Tit (0%), Marsh Tit (0%), Swift (0%), Kestrel (0%), Tawny Owl (0%), Barn Owl (0%), Blue Tit (5.6%), Pied Flycatcher (6.0%), House Sparrow (7.4%), Swallow (7.9%), Starling (8.0%), Sand Martin (10.5%), Jackdaw (15.4%), Great Tit (16.5%), House Martin (24.3%), Feral Pigeon (29.9%) and Tree Sparrow (30.0%).

Cavity-nesting birds

Bird nests built in tree-cavities sometimes teem with bugs, fleas or mites, all of which flourish and reproduce on what they can get from the occupants and their young. One such parasite is the blood-sucking Hen Flea (*Ceratophyllus gallinae*), the effects of which have been studied on Great Tits in Switzerland, although this flea is also found in the nests of other cavity-nesting birds, and occasionally also in the nests of open-nesting species. The flea usually completes 1–2 generations within the six-week nesting period of the host. Adult fleas lay their eggs in the nest material, giving rise to larvae which feed on organic matter, including faeces from the blood-feeding adult fleas, as well as the blood of their nestling and adult hosts. When the chicks fledge, any remaining larvae pupate and remain dormant for several months, before emerging to wait for the arrival of another host that enters the cavity to roost or nest (Triplet *et al.* 2002). In this way fleas can be carried by birds from one site to another, summer or winter.

When Great Tits were offered a choice on their territory of a flea-infested and flea-free nest-box, they chose the one without fleas. However, in territories where only an infested box was offered, the occupants were reluctant to accept the box, but eventually did so, with egg-laying delayed by an average of 11 days compared to birds offered a flea-free box (Oppliger *et al.* 1994). Nest desertions during incubation were significantly more frequent in infested boxes, clutch sizes were no different, but hatching success, and hence brood size, was significantly lower in infested than in flea-free nests. In another experiment, fleas were added to 20 randomly selected nest-boxes, while 14 other boxes were microwaved to kill any naturally occurring fleas (Richner *et al.* 1993). Again, it was found that fleas significantly reduced the numbers and condition of young Great Tits produced (although body condition also varied with brood size). In the flea-free boxes, 83% of hatchlings survived to fledging, compared with 53% in the flea-infested ones (see also Oppliger *et al.* 1994). At the end of the season, an average of 74 adult fleas was recovered from each flea-infested box.

The effects of fleas could be offset to some extent by abundant food. In tit habitats with low food availability, blood-sucking by fleas impaired the growth and survival of nestlings, and sometimes caused adults to desert their nests (Richner *et al.* 1993), but in food-rich habitats the nestlings could withstand the negative effects of fleas because the parents increased their food provisioning (Triplet & Richner 1997). Nestlings in parasitised Great Tit broods doubled their rate of food-begging, compared to unparasitised ones. In response, male parents in food-rich habitats increased their provisioning rates by 50%, on average, while the females showed no such adjustment (Christe *et al.* 1993). However, this increased reproductive effort by the adult males reduced their future survival and reproduction (Richner & Triplet 1999), so by working harder to raise the current brood in the presence of blood-sucking fleas, they reduced their chance of raising future broods.

Various cavity-nesting species have also been found to suffer from blood-sucking blowfly larvae (*Protocalliphora*), which attack mainly nestlings. These flies are free-living, and search out nests, laying their eggs in the nest lining soon after the chicks have hatched. The resulting larvae live in the nest material, but as they develop they periodically take substantial blood meals from the chicks, causing severe anaemia. In a study of Blue Tits in Corsica, comparing naturally infested broods with experimentally de-parasitised broods, these larvae were found to lower the growth rates, fledging mass and size (as indexed by tarsus length) of the chicks, but to cause no additional mortality, at least while the chicks were in the nest (Hurtrez-Boussès *et al.* 1997). Similar effects of blowfly larvae were recorded among Pied Flycatcher chicks in Spain (Merino & Potti 1995). In this latter study, flycatcher nestlings also suffered from mites and fleas. Over three years, mites had the most consistently harmful effects on nestling growth, while fleas were more detrimental in a cold wet year and blowflies caused mortality only in the warmest year (Merino & Potti 2006). Weather may therefore have influenced how the various parasite populations developed in different years.

In another experiment on Pied Flycatchers, one group of broods was provided with supplementary food, while a second group was treated with an insecticide to kill parasites. A third group of broods was given both treatments, while a fourth was given neither and kept as a control. The insecticide greatly reduced the numbers of blowfly larvae in treated nests. Nestlings in the group given both supplementary food and insecticide treatment achieved significantly higher growth rates and haematocrit levels than nestlings in groups that received only one of these treatments, while nestlings from control nests attained the lowest growth rates and haematocrit levels. Although nestlings in the four groups did not differ in their final body sizes, they differed significantly in their growth rates (Merino & Potti 1998).

Hirundines and swifts

Swallows and other hirundines also suffer greatly from ectoparasites, and because many raise more than one brood per year, mites, fleas and bugs tend to build up during the course of the season, so that later broods suffer more than earlier ones (Shields & Crook 1987). Moreover, some of these parasites can overwinter in and around the old nest shells, and re-infest the birds on their return to the same sites in the following spring. Numbers of some parasites can thus also accumulate from year to year and, for colonial hirundines, can sometimes make the whole site untenable (Foster 1968, Brown & Brown 1986). The birds may then abandon the site altogether for some years, but it is not recorded how often this occurs.

The Swallow has been studied in detail over many years by A. P. Møller and his colleagues, working in northern Denmark, where the commonest parasite was the blood-sucking Tropical Fowl Mite (*Ornithonyssus bursa*) (Møller *et al.* 2001). This mite has been found on many different avian host species. Its complete life cycle from egg to adult takes only 5–7 days, so 8–10 mite generations can occur within one Swallow reproductive cycle. The numbers can build up rapidly, and up to 14,000 mites have been found in one nest. Initially, the mites live in the nest lining, and feed from the soft-skinned feet of the newly

FIG 105. The Swallow *Hirundo rustica*, subject of many studies on nest parasites. (Chris Knights)

hatched chicks. When the skin on the feet hardens, the mites transfer to the body of the chicks, and are often seen among the developing plumage. Many mites are transported from the nest as the young fledge, and any left behind aggregate on the nest rim, where they may attach to any visiting Swallows. They can evidently live on free-flying Swallows and in their nests throughout the year. Nests have been found to harbour mites before the Swallows return in spring, but up to one-third of Swallows arrive from Africa already carrying mites, which can then inoculate any clean nests. Heavily infested birds show many bite wounds and become anaemic, droopy and emaciated. The mites can also act as vectors for some microparasite diseases, such as western equine virus (Møller 1994).

Summarising from the several studies on this Danish population, Tropical Fowl Mites were found to affect Swallows in the following ways: (1) on return from migration, heavily infested males had less chance of obtaining a mate than other males; (2) adults discriminated between old nests with and without mites, and egg-laying was delayed if only infested nests were available; (3) nestlings fledged prematurely from heavily infested nests, apparently in an attempt to escape the mites; (4) reproduction was delayed in the second clutch if the first clutch was badly infested with mites, because the adults usually then built a new nest for the second clutch rather than re-using the old one; (5) a smaller proportion of Swallows attempted a second brood if their first nest was heavily infested; (6) heavy infestations caused chick mortality; (7) surviving offspring weighed less than normal if heavily infested with mites; their future survival prospects would presumably therefore have been reduced (Møller 1990, 1993). In experimental nests that were treated with pesticide to kill the mites, incubation periods were slightly shorter, broods were larger and individual chicks were heavier, and more pairs went on to produce second nests, in which they produced larger clutches and broods, and heavier chicks, than the parents from untreated first nests. All these effects were statistically significant, so these blood-sucking mites clearly reduced the reproductive output of the Swallows (Møller 1993).

The prevalence and effects of mites on this Danish Swallow population changed over time. The proportion of nests infected increased from about 17% in 1982 to 66% in 1988 and then declined to about 1% in 1999. An experiment involving the addition and removal of mites, conducted in 1988, affected brood sizes and chick condition. When this experiment was repeated in 1999, the population appeared to have developed some resistance to mites, which had also become less numerous. In this later year, the proportion of eggs producing fledglings was similar for the two types of nest: 76% for nests with mites added and 75% for mite-free nests (Møller 2002b). In addition, mate choice with respect to mite loads, which was evident in the 1980s, had disappeared by 1999.

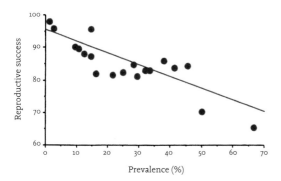

FIG 106. Breeding success (fledglings produced as a percentage of eggs laid) of Swallows *Hirundo rustica* decreases with increasing prevalence of mites. (From Møller 2002b)

Nevertheless, over the period 1962–99, annual breeding success (as measured by the proportion of eggs producing fledglings) was related to the annual prevalence of mites in this population (Fig. 106). In contrast to the effects of mites, the recorded intensities of 11 other parasites did not relate to breeding or survival of Swallows during 1983–92.

Some of this research was repeated in other Swallow populations elsewhere. In a study in Spain, nests of one group of Swallows were fumigated following completion of the first clutch, a second group after completion of every clutch they laid, while in a third group nests were kept unfumigated as controls (de Lope & Møller 1993). Overall seasonal reproductive success, measured by the numbers and quality of offspring, was larger among pairs whose every nest was fumigated than among pairs whose first clutch only was fumigated, and larger still than among pairs none of whose nests were fumigated (controls). In addition, larger numbers of subsequent clutches were laid and they were also laid earlier when all nests were fumigated than if only the first nests or none of the nests were fumigated. These findings clearly showed that ectoparasites at the levels found reduced the seasonal productivity of these Swallows.

Another interesting finding, this time from Italian Swallows, was that, under attack by ectoparasitic louseflies (*Ornithomya avicularia*), nestling Swallows grew their feathers more rapidly, and significantly shortened their time in the nest. These same nestlings gained in bone growth (tarsus length) and body weight less rapidly, so it seemed that, under the pressure of ectoparasites, they switched growth priorities from body to feathers (Saino *et al.* 1998). The young Swallows could then leave the nest earlier, freeing themselves from blood-sucking louseflies. Such differences were apparent even among nestlings from the same brood.

Chewing lice (*Hirundoecus malleus*) sometimes make holes in the feathers of Swallows. In a five-year study in Hungary, the number of holes in the flight and tail feathers averaged 28, but varied from 0 to 85 in different birds. Individuals with few holes had arrived earlier in spring than those with many holes, and began egg-laying earlier, with subsequent effects on reproduction (Pap *et al.* 2005). In addition, females that had fewer feather holes were also more likely to return in the following spring, implying that they had survived better than females with many holes. It seemed, therefore, that louse damage affected both reproduction and survival in female Swallows (males showed no relationship between feather holes and survival). However, it is hard to be sure, in a study such as this, whether poor quality feathers caused poor performance, or whether poor feathers and poor performance were both indicators of poor-quality birds, less able to cope with feather lice.

An important feature of parasite infestations, mentioned above, is that they can act in a density-dependent manner, as crowding facilitates transmission from one host to another. Increases in the numbers of parasites per nest were noted with increase in colony size in Sand Martins infested with blood-sucking fleas (*Ceratophyllus riparius*) (Hoogland & Sherman 1976), and in Swallows infested with blowfly larvae or Tropical Fowl Mites (Shields & Crook 1987, Møller 1990). Any advantage of nesting in groups or colonies was apparently offset to some extent by greater parasitism. Other aspects of these studies on hirundines are discussed in Chapter 13.

Not all studies on ectoparasites have shown adverse effects, but much may depend on circumstances at the time and on the amount of detail recorded. For example, Swifts have two main ectoparasites which are transmitted directly from parents to chicks, namely the chewing louse *Dennyus hirundinis* and the blood-eating flightless lousefly *Crataerina pallida*. In a study in Oxford, these parasites were manipulated to create two categories of broods, with light and heavy infestations. No effect on chick growth or survival was detected, even though the high loads were boosted above natural levels, and environmental conditions were poor that year (Tompkins *et al.* 1996). Similarly, Swifts parasitised by the same lousefly in Germany showed no relationship between total nest parasite load on

FIG 107. Swifts *Apus apus* have two main species of ectoparasites (a chewing louse and a flightless lousefly), which are transmitted directly from parents to offspring. (Bobby Smith)

the one hand and clutch size, brood size, nestling period or fledgling weight and size on the other (Walker & Rotherham 2010). There may, however, have been more subtle effects that were not studied, or effects may have become apparent in a different year. In the related Alpine Swift, heavy experimental infection with a related lousefly (*Craterina melbae*) showed depressed chick growth, extending the nestling period. Brood sizes were not affected, but fathers of heavily infested broods raised fewer young the following year, compared to fathers of broods that were de-parasitised the previous year (Bize *et al.* 2003, 2004). Again there seemed to be a carry-over effect of parental effort in one year affecting reproduction the next, more marked in males than females.

Colonial seabirds

Blood-sucking ticks spend most of the year in the host's nesting substrate or nearby, attaching themselves to hosts for up to a few days each year to ingest a meal, in the process sometimes transmitting microparasites (Danchin 1992). While they can be found on a wide range of birds, they cause particular problems to some seabirds which nest in the same colonies year after year, enabling tick numbers to build up to levels sufficient to cause chick mortality, as recorded in Roseate Terns and Kittiwakes (Ramos *et al.* 2001, Danchin *et al.* 1998). Among

FIG 108. Ticks in colonies of Kittiwakes *Rissa tridactyla* tend to increase with the age of the colony, and may eventually cause decline in colony size, as potential recruits settle elsewhere. (Ian Newton)

Kittiwakes, tick abundance increased with the age of a colony (Danchin 1992), and high infection rates not only affected chick survival but also resulted in colony decline through reduced recruitment and adult emigration (Danchin *et al.* 1998). Among 22 colonies of Kittiwakes in Britain, all established more than 30 years earlier, those that were decreasing in size had a higher prevalence and density of ticks (*Ixodes uriae*) than those that were increasing (Boulinier & Danchin 1996). The authors suggested a causal relationship: namely that through effects on local breeding success, ticks could deter new breeders from settling in those sites, and existing breeders from returning there, thus causing progressive declines in numbers, while colonies with lesser tick infestations continued to expand. On this view, over periods of years, tick infestations may influence local distributions and colony sizes.

In some other colonial seabirds, tick infestations sometimes lead to sudden large-scale nest desertions during a breeding season. I know of no examples from the British Isles, but some 5,000 out of a colony of 40,000 Sooty Tern pairs on the Seychelles abandoned their eggs and chicks, apparently in response to infestations of the tick *Ornithodoros capensis*. Many ticks were found in the deserted part of the colony, but few or none where reproduction was normal. The ticks were still present in the same area the following year, which the terns again avoided (Feare 1976). Similar desertions of whole or part colonies, apparently in response to heavy tick infestations, have been recorded among other seabirds elsewhere (Duffy 1983).

A well-known disease of some seabirds is puffinosis, which appears in summer among Manx Shearwaters nesting on Skomer, Skokholm and other islands off Britain, chiefly in areas of dense ground vegetation which harbour ticks. The same areas seem to be affected year after year. This disease is caused by a coronavirus which is transmitted by ticks, and causes foot blisters, conjunctivitis and paralysis (Dane 1948, Harris 1965, Nuttall *et al.* 1982). It affects mainly fledglings, killing about 75% of infected birds, but only up to 4% of overall fledgling numbers per year (Brooke 1992). It has also been recorded among Fulmars, Shags and large gulls in Orkney and Shetland, mainly in birds nesting in Shearwater colonies (Macdonald *et al.* 1967). Most infected birds die from the disease, while some birds seem to recover, but again it is unknown whether such mortality affects subsequent breeding numbers.

Whether in seabirds or land-birds, lowered production of young may have had no impact on subsequent breeding numbers if it was offset by improved survival of remaining young, as would be expected for example if breeding numbers were limited by resources. Moreover, the instances discussed above are extreme examples, and in most birds that use different sites for each breeding attempt,

FIG 109. Manx Shearwaters *Puffinus puffinus* suffer from a coronavirus disease called puffinosis. The virus is transmitted by ticks, and causes foot blisters, conjunctivitis, paralysis and sometimes death. (Laurie Campbell)

deaths from ectoparasites are much less common. However, the importance of ectoparasites may have been underestimated in those well-studied species that use nest-boxes, because most observers clean out the old nests each year, and in the process reduce the parasite levels (Møller 1989a). Among most birds in the British Isles, however, parasitism is clearly a much less widespread cause of breeding failure than is predation. Apart from causing nest desertion, parasitism seldom results in the deaths of entire broods, but predation almost always does so.

Effects on reproduction resulting from parasitism of adults

As will be clear by now, parasites can also affect bird reproduction through effects on adults. If the adults themselves are weakened by parasites, they might look after their young less well, but if the young themselves are affected, healthy parents might compensate for this, working harder to feed them better. Among other benefits, extra food provided to nestlings by their parents could compensate for blood loss or tissue damage. Parental compensation could account for studies that found little or no effect of ectoparasites on nestlings (Szép & Møller 2000). One study examined parental compensation by Blue Tits whose nests were experimentally infested with Hen Fleas. The parasites reproduced at a high rate in the inoculated nests, but the nestlings showed no reduction in growth or survival, compared with unparasitised ones. However, parent Blue Tits in the parasitised nests increased their provisioning rates by 29%, on average, but showed no obvious deterioration in body condition, compared with control birds. In this case, then, the cost of parasitism on the chicks was borne by the parents (Triplet & Richner 1997). As in the Great Tits mentioned above, this increased parental effort in one year reduced the subsequent survival (return rate) of these parents, compared to those of uninfected broods. The cost of chick parasitism was apparently borne by the parents at a later date.

If the adults themselves are weakened by parasites, this may reflect on the growth and survival of the young. Common protozoan parasites of birds include *Plasmodium, Haemoproteus* and *Leucocytozoon*, all of which are found within the blood cells and tissues of their hosts, and cause forms of avian malaria. They are transmitted from infected to uninfected birds by various biting flies, including mosquitoes, black-flies, ceratopogonid flies (biting midges or sandflies) and louseflies. They can all have negative effects on their hosts, most obviously on body condition, as found in Great Tits and others (Norte *et al.* 2009). Among House Martins, levels of infection with the blood parasite *Haemoproteus prognei* were experimentally reduced, by randomly treating adults with primaquine, while other adults were treated with an inactive liquid to serve as controls (Marzal *et al.* 2005). Treated birds subsequently had significantly fewer parasites than controls and, on average, showed increased clutch size (by 18%); hatching success (by 39%) and fledging success (by 42%). There were no effects of treatment on the quality of offspring, measured in terms of tarsus length, body mass, haematocrit or immune response. But this malarial parasite clearly reduced the breeding success of naturally infected adult House Martins.

Two kinds of *Plasmodium* and one of *Haemoproteus* were identified in blood samples taken from parent Lesser Kestrels in Spain (Ortego *et al.* 2008). Infections of male or female parent had no apparent affect on clutch size or hatching success. However, successful nests that were parented by males parasitised by one specific *Plasmodium* strain produced fewer fledglings than nests parented by males that lacked that strain. The authors suggested that parental effort was limited by this particular *Plasmodium*, but not by the other blood parasites recorded as present. In Tengmalm's Owl, high levels of *Leucocytozoon* blood parasites in the females were associated with reduced clutch size. However, this was apparent only in years of poor food supply, and no such association was apparent in years of abundant food (Korpimäki *et al.* 1993). In another study, the prevalence of blood parasites (especially *Trypanosoma avium*) in Tengmalm's Owls reduced their nest defence behaviour (a risky activity, sometimes taken as a measure of parental investment). Yet again, it seemed that adult parasitism affected parental care (Hakkarainen *et al.* 1998).

Another way in which parasites reduce the breeding success of some bird species is through effects on migration, with individuals in good condition arriving earlier in breeding areas than those in poorer condition, laying earlier and experiencing higher reproductive success. There is therefore a premium on arriving early in spring, and any factor which delays the arrival of a bird relative to other individuals puts it at a disadvantage. Early arrival dates of Swallows during spring migration were associated with low parasite burdens and strong immune responses in three populations from Denmark, Italy and Spain (Møller *et al.* 2004). One example was mentioned above, in that males with heavy infestations of chewing lice (*Hirundoecus malleus*) arrived later than other males, although no such relationship was found among the later-arriving females. Secondly, infection with blood parasites (*Haemoproteus prognei*) was associated with delayed arrival in the Spanish birds, which were the only ones with a high prevalence of these parasites. Thirdly, experimental nest infestations with the blood-sucking Tropical Fowl Mite affected the arrival date of adult males in the following year, but not of females, with arrival date being inversely related to the number of mites present. In two of three populations, males showing strong immune responses arrived earlier than males with weak responses, but again no significant relationship was apparent in females. These findings all suggest that migration can be influenced by parasite burdens; the males may have been more affected than the females because they arrive earlier, in poorer conditions.

Another instance of migration and reproduction being affected by a disease impact became apparent in some Bewick's Swans wintering in the Netherlands. Some adults caught for GPS-tagging were found to be infected by mild forms of avian influenza (strains H6N2 and H6N8). These individuals stayed longer in their wintering areas and travelled back to their Siberian breeding grounds at a slower pace than uninfected individuals, arriving too late to breed that year (van Gils *et al.* 2007). They were apparently constrained in the rate at which they could digest food, which limited the rate at which they could accumulate body reserves for the journey.

Brood-parasites

So called *brood-parasites* are other species of birds (such as cuckoos) that lay their eggs in the nests of particular host species which then raise the young. Some brood-parasites specialise on a single host species, while others use several or many. Within Europe, the Common Cuckoo exists as a number of identical-looking genetic types, each of which specialises on different host species. In Britain and Ireland, the commonest Cuckoo types concentrate respectively on the Dunnock, Meadow Pipit and Reed Warbler as hosts, but elsewhere in Europe other types specialise on White Wagtail, Redstart, Brambling and others. Each type lays an egg that is acceptable to its own host species, but the degree of resemblance between the Cuckoo and the host egg differs from one type to another. The Cuckoo's egg normally hatches before those of the host, and the young Cuckoo then tips out any other eggs in the nest, thus gaining the entire attention of its foster parents, but preventing them from raising young of their own. In one study, 19 female Cuckoos were found to lay an average of eight eggs

FIG 110. Cuckoo *Cuculus canorus*, a brood parasite of several songbird species, the main hosts in Britain and Ireland being Reed Warbler *Acrocephalus scirpaceus* and Dunnock *Prunella modularis* in the lowlands, and Meadow Pipit *Anthus pratensis* in the uplands. (Frank Snijkers)

in a season (range 2–15), each in a different Reed Warbler nest (Wyllie 1981). In 18 different studies, Cuckoos were found to affect up to 55% of host nests in particular study areas. One female parasitised a population of 36 pairs of Reed Warblers, laying 25 eggs in a season, affecting 24 of the warbler pairs, one pair twice (Bayliss 1988). In such extreme situations, Cuckoos clearly reduce markedly the seasonal productivity of their hosts, at least locally.

A second brood parasite, the Great Spotted Cuckoo, lives in southern Europe, and parasitises members of the crow family. On hatching, the Great Spotted Cuckoo does not evict its host's young, but is raised alongside them. It apparently has little effect on the breeding success of Carrion Crows, but a strong negative effect on the breeding success of Magpies, while the fledging success of the Great Spotted Cuckoo itself is twice as high in Magpie nests as in Carrion Crow nests (Soler 1990). To be suitable for any brood parasite, hosts must be of an appropriate size, and bring food suitable for the young parasite. Potential hosts vary in their susceptibility to parasitism, and some species have evolved anti-parasite behaviours, such as mobbing the parasite and ejecting strange eggs. Although only two specialist brood-parasites occur in Europe, in the world as a whole about 103 bird species are interspecific brood-parasites, comprising about 1% of all bird species (Payne 1997).

ADULT MORTALITY

Parasites and disease seem to be a major cause of adult death in only a few bird groups, notably waterfowl, in which diseases probably account for most non-hunting mortality (Bellrose 1980). In Europe, several outbreaks have killed hundreds or thousands of birds at a time, and in North America much bigger numbers of 25,000–100,000 birds at a time. Mortality resulting from parasitic diseases is also frequent among high-density stocks of Red Grouse in Britain, in the past also among Grey Partridges, and in recent years, among Greenfinches and other garden birds (Chapter 9). In these and other bird species, disease outbreaks can appear every year in one place or another, but do not necessarily kill every affected individual. Outbreaks of other diseases are rarer and more sporadic.

Waterfowl are also often infected with cestodes (tapeworms), as well as with trematodes which have molluscs as intermediate hosts. But of 475 trematode species identified in waterfowl, only 32 were found to cause pathological effects or death (McDonald 1969). Of 264 cestode species, none was normally fatal, except when infestation was so great as to block the gut (Grenquist *et al.* 1972, Persson *et al.* 1974), or when the infestation was coupled with malnutrition or other debilitation, accounting in one instance for the deaths of about 50 Mute Swans at Abberton Reservoir in Essex (Jennings *et al.* 1961).

Parasite loads affect the ability of individuals to survive from one year to the next, as already mentioned in the context of enhanced parental provisioning. In addition, some incubating Eider Ducks were treated with an anthelmintic drug to rid them of helminth parasites. Their subsequent breeding success and survival were then monitored for comparison with other females that had not been treated (Hanssen *et al.* 2003b). Birds that hatched their eggs successfully survived well whether they had been treated or not. But birds that failed during incubation subsequently survived (returned) in greater proportion if they had been treated than if they had not been treated (treated = 69%, $n = 13$; untreated = 18%, $n = 11$, $p < 0.01$). The authors suggested that the failed females were of lower quality than those that completed incubation, suffered higher costs from parasite infections, and therefore benefited more from the treatment. Several other studies, using standard measures, showed that individuals with strong immune responses survived better than average for their population (for Swallow see Saino *et al.* 1997, for House Sparrow see González *et al.* 1999).

Most studies of diseases in full-grown birds rely on pathological examination of carcasses. Some studies follow specific disease outbreaks, and are diagnostic, while others result from more general surveys intended to assess the relative frequency of different mortality causes. However, the findings from such general surveys need to be treated with caution (Chapter 3). For one thing, they usually depend on birds found dead, which are unlikely to represent a random cross-section of deaths in any wild population. Secondly, the proportion of deaths attributable to parasitic diseases varies strikingly with the thoroughness of the postmortem procedure, many studies failing to test for microparasites, especially viruses. Thirdly, predators may kill many heavily parasitised individuals before they would otherwise die, further reducing the perceived importance of disease (for examples see van Dobben 1952, Temple 1987). Fourthly, the aggregation of many macroparasites means that the small proportion of heavily infected hosts could easily escape a sampling programme. Lastly, even if a large proportion of deaths were attributable to parasitic disease, this need not tell us anything conclusive about the effects of disease on population levels, because of possible interactions with other mortality factors. The mere presence of parasites in a carcass does not necessarily imply that they were the primary cause of death.

Experiments have proved more revealing than postmortem studies about the affects of parasites on adult birds. For example, because chewing lice (Mallophaga) eat the feathers of birds, they can affect insulation. The lice are normally kept at low numbers by preening, but in experiments they can be removed completely by fumigation, enabling their effects to be more reliably assessed. Among Feral Pigeons in captivity, louse-infested birds had higher metabolic rates than cleaned ones, presumably because of poorer insulation and increased heat loss; and in the wild fumigated pigeons showed higher overwinter survival than control ones (Booth *et al.* 1993). In another experiment, survival of hen Pheasants, dosed with an anthelminthic, was about 10% higher in the three months (March–May) following treatment than that of untreated controls (Woodburn 1995). Treated hens also hatched more chicks. These birds contained various intestinal helminth parasites, most commonly the caecal nematode *Heterakis*. Studies such as these confirm that parasites of various kinds can affect individual birds adversely, but for reliable assessment of effects on population levels additional information is required. Exceptions occur in situations where so many individuals die in a brief period that breeding numbers must inevitably be reduced.

In some species, diseases are clearly more prevalent where hosts live at high densities, favouring transmission, as in various gamebirds. At least two diseases, strongylosis and louping ill, occur frequently in Red Grouse, but chiefly in populations maintained at artificially high densities. Similarly, in Red-legged Partridges studied in Spain, diseases were detected only in managed high-density populations, affecting mainly females in the breeding period (Buenestado *et al.* 2009). In these partridges, bacterial diseases caused about one-fourth of all recorded deaths, compared to almost none in unmanaged populations. High losses from disease were also noted in managed Grey Partridge populations in Italy (Meriggi *et al.* 2002). These findings might suggest that the higher densities and aggregations promoted by game management may allow disease to spread more easily than in areas where gamebirds are managed less intensively and live at lower densities. In theory, some of these diseases may then spread to other species, but I know of no examples of spread to non-game species.

CONCLUDING REMARKS

Parasites of various kinds can clearly reduce the breeding success of some individuals in wild bird populations, and also cause the deaths of some adults. These impacts vary greatly between species, with substantial breeding failures (caused by ectoparasites) occurring occasionally among some cavity-nesting passerines, hirundines and colonial seabirds. All these species require special places for nesting, and often use the same sites year after year, enabling parasite levels to build up over a number of years. The greatest mortalities among adults have been recorded among water-birds, which are susceptible to various endoparasites obtained from their food organisms, and to bacterial and viral diseases transmitted from other individuals or from their aquatic habitat.

In assessing the impacts of parasitism on a population, the same question arises as with predation: whether the resulting deaths are additive to other mortality, or compensatory so that, in the absence of deaths from parasites, a similar number of deaths would occur each year from other causes. With disease, contributing causes are often apparent. For example, individuals weakened by starvation are clearly vulnerable to disease, as are those that are crowded together in limited habitat. On the other hand, individuals that lose part of their daily food intake to internal parasites may be more prone to the effects of food shortage than other individuals that are free of such parasites. Disease should thus be seen as a response, not only to parasite infection, but to the overall condition of the host. The modifying effect of food supply on the impact of parasites on individual birds was evident in several of the studies discussed above. This makes it hard to separate the effects of disease from the food shortage or other environmental conditions that might favour it, and means that deaths from disease are often unlikely to be completely additive to other mortality (Chapter 13). Interactions between disease and predation are also likely: disease may predispose certain individuals to predation, which may in turn reduce the spread of the disease (Chapter 12).

Clearly, any parasites that affect host reproduction or mortality have the potential to influence host population levels. The questions of interest therefore are how often parasitic diseases do indeed reduce the breeding numbers of their hosts and in what circumstances. These questions lead on to the next chapter.

CHAPTER 9

Parasitic Diseases: Population Impacts

THE FACT THAT INDIVIDUAL BIRDS may die or produce fewer young because of parasitic diseases does not necessarily mean that these effects are reflected in the level of the subsequent breeding population. In some situations, losses from disease may be compensated by improved survival or reproduction of non-diseased individuals, but in other situations the disease can have additive and clear population-level effects. In fact, parasites can show similar relationships with their hosts as predators with their prey, and may cause (1) no obvious effects on breeding numbers, (2) reduced breeding numbers compared to what would otherwise occur, (3) regular fluctuations in breeding numbers, (4) irregular fluctuations in breeding numbers, associated with periodic epidemics, or (5) declines to extinction. These various situations are illustrated below by particular case studies.

NO OBVIOUS EFFECTS OF PARASITES ON HOST BREEDING NUMBERS

This is probably a common situation, but the evidence is indirect: namely that all bird species that have been studied harbour some parasites, yet in many species deaths from parasitism or disease are rare or unknown, in either chicks or adults. For example, in several studies protozoan blood-parasites were found to have no obvious effects on the body condition, survival or breeding success of individual songbirds and raptors, and in the numbers found could not have affected their population levels (Bennett *et al.* 1988, 1993, Ashford *et al.* 1990,

Weatherhead & Bennett 1991, 1992, Tella *et al.* 1996). Possibly these parasites might not always be so benign, if the more heavily infected hosts died quickly and were not represented in the birds that were sampled, or if the hosts with 'normal' levels of parasites were exposed to other debilitating influences, but the studies concerned produced no evidence for adverse impacts.

Secondly, despite harbouring parasites, the breeding numbers of many bird species are known to be limited primarily by other factors, such as food supply, nest-sites or predation. Any mortality that such species might suffer from parasitism is seemingly trivial in the overall scheme of things. Parasites might cause some deaths which are inevitable for other reasons, and could be offset by reduced mortality from other causes. Thirdly, around the world many generalist parasites have been introduced into island avifaunas along with introduced birds, yet only rarely have they been implicated in population declines of their new hosts (but see below).

LOWERING OF HOST BREEDING NUMBERS

If a parasite kills hosts in a density-dependent manner to give a stable equilibrium in which the infection rate remains constant, the host population could be regulated at a level lower than might occur in the absence of the parasite. This situation emerges as plausible in mathematical models, but to my knowledge no such stable, closely coupled interactions between a specialist parasite and its host have yet been described from birds. However, one example of population limitation by a generalist microparasite involves the louping ill flavivirus, which affects the central nervous system mainly of sheep, but also of other animals, including Red Grouse. Infected sheep often develop a characteristic louping gait, in which the front legs move forward together, followed by the back legs. Typically, about 10% of infected sheep die. This virus was probably brought to the British uplands by sheep, where it is now patchily distributed and

FIG 111. The Red Grouse *Lagopus l. scotica* suffers from two main diseases in Britain, the viral disease 'louping ill' obtained via ticks mainly from sheep, and strongylosis caused by a nematode worm ingested with the food-plants. (Edmund Fellowes)

transmitted between hosts by the Sheep Tick (*Ixodes ricinus*). The mortality that occurs in Red Grouse in areas where louping ill is now endemic is sufficient to reduce grouse to low densities, but continuing infection is dependent on the presence of sheep or other alternative hosts and on ticks as vectors (Duncan *et al.* 1979). In some areas, alternative hosts include deer and the Mountain Hare.

Although louping ill can kill adult grouse, its main effects are on chicks. In an experimental study of captive grouse, 78% of 37 experimentally infected juveniles died within six days (Reid 1975). Comparative studies on wild grouse in northern England indicated that, in areas with ticks and louping ill, chick survival was about half the level found in areas with ticks and no louping ill, or in areas with neither ticks nor louping ill (Hudson & Dobson 1991). In some areas where ticks were abundant, 84% of adult grouse had antibodies to louping ill, indicating previous non-lethal infections. Louping ill can spread in various ways. First, a tick that feeds on a host with high concentrations of virus in its blood can transmit the disease to its next host. This occurs mostly through sheep. Second, the virus can pass from infected to uninfected ticks that are feeding close to each other on Mountain Hares, but not apparently on Rabbits or deer. Third, the virus can spread from one host individual to another by droplet infection (in moisture from the nostrils), without the intervention of a tick. Droplet infection could occur among grouse chicks being covered by a parent, but this has not been proven. On hills where deer and hares are scarce, the removal or routine vaccination of sheep can eliminate louping ill from grouse stocks. Vaccination of sheep has had this effect in parts of northern England, but not in parts of Scotland where deer and hares are sufficiently numerous to sustain the disease. Despite having ticks, Rabbits and small rodents are not thought to play an important role in the persistence of louping ill.

Since the 1990s, louping ill seems to have been affecting Red Grouse in some areas where it was not previously recognised. This could be partly due to mild winters allowing better tick survival, and partly to increased numbers of hosts, notably Red Deer, or to the movement of sheep between moors in different parts of the country, thereby introducing the disease to areas previously free of it. Fencing is now sometimes used to exclude deer or sheep from valued grouse moors. In addition, killing of Mountain Hares with the aim of protecting grouse from louping ill is becoming widespread, but it is still unclear whether this process might raise grouse bags (Harrison *et al.* 2010).

Woodland gamebirds, including Capercaillie, Black Grouse and Pheasant, that were experimentally infected with louping ill virus all recovered, although some looked unwell for a few days (Reid & Moss 1980). Among open-country species, about 80% of Red Grouse died, but Scottish Ptarmigan and Norwegian Willow

Ptarmigan all died. These differences in susceptibility between species could have reflected their differing exposure to tick-borne encephalitis viruses during their evolution. These viruses and their tick hosts occur naturally throughout Eurasian woodland, so birds that live there could have developed resistance from long association. But birds of open ground, above and beyond the natural tree-line, have probably had much less contact with these viruses, so less opportunity for resistance to develop. However, the fact that some experimentally infected Red Grouse recovered from infection, while others in the wild had antibodies to the virus, suggests that the bird has developed some immunity, and with continued exposure its resistance may well increase in years to come.

REGULAR FLUCTUATIONS IN HOST NUMBERS

Both microparasites and macroparasites can induce oscillations in host abundance, through acting in a delayed density-dependent manner, in which changes in population correlate with population size, but only after a time lag (in this case of about a year: Chapter 2). The best-studied example concerns the Red Grouse as affected by the disease strongylosis, caused by a nematode threadworm (*Trichostrongylus tenuis*) which lives in the intestinal caecae of the grouse (Committee of Inquiry on Grouse Disease 1911, Hudson *et al.* 1992a, 1992b). In its moorland habitat, the Red Grouse is the only known host for this parasite, although at higher altitudes it has also been found in Ptarmigan, and at lower altitudes in Grey Partridges (see later). In some areas, these worms are found in nearly every grouse examined, often causing little harm, but when present in big numbers they can weaken and sometimes kill their hosts. The eggs of the parasite are voided with the caecal faeces (big soft droppings unlike the normal ones). The larvae hatch and, after some development, they climb to the tips of heather plants which form the main food of the grouse. In this way they pass from one grouse to another. Active third-stage larvae can usually be found on the heather plants from June to September, over which period the worm burdens of grouse increase steadily. The main damage is done by the developing larvae as they burrow into the caecal walls during their two-week development period. In autumn, many ingested larvae do not develop, but remain buried in the caecal walls in a state of arrested development (Shaw 1988). In the spring, these larvae develop simultaneously and, if they number in the hundreds or thousands, they cause massive damage. This explains why outbreaks of grouse disease usually begin in spring, although diseased birds – emaciated and scarcely able to fly – can be seen through the summer. It also explains why the same burden of worms can appear innocuous in autumn but fatal in spring. Although old birds often have many more adult worms than young birds, it is the larvae that cause the damage, so old birds suffer no more than young ones during outbreaks. Just before a population crash, Red Grouse may contain an average of around 6,000 worms per individual.

The adult worms themselves are relatively benign but long-lived, probably as long as the grouse, so infection is cumulative. Infection rates intensify year by year as the numbers of grouse rise, until eventually many grouse die from their worm burdens and the population crashes, with a consequent reduction in the numbers of the parasite. The speed of the population decline depends on whether it is due mainly to adult mortality, which can cause precipitous crashes, or to breeding failure, which causes slower declines over a year or more. As the grouse recover over a period of years, the parasites build up again, eventually causing another crash, and the cycle is repeated. Population cycles are thus thought to be produced by the effects of these parasites acting mainly on the fecundity and survival of the grouse in a delayed density-dependent manner. Transmission rates vary not only with the density of the grouse, but also with environmental conditions: wet summers are conducive to increased worm burdens, as is extensive frost-induced heather browning, which causes larvae to concentrate on the remaining green shoots selected by the grouse.

The impact of these parasites on the body weight, breeding and survival of grouse was examined in field experiments conducted over several years (Hudson 1986, Hudson et al. 1992b). The basic techniques were to catch and mark grouse at random, treat half the birds with an anthelmintic drug to reduce worm burdens and the remaining birds with water as a control, and then to monitor their subsequent performance. Overwinter weight gains were greater in treated birds than in control birds, as were their subsequent clutch sizes, hatching success and chick survival. Replication of the experiment in several other areas gave similar results, confirming that parasitism had a major influence on grouse breeding success. Moreover, in the main study area in north Yorkshire, treated birds were significantly more likely to survive from spring to the following autumn than were untreated birds. Grouse found dead on the study areas in spring generally had high parasite burdens.

These experiments clearly showed that parasites reduced the productivity and survival of individual grouse. On their own, they could not show whether parasitism affected population levels, rather than merely influencing which individuals succumbed in a population ultimately limited by other factors. They nonetheless provided a crucial strand of evidence for the hypothesis of population limitation by parasites, showing that this nematode–grouse system has the three conditions that mathematical models have shown can generate population cycles: (1) parasite-induced reduction in host breeding success, (2) parasites distributed almost at random within the host population, and (3) time-delays in recruitment to the adult parasite population owing to larval arrestment (Anderson & May 1978). Given these conditions, a mathematically simulated population would fluctuate with appropriate periodicity, with peaks every five years or so, which is what many Red Grouse populations do (Potts et al. 1984, Hudson & Dobson 1991, Dobson & Hudson 1992). Subsequent experimental work implied that the parasite may not be the only factor involved in grouse cycles, but it could be important in tipping high-density populations into decline or in amplifying cycles caused primarily by some other factor, possibly intrinsic to the population (Redpath et al. 2006, New et al. 2009).

Experimental work also provided evidence for a link between parasitism and predation (Hudson 1986, Hudson & Dobson 1991, Hudson et al. 1992b). On several moors, grouse killed by predators had higher worm burdens than grouse that survived through the summer, to be shot in the autumn. During incubation, hen grouse are thought to produce less scent than usual, making it harder for Foxes and other mammalian predators to find their nests. The scent probably arises from the caecum, which stops producing caecal faeces while birds are incubating. Wild hens that were dosed with an anthelmintic drug to reduce their worm burdens were found less often (15% of finds) by trained dogs hunting by scent than untreated hens (85% of finds). In contrast, for human observers hunting by sight, the figures were 45% and 55%. Compared with treated hens, heavily parasitised hens probably emitted more scent, making them more vulnerable to mammalian predation. In this way parasitism was a predisposing factor to death by predation during incubation. At other times of year, some heavily parasitised grouse are scarcely able to fly, making them easy for both mammalian and avian predators to catch. Parasites might also reduce the competitive ability of individual grouse, for birds without territories generally had higher worm burdens than those with territories (Jenkins et al. 1963).

Grouse disease may have reached the importance it has only because of habitat management and predator control by gamekeepers, which allows the grouse to achieve densities at which parasite transmission is enhanced. Thus, in recent studies, the presence of many heavily parasitised individuals within grouse populations was invariably associated with a scarcity of Foxes and other predators. Mathematical modelling revealed how predators, by selectively removing the most infected grouse, could allow an increase in grouse density: they effectively blocked the regulatory role of the parasites, and stopped the cycle in grouse numbers (Hudson et al. 1992b). Even if predation merely reduced the post-breeding density of the grouse, it could greatly hamper the spread of the parasite. Low levels of predation were sufficient to achieve this effect in a mathematical model, but at higher levels, predation was itself enough to reduce grouse density to an even lower average level, despite the scarcity of parasites. That the density of grouse is important in leading to population crashes was shown in experiments in which grouse were shot so heavily as to prevent a population from increasing above a particular level. The population concerned did not crash, unlike nearby populations which were allowed to increase to higher levels and then crashed catastrophically (Watson & Moss 2008).

Population cycles involving strongylosis are known among Red Grouse chiefly on wetter, western moors. On drier moors parasite numbers are too low to kill many grouse. This has been attributed to poorer survival of the free-living stages of the parasite on drier moors, for in the laboratory their survival has been found to depend on humidity as well as on temperature. On drier moors, therefore, grouse numbers may cycle from some different cause or may simply fluctuate irregularly. Elsewhere the cycles are longer and more symmetrical, as both the rise and fall take place progressively over several years. Clearly, although strongyle parasites might contribute to cycles in some areas, they are not responsible for cycles in all areas. It remains possible that their main effect is to induce crashes at high density, and thereby shorten a cycle that would still occur, but with longer periodicity, from different causes (Redpath *et al.* 2006).

Nowadays, many moor-owners regularly dose their grouse with an anthelmintic drug to try and stop the parasite from causing periodic population cashes. This is done by providing medicated grit for the grouse at various points across a moor. Like other herbivorous birds, Red Grouse naturally seek grit to aid in the digestion of their plant foods, but in this case they also take the anthelmintic which coats the grit. When this works effectively, along with good habitat management and predator control, grouse breeding success is improved, and numbers can be maintained at high level, with less marked or fewer crashes, though cycles may still be apparent (Redpath *et al.* 2006, Watson & Moss 2008).

Years ago, local outbreaks of what was apparently the same species of worm were reported in Grey Partridges, causing occasional population crashes, especially in wet years favourable to the free-living stages of the worm. However, following the massive decline in Partridge populations over most of Britain and Ireland, densities are now well below the level necessary for effective transmission of the parasite (Potts 1986). Another strongyle worm, *Syngamus trachea*, which causes 'gapes', is also frequent in Partridges, but is thought to cause only limited mortality (Potts 1986). However, this is not the case in areas where Pheasants are reared intensively, as they also host gapeworms, and Pheasants can act as a major source of infection for the more vulnerable

Partridges (Chapter 16). Gapeworms are otherwise distinguished by the fact that male and female spend all their lives attached in permanent copulation.

IRREGULAR FLUCTUATIONS IN HOST HUMBERS

Irregular declines in the numbers of some other birds are caused by periodic outbreaks of parasitic diseases, which kill large numbers of individuals in single events. These outbreaks have been recorded in a wide range of bird species, but particularly in waterfowl, which outside the breeding season often assemble in large concentrations, facilitating transmission. The most important of such diseases include avian cholera and duck plague, although both are much less frequent in Europe than in North America.

Avian cholera (or pasteurellosis) is caused by the bacterium *Pasteurella multocida*. It is highly contagious and capable of killing birds within a few hours after exposure (Friend & Franson 2002). Typically, the birds die in good condition, and sometimes literally fall out of the sky or die while feeding, with no prior sign of illness. Otherwise, sick birds often appear drowsy and can be approached closely before they attempt to flee, although some have convulsions, swim in circles or throw their heads back. These symptoms are not unique to avian cholera, however, and laboratory diagnosis is needed to be sure of the cause, the chief signs being small haemorrhages on the heart muscle and pinpoint lesions on the liver, heart and other organs. The disease is transmitted primarily by ingestion of the bacterium in food or water, but possibly also by inhalation. Susceptibility to infection, and the subsequent impact – whether chronic or acute – varies with the species, sex, age and body condition of the host, with the virulence of the particular strain of the bacterium, and with the dose and route of exposure.

Avian cholera has been recorded in more than 100 bird species, chiefly waterfowl and seabirds, but also scavengers which may be infected by feeding on diseased birds or carcasses (Botzler 1991). In North America, it is a particularly important disease of waterfowl (second only to botulism). Mortality of single individuals or small groups is reported frequently, but epidemics occur only where birds are concentrated, as in staging or wintering areas. Under these conditions, thousands of individuals can die in a short period, as exemplified by the 60,000 ducks that died at Muleshoe Wildlife Refuge in Texas in winter 1956 or the 44,000 Black-necked (Eared) Grebes that died at the Great Salt Lake in Utah in autumn 1998 (Friend 2006). Typically, the disease begins in one common host species, and then spreads to other species in the same area. Migrants can carry the disease to other sites along migration routes (Brand 1984). Wetlands can be contaminated by the body discharges of diseased birds, which include copious excretions from the nostrils and mouth. The bacterium can be found at high concentration for several weeks in waters and soils where waterfowl and other birds have died from the disease, and may persist for longer periods in healthy carrier birds, giving rise to further infections.

In Europe, several severe outbreaks of avian cholera have been recorded among Eiders, especially among incubating females using stagnant pools for drinking. One such event occurred in the southwest Kattegat of Denmark in 1996, killing at least 900 birds in late winter, and a total of 3,146 females in five local breeding colonies in spring, corresponding to 35–95% of the females present in particular colonies (Christensen *et al.* 1997). Birds seemed to have carried the disease from wintering to breeding areas. Outbreaks in Finland during 1996 and 2001 killed some 3,500–4,000 females and 400 males (Christensen *et al.* 1997, Desholm *et al.* 2002), while another on the Dutch island of Vlieland in 1984 killed 80–100 females (out of about 200), having effects on nest numbers and age structure that were still apparent five years later (Swennen & Smit 1991).

Despite the numbers of Eiders killed in these outbreaks, they probably accounted for only a small part of the overall decline of Eider populations in the Baltic region that occurred over the period concerned, entailing the loss of some 400,000 birds, mainly from food shortage (Christensen 2008; Chapter 4). Nevertheless, avian cholera outbreaks in the Baltic region have become more frequent in recent years, and could have played an increasing role in limiting Eider numbers. Other cholera incidents in the Baltic have involved Guillemots and other seabirds, killing up to 5,000 individuals (Österblom *et al.* 2004), and elsewhere deaths have occurred among Cormorants, Oystercatchers, gulls, doves, crows and sparrows. Other viral infections have been shown to kill Eider ducklings up to three weeks old, resulting in mass die-offs in Finland (Hollmén *et al.* 2002).

A different disease, duck plague, results from a herpes virus infection, also called duck viral enteritis (DVE), which is found throughout the northern hemisphere, more often in domestic than in wild ducks. Strains of the virus vary in virulence, and not all waterfowl are equally susceptible. It attacks the blood system, usually causing death within 14 days of exposure (Wobeser 1981). Sick birds seek dense cover or other darkened areas. They may exhibit extreme thirst, droopiness and a bloody discharge from the vent. The chief internal symptoms include haemorrhages throughout the body, and free blood throughout the gastrointestinal tract. Infected birds excrete the virus, so transmission occurs through contact between individuals or with a contaminated environment. Outbreaks are thought to be caused when immune birds that carry the virus shed it through faecal or oral discharge into food and water with which susceptible birds then have contact. The scavenging and decomposition of carcasses of infected birds can also contaminate the environment by releasing virus from tissues and body fluids. The virus can remain latent in carrier birds for years before stress leads to viral increase and excretion (Burgess *et al.* 1979, Friend & Franson 2002).

It appears that only waterfowl are susceptible to duck plague, and the absence of other species among the casualties is an indication that duck plague is involved. First reported from the Netherlands in 1923, the disease has since appeared at various sites across the northern hemisphere. The first recorded major outbreak in wild waterfowl occurred during the 1972/73 winter, killing an estimated 42% of the 100,000 Mallard wintering at the Lake Andes National Wildlife Refuge in South Dakota (Friend & Pearson 1973). In contrast, only 3% of 9,000 geese were affected, probably because they fed on land nearby, so were less likely to pick up the virus.

Epidemics involving macroparasites have also occurred among waterfowl. The phylum Acanthocephala contains the 'thorny-headed worms', so-called because both larval and adult stages have a retractable proboscis at the head bearing sharp hooks or spines. More than 50 different species have been reported from waterfowl. All require an intermediate host, usually a food-species of the main host, such as a crustacean. Some also occur in other birds, including raptors and passerines. Severe disease outbreaks have been reported from Eiders in many different areas, each causing marked declines in numbers. They usually correspond with periods of food stress. On the Baltic Islands of Finland, Eider numbers increased between 1920 and 1930, but in the breeding season of 1931 many females and young died from infection with the acanthocephalan worm *Polymorphus boschadis*. The numbers of Eiders then rose again, reaching their former level by 1933/34. They were then reduced by a second outbreak in 1935, which continued less severely for the next three years, by which time breeding numbers were only two-thirds and in some places only one-third of what they had been (Lampio 1946, Grenquist 1951).

FIG 112. The Eider *Somateria mollissima* plays host to several gut parasites, notably the acanthocephalan worm *Polymorphus boschadis*, which is sometimes associated with population declines. (Edmund Fellowes)

Large numbers of Eiders which succumbed to starvation in the Wadden Sea during three successive winters (1999/00 to 2001/02) were also heavily infected with acanthocephaline worms. This was partly because a shortage of mussels forced the Eiders to feed more on Green Shore Crabs, which are the main intermediate hosts for the parasite and thus acted as a source of infection (Camphuysen *et al.* 2002). Heavy infestations with the same acanthocephalan (*Polymorphus boschadis*) were also reported from Eiders found dead on the Ythan Estuary near Aberdeen during 1955–60, but effects on breeding numbers were not ascertained (Garden *et al.* 1964).

Most of the disease outbreaks mentioned above occurred sporadically, and often after long intervals. They reduced numbers so markedly that several years would have been needed for populations to recover to former levels. These populations would then be limited by other factors until the next disease outbreak. Theoretically, such events could occur so frequently that before numbers could recover to their full potential, they would be reduced again by the next outbreak. In this way, the population would fluctuate over periods of years, but never reach the levels possible in the absence of disease. Many other disease outbreaks have been recorded among wild birds, including pigeons, gulls, petrels and others, but again it cannot be more than sporadically important (Newton 1998).

Our understanding of what precipitates irregular disease outbreaks in birds is poor, but not all follow the same pattern. Some result from an unexplained appearance of a particular disease agent, others from a disease agent that normally remains latent but which becomes fatal when the birds are exposed to some other stress such as food shortage, or to crowding or other conditions that facilitate transmission. Some diseases that are not serious in the wild can kill many captive birds kept at high density in the same place for long periods. An example from poultry is Newcastle disease (fowl pest), caused by a paramyxovirus. Yet other disease outbreaks have been attributed to a genetic change in a disease organism itself – to the evolution of a new virulent strain, or of a strain that can switch from one host species to another resistant to earlier strains.

Mass mortality caused by natural toxins

Other forms of mass mortality occur in birds from time to time, as a result of toxins produced by microorganisms. A well-known example is botulism. This is a form of paralytic food-poisoning caused by a neurotoxin produced by the bacterium *Clostridium botulinum*, mostly type C strain (Kalmbach & Gunderson 1934, Sciple 1953, Friend & Franson 2002).[13] This anaerobic bacterium persists in

---

13 The *Clostridium* that causes botulism is closely related to the bacterium that causes tetanus in humans, and the botulism A toxin is popularly known as Botox or Dysport, which is used for various medical and cosmetic purposes.

spore form for years, but during warm weather it springs into life, growing well on organic matter in shallow stagnant water or mud. Birds become poisoned when they ingest the toxin-producing bacteria from the bodies of invertebrates that form their food, including maggots living on rotting vegetation and carcasses. Once affected, the birds die and support more maggots, perpetuating the outbreak. Their carcasses may then be eaten by raptors, which may in turn be affected.

Deaths from botulism have been noted in about 70 bird species in 21 families, but mostly in waterfowl and gulls. The chief symptom is a flaccid paralysis which prevents the birds from flying. Often the wings droop, the head sags to one side, and the eyelids may become encrusted. Birds die from respiratory failure or from drowning and may otherwise appear in good condition with no internal lesions (Friend & Franson 2002). Worldwide, botulism is currently the most important fatal disease of waterfowl and shorebirds, and single outbreaks occasionally kill tens of thousands of birds, with exceptionally protracted outbreaks killing up to a million in a single location (Newton 1998).

Botulism is not usually an important source of bird deaths in Britain, but in some years large numbers of gulls have succumbed, usually through feeding on rubbish dumps, where they bathe and roost in pools at which they are exposed to the bacteria or their toxins. A survey during the hot summer of 1975 revealed that more than 4,000 birds (mostly gulls) had died in this way at scattered localities, including at least 2,080 gulls in the Firth of Forth (Lloyd et al. 1976, Macdonald & Standring 1978). Many other incidents have been recorded since then, and deaths of hundreds of birds are now recorded almost annually at some colonies situated near rubbish dumps. Such frequent mortality has been held responsible for recent stepwise declines of some local colonies, especially of Herring Gulls, at various sites in Britain and Ireland (Madden & Newton, in Mitchell et al. 2004), but also of Great Black-backed Gulls at colonies in Wales (Sutcliffe 1997). These losses are trivial compared to those of waterfowl in western North America (Newton 1998).

The effects of botulism are exacerbated by droughts which cause water-birds to concentrate in larger than usual numbers on remaining shallow wetlands. The outbreak comes to an end when temperatures cool, when birds leave the site or switch to other foods, when flies stop breeding, or when water levels stabilise (Wobeser 1981). In western North America, the impact of botulism can be so substantial that after each severe outbreak the populations concerned take several years to recover their numbers. Frequent outbreaks could thus cause populations to remain for much of the time below the level they could otherwise achieve.

Another type of mass mortality, attributed to a toxin, is so-called paralytic shellfish poisoning which occurs from time to time in seabirds. The neurotoxin concerned is produced by dinoflagellate plankton species (*Gonyaulax*), whose

FIG 113. The Shag *Phalacrocorax aristotelis* is an inshore species, seldom seen far from land. It has suffered various large-scale mortality incidents caused by marine algal toxins, and others caused by strong winds and rough seas. (Laurie Campbell)

presence in abundance turns the sea surface brown or red, giving rise to 'red tides'. The dinoflagellates are consumed by plankton-feeding fish or invertebrates, especially mussels, which concentrate the poison, passing it on to birds. The toxin acts by blocking the production of nerve impulses, leading to muscle paralysis and, at higher doses, to respiratory failure. Some bird species, notably Shags, which get the toxin from contaminated fish, are much more sensitive than others, such as Eiders, which get the toxin directly from mussels. Some gulls can detect and avoid the toxin by regurgitating contaminated prey (Kvitek 1991).

Mass mortalities of seabirds in northeast England attributed to algal toxins occurred in 1968, 1975, 1984–87 and 1996–98 (Coulson & Strowger 1999). During a major incident off northeast England in summer 1968, so many Shags died that breeding numbers on the Farne Islands dropped by about 82%. However, the lesser mortality seen in other species in that year was insufficient to cause marked reductions in their breeding numbers (Coulson *et al.* 1968). Another incident was recorded in the same area in 1975, by which time Shags had recovered their numbers following the 1968 incident. This time, the population was reduced by 63%, and again many deaths of other species were recorded (Armstrong *et al.* 1978). Later incidents, in the summers of 1996 and 1997, affected mainly Kittiwakes, and in the Tyneside area some 15,000 birds died, with the largest colony (Marsden) declining by 72% between 1992 and 1998 (Coulson & Strowger 1999). During these years, many carcasses were washed up on beaches, most in good condition, but often with blood around the vent resulting from gut haemorrhage, a presumed consequence of the poisoning (Newton & Little 2009). The Kittiwakes seem to have died about 7 km offshore, in an area used for dumping human sewage, which may have stimulated blooms of toxic algae. These various incidents were relatively infrequent, and restricted to northeast England around the British Isles. Elsewhere, many ducks, cranes and seabirds have been killed, including Common Terns, Shags, Cormorants, Fulmars, Herring Gulls, Guillemots, Great Northern Divers, Sooty Shearwaters and others (Friend & Franson 2002).

Periodic blooms of algae, including true algae, dinoflagellates (protozoa) and blue-green algae (or cyanobacteria), have been reported in shallow seas and fresh waters throughout the world. Their causes are not well understood, but they may be triggered by some combination of eutrophication and water temperature. Blooms may have become more frequent in recent decades owing to run-off of fertilisers from farmland, and from other pollutant inputs, with the resulting phosphorus and nitrogen providing favourable conditions for plankton growth. Definitive diagnosis of algal poisoning in birds is difficult even with chemical analyses. Circumstantial evidence, such as the occurrence of a marine red tide in conjunction with a die-off of birds in otherwise good condition, is often used as a presumptive diagnosis.

Fungal moulds produce another type of poison. The commonest mycotoxins recorded as killing wild birds in Britain are aflatoxins, produced by some *Aspergillus* moulds that grow mainly on damp seeds. They are often associated with peanuts, killing Greenfinches and other birds at garden feeders. They are also found on cereal grains, and have occasionally killed waterfowl. They are especially likely to develop in seeds that lie around outside or are stored damp.

DECLINE TO EXTINCTION

Like other animals, birds may have little resistance to a pathogen with which they have had no previous contact. A disease may reach new areas as a result of a natural spread of the pathogen or its vectors, or through inadvertent introduction by people. In this context, alien diseases may have contributed to declines of certain endemic land-birds on oceanic islands, restricting the distribution of some and annihilating others. The best documented examples are from Hawaii, where the release of infected non-native birds, together with mosquitoes (present since 1826), led to the establishment of avian malaria and avian pox (Warner 1968). These parasites are only mildly virulent to the introduced birds, with which the pathogens have had long evolutionary associations. But they often kill the indigenous Hawaiian birds, which have little or no natural resistance. This has led to reduction in the range and numbers of many endemic bird species, which are now mainly restricted to high or dry areas where mosquitoes are absent. The extinction of roughly half the indigenous land-birds of the Hawaiian Islands since their discovery by Europeans in 1778 has been attributed mainly to these introduced diseases (Warner 1968). Nevertheless, there are yet very few examples of disease organisms limiting the areas or habitats used by birds, compared with the many examples in which predators have these effects. This could be due to the greater difficulties of recording disease effects on bird distributions, rather than their rarity in nature.

MULTIPLE PARASITES

Most of the studies discussed above were concerned with the effects of a single parasite on a host population, but in reality birds generally support several types of parasites at once, both on and within their bodies. In studies of individual parasites, the potential effects of others are unaccounted for, but a whole community of parasites may have much more impact than any one species. One study that examined several endoparasites at the same time involved Willow Ptarmigan, the continental equivalent of the Red Grouse in Britain and Ireland. In two areas of northern Norway, Willow Ptarmigan breeding density and productivity were monitored for 8 and 11 years respectively, as were their helminth parasites (Holmstad *et al.* 2005). On the basis of shot birds, 11 species of endoparasites were found. The abundance of some individual parasite species showed relationships with bird performance and population trend, but a major conclusion was that, even though some parasite species had no detectable impact on their own, they could add to the effects of others. The community of parasites had an effect on the host population, over and above their individual effects. In a later study, it was found that the intensities of two different feather lice on Willow Ptarmigan were also correlated over a number of years, both with one another and with endoparasite loads (Holmstad *et al.* 2008). This implied that variability in the parasite community was not random, but governed by changes in host susceptibility or environmental conditions that affected several parasites. They all varied in abundance from year to year, apparently in relation to the duration of snow-lie, which may have influenced their free-living stages.

SOME TOPICAL ISSUES

Diseases of garden birds
The increased feeding of birds in gardens has led to an upsurge of some diseases, and their transfer between species that would otherwise have little

close contact with one another. The concentrations of birds at regular feeding sites provide ideal conditions for the transmission of pathogens, and as with predation, householders have thereby witnessed the effects of avian diseases as never before. Several pathogens have become common in urban and suburban areas. They can be much reduced if feeders are periodically disinfected (a 1:10 dilution of household bleach and water is good for this purpose), and if spilled food and droppings are removed from around the feeders, or if the feeders themselves are shifted from time to time.

One long-standing disease of garden birds is salmonellosis, which is caused by bacteria in the genus *Salmonella*, especially *S. enterica* and *S. bongori*, each of which has many different strains. There are no distinctive symptoms, but affected birds typically fluff out their feathers and huddle, appear unsteady and uncoordinated, occasionally shivering; their eyes begin to close shortly before death, which occurs up to several days after exposure. Diagnosis requires the identification of *Salmonella* from infected tissues in conjunction with pathological findings. For garden birds, the main sources of infection are food and water, which become contaminated by faecal discharges from rodents as well as other birds. Observed mortalities mostly involve starlings, finches and doves (Kirkwood & MacGregor 1998, Friend & Franson 2002). Out of 1,477 bird carcasses found in gardens across Britain during 1999–2007, salmonellosis was diagnosed in 263 (10%) individuals of ten species, with Greenfinch and House Sparrow the most frequently infected (Lawson *et al.* 2010, 2011). Cases occurred mainly during periods of greatest feeder use, from autumn to spring, with a peak in January-February (Robinson *et al.* 2010). Away from gardens, salmonellosis has also caused mortality at various times of year among waterfowl, gulls and others that feed at rubbish dumps and sewage outfalls.

Another disease identified occasionally in garden birds is aspergillosis, caused by fungi of the genus *Aspergillus*. These form moulds on dead or decaying organic matter, including damp seeds. The spores they release are breathed in by birds and enter the lungs, from where they may be disseminated to other parts of the body, often causing death. The disease is not contagious, but reaches birds entirely from the environment. It has been known in captive birds since the early nineteenth century, and has affected oiled seabirds in rehabilitation centres. It causes occasional deaths among wild birds, including those at garden feeders, but is not usually responsible for major die-offs. Typically, affected birds are emaciated, with drooping wings, and show difficulty in breathing.

Avian pox is a common name for a mild-to-severe slow-developing disease caused by a virus which is transmitted between birds mainly by mosquitoes. It produces conspicuous blisters or wart-like lesions on bare areas, such as the legs and feet and around the bill and eyes. If the lesions are extensive enough to interfere with feeding or breathing, infected birds may become weak and emaciated, and may eventually die. Nevertheless, even heavily infected birds are known to recover if they can feed effectively, the lesions eventually shrinking to small scars. The disease has been reported from a wide range of birds, especially seabirds, gamebirds and songbirds, including in recent years tits in southern Britain. The first record from a Great Tit came from southeast England in 2006, and in subsequent years the disease spread to the north and west, as revealed by observations at garden feeders (Lawson *et al.* 2012a). Records reached a peak in August–September each year. The lesions on tits were usually larger than those on other species, looking like large ugly blisters. They were caused by a novel strain of avian pox, different from the types already found in other songbirds. However, the same strain was known from tits on the continent, so it may have reached southeast England in a bird or mosquito. Within two years of its initial

appearance, about 10% of Great Tits in Wytham Wood near Oxford were found to be infected, but fewer than 1% of other tits (Lachish *et al.* 2012b). Infected Great Tits showed reduced ability to raise young and increased mortality, compared to uninfected ones, the rates of mortality being higher in juveniles than in adults. However, at prevailing rates of infection, the disease seemed unlikely to cause decline in breeding numbers (Lachish *et al.* 2012a). In North America, too, numerous outbreaks of avian pox have been recorded at bird feeding stations. Contact transmission of the virus through infected surfaces and close association of birds using those feeders may help to transmit the disease during cooler parts of the year when mosquitoes are not active.

FIG 114. Great Tit *Parus major* showing pox lesions, which can appear as blisters, pustules or wart-like structures on the skin, mainly around the face and legs. An outbreak occurred in southern England in 2007, and spread northwards. (Jill Pakenham)

The only disease of garden birds known to have caused marked population declines in Britain is trichomonosis in finches, a disease caused by the protozoan *Trichomonas gallinae*. This organism exists as several strains of varying virulence, and was confirmed in Greenfinches by morphological and molecular evidence (Robinson *et al.* 2010). The disease was first reported as fatal to a finch in April 2005, after which it spread increasingly. Most mortality involved Greenfinches and to a lesser extent Chaffinches, with occasional House Sparrows, Bullfinches and Yellowhammers, as well as some doves. By 2007, breeding populations of Greenfinches and Chaffinches had declined in the region of highest disease incidence (the West Midlands) by 36% and 21% respectively, bringing populations well below their expected levels, and representing mortality in excess of half a million birds. In contrast, declines were less pronounced (15% and 4%) in these species in regions where the disease occurred at intermediate incidence, and less still (11% and 1%) where it was found at low incidence. Trichomonosis came to represent 68% of all deaths reported among garden birds by householders in Britain during this period, relegating salmonellosis to second position at 20%.

In later years trichomonosis spread to affect Greenfinches across almost the whole of Britain, causing an overall decline in breeding numbers of around 35% by 2009 (Lawson *et al.* 2012b). Late summer outbreaks occurred every year, with the centre of the disease shifting over time.

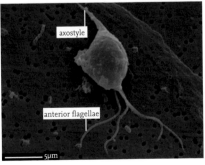

FIG 115. Above: Greenfinch *Carduelis chloris*, a victim of the protozoan disease trichomonosis which has recently affected populations over large parts of England (Keith Kirk). Right: dissected dead Greenfinch showing the cheesy lesions resulting from trichomonosis (above) and the organism itself (below) (Becky Lawson).

This was the first trichomonosis epidemic reported to affect free-living bird populations other than pigeons and doves, in which virulent strains of *Trichomonas* have occasionally caused major mortality. It is assumed that strains of this parasite passed from Collared Doves to Greenfinches at garden feeders and drinking bowls. Infection is passed directly (perhaps via saliva) from one bird to another, or from food or water which becomes contaminated by contact with the bill and mouth. Cheese-like lesions appear on the mouth and oesophagous, and infected birds appear lethargic, with fluffed plumage, and often have a wet face and vent. The doves seemed fairly resistant to the strains involved, for they showed no obvious mortality, whereas Greenfinches were highly susceptible, and sick birds were seen at many garden feeders. These events demonstrated the ability of a protozoan parasite to jump avian hosts with dramatic effects over a short period. It remains to be seen how trichomonosis develops, and what effect it will have on finch populations in the longer term. It has now been diagnosed in Greenfinches from the continent, with the first cases from Norway, Sweden and Finland in 2008, and from north Germany in 2009, with the disease spreading in subsequent years. It could have been carried there by continental Greenfinches or Chaffinches wintering in Britain and returning to their breeding areas in spring. The disease has also appeared among songbirds in North America (Anderson *et al.* 2009).

In recent years, another new disease, mycoplasmosis (or conjunctivitis), has also emerged among garden birds in North America, again chiefly in seed-eaters that use feeders. It is caused by an infection with a unique group of bacteria that lack cell walls but possess distinctive plasma membranes. They are responsible for a variety of diseases in plants and animals, and until recently were considered unimportant in birds. However, this situation changed in the winter of 1994 when eye infections in House Finches were first observed in Washington DC. They were caused by an apparently novel strain of a widespread poultry pathogen *Mycoplasma gallisepticum*. Within little over three years, mycoplasmosis spread throughout much of the eastern range of the House Finch, killing many infected individuals and greatly reducing the population (Hochachka & Dhondt 2000). The prominent field signs are puffy or swollen eyes and crusty-appearing eyelids, and occasionally birds can be seen wiping their heads on branches and other surfaces. Other symptoms of infected birds include a dried nasal discharge, and lethargy. Severely affected birds may sit on the ground, remaining after others have left, or collide with stationary objects due to impaired vision. The same disease is present in Europe, mainly among poultry and gamebirds, but has also been isolated from a Peregrine in Spain. So far as I am aware, it has not yet appeared among songbirds at garden feeders, but it could presumably do so in future.

New diseases

The examples cited above involved pathogens switching from one common host species to other new ones, a process which could have been facilitated by mutations in the pathogen. There is a long history of such processes, making the threat of new diseases ever present. Soon after people began to domesticate wild animals, they unwittingly shared with them a mix of pathogens from which new potent diseases evolved. Smallpox has been traced back to cowpox, measles probably evolved from rinderpest or canine distemper, and influenza from ancient pig diseases. One way in which new viral diseases arise occurs when, within the same animal, two different viruses invade the same cell, and during propagation, exchange genetic material with one another in a process of *re-assortment*. They can then produce a new virus which, in some instances, might be more virulent than either parent, or be able to infect a new host species formerly resistant to both parents. Moreover, the production of different strains of virus by a mixture of mutations and selection can occur much more rapidly than any co-evolutionary response in the host. As an example, consider avian influenza, which usually takes the form of an inconspicuous viral infection that is maintained in bird populations by oral or faecal routes of transmission. Avian influenza viruses have been found in at least 105 bird species, but most often in waterfowl, terns and waders (Olsen *et al.* 2006). These viruses change rapidly in nature because their genetic components continually mix in bird bodies to form slightly different subtypes. A previously unrecorded subtype (H5N1) emerged among poultry in China in 1996. It soon spread over most of Asia, and also reached Europe and Africa, mainly through the transport of poultry and poultry products (Gauthier-Clerc *et al.* 2007). The disease also passed from domestic ducks to migratory waterfowl, which suffered massive mortalities, and may have played a minor role in its spread. It caused widespread public concern because it infected some people, most of whom died.

On an alternative view, most emerging diseases are not new at all, just old diseases raised from obscurity by human action (Morse 1991). Whatever their origin, it is hard to evaluate the future threat posed by emerging diseases. One of the potentially most significant impacts of humans on diseases in wild birds is likely to stem from the massive changes in bird distributions that have followed from human activity, whether from habitat changes or deliberate translocations of species. As on Hawaii, this has brought species into contact with new pathogens, to some of which they have little or no resistance.

With or without human involvement, the mixing of bird populations at migratory stopping sites can result in the spread of infectious pathogens far and wide, continually introducing them to new areas. In addition to the spread of the H5N1 strain of avian influenza across Eurasia in 2008, this was shown in the recent spread of Lyme disease and West Nile virus around North America. Originally confined to the Old World, West Nile virus was first found in North America in 1999 and within a few years had spread widely, causing massive mortalities in crows and other birds (Rappole *et al.* 2000).

Chlamydiosis (psittacosis), caused by an intracellular bacterium called *Chlamydia psittacci*, is another avian disease that can be transmitted to people. It has been found commonly among pigeons, but also in tits, Robins, Dunnocks and others (Colvile *et al.* 2012). Pigeon-fanciers occasionally get it from their pigeons, sometimes with fatal results (Murton 1965). Some Faeroese women died in 1930, having plucked and dressed some Fulmars for subsequent eating.

Birds, people and farm animals

Other conservation problems have arisen from domestic and wild species sharing the same pathogens. In some cases, domestic livestock have been considered as a reservoir of infection for wild birds, the passage of louping ill from sheep to Red Grouse being an example discussed above. Another example involved the nematode parasite *Heterakis gallinarum* which was a carrier of the protozoan *Histomonas* causing the disease blackhead (histomonosis) in gallinaceous birds. Until the 1960s when large numbers of poultry were kept free-ranging on farmland, this parasite was frequently passed to Grey Partridges, causing substantial mortality. Now that most poultry are kept indoors, and can be treated with anthelmintic drugs, this cross-species transfer no longer occurs, removing this source of mortality from Partridges and other wild gamebirds (Potts 2012). In other cases, agriculturalists often view wildlife as a source of infection for domestic stock; and a programme of Badger control in parts of Britain was proposed in attempts to reduce the incidence of tuberculosis in cattle. When a virulent disease outbreak occurs among farm animals, the authorities often blame its arrival and spread on wild birds. Eventually the facts emerge, and often the disease can be attributed instead to movement of domestic stock or animal products. This was the case in the spread of the H5N1 strain of avian flu among poultry, and in various foot-and-mouth outbreaks among cattle.

With several such diseases, there have been contrived experiments in which birds were artificially infected with a disease and shown to be capable of transmitting it. For example, House Sparrows were infected with the causative agent of Newcastle disease, and they subsequently spread the disease to other sparrows and chickens with which they were penned. This is not to say that the same would happen in natural conditions. It has often been claimed that migratory birds, especially Starlings, brought foot-and-mouth disease from the continent to Britain. The virus does not become established in bird tissues, but Starlings that ingested the virus in contaminated food then excreted it for 10–26 hours, while it persisted for up to 91 hours on their plumage (Eccles 1939). It is conceivable, therefore, that birds could carry the virus from one farm to another, but there is no convincing evidence for this to set against the overwhelming case that people, livestock and vehicles move the virus around. In 1951, when an epidemic occurred in England, outbreaks in autumn were clustered around seaports, which was hardly consistent with the broad front migration of birds into Britain. Moreover, foot-and-mouth disease did not reach Britain during the war years 1940–44 in spite of widespread outbreaks on the continent; birds still migrated but shipping and passenger traffic were much reduced (Murton 1964).

CONCLUDING REMARKS

Despite our limited understanding of disease impacts on wild bird populations, the parallels with predation are striking. They include similar dynamic interactions between populations; the ability of generalist parasites, maintained by alternative hosts, to depress or even annihilate populations of scarcer but more susceptible host species; and the role of other stressors, notably food supply, in influencing susceptibility to parasitic diseases. Not surprisingly, then, parasites have similar effects to predators on bird populations, varying from no effect on breeding numbers, holding breeding density below the level otherwise possible, causing fluctuations in breeding densities, or causing decline to local extinction.

In most bird species, parasites seem to cause little mortality, and are much less prevalent as major limiting factors for breeding numbers than are predation, shortage of food or nest-sites. Many species might experience the occasional disease outbreak, causing heavy losses, after which their numbers take several years to recover fully, and in waterfowl in some regions outbreaks might be so frequent as to assume the role of main limiting factor. In Red Grouse, the viral disease louping ill can depress numbers in some areas, while strongylosis is involved in some cyclic fluctuations in other areas. The present level of both diseases is probably a result of human action in increasing the numbers of alternative hosts (louping ill), or in vastly improving the birds' habitat, including reducing predators, which leads grouse to achieve high densities favourable to transmission of the parasite (strongylosis).

In the studies reviewed above, microparasites were responsible for most recorded disease outbreaks which caused large-scale reductions in bird numbers, especially in waterfowl. Macroparasites more often occurred as persistent infections which reduced breeding or survival rates, but in a few species were associated with big reductions in numbers (e.g. strongylosis in Red Grouse). Impacts often varied with other stressors, particularly food shortage (e.g. Eiders and acanthocephalans).

The impact of any parasite on a population depends partly on whether the parasite influences mortality or fecundity. If individuals infected with a host-specific parasite soon die, their swift removal from the population limits the spread of the parasite. But if infected individuals do not die, but merely reproduce less well, the parasite can spread widely, eventually lowering reproduction in enough individuals to cause population decline (as with strongylosis in Red Grouse).

The role of parasites in bird population dynamics can alter with changes in the density of (1) the host and parasite species themselves, (2) alternative host species and (3) any necessary vector species, all of which influence the rate of transmission. They can also alter with changes in other environmental conditions, which affect infection and transmission rates. Some major impacts have occurred when bird species, mainly through human action, have come into contact with generalist parasites to which they have no evolved resistance. Species can be driven to low densities or even local extinction by parasites that are maintained at high densities by alternative, non-susceptible hosts. Because disease is often associated with other stressors, such as starvation or crowding, much of the mortality it causes does not necessarily add to other mortality (Chapter 13). Moreover, the effects of one parasite species might vary according to the number of other parasites the host contains, with multiple infections having more impact than single ones, an aspect largely unexplored.

In this chapter, I have been concerned primarily with the effects of disease on bird numbers, but disease organisms (like predators) could also restrict bird distributions, preventing some species from occupying large areas of otherwise suitable habitat. We would normally have no way of knowing this, except in special circumstances, as on Hawaii. Disease organisms are also likely to have marked effects on the evolution and genetic make-up of host populations (Price 1980). Throughout history, many animal and plant species have been continually afflicted with devastating disease outbreaks, leading to selection for disease resistance and, in extreme cases that left few survivors, to marked reductions in genetic variance. The importance of maintaining genetic diversity with respect to disease resistance is indicated by certain natural populations which have reduced genetic variability and apparent increased vulnerability to infectious diseases (O'Brien & Evermann 1988).

CHAPTER 10

Competition Between Species

I NTERSPECIFIC COMPETITION FOR FOOD or other resources is another
process that could limit the distribution and abundance of particular
bird species. It is one of the paradigms of ecology that, where resources
are limiting, species with identical needs cannot persist together indefinitely in
the same area. Invariably one will be better adapted or more efficient, and will
out-compete and replace the other completely. Hence, different species of birds
normally differ from one another in distribution, habitat or feeding ecology, or
in more than one of these respects (Lack 1971). They all have distinct *ecological
niches*. Such niche divergence could imply that interspecific competition has been
important in their evolution, leading to the species differences that we see today,
because any individuals that overlapped in needs too much with other species
in the past could have been eliminated by selection. However, this chapter is
concerned primarily with the largely experimental evidence that competition is
acting here and now, influencing the distributions and numbers of different bird
species in contemporary European landscapes.

Despite their ecological differences, most bird species still share part of their
food and other resources with other species, both other birds and other animals.
If such species are limited by resources, then it follows that the numbers of one
could influence the numbers of another. At the population level, competition
could thus be manifest as a reduction in the distribution or numbers of one
or more species that results from their shared use of the same resource. It may
involve resource depletion, where individuals of one species reduce the amount
available to individuals of another species. Or it may involve interference, where
individuals of one species reduce access to a resource by individuals of another
species by aggressive or other means. In any pair of competing species, it is rare

for both to be affected equally, but the winner in one situation may be the loser in another, as we shall see later.

Probably most competition between bird species involves food. The more the diets of different species overlap with one another, the greater the chance that those species will compete at some time, especially when food is short. When particular food sources are especially abundant, they may be exploited by a wide range of animals which at other times differ in their diets. For example, plagues of woodland caterpillars may be fed upon not only by the usual tits and warblers, but by a wide range of other species too, up to the size of crows. When the feast is over, they revert to their usual different foods. However, birds can also take the same foods at times when little else is available, in which case competition could be strong, between individuals of both the same and different species. Measures of dietary overlap between species only indicate the potential for competition, and not whether it actually occurs. In general, however, when food becomes scarcer in the environment, species overlap less in their feeding habits, as each increasingly concentrates on the feeding niche it is best equipped for (Schoener 1983).

To confirm the existence of competition between two species in the same area, several conditions should hold. First, they must share a common resource, taking it from the same places. This means that they have the potential to compete, but does not prove that they do so. Second, the presence of one species must reduce the availability of the resource to individuals of the other. This would confirm that one or both species is affected negatively by the presence of the other, and would also imply the operation of intraspecific competition in at least one of them.[14] Third, the survival or breeding success of the affected species should be reduced below what it could achieve in the absence of its competitor. This would confirm that individuals suffer a cost of competition. And fourth, the reduced survival and breeding success of individuals should lead to reduced distribution or density. This would confirm that one species can affect the population of another, and that competition is a factor affecting abundance. The latter two aspects are hard to demonstrate by observations alone, and experiments are usually needed to reveal any effects of interspecific competition on population levels. Several such experiments have now been done. They have entailed removing one species from an area and measuring the response in another, or manipulating a resource (such as blocking nest holes or

14 As a reminder, *intraspecific competition* is competition between individuals of the same species, and *interspecific competition* is competition between individuals of different species. Interspecific competition is unlikely to occur in the absence of intraspecific competition in at least one of the species involved, for if there were no competition of any kind, resources could not be regarded as limiting.

adding food), and measuring the response in the potential competitors. As in other field experiments (Chapter 4), the response is measured either as a before-and-after comparison or against an appropriate simultaneous control, if possible replicated in several different study plots (Connell 1983, Schoener 1983).

COMPETITION, FEEDING RATES AND ECOLOGICAL NICHES

When different species feed together on the same food, individuals of a dominant species can greatly reduce the feeding rates of individuals of subordinate species. You can see this *interference competition* at a garden feeder, where Coal Tits gain little in the presence of larger Great Tits and Blue Tits, or Siskins in the presence of larger Greenfinches. But similar interactions can be seen in a wider range of birds and situations. For example, many seabirds feed on discards from fishing boats, and around our shores Gannets are dominant to most of the others. In one study, the feeding success of Herring Gulls was found to decline in direct proportion to the number of Gannets present (Fig. 116). However, dominance relations can change with circumstance: Herring Gulls can dominate Lesser Black-backed Gulls and Great Skuas at land-based feeding sites, but are less successful than both these species in competing around fishing boats at sea (Furness *et al.* 1992). In the latter situation, Great Skuas and Great Black-backed Gulls compete for discards, and although the gull can swallow larger items, the skua is generally competitively dominant and has a higher success rate (Furness *et al.* 1992). Such interactions are often construed

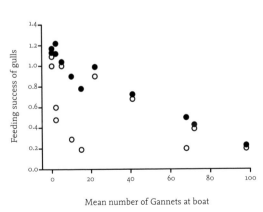

FIG 116. Mean feeding success of adult (closed circles) and immature (open circles) Herring Gulls *Larus argentatus* around fishing boats in relation to the number of Gannets *Morus bassanus* present. The measure of feeding success for each gull takes account of the number of other gulls at the boat of the same age-group. The greater the number of Gannets present, the lower the feeding success of the gulls. (Redrawn from Furness *et al.* 1992)

as competition, but they are not necessarily translated into reduced survival or reproduction, let alone reduced population level.

Experiments on niche shifts have been conducted with mixed flocks of tits and other species. In the conifer forests of northern Europe, dominant Willow Tits and Crested Tits fed mainly at favoured sites within trees, while the smaller Coal Tits and Goldcrests were relegated mainly to the outer twigs, where the risk of predation was greater (Suhonen *et al.* 1992). When the dominant species were experimentally reduced in numbers in three forest plots, the subordinate species in these plots increased their foraging in the inner canopy in comparison with three control plots (Alatalo *et al.* 1985). The segregation that normally prevailed was attributed mainly to interference, for the larger species often chased away the smaller ones. But when subordinate species were experimentally removed, so that food supplies in the outer parts of trees were less depleted, the dominant species spent significantly more time feeding there (Alatalo *et al.* 1987). So by an apparent combination of interference and depletion, the range of foraging sites used by each tit species was reduced by the presence of other tit species. It other words, it could be surmised that the each tit species reduced the amount of food available to the others.

To make sure that the foraging niche of the smaller and subordinate Coal Tit was actually the result of interspecific aggression or avoidance rather than

FIG 117. In northern coniferous forests, the Crested Tit *Lophophanes cristatus* (upper left) feeds mainly at favoured sites within the trees, relegating the smaller Coal Tit *Periparus ater* (upper right) and Goldcrest *Regulus regulus* (lower left) to the outer parts, where predation risk is greater. (Frank Snijkers (Crested Tit and Goldcrest) and Keith Kirk (Coal Tit))

by a preference for the outer parts of the tree, the foraging efficiencies of both
Coal and Willow Tits were tested in aviaries (Alatalo & Moreno 1987). Coal Tits
tended to be more efficient foragers in any part of the tree. When placed singly
in an aviary with a choice of inner and outer branches, both species collected
most of their food on the inner branches. When individuals of the two species
were placed together, the Willow Tit did not change its foraging pattern, but the
Coal Tit shifted to the outer branches. Interestingly, this move happened with
very little aggression, being caused mainly by the one species avoiding the other.
None of these experiments was designed to test whether the various interactions
between species affected subsequent survival or reproduction.

Competition between birds and ants

In woodland in summer, large numbers of ants can often be seen scurrying
from their nests on the ground over the trunks and branches, twigs and leaves of
trees in search of their arthropod prey. These are the same kinds of arthropods
as are eaten by many bird species, raising the possibility that ants and birds
may compete for food. In northern Sweden, Haemig (1992, 1994) selected pairs
of trees close to an ant colony. In each pair he applied a chemical repellent to
the lower trunk of one tree (to deter ants), while keeping the other tree as an
untreated control. Subsequent arthropod biomass was lower in the trees accessed
by Wood Ants than in trees that ants avoided. In both study years, insectivorous
birds (tits, Chaffinches, warblers, woodpeckers and Treecreepers) visited the
trees without ants more frequently and for longer periods than the trees with
ants. But Pied Flycatchers, which used the trees solely as perches for sallying to
catch flying insects, visited the trees with ants more frequently. This may have
been because ants caused some insects to fly, making them more available for
flycatchers. In a year in which seed-eating birds were abundant, these birds
showed no preference for experimental or control trees. Ants thus partially
excluded through competition birds that used similar resources to themselves,
but had no obvious deleterious effect on birds using a different resource.

Ants may have affected birds partly by reducing their shared food supply
(*depletion competition*), and partly by deterring them from feeding nearby
(*interference competition*). To explore this matter further, Haemig (1996) constructed
two artificial 'trees' in the forest, provided them with equal amounts of food
suitable for ants and birds, and placed them close to each other at equal
distances from a Wood Ant nest. Ants were excluded from one artificial tree
using the repellent, but allowed to forage in the other. After 25 visits by Great
Tits, Haemig switched the treatment between the two trees to correct for
possible location effects. In each case, Great Tits visited the tree without ants

more frequently, and for longer periods, than they visited the tree that had
ants. Furthermore, Great Tit foraging bouts on the trees with ants were shorter
when ants were more active, thus demonstrating that interference competition
from ants also influenced bird foraging behaviour. One mechanism of this
interference competition could be formic acid squirted or deposited by the ants.

In a final experiment, Haemig (1999) put up nest-boxes for tits and
flycatchers in trees with and without ants. He found that during the breeding
season interactions of Wood Ants with nesting birds differed with the level
of predation by carnivorous birds and mammals. Under low predation risk
(forest interior, low density of predators), only 8% of tits nested in trees with
ants, the remaining 92% in trees without ants. Along the forest edge, where he
counted about four times more bird and mammal predators than in the forest
interior, 45% of tits nested in trees with ants, a significant difference. For tits,
this behaviour proved to be adaptive, because along the forest edge reproductive
success was about double in the nests on ant trees compared with non-ant trees.
The interaction between nesting birds and ants, therefore, was opposite at high
and low predation risk. How ants interacted with predators was not clear, but
they evidently deterred them, to the benefit of nesting tits. This result was so
remarkable that, despite its statistical significance, one wonders if it arose by
chance. Here is a clear need for another replicated experiment.

COMPETITION AND INDIVIDUAL PERFORMANCE

Other experiments explored the effects of interspecific competition on the
breeding or survival of individual birds. In southern Sweden, Magpies and
Jackdaws fed their chicks the same sorts of food, and because chicks often
starved, food seemed to be limiting. To test for competition between these
species, Högstedt (1980) encouraged Jackdaws to nest within ten Magpie
territories by placing three nest-boxes in each, leaving ten other Magpie
territories without Jackdaws. In the second year, he reversed the treatments,
moving the boxes to those Magpie territories that had lacked them the
previous year. The same Magpie territories thus acted as experimental and
control territories in different years, which allowed for effects of individuals or
territories on performance. In both years, Magpies that had Jackdaws nesting in
their territories suffered significantly reduced breeding success. They produced
fewer young and to lower fledging weights than Magpies without Jackdaws in
their territories, the mean brood sizes at fledging being 0.33 and 1.68 respectively.
This fivefold difference resulted partly from increased chick starvation,

FIG 118. Jackdaw *Corvus monedula*, found to compete with Magpies *Pica pica* for invertebrate food-items in grassland. (Ian Newton)

presumably because of food depletion in Magpie territories by Jackdaws, and partly from increased predation of Magpie chicks by Hooded Crows. Predation increased apparently because the Magpies spent longer away from their nest searching for food and chasing Jackdaws, and their hungry chicks called more, attracting the attention of Crows. Any possible reverse effect of Magpies on Jackdaws was not measured, so it remains uncertain whether both species suffered from nesting close together, or just the Magpies.

Another experiment involved two tit species which nested in the same large wood at Wytham near Oxford, and fed their young on many of the same foods, chiefly caterpillars (Minot 1981). It had been noticed that the mean fledging weights of young Great Tits in different parts of the wood decreased with increasing local density of Blue Tits: Great Tit chicks were heaviest where Blue Tits were scarcest. So in one part of the wood, all the young Blue Tits were removed at hatching, thus reducing the food demands on the adults. These young were then added to Blue Tit nests in another part of the wood, increasing the food demands of those adults. Subsequently, Great Tit nestlings were heaviest where no Blue Tit nestlings remained, lightest where Blue Tit nestlings had been added, and of intermediate weight in the remaining area left with natural numbers. These findings thus confirmed the results from the earlier observational study. By implication, reduced pressure on a shared food supply, caused by the removal of young Blue Tits, left more food for Great Tits, whose young were then better fed. It was known from earlier studies that high fledging weight in Great Tits increased their subsequent survival chances.

Other studies elsewhere showed that Blue Tits reduced other aspects of Great Tit performance, including nestling and adult survival, and the proportion of pairs that raised second broods (Dhondt 1989). They have also shown that effects can be reciprocal, for while reducing the numbers of young Blue Tits increased the weights of Great Tit nestlings in the same area, reducing the numbers of young Great Tits increased the size of Blue Tit nestlings, presumably again through their mutual effects on shared food supplies (Török 1987).

Tits not only affect one another, for they can have negative effects on flycatchers, which also feed their young on small caterpillars. In one experiment on the island of Gotland off Sweden, the densities of Great Tits and Blue Tits were experimentally reduced to less than 10%. Collared Flycatcher pairs nesting in the same area then raised more chicks, and to greater weights, than those in control areas nearby. This held in both years of study, and in one year in one plot, the survival of adult flycatchers was also increased. Thus, those flycatchers that bred under conditions of reduced competition from tits were found to raise more young and contribute more recruits to future breeding populations than did those breeding in control plots with normal tit densities (Gustafsson 1987). The proposed mechanism was again greater access to food for the young, in both the nestling and post-fledging periods.

FIG 119. The Treecreeper *Certhia familiaris* competes with ants for food-items on the bark of trees. Experiments in which ants were excluded resulted in improved breeding success in Treecreepers. (Alan McFadyen)

In the previous section, we saw how ants could influence the feeding and nesting places of birds. Other experiments examined further the influence of ants on bird breeding. In Finland, the foraging behaviour and nest success of Treecreepers was studied in territories that varied naturally or experimentally in ant activity. As in the earlier study, both birds and ants reduced arthropod abundance, but arthropods were still more numerous on trees lacking ants, and Treecreepers fed there more often (Aho *et al.* 1997, Jantti *et al.* 2001). In territories without ants, Treecreepers started laying earlier, and nestlings were heavier with lower mortality than in territories with ants. Furthermore, in territories without ants, second clutches were larger than first clutches, while the reverse held in territories with ants. The net effect was that double-brooded Treecreeper pairs produced an average of 2.3 more fledglings to greater weight in territories lacking ants than in territories having ants. Wood Ants thus reduced the breeding success of Treecreepers, apparently by means of food depletion. Other studies of interactions between birds on the one hand and insects, reptiles or mammals on the other have provided further support for the view that competition with other organisms can frequently limit bird performance (Wiens 1989).

COMPETITION AND POPULATION LEVELS

Although the reproduction or survival of individuals may be affected by competition, as explained in earlier chapters, these effects may not necessarily influence subsequent breeding numbers, because of compensatory improvements in the survival of other individuals that escape the effects of competition. The rest of this chapter therefore concentrates on those forms of evidence that implicate interspecific competition in limiting the distributions or breeding densities of birds. It is these aspects that are most relevant in the context of population limitation.

Competition for food and feeding areas

One means by which a species can affect the distribution of another is through interspecific territorialism. Some bird species defend territories not only against other individuals of their own kind, but also against individuals of different species. This occurs where the two species in the same habitat take similar foods, so might compete with one another for the same resource. Interspecific territoriality can be inferred from examining the distribution of pairs through the habitat to see whether their territories overlap; it can then be checked by removal experiments. If removed individuals are replaced by individuals of their own species, this implies the existence only of *intraspecific* competition for territories, but if they are sometimes replaced by individuals of another species, this implies *interspecific* competition, through which one species had previously excluded the other, thus restricting its distribution.

Blackcaps and Garden Warblers are closely related to one another; both are of similar size and shape, and nest in shrubs. In Wytham Wood near Oxford, the two species held mutually exclusive territories in areas that were acceptable to both. Blackcaps arrived first in spring and established territories before Garden Warblers. When Blackcaps were removed from their territories some of the

FIG 120. Blackcap *Sylvia atricapilla* (left) and Garden Warbler *Sylvia borin* (right), two closely related species which in some areas compete for nesting territories. (Frank Snijkers)

vacancies were rapidly filled by Garden Warblers (Garcia 1983). After the removals ended, more Blackcaps arrived and settled in the area, some by displacing established Garden Warblers. The implication was that Blackcaps could dominate and displace Garden Warblers from some locations, restricting the total area and the range of habitat that Garden Warblers could use, thus reducing their overall breeding density. All this occurred in habitat suitable for both, but there may have been areas of somewhat different habitat elsewhere that were suitable for only one or other species. They do not necessarily overlap everywhere.

A similar experiment was done in Norway with two other closely related warblers (Chiffchaff and Willow Warbler) which held mutually exclusive territories (Saether 1983). In this study, removed individuals of either species were replaced by individuals of either species. Both seem to have been limited by both intra- and interspecific competition, but with neither species consistently dominant over the other. Some species pairs show interspecific territoriality in some areas but not in others. An example is the Chaffinch and Great Tit, which held mutually exclusive territories on the Hebridean island of Eigg, but overlapping territories in the more diverse habitat of nearby mainland (Reed 1982).

Other examples of interspecific territoriality recorded among European birds include the Blue Rock Thrush and three species of wheatears, all of which hold mutually exclusive territories on Aegean Islands, Reed Warblers and Sedge Warblers in England, Nightingale and Thrush Nightingale in eastern Europe, Ringed Plover, Little Ringed Plover and Kentish Plover in England, Pomarine Skua and Arctic Skua in Alaska, Golden Eagle and Bonelli's Eagle in France, and

Common Buzzard and Rough-legged Buzzard in Sweden. As far as possible, the dominant species in each pair is listed first (most references in Orians & Willson 1964, others Lack 1971, Cheylan 1973, Sylven 1979). Not all these species are necessarily interspecifically territorial throughout their mutual ranges, for the behaviour may occur only in certain areas and not others.

Some species are aggressive to a range of other species, driving them from their nesting areas; the reaction of territorial Mute Swans to smaller waterfowl provides an example (Allin *et al.* 1987). Other instances of interspecific territoriality involve the short-term defence of specific food sources, such as fruiting trees (Snow & Snow 1988). For example, Mistle Thrushes often defend individual fruit-laden trees in winter, driving away any other thrushes which attempt to feed there. It seems clear from these various findings that the presence and aggressive behaviour of one species can affect the distribution and local abundance of another.

Sometimes one species indirectly removes the food of another. Declines in the numbers of Capercaillie and Black Grouse, which have occurred in Britain during recent decades, have been attributed partly to grazing pressure from increased numbers of sheep and deer (Baines *et al.* 1994, 1995, Baines 1996). These animals at high density shortened ground vegetation, reduced the diversity of plant species, and removed most of the fresh growth. This in turn reduced the numbers of arthropods, especially caterpillars, which formed the food of grouse chicks. The survival of grouse chicks was thereby lowered, leading in turn to a decline in adult numbers. In the most heavily grazed areas, chick production by Black Grouse was much less than the 1.5–2.0 chicks per hen calculated as necessary in these areas to maintain population levels (Baines 1996). In a subsequent experiment, the numbers of male Black Grouse, counted on their display grounds, increased by nearly 5% per year on sites where sheep grazing was reduced, yet declined by nearly 2% per year on sites where it was not (Calladine *et al.* 2002). In this example, competition between herbivorous mammals and insects for the same fresh plant growth influenced the population trends of grouse. Indirectly, then, mammals and grouse were competitors. The same process involves other herbivorous birds; for example, Mute Swans by eating aquatic vegetation not only removed the food supply of other plant-eating ducks, but also the habitat of many invertebrates eaten by other kinds of ducks (Allin *et al.* 1987).

Competition between birds and fish
After the removal of fish from a 17 ha lake in southern England, submerged plant cover increased from less than 1% to 95% of the lake surface, while benthic invertebrates doubled in numbers (Giles 1992, Phillips 1992). Use of

FIG 121. Tufted Ducks *Aythya fuligula*, one of several duck species which benefit from the absence of fish from ponds, leaving more invertebrates for ducks to eat. (Richard Chandler)

the lake by avian herbivores, such as Mute Swan, Coot and Gadwall, increased in association with greater weed growth, and use by Shoveler, Tufted Duck and Pochard in association with greater invertebrate numbers. The survival of Mallard ducklings improved, and use of the lake by wintering waterfowl also rose (Wright & Phillips 1990, Phillips 1992). Such changes were not seen in other lakes nearby, whose fish populations were left intact. Similarly, in Sweden it had been observed that Goldeneyes preferred lakes without fish to those with fish, and that the diets of birds and fish overlapped. After fish were removed from one lake, and invertebrate prey species subsequently increased, more Goldeneyes were seen feeding there than formerly, and more than on an adjacent control lake (Eriksson 1979). Three to five years later, Goldeneye fledged about four times more young in the lake from which the fish had been removed than in the lake in which fish had remained. In other words, fish limited the local numbers and breeding success of Goldeneyes.

A bigger experiment was carried out over a nine-year period on a series of ponds in Bavaria, southern Germany (Haas *et al.* 2007). In each year, some of the ponds were stocked with Carp, while others were kept free of fish. Invertebrate densities and plant biomass were higher in ponds without Carp than in ponds with Carp, and water-birds (excluding specialist fish-eaters) were more abundant on ponds lacking fish. The implication was again that fish and birds competed for limited invertebrate and plant resources, and that competition favoured fish, leading to some avoidance of fish ponds by water-birds in late summer. In further experiments elsewhere, fish removal always had positive effects on birds (except for grebes and other fish-eaters), while fish addition had negative effects (Winfield *et al.* 1992, Winfield & Winfield 1994).

In conclusion, interactions between fish and water-birds are of three main types: (1) fish and water-birds may eat similar invertebrates and hence may compete for the same food supply; (2) herbivorous fish species may affect water-weeds, reducing the food supplies for herbivorous waterfowl and the habitat for the invertebrates eaten by carnivorous waterfowl; and (3) water-birds that eat fish benefit from increasing fish abundance. All experiments testing for a possible effect of interspecific competition between fish and water-birds showed an effect of fish on birds. These findings help to explain why, in some other parts of the world, as in the steppes or in the arctic, ducks are found in greatest numbers on shallow waters that lack fish, a situation that occurs because these waters periodically dry out or totally freeze in winter. Unlike fish, invertebrates can survive in the substrate or rapidly re-colonise.

Competition for nest-sites

Birds can often be seen to fight over nest-sites, larger species usually ousting smaller ones, whose breeding density may be thereby lowered. This is evident among various birds nesting in tree-cavities, among birds of prey nesting on cliffs and among seabirds on islands. Cavity-nesting species are a particularly convenient group to test for possible effects of interspecific competition on breeding density, especially if they use nest-boxes which can be manipulated in various ways, including changing the sizes of entrance holes. Most such experiments have been done in woodland areas where natural tree-cavities are scarce.

Great Tits and Blue Tits. In Wytham Wood near Oxford, the numbers of Great Tits and Blue Tits were found to be interrelated, the breeding densities of both species in different areas depending on densities of nest-boxes over the range 2–8 boxes per hectare (Minot & Perrins 1986). Over this range, both species were most numerous in areas with most boxes. At the same time, the ratio of Blue to Great Tits increased with the density of boxes, with Blue Tits breeding in greater proportion in areas where boxes were most numerous (Fig. 122). This suggested that, through competition for nest-sites, Great Tits limited the numbers of Blue Tits, and most markedly in areas where boxes were scarcest. Moreover, in areas with low densities of boxes, changes in the densities of the two species from year to year were inversely correlated, with Blue Tits increasing in years when Great Tits declined. In areas with excessively high densities of boxes, however, the numbers of both species varied in parallel. By implication, where nest-sites were limiting, the numbers of Great Tits (the dominant species) affected the numbers of Blue Tits, but where sites were not limiting no such interaction occurred, and the two species fluctuated in parallel in response to other factors.

An experiment in a German forest showed how the numbers of Great Tits and Blue Tits could be manipulated by changing the size of the entrance holes on nest-boxes (Löhrl 1977, Dhondt & Eyckerman 1980). Entrance holes of 32 mm

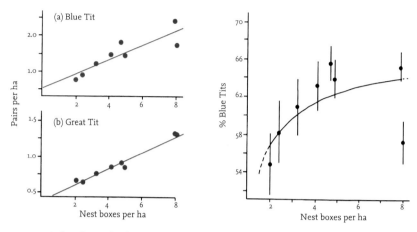

FIG 122. Left: Relationship between nest-box density and mean density of Blue Tits *Cyanistes caeruleus* and Great Tits *Parus major* in eight sections of Wytham Wood, Oxford. Regression line for Blue Tit: $y = 0.53 + 0.20x$, $r = 0.89$, $p < 0.001$; for Great Tit: $y = 0.38 + 0.11x$, $r = 0.98$, $p < 0.001$. Right: Effect of nest-box density on the mean (± SE) percentage of Blue Tits among the total numbers of both species nesting in eight sections of Wytham Wood. Regression relationships: $y = 0.67x / (x + 0.36)$, $r = 0.65$, $p < 0.05$ (one-tailed test). (From Minot & Perrins 1986)

diameter let in both species, but holes of 26 mm let in only the smaller Blue Tits. The numbers of one or both species were changed markedly over the years by appropriate manipulations, and Blue Tits bred in greater numbers in years when the dominant Great Tits were excluded by smaller entrance holes (Fig. 123).

Effects of shortage of cavities can sometimes come about indirectly, because birds often use boxes for winter roosting as well as for subsequent nesting. Blue Tit breeding density increased markedly when small-holed nest-boxes (with an entrance hole excluding the larger Great Tits) were provided, an increase that was independent of the number of large-holed nest-boxes and Great Tits that were present (Dhondt & Adriaensen 1999). This increase in Blue Tit density arose because, when small-holed cavities were available in winter, large numbers of Blue Tits used them for roosting, and these birds then stayed on to breed in the area, as discovered from their ring numbers. When adequate winter roosting sites were absent (because small-holed boxes were blocked at that time), Blue Tits did not stay in the area during winter, and in the breeding season small-holed boxes were largely unused, except for small numbers taken up by yearling Blue Tits that moved in to breed. This situation may not hold in all woods, because the numbers and sizes of natural tree-holes vary from one wood to another, and may not be limiting for one or other species.

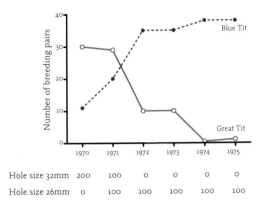

FIG 123. Numbers of breeding Great Tits *Parus major* and Blue Tits *Cyanistes caeruleus* in a 10 ha wood, Germany, 1970–75, in relation to changes in the sizes of entrance holes on nest-boxes. Holes of 32 mm admit both species, but holes of 26 mm admit only the smaller Blue Tit. Figures below the graph show the numbers of large-holed and small-holed nest-boxes present in each year. (Redrawn from Dhondt & Eyckerman 1980, based on Löhrl 1977)

Tits and flycatchers. The migratory Pied and Collared Flycatchers arrive in their European breeding areas after the resident tits have started nesting, and in these circumstances flycatchers cannot displace tits from their nest-sites. They seem therefore to be relegated to whatever sites are left over. In six forest plots in Sweden, almost all nest-boxes were occupied every year by one or other of three species. The numbers of all three fluctuated from year to year, but increases in the numbers of Great Tits and Blue Tits were accompanied by decreases in the numbers of Collared Flycatchers, and vice versa (Gustafsson 1988). The numbers of flycatchers in the plots thus depended on the numbers of tits. As an experiment, the numbers of tits in one plot were reduced in two successive years. This led to a large increase in the numbers of flycatchers, compared with those in a control plot (Fig. 124). As a further experiment in a Norwegian forest, Slagsvold (1979) blocked the entrances of all nest-boxes except those already occupied by Great Tits. In consequence, later-arriving Pied Flycatchers were completely excluded from breeding there. Males fought unsuccessfully with Great Tits for possession of boxes, while females left the area. These experiments revealed how competition for nest-sites could limit the breeding densities of flycatchers.

Fighting with Great Tits over nest-sites is generally dangerous for flycatchers, which are often killed (Löhrl 1957). On Gotland, a big island in the Baltic Sea, more Collared Flycatchers were found dead in study plots where nest-boxes were scarce than in plots where boxes were plentiful (Merilä & Wiggins 1995). In one area, 17% of breeding flycatchers were killed in fights over nest-boxes. Evidently, interspecific competition for nest-sites may constitute a significant source of adult mortality in flycatchers.

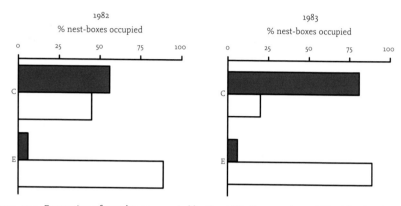

FIG 124. Proportion of nest-boxes occupied by Great Tits *Parus major* and Blue Tits *Cyanistes caeruleus* (shaded) and Collared Flycatchers *Ficedula albicollis* (open) in an experimental plot (E) where tit numbers were deliberately reduced, and in a control plot (C) where tit numbers were not reduced. The densities of nest-boxes were the same in both plots, and the differences in species occupation between plots were statistically significant in both years (1982: $\chi^2 = 12.2$, $p < 0.001$; 1983: $\chi^2 = 30.1$, $p < 0.001$). Through competition for nest-sites, large numbers of tits limited the numbers of flycatchers that could nest. (Redrawn from Gustafsson 1988)

In two experimental plots on Gotland and in two different years, nest-box densities were doubled just before the breeding season, while box density was left unchanged in three control plots (Gustafsson 1988). In a separate experiment, tits were removed as they began nesting. Both manipulations were followed by an increase in the density of Collared Flycatchers. In a final experiment, the floor area of all nest-boxes was reduced by half, causing the tits to abandon that plot altogether. However, Collared Flycatchers – which have smaller clutches than Blue Tits – accepted the modified boxes, and their numbers on that plot increased by 3–9-fold compared to the control plots. The conclusion was again that Collared Flycatchers were limited in breeding density primarily through interspecific competition for nest-sites.

Starlings and other birds. Great Tits themselves are not free from the effects of nest-site competition where Starlings occur (van Balen *et al.* 1982). In some deciduous woodland in the Netherlands, Great Tits nesting in natural holes often failed to produce young because Starlings took over the holes before the tits had finished laying. In the presence of Starlings, only 28% of the territorial Great Tits were able to nest, and of these only 40% were successful. Some of the tit pairs remained in the area without re-nesting, while others moved elsewhere, so that in the presence of nesting Starlings, Great Tit density was lowered. In one area, most large entrances of natural cavities were narrowed in March to a diameter of about 30 mm to exclude Starlings. Under these conditions, most of the Great Tits in the area could breed and most were successful. As a reciprocal experiment, the entrances of seven nest-boxes occupied by Great Tits were widened, and within two days five had been taken over by Starlings. Hence, in woods where they were common, Starlings restricted Great Tits to breeding successfully mainly in cavities with entrance holes less than 35 mm across, only a proportion of the holes that Great Tits could otherwise use. Such competition resulted in a lowering of the breeding density of Great Tits. Starlings are also known to take over old and newly excavated nest holes from Great Spotted Woodpeckers, and recent declines in Starling numbers in Britain may have been one factor promoting the recent increase of Great Spotted Woodpecker numbers (Smith 2005).

Other species. Competition for nest-boxes between Jackdaws and Tawny Owls was evident in conifer plantations in the Netherlands, but here the situation was affected by Goshawks which colonised the area part way through the study (Koning *et al.* 2009). After Tawny Owls had become established in the area, Jackdaws moved in, and proved able to take over boxes from laying and incubating owls, reducing their breeding success. Over a period of years, the number of Tawny Owl pairs able to breed successfully was inversely related to the number of Jackdaws present. Then Goshawks colonised the area, increasing from one pair in 1993 to 10–11 pairs in 1999, at which level they stabilised. As the numbers of Goshawks increased, the numbers of Jackdaws declined, apparently through predation. And as Jackdaws declined, so the breeding success of Tawny Owls improved again. Predation on recently fledged Tawny Owls by Goshawks was also substantial, but not enough to reduce Tawny Owl breeding densities. Jackdaws are also known to take over tree-cavities from Barn Owls as well as Tawny Owls. In both cases, they do so partly by dropping sticks on the brooding owl from above, as they attempt to build a nest in the cavity.

Apart from falcons, most raptors build their own nests, which can take a lot of time, and the larger species often refurbish and re-use old nests, rather than building a new one each year. In parts of the Netherlands, Goshawks and Buzzards have to compete for their own nests with the highly aggressive Egyptian Geese (Rutz *et al.* 2006). Absent in the 1970s, this introduced species increased rapidly to reach more than 5,000 pairs by the year 2000. These geese take over large raptor nests, whether occupied or not. So far, they seem not to have affected Goshawk or Buzzard breeding densities, but presumably restrict their choice of nest-sites, and may also prevent some pairs from breeding in certain years. In Britain, Egyptian Geese are still localised, but at Rutland Water they have sometimes taken over Osprey nest platforms. Elsewhere in Europe, Eagle Owls usurp large raptor nests in areas where their preferred cliff-ledges are scarce. In such areas, Eagle Owls sometimes nest on the ground, but they seem to prefer tree-nests built by large raptors, especially the Goshawk and Buzzard. In northern Germany, which is virtually cliff-free, Eagle Owls have substantial effects on the densities and productivity of Goshawk populations (Chapter 11).

Competition also occurs among birds of prey that nest on cliffs. In much of Britain, the tallest cliffs are usually occupied by Peregrines and smaller ones by Kestrels; but during the 1960s when Peregrines were reduced in numbers by organochlorine pesticides, Kestrels took over many of the vacant Peregrine sites, thereby increasing their own breeding numbers (Newton 1979). Similar examples, involving different species, have come from other parts of the world. They are not experiments in the strict sense, but they do suggest that smaller species are sometimes constrained in their nesting places by the presence of larger ones. This is another type of interaction between different raptor species, in addition to the predation of one species on another discussed in Chapter 11.

Among some seabirds, competition for nesting burrows can also be severe, both within and between species. Typically, the larger species, such as shearwaters, can evict smaller species, such as petrels. Various researchers have reduced access to nest-sites by the larger species or provided nest-boxes or smaller burrows, with the intent of benefiting the smaller species. For example, in a mixed colony of shearwaters and petrels on the Azores, nest-sites for the larger Cory's Shearwater (840 g) were limiting (Ramos et al. 1997). When 28 artificial burrows were provided for these birds, they were rapidly occupied, indicating intraspecific competition for nest-sites. Providing an additional 20 smaller artificial burrows helped smaller species, although several of these man-made burrows were later dug out by Cory's Shearwaters, which sometimes killed the occupants, as indicated by the numbers of Macaronesian (Little) Shearwaters (172 g) and Madeiran Storm Petrels (49 g) found dead near the entrances of these excavated burrows. The authors concluded that competition for nest cavities was severe both within each species and between Cory's Shearwater and the smaller species. In a later study, also on the Azores, nest-boxes were designed to exclude the larger species. Their deployment resulted in a rapid increase in the breeding numbers of Madeiran Storm Petrels by 12% in the first year and by 28% over the original colony size in the second year (Bolton et al. 2004). Furthermore, the breeding success of petrels nesting in boxes averaged nearly three times greater than that of birds in natural sites, partly because shearwaters could not excavate the box nests. The provision and manipulation of nest-sites, so as to reduce intra- and interspecific competition, clearly has potential for use in the conservation of burrow-nesting seabirds.

Reduction of breeding habitat for European Storm Petrels may also result from competition with other ground-nesters. For example, on Sule Skerry, the 300 pairs found in 2001 formed less than one-tenth of those thought to be there 15 years earlier. Since the mid-1980s, the local Puffin population increased sharply and came to occupy most of the surface of the island, continually digging and renovating burrows, and destroying petrel nests in the process. The remaining petrels became restricted to old walls and cavities under boulders at the edge of the Puffin colony. Not being very effective diggers themselves, Storm Petrels are more or less restricted to existing cavities or burrows dug by other birds or Rabbits, although they can shift soft soil.

Where they occur together, Puffins and Manx Shearwaters sometimes compete for nest burrows, and in some places Puffins have been cited as responsible for displacing shearwaters. Elwes (1869) says of Mingulay that 'about 100 years ago, however, the Puffins which before were not numerous began to increase very much and drove the Shearwaters from the holes which they occupied in the cliffs and now they have completely supplanted them.' On Skomer, each species has displaced the other, depending partly on location (Brooke 1992).

Competition for nest-sites can also influence the colony sizes and distributions of surface-nesting seabirds, with some species having an advantage over others because of their larger size or earlier arrival. In parts of Europe and North America, increases in the numbers of large gulls during the mid-twentieth century caused local reductions in the numbers of smaller gulls and terns

FIG 125. When Lesser Black-backed Gulls *Larus fuscus* (left) and Herring Gulls *L. argentatus* (right) expanded in numbers during the mid- to late twentieth century, they displaced terns from some of their nesting areas. (Edmund Fellowes and Frank Snijkers)

through use of nesting areas (Wanless *et al.* 1996, Skórka *et al.* 2005). Large gulls disrupt the nesting attempts of terns, and prey upon eggs and chicks, so that tern colonies decline and are ultimately abandoned. Gulls prefer to nest on offshore islands and sometimes displace terns to inshore islands and mainland shores where they are more vulnerable to mammalian predation. Various measures to reduce gull densities in particular areas have created space which allowed terns to return, reversing downward trends in their numbers (Kress 1983, Morris *et al.* 1992). In Britain and Ireland, most control measures have been concentrated on Lesser Black-backed and Herring Gulls, whose expanding colonies were seen to progressively displace smaller species (Coulson 1991, Wanless *et al.* 1996).

As a result of gull control and other management, the island of Rockabill in Co. Dublin currently holds the largest colony of Roseate Terns in the British Isles, some four-fifths of the total. In the late 1980s, when tern numbers were much lower on Rockabill, Herring Gulls were culled and gravel terraces were constructed on areas of bare rock and furnished with nest boxes to provide more nesting sites for Roseate Terns (Casey *et al.* 1995). Similar measures, including box provision, were also undertaken at Lady's Island Lake in Co. Wexford, and at Coquet Island in Northumberland, both of which also now support thriving colonies of Roseate Terns (Chapter 5). Other gull control has been undertaken with effect in continental Europe. For example, the culling of Yellow-legged Gulls on a remote island off Spain benefited the numbers and breeding success of the smaller Audouin's Gulls. As the larger species declined, the smaller one occupied the vacated ground (Paracuellos & Nevado 2010).

In recent years, the expanding numbers of Great Skuas on some Scottish islands have displaced Arctic Skuas from areas they formerly occupied, with consequent reductions in their numbers (Furness 1987). This occurred on Foula in the 1960s and 1970s, over most of Hermaness in the 1970s, and on Hoy in the 1980s (Phillips *et al.* 1998). By the mid-1990s, Great Skuas nested over most of the Hoy uplands, and Arctic Skuas remained only in peripheral areas, in small isolated clusters (Furness & Ratcliffe, in Mitchell *et al.* 2004). Great Skuas can kill Arctic Skuas during territorial disputes, which can have an immediate effect on Arctic Skua numbers, besides excluding them from nesting habitat. Great Skuas also compete for space with larger gull species, often killing their chicks, and eventually displacing them altogether. In other places, Cormorants have displaced the smaller Shags from some flattish nesting areas, and gulls tend not to nest close to either Cormorants or Shags (Cadiou *et al.* 2010). Competition for breeding space has also occurred between seabirds and seals, the former declining as the latter increased.

The situation in southern England regarding competition for tree-cavity nest-sites is likely to change in the years ahead as introduced Ring-necked

Parakeets continue to expand. They could then compete increasingly for nest-sites with native cavity-nesting species, but at this stage it is hard to assess their likely impacts. The same concern could be expressed over introduced Mandarin Ducks, which are capable of excluding Tawny Owls and others from potential nest-sites. Although all experimental studies of competition for nest-sites have concerned bird–bird interactions, in many regions tree-cavities are used by various other animals, from bees to bats and squirrels. Competition with other animals could thus be an additional factor influencing the densities of some cavity-nesting birds, or vice versa.

INTERACTIONS BETWEEN CAVITY-NESTING AND OPEN-NESTING SPECIES

In view of the large number of studies in which the provision of nest-boxes led to an increase in the breeding density of cavity-nesters, the question arises whether such increases have any impact on other bird species in the community – for example, through competition for food. This question was examined in six series of experiments in all of which manipulating nest-sites changed the abundance of cavity-nesters. Two of these experiments revealed no simultaneous effects on open-nesting species, one showed a decrease in open-nesting species, and three showed a increase in open-nesting species. In view of this variety of findings, it is hard to draw any general conclusions.

To begin with the studies that showed no effects on open-nesters, the first was a well-replicated eight-year study in subalpine birch forest in Swedish Lapland. In the plots where nest-boxes had been added, Pied Flycatcher density increased about 20-fold, causing the total numbers of birds in the experimental plots to almost double, while densities remained low in the control plots (Enemar & Sjöstrand 1972). Despite this massive increase in flycatchers, the density of other passerines did not decrease in the experimental plots as compared to the control plots. The implication was that increased numbers of flycatchers had no adverse effect on the numbers of other species.

In a similar study that took place near Oxford, nest-boxes in an area of broadleaved woodland were made unsuitable for three years by removing the front panel, while those in an adjacent wood were left unchanged (East & Perrins 1988). In those years in the experimental area, tits bred only in natural cavities, and the numbers of Great Tits (but not Blue Tits) were significantly reduced. No change in the numbers of open-nesters coincided with the change in tit density.

An experiment in coniferous forest in Norway gave a different outcome, in that open-nesters decreased (Hogstad 1975). In a control plot of 110 ha, in which no nest-boxes were provided, the territories of all breeding birds were mapped. In the experimental plot of 9 ha, periods without and with nest-boxes were alternated during an eight-year study, giving four years with and four years without nest-boxes. Addition of nest-boxes increased the density of cavity-nesters about 20-fold, mainly Pied Flycatchers but also Great Tits. The total number of open-nesters was reduced by about one-half in years with nest-boxes compared to years without them. After comparing annual variations in control and experimental plots, it was concluded that three open-nesting species were adversely affected by the increase in cavity-nesters, namely Chiffchaff, Willow Warbler and Chaffinch. Chiffchaffs were absent in two of the four years with nest-boxes, and Willow Warblers were absent in all four years, suggesting strong effects of competition. With only one study plot, this experiment lacked spatial replication, but the immediate changes in the breeding densities of open-nesting species in response to changes in nest-box availability in alternate years suggested a strong causal relationship.

In stark contrast, in another experiment, as the numbers of cavity-nesters were increased, open-nesting species increased too. As a forester, Wellenstein (1968) was interested in controlling insects that damage pine plantations. He used various approaches, including the provision of nest-boxes, laying out eight 1 ha plots with four different nest-box densities each replicated twice. He reported the number of broods fledged each season from the boxes, and also counted territorial open-nesting birds on the plots, making it possible to test whether variation in the abundance of cavity-nesters (caused by different numbers of occupied nest-boxes) was associated with variation in the number of open-nesters. The result was that the two sets of species fluctuated in parallel, with the largest numbers of open nesters occurring on plots with the largest numbers of nest-boxes and cavity-nesters (mostly Pied Flycatchers and tits) (Fig. 126). He suggested that this was caused by a 'social effect', later jargonised as *heterospecific attraction*.

This matter was taken further in 1988–89 when a two-year experiment was performed on six small islands in a lake in central Finland, originally planned to investigate interspecific competition. On three islands the densities of resident tits were raised experimentally (by providing winter food and nest-boxes and by releasing extra birds from the mainland), while on three other islands tits were reduced in density by removing them (Mönkkönen *et al.* 1990). In the second year, the treatments were reversed between islands, thereby controlling for possible island effects. In the event, the experimental increase in resident cavity-

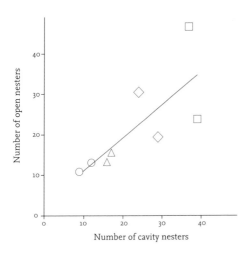

FIG 126. Number of birds nesting in replicate 1 ha plots of mixed pine–spruce forest in western Germany with different densities of nest-boxes. Circles: 9 boxes ha^{-1}; triangles: 16 boxes ha^{-1}; diamonds: 25 boxes ha^{-1}; squares: 36 boxes ha^{-1} (from Dhondt 2012, after Wellenstein 1968). Bird densities expressed as numbers per 10 ha. The results show that, as the number of cavity-nesters increased, so did the numbers of open nesters ($r^2 = 0.58$, $p = 0.028$), which the author attributed to an unspecified social effect later called *heterospecific attraction*.

nesters was accompanied by an increase in migratory open-nesting species, while no evidence was found for interspecific competition for food between the two groups. This result placed the discussion of interspecific competition in a broader context, because it seemed that interactions between species with similar resource needs could have both negative (competition) and positive (facilitation) effects (see also Chapter 11). In this example, the presence of other birds may provide a strong indicator of good habitat to newly arrived migrants unfamiliar with the area, but for heterospecific attraction to have evolved, the benefits must presumably outweigh the costs of breeding close to potential competitors (Mönkönnen & Forsman 2002).

In a later experiment, in Finnish Lapland, resident tit species were removed from four study plots before any summer migrants arrived, while in four other plots tit densities were raised by releasing the birds caught in the first four plots (Forsman *et al.* 1998). In the following year, the treatments were reversed between areas, allowing paired comparisons to be made within each plot. An index of arthropod abundance was also obtained from each plot in each year by use of sweep nets. If heterospecific attraction held, migrant densities should be higher in the years of increased tit densities, and results supported this prediction. The densities and number of migrant species were significantly higher where resident bird densities were increased than where they were lowered. At the species level, the migratory Redwing showed the strongest positive response to an increased abundance of tits. Migratory bird numbers did not vary with arthropod abundance (apart from one species out of ten, the Pied Flycatcher).

These findings were consistent with the notion that migratory species can use residents to indicate areas of favourable habitat. Year-to-year changes in food resources during the breeding season had no important effect on bird densities in these northern areas, but findings implied the importance of heterospecific attraction in structuring local bird communities.

The phenomenon of heterospecific attraction is probably most marked at high latitudes where, owing to hard winters, resident bird species may not achieve the high densities at which they would exploit to the full their potential summer food supplies. It is also at these latitudes, where summers are short, that migrants must find suitable habitat as soon as they arrive, and start nesting without delay. Further experiments are needed to find whether heterospecific attraction occurs at lower latitudes, as in Britain and Ireland.

Other experiments of this type have found consistently that increases in other species occur only at intermediate densities of tits; they do not occur at high densities, in which any benefits of settling near to tits may be outweighed by the costs of interspecific competition. In most areas where they were studied, Pied Flycatchers compete for scarce nest-sites with resident tits, so the numbers that nest in different years may be inversely related to the numbers of tits present. Yet in far northern breeding areas, flycatchers that bred in tight association with tits started nesting earlier, and had larger broods, than more isolated pairs (Forsman *et al.* 2002). This paradoxical result suggests that species interactions can switch from negative to positive, depending on circumstance, and that the co-existence of species with similar needs does not always result in competition. These ideas are explored further in Chapter 11.

EFFECTS ON POPULATIONS: LONG-TERM AND EVOLUTIONARY RESPONSES

Evidence for effects of competition on populations, as discussed above, emerged from studies lasting at most a few years, in which effects on the ecological niches, performance and numbers of individuals were measured. These effects were immediately reversed if conditions changed, but they gave evidence of competition acting here-and-now. Other types of effect occur on longer timescales, and lead to changes in geographical range (promoting differences in the distributions of species) and bird morphology (promoting differences in the ecology of species). Because of the timescales involved, these effects are not amenable to experimentation, nor are they immediately reversible. They can only be inferred from the existing patterns of distribution and ecology among related species, and so provide no more than hints about past competition. One partial exception, however, occurs when the establishment of a species in a new area (whether natural or human-assisted) is followed by reductions in the distributions or numbers of other species with similar ecology already present.

Allopatric distributions

Similar species are often *allopatric*, occupying separate geographical ranges which abut or overlap to a small extent. Some such pairs, such as the Carrion Crow and Hooded Crow, may interbreed to some extent where they meet, but others apparently do not. The fact that the different species do not spread through one another's ranges has usually been attributed to competition, with one species favoured in one region and another in the adjoining region. As Lack (1971) put it, species inhabit separate but adjoining ranges where (1) they have such similar ecology that only one of them can persist in any one area, and (2) each is better adapted than the other to part of their combined ranges. Competition is the more likely explanation if the zone of contact between them does not correspond with an obvious change in habitat.

Boundaries between pairs of allopatric species are seldom abrupt, but occur as an overlap zone, in which species gradually replace each other in similar habitat. In continental Europe, this situation is exemplified in varying degrees by Chaffinch/Brambling, Crested Tit/Siberian Tit, Curlew/Whimbrel, and Red-

FIG 127. Chaffinch *Fringilla coelebs* (left) and Brambling *F. montifringilla* (right), two closely related species which replace each other in the northern boreal forest, the former occurring in the south and the latter in the north. (Frank Snijkers)

necked Phalarope/Grey Phalarope. In each pair, the first-named species breeds mainly south of the other, and their zone of overlap shifted northward during the twentieth century, coinciding with climatic change. Such boundary changes thus implicate environmental factors in influencing the competitive balance between related species in similar habitats (Lack 1971). Competition could be involved in limiting many bird ranges, but the evidence is circumstantial, and alternative explanations of the findings are hard to eliminate. Because the outcome of competition is likely to be influenced by other factors, we should expect that the boundaries between apparent competitors would move as climate and other conditions change.

For some species, competition may not be *direct*, involving a single closely related congener, but *diffuse*, involving several species, not all of which may be closely related. Such diffuse competition is hard to detect, because we often have little notion of which species the competitors might be. But the idea is that the community of species present in an area divides up the feeding opportunities in such a way that an invader would have to displace several of them from parts of their niches if it were to survive there. We can only surmise the existence of diffuse competition in special circumstances, in localities where whole constellations of species are missing, and range (or niche) expansions occur in remaining species that have no clear single-species competitor. Examples are provided by the many species that occupy wider niches on islands, where potential competitors are fewer, than on mainlands, an example being the Coal Tit on Gotland, as described below (Lack 1971, MacArthur 1972).

Competitive release

Some potentially competing species occur in some areas together (*sympatry*) and in other areas alone (*allopatry*). Evidence for competition comes from niche contraction where the species occur together, or from niche expansion where they occur alone (known as *competitive release*). Many closely related species of bird that occupy mainly different geographical ranges diverge in habitat or feeding habits only in the overlap zone where they occur together (Lack 1971). For example, throughout its wide European range, the Chaffinch breeds in both coniferous and broadleaved woods. On the islands of Gran Canaria and Tenerife, however, it is replaced in pine forests by the Blue Chaffinch. This is the only part of the range of the Chaffinch where a second chaffinch species occurs and the only place within its range (including some other Canary Islands) where it does not breed in pine forest. Similarly, two species of nightingales breed in thickets in Europe, the Nightingale in the west and southwest and the Thrush Nightingale in the east. They replace each other geographically, except in parts in eastern Europe where their ranges overlap. Only in this overlap zone is the Nightingale restricted to drier and the Thrush Nightingale to wetter habitats of the same general type (Lack 1971). In these and other species pairs, the differences in ranges, and in habitats in the zone of overlap, have been attributed to competition. They again indicate how the presence of one species in an area might restrict the distribution and numbers of another through niche contraction.

Turning now to niche expansion, when a species is missing from a locality where it would be expected to occur, its place is sometimes taken by another species, found elsewhere in a different kind of habitat. The House Sparrow and Tree Sparrow present a complicated example (Summers-Smith 1988). In the west of their joint Palaearctic range, the House Sparrow occupies towns and villages, in close association with people, while the Tree Sparrow occurs in the countryside. But in southeast and eastern Asia, where the House Sparrow is absent, the Tree Sparrow occupies the towns and villages. In between, the separation is less clear-cut: in some regions the Tree Sparrow occupies the towns and the House Sparrow the rural areas, while in other regions the situation is reversed. The general trend, however, is for a change from House Sparrow to Tree Sparrow in the towns, as one travels from west to east across Eurasia, and as other conditions change. Moreover, in much of the Mediterranean region, where both these species are absent, the Spanish Sparrow takes over the urban niche. In eastern Sardinia, where the Tree Sparrow has recently colonised, it has displaced the Spanish Sparrow from built-up areas. In a sense, such examples provide natural experiments on the role of competition. But one can never be sure that some other relevant factor does not differ between areas, besides the presence or absence of a potential competitor, and accounts for the pattern.

Examples of a related phenomenon, *character release*, are provided by the European tits. Particular species diverge from the usual morphology of their species only in small parts of their range where competitors are absent. On the Swedish mainland Great, Blue, Willow, Marsh and Crested Tits all co-exist with the socially subordinate Coal Tit. On the Baltic island of Gotland, Willow, Marsh and Crested Tits do not breed, and the Coal Tit is the only small species present. On this island, the Coal Tit has expanded its foraging niche, feeding more on the inner parts of trees, while on the mainland, where it is constrained by the presence of the other species, it feeds mostly on the outer parts of trees and on needles. It also occurs at much greater density than on the mainland. This example of ecological release has also led to an evolutionary change: Coal Tits on Gotland are considerably larger and have heavier bills than their counterparts on the mainland (Gustafsson 1988). They thus illustrate the effects of release from interspecific competition on body form and foraging behaviour. A similar effect is seen in Irish Coal Tits, which show greater sexual dimorphism in bill size and shape than British ones, again associated with fewer competing species in Ireland (Gosler & Carruthers 1994). In this instance, the sexes segregate more in feeding behaviour where they are less constrained by related species (Marsh and Willow Tits being absent from Ireland). Such patterns are repeated in other tit communities elsewhere in Europe, in that the absence of any one species is commonly associated with a morphological change in another, with small species becoming larger than elsewhere (Lack 1971, Dhondt 1989). Because birds overlap in diet with a wide range of animals, not all character shifts necessarily occur in response to other birds.

CONCLUDING REMARKS

Because different animals overlap in their resource needs, and resources are often limiting, we would expect that species would often compete with one another, and that the numbers of one would influence the numbers of another. The existence of competition among different bird species is suggested by their distribution patterns, and by their feeding and nesting habits, and confirmed by large numbers of experiments. Some of the field experiments are among the best yet conducted on free-living birds, as they had both replicates and controls, and some lasted for several years. As a result, the findings are unambiguous. The removal of one species (or group of species) from an area has repeatedly led to an expansion in the niche of another (or several others), to an improvement in its survival or breeding success, and sometimes to an increase in its numbers or distribution. The latter provides unequivocal evidence that the presence of one species in an area can depress the density of another that shares the same resource.

Depending on circumstances, one species can exclude another completely from an area, or the two may co-exist using different parts of a resource. One species can remove part of a food supply that would otherwise be available to another, or through aggressive and other means it can restrict access to a food source by another. Dominant species can also pre-emptively occupy the best nest-sites, or steal occupied sites by expelling another (usually smaller) species. Where nest-sites are few, the population trends of competing species may sometimes vary in inverse relation to one another, with the subordinate species increasing as the dominant one declines. Similar evidence of interspecific competition has also emerged from studies on other organisms. They have shown that depletion and interference competition are widespread among both plants and animals, and that one of a pair of competing species is usually affected much more than the other. In these respects, then, birds are similar to other organisms.

Which of two species fares best in a competitive situation varies with circumstances, the type of competition (whether by interference or depletion), and the resource involved. For example, where Great and Blue Tits fight over localised resources, such as nest-sites accessible to both species, the larger Great Tit has the upper hand, and can reduce the local breeding density of Blue Tits (by aggressive means, interference competition). But where the two species depend in summer on the same caterpillar supply, the smaller Blue Tit can remove smaller caterpillars before they reach a size favoured by Great Tits, and thus lower the breeding success of Great Tits (by non-aggressive depletion competition) (Dhondt 1989).

Although the reproduction or survival of individuals may be affected by competition, as explained above these effects may not always reduce the subsequent breeding numbers because of compensatory improvements in the survival of other individuals that escape the effects of competition. But, as with any other limiting factor, competition may still affect the genetic composition and evolution of the population, by selecting for individuals with inherent attributes that reduce the impacts of competition. In other words, when individuals with different heritable traits respond in different ways to interspecific competition, this competition may constitute an important selective force. It might, for example, influence the bill structure of a species if this led to it dealing more efficiently with foods also taken by its competitors. This is the mechanism by which divergence in bill or body size is thought to have evolved in isolated populations in the absence of one or more competing species, as in the island tits mentioned above. These evolutionary effects of competition would be expected to occur over much longer timescales than most of the effects discussed in this chapter. They match the evolutionary responses of birds to other limiting pressures, such as predation and parasitism, aspects discussed in Chapters 12 and 13. Regardless of its evolutionary effects, however, it is clear that interspecific competition does indeed reduce here-and-now the numbers and distributions of many bird species, including some widespread and familiar ones.

CHAPTER 11

Interactions Between Different Limiting Factors

I N EARLIER CHAPTERS, the main factors limiting bird numbers, whether resources or natural enemies, were discussed for the most part as though they acted separately. While changes in the densities of many bird populations do indeed seem to be influenced primarily by changes in one major limiting factor, it is also clear that different limiting factors can sometimes act together to influence bird numbers and that their effects are not always straightforwardly additive. Sometimes, one factor might enhance the effect of another, so that their combined impact on population levels is greater than the sum of their individual effects. At other times, one factor might reduce the effect of another, so that their combined impact is less than the sum of their separate effects. It is only in recent times that such interactions have been studied in detail, providing some fascinating insights. This chapter considers the interplay between different resources and between different predators in influencing bird numbers, while the next two chapters examine the interactions between predators and resources, and between parasites and resources.

When studying changes in bird numbers, field biologists often find it hard to distinguish the effects of various factors that might have been involved. Take, for example, the Eider population of the Baltic region which around 1990 numbered around 1.2 million individuals (Christensen 2008). Although up to 180,000 birds were shot annually, numbers increased rapidly during the 1970s and 1980s, associated with an increased food supply (mainly mussels and other shellfish), which followed the growing input of fertilisers, sewage and other waste to coastal waters. The growth in Eider numbers also coincided with a period when a major predator – the White-tailed Eagle – was extremely scarce.

From around 1990, however, the overall population began to decline, with about a third of the birds being lost over the following decade. This decline coincided with heavy harvesting of mussels by fishermen, causing mass starvation events among Eiders (Chapters 3 and 4), accompanied by a series of major disease outbreaks (mainly avian cholera), and intense infections of acanthocephalan gut parasites (Chapter 9). Numbers of White-tailed Eagles also recovered at this time, and American Mink colonised some of the Eiders' nesting areas, becoming serious predators on the birds and their eggs. This made it hard to find whether the decline in Eider numbers was caused by a series of unrelated events which happened to coincide, or an underlying food shortage which led not only to starvation but also to increased susceptibility to parasites, pathogens and predators. Body condition of individual Eiders decreased during the period of population decline, presumably reflecting food shortage, but also affecting their immune response, an aspect to which we can return later. Shortage of mussels also led to Eiders taking more crabs, the main source of acanthocephalan parasites. Whether predators had any significant role in these changes is not clear, but the scale of human hunting fell to half its previous level (owing mainly to fewer hunters). Because the Eiders were so numerous and widely dispersed over a large area of sea, experiments were not feasible, making it harder to

FIG 128. The White-tailed Eagle *Haliaeetus albicilla* preys upon Eiders *Somateria mollissima* and other large water-birds, as well as fish. (Laurie Campbell)

assess the role of different limiting factors and the interactions between them. This story provides an example of the kinds of problems which often confront researchers attempting to understand changes in bird populations, when several factors change simultaneously. It also brings us to the problem of the interrelationships that can occur between different limiting factors.

INTERACTIONS INVOLVING DIFFERENT RESOURCES

For breeding, birds require both food and nest-sites, and the nesting densities of many species are limited by one or the other, whichever is in shortest supply. For some species certain regions may offer abundant food but few nest-sites, while other regions may offer plenty of nest-sites but little food (Newton 1979). Over much of its range, the Peregrine nests on cliffs. It breeds in those parts of Britain where cliffs are available, where its densities there are related mainly to food supply (Ratcliffe 1980). For a long time the Peregrine was effectively absent from the rest of the country – mainly inland lowland areas – where cliffs (or quarries) were lacking, but where potential prey were plentiful. In recent decades, however, the situation has changed, as Peregrines have begun to nest increasingly on churches and other tall buildings in cities. This new behaviour has enabled the species to colonise lowland areas not previously available to it, but it is still largely absent from the land-areas separating towns and cities which lack acceptable nest-sites of any kind. In other words, this species is limited in the extent to which it can exploit a widely distributed food supply by a restricted distribution of suitable nest-sites.

Colonial species are often confined to isolated patches of nesting habitat, which can lead to depletion of food supply near the colonies, while food remains abundant further away, beyond the regular foraging range. It has been argued that some seabird populations, nesting on isolated islands, may be regulated in the breeding season by such localised competition for food, which limits the potential production of young (Ashmole 1963). On this argument, population limitation is achieved not by nest-sites alone, nor by food supply alone, but by a combination of the two. Although individual birds might survive by feeding further afield where food supplies may be less depleted, they could not reproduce there, owing to lack of nest-sites. Of course, species differ in how far they range from their colonies, and in the seas around Britain and Ireland, Shags and Black Guillemots forage mainly within a few kilometres of their nest-sites, while Gannets and Manx Shearwaters range up to several hundred kilometres. Such long-distance foraging requires special adaptations in both the adults and their chicks, and has considerable costs in terms of time and energy. These constraints apply only to breeding birds, which must continually return to their nests, and not to non-breeding birds, which are free to range over much wider areas and may never reach the densities at which food would become limiting. In such situations, it is the restriction in productivity at colony sites which inhibits further population growth.

As yet, evidence for this means of population regulation, entailing an interaction between localised colony-sites and widespread food supply, is entirely circumstantial. Nevertheless, studies on some seabird species gave results consistent with this idea: (1) the size of particular colonies declined with increase in the number of other colonies (and individuals) in the surrounding area, suggesting density-dependent regulation of colony sizes (Fig. 129); (2) breeding success and fledgling weights were lower in larger colonies, suggesting local competition for food (Birkhead & Furness 1985, Gaston 1985, Hunt et al. 1986); (3) the density of prey fish was lower near the colonies than further away, suggesting prey depletion (Birt et al. 1987); and (4) occasional mass breeding failure was observed at colonies when food was scarce in the vicinity, but known to be abundant beyond the foraging ranges of the birds (Chapter 4). We would not of course expect all colonies to be close to the food limit at any one time.

Similar localised access to a widespread food supply occurs in deserts, where the need to drink restricts most bird species to feeding within flight range of a water source, either year-round or in the driest season. This restriction may in turn lead to depletion of local food supplies, with effects on bird numbers, while in more distant areas food is present but out of reach. The actual foraging range again varies between species, depending on their flight capabilities and drinking frequencies. Lack of drinking water is not a constraint expected in Britain and Ireland, but in arid parts of the Mediterranean region the availability of surface water may clearly influence the distribution of some bird species, as shown for the Red-legged Partridge (Borralho et al. 1998).

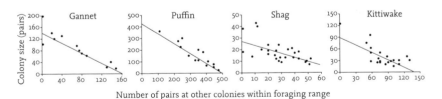

FIG 129. Relationships between sizes of long-established seabird colonies around Britain and the total number of other pairs at other colonies within the foraging ranges of the species concerned. Colony sizes expressed as square root values, and foraging ranges taken as 100 km for Gannet Morus bassanus, 150 km for Puffin Fratercula arctica, 30 km for Shag Phalacrocorax aristotelis and 40 km for Kittiwake Rissa tridactyla. (From Furness & Birkhead 1984)

Other familiar examples of birds whose foraging range is restricted by water, but in a different way, are provided by geese and other waterfowl, which need the safety of water-bodies for roosting, but fly out each day to feed on farmland within range of their roosts. Those species that can habitually commute further than others gain access to wider areas. For example, Pink-footed Geese in eastern Scotland regularly flew up to 20 km between their roosting and feeding sites, whereas Greylags fed mainly within 2 km of their roosts (Newton *et al.* 1973).

Likewise, in open land, some species may be restricted in distribution by their need for trees or cliffs for nesting and roosting, leaving intervening areas largely unexploited. Such focal-point regulation of bird numbers, amid a widespread food supply, may be the norm in many types of habitat. In effect, one patchy resource (nest-sites or roost-sites) permits only patchy exploitation of a second more widespread resource (feeding sites), thus preventing the full utilisation of a potential food supply.

INTERACTIONS INVOLVING DIFFERENT PREDATORS

Different species of predators might compete with one another by eating the same species of prey, but they also interact in other ways. So-called *intra-guild predation*, in which one larger predator kills and affects the numbers and distributions of smaller ones, is becoming increasingly apparent in western Europe as large birds of prey are recovering from past human persecution. One example unfolded over a 23-year period in Kielder Forest in Northumberland, where Goshawks first bred in 1973 and then increased steadily until 1989, after which their numbers stabilised at around 20 pairs (Petty *et al.* 2003). Goshawks killed many adult Kestrels in early spring, and were held responsible for a progressive decline in Kestrel breeding numbers. The larger species removed increasing proportions of Kestrels year by year as their numbers declined, making the predation *inversely density-dependent*. To judge from prey remains, Goshawks killed more Kestrels each spring than were recorded at any one time in the area, so it seemed that immigrants were being taken continually as they moved in. The total numbers killed were estimated to average 115 per year, whereas the area at no time supported more than seven nesting pairs. Short-eared Owls, which also hunt voles in the daytime and fall prey to Goshawks, declined over the same period, whereas Tawny Owls and Long-eared Owls, which hunt voles by night (and are therefore much less vulnerable to diurnally hunting Goshawks), did not decline. These and other small raptor species formed nearly 5% of more than 5,000 Goshawk prey remains examined in the area. This study thus provided circumstantial evidence for the role of predation in structuring raptor communities by limiting the densities of some smaller species. But the story does not end here.

The presence of such a large and effective predator is likely to have had cascading effects down through the food-chain, and not all species may have fared badly. Goshawks are known to reduce the densities of corvids and squirrels, which are major predators of the eggs and chicks of other bird species. To find whether the presence of Goshawks led to reduced predation on nest contents of birds in northern Finland, artificial nests containing quail eggs were placed at distances of 50–2,500 m from various Goshawk nests (Mönkkönen *et al.* 2000). In spruce forest, predation on these artificial nests increased with increasing distance from a Goshawk nest, implying that egg predators (such as Jays and Red Squirrels) had been reduced near Goshawk nests. Whether this actually benefited any other birds nesting close by was not shown, but the possibility remains.

The Goshawk itself is not immune to significant intra-guild predation. In Holstein in Germany, a Goshawk population was monitored before and after the area was colonised by Eagle Owls (Busche *et al.* 2005). These owls were first found

breeding in the area in 1988, and within two years Goshawks began to decline, reaching only one-third of their former numbers 12 years later. By then, most of the original Goshawk nests had been taken over by Eagle Owls. No Goshawk built a new nest within 500 m of an established Eagle Owl nest, and at greater distances Goshawk nesting attempts often failed, mainly through owl predation on chicks. The same trends occurred in other European areas recently colonised by Eagle Owls.

Similar effects of Eagle Owls occurred on Black Kites studied in eight different areas of the Italian Alps (Sergio *et al.* 2003). These effects were most severe in areas of high owl densities. The owls took both adult and nestling kites, especially when the two species nested within 2 km of one another. Kite productivity declined steeply with proximity to an Eagle Owl nest, and no Kite pair raised young within 1 km of an owl nest. Not surprisingly, kite

FIG 130. The Eagle Owl *Bubo bubo* is a powerful predator which can limit the numbers of some other raptors. It long since disappeared from Britain, but now breeds again in small numbers. (Laurie Campbell)

territories near to Eagle Owl nests were abandoned frequently, but they were often soon re-occupied, so that the two species continued to co-exist in the same areas. Overall, despite the presence of Eagle Owls, Black Kites seemed to be attracted to particular areas by a rich food source, but reduced their predation risk by nesting on the edges or in the spaces between Eagle Owl territories. Nevertheless, this behaviour did not provide complete protection (Sergio *et al.* 2003).

In the same areas of the Italian Alps, the diversity of nocturnal raptors was positively related to Eagle Owl density (Sergio *et al.* 2007). As the density of Eagle Owls increased between areas, so did the diversity of other owl species rarely eaten by Eagle Owls. The authors hypothesised that Eagle Owls depressed the density of aggressive mid-sized species, such as the Tawny Owl, which actively preys upon and competes with smaller owl species. An abundance of Eagle Owls could thus have released the pressure of predation and competition on smaller owl species, ultimately resulting in a more diverse assemblage. All these studies were observational and based on correlations, so should be interpreted with caution. However, they were repeated in different areas, highlighting the potential for intra-guild predation to affect the diversity and structure of whole communities (for effects of Goshawks on an interaction between Tawny Owls and Jackdaws see Chapter 10).

The relationships between the small Tengmalm's Owl, the larger Ural Owl and the still larger Eagle Owl were studied in western Finland (Hakkarainen & Korpimäki 1996). All three species ate rodents, but in addition Tengmalm's Owl was often eaten by the Ural Owl, which was in turn often eaten by the Eagle Owl. Tengmalm's Owls nested in cavities (or boxes) with entrance holes too small for both the larger species. Nest-boxes that were suitable only for Tengmalm's Owls were placed in areas lacking both the other species (as the control), and also within Ural Owl territories and within Eagle Owl territories. Boxes in areas with neither larger species or with Eagle Owls only

FIG 131. The Tawny Owl *Strix aluco* can limit the numbers of smaller owls, but can itself be limited by larger owls. (Richard Chandler)

were used significantly more often than boxes placed within Ural Owl territories. It appeared that Tengmalm's Owls may have perceived Ural Owls as their more significant predator. Most of the Tengmalm's Owls that did nest in Ural Owl territories failed before egg-laying, and those pairs that reached the egg stage laid an average of 11 days later than their equivalents in areas lacking Ural Owls. In addition, male Tengmalm's Owls at these nests were younger, on average, than males elsewhere and were more often paired with young females. These findings would have been expected if Ural Owls were preying upon Tengmalm's Owls in their territories, and if some of the birds they killed in early spring had been replaced by others. In any case, Ural Owls seemed to deter Tengmalm's Owls from settling in some otherwise suitable habitat, and thereby limited their breeding densities. Studies elsewhere have shown that Ural Owls are even more significant predators of Tawny Owls and can totally exclude them from some areas, and the same holds for the effects of Tawny Owls on Tengmalm's Owls (Vrezec & Tome 2004). Could the abundance of Tawny Owls across all wooded parts of Britain result from the absence of Ural Owls, and also explain the absence of Tengmalm's Owls here? Tengmalm's Owls have turned up in Britain from time to time, but have not become established.

Many other examples of one predator species affecting the numbers and distribution of another have emerged from studies in continental Europe. They include Goshawk affecting Red Kite, Black Kite, Buzzard, Honey-buzzard, Sparrowhawk*, Hobby* and Kestrel*; Golden Eagle affecting Peregrine and Buzzard; Eagle Owl affecting Booted Eagle*, Peregrine, Buzzard*, Black Kite*, Goshawk* and Tawny Owl*; Ural Owl affecting Tawny Owl and Tengmalm's Owl; Tawny Owl affecting Tengmalm's Owl*; various raptors affecting Lesser Kestrel; and Pine Marten affecting Hawk Owl, Tengmalm's Owl and Pygmy Owl (mainly Sergio & Hiraldo 2008, also Rutz et al. 2006). In most of these examples, the smaller species avoided settling near the larger, or moved to avoid it, leading to territory abandonment or reduced occupancy, and at least in those species marked with an asterisk it led to an overall reduction in breeding density. Examples of intra-guild relationships seem consistent across wide geographical areas. These European studies give some idea of the impact that Eagle Owls are likely to have on other birds of prey, if they become widely established (or re-established) in Britain. At the least, we can expect declines in the populations of medium-sized raptors, such as Buzzards and Peregrines, and possibly also in some other species. What effects, if any, Eagle Owl predation may have on the prey populations of the medium and smaller raptors remains to be seen.

Intra-guild predation has implications for game management, because where large predators are left alone they could reduce the numbers of the

mid-sized ones that have most impact on gamebirds. For example, Golden
Eagles eat substantial numbers of foxes, corvids and medium-sized raptors, such
as Hen Harriers. It has been suggested, on the basis of distributional data, that
the presence of a pair of Golden Eagles on a grouse moor could be beneficial
because they kill or keep away other species of predators, and could thereby
reduce the overall impact on game stocks (Fielding *et al.* 2003). The numbers of
grouse that the Eagles themselves eat are small compared to the numbers eaten
by all the other predators. Similarly, it was calculated from studies in northern
Europe that, where Goshawks were not killed by gamekeepers, they would
remove enough corvids to increase the production of young grouse, giving a
net gain in grouse even though the Goshawks would take some of the grouse
themselves (Milonoff 1994).

FEEDING ASSOCIATIONS

Species that eat the same type of food as one another, and are limited by it, can
be expected to compete, and the numbers of one may affect the food supply,
and hence the numbers, of another (Chapter 10). However, the interaction is
not always negative, because some species benefit from others exploiting the
same resource. Some seabirds associate with cetaceans or predatory fish, which
drive small fish to the surface where they become available to the birds. Both
under-water and over-water predators may benefit from this association, because
attempts to avoid one predator may expose the prey to a second. Some vultures
find their food mainly by watching other vulture species, and many other birds,
from gulls to raptors, sometimes pirate food from other birds (Brockman &
Barnard 1979). Skuas and others specialise in robbing other seabirds of the fish
they have caught. In northern Britain, Arctic Skuas rob mainly smaller seabirds,
such as terns and auks, for small fish such as sandeels, while Great Skuas rob
larger victims, such as Gannets and large gulls, for bigger fish.

These latter relationships appear markedly asymmetric, in that one species
benefits greatly at the expense of the other, and may be largely dependent on
the other for its livelihood. Over a 21-year period, fluctuations in the numbers
of Arctic Skuas on the island of Foula (Shetland) paralleled similar fluctuations
in their main food providers, which were Arctic Terns (Phillips *et al.* 1996). In
later years (mainly 2001–04), when a general decline in sandeel abundance led
to massive breeding failures in Arctic Terns, Kittiwakes, Guillemots and others,
Arctic Skua populations suffered similar declines (Caldow & Furness 2000). In
the same way that other seabirds can switch to alternative prey items, when their

FIG 132. The Arctic Skua *Stercorarius parasiticus* exists in the breeding season mainly by robbing other smaller seabirds of their prey. It has been declining rapidly in recent years, in association with the decline in Lesser Sandeels *Ammodytes marinus*, its main food. (Laurie Campbell)

favoured prey is scarce, Arctic Skuas made similar switches in victim species (Phillips *et al.* 1996). They got most of their food from Arctic Terns in the mid to late 1970s, from Puffins during the mid to late 1980s, and from Guillemots in 1989. But in 1991, when sandeels were again more abundant, they reverted mainly to Arctic Terns as their main providers.

While some species clearly benefit from robbing others, the costs to the victims can be substantial, as reflected in reduced production of young (as shown for Puffins robbed by Herring Gulls: Nettleship 1975). This contrasts with some other well-known associations between species in which there is no obvious cost to the provider species. For example, when Cattle Egrets associate with cattle and

FIG 133. Herring Gull *Larus argentatus* in the act of robbing a Puffin *Fratercula arctica* of its food. (David Boyle)

other large grazing mammals, exploiting the insects they disturb, there seems no obvious cost or benefit for the cattle.

Another type of association in which the presence of one predator may facilitate predation by a different predator occurs when one species puts birds off their nests, exposing the contents to another. An example concerns White-tailed Eagles hunting incubating Eiders on islands off Finland (Kilpi & Öst 2002). The eagles can readily take ducks nesting in open situations, but have more difficulty grabbing ducks nesting under bushes or trees. They nevertheless attempt to flush such birds off their nests, many of which escape, but for a time their eggs are exposed to crows and gulls, which are then responsible for most of the nest failures. In this example, eagles have both direct and indirect effects, and habitat structure influences the interaction between the different predators and their prey. Similarly, where livestock are kept at high densities on grassland, many eggs are lost to trampling (Beintema & Muskens 1987); but in addition, as incubating birds are continually flushed, eggs are repeatedly exposed to opportunist predators such as crows (Hart *et al.* 2002).

NESTING ASSOCIATIONS

While some birds gain food through thieving, others gain protection by nesting close to more aggressive species, such as Fieldfares, Lapwings, terns, gulls or falcons, which drive away predators. Most such relationships seem one-sided, in that one species gains protection from another, but gives little in return. For example, some ducks nest within colonies of Black-headed Gulls, providing that the ground cover is sufficient to hide their own nests. The gulls keep away other more skilled egg finders, such as crows, thus conferring protection on the ducks. On an island in Loch Leven in southeast Scotland, Tufted and other ducks nesting in a gull colony were significantly more successful than those nesting outside, and those nesting within the middle of the colony were more successful than those on the edges (Newton & Campbell 1975). The colony was preferred over surrounding areas of similar vegetation, and densities of up to 215 duck nests per hectare were recorded there. Similar findings emerged from a study of Tufted Ducks and Pochards nesting in gull colonies in central Finland (Väänänen 2000).

Other well-known protective associations involve Arctic-nesting geese, some species of which nest for preference near Peregrines or Snowy Owls. The breeding success of Red-breasted Geese nesting in association with Peregrines was studied in Siberia, where the main predator on the goose eggs was the Arctic Fox (Quinn & Kokorev 2002). The risk of egg predation for geese within colonies rose with increasing distance from a Peregrine eyrie but declined with increase in colony size. Predation risk from the falcons themselves was low, although the risk of being harassed was high, leading some geese nesting nearest to falcons to desert their nests.

There is little evidence to suggest that the protective species have either benefits or costs from the association, but this aspect has not been well studied. The presence of many geese near a Peregrine nest may attract Foxes, making the job of nest defence more demanding for the falcons. One example of mutual benefit in a nesting association in the subalpine birch woods of northern Europe involves Fieldfares and Merlins, both of which defend their nests vigorously (Wiklund 1982). Over a ten-year study, Fieldfares that nested in colonies were generally more successful than those that nested solitarily, but both Fieldfares and Merlins achieved higher nest success when nesting close to one another than when nesting separately and alone. Fieldfares apparently chose to nest near Merlins, which had already laid eggs when the thrushes started nest-building. Another species which breeds better in groups than solitarily is the Lapwing, again because of their communal nest defence, several pairs acting together being more successful at driving away predators than a single pair acting alone (Seymour *et al.* 2003). In addition, Meadow Pipits and Yellow Wagtails that settled close to Lapwings showed significantly higher nest success than other pairs nesting away from them (Eriksson & Götmark 1982).

In addition to the above examples, Woodpigeons have been found nesting within a few metres of Kestrels in Denmark, Hobbies in the Netherlands, and Black Kites in Spain (Cain & Hillgarth 1974, Bijlsma 1984, Bang *et al.* 2005). In the Netherlands, the breeding of Woodpigeon pairs was synchronised with

FIG 134. Familiar winter visitors to Britain and Ireland, back in their breeding areas Fieldfares *Turdus pilaris* often nest in loose colonies, and join together to drive away predators. (Alan Martin)

the breeding of Hobbies, resulting in an almost doubling of Woodpigeon nest success compared to pairs nesting away from Hobbies. On farmland in Poland, Skylarks nested at highest density near Ravens, apparently because Ravens kept away other more significant nest predators (Tryjanowski 2001). All these associations seemed to occur from choice, and not merely because the species involved shared the same habitat. In addition, small passerines often nest successfully in the lower parts of big raptor nests. For example, in various active Goshawk nests in Schleswig-Holstein, a total of 14 nests of Treecreepers were found over a period of years, plus 11 nests of Starlings, two of Redstarts and one of Coal tits, together with one roosting bat (Looft & Biesterfeld 1981). It may be assumed that all these birds gained some protection from their Goshawk host.

FISHERIES AND SEABIRDS

Similar interactions between species are illustrated by the effects of human fishing, which can lead to either increases or decreases in seabird numbers, depending on circumstances. Many scavenging seabird species have increased in numbers because the offal and discards thrown overboard have provided a massive new food supply, resulting from fisheries bringing to the surface large amounts of fish material that would otherwise remain inaccessible to birds (Chapter 4). The Fulmar, Gannet, Great Skua and large gulls are the major beneficiaries around Britain and Ireland (Fisher 1966, Furness *et al.* 1992, Reeves & Furness 2002, Furness 2003, Votier *et al.* 2004b). At some colonies, discards or offal comprise the bulk of the chick diet. Further south, in the Benguela Current off southwest Africa, where some of our seabirds spend the winter, similar benefits accrue. In this productive area, seabird densities increased by eight times over a 30-year period following the establishment of a trawl fishery, with birds again benefiting from the discards (Abrams 1985). When winding in the nets, such trawlers were typically accompanied by more than 1,000 birds, with very few seen elsewhere.

In addition, the removal for human consumption of large predatory fish has probably led to an increase in the abundance of small fish (such as Sprats and sandeels) suitable for seabirds to eat. The evidence is correlative, with the smaller species increasing as the larger declined, but the same linked trends occurred at different times in different regions (Sherman *et al.* 1981, Furness 1982). Around Britain and Ireland, the increase in small fish may have facilitated the growth of many seabird populations during the 1950s–1980s (Chapter 4). However, recent human overfishing of sandeels, coupled with oceanographic changes and partial recovery of some predatory fish populations, have resulted in the collapse

FIG 135. Fishing boat with accompanying gulls, which benefit from the waste thrown overboard. (Chris Knights)

of some sandeel stocks. This has led in turn to population crashes in several seabird species around northeast Britain, including Arctic Terns, Kittiwakes and others, some declining by more than 50% within a few years, implying increased mortality as well as breeding failures (Chapters 4 and 15).

These examples indicate the effects on populations of competition and food enhancement, and also show how the removal of certain organisms (such as large predatory fish) from an ecosystem could have repercussions through the whole system. It has the same effects as the removal of large predators from some terrestrial habitats, discussed above.

CONCLUDING REMARKS

Some of the interactions that can occur between different resources and between different predators can clearly influence the population sizes and distributions of birds. Some of the relationships that have emerged were counterintuitive, such as the localisation in one resource limiting access to another, one predator increasing prey availability for another, or limiting the numbers of another predator, which thereby allows yet smaller predators to establish themselves, with cascading effects down the food-chain.

The phenomenon of *focal-point* population regulation occurs where birds are concentrated in specific localities by their need for nest-sites, cover or water. This can lead to heavy exploitation of the local food supply, while further away food remains abundant and largely unexploited. In such cases, species can be limited in distribution and abundance by whichever resource is in shortest supply.

While certain species can indirectly reduce the numbers of their competitors through their effects on shared resources, predators or parasites, others can make more of a shared resource available to their competitors. Examples include the terns and other small seabirds that make fish available to food-robbing skuas. Commercial fisheries have affected seabird numbers either negatively by removing food supplies or positively by providing new food sources (in the form of offal and discards). These examples illustrate the range of interactions that can occur between different predators (including humans) exploiting essentially the same resource.

Other examples of such interactions come from intra-guild predation, which is widespread among raptors and owls. It seems that many raptors, so often studied because of their perceived effects on other bird species, are themselves limited in intact communities partly by predation. Responses by smaller to bigger species include spatial avoidance, reduced site-occupancy and reduced breeding success and survival, all leading to reduced populations. Intra-guild predation may thus have the potential to structure raptor communities, thereby affecting prey species lower in the food-chain. The term *meso-predator release* has been used to describe the situation where the removal of top predators by humans has allowed populations of smaller predatory species to expand, with effects on their prey.

Such intra-guild relationships are not confined to birds. In both Europe and North America, the destruction of large mammalian predators, such as Wolves, has allowed smaller ones, such as Foxes, to increase, affecting populations of ducks and other ground-nesting birds (Greenwood *et al.* 1995). The truth of this statement is shown in areas where Wolves or Lynx have been allowed to return, resulting in declines in Fox numbers, and reduced predation on ground-nesting birds. The lessons from these studies are not merely that one predator can control the numbers of another, but that effects can ripple down to other species lower in the food-chain (see also Chapter 4, Estes *et al.* 2011).

Experiments on other organisms, including invertebrates, have shown that predator removal can sometimes lead to marked increases in the numbers of some prey species, but at the expense of others that share the same resources (Sih *et al.* 1985). The implication is that, by depressing populations of competing species below the levels at which they would be limited by resources, predation can allow certain species to co-exist that would otherwise be incompatible. In other words, predation can influence overall species diversity. Although such situations have been well studied in other animals, especially marine communities, I know of no well-documented examples from among birds.

CHAPTER 12

Interactions Between Predators and Resources

P REDATORS HAVE OTHER EFFECTS on their prey than simply eating them. They have indirect effects, influencing where prey individuals feed, sleep and nest. The mere presence of a predator constrains the prey to using only part of the space and other resources otherwise available to it. Taking these non-lethal effects into account, predators have much greater impacts on prey populations than is evident merely from the numbers killed. Without the constraints imposed by predators, many bird species could make use of a wider range of sites, and probably thereby achieve greater numbers. All bird species are affected in some degree by risk of predation. Every predator has its own predators and every prey is in turn a predator on something else, whether plant or animal. The interactions between resources (food and nest-sites) and predation are explored in this chapter, assessing how they influence the behaviour, habitat use, body condition, distribution and ultimately the numbers of birds.

Any anti-predation behaviour of birds, from vigilance to avoidance, has costs. It takes time that might otherwise be used for foraging or other useful tasks, and it reduces the number of places that birds can safely use. Yet birds almost always show some form of anti-predator behaviour, for any individual that ignored the risk of predation would soon die. Moreover, birds in a group normally conform in their anti-predator behaviour, each individual reacting like the rest, for any bird that did something different (such as staying when the rest flee) could be rapidly targeted, thereby removing any benefit it might otherwise gain from group-living.

Part of the anti-predation behaviour of birds is innate – a product of evolution, resulting from predation on previous generations – while another part is learnt, either by direct experience or from other individuals. Thus, the habitat preferences and general wariness of birds are largely genetically controlled, and persist for generations even in the absence of predation. Equally, the role of learning is evident in birds that are raised in captivity and show much less fear of people than their wild relatives do. It is also readily apparent by comparing the behaviour of birds in the countryside where they are shot at, with that of their equivalents in towns where they are not. Woodpigeons are clearly much tamer in parks and gardens than in farmland, and Greylag Geese are notoriously wary when feeding in cropland but are tame enough to be fed by hand in town parks. Admittedly, these are mostly different individuals of the same species, but their widespread occupation of parks has occurred only since the nineteenth century. An ability of individuals to adjust to prevailing threats is also evident in wildfowl and other hunted species which soon learn the places and times of year when they are shot (hunters often comment that quarry species seem to become tamer when the shooting season has ended).

But even the hard-wired, genetically controlled responses can be changed over the generations by natural selection, if species find themselves in predator-free environments. This is shown by birds that have colonised oceanic islands which lack mammalian predators. Many such species have lost the inherent fear of predators shown by their mainland ancestors, allowing a close approach by people and introduced predators, and nesting in unsafe places. Some species on islands have also lost the power of flight, no longer needing it to escape.

THE STARVATION/PREDATION TRADE-OFF

Predators can accentuate food shortage in their prey when their attacks discourage prey from feeding in places where they are at high risk, or by disturbing them so often as to reduce the time they have to feed. A person walking over a coastal mudflat can interrupt the feeding of thousands of birds, as can a Peregrine flying over. Such disturbance stops birds from feeding for a period, and if they take flight it also raises their energy expenditure. Once attacked by predators, many birds take time before they start to feed again, and then spend more time on the alert. In flocks of small birds, return times after an attack can be as little as a few minutes, but other birds stay hidden for much longer, losing precious feeding time. In extreme cases, persistent disturbance can effectively exclude birds from feeding in places they might otherwise use, thus reducing the total habitat and food available to them (Cresswell 2008). The effects of continual disturbance can be especially serious during cold weather, when birds may in any case be struggling to obtain enough to eat (McGowan et al. 2002, Stillman & Goss-Custard 2002). On short winter days, Yellowhammers reduced the time they spent looking around in order to increase the amount devoted to feeding, thereby increasing their risk of predation (van der Veen 2000). At these times, birds favour feeding over vigilance presumably because, without food, death from starvation is inevitable, but death from predation is never inevitable, because a bird may not be attacked and, if attacked, it may escape.

Food shortage might thus increase the risk of predation by forcing birds to feed in less safe places or for longer each day, or to spend less time on vigilance. Conversely, predators might increase the risk of starvation by deterring birds from feeding in food-rich sites if they are unsafe. Individuals therefore face a starvation/predation trade-off, and ignoring one may bring greater risks from the other. There is nothing surprising in this, for all animals have evolved to live with the risk of starvation, and most also with the risk of predation.

The role of food supply in influencing predation rates was confirmed incidentally during some food-provision experiments. For example, the supplementary feeding of tits in the wild led to improved overwinter survival, partly through reduced predation losses (Chapter 7). The extra food enabled birds to spend more time than otherwise in safer sites, and on vigilance behaviour, thereby reducing their predation risk (Jansson *et al.* 1981). This opens the possibility that the use of seed-feeders in gardens also reduces the feeding periods of birds, and that part of the numerical increase in some tits and finches over recent decades may be due to reduced predation in addition to increased food supply, but I know of no relevant studies.

It is not only the amount of food that influences predation risk, because birds take longer to obtain their daily needs from some kinds of food than from others, which influences their exposure times. For example, some bird species prefer to eat seeds in winter, but can also subsist on green leaves. The Grey Partridge is one such species, but it needs 24 times longer to obtain its daily ration from wheat leaves than from wheat grain (Potts 2012). At a benign 15 °C, this amounts to about six hours of feeding compared with 15 minutes, with the rest of the day in the non-breeding season mainly spent hiding in cover. In this way, feeding conditions can greatly influence predation risk. The sections below, discussing habitat use, time budgets, body condition and human disturbance, can all be considered as aspects of the starvation/predation-risk trade-off.

HABITAT USE

The structure of the habitat, and the shelter it provides, can influence the densities at which birds settle (including territory sizes), as well as their feeding efficiency and predation risks. For many bird species that both nest and forage within their territories, it is hard to evaluate the separate influences that predation risk and food supply have on habitat selection. In Grey Partridges on English farmland, the amount and disposition of cover had a marked influence on territorial spacing regardless of food supply, with pairs occupying larger areas where cover was sparse (Jenkins 1961). But for some other species in which nesting and feeding occur in different habitats, cover seems paramount in the selection of nesting places. The evidence for this view is largely indirect, in that the habitat preferences of particular species relate to cover rather than food supply, and, through reduced predation, breeding success improves with quality of nesting cover. Given a choice, some species prefer to nest in thorny or spiny vegetation, which gives more protection than other cover.

The smaller the amounts of nesting cover in any landscape, the easier it is for predators to find nests and the higher their foraging success. Increased predation on the eggs of several ground-nesting species in recent decades has been attributed to destruction of cover (Chapter 7; for Grey Partridge, see Potts 2012; for various ducks, see Greenwood *et al.* 1987). Conversely, habitat structure can influence the ability of predators to exploit their prey. For some raptor species, the presence of cover or of suitable perches in open land can facilitate prey capture. To test the idea that shortage of hunting perches limited the use of open areas by raptors, man-made perches (posts) were provided on 11 clear-cut forest areas, while 11 other areas served as controls (Widén 1994). Foraging raptors used experimental clear-cuts significantly more than control ones, and usage changed accordingly when the perches were switched between areas. By implication, perch provision increased both food availability for the raptors and predation risk for their prey.

Particular species are more likely to suffer predation in some habitats than in others. But the habitats that give most security are not necessarily those that offer most food. How then does the bird prioritise between safety on the one hand and food abundance on the other? Studies on some species have shown that, providing that individuals can get enough food for their day-to-day maintenance, they prefer safe places over dangerous ones, even though the latter may offer better feeding. Moreover, birds compete over the safer places. Such competition is evident in the relationships between species, and also between different individuals of the same species. Among feeding flocks of tits in northern Europe, the dominant Willow Tits and Crested Tits fed mainly on the insides of trees, forcing the subordinate Coal Tits and Goldcrests to the outer twigs, where the risk of predation was greater (Chapter 10). Over winter, much larger proportions of the subordinate than the dominant species were killed by Pygmy Owls, their main predator in these areas (Suhonen *et al.* 1992).

FIG 136. The Redshank *Tringa totanus* can be subject to heavy predation by Sparrowhawks *Accipiter nisus* and other raptors on winter coastlines. (Richard Chandler)

The role of competition within species can be illustrated by findings from Tyninghame Bay in the Firth of Forth, where wintering waders were frequently attacked by Sparrowhawks operating from bushes near the shoreline (Cresswell 1994, Whitfield 2003c, Cresswell & Whitfield 2008). For Redshanks, saltmarsh areas near the bushes offered more food but more chance of being killed, whereas the safer intertidal flats further out offered less food but a better chance of detecting and escaping approaching Sparrowhawks. In practice, adult Redshanks chose the distant mudflats, where predation rates were lower, whereas through competition for these more secure sites, most young Redshanks were relegated to the less safe areas offering more food. A Redshank in a food-rich area could attain twice the feeding rate as one in a food-poor area, but was five times more likely to be killed by a Sparrowhawk. It seemed that the more dangerous saltmarsh habitat was used only when the birds could not meet their energy needs on the mudflat, or when they were deterred from feeding there by more dominant individuals. This example illustrates a general point, that the quality of any feeding area is enhanced by food abundance but reduced by high predation risk.

When Sparrowhawks attacked Redshanks from shoreline bushes, their chance of making a capture declined exponentially with increasing distance from the bush out to about 30 m, beyond which there was little change in the chance of capture (or in the risk for the Redshank). Interestingly, Redshanks used areas more than 30 m from the bushes, mainly in accordance with the food they offered, preferring the most profitable areas; and it was chiefly in cold weather (below about 5 °C), with increased food needs, that Redshanks fed closer to the bushes. By avoiding proximity to bushes at other times, Redshanks shunned 26% of the available food-rich habitat (Cresswell *et al.* 2010). At night, when Redshanks could still feed, some individuals were killed in the same areas by Tawny and Long-eared Owls. So the risks of feeding near bushes held both day and night.

Redshanks fed either singly or in small flocks. When feeding near to the bushes, an individual's chance of being killed by a Sparrowhawk declined with increasing flock size; each individual gained both from the greater overall vigilance provided by a flock, and from the *dilution effect* – in that the larger the flock, the less the chance of any one individual being caught. For Redshanks, as in many other birds, there was safety in numbers.

Prevailing weather added another twist to the story (Hilton *et al.* 1999). Extreme cold resulted in Redshanks using the saltmarsh more, feeding closer to cover in order to gain access to more food. Low temperatures presumably raised the metabolic needs of Redshanks, thus increasing their willingness to accept higher predation risks in return for greater foraging success. Not surprisingly, Sparrowhawks had better hunting success in these conditions. On the other hand, Redshanks responded to rain by foraging in areas that reduced their predation risk, perhaps because rain may have made an approaching hawk harder to detect, but in these conditions Redshanks made more false-alarm flights, wasting time and energy. These findings suggested that weather may influence habitat choice through its effects on the relative risks of starvation and predation. In addition, Redshanks reacted strongly to Sparrowhawk activity, using the saltmarsh less and foraging further from cover, on days when attack rates were high.

Sparrowhawks tended to hunt Redshanks on the basis of their vulnerability, rather than their abundance (Quinn & Cresswell 2004, 2006). While the vulnerability of Redshanks decreased with increasing group size and distance from cover, grouping reduced the feeding rate of Redshanks because it led to more interference between individuals. Increased starvation risk in midwinter meant that Redshanks were forced to feed on highly profitable prey, *Orchestia* amphipods, which responded to the proximity of Redshanks by retreating into the mud beyond reach. This meant that, when feeding on *Orchestia*, Redshanks were forced to feed vulnerably, widely spaced and close to predator-concealing cover. It was these constraints – limiting the ability of Redshanks to feed in large, dense flocks away from cover – that ultimately led to their deaths. Redshanks therefore exemplified not only how predation increased through starvation risk, but also how other constraints prevented Redshanks from making the most of their anti-predation behaviour. Mortality was increased both by cold weather and by low population densities (Minderman *et al.* 2006).

Many other shorebirds of coastal mudflats prefer to feed in the open where they can see a predator approaching in time enough to flee, relying on speed and manoeuvrability. The distance from shore at which different species feed

FIG 137. When attacked by a Peregrine *Falco peregrinus*, shorebirds tend to bunch together in tight flocks, twisting and turning at high speed, confusing the predator and preventing it from singling out a victim. (Chris Knights)

apparently influences the rates at which they are killed by raptors, as shown by a study on the Banc D'Arguin in Mauritania, a huge intertidal area where many European shorebirds spend the winter (van den Hout *et al.* 2008). In this region, the main predators were three falcon species (Lanner, Barbary and Peregrine), which used the low dunes bordering the mudflats from which to launch surprise attacks on inattentive prey. Here again, shorebirds were safer in larger flocks, which tended to be attacked less often. Furthermore, species that foraged relatively close to shore and in small flocks were preyed upon more often than expected from their relative abundance. In three species, Knot, Bar-tailed Godwit and Dunlin, juveniles were more vulnerable than adults. And of the Knots, it was predominantly young birds that fed inshore, apparently excluded from the safer areas further out by competition with dominant adults. On average, juvenile Knots, using riskier habitats, were ten times more likely to be killed than adults (1% compared to 0.1% of the total present).

For many other birds of open land, cover represents a threat that could conceal predators. Such species may increase their vigilance, and hence lower their food intake, when feeding close to cover (Metcalfe 1984). In one study, wintering Skylarks preferred to feed in the middle of fields, and only when food was depleted there did they move closer to hedgerows (Robinson & Sutherland 1999).

Some birds of open country avoid nesting near hedgerows or trees which might harbour predators such as crows, which often watch from treetops. This is true, for example, for Lapwings nesting in farmland, and in one study nests that were more than 50 m from a field boundary survived better than nests that were closer (Sheldon *et al.* 2007). Two ground-nesting passerines, the Skylark and Yellow Wagtail, were also found to experience higher rates of nest predation with increased proximity to field boundaries, although the exact nature of the relationship differed between species and, in the case of the Skylark, also with boundary type (Morris & Gilroy 2008). Most nest losses were attributable to predation. In one year, video cameras deployed at Skylark nests showed that all recorded predation was by mammals of various species, and that these were most active in or around grassy field margins. In general, then, these ground-nesting species of open land do best in wide open landscapes devoid of trees and shrubs.

Cover and escape behaviour

In open landscapes, cover can be either dangerous (allowing predators to sneak up unseen), or protective (providing a refuge from predators), depending on the species and its escape responses. Some bird species, such as House Sparrows, rely for escape on dashing into cover. Such species seldom forage far from cover, and distant food may be unavailable to them. The proportion of time they spent on vigilance was found to increase with distance from cover, which reduced their food-intake rates and again rendered parts of the habitat unusable (Barnard 1979, 1980, Caraco *et al.* 1980, Elgar 1989). This interaction between habitat structure and predation pressure can limit the proportion of habitat that birds can exploit, and effectively limit their numbers below what the total potential food supply would permit. It provides another example of focal-point exploitation of widespread food supplies.

With the depletion of food near to cover, competition may become more intense, forcing some birds to feed further from cover and increasing the numbers caught by predators. In an area in northeast Scotland, Bullfinches normally fed close to bushy cover, venturing further away mainly in December–February, when they sought heather seed on open moorland (Marquiss 2007). At these times, when far from the cover of trees, they fed in much larger groups than usual. To judge from plucked remains of Bullfinches killed by Sparrowhawks, this was the main period of predation on full-grown birds. These seasonal patterns of foraging behaviour and predation suggested that Bullfinches were vulnerable when a limited choice of food obliged them to feed far from cover. In the presence of their predators, therefore, Bullfinches seemed limited as much by landscape structure as by the abundance of key food-plants.

FIG 138. The Bullfinch *Pyrrhula pyrrhula* obtains most of its food within or near the cover of trees and bushes, but ventures further from cover at times of shortage. (Alan Martin)

These findings supported the idea that changes in the status of Bullfinches in southern England from the 1950s to the 1990s could have been caused indirectly by changes in the status of Sparrowhawks (themselves resulting from changes in the use of organochlorine pesticides). When Sparrowhawks disappeared from most of southeast Britain during the organochlorine era, Bullfinches became very numerous, and were often seen far from cover on open land, where they could feed without serious risk of predation (Newton 1967). But in later years, as Sparrowhawks returned, Bullfinches again became restricted to feeding within a few metres of cover and declined in numbers. In this way, by influencing the distance from cover that Bullfinches were prepared to feed, Sparrowhawks could have indirectly affected the amount of food available to them in winter, and hence their numbers. It is a situation in which change in cover, food or predation could have influenced Bullfinch numbers. Other work had indicated that Bullfinches were limited by winter food, at least in woodland (Newton 1967).

In an experiment, peanut-laden feeders were placed at different distances from a hedgerow, and their use was monitored by the rate of food removal (Cowie & Simons 1991). Total food consumption at feeders close to cover was double that at feeders only 7.5 m away from cover. House Sparrows fed only near cover, Blue Tits mainly near cover, but Greenfinches fed frequently at greater distances, though still relied on cover for escape. To examine the effect of dominance hierarchies on predation risk, Hinsley *et al.* (1995) examined the ages and sexes of Great and Blue Tits visiting two peanut feeders placed at different distances from cover, along with the success of Sparrowhawk attacks. One feeder was hung 6 m from a thick hawthorn bush, largely impenetrable to Sparrowhawks, and another was hung from some open birches easily penetrated by Sparrowhawks and 49 m from the nearest safe cover. The two feeders were 55 m apart. The study was continued over two winters, and samples of tits were caught at both feeders using mist nests. In both species, juveniles were subordinate to adults. Combining the results from both species in both years, 40% of tits trapped at the

Great Tits *Parus major* and Blue Tits *Cyanistes caeruleus* prefer to use feeders hung near cover, into which they flee on the approach of a Sparrowhawk *Accipiter nisus*. (Jill Pakenham)

feeder close to cover were adults, compared with only 17% at the feeder further from cover. No difference in sex ratio was noted between birds at the two feeders. Of 62 Sparrowhawk attacks observed at the feeder near cover, only three (5%) resulted in the capture of a tit, while of 52 attacks seen at the feeder far from cover, at least 11 (21%) resulted in a capture, and another 13 (25%) resulted in a chase which may have ended in an unseen capture. In other words, adult tits fed mainly at the safe feeder, where Sparrowhawk attacks were rarely successful, while subordinate juveniles were mainly relegated to the more exposed feeder, where Sparrowhawk attacks were much more often successful.

Studies on Willow Tits in Norway also showed that feeding site and anti-predator behaviour were related to social rank (Hogstad 1988). Three winter groups were studied, each of six birds, including an adult pair, two juvenile males and two juvenile females, with the following dominance order: adult male > juvenile male 1 > juvenile male 2 > adult female > juvenile female 1 > juvenile female 2. The proportion of time these birds spent scanning for predators increased with distance from cover, and at any given distance adults scanned more than juveniles. Given a choice of feeders placed at one, three, five, ten and 20 metres from the forest edge, the tits preferred feeders closer to cover. Low-ranking individuals used feeders further from cover because higher-ranking ones prevented them from using closer feeders. When only the 10 m and 20 m feeders were baited, only low-rank juveniles visited them, subordinate females more than subordinate males. These juveniles increased their use of exposed feeders during very cold periods, suggesting that they were prepared to take greater risks then. In addition, after birds at a feeder were exposed to a stuffed predator, the sequence with which they returned to the feeder was correlated with dominance status, with the juveniles first, indicating that, in their need for food, they took greater risks than the adults. These experiments clearly showed the importance of dominance status in competition for safer feeding sites.

Flocking, vigilance and vulnerability

As indicated above, the need for vigilance in the presence of predators is influenced by flocking, as well as by habitat structure. Many birds spend less time on scanning when feeding in flocks than when feeding alone, benefiting from the wariness of others. Vigilance behaviour was studied in 123 radio-tagged Grey Partridges at 20 English farmland sites that differed in habitat structure and predation risk (mainly from raptors, especially Sparrowhawks) (Watson et al. 2007a). Partridges suffered least predation when they were in larger groups, and in more open habitat with short vegetation, where they could both feed efficiently and detect approaching predators in time to react. Individual Partridges spent more time on the alert when they were in small groups or in tall vegetation, as opposed to larger groups or short vegetation. This extra vigilance reduced predation, but did not prevent it altogether. It was in late winter and early spring that Partridges suffered most predation from raptors, after they had switched from coveys to individual pairs spaced across the landscape, and when cover was at its seasonal low. Having given up the advantage of group-living, the birds were then at their most conspicuous and vulnerable. Only when crop vegetation was tall enough to give canopy cover did vigilance against raptors become largely unnecessary.[15]

By reducing the need for individual vigilance, flocking can also increase feeding rates, providing that the birds, feeding close together, do not interfere with one another. Among Goldfinches, the rate of individual food intake was found to increase markedly with group size, at least up to eight individuals. Birds in groups of eight or more ate over twice as many seeds per minute as singletons. Usually the birds fed among tall herbs where visibility was limited, but when feeding in more open sites, such as freshly mown fields, group-feeding individuals increased their feeding rate even further, sometimes up to seven times the solitary feeding rate (Glück 1986). Relationships between scanning and group size have been noted in many other bird species (Barnard 1979, Benkman 1997), as have relationships between scanning, cover and visibility, with birds spending more time on the alert in places where their visibility was restricted (Metcalfe 1984, Whittingham et al. 2004). This is another way in which the risk of predation, interacting with habitat structure and group size, influences feeding rate and hence starvation risk.

---

15 Not all vigilance in birds can be attributed to anti-predator behaviour, as some territorial species also spend much time scanning for intruders, driving away any individuals of their own species that encroach on their territories. This behaviour is common in territory-holding Grey Partridges even in areas with very few predators (Jenkins 1961), although in many situations territorial birds presumably watch for predators and conspecific intruders at the same time. Other species, including crows, shrikes and raptors, can watch for predators, intruders and prey items at the same time.

The main benefits of flocking (more eyes on the job and the dilution of capture chances) also accrue from feeding in mixed flocks with other species, but the mutual benefits are not always equal. Some species are naturally more vigilant than others, or feed in situations that offer a better view, and some are more easily caught than others. Other things being equal, the ideal partner species in mixed flocking would be one that is both more vigilant and more easily caught.

A close association between Dunlin and Golden Plover was noticed long ago, with the Dunlin referred to as the 'plover's page' (Thompson & Thompson 1985). This association was apparent even in the breeding season, when observations revealed that the Dunlin used the plover for early warning (rather than the other way round), and that individual Dunlin spent less time on vigilance when feeding near plovers than near other Dunlins. As another example, Black-headed Gulls, Lapwings and Golden Plovers were studied as they fed together in winter pastures. The gulls usually responded to approaching danger soonest, thereby alerting the plovers, and when gulls did not take off the plovers remained feeding. However, while the plovers gained from the greater vigilance of the gulls, they incurred a cost through food-robbing (Thompson & Barnard 1983).

The fact that several factors can influence the vulnerability of a species to predation was shown by attacks of trained Goshawks on Woodpigeons, in which flock size, habitat, time of day and physical condition all played a role (Kenward 2006). From 74 attacks on flocks, 19% resulted in a capture, whereas from 18 attacks on single pigeons 78% were successful. Attack success decreased with increase in flock size, chiefly because pigeons in large flocks detected the hawk and took flight earlier. The amount of cover in the habitat affected attack success because pigeons feeding in short-grass fields usually detected the hawk and took off earlier than those feeding in taller crops, such as kale. In addition, attacks were about three times more successful in the last hour before sunset than earlier in the day, possibly because the pigeons were feeding hard then to fill their own crops before roost, and were less airworthy with full crops. Also, pigeons caught by surprise on the ground, or soon after take-off, showed no difference in body weight from birds shot from flocks, whereas pigeons caught after a chase were usually in poorer condition, emaciated or diseased, being caught because they were unable to keep up with the flock. It was in a chase attack that the body condition of the prey made a difference to its chance of being caught.

While many Woodpigeons caught by Goshawks were in poor condition following a chase, this was not true of Pheasants, which had different escape tactics, dependent on a quick run into cover. In this situation, the success rate of Goshawks increased with the distance of the Pheasant from cover, so the pressure on Pheasants was to feed as close to cover as possible. On an estate

where Pheasants were reared in large numbers, they seldom fed more than
10 m from cover, and only 4% of 79 Goshawk kills were more than 5 m from
cover. In this situation, there was no chance for a flying chase in which selection
for weakness might have occurred (Kenward 1977). Female Pheasants, being
much smaller than males, were easier for Goshawks to kill and were apparently
favoured where an abundant choice was available. However, where Pheasants
were sparse, Goshawks took whichever sex they could get.

In general, then, in their escape tactics, one can divide many birds into either
cover-dependent or cover-shunning (open-land) species. The former are reluctant
to venture far from cover to feed, and they suffer from food depletion near cover
but experience greater predation further away, as exemplified by House Sparrows,
Bullfinches, Pheasants and others discussed above. The cover-shunning species
feed for preference in the open, and as food is depleted they move closer to cover,
where predation risk is greater; to escape predation they rely either on crypsis
and 'freezing' (such as Skylark, Meadow Pipit and Wheatear) or on early detection,
agility and speed (such as many shorebirds). Different predators exploit different
situations, with Sparrowhawks and Goshawks posing the greatest threats to
birds near cover, and falcons and harriers to birds in the open. In the absence
of predators, all these prey species could probably exploit a much greater
proportion of the landscape than they do in the presence of predators. Reduced
predation risk is a situation that many species in Britain and Ireland experienced

FIG 140. The Meadow Pipit *Anthus pratensis* nests in the open, away from trees or bushes,
and usually 'freezes' on the approach of a predator, remaining motionless and relying on
its camouflage to avoid detection. Similar behaviour is shown by other birds of open land,
including the Skylark *Alauda arvensis* and Wheatear *Oenanthe oenanthe*. (Keith Kirk)

from the mid-nineteenth century into the mid-twentieth century, when predators were greatly reduced over much of the landscape by gamekeepers.

It may be misleading to divide all species neatly into cover-dependent and cover-shunning, because some species can switch their behaviour according to the risks involved. Living entirely on the ground, Grey Partridges change their behaviour between day and night, in line with the activity rhythms of different predators. During the day, Partridges spend as much time under the canopy of tall herbaceous cover as feeding needs permit, hiding from raptors which hunt by sight. But at night, when raptors are inactive, Partridges roost away from cover far out in short-vegetation fields, where they can best detect approaching Foxes, which hunt largely by scent (Potts 2012). Among isolated pairs, male and female lie side by side, but head-to-tail, to give all-round visibility. If food permits, Partridges squeeze their feeding into the two switch-over periods, around dawn and dusk, times when both day and night predators are least active. It seems that predation avoidance largely governs their daily lives.

Habitat and predation

The nature of habitat can thus influence the vulnerability of prey, because it affects the ability of the prey to hide, to detect an approaching predator or to escape if attacked. Levels of predation can change, even if predator numbers remain constant, when habitats are modified in ways that make prey more or less vulnerable. Various such structural changes have occurred on farmland in recent decades, and have been suggested as one cause of declines in some farmland birds. Many species are known to have higher nest success in dense than sparse cover, and the general tidying up and more intensive use of the countryside over recent decades has clearly reduced the amount of nesting cover available to some species, not least by the removal of hedges and other field boundaries. Restriction of habitat area can lead to increasing nest density in remaining patches. For example, Grey Partridges nest mainly in field boundary vegetation, and the smaller the amount of field boundary per unit area of farmland, the more concentrated are the Partridge nests. With reduced habitat to search, these nests are more readily found by Foxes and other predators. Other species which nest on open ground, such as Lapwing and Stone-curlew, often concentrate on patches of fallow land, raising the nest density above what would occur if more of the total spring landscape were fallow, as occurred in the past. Moreover, those Skylarks which attempt to use winter-sown crops tend to nest in the sparser vegetation along tractor tramlines, and consequently suffer high predation rates, possibly because predators such as Foxes hunt along the tramlines (Donald *et al.* 2002). All these examples show the role of vegetation structure in influencing habitat selection and predation risk.

Landscapes of contoured predation risk

By their mere presence, then, predators may limit the distributions of some bird species, which avoid areas of high risk, and thus surrender part of their resource base, whether food or nest-sites which would otherwise be available. For part of each year, the breeding sites of predators may increase predation risk nearby, with obvious effects on the distributions and numbers of their prey. Several bird species have been found to settle at lower density near to raptor nests than further away. One example concerns Kestrels in western Finland, for which nesting locations in open farmland were pre-determined by the provision of nest-boxes (Suhonen *et al.* 1994). Kestrels were summer visitors to the area, hunting small birds (as well as rodents), mostly within 1 km of their nests. Small migrant bird species that arrived after the Kestrels settled at lower density near Kestrel nests than further away, the pattern being especially marked in Skylarks. But no such pattern occurred in small resident species that were already settled when the Kestrels arrived, or in larger species unaffected by Kestrels. Similar avoidance of the vicinity of Merlin nests by songbirds was noted in Canada (Sodhi *et al.* 1990), of Peregrine nests by various songbirds in Greenland (Meese & Fuller 1989), of Sparrowhawk nests by songbirds in Finland (Forsman & Mönkkönen 2001, Thomson *et al.* 2006), of various predator nests by meadow birds in the Netherlands (van der Vleit *et al.* 2008), and of Great Grey Shrike nests by Skylarks and Whinchats in Poland (Hromada *et al.* 2002). But these observations did not reveal whether any songbirds were prevented from breeding altogether by the presence of predators or whether they simply settled elsewhere. They did indicate, however, that predators, by their mere presence, lowered the attractiveness of certain localities, and thus influenced local prey densities.

In a further study, the settlement patterns of summer-visiting Pied Flycatchers were examined in central Sweden in relation to the locations of diurnally hunting Pygmy Owls (80% songbirds in diet) and nocturnally hunting Tengmalm's Owls (36% songbirds in diet). Flycatchers strongly avoided Pygmy Owls, occupying 42% of nest-boxes in areas with Pygmy Owls, against 92% of boxes in areas lacking Pygmy Owls, but no difference was apparent with Tengmalm's Owls (80% and 80% respectively). This finding suggested that Flycatchers distinguished between the two predators, avoiding the dangerous Pygmy Owl, but paying little attention to the less dangerous Tengmalm's Owl (Morosinotto *et al.* 2010). Those flycatchers that did nest near Pygmy Owls took longer to build their nests than others, showed an average 4-day delay in egg-laying, and laid smaller clutches (controlling for lay date). No such delay or reduced clutch size was seen in flycatchers nesting near Tengmalm's Owls.

Predators do not necessarily breed in the same localities every year, and their movements can bring about changes in the spatial settling of prey species. In a three-year study, occupation of Red-backed Shrike territories in Sweden increased with distance from the nearest Magpie nest (Roos & Pärt 2004). Over the three years, changes in the distribution of Magpies and Hooded Crows affected the spatial distribution of occupied shrike territories. This contrasts with the situation described in the previous chapter, in which some bird species actually prefer to nest near predators, if by so doing they gain protection from other more significant predators.

Nest-sites and predators

To protect their nests from predators, some bird species rely on camouflage, others on dense cover, and yet others on relatively inaccessible sites, such as high trees or cliffs, which give security at least against some mammalian predators. However, species that normally use only secure sites sometimes use less safe sites in areas that lack mammalian predators. Consider for example Peregrines, not as predators but as prey. Throughout their range, Peregrines nest mainly on cliffs, which protect them from mammalian predators, including humans. But in areas where natural predators and people are few, Peregrines will accept lesser crags, earth slopes or even low mounds on flat ground or in bogs (Newton 1979). In recent years, Peregrines in Britain have occasionally nested on slopes or level ground, but the habit has not persisted, presumably because such nests usually fail through predation. It is seemingly the risk of predation that restricts the variety of places where Peregrines are prepared to nest, and thus limits their distribution and numbers.

The nest-site preferences of other raptors are also related to predation risks, with species accepting ground sites only where mammalian predators pose no threat (Newton 1979). The minimum requirements of security sometimes change with time as disturbance and predation pressures change. In some parts of the world, Ospreys nest on the ground on offshore islands lacking mammalian predators, but they disappeared from a treeless island off California following its colonisation by Coyotes (Newton 1979). Individuals in many populations occasionally attempt to nest in less safe sites but seldom succeed. But if they do succeed, the habit might then spread and lead to local expansion in distribution and density. For example, among Kestrels on Orkney, the first ground nest was recorded in 1945. The habit then spread rapidly and, once a site was established it remained in continuous occupation so that, by 1955, 19 such sites were known, all in tall heather, in cracks in banks or Rabbit holes (Balfour 1955). This enabled Kestrels to occupy areas not otherwise available, and thereby increase their numbers.

FIG 141. Kestrels *Falco tinnunculus* usually nest high on cliffs or trees, but on islands lacking mammalian predators they also nest on the ground, as occurred commonly on Orkney in the mid-twentieth century. (Peter Beasley)

Almost certainly, the same applies to other birds (see also Chapter 5). Many species that nest high on cliffs or trees in mainland Britain, including Hooded Crows, Grey Herons, Buzzards and others, often nest on the ground on offshore islands that lack mammalian predators. Similarly, on the Dutch island of Vleiland, despite its 300 ha of pine plantations, some Woodpigeons, Stock Doves, Kestrels, Great Tits and Redstarts nest on the ground (Spaans & Swennen 1968). Yet on the nearby mainland, where mammalian predators are numerous, all these bird species nest entirely in trees.

There are thus indications that the types of nest-site used by particular bird species are not fixed, and that minimum requirements (in terms of security) can alter in response to changes in disturbance and predation pressures (Chapter 5). In this indirect sense, mammalian predators are responsible for restricting the breeding density of their avian prey species in areas where safe sites are scarce, for if it were not for their predators, many bird species might accept less safe sites, and thereby breed in greater numbers.

Seabirds provide more examples, nesting on offshore islands partly to avoid mammalian predators. However, many islands are now unsuitable for certain species because they have been colonised by introduced rats and other predators, which eat the eggs and chicks. But on islands where such predators have been removed, seabirds have returned, reacting rapidly to the changed conditions (Chapter 7). Once again, the implication is that predators can influence prey distributions, and thereby limit their overall population levels, even though not a single adult in a secure site may die of predation.

While some bird species rely on nesting in safe places to raise their young under reduced predation risk, other species rely on camouflage, distraction displays or other defence behaviour. However, these strategies also carry risks: camouflage means that the female must sit tight – so tight that she risks being caught on the nest – while distraction and defence behaviour carry similar risks because they involve closer proximity to a predator than usual.

In many bird species, individuals are more likely to change their nesting places after a nest failure than after a success – the failure indicating that the site is unsafe (Newton 2008). After persistent predation of their eggs and chicks, ground-nesting colonial birds, such as terns, sometimes shift en masse to a new site, and in time these continual shifts can lead to a build-up of birds in the safest places, as less secure sites are progressively abandoned. Instead of being widely distributed in scattered small colonies, the species becomes concentrated in a small number of bigger safer colonies. Such a process occurred among terns and gulls suddenly exposed to predation by introduced American Mink on various islands off western Scotland. Following a Mink eradication scheme, the larger recently formed colonies began to disband, and former smaller colony sites were re-formed (Chapter 7). Presumably the concentration of so many birds in a few safe places brings disadvantages, such as increased competition for local food supplies, longer commuting distances to former foraging areas, or increased parasitism. Nevertheless, it exemplifies how predation pressure can alter the distribution and behaviour of a population, with possible repercussions on the action of other limiting factors.

Another form of interaction between habitat and predation involves the apparent long-term memory of predators. During a study of Tengmalm's Owls, the risk of nest predation by Pine Martens was related to the age of the nest-box, and was higher in boxes where the previous nest was preyed upon than in boxes where the previous nest was successful. Sonerud (1993) relocated a randomly selected half of a sample of 12-year-old boxes, and then some years later relocated the other half. In both cases, predation on owl nests was significantly reduced in the relocated boxes but unchanged in the unmoved ones (22% vs. 83%). He thought that Pine Martens remembered nest-sites where they had found a meal. The same phenomenon may explain why Black Woodpeckers that excavated a new cavity suffered lower nest predation than those that re-used an old cavity from the previous year (Nilsson et al. 1991). These findings imply that, when nest-sites are sufficiently plentiful to enable individuals to move around, predation may be lower than when such sites are less abundant, forcing birds to re-use the same sites year after year. This is equivalent to the situation involving the build-up of arthropod parasites in frequently used nest-sites (Chapter 8). It is not enough for nest-sites to be sufficient for users; they must be much more than sufficient if the rates of predation and parasitism are to be kept low.

TIME BUDGETS AND CHICK NEGLECT

In the breeding season, food shortage can lead to predation of chicks by causing adults to spend more time foraging rather than guarding their young. This has been seen in such diverse species as raptors, gulls, skuas, crows and smaller passerines. When supplementary food was placed near the nests of Magpies and Carrion Crows, larger numbers of young were raised than at other nests, not because the young were better fed, but because they suffered less predation (Yom-Tov 1974, Högstedt 1981; Chapter 3). The extra food enabled the parents to spend more time near the nest, better placed to protect their chicks against raids by other birds. In such cases, then, food shortage and predation can again interact to influence nest success or survival. Similarly, adult Guillemots do not normally leave their chicks unattended, at least one parent usually being present. Yet in 2007, when food was very scarce at some North Sea colonies, both partners of many pairs foraged simultaneously. With half the nests left unattended, unprecedented numbers of chicks were killed by neighbouring Guillemots (Ashbrook et al. 2008). Chick losses in similar circumstances have also been described among gulls and skuas (Oswald et al. 2008). When sandeels were in short supply, Arctic Skuas spent longer away from their territories, searching widely for feeding opportunities, and were thus less able to defend their chicks against others of their species, as well as Great Skuas. Their breeding success was thereby much reduced (Caldow & Furness 2000, Davis et al. 2005). Although colonial breeding is normally considered advantageous for seabirds, scarcity of food exposes the disadvantages.

Long parental absence is not the only means by which food shortage is translated into greater predation of chicks. When they are hungry, nestling birds tend to beg more, creating more noise and thereby drawing attention to themselves (for Great Tit, see Perrins 1979; for Magpie, see Redondo & Castro 1992; for Corn Bunting see Brickle et al. 2000). The young of precocial species get their own food, but when hungry they tend to move around more in search of it, becoming more visible to predators. This has been repeatedly shown in gallinaceous gamebirds (Green 1984, Warner 1984, Rands 1986), and also in waterfowl (Hunter et al. 1984) and waders, including Oystercatchers (Ens et al. 1995). In one study, Eider ducklings were often eaten by Herring Gulls, but in numbers that varied greatly from year to year; in some years practically all the ducklings were swallowed during their first ten days of life (Swennen 1989). It transpired that gull predation was heaviest in years when the small ducklings were already weakened by food shortage, partly because they did not then respond appropriately to alarm signals from the adult females. Similar correlations occur between the condition of young birds and their susceptibility to parasites (Chapter 13).

BODY CONDITION AND FAT CONTENT

Apart from behaviour, which is the most immediate way in which birds can cope with predation risk, individuals can also adjust their body composition. While feeding during the day, small birds lay down body-fat for use overnight, typically carrying more fat in winter when nights are longer and colder (Evans 1969, Newton 1969, Biebach 1996). For any given temperature, the greater its fat reserve, the longer a bird can resist starvation. However, extra body reserves have costs, one of which is reduced flight efficiency, which in some species could increase predation risk. Among small birds exposed to simulated raptor attacks, even slight differences in body weight reduced the take-off angle, acceleration and manoeuvrability during flight (Witter *et al.* 1994). Blackcaps in captivity were exposed to simulated predator attacks and filmed as they attempted to flee. It was found that individuals carrying a fuel load equivalent to 66% of lean body mass (the most recorded in this species) suffered a reduction of 32% in angle of ascent and 17% in velocity compared with lean Blackcaps (Kullberg *et al.* 1996). Adverse effects of migratory fattening on flight performance have also been recorded in captive Robins, Sedge Warblers and other species exposed experimentally to simulated predator attacks (Lind *et al.* 1999, Kullberg *et al.* 2000). During the course of a single day, in experimental conditions, a typical 7% gain in body weight caused a 30% increase in the time taken for a small bird to reach cover (Metcalfe & Ure 1995). Another cost of body-fat is the extra time and energy needed to maintain it and to carry it around, for which fat birds need to feed more.

Because fat reserves have costs as well as benefits, the levels found in individuals could represent another trade-off between the risks of starvation and predation (Lima 1986, McNamara & Houston 1990). In poor foraging environments (with low or unpredictable food availability), birds would be expected to have higher body mass owing to fat reserves accumulated as protection against increased starvation risk. On the other hand, under frequent attack by predators, birds would be expected to have reduced fat levels so as to increase their likelihood of escape. Birds can reduce their chance of capture either by feeding in safe places where there is little chance of being attacked or, if they are forced to feed in unsafe places, by reducing their risk of capture when attacked. It is this situation which favours reduced body mass. In the absence of predation risk, much of the cost of high body mass is removed, and birds can therefore be heavier (as found for example on predator-free islands, or at times when local predators are absent: MacLeod & Gosler 2006).

Remarkably, during a 15-year period when Sparrowhawks were absent from southeast England (through pesticide poisoning), Great Tits in that region became significantly heavier (fatter) (Fig. 142). When hawks recovered in numbers the tits became significantly lighter again (Gosler *et al.* 1995). These changes were evident in the body-weight values for Great Tits submitted by bird-ringers from many different localities. But no such changes occurred in Great Tits in western districts where Sparrowhawks were present throughout, nor in a second species, the Wren, which was less often killed by hawks. Again the implication was that tits regulated their own fat contents at some compromise level, depending on the relative risks of starvation and predation. Assessing whether starvation or predation is the major cause of winter mortality in small birds is therefore not always straightforward. Individuals could die of predation because, to protect themselves against starvation, they reduced vigilance to feed harder or accumulated extra body-fat which made them less manoeuvrable in a chase.

The effect of experimentally altering the perceived (but not the actual) risk of predation on the fat reserves of wild Great Tits was studied at a winter feeding

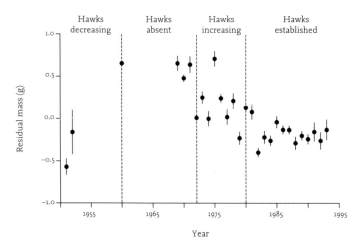

FIG 142. Changes in the body mass of Great Tits *Parus major* in Wytham Wood, Oxford, 1951–93. Points shown are means and standard errors, after correction for body size, time of day and ambient temperature. Great Tits were significantly heavier during the years when Sparrowhawks *Accipiter nisus* were absent. (From Gosler *et al.* 1995)

site (Gentle & Gosler 2001). The perceived predation risk was alternated between 'safe' and 'risky'. Increasing the perceived risk of predation from 'safe' to 'risky' involved 'swooping' a model Sparrowhawk over the feeder at four unpredictable times each day, using a remote mechanism. The experiment appeared successful in altering the perceived risk of predation, because Great Tits carried significantly reduced fat reserves during the 'risky' treatment. Furthermore, dominant individuals reduced their reserves more than subordinates. As birds returned to feeders within seconds after a mock predator 'attack', the reduction in fat reserves could not be attributed to an interruption in feeding.

Beginning with the widespread colonisation of cities by Sparrowhawks from the 1980s, urban House Sparrows showed reduced body mass (MacLeod et al. 2006). While lessening their vulnerability to predation, this change may have increased their vulnerability to starvation; but whatever the underlying cause, House Sparrows have declined greatly in numbers over recent decades, in towns as well as countryside (Chapter 7). Change in body weight in relation to changing predation pressure is not just a feature of small songbirds. The midwinter body weights of Golden Plovers in the Netherlands were found to have declined over a 20-year period, which coincided with an increase in the numbers of Peregrines and Goshawks, the main predators of wintering plovers (Piersma et al. 2003).

If body reserves are viewed as a compromise between the risks of starvation and predation, several puzzling facts about the fat levels of small birds can be more readily explained. These include the tendencies for birds to carry less body-fat at times of year when food is plentiful than at times when food is scarce, for fat reserves to increase with reducing day-lengths (and lengthening nights), to increase with reducing temperatures and reducing predictability of food supplies, as found in many species (Biebach 1996). It also explains why subordinate juvenile birds (which have most difficulty in obtaining food) often carry more fat than dominant adults in the same areas (as found in Great Tits and others: Gosler 1996). Competing with dominant adults, juvenile birds cannot always be sure of getting enough food, so an extra body reserve could help. In similar vein, among Coal Tits caught in winter, transient individuals were found to carry more fat than residents, a result expected because residents have priority of access to food sources and better knowledge of where they are (Broggi & Brotons 2001). It is not just reduced access to food that matters, but also interrupted feeding, as submissive individuals may gain access to food only at long and irregular intervals, another factor favouring large fat reserves.

Using data collected by bird-ringers from 11 different regions of Britain over nine years, the winter body masses of Starlings were examined in relation to measures of starvation risk, predation risk and population trend (MacLeod *et al.* 2008). Mean body mass varied as predicted, being lower in circumstances when foraging conditions were judged more favourable and when predation risk was higher. Regional populations that were declining the most steeply had higher body mass, which was taken as indicative of a poor foraging environment, leading to lower relative survival. It may seem counterintuitive that birds declining in numbers owing to declining food supply should show higher-than-usual body weights; but this is what the findings from many species now show, and it is explicable on the basis of starvation/predation risk management. Obviously, these relationships could not hold once starvation had set in, but in small birds the time between health and death from starvation spans at most a few hours, so that starving birds are seldom represented in samples of trapped individuals. For the most part, the weights obtained from trapped birds can be considered 'normal', and not representative of starving individuals.

The importance of unpredictability in food supply was shown experimentally in captive Knots which were offered food either on a continuous basis or at random moments in time (Piersma & van Gils 2011). These feeding regimes were maintained for about ten weeks and gave clear-cut results: Knots that had food continuously available were always about 5 g (3–4%) lighter than Knots whose food was taken away unpredictably, at irregular intervals.

If birds had to feed all day to get enough food, they would have little choice in their feeding times. But if they could meet their food needs in only a part of the day, they could choose when to feed. Starvation risk could then be minimised by gaining mass in the morning, thus ensuring against unpredictable feeding conditions later in the day, while predation risk could be minimised by remaining light and agile for most of the day, and feeding mainly in the evening just before roost. This matter was examined in Blackbirds on the basis of around 17,000 body weights obtained over a period of years by bird-ringers who recorded dates, times of day and other details (MacLeod *et al.* 2005a). In the short days of winter, when food was relatively scarce, most of the daily weight increase did indeed occur in the morning, with little further rise in the afternoon, as expected on a strategy of minimising starvation risk. However, under the longer days of August–November, the birds showed two periods of mass gain, one soon after dawn and a bigger one just before dusk, which was deemed consistent with minimising predation risk. It seemed that the pattern of daily fattening changed with the seasons in line with the expected change in relative risks. In a further study, an automated identification and weighing system was used to monitor the body mass of wild Great Tits at feeders, while simultaneously manipulating their perceived predation risk using a model Sparrowhawk (MacLeod *et al.* 2005b). The tits were found to alter their pattern of daily feeding in response to heightened predation risk, delaying mass gain until later in the day. But such flexibility is possible only where food is sufficiently plentiful to allow birds choice in when they feed. An earlier study of Bullfinches showed that, from autumn to spring, weight gain occurred at a similar rate throughout the day, so perhaps Bullfinches had to feed more consistently through the daylight hours to obtain their daily needs (Newton 1969). They also fed near cover, which offered more protection from Sparrowhawks.

In preparation for long migratory flights, birds can accumulate much bigger fat reserves than in winter, bringing additional predation risks. Striking effects of migratory fattening on flight performance have been measured in captive Blackcaps, Sedge Warblers, Robins and other migrants exposed to simulated predator attacks (Kullberg et al. 1996, 2000, Lind et al. 1999).

Not all birds suffer from extra weight, however, because not all depend on agility to escape predation. For example, Wheatears simply hide behind a stone when a hawk passes, or 'freeze' to avoid detection. On seeing a Sparrowhawk, Wheatears studied on Heligoland Island remained 'frozen' for between 1 and 17 minutes, but occasionally for up to 33 minutes. They thereby avoided predation but lost potential feeding time, which reduced their fattening rates (Schmaljohann & Dierschke 2005). In this situation, lighter Wheatears were significantly more likely to be captured than heavier ones, possibly because the lighter ones were feeding harder and were less watchful (Dierschke 2003). Similar patterns were found in 11 species of other migratory songbirds stopping on Heligoland: the body weights of individuals caught by local cats or raptors were lower than those of birds trapped for ringing purposes (Dierschke 2003). Of those birds that had been ringed and weighed already, the cat victims were among the lightest 20% of their species at the time of ringing. The lightest individuals were most vulnerable to predation, probably again because they took more risks, spending less time on vigilance or feeding in less safe places. In another study, it was noted that falcons caught the lighter individuals from among wader flocks (Bijlsma 1990).

The relationships discussed so far were based primarily on correlations, with occasional field experiments (e.g. Gentle & Gosler 2001, MacLeod et al. 2005b), but studies on captive birds have revealed that birds can change not only their fat levels in response to predation risk, but also their muscle mass, as measured using an ultrasound device. In an indoor experiment, Turnstones were exposed to daily but unpredictable disturbances by either a gliding Sparrowhawk model or a Black-headed Gull model (van den Hout et al. 2006). Over a few days, the birds increased their pectoral muscle mass upon exposure to the raptor and decreased their muscle mass on exposure to the gull (van den

Hout *et al.* 2006). The same experiment on Knots showed that over a few days this species responded to exposure to the model raptor by reduced body mass, rather than by increased muscle mass, retaining a more or less constant pectoral muscle mass. This difference between species could be linked to their different feeding habitats. Turnstones that feed on the shore need speed to get away, and larger muscles enable the birds to accelerate rapidly from a surprise attack by a Sparrowhawk approaching from cover. In contrast, Knots on the open mudflats need agility to escape. They have more time between detection and attack, and acceleration may not be their first priority: they cluster together, performing synchronised erratic flights that confuse an approaching predator, and this behaviour requires high turning manoeuvrability. Under these conditions, it is better to reduce body mass, since being lighter reduces inertia, allowing tighter turning angles (van den Hout *et al.* 2010). It seems that flight efficiency to escape predators means different things to different prey species, according to their mode of escape, and they can adjust their body structure accordingly. But of course, there are always trade-offs that could increase their starvation risk.

A starving bird uses first its fat reserves, then its body protein, which it can get from different organs. Should it sacrifice its flight capacities or its food-processing capacities, or both at the same time? Analysing the composition of 103 Knot bodies provided an answer for this species (Dietz & Piersma 2007). These birds had all been collected in the Netherlands in winter, and had either died from starvation during severe weather or from accidents during normal weather. All organs measured (gizzard, liver, intestines, pectoral muscles, leg muscles) were smaller in the starved birds than in the non-starved ones, but the reductions were much greater in the pectoral muscles (roughly 60% decline) than in the gizzard (21% decline), especially with respect to the reduction in total body mass (33%). In fact, the starved birds had gizzards just big enough to balance energy income with energy expenditure on a daily basis. So the capacity to process food at this stage appeared more important than preventing capture and being eaten. This made sense for the reason mentioned earlier, that impaired escape abilities need not lead to death so long as there is no successful predator attack, but reducing digestive capacity would surely lead to death.

The findings presented above strongly imply that birds can somehow manage their body weights and body composition according to a continually changing balance between perceived starvation and predation risks. How they assess these risks, or make these adjustments in body composition, is as yet unknown; but despite such adjustments, many birds still die from starvation or predation, testifying to the continuing influence of selection pressures to minimise these risks.

HUMAN DISTURBANCE

The customary wariness of birds towards people is presumably a result of past human hunting, in that any birds that did not take evasive action would have died. Apart from killing them, people have the same indirect effects on birds as do natural predators, disrupting their feeding and other activities, and increasing their energy expenditure through flight. People may also prevent birds from using some potential feeding areas, or cause them to forage in places where their intake rates are lower or their risks are greater. Any keen observer will have noticed that: (1) some bird species are more sensitive to human presence than are others, and fly at greater distances; larger species that are frequently shot are especially wary; (2) individuals of most species can habituate to predictable and benign disturbance, yet remain sensitive to unpredictable or damaging disturbance (such as shooting); (3) most species respond to people more than to other forms of disturbance, such as cars or aircraft; (4) most quarry species are more sensitive (flying at greater distance from the source of threat) in seasons or in areas where they are shot at than in seasons and areas where they are protected; and (5) human presence can prevent some species from using certain areas altogether. Birds evidently respond continually to potential predation risk, altering their behaviour, and hence the range of areas they can use and the resources available to them. If human presence prevents birds from fully exploiting the available resources, it could affect their population levels. As with natural predation risk, this makes disturbance equivalent in its effects to habitat deterioration or loss.

In most cases, human disturbance probably has only temporary and insignificant effects on birds, but it may in some circumstances lead to reduced food intake, reproductive success or survival, which in turn may reduce the population level. Most studies of the effects of disturbance on birds have measured only changes in behaviour, and few have explored the consequences to individuals and population levels. One method of assessing the behavioural response is by measuring the distance at which a bird flees as it is approached by a person. This distance can vary according to the availability of alternative feeding places nearby, and the nutritive needs of the individual concerned. It is obvious to any bird-watcher that, during periods of severe weather or food scarcity, birds allow themselves to be approached more closely than usual before fleeing, a finding confirmed experimentally (Beale & Monaghan 2004). Two approaches have been taken to assess more substantial disturbance effects: either mapping the distribution of birds before, during and after periods of disturbance, or comparing the numbers of birds across a series of areas exposed to different levels of disturbance.

Many studies concern waterfowl, which, through human activities such as boating, may be totally excluded from some otherwise usable habitat. Fishermen on banks and in boats were found to affect the number of ducks using part of Grafham Water in southern England (Cooke 1975). Pochard and Coot almost entirely avoided the area when fishermen were present, but these and other species used the area heavily after mid-October when fishing stopped. Similarly, some areas open to hunters remain virtually unused by waterfowl until after the end of the shooting season (Fox & Madsen 1997). The guns normally used against waterfowl have an effective killing range of 30–40 m, but birds react to gunshot as far away as 80 m, and some can be disturbed at distances up to 500 m (Madsen 1995). In areas open to hunting, ducks often redistribute themselves after the end of the shooting season. For example, during shooting on Lough Neagh in Northern Island, most diving ducks (Pochard, Tufted Duck and Scaup) fed more than 500 m out from the shore, but when shooting ended many birds moved closer inshore (Evans & Day 2001). Such distributional changes may be unimportant to the overall population level if they simply alter the dates at which particular foraging areas are exploited, but they could reduce the population level if they prevent birds from fully exploiting potential food supplies or cause them to feed in other areas with greater risk from natural predators.

In one study, disturbance effects of shooting were examined by setting up experimental reserves in two Danish coastal wetlands (Madsen 1995). Over a five-year period, these reserves became important staging areas for coastal waterfowl, and the national totals of several species were increased as more birds remained there. Hunted species increased the most, some 4–20-fold according to species, while non-hunted species increased 2–5-fold. Furthermore, most quarry species

FIG 143. Pochards *Aythya ferina* are especially sensitive to human disturbance in their feeding areas. (Alan Martin)

stayed in the area for up to several months longer each winter than in earlier years. No declines in usage were noted in other areas still open to wildfowling, so the accumulation of birds in the reserves was attributed to the stopping of birds that would otherwise have migrated further south. One consequence of this build-up of birds was a greater depletion of the local food supply, especially eelgrass (*Zostera*). A further study on two coastal wetlands in Denmark examined the effect of restricting shooting to the evenings only, rather than all day, but this made little difference to the tendency of the ducks or Snipe to leave the area (Bregnballe *et al.* 2004).

Other studies have confirmed that autumn hunting can encourage waterfowl to migrate earlier than they otherwise would. In a study in central Finland over several years, the numbers of Mallard and other ducks fell by more than 90% immediately after the start of the hunting season. Most birds left the area completely, and remaining birds concentrated in protected areas (Väänänen 2001). Similarly, among Pink-footed Geese on a major staging area in Denmark, the start of hunting resulted in almost the entire population moving on to the Netherlands within one day (Madsen & Jepsen 1992). Likewise, mass departures of Greylag Geese from Norway occurred in the first few days of hunting, and were ascribed to the disturbance involved (Follestad 1994). Probably most of these birds would have soon left anyway, but hunting was sufficient to trigger their departure prematurely.

In all these various studies, therefore, hunting disturbance emerged as a major factor influencing the distribution of waterfowl, at both local and regional scales. Hunting also led to increased turnover in the waterfowl of disturbed sites, as individuals stayed for shorter periods than in undisturbed sites, an effect especially evident at migratory stopover sites (Tamisier *et al.* 2003). These findings provided yet further evidence that birds select their feeding areas by balancing the benefits of food abundance and predator avoidance. By implication, to obtain a given intake rate, higher food densities would be required at a disturbed site than at an undisturbed one. And of course, the risk of being killed is also greater at the disturbed site. Clearly, the full potential of many wetlands to support waterfowl is not reached because of the disturbance caused by human activities, especially hunting (Tamisier *et al.* 2003). On large water-bodies, provision of areas where waterfowl can feed, loaf and roost is important if local numbers are to be maintained. When not threatened by predation and disturbance, waterfowl sometimes roost in their feeding areas, but otherwise they flight to safer areas elsewhere.

Attempts were made to quantify the effects of disturbance on Pink-footed Geese wintering in an area of southeast England where they fed mainly on the

FIG 144. Pink-footed Geese *Anser brachyrhynchus* in winter fields. (Chris Knights)

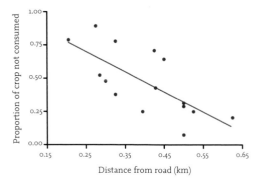

FIG 145. The percentage of waste sugar beet biomass eaten by Pink-footed Geese *Anser brachyrhynchus* in relation to distance from the nearest road. Each point refers to a separate field. Studies of this type help to quantify the effects of disturbance on the birds' ability to exploit a food supply. The wariness of the geese themselves varied largely with prevailing shooting pressure. (From Gill *et al.* 1996)

post-harvest remains of Sugar Beet (Gill *et al.* 1996). The geese were often shot, so were wary, especially when feeding close to roads. By measuring the biomass of waste beet fragments before and after the geese had fed, it was discovered that smaller amounts of beet had been eaten in fields near to roads than in fields further away (Fig. 145). The total number of bird-days for each field depended both on its initial content of beet remains and on its distance from a road. If all fields were exploited by the geese to the level of the least disturbed fields, many more geese could have been sustained in the area over winter. The reduction in use of these feeding grounds caused by disturbance was quantified by translating the biomass of food not consumed into the number of birds that this food could have supported (some 80% more than the number found). Admittedly, if the geese were really hungry they might have become less wary, but they would then increase their risk of being shot. This was another example in which the effects of hunting on a population extended well beyond the numbers killed. The approach allowed both quantification of the effect of disturbance on numbers at a local scale, and exploration of the potential consequences of changes in disturbance on the size of the overall population. In a second study, the impacts of disturbance by farmers on spring fattening of Pink-footed Geese were examined. On undisturbed sites in northern Norway, the geese rapidly put on weight, whereas in disturbed sites they did not. Subsequently, geese that had fed in undisturbed sites produced more young per female, and survived in greater proportion, than geese from disturbed sites (Madsen 1995). This is one of the few studies in which the effects of disturbance on reproduction and survival were assessed, together with the repercussions on population trends.

The Black-tailed Godwit is thought to be especially sensitive to human disturbance while breeding. In an experimental study in a Danish nature reserve, bird behaviour and breeding densities from two baseline years were compared with those in three experimental years with two levels of human disturbance (two and seven walkers per day respectively) (Holm & Laursen 2009). Godwits mobbed natural predators as well as walkers, and made some apparent 'false alarms'. But they flew and showed mobbing behaviour significantly more often when disturbed by walkers than when not. On average, the duration of simultaneous flights by both members of breeding pairs was greater when they were disturbed, leaving nests open to predation. Disturbance levels of seven walkers per day affected territory densities up to 500 m from the routes taken by the walkers, causing effective habitat loss to breeding godwits. This sensitivity to disturbance may help to explain why Black-tailed Godwits have disappeared from many otherwise suitable breeding areas in western Europe.

FIG 146. Black-tailed Godwit *Limosa limosa* in summer (left) and winter (right). (Frank Snijkers and Richard Chandler respectively)

In contrast, no adverse effect was noted on the numbers of Black-tailed Godwits at various wintering sites in southeast England, at least not at the prevailing levels of disturbance (Gill et al. 2001). The birds flew when approached, but generally returned and fed there at a later time, so that food supplies were used just as much as those elsewhere. This does not necessarily hold for other shorebirds, however, for several studies have shown lower numbers in disturbed than undisturbed sites (Klein et al. 1995). Even if they do not flee from disturbance, waders reduce their feeding rates in the presence of people nearby (Yasué 2005).

If the response of foraging birds to disturbance results from a trade-off between predation and starvation risks, birds would be expected to vary their response to disturbance according to prevailing threats and food needs. Anyone can see how waterfowl are generally tamer in nature reserves than outside where they are shot at, and how birds are generally tamer in hard weather, when it is difficult for them to get food. Some species show systematic seasonal changes in their response to disturbance. For example, as autumn turns to winter, the energy needs of Oystercatchers increase while feeding conditions deteriorate. Birds then approach disturbance sources more closely than before, allow people to approach more closely, and return more quickly after fleeing (Stillman & Goss-Custard 2002). Similarly, waterfowl become much more wary when they are flightless during moult than at other times, restricting their activities to safe areas, and in the case of geese feeding only near to open water to which they can escape by running (Fox & Kahlert 2000). These behavioural changes again represent adjustments to prevailing threats and food needs.

Another effect of human disturbance is to facilitate natural predation. In one Finnish study, only about 40% of Velvet Scoter ducklings survived to three weeks old, because many were eaten by gulls (Mikola et al. 1994). Predation was greatly influenced by disturbance from passing boats, which caused the broods to scatter. Gull attacks were 3.5 times more frequent in disturbed than undisturbed situations, and broods disturbed more often than average ended up smaller than average. Similarly among Herring Gulls, hatching success on different islands was related to different levels of human disturbance, which caused adults to leave their eggs exposed to other gulls and to the sun, which overheated embryos (Hunt 1972).

Studies of the effects of human disturbance on wildlife provide useful parallels with the non-lethal effects of natural predators. They are also of direct relevance to wildlife conservation, as human disturbance in rural areas continues to rise. As with predator disturbance, the critical question is whether human disturbance results in lower overall population sizes. For some species, such as the Ringed Plover, it surely does, for this species once bred on sandy beaches all around the British Isles, but has now gone from those heavily used by holiday makers. On one 9 km stretch of Norfolk beach, where the species still persists, studies indicated that, if the numbers of people were to double, the Ringed Plover population would decline by a further 23%. On the other hand, if nest loss from human activity was prevented (for example by fencing nests), the Ringed Plover population would rise by 8%, and if people were totally excluded, the population could increase by 85% (Liley & Sutherland 2007).

Another beach-nesting species which has declined in recent decades at least partly through human disturbance is the Little Tern (Ratcliffe *et al.* 2000). Estimates from colonies throughout Britain between 1990 and 1998 showed that overall annual productivity fluctuated between 0.19 and 0.70 (median 0.45) chicks per pair, too few to maintain the overall population level (Ratcliffe 2003). This low breeding success was due partly to human disturbance, coupled with predation. The problem was partly solved by the use of electric fencing around colonies and by 24-hour wardening, but avian predators continued to take chicks at some colonies. At Britain's largest colony of around 200 pairs, at Great Yarmouth, Kestrels were seen to take 526 Little Tern chicks in one season.

The Nightjar is another ground-nesting species that seems vulnerable to disturbance. Its favoured places on the heathlands of southern England are popular with dog-walkers and others, and the effects of too many people were reflected in the numbers of Nightjars found on 36 different patches of heathland in Dorset (Liley & Clarke 2003). On the most disturbed patches, suitable in other respects, Nightjars were absent altogether. Similarly, on 16 heathland sites suitable for Woodlarks, the proportion of unoccupied habitat was greatest on the most disturbed sites, and was reduced below 50% at around eight disturbance events per hour (Mallord *et al.* 2007). The impact of disturbance depended not just on the numbers of people, but also on their distribution. Where access was managed – for example by footpaths – a doubling of visitor numbers would have had little further effect on Woodlarks, but the same numbers of people distributed across all sites would have led to major negative effects on the overall population. Production of young was reduced by 17% compared with that predicted in the absence of disturbance. These studies indicated that the presence of people reduced the carrying capacity of heathlands for localised breeding birds.

Many studies of disturbance have been conducted by researchers during the course of their other work. Most record no effects on free-flying birds, other than causing them to move away for a period, but some colonial birds, such as terns, seem particularly sensitive to human presence early in the season, when they are settling in their nesting areas. Repeated disturbance at this stage can cause whole colonies to disband and move elsewhere, but there is not necessarily any effect on their subsequent productivity. Other studies, later in the nesting cycle, have recorded a reduction in breeding success with increased frequency of visits and nest inspections by observers. Often this occurs in nesting colonies because, when adults are flushed from their nests, marauding crows or gulls can grab the eggs or chicks. Without human presence, this could not happen to the same extent. Researchers generally behave so as to minimise such losses.

Among other studies on the effects of observer visits to bird nests, half reported some reduction in nest success, due mainly to increased predation, while the other half noted no effect (Götmark 1992). A later review of 18 further studies revealed that observer activity did not increase subsequent predation of nest contents, and in some species it reduced the risk (Ibáñez-Álamo et al. 2012). In these latter cases, the presence of a person, or his scent, near a nest may have deterred predators from approaching the site. Findings varied with the type of bird, the type of nest-site and the type of predator, with mammalian predators (relying largely on smell) reacting differently from avian predators (relying on vision).

Some bird species seem reluctant to feed or nest near roads. In the Netherlands, Lapwings were found at lower breeding densities within 560 m of busy roads than on similar grassland further away. The equivalent figure for Black-tailed Godwits was 940 m, and for Oystercatchers 3,530 m. Clearly, these species varied in their sensitivity to traffic, the roads concerned carrying around 50,000 vehicles per day (Reijnen et al. 1996). Other species seem less sensitive, as indicated by the Carrion Crows that nest in roadside trees and habitually feed from road kills.

Despite their general sensitivity to disturbance, some birds can become accustomed to regular human presence, providing it is benign, and allow a much closer approach. Look at many town birds, compared with their counterparts in the countryside. Even seabirds nesting on offshore islands can get used to people nearby. For example, on the Farne Islands, which receive frequent boat-loads of tourists, seabirds tolerate a much closer approach than at less visited sites. Birds can habituate to human presence that they learn is non-threatening.

CONCLUDING REMARKS

Predators can clearly have much bigger effects on bird populations than expected from the numbers killed. They restrict the range of nest-sites and foraging places that prey species can use, the amount of time they have available for foraging (constrained by vigilance and fleeing) and the body reserves they can afford to carry (constrained in some species by the need for agility). Some aspects of bird behaviour and body composition can be understood in terms of shifts in the starvation/predation trade-off, continually adjusted according to prevailing conditions. This supposed trade-off also throws a different light on the notion of *compensatory* mortality. When individuals in a poor condition that 'would have died anyway' are killed by predators, this could be interpreted as evidence for the relative unimportance of predation. But the presence of predators may have led the birds to reach poor condition in the first place, through restricting their foraging options. We could thus view such mortality, not as compensatory, but as a consequence of non-lethal predator effects on foraging rates (Cresswell 2008). Much of our current understanding of predation risk is based on systems where lethal effects dominate, but these may not be typical. The same holds for human hunting, whose effects extend well beyond the numbers of birds killed. Clearly, non-lethal effects of predation are an important ecological fact of life, and paradoxically they may be greatest in species which suffer least predation, these being the ones that pay in other ways, being more restricted in their living space and behaviour.

Direct and indirect effects of predation differ in another important respect: the one varies in relation to the number of predators present, the other does not. Kill rates on a prey population normally rise with increase in the numbers of predators present, and relatively large numbers of predators are usually needed to hold a prey breeding population below the level it could otherwise achieve. This is not true for indirect effects, in which only an occasional encounter with a predator is enough to influence the behaviour of a very large number of prey individuals. Among birds that feed in flocks, one attack is sufficient to alert the entire flock to the presence of a predator in the vicinity, even though the entire flock may escape. Among solitary species, the effect of a failed attack can have repercussions for others, via the 'predator pass-along effect' (Lima 2002). Individual prey that successfully evade a predator's attack pass the predator along to other prey individuals, who then in turn also experience the predator, thereby increasing the perceived risk among the whole population. In other words, mortality per se is a poor predictor of predation danger as perceived by prey, and it is this perception which seems to have most influence on prey behaviour. Low predation rates do not necessarily indicate that predators are unimportant to the performance of individuals or to the population dynamics of prey species.

Predators increase habitat heterogeneity because they are present in some places and not in others. We can imagine a 'landscape of fear', a contoured map of predation risks, with some species shunning cover which can hide predators, and others using cover as a safe retreat. For the latter species, such as the House Sparrow and Bullfinch, patches of shrubby cover provide oases of security in a generally dangerous landscape. Food supplies are therefore most heavily exploited near cover, and away from it, become progressively less exploited, reflecting increasing danger from predation. Birds can therefore die in the presence of plenty, either from starvation or from food-related predation.

When predation risk is generally low, we can expect that variations in bird densities across a landscape will relate primarily to food, but where starvation risk is generally low, we can expect that they will relate more to predation risk, with avoidance of dangerous places even if they are rich in food. Seasonal changes in the starvation/predation trade-off would be expected to result in seasonal shifts in the distribution patterns of birds across a landscape.

Dangerous places, which are used under duress, remain dangerous partly because only a few individuals normally feed there at any one time, which further increases their vulnerability. In situations which force many birds there at the same time, such as a sudden snowfall or a large arrival of migrants, predation risk for the individual is reduced, owing to the greater security provided by larger numbers. Dangerous areas thereby become less dangerous, but this is dependent on unusual circumstances. Hunting conditions for predators may still be good there, but the risk for the individual prey is reduced by a large influx.

Some people have doubted that disturbance by people or predators could have such marked impact on bird populations, because few, if any, birds are killed. However, mortality is not the relevant measure here. Natural selection acts on individuals, not on populations, and the question is how much higher the mortality risk would be on any individuals that did not adopt precautionary measures. To take a human analogy, relatively few people are killed by traffic in cities, and traffic deaths are clearly not significant in limiting human numbers. But the existence of this risk is enough to affect the behaviour of almost everyone. Any person who habitually disregarded traffic would soon face premature death. The same holds for birds that do not take precautions against predation, even though taking such measures can cost them dearly in other ways.

These costs can eventually bear on long-term survival and reproduction. Avoiding predators can come at the expense of foraging opportunities: time dedicated to vigilance during foraging cannot be spent on searching for food; flocking has obvious benefits, including shared vigilance (freeing time for foraging), risk dilution and predator confusion, but it may also result in competition, depressing food intake. In most of these cases, the bird pays a price for its safer life. This is the hidden cost of predation, which at the level of the individual can be expressed in terms of loss of energy and hence in individual performance, and at the level of the population in terms of lost resources and hence in population size and distribution.

CHAPTER 13

Interactions Between
Parasites and Resources

L IKE PREDATORS, PARASITES HAVE both lethal and non-lethal effects on bird populations. The extent to which they reduce the breeding success and survival prospects of individuals varies with nutrition and other potential limiting factors. Not only are many internal macroparasites transmitted via food, but once established within their hosts, they commandeer, directly or indirectly, part of the host's nutrient intake for themselves. It may thus be expected that, in order to perform at the same level, a bird with gut parasites needs to eat more than one without them, or that, on the same amount of food, a bird with parasites would perform less well than one without. Birds with many parasites are more likely to die during periods of food shortage, or reproduce less well than those with fewer (Chapters 8 and 9). The same points hold for birds adversely affected by microparasites, whether bacteria, protozoa or viruses. The main defence that a bird has against parasites is provided by the immune system. Studies on birds have provided some important evidence for the adaptive value of this system, previously no more than an unconfirmed assumption. Such studies have shown the influence of body condition on the immune response and the nutritional costs involved. They have also demonstrated the role of external factors in influencing parasite transmission and the resulting frequency and severity of disease outbreaks. These aspects form the subject of this chapter.

The transmission of any parasite that is passed directly from one host to others without a vector is affected by the density of those hosts, which can in turn be influenced by prevailing conditions, including other limiting factors. In the past, the strongyle parasite *Trichostrongylus tenuis* caused occasional crashes in Grey Partridge populations in Britain, especially in wet years, but as the densities of Partridges have declined in recent decades through other causes, the parasite has ceased to be important (Potts 1986). In the Red Grouse, the same parasite became important from the late nineteenth century, once habitat management and predator removal had led to greatly increased Red Grouse densities (Committee of Inquiry on Grouse Disease 1911). Similarly, changes during the twentieth century in the conditions in which waterfowl live have increased the prevalence of various diseases, especially in North America (Friend 1992, Friend & Franson 2002). Being gregarious for much of the year, waterfowl lend themselves to the transmission of infectious agents, especially in the non-breeding season when they gather in large concentrations. Through the destruction of natural wetlands and the creation of refuges, some species are being increasingly concentrated in fewer places. And because of artificial feeding they now remain in certain refuges for longer each year than formerly, further raising the opportunities for pathogen outbreaks to occur. Droughts accentuate this crowding by further diminishing the area of wetland habitat. Little wonder that the first known outbreaks of two virulent diseases of waterfowl (avian cholera and duck viral enteritis) occurred on North American wetland reserves (Friend 1992). Avian cholera has since become a major limiting factor, periodically reducing waterfowl numbers in several parts of the world (Chapter 9), and spreading far and wide as infected birds migrate (Brand 1984). Changes in the conditions that favour the development and spread of pathogens have almost certainly influenced the proportion of waterfowl deaths from disease, and their importance in limiting populations, compared with earlier times, although these diseases are much less obvious in Britain and Ireland than in some other regions. Many other parasitic diseases, which have largely disappeared from bird populations or appeared only in recent years, are associated with changes in the densities of hosts, alternative hosts or vectors, or with changes in other environmental conditions that affect transmission.

COSTS OF ANTI-PARASITE MEASURES

Like anti-predator behaviour, anti-parasite behaviour has costs, so trade-offs are involved. The immune system produces antibodies against any infective agent, reducing its effects. As a reminder from Chapter 8, the immune system has two main components: one gives general protection against any foreign invader of the body, and the other is an induced response that develops on exposure to specific infections. On the second system, once immunity against a particular pathogen has been acquired, it usually remains effective for the rest of the host's life. Immune responses are thus generally beneficial to an individual, but their development requires resources which might otherwise go to some other purpose, such as body maintenance, growth or reproduction. In stressful circumstances, an individual might be unable to produce an immune response, so succumbs to a parasitic disease. In the same way that birds face a starvation/predation trade-off, therefore, they also face a starvation/disease trade-off. Immune defence is also *condition-dependent*, and well-fed birds in good body condition are better able to mount an effective immune response than those in poor condition, which therefore more often succumb to disease. Some experimental evidence for these statements is summarised below.

Studies of immune defence in adult birds

To test whether an immune response per se is costly, individual Collared Doves were inoculated with 'foreign material' in the form of sheep red blood cells (SRBC), and were later checked for the development of appropriate antibodies in the blood. In addition, their metabolic rates were assessed from their oxygen consumption as measured in an open-circuit respirometer (Eraud *et al.* 2005). In the inoculated birds, antibody production against SRBC was accompanied by an average 8.5% rise in metabolic rates about seven days later, compared to those of saline-injected control birds. Those individuals that responded most strongly to SRBC lost more body weight during this period than others, despite an unlimited food supply. These findings were taken to reflect the metabolic costs of producing an immune defence against SRBC, supposedly mimicking the costs of combating a pathogen, although in this case no pathogen was involved.

In a similar field experiment, male Great Tits that had been injected in winter with SRBC and mounted an immune response showed, in the following week, nearly 9% higher basal metabolic rate, 37% higher heterophile-to-lymphocyte ratios (leucocytic stress indices), and about 3% (0.5 g) loss of body mass compared to sham-injected control birds (Ots *et al.* 2001). As in the Collared Doves above, it seemed that the immune response had raised energy expenditure and lowered body condition. In another experiment, an antibody response was induced in female Blue Tits by immunising them with human non-pathogenic diphtheria-tetanus vaccine, and the rates at which they fed their chicks were then compared with those of saline-injected controls (Råberg *et al.* 2000). Vaccinated females reduced their chick provisioning rates – thus demonstrating a cost of the immune response as measured by parental effort – while the control birds showed no such reduction. In another study, Pied Flycatcher females were immunised with similar vaccine, and an immune response was confirmed from the presence of appropriate antibodies in blood samples. These females decreased both their feeding effort and their investment in self-maintenance (tail feather growth); they also produced fewer and poorer-condition nestlings than control females injected with harmless saline (Ilmonen *et al.* 2000). These findings again revealed that an immune response per se (without any additional pathogen effects) lowered a bird's performance, at least in the short term.

In another experiment, during the laying of the first clutch, adult House Martins were injected with either Newcastle disease virus (NDV) or saline (Marzal *et al.* 2007). At the time of injection, blood samples were taken for assessment of parasites and leucocyte levels. The clutch was then removed to induce re-laying. The experimental treatment reduced the frequency of re-laying, and infected birds that did re-lay laid later and produced smaller broods than control birds. Between the time of injection and the second blood sampling, nine days after hatch, NDV had stimulated the non-specific (humoral) part of the immune system, and leucocyte counts in blood samples from experimental birds had risen significantly, compared to those from controls. Treated birds also had significantly increased numbers of chewing lice on their feathers, compared with controls. In contrast, the quality of nestlings in terms of their body size, body mass and T-cell-mediated immune response did not differ significantly between treated and control parents. Overall, however, in adult House Martins the production of an appropriate immune response to NDV was costly, as it reduced their seasonal fecundity. But no such result was found in Starlings, which produced an antibody response to inoculation with SRBC, but showed no difference in subsequent reproductive success from other females injected with saline (Williams *et al.* 1999). So in these birds the cost of producing an immune response was not reflected in reduced reproduction.

While some studies showed that mounting an immune response can affect reproduction, partly through reducing parental effort, others revealed that parental effort can itself affect susceptibility to a pathogen. This would be expected if there was a trade-off between investment in reproduction and immune defence. In one experiment, some female Collared Flycatchers were immunised with NDV three days before hatch; one group was given enlarged broods to feed by adding two chicks, another had reduced broods by subtracting two chicks, and a third group had normal-sized broods. Those females with enlarged broods proved less able to produce specific antibodies against NDV than the other females. They showed higher intensities of *Haemoproteus* blood parasites (counted in blood smears), and survived significantly less well to the next year (Nordling *et al.* 1998). Only about 20% of the heavily infected females were present in the local breeding population next year, compared with 40% of other females. It seemed that increased parental effort had limited the ability of females to produce an immune response, so that they then suffered from increased parasite infection and reduced survival.

Following manipulation of the brood sizes of Great Tits, the rates of chick provisioning by parents were measured, along with the prevalence of naturally occurring parasites in blood smears (Richner *et al.* 1995). Males with enlarged broods showed significantly higher rates of food provisioning, but at the same time almost double the rate of malarial (*Plasmodium*) infections than males feeding smaller broods. In contrast, females with enlarged broods showed no change in chick feeding rates or in malarial infections, the entire cost of a bigger family being borne by the male. Moreover, from among unmanipulated Great Tits, only 14% of infected males were still present in the local breeding population the following year, compared with 57% of non-infected males, a highly significant difference. By implication, males had apparently paid the cost of malarial infections by surviving less well subsequently, perhaps partly because they had been unable to limit their malarial parasites.

The association between feeding conditions and susceptibility to blood parasites was investigated in the vole-eating Tengmalm's Owl, but in years with different levels of food supply (Ilmonen *et al.* 1999). In a poor vole year (1993), when food for owls was relatively scarce, almost all breeding Tengmalm's Owls contained *Trypanosoma avium* in their blood, whereas in a good vole year (1994) only a few owls were infected, and in a moderate vole year (1995) intermediate numbers. In the same moderate vole year, high parental effort in raising large broods was associated with poorer body condition and increased blood parasites in both sexes, whereas in the good vole year no such association was found. In two further years of relatively low vole abundance (1996, 1997), the researchers tested whether supplementary food would lead to reduced parasite burdens. In accordance with the annual differences, trypanosome prevalence was indeed lower among supplemented than control females in each year. These findings again supported the notion of a trade-off between parental effort and immunocompetence, but showed also the importance of the food supply in the ability of individuals to combat blood parasites. It could be assumed that the owls were continually infected with blood parasites, as least during the summer months when insect vectors were active, but the extent to which the parasite population developed in the blood was related to the nutritional condition of the owls. The owls were better able to protect themselves when they were well fed.

Studies on Eider ducks in northern Norway also revealed how the immune response of a bird to an infection could be influenced by its general body condition, in turn dependent partly on feeding conditions. Eiders are normally long-lived. They suffer from a range of parasites and pathogens, against which individuals are normally capable of mounting an effective immune response, though sometimes at the cost of reduced growth and survival (Hanssen *et al.* 2003b, 2004). Female Eiders normally accumulate large body reserves before egg-laying, increasing in weight by up to 40%. They survive on these reserves during the three weeks of incubation. If the females are in good enough condition after hatch, they look after their young, but if not, they desert their young, which join a crèche of other (mainly deserted) ducklings, whose survival rate is usually very low. Indications of immunosuppression (low lymphocyte levels in blood) were seen in female Eiders of low body mass late in the incubation period and also in females that subsequently abandoned their broods (Hanssen *et al.* 2003a). These findings suggested that, when stressed by breeding, female Eiders avoided producing a costly immune response that would further jeopardise their energy balance. They got round the problem by deserting their eggs or young in order to devote more attention to their own condition. Although females with reduced lymphocyte levels more often deserted their young, they then had greater return rate the following year. It seemed that immunosuppression, as indicated by low lymphocyte levels, was a reproductive cost that females could partly allay by abandoning their young.

An experimental study by the same team involved injecting incubating female Eiders with three different non-pathogenic antigens, namely SRBC,

FIG 147. Female Eider *Somateria mollissima* with duckling crèche. (Edmund Fellowes)

diphtheria toxoid and tetanus toxoid, or with saline as a control (Hanssen *et al.* 2004). Responses were measured by checking for antibodies in the blood 7 and 15 days later. In those females that did not produce a humoral immune response against SRBC, the return rate to nesting areas the next year was 72%, whereas in those females that did show a response the return rate was 27%. By implication, the birds that mounted an immune response paid a cost in reduced subsequent survival. Moreover, responding against diphtheria toxoid while also responding against SRBC led to a further reduction in return rate. Similar results were obtained independently in two different years, again implying greater mortality (in this study non-breeding and dispersal could be ruled out as the cause of low return rates). This was the greatest cost in survival terms yet recorded for an immune response in birds, and may explain why individuals show little or no immunity when under stress or malnourished, allowing infections to run their course unchallenged.

These various studies imply that, during the breeding season, producing an immune response to infections can have serious costs for female Eiders in terms of their subsequent survival and reproduction. There is, however, an important point to bear in mind in experiments involving toxoids rather than live pathogens. Unlike a live pathogen, a toxoid is non-replicating, so will eventually disappear from the body, whether or not an immune response is mounted. This may explain why the cost (in survival terms) appeared to be higher in birds that showed a response than in those that did not.

In addition to the effects of body condition described above, the hormonal changes associated with reproduction can lead to immunosuppression (Deerenberg *et al.* 1997). Male Swallows implanted with the reproductive hormone, testosterone, showed an initially reduced immune response, as measured by immunoglobulin levels, and had developed higher intensities of parasite infestations (four ectoparasites) by the time of recapture than control males (Saino *et al.* 1995). In addition, some birds, when working to feed young, sacrifice not only their own body condition as described above, but also their maintenance activities, such as feather care, which enables ectoparasites to build up (Clayton 1991). These various responses to parasites provide additional costs to reproduction which have seldom been measured.

Energetically costly processes, such as maintaining strenuous exercise or body temperature in cold weather, are also thought to suppress immune function (Svensson *et al.* 1998). In winter, some Blue Tits were caught from the wild and kept in temperature-controlled aviaries. They were immunised with diphtheria-tetanus vaccine, and divided into two groups. One group was kept at high temperature (20 °C) and the other at low temperature (4 °C by day and −15 °C by night). Birds in the latter group showed much weaker immune responses, suggesting that the extra metabolic cost of keeping warm compromised their immune capability. By implication, cold winters could suppress the immune responses of birds and thus could affect their disease risks and survival rates.

Studies of immune defence in nestlings

As it goes through life, each individual acquires immunity to one pathogen after another. The first infection of each may be costly, but because of acquired immunity, subsequent infections can be contained at much reduced cost. On this basis, a newly hatched bird should be more vulnerable to pathogens than older birds, because it has little or no acquired immunity.[16] Nevertheless, like adult birds, nestlings must presumably strike a balance, as they face a trade-off between investment in body growth and immune defence. In wild nestlings of several species, the manipulation of parasite loads showed that nestling immunocompetence and growth made competing demands, and that an investment in immune defence resulted in a reduction in growth or a longer growth period (which could in turn increase the risk of mortality from other causes) (Saino *et al.* 1998, Szép & Møller 1999). Moreover, both immunocompetence and survival prospects were greater in well-fed than in starving individuals.

As in experiments on adult birds, some researchers used a non-pathogenic material to assess the cost to nestlings of the immune response itself, without the addition of a virulent pathogen. Among natural broods of Swallows, the body mass, body condition and immune response (T-cell-mediated) of chicks were all negatively related to brood size (lower in chicks from large broods), and positively related to parental feeding effort (greater in chicks which received most feeds). Moreover, chicks in experimentally enlarged broods received less food per individual, and had a lower immune response and body mass, than chicks in experimentally reduced broods. However, chicks provided with a small amount of extra protein-rich food (minced beef heart) showed a greater immune

---

16 Humans and some other mammals can acquire some immunity from their mothers, through the placental blood supply and milk. While these routes are not open to birds, chicks can get specific antibodies from their mothers via the egg yolk. This was implied in Swallows, in which antibodies to Newcastle disease virus were detected in the yolk of eggs laid two weeks after the females had been inoculated with this vaccine (Saino *et al.* 2002b), and further evidence is available for other species (Gasparini *et al.* 2007) Other potential routes for transference of antibodies from parents include various secretions given with food, including the crop-milk of pigeons and flamingos, the stomach oil of petrels or the watery drool of some raptors, but I know of no studies to test this possibility.

response, but no greater body mass, than young which received no beef. This study further supported the notion that the nutritional needs of growth and parasite protection compete, and that well-fed chicks do better in both respects (Saino *et al.* 1997). Due to limitations of time and nutrition, investments in one direction necessarily curtail investments in another direction.

By manipulating the brood sizes of Swallows, it was found that chicks in enlarged broods were not only lighter in weight than those in reduced broods, but also hosted more mites (Saino *et al.* 2002a). Chicks in enlarged broods had lower immune response than nestlings in reduced broods. The authors suggested that nestlings in enlarged broods, receiving less food per individual, had depressed not only body growth but also immunity, which may in turn have led to the larger mite infestations.

Other studies on various species have confirmed that food supply can influence the ability of nestlings to withstand parasitism, the effects of which may be greater in years or habitats with poor food supply than in years or habitats with good food supply (Moss & Camin 1970, Triplet *et al.* 2002). Effects can also be greater in the last-hatched (least well-fed) chick than in the other chicks within a brood (Arendt 1985). In addition, a trade-off between growth and immunity has been implicated in several species studied (for Swallows see Saino *et al.* 1998, Merino *et al.* 2000; for Sand Martins see Szép & Møller 1999; for House Martins see de Lope *et al.* 1998; for Magpies see Soler *et al.* 2003). What is still uncertain, however, is the extent to which the types, intensities and range of parasite species influence whether a response is mounted, and the strength of that response. Where nutrients are limited, nestlings might devote more resources to their immune system only when the benefits are high, as in situations of high parasitism or particularly virulent parasites (de Neve *et al.* 2007), but so far this aspect has been little studied.

Species differences in immunocompetence

Two organs in birds are particularly concerned with immune defence. The bursa of Fabricius is a diverticulum of the cloaca which produces antibodies in young birds but regresses before sexual maturity (Toivanen & Toivanen 1987). Its relative size reflects the current state of infection of young birds and their ability to raise an immune response when in the nest and in the immediate post-fledging period (Glick 1983). The spleen is a lymphoid organ that in birds lies on the right side of the junction between the proventriculus and the gizzard (Rose 1981). It is a major (but not the only) site of lymphocyte production, providing the B-cells and T-cells that are involved in immune responses. These lymphocytes comprise about 85% of spleen volume, and the rest consists mainly of macrophages and plasma cells, which also function in immune defence (Rose 1981). The size of the spleen in adult birds reflects the current state of parasitic infections and perhaps also the ability to raise a future immune response. Individual birds with heavy parasite infections have been found to have a larger bursa of Fabricius or spleen than healthy individuals (Glick 1994). The size of both organs has therefore been used as a measure of immune function in different species.

In theory, bird species which suffer most from parasites should invest most in immune function. This prediction was tested by using published measures of parasite-induced nestling mortality as an estimate of the cost of parasitism in different species, and the relative size of the spleen in adults of those same species as an estimate of their investment in immune function. Comparing 21 bird species, a significant relationship emerged between parasite-induced mortality and relative spleen size, those species suffering the greatest losses as nestlings having the largest spleens. This relationship accounted for a third of the variance, even after controlling for some potentially confounding variables (Møller & Erritzøe 2002). It was consistent with the notion that the level of investment in immune function in different bird species was related to the level of threat that parasites posed (as judged by the scale of parasite-induced nestling mortality). However, it was unclear whether the most vulnerable species had a naturally larger spleen as an evolved response, or whether they developed a larger spleen in earlier life as a result of direct exposure to greater parasite loads.

In addition, within each of 20 species studied on the basis of found carcasses, the spleen was found to be larger in individuals that were parasitised or diseased than in individuals of the same species that had died from some other cause (Møller et al. 1998). The enlarged spleen was interpreted as a response to parasitic disease. But there was also an association within species between spleen size and body condition, with individuals in better condition having a larger spleen (apparent in all species, statistically significant in 11). In other words, within species the size of the spleen varied both with the body condition of the individual and with its current status with respect to disease. So between them, these two studies indicated that: (1) spleen size varied between species in line with losses to parasitism, and (2) spleen size varied within species, being greater in diseased than non-diseased individuals, and greater in individuals in good than poor body condition.

Differences in parasite effects between species depend partly on host behaviour, as is illustrated by different species of swallows and martins, some of which nest solitarily and others in small or large colonies (Møller et al. 2001). Among these birds, the impact of parasites on host reproductive success was found to increase with the degree of coloniality, but in highly colonial species the cost of parasitism was countered by high immune responses. Investment in immune function was particularly strong in nestlings, and among social species this investment was associated with a relatively prolonged period of development. Thus, highly social species of swallows and martins may cope with strong pressure arising from parasites by investing heavily in immune function but at the cost of a prolonged nestling period. This could be viewed as an evolved response.

In another study, the sizes of the bursa of Fabricius and spleen were compared between pairs of bird species that were either hole-nesters or open-nesters, or colonial or solitary nesters, respectively (Møller & Erritzøe 2002). Both organs were consistently larger in hole-nesters than in open-nesters, and similarly in colonial than in solitary nesters. Again, it was hard to know whether these differences were inherent or individually developed in response to past infections.

So far, most studies of ecological immunology have considered only single aspects of immune function, but it seems that different aspects (such as the humoral and cell-mediated systems: see Chapter 8) do not necessarily respond at the same time to the same challenge. The different components of immune defence may differ in their running costs, with the more expensive system used only when necessary. Species that host particularly virulent parasites may thus face greater costs. Birds that scavenge at carcasses, and could thereby encounter many virulent parasites, have larger spleens for their body size and greater blood leucocyte concentrations than closely related non-scavengers (Blount *et al.* 2003). They also have relatively greater proportions of phagocytic leucocytes than lymphocytes in their blood, suggesting robust front-line defences that could reduce the need for more costly lymphocyte-dependent responses. In line with this view, following experimental inoculation with phyto-haemagglutinin (PHA)[17] and sheep red blood cells (SRBC), scavengers produced significantly larger humoral immune responses, but not cell-mediated responses, than non-scavengers. These results suggest that single measures of immune defence may not necessarily reflect the overall immune response of a bird, or entirely reveal the likely costs involved. Defences may vary between species, according to their patterns of risk.

Seasonal changes in immune responses
In association with seasonal changes in the impact of parasites, or in body condition, host species often show seasonal changes in immune function. Many

---

17 Haemagglutinin is a substance that causes red blood cells to agglutinate; phyo-haemagglutinin is a plant product (a lectin) which has the same effect, and can therefore be harmful to birds and mammals: see Box 4, in Chapter 8.

ectoparasites time their reproduction to that of their hosts, so that immune responses tend to be strongest in the breeding season. For example, a large increase in spleen mass (by 22% on average) between the non-breeding and breeding seasons was recorded across 71 different bird species, and a seasonal increase (by 15% on average) in T-cell-mediated immunity across 13 species (Møller *et al.* 2003). However, the extent of these seasonal changes in immune parameters differed significantly between species, with cavity-nesters having a larger increase in immune response during the breeding season than open-nesters, fitting the fact that cavity-nesters generally suffer more from nest parasites (Chapter 8).

It seems, then, that both the immune demands of birds and their ability to mount responses fluctuate during the year. In Great Tits, the proportion of lymphocytes in the blood was found to reach a peak in July each year, during moult (Pap *et al.* 2010). Haematocrit[18] values reached their lowest levels at this time, having declined from spring through summer, only to climb again during autumn and winter. Both these measures implied that the moult, following immediately after breeding, was a period of major stress in these birds. But changes in the ability of birds to mount an immune response can occur over much shorter periods, depending on other stresses. For example, using PHA skin tests, parent Kittiwakes on Svalbard showed a significant decline in cell-mediated immune responses from the time of hatching until the chicks were 15 days old. This was a period when both parents experienced a big increase in foraging demands, during which they would be likely to suffer declines in body condition and immune capability (Broggi *et al.* 2010).

As the breeding season progresses, many insectivorous birds face a declining food supply, and an increasing onslaught from ectoparasites, whose numbers gradually build up. One might expect, therefore, a shift in the trade-off between growth and disease resistance between early and late broods in multi-brooded species. This question was investigated in Swallows, in which nestlings from second broods were found to mount stronger T-cell responses to a challenge with a novel antigen (PHA), but had lower rates of weight gain, than nestlings from first broods (Merino *et al.* 2000). In addition, broods in which at least one nestling died had lower T-cell-mediated immune responses, but not lower rates of weight gain, than broods without mortality. These findings suggested that nestling deaths occurred through an inability to defend themselves against parasites rather than an inability to grow. All these various experiments again point to a trade-off between growth and immune defence,

---

18 The packed cell volume, or percentage volume of red blood cells in liquid blood.

the balance of which may change during the course of a year, or even during the course of a breeding season, as food supplies or food demands change (or parents work harder to obtain them).

POLLUTANTS AND IMMUNE DEFENCE

The immune system of birds can also be suppressed by certain pollutants, which could thereby increase susceptibility to parasitic disease. Mallards which were experimentally dosed with PCBs, DDT, dieldrin or selenium showed reduced resistance to a duck hepatitis virus (Friend & Trainer 1970, Whiteley & Yuill 1991), while Mallards exposed to petroleum oil had decreased resistance to avian cholera. In other experiments, many chemicals that occur in the modern environment have also reduced the resistance of laboratory animals to viral, bacterial or macroparasite infections. The list of implicated toxicants includes organochlorine, organophosphate or carbamate pesticides, halogenated aromatic hydrocarbons and heavy metals, such as arsenic, cadmium, lead, zinc and mercury (Whiteley & Yuill 1991). However, it is hard to assess reliably the immunological impacts of these pollutants in nature.

PARASITES AND PREDATORS

Over a long period in Denmark, Sparrowhawks and Goshawks were found to prey heavily on bird species that were also most prone to infection with protozoan blood parasites (Møller & Nielsen 2007). This finding held after allowing for potentially confounding variables, such as the body sizes and breeding densities of the species concerned, as well as their breeding sociality and phylogenetic relationships. Infections may have predisposed these species to predation, but by concentrating on vulnerable species these predators may have incidentally reduced the transmission of the parasites to other species.

Within species, other possibilities occur. For example, if predators selectively removed diseased individuals as they appeared in populations, they might thereby help to suppress epidemics, and thus contribute to the maintenance of prey numbers. An example of such selective predation, discussed in Chapter 7, involved Red Grouse, in which nesting females killed by predators had contained more parasites on previous examination than nesting females that were not killed in this way (Hudson & Dobson 1991, Hudson et al. 1992a). Heavily parasitised birds may have had a stronger odour, enabling Foxes to find them on the nest more easily. Mathematical models indicated that small numbers of predators selectively removing heavily infected individuals could allow Red Grouse density to increase because the predators effectively reduced the regulatory role of the parasites. However, the level of predation had to be just right, because at higher levels it could itself suppress the grouse population (Chapter 9).

Further evidence that predators can selectively remove diseased individuals came from a study in which birds brought in by domestic cats were compared with birds of the same species that had died from causes other than predation (Møller & Erritzøe 2000). Taking the spleen as an important organ of immune defence, in 16 out of 18 songbird species, prey individuals had smaller spleens than non-prey, significantly so in four species. This implied to the authors that birds killed by cats had weaker immune systems. The two samples did not differ in other respects – month of death, age or sex, body or liver mass, wing or tarsus length. These findings implied that cats selectively removed those individuals most vulnerable to parasitic diseases. Amongst other animals, there are examples of parasites making infected prey more prone to predation, either by weakening them or by affecting their behaviour (Coombes 1996). These various studies illustrate how parasites can influence predator–prey relationships. In addition, predators or parasites might increase the numbers of some species by killing their competitors, thus making more resources available (Chapter 10).

Investment in immune function can apparently be compromised in birds seriously exposed to predation risk (Navarro et al. 2004). Captive adult House Sparrows were randomly exposed to either a cat (predator) or a rabbit (non-predator) for six hours, during which time the experimenters assessed the birds' ability to respond (by a T-cell-mediated reaction) to a challenge with PHA. In two different experiments, sparrows exposed to the cat showed a significant reduction, on average 18% and 36%, in T-cell responses compared to sparrows that were exposed to the rabbit. Secondly, in a field experiment with House Sparrows exposed to a Barn Owl or Rock Dove placed next to a nest-box during egg-laying, the researchers found a mean reduction of 20% in T-cell-mediated response in birds exposed to the owl, compared to those exposed to the dove. In a third experiment, House Sparrows were exposed to either a Barn Owl or a Rock Dove, and development of malarial infections was recorded during the following six weeks. Individual sparrows exposed to the owl had a higher prevalence and intensity of *Haemoproteus* infection than did control individuals exposed to the dove. It seemed that exposure to predators reduced the ability of House Sparrows to cope with parasites. This effect could have been mediated via stress hormones, such as adrenaline, which are known to suppress the immune responses of birds and other animals (Apanius 1998, Wingfield et al. 1998).

PARASITES AND NEST-SITES

Many arthropod parasites depend for their transmission largely on birds
using the same nest-sites in successive years (Chapter 8). Occupants can
therefore be re-infected afresh each year from the parasites (including eggs
and larvae) left from the previous year. Such carry-over occurs chiefly in birds
which use scarce but relatively secure sites, such as tree-cavities or cliff-ledges.
Individuals of many such species, when given the choice, change their nest-
sites from year to year, breaking the line of transmission. But where nest-sites
are scarce, individuals may be forced to use the same sites in successive years,
with immediate re-infection, or may be discouraged from breeding altogether.
In contrast, solitary-nesting birds that use more commonly available but less
protective sites, such as on the ground or among the branches of bushes
and trees, can nest in a different place each time. They may therefore suffer
less ectoparasitism but, because their nests are more accessible, they may
experience greater predation risk (Chapter 6). Heavy infestation with external
parasites is one of the trade-offs in using predator-secure but rare nest-sites.
The availability of appropriate nest-sites could thus influence the general level

FIG 148. Osprey *Pandion haliaetus*, one of many large raptor species in which individuals
return to the same nest in successive years. (Laurie Campbell)

of ectoparasitic infestation in bird populations, with lower average infestation rates in areas where nest-sites are sufficiently plentiful to allow birds to change their sites from year to year, although I know of no attempt to test this idea. The important points are that scarcity of prime nest-sites, by leading birds to use the same sites repeatedly, could enhance parasite effects, and parasites could further enhance the nest-site shortage through rendering some sites temporally uninhabitable. This process could affect colonial species, as well as solitary-nesting ones (Chapter 8).

A related problem occurs in some large birds of prey, such as Ospreys and eagles, which build such huge nests that they can seldom complete a nest in time to lay eggs in the same year, so refurbish an old nest instead. Use of the same nest in successive years presumably allows ectoparasites to build up, but some species reduce this risk by adding aromatic greenery to their nests, and by having two or more alternative nests within their territories that can be used in different years. This is dependent on more than one suitable site for nest-building being available within the territory, and this is not always the case, especially in cliff-nesting species.

HABITAT AND DIET EFFECTS

In any bird species, disease risk is often related to habitat features, and not only through food supply. This is because the parasites themselves, or their secondary hosts or vectors, require specific habitats. For example, in a study of Eagle Owls in central Spain, the number of parasite species, concentrations of white blood cells (indicating immune defence) and the prevalence of the blood-sucking fly *Carnus haemapterus* were all high in broods close to watercourses, while the prevalence of blood parasites transmitted by black-flies increased with the amount of forest in the surrounding area (Ortego & Espada 2007). In addition, fledglings in nests located in more diverse habitats, presumed to support a greater range of parasite and vector species, had higher prevalence of blood parasites and higher white blood cell concentrations than fledglings in more uniform habitats. These findings indicate that, where vectors are involved in parasite transmission, habitat conditions for the vectors can influence the levels of parasitism in hosts.

Many parasites have as intermediate hosts creatures that are eaten by birds. If birds avoided eating these species they could thereby avoid the parasites. Earthworms, slugs and snails are important sources of the nematode *Syngamus trachea* which causes 'gapes' in gamebirds. These items are eaten by Grey Partridges much less often than expected from their availability, compared to other invertebrate food-items (Potts 2012). Could the risk of parasitism be one reason for this avoidance, or is there another reason? This type of situation gives the potential for another trade-off, with starving birds being obliged to accept potentially dangerous prey items that they would normally avoid. To my knowledge, this situation remains unexplored.

CONCLUDING REMARKS

It is clear that pathogens – like predators – can have much more effect on the numbers and distributions of species than is evident from the numbers killed. They do so mainly by reducing reproduction, and deterring individuals from nesting in certain places, even in the presence of abundant resources. The transmission and prevalence of some parasitic diseases are greatly influenced by the densities of hosts, alternative hosts and vectors, as well as by prevailing environmental conditions, including the presence of predators (Chapter 8). Moreover, individuals and species with high levels of parasitism can show increased risks of predation.

Because birds can be identified individually by ringing, and then caught and re-caught at later dates, pathogen and parasite impacts have been studied in birds in ways not possible for most other wild animals. This applies particularly to the immune response, and its dependence on nutrition and body condition. Producing an immune response is costly in its resource needs, and may have consequences in reduced survival or breeding success, so yet again the bird faces a trade-off, whether to suffer the costs of the immune response or the parasites. The choice is clearly influenced by the nutritional condition of the bird itself, and may also depend on the virulence of the parasite. Some studies showed that adult and nestling birds that were able to mount a strong immune response against a novel antigen subsequently survived better than the average for their population (Saino et al. 1997, González et al. 1999, Møller & Saino 2004). Other studies showed that birds which mounted such a response then showed lower growth or survival (Saino et al. 1998, Hanssen et al. 2004). Presumably much depended on the nutritional condition of the individuals concerned. Some of the carry-over effects of breeding, reflected in reduced subsequent survival, may be mediated through these immune or disease costs. Put bluntly, any bird that sacrifices immune defence in order to feed its young risks the development of its parasite populations to a level at which they later kill it.

An unexplored aspect is whether the act of combating one virulent parasite, such as a malaria-causing protozoan, affects the ability of a bird to combat another at the same time. Multiple infections may have been another reason why some experimental birds failed to mount an immune response to an artificial infection. Such birds may already have been fighting other infections unknown to the researcher, and unable to take on another.

Parasite infections often increase in birds that are breeding (Møller 1993, Norris et al. 1994). The problems of returning to nest-sites used in previous years, and the energy costs of feeding chicks, have already been discussed, but other aspects of breeding may also increase susceptibility to parasitism. These aspects include the endocrine changes involved in reproduction and the loss of body condition that often occurs during the rearing of young, as birds sacrifice their own body maintenance for the sake of their offspring. In the same way that the anti-predator behaviour of birds appears flexible, in that it can be varied by individuals according to the prevailing threat that predators pose, the same may be true of anti-parasite measures, especially the immune response. It is probably in conjunction with other limiting factors, especially nutrition, that most parasites affect bird populations. Nevertheless, steroid hormones, whether related to stress (corticosteroids) or sexual activity (testosterone and oestrogen), can also suppress the immune system, making birds and other animals more vulnerable to their parasites (Apanius 1998, Wingfield et al. 1998).

The immune system has of course been studied much more in people than in birds, but parallels occur (Lochmiller & Deerenberg 2000). In both groups, the parasites themselves, or the immune responses to them, have costs which can sometimes be lethal. From studies on humans, the cost of an immune response stems partly from raising the body temperature (which requires a 10–15% increase in basal metabolic rate for every 1 °C rise), and partly from repairing damaged cells and tissues. These responses are often undertaken under reduced food intake, as many infections bring lassitude and loss of appetite. They are therefore accomplished partly from the breakdown of body tissues, including protein, so can only be achieved at the expense of other processes. People exposed to diseases show similar responses to those shown by birds, for example the enlargement of the spleen in response to malarial infections (the spleen functioning to remove infected red cells from the bloodstream) and the loss of weight under certain infections (which require replacement of damaged tissues). In some sick people, with all the costs included, the resting metabolic rate can be up to four times higher than normal. These aspects are as yet unstudied in birds, but at least we know that parasitic diseases do not affect birds in isolation from other environmental conditions, and that they often act in association with other limiting factors, especially food supply.

CHAPTER 14

Weather

W EATHER CAN AFFECT BIRD NUMBERS indirectly through its influence on habitats and food supplies, and partly through its direct effects on bird survival, breeding and movements. Prolonged periods of regional severity, such as hard winters or dry summers, affect most bird species by reducing food availability. But episodic events, such as severe storms, can kill many birds directly, as well as damaging their habitats and food supplies. During migration, extreme weather can kill birds in flight, or cause them to drift far off course. In theory, birds could be influenced by weather at any time of year and by any climatic extreme, whether hot or cold, wet or dry, wind or fog. Unlike other limiting factors, extreme weather events, whether prolonged or episodic, tend to occur irregularly, and after each such event depleted populations may take years to recover. Such extreme events can thus have a big influence on mean population sizes, as well as on year-to-year fluctuations. This chapter is concerned with these various weather impacts on bird populations, while the longer-term effects of climatic change are discussed in Chapter 15.

In the British Isles, the dominant seasonal weather variable is temperature, and marked declines in bird numbers often occur during long periods of snow and ice. At lower latitudes, the dominant weather variable in many regions is rainfall, with major increases in bird populations occurring in association with wet periods which stimulate plant growth and animal reproduction, with declines during droughts. Dry periods may also increase the risk of fire, which can damage habitats, affecting bird populations for years to come. In Britain and Ireland, wild fires affect mainly heathland, and then usually at intervals of many years. In contrast, fires feature prominently in the lives of our summer migrants which winter in the arid zones of Africa, where natural fires occur every year.

TOLERANCE LIMITS AND BEHAVIOUR

Birds are well suited to resist the changes in temperature and rainfall to which they are usually exposed. They are warm-blooded, well insulated, relatively waterproof and mobile. They also have some behavioural control over thermoregulation – for example, by sleeking or fluffing their body-feathers.

Direct effects of weather result partly because, being warm-blooded, birds must maintain a high and constant body temperature, which entails a high metabolic rate and frequent access to food. Within a certain range of ambient temperatures, called the thermoneutral zone, birds can maintain their body temperature at minimal cost. But as air temperatures fall below this zone, birds must burn ever more energy to keep warm; and at temperatures above this zone, they must expend energy (and water) to keep cool by panting. However, species of birds differ in the range of temperatures spanned by their thermoneutral zone, according to the environments in which they normally live. Some species can better stand extremes of heat and others extremes of cold. Some of the adaptations underlying these species differences are physiological, such as metabolic rate, and others are morphological, such as plumage insulation.

Similarly, most birds can withstand some wetting of their feathers (some aquatic birds more than most), but torrential rain can soak their plumage, so that its insulating air-layer is lost and the bird may die of heat loss. Young birds are most vulnerable to weather extremes before they can thermoregulate, when they mainly rely on their parents to keep them warm, cool or dry. A small number of bird species, such as swifts and hummingbirds, can become torpid at night or other cold times, greatly lowering their body temperature and energy expenditure for limited periods.

We can all see how birds behave so as to reduce the metabolic costs of extreme cold. They might, for example: (1) select warmer places within their habitat, (2) reduce energy-demanding activities not concerned with feeding, (3) increase the time spent feeding or, if the metabolic costs of feeding at low temperatures exceed the gains from food obtained, they may (4) cease feeding altogether and rest. This last behaviour is seen mainly in large birds, such as waterfowl, but can only be short-term, as it depends on using body reserves. In addition, most birds seek sheltered places for overnight roosting and, in cold weather, some species, such as Wrens and Long-tailed Tits, roost communally, huddled together for warmth. Grouse use snow as insulation against the cold when resting and roosting, by digging bowls where they sit with their backs to the open sky, or by burrowing underneath the snow surface to create a short tunnel, and sealing the entrance by kicking back excavated snow. This behaviour has been seen in all the four grouse species that occur in the British Isles, and birds may spend long periods resting in their snow bowls or burrows by day, protected against the cold and largely or entirely hidden from predators (Watson & Moss 2008). Grey Partridges also make use of snow bowls in severe conditions.

Birds cope with extreme heat by panting, losing heat as water evaporates from the inside surface of the opened mouth. The resulting water loss can sometimes result in death from dehydration (McKechnie & Wolf 2010). Nestlings are less able to regulate body temperature than full-grown birds, so inside closed nests on hot days, eggs and chicks can soon overheat. Parents with open nests exposed to the hot sun often stand over their eggs or chicks to shade them, and some species, such as sandgrouse, also bring water to their young.

GENERAL EFFECTS OF PROLONGED EXTREMES

Although birds are continually affected by weather, it is the prolonged extremes that have most impact on populations, whether hard winters or cold wet summers. In general, the more extreme and long-lasting the conditions, the greater the range of species affected. The foraging success of some bird species is so much influenced by weather that annual variations in relevant climatic variables can promote annual variations in survival, breeding and population levels, as shown by the examples in Figures 149 and 150.

Winter cold

During the twentieth century, the winters of 1916/17, 1939/40, 1946/47 and 1962/63 were exceptionally severe. The last of these was the worst, both in the degree of cold and the duration of snow lie, which lasted as little as ten days on some southwest coasts but up to 70 days over other lowland areas, while the sea froze in the Wash and the Thames estuary.[19] More localised or briefer periods of extreme severity also occurred in the winters of 1928/29, 1978/79, 1981/82 and 1985/86, while in the early twenty-first century severe cold spells occurred in the winters of 2009/10 and 2010/11. These different winters varied in the duration of frost and snow periods, in the lowest temperatures reached, in snow depths, in the numbers of glazed frosts, and in the extent to which freshwater and saline habitats froze, all of which influenced the range of bird species affected. Not surprisingly, long unbroken periods of frost or snow had more impact on bird populations than did several shorter periods interspersed with mild spells.

---

19 Sea water usually freezes at around –2 °C, as opposed to 0 °C for fresh water, but agitation of the water surface can reduce both these values.

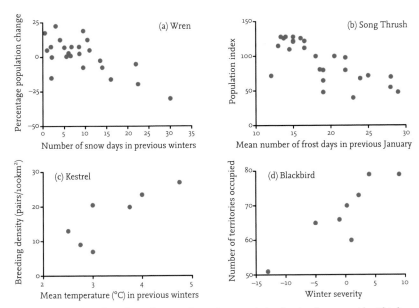

FIG 149. Examples of weather effects on the spring population levels of some resident birds. Each point refers to a different year.

(a) Relationship between the extent of population change between successive breeding seasons for Wrens *Troglodytes troglodytes* in woodlands and the number of snow days in the intervening winter, England ($r = 0.71$, $p < 0.01$). (From Greenwood & Baillie 1991)

(b) Relationship between the population level of Song Thrushes *Turdus philomelos* on British farmland each spring and the number of freezing days in the preceding January, given as an average from 20 weather stations ($r = 0.75$, $p < 0.001$). (From Baillie 1990)

(c) Relationship between the breeding density of Kestrels *Falco tinnunculus* in south Scotland and the mean temperature of the preceding winter ($r = 0.51$, $p < 0.05$). (From Village 1990)

(d) Relationship between spring numbers of Blackbirds *Turdus merula* in part of the town of Lund, south Sweden, and the severity of the preceding winter weather (as measured by the deviation of the mean temperature during November–March from the long-term mean for the period) ($r_s = 0.86$, $p < 0.01$). (From Karlsson & Källander 1977)

In the British Isles, the effects of hard weather on birds are plain for all to see. Typically, at the start of a cold snap with snow, large-scale 'weather movements' occur, as birds of several ground-feeding species leave for warmer climes, while others from even colder regions move in. Thousands of larks, thrushes, Lapwings and others can be seen overhead as they fly south or southwest. Such movements are also apparent from subsequent ring recoveries, which come in greater proportion than usual from the furthest parts of the

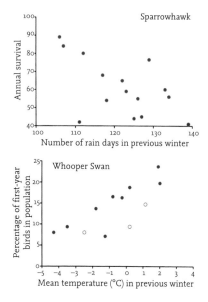

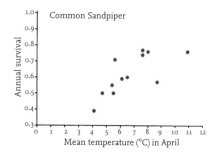

FIG 150. Examples of weather effects on bird survival and breeding success.

(a) Winter weather and survival. Relationship between the annual survival of Sparrowhawks *Accipiter nisus* and winter (October–April) rainfall, south Scotland (logistic relationship: y (%) = 100 exp (4.31 – 0.033r)/[1 + exp (4.31 – 0.033r)], $p < 0.05$). (From Newton et al. 1993)

(b) Spring weather and survival. Relationship between the annual survival of Common Sandpipers *Actitis hypoleucos* and temperature in the latter half of April, soon after arrival in breeding areas, northern England, 1977–89 (y = 0.074x + 0.40, r = 0.82, $p < 0.001$). Birds suffered higher mortality than usual in years when snowstorms occurred in the days following their arrival, so that breeding densities in these years were much reduced. (From Hollands & Yalden 1991)

(c) Winter weather and breeding. Percentage of first-winter birds among Whooper Swans *Cygnus cygnus* in south Sweden in January 1967–78 shown in relation to mean temperatures for the preceding December–March in south Sweden (r = 0.76, b = 2.05, $p < 0.01$). Open circles denote winters after a cold spring in the Siberian breeding areas. (From Nilsson 1979)

wintering range (Holgersen 1958, Baillie et al. 1986). Many of our Lapwings reach Spain at such times, where the species is known as *Avefría* ('bird of the cold'), while others take refuge in Ireland. Although such birds may escape the worst of the weather by moving further south than usual, ringing has confirmed that they may still suffer greater mortality than usual. Not all individuals manage to find milder areas, and those that do are often present in large concentrations, presumably increasing the pressure on local food supplies. Their hunger and unfamiliarity with the area seem to make waterfowl and waders in these circumstances more vulnerable to human hunters, who increase the losses still further. Moreover, as weather severity increases with elevation, many species move to lower ground within Britain, but among those that stay, impacts are generally greater on higher ground (Fig. 151).

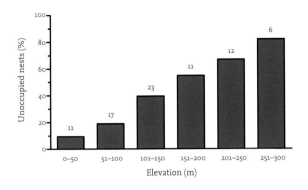

FIG 151. The loss of breeding Barn Owl *Tyto alba* pairs at 80 nest-sites in southern Scotland following the severe winter of 1978/79. Those at the highest elevations suffered the greatest losses. The numbers of nests are shown above the columns. (From Taylor 1994)

As the cold continues, birds become increasingly concentrated wherever food remains available, and bigger numbers than usual appear around houses and sea-coasts. These are the times we most often see Fieldfares and Redwings in gardens, gleaning any remaining apples, with Reed Buntings and other unexpected visitors around garden feeders. Many birds become tamer than usual at such times, as they sacrifice safety for food; they often forage for longer each day, and some normally nocturnal species, such as the Barn Owl, may hunt by day. Water-birds are sometimes found frozen to the ice on ponds, and land-birds to the branches on which they have roosted; while others have ice on their feet or plumage. Many more birds than usual are found dead or dying, enough to attract public concern, and by the following spring, when breeding begins, some resident species appear scarcer than usual (Jourdain & Witherby 1918, Ticehurst & Hartley 1948, Dobinson & Richards 1964, Cawthorne & Marchant 1980, Marchant *et al.* 1990, Greenwood & Baillie 1991).

While many birds leave Britain during cold weather, other birds from further north or east may move in. This is especially noticeable in species that normally occur in small numbers. One such event occurred in January–February 1979, when a period of very cold weather hit the Baltic and North Sea coasts. The weather in Britain was less cold, and large numbers of additional waterfowl arrived in southeast England, including Red-necked Grebes, Smews, Red-breasted Mergansers, Goosanders, and also predators such as Hen Harriers, Long-eared and Short-eared Owls (Chandler 1981, Davenport 1982). Similarly, during the early winter of 2010/11, with heavy snow and freezing temperatures in western Europe, thousands of extra geese, ducks and waders poured into southern Britain. No fewer than 72,000 Lapwings and 50,000 Wigeon accumulated on the Somerset Levels alone, the largest totals ever recorded for this site. The numbers of some bird species in Britain in different winters may thus depend more on conditions on the continent than in Britain itself.

The ability of any species to withstand a cold snap depends partly on its size, as larger species have relatively more body reserves, and need to devote a smaller proportion of their daily energy intake to keeping warm – because of their reduced surface area to volume ratio (Blem 1990, Cawthorne & Marchant 1980). With increasing body size, therefore, the safety margin for survival without feeding increases and the impact of cold weather lessens (Figs. 153 & 154). The most vulnerable species in Britain and Ireland, which suffer the most marked declines during cold spells, include the Goldcrest, Long-tailed Tit, Treecreeper, Dartford Warbler, Bearded Tit and Wren, all of which weigh less than about 10 g, followed by the Stonechat, which is somewhat larger. In winter, such small birds are unlikely to last more than a day without food, medium-sized species

FIG 152. Four small bird species which suffer high mortality during hard winters. Upper left: Bearded Tit *Panurus biarmicus* (Frank Snijkers). Upper right: Long-tailed Tit *Aegithalos caudatus* (Edmund Fellowes). Lower left: Wren *Troglodytes troglodytes* (Frank Snijkers). Lower right: Stonechat *Saxicola torquatus* (Edmund Fellowes).

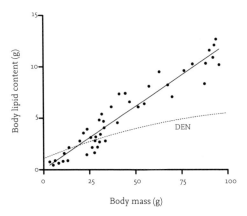

FIG 153. Mean lipid weight in relation to total body weight among wintering songbird species. Each dot refers to a different species. The dashed line shows the lipid equivalent of the daily energy need (DEN, assuming 1 g of lipid yields 37.7 kJ), and indicates that the safety margin of surplus fat increases with body size. In other words, larger species could survive for longer without feeding than small ones (some of which can survive some degree of reserve deficit by nocturnal torpidity). (Modified from Blem 1990)

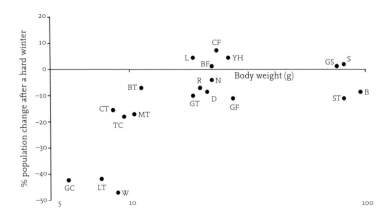

FIG 154. Percentage changes in woodland bird populations in Britain between 1978 and 1979 (a hard winter), shown in relation to the body weights of the species concerned. More species decreased than increased, and the most marked decreases occurred in the three species of lowest body weight. B, Blackbird *Turdus merula*; BF, Bullfinch *Pyrrhula pyrrhula*; BT, Blue Tit *Cyanistes caeruleus*; CF, Chaffinch *Fringilla coelebs*; CT, Coal Tit *Periparus ater*; D, Dunnock *Prunella modularis*; GC, Goldcrest *Regulus regulus*; GF, Greenfinch *Carduelis chloris*; GS, Great Spotted Woodpecker *Dendrocopos major*; GT, Great Tit *Parus major*; L, Linnet *Carduelis cannabina*; LT, Long-tailed Tit *Aegithalos caudatus*; MT, Marsh Tit *Poecile palustris*; N, Nuthatch *Sitta europaea*; R, Robin *Erithacus rubecula*; S, Starling *Sturnus vulgaris*; ST, Song Thrush *Turdus philomelos*; TC, Treecreeper *Certhia familiaris*; W, Wren *Troglodytes troglodytes*; YH, Yellowhammer *Emberiza citrinella*. (Redrawn from Cawthorne & Marchant 1980)

(of around 300 g) might survive for several days, while large geese and swans can last for two or more weeks. We can therefore expect that short periods of hard weather will kill mainly small birds, but that as the cold continues, larger species will form increasing proportions of the casualties. For obvious reasons, though, most of the carcasses that are found in hard winters are of larger, more conspicuous species (Dobinson & Richards 1964).

Among small birds, ground-feeders generally fare worse than tree-feeders, and insect-eaters fare worse than seed-eaters. The most marked population declines recorded in Britain after hard winters involved the small insectivorous birds mentioned above. Two successive cold winters (1961/62 and 1962/63) reduced the numbers of Dartford Warblers, which were in any case restricted to a few parts of southern England, by 98% (457 to 11 pairs: Gibbons *et al.* 1993). It is not hard to imagine that, if the next winter had also been severe, this species could have been obliterated altogether from Britain. In fact, the following winters were much milder, enabling Dartford Warblers to increase from the 11 pairs in 1963 to over 3,200 in 2006, accompanied by a large expansion in distribution north to Staffordshire (Wotton *et al.* 2009). Larger ground-feeding species, such as Song Thrush and Lapwing, showed marked declines in some hard winters but not in all, while some aquatic species, such as Grey Heron, Kingfisher and Moorhen, declined in all severe winters. Among coastal waterfowl, the Shelduck appeared particularly susceptible, and among coastal waders, the Redshank and Oystercatcher (Davidson & Evans 1982, Atkinson *et al.* 2003, 2005). Large birds such as Mute Swans are not immune to starvation, and many were found dead in winters when ice covered their shallow-water feeding areas for weeks at a time. The numbers in Britain fell by about 25% over the two icy winters of 1961/62 and 1962/63.

FIG 155. The Dartford Warbler *Sylvia undata* almost disappeared from Britain during the hard winters of 1961/62 and 1962/63, but subsequently recovered and expanded its range, reaching more than 3,200 pairs by 2006. (Alan Hale)

Different species are also affected by different aspects of weather, depending on how they get their food. For example, in the canopy-feeding Blue Tit, survival declines with increase in the number of cold wet days during winter, in the ground-feeding Robin and Dunnock with the number of snow days (Robinson *et al.* 2007). Among Treecreepers mortality rates rise with increasing winter rainfall (particularly in January), possibly due to heat loss as a result of their breast feathers becoming soaked from brushing against wet treetrunks (Peach *et al.* 1995). In general, canopy-feeders are particularly affected by glazed frosts. Among shorebirds, some species are affected by the freezing of salt water within mudflats, which prevents them from probing for food, and others are affected by strong winds which interfere with their surface feeding (Dugan *et al.* 1981). Different responses to the same conditions provide one reason why different bird species in the same region do not necessarily fluctuate in synchrony from year to year. Moreover, many species may be more vulnerable to severe weather in years when their food is scarce, being better able to withstand extremes in years when food is plentiful. This is evident, for example, in species which feed on variable tree-seed crops, such as Nuthatch and various tits (Perrins 1979, Nilsson 1987, Matthysen 1989). Birds may also be more affected by cold snaps that occur near the end of winter, when most food has been eaten, than near the start when food is still abundant. Daylength also influences the situation, with the short days of midwinter greatly reducing the time available for feeding by most birds. Some species, such as Grey Partridges, can dig through shallow snow to access food, but if this snow is topped by hard ice, this becomes impossible, and they can die of starvation. For these various reasons, the same species may be affected in some winters of severe weather but not in others.

During cold weather on the Wash in February 1991, many waders perished. Approximately 2,500 carcasses were collected, including Oystercatchers, Grey Plovers, Knots, Dunlins, Curlews and also Redshanks, of which about two-thirds of the wintering population were calculated to have died (Clark *et al.* 1993). The heaviest losses fell during a period when high tide occurred around the middle of the day, giving the maximum reduction in potential feeding time. Although some species can feed at night, their intake rates are lower then. On both the Wash and the Dutch Wadden Sea, Oystercatchers suffered heavy mortality in two cold winters when their main food-items – cockles and mussels – were scarce. It was the combination of frozen mudflats and scarcity of both main prey species that killed so many birds, with thousands of emaciated carcasses found (Camphuysen *et al.* 2002).[20]

---

20 Elsewhere in Europe, where snow and ice persist into spring, the fate of bird populations can be influenced by the number of days that water remains ice-covered (for Mute Swan in Denmark see Bacon & Andersen-Harild 1989; for Coot in Netherlands, see Cavé & Visser 1985; for Dipper in Norway see Saether *et al.* 2000), or the date in spring that water becomes ice-free (for Wigeon in Iceland see Gardarsson & Einarsson 1997; for Eider in Finland see Lehikoinen *et al.* 2006).

While many resident species suffer from hard winters, summer visitors, which winter in the tropics, may benefit on their return to northern breeding areas from the shortage of local competitors. The larger than usual numbers of Pied Flycatchers that are said to have nested in Britain in 1917 and 1947 supposedly benefited from the greater availability of nest-cavities in those years, resulting from the scarcity of resident tits caused by preceding hard winters (Elkins 2004).

Loss of body condition

To judge from their corpses, small birds usually lose up to about a third of their body mass during starvation, while larger birds (thrushes to waterfowl) can lose up to a half. By this stage, practically all body-fat has been used, together with some protein, as shown by their emaciated breast muscles (Harris 1962, Hope Jones 1962, Marcström & Mascher 1979, Davidson & Evans 1982). However, during severe cold birds might die either from starvation or from hypothermia (equivalent to death from 'exposure' in humans). Starvation results from insufficient food, so that a bird's initial body reserves are gradually used up to the point of death. Hypothermia occurs under extreme heat loss, when the bird has sufficient body reserve, but cannot metabolise it fast enough to keep warm, so that it dies through chilling.

This difference may explain why the carcasses of birds that have starved in milder climates are lighter in weight than those of similar birds that have died in colder or more exposed conditions (Davidson & Evans 1982, Piersma & van Gils 2011). The birds in milder climates could meet their energy need on protein breakdown and therefore survive for longer than birds in colder climates which died from chilling long before they had used all available body protein. Knots starving in a typical west European winter had 25 g more fat-free mass left than conspecifics that died in Africa. Similarly, Oystercatchers wintering in northeast Scotland died at 30–50 g heavier (with almost no fat left) than individuals wintering in the milder Wadden Sea, and Redshanks in southeast England died an average of 5 g heavier in one cold snap than those that died in a less cold one. In each case, the assumption would be that birds in the colder climate died from chilling before they could use all their available body reserve, whereas those in the milder climate could survive until their body reserve was exhausted.

Summer rain

Prolonged rain prevents parent birds from foraging efficiently, which can lead to reduced growth and survival of nestlings, even those snug within tree-cavities, such as Pied Flycatchers (Siikamäki 1996). It sometimes leads to the production of fault bars on the feathers of nestlings, lines of weakness at which the feathers may subsequently break, affecting the bird until the next moult. Rain also washes insects out of the air and off vegetation, reducing the food supply for a wide range of insect-eating birds from hirundines to warblers. As I write this chapter at the end of the wettest summer for more than 100 years (2012), BTO surveys indicate that many birds have done badly. Among various songbird species, productivity was reduced by one-third to two-thirds compared to five-year average values. Eight warbler species had their worst breeding season for at least 30 years, and resident caterpillar-feeders, such as Great and Blue Tits, produced fewer fledglings per breeding attempt. This would have been expected from wet years in the past.

Wet summers can be disastrous for species such as the Swift, which raise their young on flying insects. The resulting food shortage leads to delay in egg-laying and incubation, to egg desertion, small clutches, poor nestling growth and starvation, in some years in northern Europe causing almost total breeding failure (Koskimies 1950). This occurs even though the young can lower their body temperatures and remain torpid for long periods. Similar detrimental effects of rain have been noted among Alpine Swifts in central Europe, although the young reduced their body temperatures by as much as 18 °C to lessen their energy expenditure during periods of deprivation (Bize et al. 2007).

Birds of prey also seem particularly vulnerable to wet weather, which affects breeding by reducing the food supply, suppressing hunting behaviour or prey availability, and in some cases also by soaking the nest contents, so that eggs or chicks die of chilling. Negative relationships between annual breeding success and prevailing rainfall have been noted in a wide range of raptors, including Kestrel, Peregrine, Buzzard, Honey-buzzard, Red Kite, Sparrowhawk, Goshawk and various harriers (Cavé 1968, Schipper 1979, Davis & Newton 1981, Newton 1986, Mearns & Newton 1988, Kostrzewa & Kostrzewa 1989, Village 1990, Bradley et al. 1997). In some species, such as the Peregrine, weather around the time of hatch seems especially important in influencing overall annual productivity (Mearns & Newton 1988).

Cold drenching rain in summer can sometimes cause nest flooding, but perhaps has its greatest impact on the recently hatched young of gamebirds and waders, whose chicks are active from the time of hatch. Wet vegetation makes it hard for chicks to obtain enough food without getting soaked or risking hypothermia, and poor chick survival in such conditions has been recorded in a wide range of species, including Grey Partridge, Ptarmigan, Red Grouse, Avocet and others (Jenkins 1961, Watson et al. 2000, Hötker & Segebade 2000). This mortality is sometimes sufficient to cause declines in subsequent breeding numbers, as found in Black Grouse and Capercaillie (Moss et al. 2001).

But not all bird species in an area are affected adversely by rain. Unusual wetness through the spring and summer can benefit worm-eating species, such

FIG 156. The Rook *Corvus frugilegus* benefits from damp ground in which it can easily obtain earthworms and other prey, but suffers heavy mortality during summer droughts when its invertebrate food becomes less available. (Edmund Fellowes)

as the Blackbird and Rook, which probe for food more easily in damp ground (Lack 1966, Dunnet & Patterson 1968). Some wetland birds can benefit from the high water levels of wet years, partly because of the increased area of shallow water available. However, marked and rapid fluctuations in water levels can cause flooding of the nests of low-nesting species, those around shorelines and on low-lying islands being especially vulnerable.

Summer warmth

It is easy to imagine that many birds would benefit from warm dry weather when breeding. Not only does this allow the adults to hunt efficiently for all of every day, but it reduces the need for brooding of the chicks to keep them warm. Not surprisingly, then, many bird species breed better in warm dry summers than in cold ones, although some species seem more dependent than others on summer warmth (Crick 2004). For example, in the small population of Golden Orioles nesting in East Anglia, the cause of many nest failures was poor weather in June, with productivity averaging three times greater when June was warm and dry than when it was cold and wet (Milwright 1998). These findings were perhaps not surprising, considering that these birds fed mainly on the adults and larvae of butterflies and moths, and on adult bumblebees. Other insectivorous species which benefit from warm dry weather during the nestling period in continental Europe include Red-backed Shrike and Hoopoe (Hušek & Adamik 2008, Arlettaz *et al.* 2010).

Similar findings emerged for Woodlarks studied in East Anglia (Wright *et al.* 2009). These birds laid earlier and larger clutches in years when temperatures were high and rainfall low in the pre-laying and laying periods (taken for each

FIG 157. The Woodlark *Lullula arborea*, a heathland species which breeds best in warm dry summers. (Chris Knights)

nest as the period from four days before laying to clutch completion). The birds also showed higher nest success when temperatures were high during the nestling period, and had more nesting attempts in warm years than in wetter ones. However, in this study, weather had less effect than nest predation on annual productivity.

Some bird food organisms, such as most insects, do well in warm weather, and are more abundant and active then, increasing the food available for many birds. However, for birds that depend on larval insects, such as caterpillars, warm weather brings problems because larval development is temperature-dependent. This means that hot summers can speed the development of larvae, reducing the period over which they are available and over which nestling birds can be efficiently raised. For example, Winter Moth caterpillars, which are a major food of tits and other birds in oak woodland, remain available for up to 40 days in cold springs, but for only about 20 days in warm springs. In some regions, this may reduce the ability of some insectivores, such as tits, to raise second broods, or to attempt a second nest after failure of the first (Chapter 15).

Heat and drought can also dry out the soil, killing soil-dwelling invertebrates, or causing them to retreat downwards beyond the reach of probing birds. The breeding seasons of species that eat these creatures may therefore be curtailed in dry summers, reducing the numbers of broods that can be raised by thrushes and the numbers of repeat nesting attempts by waders, such as the Snipe (Lack 1966, Green 1988b). Dry summer soil-conditions were also associated with reduced survival of adult Song Thrushes (Robinson *et al.* 2004), and with reduced body weights of adults and chicks (Gruar *et al.* 2003). Nevertheless, Song Thrushes

FIG 158. The
Song Thrush *Turdus
philomelos* suffers from
winter cold and from
summer drought,
both of which make
earthworms and other
small prey less available.
(Edmund Fellowes)

can still break open snails during dry periods, a facility that closely related
Blackbirds lack. In addition, the midsummer drought, when earthworms retreat
deeply into the soil, causes much mortality in Rooks, especially among young of
the year (Dunnet & Patterson 1968). By breeding early in spring, Rooks avoid the
midsummer drought, but they cannot avoid its effects on their fledged young.

The effects of weather in the breeding season can also carry over into the later
life of chicks. Among Choughs nesting on the island of Islay off western Scotland,
the average number of young produced per breeding attempt varied between
years, associated with weather in the months before breeding. Productivity

FIG 159. The Chough
Pyrrhocorax pyrrhocorax,
whose breeding is
greatly influenced by
the amount and timing
of rainfall and its effect
on invertebrate food
supplies. (David Boyle)

increased with rise in preceding late-summer (July–September) temperatures and decreased with preceding late-winter (January–March) rainfall (Reid *et al.* 2003). These two weather variables, which influenced the availability of invertebrate prey in the soil, explained 60% of the variation in mean annual breeding output. Moreover, cohorts fledging in years of favourable weather conditions were more likely to survive to breeding age and have longer breeding lives and greater lifetime reproductive rates than cohorts fledging under poor conditions.

While warm dry weather during nesting benefits many birds in Britain, some also suffer directly from too much heat. Great Skuas breed only in the most northern parts of Britain, and the extent to which they can spread south may be limited by summer temperatures (Furness 1987). They appear especially stressed while incubating on warm sunny days, and frequently leave the nest to bathe in fresh water nearby, apparently to cool down. When air temperatures surpass 14 °C and food is scarce, adults are especially likely to be absent from their nests, which leaves unprotected chicks vulnerable to fatal attacks from neighbouring pairs. Fewer chicks have survived in such years (Oswald *et al.* 2008). In other species too, heat may affect parental behaviour, reducing the time and energy spent on foraging, as suggested for Pied Flycatchers nesting at the southern end of their range in Spain (Sanz *et al.* 2003). Effects depend on the species, and on the temperatures involved.

I know of no well-documented examples of birds succumbing to hyperthermia in the British Isles, but among Lesser Kestrels in Portugal a rare spell of hot weather in 2009 killed 22% of chicks in artificial nest-sites (Catry *et al.* 2011). On three days, the maximum outside temperatures exceeded 39 °C, the normal body temperature of birds. Some young chicks perished inside their nests, due to acute hyperthermia and dehydration, while some older ones left their nests prematurely and died on the ground. Among survivors, growth rates were reduced, as was body condition at fledging. Wooden nest-boxes attained the highest temperatures, those facing south exceeding 55 °C, clay pots reached lower temperatures, and wall cavities lower still. Under high temperatures, no effects were noted on adult hunting or prey deliveries at nests, and nestling deaths were attributed entirely to overheating. In the hot climate of Israel, heat waves caused hyperthermia or mortality of entire broods of Kestrels and Barn Owls in nest-boxes (Meyrom *et al.* 2009). And in the same area, Barn Owls preferred to use cooler boxes, where they also produced more fledglings per attempt than in warmer ones (Charter *et al.* 2010).

The influence of weather on bird breeding cannot always be judged by its effects at the time. In temperate regions, aerial insect-feeding birds breed most successfully in warm dry summers, but if every summer were dry, the lack of

FIG 160. House Martin *Delichon urbicum* collecting mud for nest building. (Chris Knights)

rain would in time reduce insect supplies, with eventual effects on nest success. Similarly, the small chicks of many waders and gamebirds survive best in dry weather, but they depend on rainfall in preceding months to provide their insect food (Moss 1986). Further south, in semi-arid environments, rainfall in winter and spring has generally beneficial effects on bird breeding, through promoting plant growth, and an abundance of the insects and other small creatures that birds eat. Such effects have been documented in some birds of prey, for example, including Lesser Kestrels in Spain and Common Kestrels on the Canary Islands (Rodriguez & Bustamente 2003, Carillo & Gonzales-Davila 2010). Among Lesser Kestrels, winter–spring rainfall has a generally positive effect on breeding, including the body condition of growing chicks. However, rain during the nestling period has a negative effect on chick survival, presumably by reducing the ability of the parents to hunt (Rodriguez & Bustamente 2003). Finally, drought can also affect birds in less obvious ways, such as by influencing the availability of mud which House Martins and other species need for their nests.

WEATHER AND POPULATION DYNAMICS

In the ways described above, annual variations in weather can cause annual fluctuations in the breeding numbers of many birds, through effects on survival or breeding success (Saether *et al.* 2000, 2004, Saether & Engen 2010). Evidence for effects of winter weather on survival rates comes mainly from passerines and other birds that raise their young in nests, whereas evidence for effects of summer weather on production of young comes mostly from waders, ducks and gallinaceous birds. In these latter species, under the care of their parents, the young forage for themselves from soon after hatch but need brooding periodically to keep warm and dry. However, there are exceptions to these generalisations.

The year-to-year fluctuations in some British bird populations, based on data from the Common Birds Census, were examined in relation to weather at different times of year (Greenwood & Baillie 1991). In about one-third of 39 songbird species examined, the annual population changes showed significant relationships with some aspect of winter (November–February) weather, either mean temperature or the number of snow or frost days, with marked declines in harsh conditions. In three species the annual population changes were related to summer (May–June) weather, as they benefited from warmth or reduced rainfall. Only one species apparently benefited from relatively high spring (March–April) temperature, and none showed any relationship with August–October weather. Subsequent studies have tended to confirm the importance of winter and summer weather.

Mean winter temperature had a large influence on the year-to-year breeding densities of Dippers in southern Norway, through its effects on survival (Saether et al. 2000, Loison et al. 2002). Several studies of Great Tits have revealed the importance of temperature in the non-breeding season, but at different months in different populations, habitats or study periods (Slagsvold 1975, von Haartman 1973, O'Connor 1980, Orell 1989). In general, the effect of weather on the population dynamics of Great Tits increased with latitude, presumably reflecting the effects of harsher winters further north (Saether et al. 2003). In Wytham Wood near Oxford, the highest correlation coefficients between breeding numbers and temperatures related to late winter and early spring, when food was probably at its seasonal scarcest (Slagsvold 1975). Other analyses have revealed effects of winter cold on the year-to-year fluctuations of Goldfinches and Skylarks in Britain (Eglington & Pearce-Higgins 2012), and also of Kestrels in Britain and Germany (Village 1990, Kostrzewa & Kostrzewa 1991).

In some bird populations studied over long periods, weather both inside and outside the breeding season had marked effects. This was true, for example, in House Martins studied during 1967–76 in a village near Stuttgart in Germany (Stokke et al. 2005). Annual nest counts showed that numbers dropped markedly in association with two extreme weather events. In 1969 a period of cold wet weather in the breeding season reduced breeding output and hence population size the following year, while in 1974 birds were affected by extremely cold weather during autumn migration. In this year, hundreds of thousands of House Martins, including migrants from other regions, were found dead and dying in the Swiss Alps and surrounding areas, as victims of extreme cold and snowfall in late September and early October. Over the whole ten-year period, temperatures in breeding areas, together with the density of the population, explained a significant proportion of the annual variation in juvenile survival, while conditions on autumn migration had significant effects on adult survival. Weather conditions thus affected the two age classes in different ways, and in breeding areas only juveniles were influenced by factors that acted in a density-dependent manner, such as food supply.

Allowing for other limiting factors

Because weather is only one of several factors influencing annual changes in breeding numbers, its effects become apparent to the ordinary observer only in the most extreme years, as in the House Martins above. However, statistical analyses of annual measures of breeding numbers, survival or breeding success can reveal effects when they are less immediately obvious. In some bird species, effects of weather are evident on breeding numbers alone, in others on change in breeding numbers from the previous year, and in yet others only after allowing for the year-to-year variations in population density, which influence the action of density-dependent factors.

Among studies in the latter category, Sparrowhawk breeding numbers in an area of south Scotland fluctuated only between 29 and 39 pairs over a 25-year period, with no long-term trend. Some 60% of the annual variation in breeding numbers was attributed to density-dependent factors, including competition for potential nesting territories, but another 10% was attributed to spring (March–April) weather. Dry springs had a positive effect on breeding numbers, and wet springs a negative effect (Newton 1986). No effects of weather at other times of year were detected. Among Golden Plovers breeding in the southern Pennines, fluctuations were greater, varying between 5 and 30 pairs over a 24-year period, but again with no obvious long-term trend (Yalden & Pearce-Higgins 1997). Some 27% of the variation in annual changes was explained by density-dependent factors and an additional 15% by winter weather, as measured by mean monthly air temperatures over the period November–February. No effect of summer weather on breeding numbers was apparent over the years involved, but this became apparent in later years, as droughts became more frequent (Chapter 15).

In the Wren, 82% of the variation in year-to-year changes in breeding numbers in a wood in southern England could be explained by density in the preceding breeding season (which accounted for 23% of the variation) and the number of days with snow lie in the intervening winter (which accounted for the remaining 59%) (Newton *et al.* 1998). Similar findings for Wrens emerged at another study site over a different time period (Peach *et al.* 1995). By implication, for any given population density, more Wrens were lost in snowy than in mild winters, and for any given duration of snow lie, a greater proportion of Wrens were lost in years of high than low densities. Similarly, among Song Thrushes in Britain, during the period 1962–76, 90% of the variance in year-to-year changes in breeding numbers could be explained by population density in the preceding year coupled with the number of freezing days in January. The relationship became less marked in subsequent years, when a long-term decline set in, caused by other factors (Baillie 1990). A later analysis for the years 1964–2000 showed that the annual survival of first-year Song Thrushes was correlated with the length of the longest run of winter frost days (Robinson *et al.* 2004).

Species wintering in Africa
In regions of low rainfall, such as much of Africa where many of our summer visitors spend the northern winter, water is a major limiting factor for plant growth, and hence for insect populations. Annual variations in rainfall thus cause marked variations in bird food supplies, as well as in the amount of wetland available to water-birds. In consequence, local bird populations usually increase during wet periods and decrease during dry ones, and several dry years in succession can devastate the populations of most species. In this way, through affecting food and water supplies, rainfall (rather than temperature) becomes the major ultimate determinant of bird numbers.

FIG 161. Sedge Warbler *Acrocephalus schoenobaenus*, which fluctuates according to rainfall in the Sahel zone of Africa where it spends the winter. (Richard Chandler)

Effects extend to the many Eurasian species which spend the northern winter in the Sahel zone and other arid parts of Africa. In the Sedge Warbler, for example, both annual survival and spring population levels, as measured in Britain in the years 1969–84, were linked to annual rainfall in the western Sahel zone where this species winters (Fig. 162). Likewise, the numbers of migrant herons counted at colonies in the Netherlands and France each year were correlated with water discharges through major rivers (reflecting rainfall) during the previous year in west African wintering areas (Fig. 163). In addition, overwinter survival rates of Purple Herons, White Storks, Lesser Kestrels (first-year birds

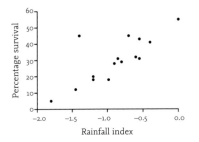 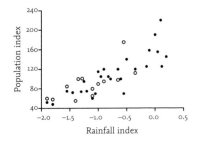

Rainfall index   Rainfall index

FIG 162. Relationship between (a) annual survival of Sedge Warblers *Acrocephalus schoenobaenus* at various sites in Britain or (b) annual spring population index in Britain, and preceding annual rainfall in the Sahel zone of Africa, where Sedge Warblers spend the winter, 1969–84. Symbols reflect different counting programmes: closed symbols, BTO Common Birds Census; open symbols, BTO Wetland Bird Survey. (From Peach *et al.* 1991)

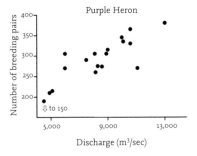 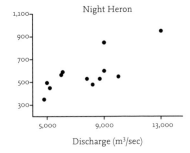

Discharge (m³/sec)   Discharge (m³/sec)

FIG 163. Relationship between the numbers of migrant herons nesting at colonies in western Europe and wetland conditions in wintering areas in west Africa during the preceding year. Purple Herons *Ardea purpurea* were counted at one major colony in the Netherlands, and Night-herons *Nycticorax nycticorax* at several colonies in southern France. Wetland conditions were measured as the maximum monthly discharges through the Senegal and Niger rivers. Both relationships were statistically significant, with herons being more abundant following wet years in their wintering areas (on Kendall's rank correlation test, $p < 0.005$). (From den Held 1981)

only), Whitethroats, Willow Warblers, Swallows and Sand Martins have shown similar correlations (Winstanley *et al.* 1974, Cavé 1983, Dallinga & Schoenmakers 1989, Møller 1989b, Kanyamibwa *et al.* 1990, Baillie & Peach 1992, Bryant & Jones 1995, Peach *et al.* 1995, Mihoub *et al.* 2010). In all these migratory species, climatic conditions in wintering places several thousand kilometres south of the breeding areas affected the spring population levels seen in Europe. From the 1960s to the late 1980s, rainfall in west Africa was below average, and many of our summer migrants that wintered or passed through the drier regions showed net population declines over this period. However, most of them recovered in the 1990s, as rainfall generally improved and drought years became fewer.

The White Storks breeding in Europe show a migratory divide, those from western Europe crossing at Gibraltar to winter in west Africa and those from eastern Europe travelling round the east side of the Mediterranean to winter in east Africa. Correspondingly, annual changes in the numbers of White Storks breeding in Alsace (France) during 1948–70 were correlated with annual rainfall in west Africa, while annual changes of storks breeding in parts of Germany during 1928–84 were correlated with rainfall in east Africa (Dallinga & Schoenmakers 1989). In years with high winter rainfall, storks also arrived earlier in their breeding areas and a higher proportion of pairs produced young.

WEATHER, BODY RESERVES AND BREEDING IN LARGE WATERFOWL

Large waterfowl nesting in the Arctic depend chiefly on body reserves accumulated in their wintering and migration areas to produce and incubate their eggs (Chapter 3). Before the final stage of migration to breeding areas, weight gains of 30–50% have been recorded, females accumulating more extra fat and protein than males. The birds often arrive when their breeding areas are still snow-covered, and lay their eggs as soon as bare ground is exposed.

In the accumulation of the necessary body reserves, the birds are influenced by weather conditions on wintering and staging areas, and in their subsequent breeding success by weather in nesting areas. Among Whooper Swans wintering in Sweden, the proportion of young among winter flocks was correlated with the severity of weather in both the preceding winter (assumed to influence the body reserves of females, Chapter 3), and the preceding spring on the Siberian breeding grounds (assumed to influence the use of reserves) (Fig. 150c). Overall, 58% of the variance in breeding production between years was attributed to previous winter weather in Sweden and 32% to spring weather in Siberia. Declines in breeding success after hard winters have been documented in several other species, including Mute Swan, Barnacle Goose and Eider (Cabot & West 1973, Nilsson 1979, Bacon & Andersen-Harild 1989, Lehikoinen *et al.* 2006).

The breeding success of Barnacle Geese, and hence their autumn population sizes, were influenced by temperatures both in wintering areas in Britain and in breeding areas in Svalbard (Trinder *et al.* 2009). Winter temperatures are likely to have influenced the body condition of the adults, an effect carried over to the breeding season (as described in Chapter 3), while May temperatures in breeding areas affected the timing of the spring thaw, and hence the timing of breeding. In addition, breeding success was also reduced according to the number of days with strong crosswinds during the migration period, presumably through increasing the energy demands of migration and depleting the all-important body reserves.

It is not surprising that, in Arctic-nesting geese, marked annual variations in breeding success are associated partly with variations in the spring weather on breeding areas. When the geese arrive in the Arctic, food is largely unavailable, and in years when snow melt is late, the birds use more of their body reserves than usual for survival. This can prevent some females from laying and reduces the clutch sizes of others, leading to a general reduction in breeding success (Barry 1962, Newton 1977, Davies & Cooke 1983). The females are solely responsible for incubation, and if their reserves run out, many desert their nests to feed, leading to further reduction in breeding output. Among some populations of Brent Geese and Snow Geese, for example, the proportion of young in winter flocks has varied from less than 2% after late springs to more than 50% after early springs (Newton 1977). Similarly, the proportions of breeding Barnacle Geese that produced young in Svalbard were 60–80% in early seasons and 15–25% in late ones (Prop et al. 1984).

Similar relationships between winter/spring weather and breeding success hold for some species of ducks, such as the Eider, in which females also rely heavily on body reserves for egg production and incubation (Parker & Holm 1990). At high latitudes, many waders also fail to breed in late springs, returning to their wintering sites weeks ahead of normal (Tate 1972, Green et al. 1977). The scarcity of young means that wintering numbers tend to be low in those years.

EPISODIC WEATHER EVENTS

Depending on the region, storms of one sort or another can occur at any time of year, and hence can affect birds at any stage of the annual cycle. Their unpredictability means that their effects are hard to document, because it is largely a matter of chance if they hit localities where bird counts were made beforehand, for comparison with counts made after the storm. However, it has sometimes been possible to compare bird numbers after the event in affected and unaffected areas, as in some of the examples below.

Spring snowstorms. Cold snaps, with heavy snow, sometimes occur after birds have started nesting. As expected, mortality and breeding failures are greatest in small species, especially in recently returned migrants affected by lack of insects. Small species that use holes and other protected sites fare better, as do

FIG 164. The breeding numbers of Common Sandpipers *Actitis hypoleucos* in the southern Pennines were for several years related to April temperatures, around the time of arrival from spring migration (see Fig. 150b). (Edmund Fellowes)

some larger species (such as ducks) which can continue incubating through the snow. Birds at the laying or hatching stages are particularly vulnerable, as are those with small chicks (Bengston 1963, Pulliainen 1978, Ojanen 1979).

Among Common Sandpipers, which migrate from Africa to breed in Britain, annual survival fluctuated in one area according to the weather in April, when they arrived (Fig. 150b). Over 13 years, the mean annual survival of ringed birds was 79%, but following late snowstorms in 1981 and 1989 survival fell to 39% and 50%, respectively. This was associated with a drop in breeding pairs from 21 to 14, and from 20 to 12. Recovery in breeding numbers was slow, with annual increments of only 1–2 pairs (Hollands & Yalden 1991). Similarly, in the spring of 1966, frost and snow on 11–17 April caused massive mortality of newly arrived Lapwings across southern Sweden and Finland, with reductions in populations amounting to 30–90% in different regions (Vespäläinen 1968, Marcström & Mascher 1979).

Summer rainstorms. One violent storm in Essex in September 1992 produced hailstones up to 5 cm across. After this event, 3,238 bird corpses were found at Foulness, mainly gulls, waders and gamebirds, many of which had broken wings, legs, skulls and bills (Adcock 1993). Elsewhere, rainstorms have killed many young birds, especially when they occurred soon after hatch, as illustrated by the 90% chick mortality recorded at a Herring Gull colony (Threlfall *et al.* 1974). In addition, flooding and wave action resulting from rainstorms has often destroyed the nests of aquatic birds over wide areas (Harris & Marshall 1957). Spring flooding delayed the onset of breeding of Snipe on the Nene Washes by up to 70 days, greatly reducing their opportunity to produce young that year (Green 1988b). Even Peregrines and other raptors are not immune to the effects of rainstorms, which can sometimes flood their nest ledges, killing the chicks (Bradley *et al.* 1997).

Winter storms. During a severe windstorm and saltwater flooding in January 1953, much forest and reedbed habitat was destroyed in southeast England, and the Bearded Tit population (then confined to southeast England) fell by 44% between the breeding seasons of 1952 and 1953 (Axell 1966). Years later, a similar

FIG 165. Snipe *Gallinago gallinago* breeding is dependent on soil conditions. Spring flooding can delay the start of breeding, while drainage or summer drought can advance the end of breeding. (Alan Martin)

event affected Bearded Tits at Leighton Moss in northwest England (Wilson & Peach 2006). Adult numbers had increased threefold (from 60 to 180 individuals) between 1992 and 2000, but declined by 94% during the winter of 2000/01. This population crash was associated with a prolonged flood of the reedbed litter layer, the main winter foraging habitat of Bearded Tits, followed immediately by cold weather. At the end of the flood, Bearded Tits weighed 20% less than during previous winters. Similarly, following a severe wind storm in Belgium in January 1990, about 62% of Crested Tits in a study population died and many of the surviving ringed individuals were blown up to a few kilometres from the area (Lens & Dhondt 1992). Gales can also damage habitats, especially forest, which can take many years to recover, so that the total effects on the avifauna exceed those resulting from immediate mortality.

Whether snow, rain or wind, severe storms occur sporadically, and usually affect some tens, hundreds or thousands of square kilometres at a time. As illustrated above, they can cause severe losses of a wide range of bird species, either of full-grown birds or nests with eggs and chicks, sometimes resulting in substantial declines in local populations.

Weather on migration

The sections above have been concerned mainly with weather effects on winter survival and summer breeding, but migrants suffer additional hazards. During migration, birds may encounter fog, which can hinder their navigation, unfavourable winds, which can slow their progress or blow them off course, or heavy rain, which can soak them. Such conditions can cause heavy losses among migrants, especially over water, and such mortality is sometimes reflected in reduced breeding densities. Fog can also cause birds to collide with tall structures, such as communication masts, adding further mortality (Newton 2008).

Seabird wrecks

Seabirds are also vulnerable to episodic weather events, such as strong or persistent storms, at whatever time of year they occur. In the breeding season, storms or high spring tides can result in nests at low elevations being washed away (notably the beach nests of Little Terns), and even the lower nests of cliff-nesters. Torrential ran also can flood the nest chambers of burrow-nesting species, such as Puffins, with chicks being drowned or forced out to be killed by gulls.

Outside the breeding season, prolonged gales bringing rough seas and turbid waters can make feeding difficult, and sometimes result in high mortality among exhausted seabirds. This is evident in so-called *wrecks*, when many birds are washed ashore or blown inland by onshore gales. Such wrecks have been recorded in various parts of the world, but affect some species more than others, depending partly on how close to land they feed. Usually, the birds found dead are thin, indicating starvation. Some of the biggest wrecks recorded around Britain and Ireland include the following:

* In September 1969, over 12,000 seabirds (mostly Guillemots) were washed ashore in the Irish Sea. This event, which occurred when birds were moulting, was attributed to a combination of stresses, including poor weather (and associated food shortage) and contamination with organochlorine pollutants, especially PCBs (Holdgate 1971).
* In February 1983, following a week of severe winds, 34,000 seabirds were found dead on the east coast of Britain (Underwood & Stowe 1984). They included Razorbills (16,000), Guillemots (12,200), Puffins (1,600) and Little Auks (1,200).
* On 15–16 October 1987, unusual numbers of pelagic seabirds were borne inland. They appeared to have been displaced northward from feeding areas in the Bay of Biscay, and to have travelled in the eye of a storm towards land where, on meeting strong winds, they were carried far inland. Many were subsequently found feeding, apparently in good condition, on lakes and reservoirs (Elkins & Yesou 1998). They included up to 550 Sabine's Gulls and 200 Grey Phalaropes, which would have been migrating at the time.
* In February–March 1994, during 22 days of strong onshore winds, more than 50,000 birds were washed onto the east coast of Britain, mainly Guillemots, Shags and gulls (Harris & Wanless 1996).

This last event caused the deaths of an estimated 20,000–50,000 Guillemots and 3,000–5,000 Shags (Harris & Wanless 1996). It had no detectable effect on local Guillemot breeding numbers, but caused a massive decline in Shag breeding numbers. The species difference occurred because the mortality affected a smaller proportion of the Guillemots in the area, and mainly immatures, whereas in Shags it affected a larger proportion, and similar numbers of adults and immatures. On the Isle of May, occupied Shag nests fell from 715 in 1993 to 403 in 1994, and hardly any non-breeding adults were seen at the colony in 1994. In that year, the return rate of ringed adult Shags dropped to 13% (compared with 75–82% in previous years) and the breeding population sank to its lowest level in 35 years. This event wiped out in a few weeks a net increase which had occurred over this whole 35-year period. During the study, there were three major population crashes, in 1975–76, 1993–94 and 2004–05, with numbers rising steadily between times (Frederiksen *et al.* 2008). Shags depend on clear water to find their food, and storm conditions make the water turbid. Wind and rain also make it harder for Shags to dry their plumage, which is not fully waterproofed, and which is constantly drenched from waves and spray. In contrast, Guillemots feed further from shore, in deeper less turbid waters, and are better waterproofed.

Other smaller wrecks around Britain and Ireland have involved various species. Overland wrecks of Leach's Petrels occurred in the autumns of 1891 and 1952, affecting birds en route to wintering areas (Boyd 1954). In 1952, at least 6,700 birds were picked up dead or dying in the British Isles, while others were found as far inland as Switzerland. Small numbers of Storm Petrels were also involved. Wrecks of Little Auks, involving hundreds or thousands of individuals, occurred in 1895, 1900, 1910, 1912, 1950, 1953 and 1983 (review in Newton 1998); while a wreck of Fulmars occurred around February 1962, with some 849 carcasses reported mainly from eastern Britain (Pashby & Cudworth 1969). Wrecks of Guillemots have occurred fairly frequently, with 13 recorded in Shetland alone between 1979 and 2002, and eight elsewhere in Scotland between 1968 and 2000 (Harris & Wanless 2007). All these various events occurred in winter (November–March), and probably involved mainly migrant birds from distant colonies. Juveniles predominated, and many appeared in poor condition, but it was never certain whether poor condition predisposed birds to the effects of strong winds, or whether the winds caused the poor condition by preventing feeding.

It is curious, if such wrecks are primarily storm-induced, that some consist overwhelmingly of one species. This could be because one species predominates in the area at the time, or because predisposing factors, such as prior food shortage, affect one species more than others. Although large numbers of birds are sometimes involved, it is often unclear which breeding populations they represent (in winter they could include migrants from several breeding areas). The fact that seabird populations usually contain large numbers of non-breeding immatures, from which replacement breeders could be recruited, may help to minimise the impact on breeding numbers.

THE NORTH ATLANTIC OSCILLATION

The discovery of a large-scale climatic phenomenon – the North Atlantic Oscillation (NAO) – has proved useful in assessing climatic influences on bird populations, for it is sometimes easier to find links between bird demography and this crude index of prevailing weather than between demography and more precise measures such as local temperature or rainfall. The NAO operates over a wide area, so can be used to reflect conditions on migration routes as well as in specific breeding and wintering areas. It varies according to the pressure differential between tropical and polar air masses, with positive values when these differentials are higher than normal and negative values when they are lower (Hurrell et al. 2003). In northern Europe, positive NAO values are associated with warm, wet and stormy weather, and negative values with colder and drier conditions. In southern Europe, the same index produces the opposite conditions. The NAO fluctuates annually but tends to remain in one phase for several years at a time. In 1950–80 there were many negative years, with fewer subsequently, although the lowest of all values was in winter 2009–10. Through its effects on local weather, the NAO would be expected to affect both land-birds and seabirds. It could also influence migrants travelling up through Europe in spring which, under high NAO indices, would encounter first conditions of low precipitation and temperatures in southern Europe, followed by heavy precipitation and relative warmth in the breeding areas of northern Europe.

Not surprisingly, then, the NAO can often explain some of the annual variation in bird numbers, breeding or survival rates. For example, the annual survival of five out of ten passerine species in Britain over the period 1966–2001 was correlated with the strength of the NAO (Robinson et al. 2007). In most such species, first-year survival was affected more than adult survival. In four species of grouse in Scotland, the annual numbers shot on various moors (mainly reflecting previous breeding success) were correlated with the NAO index, probably because warm dry summers favoured good breeding (Watson & Moss 2008). Among Swallows, significant differences in reproductive performance emerged over the years – particularly in the relative performance of first and second broods – that could be related to changes in weather patterns as reflected in the NAO index (Møller 2002a).

OCEANIC CONDITIONS

Changes in currents and surface temperatures

Changes in currents or sea-surface temperatures that are associated with the NAO index can have huge impacts on seabird populations by affecting their food supplies. For example, in northwest Britain, over a 33-year period, a correlation emerged between the breeding performance of Kittiwakes, the abundance of Herrings, zooplankton and phytoplankton, and the frequency of westerly winds (Aebischer *et al.* 1990). All declined at a similar rate from the 1950s to reach a trough around 1979–80, and then recovered somewhat. Although the mechanisms were unclear, the existence of such correlations again pointed to some underlying oceanographic-climatic influence, whose effects were felt through organisms at different trophic levels.

In the northeast Atlantic and North Sea, positive NAO values are associated with warm sea-surface temperatures, lower abundance of zooplankton, and reduced numbers of sandeels. These conditions influence all the species that depend on sandeels, as reflected in their lower survival or reproductive rates (Chapter 4). In addition, among Fulmars nesting on Eynhallow in Orkney, the likelihood of individuals returning in a later year was lower in years of high NAO index, as was their hatching and fledging success (Thompson & Ollason 2001). Although Fulmars were not dependent on sandeels, it seemed that their survival and breeding also varied with oceanic conditions.

While the food-species of some seabirds decrease under increasing sea temperatures, the food-species of other seabirds decrease under decreasing sea temperatures. For example, in Pembrokeshire in 1991, many Cormorants made no attempt to breed. This followed a period of abnormally cold and persistent northerly winds during April and early May, which, it was suggested, confined fish to deep water beyond the reach of Cormorants (Debout *et al.* 1995). The same occurred in Norway, where the numbers of breeding Cormorants were markedly reduced in 1986–87, following winters with low sea temperatures, and low numbers of Capelin and other suitable fish. Positive correlations have been found in Norway between sea temperatures in December and the numbers of Cormorants wintering and also breeding in the following spring (Debout *et al.* 1995).

Year-to-year fluctuations in the breeding of some seabirds in other regions have been linked with sea-surface temperatures, and at high latitudes with the timing of ice break-up. There can be no doubt, then, that seabird populations in many regions are from time to time greatly influenced by the food shortages caused by changes in currents, winds and sea temperatures. These aspects are discussed further in the next chapter.

SELECTIVE MORTALITY IN WEATHER EVENTS

Extreme weather, leading to bird deaths and population declines, clearly does not affect a random cross-section of birds in the area at the time. Some species are more vulnerable than others and, within species, some sex- and age-groups are affected more than others. During the hard winter of 1962/63, Shelduck and Wigeon females died in greater proportion than males (Harrison & Hudson 1964). And in the cold of February 1991, mortality among shorebirds in southeast England was weighted towards males in at least three species, towards juveniles in at least one, and towards smaller individuals in five other species (Clark 2009).

In certain species, individuals of a particular size and shape die in greater proportion than others. An early and now famous example involved some House Sparrows which died in a severe storm, and were found to differ in weight and measurements from those that survived (Bumpus 1899). In a more recent study, the mean body size (as assessed by sternum length) of Sand Martins nesting in Britain was found to vary over the years, according to rainfall in their African wintering areas (Bryant & Jones 1995). Drought years were followed by reductions in mean body size, and wetter years by increases. These changes again resulted from selective mortality, as shown from ringed birds, and because body size is partly under genetic control, such events could exemplify natural selection in action.

As well as being emaciated, hard-weather victims are often found to be parasitised, injured or incapacitated in some other way. For example, among Oystercatchers that died during a cold spell in the Netherlands, about 61% were handicapped by anatomical deviations (such as curved or crossed mandibles), a significantly greater proportion than in the population at large. These birds had survived normal circumstances, but succumbed at a time of stress. Of the remaining birds that died, 19% of those older than one year were still in moult, two months later than normal. Although this incident provided another striking example of selective mortality, the abnormalities were not necessarily under genetic influence, so the removal of these birds need not have affected the genetic composition of the population (Swennen & Duiven 1983).

CONCLUDING REMARKS

Britain and Ireland are blessed with a relatively mild climate which, although highly changeable, is mostly free from the extremes encountered in other parts of the world. Weather effects are thus less severe than elsewhere, but still have marked effects on many bird populations. Some of the extreme weather events described above lasted no more than a few hours, while others lasted for several days or weeks, and sometimes occurred in successive years. They also varied in spatial extent, with some short-lived storms affecting only a few tens or hundreds of square kilometres, while severe cold or drought sometimes affected most of the country and neighbouring parts of the continent. The most obvious extreme weather events affecting birds in Britain are periods of severe frost and snow in winter and, in a smaller range of species, periods of extreme drought or extreme rainfall in summer.

In species whose numbers are affected by weather events, we can envisage three scenarios, depending on the frequency and severity of extreme events relative to the recovery rates of the populations concerned. Where such events cause big reductions in numbers but at long intervals, the population may recover from each event within a few years, so that for most of the time its numbers are limited by other factors. This type of pattern is exemplified by the Grey Heron, whose numbers in Britain are periodically reduced by hard winters. In the last 100 years, hard winters have mostly occurred at intervals much longer than the 1–3 years taken for Heron numbers to recover, so that the periodic reductions in numbers were interspersed by periods of recovery and relative stability (Fig. 5d).

The second scenario is where extreme events occur at such frequent intervals and cause such heavy losses that a population can never recover fully from one event before it is reduced by the next, giving an irregular saw-tooth pattern of fluctuations over periods of years. The population is then limited primarily by successive catastrophes, and can never reach the level that it might achieve if such events were less frequent or absent. This type of pattern is shown by the several bird species, such as the Stonechat or Dartford Warbler, which seem to be affected by any snow period of whatever duration. Numbers typically show occasional years of abrupt decline, each followed by several years of continuous increase, but never seem to reach a level at which they would stabilise, except in particular localities. Their numbers are thus presumably for most of the time well below the level that the local environment would otherwise support.

In the third scenario, severe events follow one another so rapidly and each time cause such heavy losses, that the species dies out from the area concerned. We cannot expect to observe this pattern frequently, but two successive hard winters almost eliminated the Dartford Warbler from Britain in 1961–63 (see above). The same pattern could well apply to many other resident species at their northern range boundaries which shuttle north and south over periods of years, depending on the severity of the winters. On this view, several species, such as the Green Woodpecker and Nuthatch, could extend further north in Britain if winters there became generally milder, and both these species have indeed spread north in recent years (Chapter 15). Winter severity is of course a relative measure, and what would eliminate one species need have no marked effect on another.

Prolonged periods of severe weather, and brief storms of one sort or another, have sometimes caused reductions of more than 90% in local population levels, exemplified in Britain by the Dartford Warbler, Bearded Tit and others. Similar events in the breeding season have also caused widespread breeding failures. Where habitat damage occurs, recovery of the bird population depends on the rate at which the habitat itself recovers, until which stage different species may be favoured. Similarly, shifts in ocean currents or sea-surface temperatures can cause substantial changes in seabird populations, mainly through effects on food supplies. Recovery from such extreme events can also take up to several years or decades (as in Shags).

Mortality resulting from sudden storms is almost certainly density-independent, for it occurs within a few hours, with little or no opportunity for competition. In contrast, during prolonged periods of severe weather, which lead to food shortage, the opportunity for competition during the event is much greater, so that initial density may influence the proportion of birds that die. This was evident in those studies in which annual population changes were shown to change in relation to the initial population density as well as in relation to weather.

Although the timing of extreme weather events is largely unpredictable, small birds with short lifespans are unlikely to experience more than one in their lives, and several generations may pass without any. In the same area, individuals of larger, long-lived species can expect to experience one or more extreme events during their lives, and few if any generations can escape them altogether. Severe weather events usually kill a non-random sample of the local avifauna, and of particular species. It is perhaps not surprising, therefore, that when extreme events occur they weed out vulnerable individuals, and in short-lived species sometimes lead to measurable morphological change in the population. With the changing climate in Britain and Ireland, and the projected increasing frequency of severe weather events, opportunities will abound in future for ornithologists to learn more about their effects on bird populations.

CHAPTER 15

Climate Change

L ARGELY DRIVEN BY HUMAN ACTIVITY, the global climate is now changing. The issues are becoming increasingly familiar to all of us. The main known cause is the release of 'greenhouse gases' into the atmosphere, which reduce natural heat radiation from the earth, enabling the planet surface to warm. The most significant of these gases is carbon dioxide, whose concentration in the atmosphere rose by 39% from pre-industrial times to 2010 (from about 280 to 390 parts per million). This rise is occurring mainly through the burning of fossil fuels, both coal and oil. Other increasing greenhouse gases, such as methane and nitrous oxide, have even stronger heat-trapping properties, but occur at much lower concentrations.

On a global scale, continuing deforestation is contributing to the problem. This is partly because trees hold more carbon per unit area than smaller plants, so release more when they are burnt, and partly because living forest converts carbon dioxide to oxygen more rapidly than does any other vegetation. So as forest areas shrink, ever less carbon dioxide is removed naturally from the atmosphere. Furthermore, as the earth becomes warmer, permafrost melts and peat deposits dry, enabling more stored methane to escape and more stored carbon to oxidise to carbon dioxide.

As a result of these processes, the mean global temperature rose by 0.74 °C during the last century, mainly in the latter half. Since the 1980s, each decade has been warmer than the previous, with 2001–10 the hottest on record. However, warming has not occurred to the same extent everywhere, nor evenly through the year. It has been greatest at high northern latitudes, and greater in winter and spring than in summer and autumn (Houghton *et al.* 2001). In some places, temperatures have even decreased, in association with changed air circulation patterns. Alterations have also occurred in the frequency of extreme weather events, whether heat or drought, storm or flood. The area of Arctic sea ice is shrinking rapidly, the Greenland and Antarctic ice sheets are melting and contracting, and most montane glaciers are also retreating. Owing to the expansion of sea water induced by greater warmth, together with increased ice melt, sea-levels are gradually rising, endangering many low-lying coastal areas and islands.

OCEANIC CHANGES

Over the past 50 years, the oceans have restrained global temperature rise by absorbing more than an estimated 93% of the heat added to the climate system. Nevertheless, as a worldwide average, sea-surface temperatures increased by 0.68 °C during the period 1991–2004 (Rayner *et al.* 2006). Increasing atmospheric carbon dioxide levels are also acidifying sea water. In the last 200 years, the oceans are thought to have absorbed about one-half of all anthropogenically produced carbon dioxide, which is present in surface waters as carbonic acid. This has resulted in a decrease of 0.1 pH units in surface waters since pre-industrial times, equivalent to a 30% rise in acidity (the concentration of hydrogen ions). Because corals, molluscs and other marine organisms have greater difficulty in incorporating calcium compounds into their skeletons in acid conditions, this change threatens many species with calcareous shells, including some plankton. In many regions, corals are already affected, and some biologists believe that the acidification of sea water will have greater effects on marine life than climate change itself.

Climate influences the abundance and distribution of phytoplankton, on which all marine life ultimately depends. In eight out of ten ocean regions, including the northeast Atlantic, phytoplankton production has declined over the past century, in step with rising sea-water temperatures and changing oceanic circulation patterns (Boyce *et al.* 2010). Global warming has thus reduced overall marine primary productivity over wide areas, affecting the whole food-web from the timing, abundance and distribution of phytoplankton blooms, through zooplankton and fish up to seabirds and other top predators. Plankton species have made some of the fastest apparent responses to climate change. Range boundaries of some northeast Atlantic copepod species have shifted northwards by more than 1,100 km over the past half-century, and dramatic shifts in their timings and distributions may have underpinned the recorded disruptions of some North Sea food-webs (Edwards & Richardson 2004).

BIRD RESPONSES

In theory, birds could respond to changing climate in four ways: (1) they could adapt facultatively, adjusting their behaviour within its pre-existing limits to cope with changing conditions; (2) they could adapt by evolutionary change, which would entail genetic modification under the action of natural selection; (3) they could change their distributions and migrations so as to remain within regions of favourable climate and other conditions; (4) they could respond insufficiently in any of these ways, and so decline to extinction in at least some parts of their range.

In the past, in post-glacial periods, change in distribution was the most obvious response of plants and animals to ameliorating climate, as species spread northwards across Europe, following the retreat of the ice. Many species became extinct at such times, although this is better established from the fossil record for mammals than for birds. The amount of genetic change was presumably limited, if the species were to remain essentially unchanged and not evolve into something different. And before a species could evolve substantial modification in a changing area, it was likely to be supplanted by competing species already equipped with adaptations appropriate to the changed conditions. Given that the current pace of climate change is greater than in any previous glacial times, rapid adaptation is perhaps even less likely than in the past. We will return to this aspect later.

In studying the effects of changing climate on bird populations, we might therefore expect to find changes in: (1) the timing of seasonal events, such as migration and breeding; (2) reproductive or survival rates, which may or may not lead to changes in population levels, depending on their net effects; (3) numerical changes, with populations declining in southern or lower-altitude parts of

FIG 166. The Little Egret *Egretta garzetta* has colonised Britain since the 1980s (with the first breeding record in 1996), and has since expanded over much of southern Britain and Ireland, numbering more than 800 pairs in 2010. (Richard Chandler)

their existing range and increasing in northern or higher-altitude parts; or (4) distributional changes, as species move to higher latitudes or altitudes. In recent decades, all these types of change have been recorded among the land-birds and seabirds of Britain and Ireland.

THE TIMING OF SEASONAL EVENTS

For more than 200 years across Europe, amateur naturalists have recorded the timing of various spring events, such as the bud-burst and flowering of trees, the first calling and spawning of frogs and toads, the first emergence dates of insects, and the first arrival, song or egg-laying dates of birds.[21] Such striking events are easy for an observer to detect and record. They have been described in many individual studies, scattered through the scientific literature. One detailed analysis attempted to pull together all known information from 21 European countries, and look for common trends. This enormous body of data, encompassing 561 plant and animal species, revealed that the timing of spring events had advanced by an average of 2.5 days per decade in Europe during the period 1971–2000 (Menzel et al. 2006). Other data compilations showed much the same for North America. One was based on 64 studies, encompassing nearly 700 plant and animal species, and revealed an average advance of 5.3 days per decade over the period 1951–2001 (Root et al. 2003). Another, embracing 172 species of plants, birds, butterflies and amphibians from various parts of the world, gave a mean advance of 2.3 days per decade over periods of 16–132 years (Parmesan & Yohe 2003). Although differing in detail, these various studies all gave a strong signal that climate warming has affected plant and animal life across much of the northern hemisphere, and in the direction predicted.

Another important finding was that spring warming has not affected all species in the same area to the same degree. Some have advanced more than others. This fact has important implications for the relationships between species, whether predators and prey, parasites and hosts, or competitors, because it could disrupt existing relationships or lead to the formation of new ones. One reason for such variability among species is that, while birds themselves are warm-blooded and can regulate their body temperature, the plants and invertebrates on which many birds depend are not. Their biochemical and

---

21 The oldest known set of records from Britain was started by Robert Marsham, who began meticulous recordings of 27 'indications of spring' on his Norfolk estate in 1736. His descendants continued his work until 1958, creating Britain's longest single-site phenological record. Phenology is the study of the seasonal timing of biological events.

physiological processes may occur 2–3 times more rapidly for every 10 °C temperature rise. As a presumed result of climate warming, plants begin their leaf and flower development earlier in the spring. Hence, the food of herbivorous insects is available earlier and their larvae are expected to develop earlier and more rapidly, and emerge as adults earlier in the year than in the past. Caterpillars and other larval insects may therefore become available to birds earlier than before, but remain available for a shorter period each year, while the reproductive timing of their warm-blooded avian predators may change to a considerably lesser extent. We will return to this question of mismatch later.

To many ornithologists, the most obvious manifestations of climate change are in the timing of bird migration and breeding. Some migrants are arriving earlier in spring than in the past, and some are also departing later in autumn, spending longer each year in their breeding areas (Lehikoinen *et al.* 2004, Newton 2008). Both migratory and resident species are also starting to breed earlier in spring than in the past (Crick *et al.* 1997, Thackeray *et al.* 2010). However, these changes in timing are important in our present context only if they affect reproductive or survival rates, and thereby influence population levels.

Migration dates
The timing of spring migration closely follows weather patterns, and birds generally arrive in their breeding areas earlier in warm springs than in cold ones (Fig. 167). This is possible largely because, after winter dormancy, plant growth and animal life develop earlier in warm springs, providing an earlier food supply for migrating birds. An earlier food supply enables birds to accumulate the body

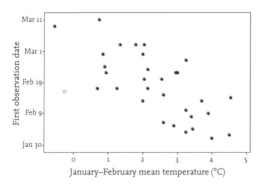

FIG 167. First observation (= arrival) dates of Oystercatchers *Haematopus ostralegus* in nesting areas in mid-Deeside, northeast Scotland, in different years in relation to mean January–February temperatures. In line with this statistically significant relationship, arrival dates became generally earlier over the study period (1974–2010) in association with gradual warming, but the last year of the study (2010, shown by an open symbol) was exceptionally cold. (From Jenkins & Sparks 2010)

reserves for each successive stage of their journeys earlier than in colder years. For the same reason, individuals can also survive at earlier dates in their breeding areas than is possible in cold springs. In addition, under warmer weather, the energy needs of the birds themselves are reduced, allowing more of their energy intake to be devoted to migration or reproductive development.

As springs have become warmer over the years, migration dates have become earlier. In one detailed review, incorporating past records for 19 countries mainly in Europe and covering the period 1950–2009, the first arrival dates of birds became earlier, on average, by 2.8 days per decade (based on 440 species), and mean or median arrival dates by 1.8 days per decade (based on 214 species) (Lehikoinen & Sparks 2010). It was not obvious why the two figures differed, but different numbers of species were involved, and the first dates for each year were inevitably based on small numbers of birds, perhaps in some years just single individuals, while the mean dates involved large numbers. Among the individual data series, 82% pointed to earlier first arrival dates, and 76% towards earlier mean or median arrival dates. But in Britain and Ireland, almost all the species for which reasonable samples were available showed earlier mean arrival dates, some having advanced by as much as two weeks in 50 years. These changes were more apparent in the earlier-arriving short-distance migrants, travelling entirely within Europe, than in the later-arriving long-distance migrants returning from Africa, but the extent of advance in arrival rates was also related to feeding habits. We will return later to the reasons for these differences. Similar findings emerged for North America and Australia, but the recorded rates of change varied between studies, according to location, timing and species composition.

Spring arrival dates depend not just on conditions in breeding areas, but on conditions along the whole migration route from wintering areas, and sometimes birds can be delayed en route, so that their arrival in breeding areas shows no advance. A long-term study of Swallows in Denmark revealed a significant change in the mean spring arrival date over 32 years (Møller & Merilä 2004). But the best predictor of arrival date was not the climatic conditions in the Danish breeding areas, but the conditions in Algeria, North Africa, during spring migration. This was the area where Swallows refuelled after their gruelling northward journey over the Sahara. Analyses based solely on weather conditions in the breeding area (as in most studies) would be unable to reveal such carry-over effects from spring migration. Similarly, analyses solely in terms of temperature take little account of other weather variables that affect migration, such as wind and rain. Nevertheless, there is abundant evidence from many species that individuals migrate more rapidly and arrive earlier in breeding areas in warm springs than in cold ones, and that arrival dates have

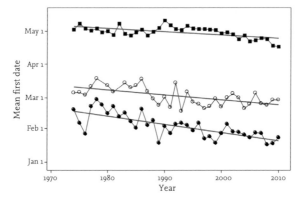

FIG 168. First song or arrival dates for various species in mid-Deeside, Scotland, showing mean values for 16 resident species (filled circles), 10 short-distance migrants (open circles) and 12 long-distance migrants wintering in Africa (filled squares). Regression lines superimposed in grey; all downward trends were statistically significant. Over the period 1974–2010, the first song/arrival date of 38 species tended to become earlier, with the average advance being 25 days over the 37 years of study (or 7 days per decade). Change was greater in the dates of first song of resident species than in the dates of first detection of short-distance and long-distance migrants. Relationships with temperature were apparent, but were statistically significant for fewer than half the species. (From Jenkins & Sparks 2010)

advanced over recent decades (Lehikoinen *et al.* 2004, Newton 2008). Examples of advancing arrival dates in northeast Scotland are shown in Figure 168.

The fact that short-distance migrants have advanced their spring arrival dates more than long-distance ones may be due to several reasons. First, short-distance migrants tend to migrate earlier in spring, and temperatures have risen more in early spring than in late spring, so short-distance, early migrants would be expected to have advanced more. Secondly, the nearer to breeding areas that birds winter, the more likely is the weather in wintering areas to be correlated with weather in breeding areas, so an earlier spring in wintering areas could stimulate migration to reach an earlier spring in breeding areas. In contrast, long-distance migrants wintering south of the Sahara in Africa can have little clue from their wintering areas of how conditions are developing in breeding areas, more than 1,000 km to the north. Experiments have revealed that such birds use an 'internal clock', coupled with daylength change, to time their departure from wintering areas. This response is presumed to have evolved over long periods of time in order to get the birds to their breeding areas in time to take advantage of the seasonal surge in food supplies there (Berthold 2001, Newton 2008). The assumption is that this innate system can be changed only slowly over the generations by natural selection acting in European breeding areas to influence the date of departure from African wintering areas. Thirdly, long-distance migrants may be unable to advance their arrival dates in most years because conditions en route prevent an earlier or faster migration. A particular problem, mentioned already, is that spring conditions have not changed by the same amount everywhere, but have advanced more in some northern regions than in southern regions through which the migrants have to pass.

In these various ways, migratory behaviour could constrain the ability of some bird species to respond fully to rapid changes in climate. Among 100 European species of migratory birds, earlier timing of spring migration was associated with stable or increasing populations over the period 1990–2000, as judged from national count data (Møller *et al.* 2008). Yet among species that did not change their spring migration timing, or even delayed it, populations declined. This may be because migratory species which are unable to advance their arrival date in response to spring warming are now arriving too late to fully exploit changed timings of their food supplies in breeding areas, an aspect discussed in detail later. On this basis, ongoing climate change could be affecting populations of migratory bird species more adversely than resident ones.

Turning to autumn, while in some parts of Europe temperatures at this time of year have risen in recent decades, in other parts they have not. Nevertheless, some species have advanced their departure dates, while others have delayed them (Jenni & Kéri 2003, Lehikoinen *et al.* 2004, Sokolov 2006). In many songbird species, mainly long-distance migrants that produce only one brood per year, the whole cycle of events has been brought forward, so that after earlier arrival in spring, birds then breed earlier and can depart earlier in autumn. The timing of autumn migration may then be better linked to temperatures in spring than to temperatures in late summer when the birds leave (Sokolov 2006). But by leaving earlier, migrants can get to the Sahel zone of Africa in time to experience more of the benign wet season there before the dry season sets in. In other species, mainly short-distance migrants that can raise more than one brood in a season, the timing of autumn migration has become delayed in recent years, as the birds have begun to spend longer in their breeding areas, perhaps in some cases raising an extra brood. In England, over a 50-year period, common species that changed their migration dates were estimated to be arriving 12 days earlier and departing 8 days later, giving 20 extra days in breeding areas (Sparks *et al.* 2007).

Breeding

As with migration dates, many birds begin to lay their eggs earlier in warm springs than in cold ones, and in parallel with springs becoming generally warmer in recent decades, laying dates have advanced (Parmesan & Yohe 2003, Dunn 2004). Again the magnitude of this response has varied between species, depending partly on the extent of temperature change during their particular laying period in the region concerned, on their diet and body size, on the number of broods per year, and on the timescale over which individuals accumulate resources for breeding. Most bird species depend on food consumed as the eggs are formed, but some large birds, such as some Arctic-nesting waterfowl, form their eggs largely from body reserves accumulated beforehand in wintering and migration areas (Chapter 3). Reliance on long-term body reserves reduces their dependence on food availability at the time of egg-laying.

In a review of published studies, some 79% (45/57) of mainly European bird species laid earlier in years with higher air temperatures in the breeding areas (Dunn 2004). About 60% of these species also showed a significant trend towards earlier laying in recent decades. Among British birds, over the 25-year period 1971–1995, some 30% (20/67) of species examined tended towards earlier laying (Crick *et al.* 1997). On average, eggs were laid about 8.8 days earlier at the end of the study than at the start, an advance of 3.5 days per decade. In a subsequent study, it emerged that 19 of 36 species in Britain were breeding earlier in the 1990s than in the 1960s and 1970s, and of these 19 species, 17 also showed negative correlations between laying dates and March–April temperatures (Crick & Sparks 1999). The advancement in laying averaged three days earlier for every 1 °C rise in the mean March–April temperature (range 1.1–5.5 days per °C according to species).

As expected from these relationships, some species have shown correlations between laying dates and the North Atlantic Oscillation (NAO) index – for example, the Collared Flycatcher (Przybylo *et al.* 2000). In addition, numerous studies have shown that seabirds, as well as land-birds, tend to breed earlier in warmer springs. Research on individually marked Guillemots on the Isle of May revealed that particular females tended to lay earlier following mild winters, as indicated by the winter NAO index (Frederiksen *et al.* 2004a). Among Guillemots on Skomer Island off Wales, despite annual variations, laying dates advanced by about two weeks over a 30-year period (Votier *et al.* 2009).

The widespread correlations found among birds between laying dates and air temperatures could have arisen in several ways. Temperature may have directly affected the energy demands of birds, which, being less in warmer weather, allowed more of their daily nutrient intake to be devoted to egg production, rather than to daily maintenance. Alternatively, greater warmth may have influenced the development of their food supplies, particularly insects and other 'cold-blooded' organisms. Both of these effects may in turn have influenced the ability of the females to produce eggs. The fact that some bird species seemed not to respond to temperature could have been due to their food supplies or laying dates being less influenced by local temperatures than by other factors, to insufficient advance in migration dates, or to small samples or insufficient years to detect a statistical effect. Under experimental conditions, temperatures in the presence of plentiful food had no effect on the earlier stages of gonad development in spring. On the other hand, warmer conditions led to earlier testes regression and moult at the end of the breeding season in Starlings, Greenfinches and Great Tits, thus reducing the maximum period over which breeding was possible (Dawson & Visser 2010).

Several bird species have been studied simultaneously by different observers at widely separated localities across Europe. Among *Ficedula* flycatchers, the extent to which laying dates had advanced over the years varied according to the degree of spring warming, and laying dates showed no obvious advance in areas with no obvious warming (Both *et al.* 2004). Among Great and Blue Tits, the relationship between advance in laying dates and spring warming was less consistent, apparently because other factors also influenced laying dates (Visser *et al.* 2003). In Great Tits, the greatest advances in first egg dates occurred in populations that showed the greatest decrease over time in the proportions of second broods, but the reasons for this relationship are unclear.

The mismatch problem

Many birds are now able to breed earlier than in the past probably in part because their food supplies are developing earlier in spring, as mentioned above. However, an unexpected response to climate warming concerns the growing mismatch between the timing of bird breeding and food supplies. This applies particularly to woodland insectivores, such as tits and flycatchers that eat defoliating caterpillars. Under warmer springs, these caterpillars hatch and grow earlier and more rapidly than in the past, making them available for a shorter period. The breeding dates of birds which eat caterpillars are also earlier, but in some populations, egg-laying dates have advanced less than the caterpillars themselves. The result is that many pairs now miss the main peak in their food supply on which they raise their chicks, and their breeding output is much reduced. For example, in the Hoge Veluwe in the Netherlands, Great Tits feed their young mainly on Winter Moth caterpillars, which in turn feed on the leaves of oak trees. The caterpillars hatch just as the oak buds are opening, and their development takes about 3–5 weeks (depending on prevailing temperatures), after which they pupate in the soil, and become unavailable to tits. Over recent decades, bud-burst and the peak in caterpillar biomass has advanced by about eight days per decade, but the laying dates of resident Great Tits by only two days per decade (Visser *et al.* 1998, 2003). One reason is that temperatures from February onwards affect bud and caterpillar development, but Great Tits respond to temperatures only from around mid-March, and temperatures in the earlier period have changed more than those in the later period. Nevertheless, despite some reduction in breeding output, Dutch Great Tits have as yet shown no sign of population decline. This is probably because their numbers are much more affected by winter conditions than by summer conditions (Chapter 4).

In contrast to the Netherlands, Great Tits nesting in Wytham Wood near Oxford advanced their laying dates more strongly than the peak time of their caterpillar prey (Cresswell & McCleery 2003). In the past, they had always bred late relative to the food peak, but they are now better synchronised, and their breeding success has improved over the years. Why one situation prevails in the Netherlands and another in England remains unclear, but in a third area in central Europe the laying dates of Great Tits advanced over a 40-year period very much in synchrony with the caterpillars (Bauer *et al.* 2010). Evidently the situation has varied from region to region. In many bird populations some individuals always bred much later than the rest, so were always 'mistimed' with the food peak, and often failed to raise young. The new situation is that, under climate warming, most or all individuals in some populations have become mismatched, in a way that causes a marked decline in the breeding output of the overall population. The crucial question has become not whether birds have advanced their breeding in response to climate warming, but whether they have advanced it sufficiently to keep up with the insects and other cold-blooded creatures on which they depend (Visser & Both 2005).

Migrants, such as the Pied Flycatcher, are absent from their breeding areas in early spring, so cannot respond to conditions there at that time of year. Although in areas where spring has advanced they are arriving earlier, this may again not be early enough for the food supply. This was clearly seen in a Dutch population of Pied Flycatchers, which over a period of years advanced their egg-laying by about one week, partly by reducing the time interval between arrival and laying (Both & Visser 2001). However, caterpillar development in the same area over the same period advanced by about two weeks, reducing the synchronisation between the nestling period and the food peak. In consequence, breeding output declined, as did subsequent breeding numbers. Population decline occurred most dramatically in rich deciduous woods, but no obvious trend occurred in mixed woods or in pure pine forests. In the deciduous woods the food peak had become earlier and shorter, while in mixed and pine forests the food peak had also become earlier but was generally later and broader than in deciduous areas, involving largely different species of caterpillars. In extreme years, chicks in some

FIG 169. Pied
Flycatcher *Ficedula
hypoleuca* chicks
now hatch in some
regions later than their
potential food peak,
causing population
decline. (Keith Kirk)

populations hatched an average of ten days after the caterpillar peak. Among
nine areas across the Netherlands during 1987–2003, the greatest population
declines occurred in areas where food peaks were earliest, and where the birds'
laying dates responded most weakly to temperature rise. Some populations
declined by about 90%, while in areas where food peaks were latest, declines were
much less, around 10% (Both *et al.* 2006). Pied Flycatchers in Britain have also
declined, but again by different amounts in different areas.

The mismatch problem reveals a subtle and indirect way in which change
in spring temperatures can alter the abundance and distribution of bird
populations. Clearly, long-distance migrants are likely to have the most difficulty
in maintaining synchronisation with their food sources. They normally arrive
in breeding areas shortly before they start nesting, which constrains their ability
to advance their egg-laying. It is in fact some of the Eurasian–African migrants
which are latest to arrive in their breeding areas that have shown least change in
their spring arrival dates over the years, and also some of the greatest population
declines (Møller *et al.* 2008). This is true for forest- and scrub-nesting species, but
not for marshland species, whose food supplies remain plentiful over a longer
period each year, without the short peak characteristic of woodland caterpillars
(Both *et al.* 2010). Reed and Sedge Warblers have shown no obvious declines since
1990, and in some regions have increased over this time.

Most studies of the mismatch problem have so far concerned passerines, but
some non-passerines have been affected too, and it is not always a case of young
birds hatching too late for the prey. For example, a study of Golden Plovers and
their cranefly prey was conducted in the southern Pennines, at the south end
of the species' breeding range (Pearce-Higgins *et al.* 2005). Recent laying dates
were correlated with March–April temperatures, and also with March rainfall,

but the emergence dates of adult craneflies (from larvae overwintering in the peaty soil) were correlated with May temperatures. On the basis of relationships studied in recent years, and models of future climate change, the mean laying dates of Golden Plovers are predicted to advance by about 18 days by the last third of the present century, but cranefly emergence by about 12 days. If this situation materialises, Golden Plover chicks will be hatching well before their current main food-species is available for them. This study illustrates how ideas developed from existing correlations may be examined on the basis of predicted future climate. Further examples of this approach are given later, mainly in the context of distributional changes.

Another example of a mismatch is provided by the Black Grouse in Finland (Ludwig 2009). These birds are resident, and have declined in recent decades, mainly due to poor reproduction, for which predation has often been blamed. They have responded to spring warming by laying earlier, which results in an earlier hatch. However, temperatures at the time the young hatch in early summer are not warmer than in the past (in some years colder), and so newly hatched chicks increasingly face relatively cold post-hatching conditions. This is a critical time, and chicks (which feed themselves initially on caterpillars and other insects) now suffer increasingly higher mortality apparently because they hatch 'too early'. They have greater energy demands because they need to keep warm and, because insects are less active, they may need to move around more to forage, increasing their vulnerability to both hypothermia and predation. Productivity and adult numbers of Black Grouse have therefore declined since the 1970s, and former cyclic fluctuations in numbers are no longer evident.

Change in laying dates is not the only means by which birds could achieve greater synchrony with their food supply. They may adjust the number of broods raised per season, reducing two to one, thereby optimising the timing of the entire annual cycle. This may have happened in some of the Great Tit populations mentioned above. But many small birds still produce more than one brood per season if conditions are right. In Poland, Reed Warblers arrive from migration and start their first clutches two weeks earlier than they did in the 1970s. And whereas during the 1970s and 1980s at most 15% of pairs produced a second clutch, up to 35% did so during 1994–2006. Their lengthened breeding season, along with other beneficial habitat changes during warmer years (such as the earlier growth of reeds that support nests), allowed these warblers to produce more offspring per year (Halupka et al. 2008).

In most of the available examples, from birds to marine plankton, the phenology of predatory species has shifted to greater or lesser extent than that of their food organisms. This was apparent, for instance, among 726 different species examined at different tropic levels and across terrestrial, freshwater and marine environments around Britain (Thackeray *et al.* 2010). Evidently, many predator–prey systems are becoming mistimed by climate change (Visser & Both 2005).

Another type of mismatch has been described in some Arctic regions, where the spring break-up of sea-ice now occurs about three weeks earlier than in the 1970s. This is causing Polar Bears to appear on land earlier than before, well within the bird nesting season, and leading to locally catastrophic levels of egg predation among geese and seabirds. The bears are mismatched with their traditional diet of seal pups, but newly 'matched' with the egg season of birds. Some bears have been seen consuming dozens of goose clutches in a single day, with up to several bears in a colony at the same time. Predation is accentuated by the fact that geese have been spreading northward in recent decades, bringing them more than ever within the range of Polar Bears (P. A. Smith *et al.* 2010). Potential effects on breeding numbers have not yet been assessed, but on recent predation rates, Snow Geese on the Cape Churchill Peninsula of Hudson Bay are projected to decline (Rockwell *et al.* 2011). Polar Bears have also been filmed climbing cliffs for seabird eggs and chicks.

CHANGES IN POPULATIONS

At its simplest, we might expect that what we regard in the British Isles as southern species would increase and spread under a warming climate while northern species would decline and contract. Species are thus likely to show contrasting trends in different parts of their geographical range, even in the north and south of Britain.

Land-birds

In Chapter 14, we saw that many land-bird bird species in Britain decline during hard winters and other weather extremes, and then increase until the next severe event, when they decline again. If hard winters become less frequent in future, the population would suffer fewer weather-induced declines, so could remain for longer periods near capacity level. Its average level would thus be higher. On the other hand, if severe events became more frequent, populations could remain at lower levels for much longer, and could even decline to regional extinction. It was apparently the high frequency of hard winters which formerly limited the numbers and northward expansions of some bird species in Britain, including the Dartford Warbler, Bearded Tit and Green Woodpecker, all of which have expanded northward in recent years as winters have mellowed.

It is less easy to envisage how populations at the southern end of the breeding range might decline and eventually disappear, causing the southern range boundary to retreat northward. However, some species are already declining disproportionately in southern parts of their breeding range, and in a few the mechanisms have been studied. One such species is the Golden Plover, mentioned above (Pearce-Higgins *et al.* 2010). As well as a growing mismatch with the food supply, another potential mechanism of population decline has emerged. Formerly, severe winter weather was the dominant constraint on this plover population, but as winters warmed, the negative effects of hotter summers on breeding became a more significant influence. The annual productivity of Golden Plovers in the southern Pennines was correlated with the abundance of adult craneflies which emerged in May–June, providing a major food source for chicks. The chicks survived better in years when there were lots of craneflies (Pearce-Higgins & Yalden 2004). However, high summer temperatures dried out the surface layers of the peat, killing young cranefly larvae, and resulting in fewer adult craneflies emerging the following year. Few plover chicks then survived to fledge, and breeding numbers the next year declined. In consequence, year-to-year changes in Golden Plover breeding numbers became correlated with August temperatures nearly two years earlier (Pearce-Higgins *et al.* 2010). Broadly speaking, in years when the mean August temperature exceeded 18 °C plover breeding numbers the spring after next declined, whereas when the mean August temperature was less than 18 °C, breeding numbers the spring after next increased.

Climate models predict a steady increase in August temperatures over the next 100 years which, depending on the magnitude of climate warming, could bring a significant risk of local extinction for Golden Plovers. Direct effects of climate warming on cranefly populations may therefore cause northward retraction of Golden Plovers, a trend also predicted from other data (see later). Moreover, craneflies are important food-items for many other upland birds, which could also be affected. On the area where this study

FIG 170. The Golden Plover *Pluvialis apricaria* is declining at the southern end of its breeding range in Britain, probably in association which climate change, which affects its summer food supply. (Edmund Fellowes)

was made, the problem was exacerbated by the digging of drainage channels through the peat (done in the supposed interests of sheep), but blocking these channels allowed the peat to re-wet, giving better survival of cranefly larvae (Carroll *et al.* 2011). As in many situations, human land-use practices had exacerbated an effect of climate change. Chironomids and earthworms are also important in the diets of many upland birds. Like craneflies, they are influenced adversely by heat and drought, so ditch-blocking to re-wet peaty soils could do much to help several upland bird species into the future.

A similar approach was used to explore a recent decline in the Ring Ouzel in Britain, a summer visitor to our uplands which winters mainly in the Atlas Mountains of Morocco (Beale *et al.* 2006). In the Moorfoot Hills, breeding numbers changed from year to year in relation to temperatures and rainfall in the preceding summer, after breeding, and also in relation to rainfall in the wintering areas 24 months previously, coinciding with the period of juniper flowering (juniper berries being a major winter food). High temperatures and intermediate rainfall in Britain, and high spring rainfall in Morocco 24 months previously, all had negative effects on Ring Ouzel breeding numbers. All these weather variables have changed in recent decades in a way that would be predicted to cause a population decline in Ring Ouzels. A mathematical model based on recent data predicted a decline of about 3.6% per year, about three times larger than the observed rate, but nevertheless it did suggest that changing weather may have been involved. Breeding success itself showed no relationship with weather, but hot weather in late summer in Britain may have affected the post-breeding survival of the birds, while higher rainfall in Morocco may have affected winter survival, in both cases through reduced food supplies.

Understanding the relationships between bird numbers and distributions on the one hand and weather and land use on the other has led to the use of models to predict the likely future population trends of various other land-bird species breeding in Britain. On the basis of such models, two northerly species, the Curlew and Meadow Pipit, were predicted to greatly decline in the coming years, and two southerly ones, the Green Woodpecker and Nuthatch, to greatly increase (Renwick *et al.* 2012).

Marked population cycles of lemmings and voles have been an important feature of northern forests and tundras for as far back as records go. With shorter and warmer winters since the 1980s, these cycles have begun to fade out in some regions, giving lower and more stable rodent populations similar to those previously found only at lower latitudes, but the exact mechanism probably varies between regions and between rodent species. Lemmings can live under the snow pack where ground warmth melts a narrow layer of light and fluffy snow. This creates space for lemmings to move about, feeding on ground vegetation, while insulated from the cold and concealed from most predators. In Norway, a shorter snow period now limits the time that lemmings can spend in their safe sub-snow labyrinths, and warmer temperatures promote alternating freeze–melt cycles, creating an icy ground layer that impedes access to the moss that lemmings eat. Less insulated from cold, less able to access food and more vulnerable to predators, lemmings in some areas no longer produce the large-scale population peaks on which so many predatory mammals and birds depend (Ims *et al.* 2008). In the same regions, voles which feed on more erect vascular plants continue to cycle, but the cycles are longer and less pronounced than in the past. The same has happened over much of the Fennoscandian boreal forest, where a dampening of rodent population cycles was first recorded (Hörnfeldt 2004, Ims *et al.* 2008). The average level of vole populations has therefore declined over the years, as have the numbers of several predators, including owls (Hipkiss *et al.* 2013). In Britain, similar changes emerged during studies in the Kielder Forest region of northeast England. Over the period 1984–2004, the peaks in vole numbers became gradually less marked and more localised, before disappearing altogether. With less snow and shorter winters, voles could not increase over winter to the same extent as in the past, and towards the end of this period spring numbers showed relatively little year-to-year variation (Bierman *et al.* 2006).

Voles and lemmings have huge impacts on entire ecosystems, affecting their predators and the other animals eaten by these predators, and thereby imposing a cyclic pattern on a wide range of other birds and mammals (Chapter 4). Several avian predators depend primarily on the spring peaks in vole numbers to reproduce, including Short-eared and Long-eared Owls, while many other species, such as Kestrel and Barn Owl, breed better in years of vole peaks than in other years. The fortunes of many waterfowl, waders, grouse and others are indirectly bound to the cycles in small rodents, all these species gaining relief from predation and increasing in numbers in years of rodent peaks. In Fennoscandia and eastern Greenland, the collapse of lemming cycles has been accompanied by reduced occurrence of Snowy Owls and other rodent predators (Ims & Fuglei 2005, Gilg *et al.* 2009). Hence, under climate warming, one of the most familiar features of northern regions seems to be disappearing, or at least retreating northward, with huge effects on the wide array of species dependent on it.

Changing climate can also affect relationships between hosts and parasites which depend on synchrony. One species that may have been affected in this way is the Cuckoo, in which different genetic types specialise on different host species (Chapter 8). Among these host species, residents and short-distance migrants have advanced their laying dates in response to climate change more than long-distance migrants, including the Cuckoo itself. Because different parts of Europe have shown different degrees of climate warming, Møller *et al.* (2011) argued that the use of residents or short-distance migrants as hosts should have declined in areas with greater increase in spring temperature. This seems to have happened. Comparing the relative frequency of parasitism of the two host categories in 23 European countries before and after 1990, it emerged that parasitism of residents and short-distance migrants had decreased, relative to parasitism of long-distance migrants. Cuckoos have declined greatly in western Europe in recent years, but those genetic types specialising on long-distance migrants may have been affected less than others. This may not apply to Cuckoos in Britain, in which numbers nesting in the north have remained fairly stable in recent decades, while numbers in the south have decreased by more than two-thirds since 1980. The northern birds depend mainly on Meadow Pipits, which are short-distance migrants, while the lowland ones depend mainly on Reed Warblers and Dunnocks, which are long-distance migrants and residents respectively. Clearly, more research is needed to understand the population changes of Cuckoos and the extent to which climate warming is involved.

One difficulty in assessing the effects of climate change on bird populations is that other factors of likely importance may change at the same time as climate, particularly other human impacts. The problem therefore is to separate the role of changing climate from the role of changing land-use practices (or fisheries practices in the case of seabirds). The effects of climatic factors on year-to-year changes in bird numbers can often seem large in species whose habitats have remained relatively stable in recent decades, whereas in species whose habitats have changed (such as many farmland birds) the effects of weather are largely swamped by the effects of habitat change (Eglington & Pearce-Higgins 2012). Similar problems occur in separating the roles of different drivers of population change in seabirds. Many such species around Britain have declined in numbers, along with fish stocks, but it is not always clear how much the decline in fish stocks is due to climate-driven oceanic changes and how much to change in fishery practices.

Seabirds

For the most part, the present seabird communities of Britain and Ireland are adapted to cold-water conditions, and warming seas could bring changes in prey populations thereby affecting their predators. Much will therefore depend on how sensitive the prey species are to changes in marine conditions, and whether alternative prey are (or will become) available (Wanless 2007). Marine biologists have paid particular attention to sea-surface temperatures (SSTs), which can be readily measured, but are influenced more by water currents than by local air temperatures. Such changes in the marine environment also affect storm frequency (and thus the build-up of primary production), as well as the timings of seasonal temperature and salinity changes. Given these complex changes, and uncertainties over prey supplies, it is hard to predict how different seabird species might be affected in years to come.

Some changes are already occurring. In the northeast Atlantic, particularly in northern parts of the North Sea, the Lesser Sandeel is a vital prey species for many seabirds in the breeding season (Chapter 3). Sea temperatures in the northeast Atlantic, and around British and Irish coasts, have risen by approximately 0.2–0.8 °C per decade since the 1980s, most rapidly in the southern North Sea and English Channel (Hughes *et al.* 2010). Over the past 50 years, the annual average 10 °C isotherm of sea water has shifted north from southern Britain to southern Norway. This warming has apparently changed the abundance and species composition of plankton, particularly copepods, producing conditions that are unfavourable for sandeels, and thus for a wide range of seabirds (Chapter 4; Frederiksen *et al.* 2004b, 2006, Harris *et al.* 2005, Votier *et al.* 2005, Grosbois & Thompson 2006). The recent catastrophic breeding failures of seabirds at North Sea colonies evidently arose from problems lower down the food-chain, as sandeels as well as birds were starving (Chapter 4).

At the Isle of May, off southeast Scotland, the breeding outputs of three seabird species (Kittiwake, Shag, Razorbill), which rely on one-year-old sandeels, were positively related to the biomass of larvae one year earlier. Abundant larvae usually led to abundant one-year-old fish a year later. Sandeel abundance was in turn related to SST, being lower in warmer years. In warm years, there appeared to have been a change in the plankton that sandeels feed on, from cold-water to warm-water species. The reduction in sandeel recruitment was especially noticeable in the southwest North Sea, where Lesser Sandeels are near the southern limit of their distribution (Arnott & Ruxton 2002). Shortage of sandeels affected both the annual adult survival and breeding success of Kittiwakes, with a one-year lag in the relationship with breeding success (Frederiksen *et al.* 2004b, 2007). However, in Guillemots, which bring only one much larger fish at a time to their young, breeding output was better correlated with the size of the fish than with their abundance (Frederiksen *et al.* 2006).

In addition to these natural events, Kittiwakes on the Isle of May bred less successfully and survived less well in years when a sandeel fishery was operating within 50 km of the colony. Closure of the fishery in 2000 led to significantly improved Kittiwake breeding output and survival, but only temporarily, because sea temperatures continued to rise and sandeels to decline. Sandeel shortages also occurred around Orkney and Shetland, where several seabird species were affected (Chapter 4). The annual survival of adult Puffins was also reduced in years of high SSTs. Puffins have more restricted wintering areas than Kittiwakes (Harris *et al.* 2005), but in recent years east-coast Puffins have begun to expand out of the North Sea into the east Atlantic to winter, a trend that could have been driven by food changes (Harris *et al.* 2010).

The same conditions that are detrimental to sandeels may favour other fish, which at least some seabirds may be able to exploit. Surveys showed a dramatic increase in Snake Pipefish from about 2003, as part of a general spread of Atlantic shelf species into the North Sea. Some seabird species have been recorded bringing pipefish to their chicks at colonies around Britain, and also feeding on them outside the breeding season. However, pipefish have a rigid bony structure that makes them difficult for birds, particularly chicks, to swallow, and there are numerous records of chicks choking to death, or being unable to swallow pipefish brought by their parents. It thus seems unlikely that pipefish could become a viable alternative food source for any seabird species. Their presence in such numbers in British waters was short-lived, however, for after a few years they declined in the diets of seabirds.

Because seabirds are long-lived, with low reproductive rates and long-deferred maturity, changes in their population sizes tend to be slow. Nevertheless, some dramatic declines in British seabirds have occurred since the 1990s, with some colonies declining to less than half their former level in 20 years, as described in Chapter 4. But there have also been marked regional variations, with the biggest declines in numbers and productivity in the north of Britain, particularly around Orkney and Shetland. Sandeel distribution in British waters is patchy, and the differing fortunes of these various stocks linked to changing oceanic conditions have apparently underpinned the pronounced geographical variation in breeding success observed in Kittiwakes and other seabirds that rely on this species (Wanless 2007).

Climate warming is also predicted to bring more storms. Around Britain, Shags are especially sensitive to such events because they feed mainly in coastal waters and can be badly affected by strong onshore winds. Survival is reduced in wet and windy winters, in some of which mass mortalities have occurred (Chapter 17). Simulation modelling indicated that, under the more frequent climatic extremes predicted under climate change, Shags could in time disappear from eastern Britain altogether (Frederiksen *et al.* 2008). Increased storm frequency in late spring and summer could also affect open cliff-nesting species, such as Kittiwake and Guillemot. These are further predictions based on existing data that time may test.

In earlier decades, the breeding success in many North Atlantic seabirds showed a positive relationship with SSTs, but now the relationship is negative, reflecting the different range of SSTs encountered during the different periods, initially lower than in more recent years (Hamer 2010). In addition, the same oceanographic change can have opposing effects on different demographic measures. Several North Atlantic seabird species showed a positive relationship between breeding success and SSTs (Sandvik *et al.* 2008), but a negative relationship between adult survival and SSTs, often with a lag of one or more years (Sandvik *et al.* 2005, Votier *et al.* 2005). The relative strength of these two relationships presumably influenced the trend in breeding numbers

CHANGES IN GEOGRAPHICAL DISTRIBUTIONS

One of the most obvious ways in which organisms might respond to climate change is by changing their geographical distributions. They may withdraw from regions where climate is becoming less suitable, and expand into regions becoming more suitable. Under a warming climate, organisms would be expected to shift towards higher latitudes and higher altitudes, a process resulting from increase and expansion at the advancing range margin and decrease and shrinkage at the retreating margin. Biologists have again combined information on recent distributional changes from many plants and animals to assess general patterns. One such large-scale analysis, covering 99 species of birds, butterflies and alpine plants, revealed substantial range shifts during the late twentieth century, averaging 6.1 km northward per decade or 6.1 m upslope (Parmesan & Yohe 2003). Among species whose distributions changed, 81% were in the direction predicted from climate warming. Other large-scale analyses

FIG 171. The Kingfisher *Alcedo atthis* suffers heavy mortality during hard winters in which fresh waters are frozen for long periods, but in runs of years with milder winters it increases and spreads northwards, extending its breeding range in Britain. (Frank Snijkers)

gave similar results, providing other general signals of the biological impacts of climate change (Root *et al.* 2003, Hickling *et al.* 2006).

Among the bird populations of Britain and Ireland, such distributional changes are well under way, supporting predictions. Some species found most abundantly in southern Britain have become commoner within their existing range and have spread northwards in recent decades. Examples among resident species include the Dartford Warbler, Nuthatch, Bearded Tit, Jay, Kingfisher, Green Woodpecker and Barn Owl, and among summer migrants the Reed Warbler and Hobby. Other species have colonised Britain from further south in Europe and are gradually spreading northward. Such species, with their first year of recorded breeding, include: Black Redstart (1923), Little Ringed Plover

FIG 172. Four species that colonised Britain during the twentieth century. Upper left: the Little Ringed Plover *Charadrius dubius* was first recorded nesting in 1932, and had reached more than 700 pairs by 2010 (Richard Chandler). Upper right: the Firecrest *Regulus ignicapilla* was first recorded nesting in 1962, and by 2010 was thought to number more than 1,000 pairs (Chris Knights). Lower left: the Cetti's Wabler *Cettia cetti* was first recorded breeding in 1972, and was estimated to number nearly 2,000 pairs in 2010 (Frank Snijkers). Lower right: the Mediterranean Gull *Larus melanocephalus* was first recorded nesting in 1968, and had reached more than 1,000 pairs in 2010 (Alan Hale).

FIG 173. Spoonbill *Platalea leucorodia*, a former breeder in Britain which ceased to breed before the nineteenth century, but has recently begun to nest again in small numbers, mainly in East Anglia. (Chris Knights)

FIG 174. The Cattle Egret *Bubulcus ibis* was recorded as breeding in Britain in 2008, but under climate warming it could soon establish itself as a regular breeder. (Alan Martin)

(1938), Firecrest (1962), Mediterranean Gull (1968), Cetti's Warbler (1972) and Little Egret (1996). Other species, currently found mainly further south in Europe, could colonise and breed in Britain in the coming years. Some likely candidates have already bred on one or more occasions, including the Cattle Egret (first recorded nest in 2008), Purple Heron (first recorded nest in 2010), Great White Egret (first recorded nest in 2012), Little Bittern (confirmed breeding 1984 and 2010), Spoonbill (from the 1980s), Black-winged Stilt (occasional breeding since nineteenth century), Yellow-legged Gull (first recorded nest in 1995), Hoopoe (occasional breeding since nineteenth century) and Serin (first recorded nest in 1967); while others that are expanding in Europe and could nest in Britain at any time soon include the Glossy Ibis, Black Kite, Icterine, Melodious and Fan-tailed Warblers. On the other hand, other species now restricted to the south of Britain, such as Nightingale and Turtle Dove, show no sign of spreading north, but these species are in rapid decline for reasons apparently unconnected with climate in their breeding areas.

Species likely to retreat under continued climate warming include those northern species for which Britain and Ireland lie in the southern parts of their breeding range, or which are found further south chiefly at high altitude. Such

FIG 175. Two species of the high mountaintops considered especially vulnerable to climate warming. Left: Dotterel *Charadrius morinellus* (Laurie Campbell). Right: Snow Bunting *Plectrophenax nivalis* (Edmund Fellowes).

species include widespread but declining ones, such as Ring Ouzel, Curlew and Golden Plover, more localised ones, such as Redwing, Common Scoter, Red-necked Phalarope, Whimbrel, Arctic Skua, and some rare and occasional breeders, such as Purple Sandpiper, Temminck's Stint, Wood Sandpiper, Shore Lark, Red-spotted Bluethroat, Brambling and Lapland Bunting. The high mountain areas on which Dotterel and Snow Bunting breed are some of the habitats considered most threatened by a warming climate, which puts these species at especially high risk. However, the degree to which any species will respond to climate warming is far from clear, especially because some are currently in decline for other reasons.

Species mentioned above are the most obvious examples, but many others have shown some distributional change in Britain and Ireland over the last fifty years. Details may be seen in the successive atlases of bird breeding distributions compiled by the BTO. Putting together the maps for different species, it is also apparent that the total numbers of breeding species have increased over much of the country during this period, although only part of this increase is likely to be due to climate change. Some is due to expansions of species previously reduced by human persecution (Chapter 17). More detailed analyses have been done in recent years. For example, over the 13-year period 1994–2006, under rising average temperatures, bird diversity increased across much of Britain, with the numbers of species per unit area increasing in all main habitats, but especially in upland areas (Davey *et al.* 2011). This trend was largely driven by range expansions of generalists (species widely encountered across a range of habitats), whilst many specialists (species with more specific habitat requirements) became less common. As a result, the bird communities in different locations and habitats became more species-rich, but also more similar to one another.

Changes have also occurred among wintering birds. Some species that were formerly wholly or largely migratory are now wintering in Britain and Ireland in increasing numbers, including the Lesser Black-backed Gull, Blackcap and Chiffchaff. The strong implication is that all these species were formerly limited by winter climate or its influence on food supplies. But while these species are increasing in Britain and Ireland, others are declining here for essentially the same reason – they are wintering nearer to their breeding areas. In particular, the numbers of some waterfowl and waders, especially those coming from northern Eurasia, are beginning to fall as the climate in western continental Europe ameliorates. This is enabling increasing numbers to shorten their migrations and winter nearer to their continental breeding areas, visiting Britain only in severe weather. The centres of gravity of their wintering populations in Europe have shifted northeast by about 115 km (MacLean *et al.* 2008). Even within Britain, the proportions of shorebirds wintering on western estuaries have declined since the 1970s, while those on eastern estuaries have increased. In addition, a shortening of migration distances has been described from ring recoveries among many bird species from Britain, Germany and the Netherlands (Wernham *et al.* 2002, Fiedler 2003, Visser *et al.* 2009). On the other hand, some European species whose breeding ranges have spread northward have kept the same wintering areas, which required a lengthening of migration distances, in some cases by up to 1,000 km (Newton 2008). Similar trends have occurred in North America, where many bird species are now wintering at higher latitudes than previously (La Sorte & Thompson 2007).

Although regional bird communities are clearly changing under a warming climate, in at least some regions they are changing less rapidly than expected from climate itself, implying a lag in response times. From counts of birds at many different localities in France, it was examined how bird communities change from south to north across the country. It was also calculated how average March–August temperatures changed over the same distance. Over the 18-year period 1989–2006, bird communities in 722 lowland localities changed in composition by an average amount that would have been equivalent to a 91 km shift in latitude, while average temperatures at those localities changed by an average amount equivalent to a 273 km shift in latitude (Devictor *et al.* 2008). In a sense, then, changes in bird communities could be said to be lagging behind changes in climate to an extent equivalent to a 182 km shift in latitude.

The rates of spread of birds, like those of other organisms, are limited by their reproductive and dispersal rates. Species do not normally spread together as a community, but individually, each at its own pace, so that communities change or build up slowly over time. This was the situation in post-glacial times, with species spreading northward at their own individual rates, as revealed by the pollen and fossil records (Newton 2004).

Recent range changes by no means represent a new phenomenon. From the beginning of detailed ornithological recording in the nineteenth century, range changes in birds have been repeatedly documented. For example, over the period 1850–1950 at least 38 bird species expanded northwards through Finland, associated mainly with increasing temperatures, but also with human land-use practices (Kalela 1952). These trends continued, and over a more recent 12-year period (1974–79 to 1986–89), 116 species breeding in southern Finland had extended northwards by an average of 19 km (about 16 km per decade), whereas 34 more northerly species, bounded at their northern edge by lack of suitable habitat, had shown no such extension (Brommer 2004).

A wide variety of other animals has also spread northward or upward in Britain in recent decades (Hickling *et al.* 2006). Upslope shifts are difficult to detect in Britain because the altitude range is relatively small, but in the Italian Alps most bird species shifted upward during 1994–2005, and in the Swiss Alps upslope expansions at the upper boundary or retractions at the lower boundary were recorded in about one-third of 95 species examined over short periods between 1999–2004 and 2004–07 (Maggini *et al.* 2010, Popy *et al.* 2010). These shifts were consistent with the effects of climate warming, but other explanations could not be excluded. On a wider scale, Burton (1995) documented range changes during the twentieth century among 424 European bird species, when 195 species advanced to the north and 64 to the west, while 56 retreated to the south and seven to the east. He attributed almost all these changes to climate, but did not consider other likely factors, such as change in land use. The distributions of birds change for various reasons, and we must be careful about attributing them all uncritically to climate change.

GLACIAL CHANGES

During the last two million years, the earth has seen around 20 different glacial periods, as it successively warmed and cooled in association with changes in its orbit and axis with respect to the sun. These changes produced global average temperature differences of about 5 °C between the coldest and warmest periods on cycles of roughly 100,000 years.[22] Following the last glaciation, almost the entire avifauna of Europe would have spread northwards, as vegetation re-colonised areas previously under ice. Understanding the effects of past climate changes on flora and fauna has achieved special significance in light of the current climate change.

In the most recent post-glacial period, the mean rates of spread of various tree species, estimated from the pollen record, mostly lie in the range 200–400 m per year, though mean rates up to 2 km per year occurred occasionally (e.g. Davis 1981, Huntley 1991, King & Herstrom 1997). These rates were species-specific, but lagged behind the rate of climate change, presumably because they were constrained by other factors, such as the dispersal rates and generation times of the tree species themselves. The rates of northward range shift in various plants and animals, recorded over recent decades and mentioned above, fall fairly centrally within the range of values recorded for post-glacial times.

However, under current global warming, July isotherms are expected to advance northward at 4–5 km per year. If trees were to keep up with this rate, they would need to migrate 10–25 times faster than typical post-glacial rates, and at least twice as fast as the fastest post-glacial rates. It is therefore hard to predict the effects of further warming on plant and animal distributions, because the lag may be much greater than in the past. They also now lack continuity of suitable habitat through which to spread, because, in contrast to post-glacial times, places where native plants could grow are now much fragmented by human land use, making dispersal much more difficult.

ADAPTATION

In the past, as emphasised already, the major response of animals to changing climate was change in distribution, as species followed the gradual shifts in climatic and ecological conditions. All animals can survive in a range of different conditions, through existing flexibility in their physiology and behaviour, but, beyond certain limits, genetic changes would be necessary if they were to cope with further extremes. Such changes are likely to include modifications in their

---

22 If glacial cycles proceed inexorably, and the peak of the current interglacial has passed, we could now be heading for the next glaciation, but on a much longer timescale than recent global warming. Recent warming is evident on short timescales of decades, and sits upon the much longer-term glacial cycles of around 100,000 years. However, appropriate changes in the earth's orbit and tilt, needed to initiate the next glacial period, are not predicted to occur until about 60,000 years from now.

physiology, cold or heat tolerance, migratory and other behaviour, and minor changes in their morphology, such as body size and colouration. If these changes had occurred in the past, they would be difficult or impossible to detect in the fossil record. However, at the present time, bird species commonly show clines in physiology, photoperiod responses,[23] migratory behaviour, body size and plumage colouration across the range, with individuals becoming slightly larger in colder areas, and paler in snowy or desert areas. If in a given area, climate became warmer, body size, for example, would be expected to decline. Several studies have documented changes in the body sizes in various British and European birds during the twentieth century, as reflected in various measurements (Yom-Tov & Yom-Tov 2006, Yom-Tov et al. 2006, Moreno-Rueda & Rivas 2007). However, not all these changes involved declines, and among those that did, it was not possible to separate changes due to immediate environmental influence (such as reduced nutrition during growth) from those resulting from genetic change (Yom-Tov & Geffen 2011).

Another way in which birds could adjust to changed climate is through change in their migration and breeding dates, as described above. But because the same individuals can adjust their arrival or egg-laying dates to conditions in particular years, this can be regarded as a facultative response to prevailing conditions, giving birds some flexibility to cope with variable conditions. The increasing earliness recorded in many species in recent years may therefore have occurred largely within this pre-existing flexibility, requiring no genetic change to promote earlier arrival or egg-laying. This was the conclusion arising from recent studies on tits, even though the degree of flexibility may itself have been under genetic influence (Nussey et al. 2005, Charmantier et al. 2008). There may be limits to this flexibility, however, and if climate continues to change, some genetic change may be necessary for birds to cope with even greater change in spring temperature. Migration and breeding dates are known from research on several species to be under genetic as well as environmental influence, and if birds are no longer laying early enough to make the best of their food supply, earlier arrival or laying should be favoured by natural selection, until a match was restored. The unresolved question is whether birds can make this evolutionary change rapidly enough to prevent them from disappearing before sufficient change could develop.

Evidence for a genetic change in migration emerged from samples of Blackcap nestlings collected randomly in south Germany, hand-reared and tested

---

23 Birds use prevailing daylength changes to time their annual-cycle events, such as breeding and migration. So if species extend into different latitudes, they have to change their photoperiod responses too, in order that their annual cycles become re-adjusted to the different conditions in the newly colonised range.

in uniform conditions each year over a 13-year period (Pulido & Berthold 2004). In successive samples of birds, the amount of autumn migratory behaviour was shown to gradually decline towards a later onset and reduced activity. These changes persisted in young bred from these birds, showing that the behaviour was inherited. They were precisely the changes expected under the action of natural selection in an ameliorating climate, with the population becoming less migratory over time. Evolutionary changes in the timing of spring migration have also been demonstrated in wild birds subject to extreme weather events which selectively killed earlier-arriving individuals, leaving the later-arriving ones to breed in subsequent years (Brown & Brown 2000). However, although some evolutionary changes in bird populations, consistent with those expected from current climate change, have been recorded in recent years, they could all be regarded as minor adaptive adjustments to climate change, compared to the extensive distributional changes known from the past.

THE YEARS AHEAD

Changes in climate and bird populations in the recent past have been measured with reasonable accuracy, but this leaves open the matter of what will happen in future. Will previous changes simply continue in the same direction, will they speed up, or will some different changes occur? Much is likely to depend on the degree of reduction in greenhouse gas emissions that can be achieved. According to climate scientists, if carbon dioxide emissions were to stop now, global warming would still continue beyond 2050.

With no curbing of emissions, atmospheric carbon dioxide concentrations are projected to exceed 400 ppm by the end of this century, and global temperatures to rise by a further 1.8–4.0 °C (IPCC 2007). These temperature rises are similar to the global average that marked the end of the last glaciation, and, as at that time, future warming is likely to be greatest at high northern latitudes, and greater over land than sea. Areas affected by drought are likely to increase in mid-latitudes, including much of southern Europe. Sea-levels will continue to rise, reaching around 28–42 cm higher than in the 1990s. The associated increases in wave heights and tidal surges are expected to inundate large areas of coastal habitat around the world, including many fertile delta regions and low-lying islands. In the seas, we can also expect shifts in water temperature, surface salinity, currents and nutrient availability, as well as increased acidity.

For Britain and Ireland, the predictions are that by 2080 (and relative to the 1961–90 means): average temperatures will rise by 2.0–3.5 °C, annual precipitation will fall by up to 15%, and snowfall by 30–90% (Hulme *et al.* 2002, UJCIP02 scenarios). Changes will be most marked in southeast England, where mean summer temperatures will rise by 5 °C, summer rainfall will decline by 50%, and winter precipitation will rise by up to 30%, giving less rain over the year as a whole. Sea-levels will rise between 26 and 86 cm, and sea temperatures will continue to increase, with the English Channel in summer becoming 2–4 °C warmer. In addition, over large parts of the country, soil moisture will fall by 40% in summer.

We can also expect a general increase in the frequency and severity of storms (especially in spring and autumn), summer droughts, winter floods and storm surges, with extremely high sea-levels occurring 10–20 times more often in the 2080s than in the recent past. Rising sea-levels are likely to cause severe habitat loss in coastal areas, with the heaviest impacts on intertidal habitats, saltmarshes and sandy beaches. The natural processes of flooding, erosion and deposition could change the shape of estuaries and mudflats, and generate new areas of coastal habitat in some places. However, most of the coastlines of Britain and Ireland are fixed by natural cliffs or artificial embankments, limiting the extent to which these natural processes can occur.

Meanwhile, the acidification of sea water can only continue, and if too little is done to curb the output of carbon dioxide and methane, the pH of sea water, already down by 0.1 units, is predicted to drop by up to another 0.4 units by the end of this century (Orr *et al.* 2005). There are also likely to be some significant changes in the circulation of water within the oceans. The implications of such changes are much less clear, but they are of particular relevance to the British Isles, whose present mild climate is largely due to the warming influence of the Gulf Stream. If this major current were to weaken or change course, as some models have predicted, this could swing our climate to colder, giving us conditions similar to Labrador on the opposite side of the Atlantic. Whatever changes materialise, current interest centres on predicting the effects of climate warming on fauna and flora, and on minimising its adverse impacts.

Climate envelope models

Some researchers have attempted to predict how species distributions might change by use of *climate envelopes* (see particularly Huntley *et al.* 2007). The method consists of calculating the span of climatic conditions embraced by the known geographical range of a species (its climatic envelope), and then using climate models to predict where this same range of climatic conditions might lie at some future date, perhaps 100–200 years from now, and assuming that the species will move accordingly.

Such methods have obvious drawbacks (Huntley & Green 2011). For one thing, factors other than climate influence the distributions of species, including human land use and suitability of habitat, or excessive persecution. The current ranges of many species may therefore be much smaller than climate alone would permit, and in this case the calculated climatic envelope may be too restricted. Similarly, the areas of projected future suitable climate may contain parts that are unsuitable for some species for reasons other than climate. In addition, not all species may be able to disperse and reach all the places where models suggest that future climate is suitable. So, in forecasting the future range changes of individual species, such climate-based models may prove to have shortcomings, especially for species likely to have large man-made gaps in their current or future ranges, such as some raptors. Lastly, the calculation of climate envelopes is based on information on occurrence, not on abundance, so the method gives no clear way of predicting population changes independently of distributional changes, and it also makes no prediction of the timescale on which changes might occur.

Nevertheless, by determining the climate envelopes of the 1980s ranges of European birds, it is instructive to estimate the extent to which these ranges might shift under different scenarios of climate change over the rest of this century (Huntley *et al.* 2007). Taking a 'middle-of-the-road' estimate for the future European climate,[24] the breeding ranges of European bird species would shift, on average, 545 km to the northeast by the end of the century, but some range boundaries for some species could shift as much as 1,000 km. Northern, eastern and western range boundaries would be likely to shift mainly in response to temperature, but southern boundaries in some species mainly in response to greater aridity. Although the future ranges of some species could be larger than their recent ones, most are likely to be smaller, and overall, bird ranges are predicted to shrink by an average of one-fifth of their recent size. For six species which currently breed in Europe, suitable climatic conditions could vanish from the entire continent. Modelling further suggested that species will respond individually: no two species have identical ranges in Europe now, and this is still likely to hold by the end of the current century.

For all 426 species considered by Huntley *et al.* (2007), overlap between present and future ranges averaged 39%, but for 51 species the overlap could be 10% or less, and for 27 species there may be no overlap. In other words, the future potential ranges of 27 species may be totally different at the end of the century from what they are now. The likelihood of extinction is perhaps higher than average for those species with little or no overlap between their current

---

24 Based on the B2 emissions scenario of the Hadley Centre and the HadCM3 climate model.

and projected ranges. Across the continent, on these projections, average species richness would decline by 8.6% or more, depending on how effectively birds can disperse to suitable areas, although in some regions, such as most of Britain, species richness is likely to rise.

Effects of climate change are also likely to be severe on long-distance migrants that winter in Africa south of the Sahara. If their breeding ranges in Europe move north or northeastwards, migration distances are likely to lengthen, and any further desertification in north Africa will worsen the journey. In various *Sylvia* warblers, potential breeding ranges were predicted to shift northwards under climate change, whereas potential non-breeding ranges showed no consistent directional shift (Doswald *et al.* 2009). In some such species, potential future ranges were predicted to become larger, but in others smaller, while overlap between recent and predicted future ranges was generally low, averaging less than 36% for both breeding and wintering ranges. Migration distances in *Sylvia* warblers would be expected to increase, on average, by about twice as much in trans-Saharan migrant species as in short-distance migrants. For this and other reasons, long-distance migratory *Sylvia* species are likely to suffer more from climatic change than related species that are resident or short-distance migrants.

How will climate change affect the all-important Sahel zone to the south of the Sahara desert? Some climate models predict more rain, while others predict less. Increasing drought has harmful effects on birds wintering in this zone, and probably also on others migrating through in spring at the driest time of year. Together with the rapidly escalating human impacts through most of Africa, it is hard not to be pessimistic about the future of birds that winter there. However, shifting northwards under climate change may enable some species to winter in southern Europe, rather than in sub-Saharan Africa, and this would eliminate the tough desert crossing and reduce the overall length of the journey. Several species which seemingly once wintered entirely south of the Sahara are now wintering in increasing numbers in southern Spain, including the Yellow Wagtail, Lesser Kestrel and White Stork, indicating that such a change is already under way.

Although climate envelope models may not give a wholly accurate forecast of eventual changes in species distributions, other findings are consistent with their predictions. Two studies indicated that some of the variation in the population trends observed among species since 1980 was related to trends in climate suitability as estimated from climate envelope models. Broadly speaking, those species for which climate was judged to have most improved were those that had undergone the most marked increases in populations (mainly southern species), while those for which climate was judged to have most deteriorated

FIG 176. The White Stork *Ciconia ciconia* has begun to winter in increasing numbers in southern Spain, eliminating the journey to Africa. (Frank Snijkers)

were those that had undergone the most marked declines (mainly northern species). Other studies gave similar findings, in that species that live under relatively cool conditions showed the sharpest downward trends in recent years. This finding emerged from studies of 71 species in France and 110 species across Europe examined over the period 1980–2005 (Jiguet *et al.* 2007, 2010). The advantage of using population trends as a measure of climate warming effects is that they tend to change along with climate, but ahead of change in geographical range, which lags behind change in climate.

The effects of climate change on many bird populations and distributions are likely to be indirect. They may operate through altered habitat or food availability, abundance of competitors, disease or predation risk. Human land use is also heavily influenced by climate, and many indirect effects of climate change are likely to operate through enforced changes in agriculture, forestry or water management. Future changes in human land use form a major uncertainty in predicting future effects of climate change on birds. Almost certainly, some species will behave in unpredicted ways, the response of each species reflecting its unique ecology, habitat and life history. In migratory birds especially, dependence on multiple locations means that global warming could affect their populations in various ways.

Problems of spread

The highest predicted extent of global warming during the current century is equivalent to the amount that occurred in the past between a glacial and interglacial period, yet the rate of this predicted change is ten or more times greater. To judge by their recent performance, some bird species may be able to spread north or northeast at a rate that matches the change in climate, providing that habitat is already available beyond their existing range (as for Little Egret and Kingfisher). Difficulties will occur for species that require special habitats and food which may become available only as appropriate plants and animals spread from further south. Many such plants and animals may be unable to spread fast enough to keep up with climate change (as already demonstrated), and some may decline or become regionally extinct as a result. Their passage through modern landscapes is anyway likely to be impeded by human land use. With most of the land surface under farm crops or concrete, the opportunity for trees and other plants to spread naturally is much curtailed, compared with post-glacial times. Much of Europe no longer provides any broad-front dispersal route, but at best a series of narrow interrupted corridors and stepping stones of suitable habitat. This means that, for many organisms, response to climate change by movement may be inadequate or prevented. Some plant and animal species are likely to remain stranded in areas of decreasingly suitable habitat, unable to disperse fast enough or far enough into more appropriate areas. This dispersal problem could lead to a much greater number of regional extinctions than have occurred over equivalent periods in the past. Although many animals are more mobile than plants, they are still tied to areas of suitable vegetation. Those on oceanic islands, mountain tops or the northern edges of land-masses may have nowhere to go.

In Britain and Ireland, as opposed to Europe as a whole, the numbers of breeding bird species are likely to rise further in the years ahead, as gains exceed losses, continuing recent trends. For wintering birds under continued warming, it is harder to predict the net trend, for some breeding species which now migrate may become more sedentary, while others that now winter here may begin to remain further north or east, as is already occurring (Newton 2008, 2010).

Diseases

Much speculation has centred on how disease impacts will alter under climate change, as some species could come into contact with pathogens that are new to them and to which they have no natural immunity. Over a 38-year period (1971–2008) in Denmark, as spring–summer temperatures and rainfall rose, mosquitoes and black-flies emerged progressively earlier in spring, and various parasites of Swallows changed in relative abundance and virulence (Møller

2010). Tropical fowl mites decreased in abundance and effects, while louseflies increased in association with the earlier breeding of their hosts. Two kinds of blood parasites also increased during the study period. Yet despite these changes in the composition of the parasite community, no significant change in the overall breeding performance of Swallows was recorded.

Not all changes are likely to be so benign. Mosquitoes are gradually spreading northward and upward, becoming more active, and bringing new diseases to species with no previous exposure (Gaston *et al.* 2002). Avian malaria and avian pox are diseases dependent on mosquito vectors that have caused extinctions of endemic bird species on Hawaii and elsewhere, and are now becoming generally commoner in many regions (Garamszegi 2011). Both have long been established among British birds but seldom cause serious disease, although a virulent strain of avian pox (a viral skin disease) has increased in recent years. It was observed among tits in southeast England in 2007, and then spread north (Chapter 9).

The development rates of free-living stages of macroparasites are sensitive to temperature, and for many species weather plays a role in survival and ease of transmission. Take the two main diseases currently affecting Red Grouse, caused by the caecal threadworm and louping ill virus (Chapter 9). Milder and wetter weather might facilitate the transmission of both, by promoting better survival of the free-living stages of the threadworm and of the ticks which transmit louping ill. Conversely, warmer and drier conditions might reduce transmission rates by making worm larvae and ticks more prone to desiccation. Unlike a few decades ago, ticks now appear on host species in every month of the year, and louping ill appears to be spreading among Red Grouse populations (Watson & Moss 2008). Further spread of ticks and louping ill to the high mountain tops could be disastrous for the ill-prepared Ptarmigan, which has no natural immunity to the virus. Pathogens can spread rapidly, but host species need time to build up resistance and, until they do, they are likely to decline, possibly to the point of regional extinction. It is a race against time, the outcome of which depends on whether enough individuals acquire resistance before the species disappears altogether from the region concerned.

CONCLUDING REMARKS

Climate warming over the past half-century has clearly affected plant and animal populations in predicted ways, with birds showing changes in migration and breeding dates, and in numbers and distributions. Less predictably, phenological changes have brought some mismatches between bird breeding and food supplies, as different kinds of organisms have responded at different rates to spring warming. Consequent reductions in reproductive rates have sometimes been sufficient to cause population declines in some bird species. Through their sensitivity to weather, birds have become useful indicators of biological effects attributable to climate change, and more is known about their responses than those of most other animals. A note of caution is necessary, however, for almost all our information in this area is based on correlations between changes in bird performance and changing climate variables. We have only limited opportunity to test for causal relationships or for potential confounding effects of other factors.

This book has been mainly concerned with studies from the 1950s on, assessing the effects of various limiting factors. Most of the changes in bird population levels examined over this period were clearly linked to effects of food supplies, nesting sites, predators and parasites, with human land use (as it affects these limiting factors) as the main driver of many long-term trends. Weather effects evident over most of this period were manifest chiefly in hard winters, when they influenced the food supplies and survival rates of birds. Yet since the 1980s, weather effects – initially largely hidden by other factors – have become increasingly apparent, affecting mainly phenology, and latterly also population and range changes. Nevertheless, over this whole period from the 1950s, no-one could reasonably claim that climate warming has been the major cause of bird population changes in Britain and Ireland. Alongside other influences, such as human land-use or fisheries practice, its effects have been small but growing. They can be expected to grow massively in future as warming gathers momentum.

For at least the past 2.5 million years, climate has always been changing between warm and cold periods. Many plants and animals have survived these changes, but the fossil record reveals that others disappeared, either totally or from western Europe. Regional extinctions could be greater in the years ahead, partly because climate is changing more rapidly than in the past, and partly because of the difficulties that plants and animals have in spreading through landscapes dominated by human use. Obvious mitigating measures could include joining together existing patches of natural and semi-natural habitats to produce habitat corridors through which plants and animals can spread naturally, or deliberately moving plants and animals into areas where conditions are becoming favourable. The coming decades will be an interesting time for naturalists, as all kinds of changes occur within wildlife communities. Not all are likely to result from climate change, and many could result from human land use and other activities, including the development of alternative sources of energy. Separating the effects of climate change from those of other anthropogenic impacts will not always be easy.

CHAPTER 16

Managed Hunting

B
Y KILLING BIRDS, PEOPLE CAN influence wild populations in the
same ways as can natural predators. However, because most human
populations no longer depend on wild prey, numbers of people do not
decline in response to the over-kill of wild species. Aided by technology, people
have unprecedented powers to reduce or eliminate birds and other wildlife not
just through habitat destruction, but also through culling at a rate that exceeds
their natural replenishment. In the past, over-hunting greatly reduced the
numbers of many kinds of birds in Britain and Ireland, including waterfowl,
waders, seabirds and birds of prey, eliminating a few species totally (Chapter
17). Population increases in many of these species during the twentieth century
may therefore represent recoveries from past over-kill. Overexploitation was
widespread, and the main exceptions were gamebirds, which, at least from the
mid-nineteenth century, were managed by landowners specifically for sustainable
hunting. Nowadays, most killing of birds occurs through recreational hunting or
for crop protection, or as incidental to some other activity, such as fishing. This
chapter considers sustainable game management, while other killing of birds is
discussed in Chapter 17. Like the rest of this book, these chapters are concerned
mainly with the situation in Britain and Ireland.

GAME MANAGEMENT

In Britain and Ireland, the right to hunt game has long been vested with the
landowner. This contrasts with the situation in some other parts of Europe where
land ownership does not extend to the game upon it. Beginning in the nineteenth

century, with game more important to many landowners than agriculture, game shooting became highly competitive, and bag sizes (numbers shot) became paramount. Land was managed largely for the game it could support. In the 1840s, the change from muzzle-loading to faster breech-loading guns paved the way for a different kind of shooting, in which wave after wave of birds could be driven over the stationary guns, presenting large numbers of challenging targets. Everything possible was done to increase the densities and productivity of the chosen species, from habitat management to predator removal, the aim being to produce as large a sustainable harvest as possible. In so-called *driven shooting* birds are pushed over the guns by a line of beaters, flushing the birds forward. Driven shooting is considered feasible for Grey Partridges at post-breeding densities exceeding about 120 birds per km^2, and for Red Grouse above about 60 birds per km^2 (Hudson 1992, Potts 2012). The alternative to driven shooting, feasible at much lower bird densities, is *walked-up shooting*, in which birds are usually found by dogs, and shot as they take off. Owing to the effectiveness of dogs, it is easy to over-shoot a population by this method, leading to its long-term decline.

Along with other field sports, game shooting has helped to shape the countryside, with many lowland woods planted as Pheasant coverts and upland heather moors managed specifically for Red Grouse.[25] Such land management benefited many other species too, which flourished alongside game, but exceptions included the predatory species deliberately killed to benefit game. The practice of game management, especially predator control, was vested in gamekeepers, specifically employed for the purpose. In 1911 the numbers of house-holding gamekeepers in Britain, according to the national government census, reached 23,056, but beginning with the First World War (1914–18), their numbers progressively declined. By 1951 they reached only 4,391 and by the 1990s probably around 2,500 (Tapper 1992). According to the National Gamekeepers' Organisation, numbers had risen to about 5,000 in 2010, largely associated with a growth in Pheasant rearing.

---

25 Since Victorian times the Red Grouse has been among Britain's most economically important gamebirds. Grouse shooting, along with deer stalking, are Britain's equivalent of big game hunting, generating important income for landowners, and conferring status on the participants. Grouse numbers across much of upland Britain started to decline from about 1880. The concern was such that in the early 1900s Lord Lovat and other moor owners established a Committee of Inquiry on Grouse Disease, which stimulated new research, becoming one of the first population studies of birds: *The Grouse in Health and Disease* (1911). Further declines led to two additional detailed and long-term studies on the species: one from 1956 by the Nature Conservancy and led initially (1956–66) by David Jenkins and latterly (1966–90) by Adam Watson (continued for some further years by Robert Moss and others); and another from 1978 by the Game Conservancy led by Peter Hudson. Both studies continued to beyond the end of the twentieth century, making the Red Grouse one of the most thoroughly studied of all birds.

FIG 177. The Grey Partridge *Perdix perdix*, a former major gamebird in lowland Britain, now much reduced, mainly as a result of agricultural changes. (Frank Snijkers)

The excess and inequity of some past bags would probably cause outrage today. For example, at his Elveden Estate in Suffolk, the Maharajah Duley Singh single-handedly shot 780 Grey Partridges in one day, and on moorland at Blubberhouses in Yorkshire Lord Walsingham killed 1,070 grouse in a day, at an average of 2.3 birds per minute, using 1,510 cartridges and four shotguns, and assisted by two loaders and 40 beaters. The day record for a party of hunters shooting Grey Partridges was 2,069, on an estate in Lincolnshire in October 1952, and the day record for a party shooting Red Grouse was 2,523 in seven drives on Roan Fell near Langholm in Dumfriesshire in 1911. On this occasion, shooting had to stop because the party of eight ran out of cartridges around midday, but they thought they could have shot at least another 300 brace. Over the season as a whole, some 29,092 birds were shot and retrieved on this moor. Although bags of this size are probably unattainable for these species in today's landscapes, the competitive spirit still prevails, and the value of sporting land, and the shooting rents that can be charged, are largely dependent on the average numbers of birds that can be shot per year.

The heyday of game shooting based entirely on wild-bred birds was in the late nineteenth and early twentieth centuries, but even today some sizeable bags can still be obtained. They are achieved mainly using Pheasants and Red-legged Partridges which are reared in captivity and released in summer in preparation for each year's shooting season. Neither species is native to Britain and Ireland, but both now have long-established feral stocks (Box 5). Shooting parties pay

Box 5. The main non-native gamebirds in Britain and Ireland

Some introductions of the Pheasant to Britain may date back to Roman times, and the species was apparently widespread by the fifteenth century. It occurs naturally in a wide area across southern Asia. Up to 31 different subspecies have been described from different parts of the natural range, and several have been introduced to Britain. The subspecies *Phasianus c. colchicus*, found naturally in Armenia and Georgia, was probably the first to be released, followed in 1785 by the Ring-necked form *P. c. torquatus* from eastern China, and later by other types from elsewhere, all of which are now intermixed. In its natural habitat, the species is found in dense vegetation around forest edges and reedy wetlands, but in Britain it occurs mainly in wooded farmland. In the early twentieth century, prior to large scale put-and-take releases, the self-sustaining wild population provided around 15% of lowland game bags in Britain, but by the 1980s Pheasants had risen to form more than half of lowland game shot, increasing through releases, as the Grey Partridge continued to decline. Over this period, the average bag of Pheasants on shooting estates increased from around 25 birds per km^2 in 1900 to around 150 per km^2 ha in the 1980s (Tapper 1999). Developments in the poultry industry, involving artificial incubation, brooder units and pelleted food, made large-scale artificial rearing possible, bringing the sport of Pheasant shooting to a wider range of people, though not without environmental costs (see text). Against a background of widespread large-scale releases, it is hard to estimate the wild population of Britain, but it could be around 1.8–1.9 million females, probably in decline (Park *et al.* 2008). They should be set alongside the estimated 35 million artificially-reared birds now released annually in Britain, so that the species is currently found over most of lowland Britain and Ireland.

The Red-legged Partridge (or Red-leg) was introduced from southern France to East Anglia before 1770, from which it spread slowly, achieving its current distribution (of wild stock) in the 1930s. The species thrives on dry sandy soils and breeds best in areas of high summer temperatures. It has been less susceptible than the native Grey Partridge to the reduction in insects caused by pesticide use on arable land, because its chicks consume more seeds and vegetable matter, even shortly after hatching. The hen commonly lays two clutches, leaving one for the cock and incubating the second herself. This habit made the Red-leg attractive for rear-and-release purposes. However, in the late 1960s, game farmers discovered that the closely related Chukar Partridge and Chuckar/Red-leg hybrids were even more prolific in captivity, so switched mainly to these for release purposes (Tapper 1999). The first were put out in 1970, and they soon became popular throughout lowland Britain, being released in many areas where they could not otherwise persist. Despite their performance in captivity, they bred much less well than Red-legs in the wild, and hybridised, threatening the purity of the original Red-leg stock. High levels of shooting also induced an unsustainable mortality on wild Red-legs. For these reasons, the releasing of Chukars and Chuckar/Red-leg hybrids was banned in 1992, and from then on releases were restricted to pure Red-legs. Because of the current scale of releases, which are estimated at about six million per year, it is hard to assess the current status of the wild Red-leg, except between the broad limits of 72,000–200,000 pairs (Park *et al.* 2008). Wild Red-legs are now widespread in lowland Britain, but absent from the northwest, and are still rare and localised in Ireland. Released birds are found much more widely.

FIG 178. The Pheasant *Phasianus colchicus*, an introduced species which, because of artificial rearing, has become the major gamebird of lowland Britain. (Alan Martin)

heavily for a '500-bird day'. In addition, small-scale releases of the native Grey Partridge are made in some parts of Britain, but less successfully (Tapper 1999).

Changes in game bags between the periods 1900–10 and 1980–89 reflect the changes in game management and populations that occurred then (Tapper 1992). Over that time, average Pheasant bags, in terms of numbers killed per km², more than tripled. This was helped by the fact that, whereas in the past all Pheasants were wild-bred, in the later period more than 80% were reared in captivity and released. The same held for Red-legged Partridges, in which bags increased nearly 12-fold over the 90-year period. For the Grey Partridge, which does not lend itself to rear-and-release, bags fell by four-fifths in this time, leaving only a minority of estates where Grey Partridges were still shot. They virtually disappeared from much of the countryside, mainly because of unfavourable agricultural practices (chiefly pesticide use: Chapter 18), most landowners being obliged to sacrifice Grey Partridges for agricultural profitability. It was largely because of this change that lowland shooting switched in the 1970s and 1980s from wild Grey Partridges and wild Pheasants to artificially raised Pheasants and Red-legged Partridges. Another advantage of switching to pen-reared birds was that predation was greatly reduced, even in the presence of generally increasing predator populations.

Over the same nine decades, bags of Woodcock increased by more than fourfold, while bags of Snipe declined by three-fourths. For both species, winter visitors probably made up most of the kill, as local breeding populations declined over this period, mainly through land-drainage. In the uplands, bags of Red Grouse fell to less than half, bags of Black Grouse to about one-twentieth, and Capercaillie to about one-fortieth. None of these upland species can be artificially reared in large numbers, and again all have declined mainly through the changes and intensification of land use (Chapter 4). The last century thus saw substantial declines in many wild populations of gamebirds and also in shooting bags in Britain and Ireland (Tapper 1999). Despite these changes, a survey in 2004 revealed that around 600,000 people participated in the shooting of lowland game species, and around 47,000 people in grouse shooting (PACEC 2006).

The Woodpigeon is unusual in Britain in being considered as both agricultural pest and game. It is not managed in the same intense way as gallinaceous birds, but most of those shot enter the human food-chain. The same holds for those waders and waterfowl that are still shot under game legislation (listed in Chapter 17).

The same species may be classed as game in one country but not in another. For example, the Rabbit is considered a major game species in southern Europe, and predators are persecuted for eating them, whereas in Britain and Ireland Rabbits are considered as pests, and anything that kills them is welcomed, providing that it does not also eat gamebirds. On the other hand, auks are protected in Britain and Ireland, but have been treated as game elsewhere. In the recent past, shooting in Norway and Denmark has killed many Guillemots and Razorbills from British and Irish colonies. In Norway, some 30,000–40,000 auks were shot each winter in the 1970s, an activity that was banned in 1979 (Barrett & Vader 1984). While protected in Britain and Ireland, sea-ducks are still fair game in Denmark, with tens of thousands of Eiders being killed each year. Many British-bred Lapwings and other waders are killed in France, and Turtle Doves are still shot in large numbers as they migrate through France and other Mediterranean countries in autumn.

PRINCIPLES OF GAME MANAGEMENT

The ideal of game management can be illustrated by an analogy with banking. Imagine that a person has a certain capital investment sufficient to enable living indefinitely on the annual interest. If that person overspends, taking not only the interest but also some of the capital, the investment would progressively decline, providing less and less interest until the entire sum had been frittered away. In hunting, the exploited population can be regarded as an investment. The ideal is to take as large a bag as possible each year without causing population decline, adjusting the annual take to changes in the reproductive rate. Once the annual take comes to exceed the surplus that the population can produce using its own reproduction (the interest), decline sets in, and if this situation continues it can lead to elimination of the entire stock (the capital).

The impact of hunting on any wild species therefore depends greatly on whether that species is managed as a sustainable resource, as in resident gamebirds on some private estates, or whether it is hunted on a free-for-all system where anyone can kill whatever number they can get. By manipulation of habitat, disease and natural predation, densities of some managed gamebird species have been increased well above the level they could otherwise achieve. With careful control of hunting, they have continued to provide large annual 'harvests' for long periods, on some estates for more than 150 years. Where this system has failed, and gamebird populations have declined, this can usually be attributed to land-use changes and poor habitat management (Potts 1986). In contrast, species hunted on a free-for-all basis have almost always declined, causing breeding populations to fall well below the level that the habitat could support. The truth of this statement is evident in the fact that, whenever hunters gained unrestricted access to previously unexploited populations, these populations usually declined rapidly, recovering only if some measure of protection was later imposed. Migratory waterfowl in Europe were hunted in this way until the mid-twentieth century, but all have increased greatly in recent decades following the creation of reserves, the enactment of protective legislation and greater restraint by the hunters themselves (Chapter 17). The extent to which bird populations can be maintained in the face of open hunting depends largely on the extent to which regulations, such as closed seasons and bag limits, can be introduced and enforced over wide areas, as discussed later.

Harvesting theory
In managed wild game species, therefore, the aim is to crop the population, removing some individuals each year and leaving others to reproduce and provide future harvests. The ideal of taking as many individuals from the population each year as is possible without causing sustained decline in breeding numbers can be achieved most effectively: (1) if hunting is concentrated in the immediate post-breeding period, when numbers are at their highest, and (2) if hunting losses are then entirely compensated by reduced natural losses over winter or by improved reproduction the following spring, so that by the next hunting season numbers are fully restored. If this were so, the population could be harvested at a certain level indefinitely, causing no long-term decline. Experience has shown, however, that this ideal is hard to achieve, and that it is easy to overexploit a population, causing it to decline over the years.

Sustained harvesting depends on the fact that depleted populations can quickly restore their size, through density-dependent changes in births or deaths. The maximum sustainable yield (MSY) can be defined as the highest harvesting rate that the population can match year after year with its own recruitment. The MSY, then, represents the balance between overexploitation and underexploitation. It is most readily found by trial and error, checking the effects of different levels of harvest on the population trend, and then setting each year's bag on the basis of experience. Among gamebirds, MSY values tend to be highest in populations that are managed, with predator control leading to enhanced production of young, and a high post-breeding density. However, MSY values would also be expected to change through time, as other conditions change.

Among wild game species, therefore, an important question concerns the extent to which mortality from hunting is additive to natural mortality, rather than compensatory. If hunting mortality were additive, previously stable populations could decline when hunted, but if it were strongly compensatory they could maintain their numbers. For hunting loss to be offset by reduced natural loss before the start of breeding, three conditions must normally be fulfilled: (1) the hunting loss must be less than the natural loss; (2) the natural loss must be density-dependent; and (3) the hunting loss must occur before or during, but not after, the main period of natural loss. Thus, if hunting is concentrated in autumn, there is then ample time for at least some compensation through reduced natural loss before the next spring. But if hunting is concentrated in late winter or spring, when much natural mortality has already occurred, then it may add to natural mortality, resulting in population decline. As an example, the shooting of 40% of Ptarmigan in autumn caused no obvious decline in breeding numbers compared with control areas, but the shooting of 40% of spring numbers led to a big decline in breeding numbers (McGowan 1975). It is for this reason that most hunting seasons for birds are set to begin in the immediate post-breeding period and end well before the start of the next breeding period, game managers having long ago realised the benefits.

In some studies, attempts have been made to calculate the MSY, and to measure to what extent hunting at a given level added to the natural annual mortality. Among Red Grouse at Glen Esk in Scotland, shooting at 30% of the post-breeding numbers was entirely compensated by reduced natural loss, causing no depletion in breeding stock (Jenkins et al. 1963). In fact, this Red Grouse population at the time appeared to be underexploited, and more birds could have been shot without affecting breeding numbers. For managed Grey Partridges in England during pre-pesticide times, prevailing hunting mortality at 30–45% of post-breeding numbers was largely (but not entirely) offset by reductions in natural mortality (Jenkins 1961, Potts 1986). To achieve such figures, it was necessary to shoot so as reduce breeding numbers somewhat below the maximum level possible. This had the effect of raising breeding success (which was density-

FIG 179. The Red
Grouse *Lagopus l.
scotica*, a famous
denizen of heather
moorland, and the
most celebrated
gamebird of Britain
and Ireland. The
opening of its shooting
season, on 12 August
each year, is eagerly
anticipated by the
seasonal closure
of Parliament.
(Edmund Fellowes)

dependent), to give a larger post-breeding population than otherwise possible.
Other estimates of MSY gave 29% for wild Mallards in Britain and 20% and for
female wild Pheasants (Hill 1984, Robertson & Rosenberg 1988). However, such
figures might not hold in other populations of these species, subject to different
breeding and natural mortality rates and, in general, partial compensation of
hunting losses by reduced natural losses appears to be the most frequent finding
to emerge from studies on managed populations (Nichols *et al.* 1984, Nichols 1991).
The fact that some bird populations increased after hunting was reduced implies
that shooting at the previous level was at least partly additive.

Whether from human hunting or natural predation, it is usually hard to
judge whether compensation is total or partial, for one never knows (except by
experiment) what the breeding population might have been in the absence of
these losses, only how it compares with previous figures. Also, while in some
species compensation might occur by spring, when remaining birds start to
nest, in others it may not be apparent until late summer, after reproduction
has occurred. Moreover, some bird species suffer such heavy mortality
during hard winters that recovery of numbers may take several years, with
compensatory change in demographic parameters occurring over this whole
period. The important point is that, in testing for the extent of compensation in
demographic measures, it is important to acknowledge the time period involved.
To be useful in game management, total (or almost total) compensation for
shooting losses must occur before the next shooting season, whether through
reduced natural losses or improved reproduction.

Studies on several species have shown that, up to a certain level, hunting itself could be density-dependent, removing a larger proportion of individuals from high-density populations (for Grey Partridge see Potts 1986, for Mallard see Schifferli 1979). In other words, mortality from hunting can be regulatory in its effects, providing some safeguard against over-hunting.

In widespread species, MSYs can be higher if cropping is restricted to particular localities than if it is undertaken over large areas. This is because, within small areas, immigration can help to replenish depleted local stocks but, as hunting is expanded to wider areas, immigration becomes progressively reduced. On this same basis, one proven method of protecting hunted bird species involves the establishment of refuges in which hunting is barred. This reduces the overall hunting pressure on a population without the need to alter other regulations, and can help to sustain stocks, thereby supporting a larger harvest in the longer term. Such refuges can work well for species that concentrate at high densities, such as breeding seabirds or wintering waterfowl.

Similar principles apply to pest control, although the objective here is quite different: to reduce the population in order to lessen the damage to crops or other resources. If the damage is seasonal, it can be lessened if the population can be reduced substantially before the damage begins. But to reduce the population in the longer term, the number of individuals killed per year must exceed the ability of the population to compensate through improved survival and reproduction of the remaining birds, or through sustained immigration. In other words, the mortality inflicted must be additive. The killing must also be continued year after year if numbers are to remain low, for relaxation of control efforts can quickly lead to population recovery. This is why pest control is normally an ongoing commitment, at which many people can earn a living.

Selective hunting

In some gamebirds, shooting can be directed to certain types of individuals, so as to minimise the effect on next year's harvest. For example, in polygynous pheasant and grouse species, preferential harvesting of males can substantially increase the MSY, providing that the reproductive rates of surviving females are unaffected. In one study, shooting that pushed the adult sex ratio in Black Grouse to 2:1 in favour of females caused no reduction in their subsequent reproductive rates (Ellison et al. 1988). In Pheasants, productivity and numbers have been maintained with post-hunt ratios as distorted as one male per ten females (Ball 1950, Allen 1954). In Capercaillie in parts of Europe, it was in the past usual to shoot some cocks at their display grounds in spring, smaller numbers being sufficient to fertilise all the hens. This type of management is

FIG 180. Black Grouse *Tetrao tetrix* male in display. This species is polygynous and the sexes can be readily be distinguished, which enables the males to be shot and the females to be left, thereby minimising the effect of shooting on the subsequent production of young. (Edmund Fellowes)

feasible in polygynous gamebirds, because the larger, more colourful males can be readily distinguished by hunters. In monogamous bird species, the two sexes need to be present in equal numbers, and in any case cannot easily be distinguished when on the wing, so managed differential hunting of the sexes is then impracticable.

Other losses

In setting bag limits, it is important to allow for all mortality associated with the harvest. The numbers of birds killed and retrieved are measurable, but form only part of the total, as other birds are hit and die later. In North America, most estimates of this 'cripple loss' in waterfowl are around one-fifth of the number retrieved, but have ranged between about one-tenth and two-fifths in different studies (Nieman *et al.* 1987). An exceptional loss was recorded among Eiders off Denmark, where it was estimated that, owing to long-range shooting, for every bird shot and retrieved, another was wounded. This loss was reduced when hunters were persuaded to forgo shooting at distant quarry (Holm & Haugaard 2013).

Other losses associated with hunting are hard to estimate because they result from the methods used and can affect both hunted and non-hunted species. An obvious example is the ingestion of spent lead shot by some species, which can continue for years into the future (Chapter 19). In setting harvest levels, allowance should ideally also be made for additional human-induced mortality not associated with hunting. For instance, large numbers of gallinaceous and other birds may die from collisions with fences or overhead wires. From sample counts of carcasses under sections of power line that ran through suitable habitat in Norway, the annual loss from collisions was estimated at about 20,000 Capercaillie, 26,000 Black Grouse and 50,000 Willow Ptarmigan (Bevanger 1995). These numbers were equivalent to about 90%, 47% and 9% of the annual hunting harvest of these species, but unlike the harvest, these losses occurred year-round including spring, so their effects on population levels are likely to have been greater. In Scotland, tall fences erected to exclude deer from conifer plantations proved hazardous to Capercaillie, killing enough in some areas to cause population declines even in the absence of hunting (Watson & Moss 2008). Similarly, from a wintering population of 450,000 Eiders off Denmark, 140,000 (31%) were shot each year, but another 28,000 (6%) were killed by oil pollution, bringing the total loss caused by humans to 37%, which was judged at the time to be unsustainable (Joensen 1977).

MULTI-SPECIES PROBLEMS

Developing a good harvesting strategy is difficult enough where species can be hunted individually, but much more difficult where several species are hunted together, as in duck shooting in some areas, especially if the hunters cannot

FIG 181. The Teal *Anas crecca*, a small fast-flying duck which is a favourite quarry of wildfowlers. (Edmund Fellowes)

distinguish between species. This difficulty is worsened by the fact that many birds are shot in the poor light of dawn or dusk. The main problem is that species in the same area differ in their vulnerability, so some can be shot to the point of rarity while others remain common enough to encourage continued shooting. At Loch Leven in southeast Scotland, during the 1970s ducks were shot as they passed over hunters in the dim light of dawn. This led to over-shooting of Gadwall and Teal, and to under-shooting of the more numerous Mallard, which were more wary. Over a period of years, Gadwall and Teal numbers declined at this site, while Mallard numbers did not (Allison *et al.* 1974). Similarly, over-shooting can have disastrous effects on remaining wild Grey Partridges when they are caught up in drives of released Red-legged Partridges and shot inadvertently (Aebischer & Ewald 2004). This is despite the fact that, on any mixed shoot, smaller proportions of available Grey than Red-legged Partridges are shot.

PRIVATE AND PUBLIC SHOOTING

In large parts of the world, many bird populations are not hunted sustainably, but on the basis of tradition, need or greed, with no restraints applied. In areas where hunters are sparse relative to the numbers of birds available, or use primitive methods, unrestrained hunting may be acceptable, because it harvests well below the MSY. But nowadays, with modern weaponry, most widely exploited bird populations are unlikely to persist unless harvesting is controlled in some way. If it is not, individual hunters may raise their share of the harvest to excessive levels.

In more general terms, overexploitation of bird and other animal populations usually results when, through lack of 'ownership', several interest groups have unrestricted access to the same population. No one group is prepared to limit its take, because this would merely leave more for the others. The system then operates on the basis of competing greed, what Hardin (1968) called the *tragedy of the commons*. Hardin (1968) used the analogy of a publicly owned pasture (common land) in which sheep or cattle owners have free and unrestricted access to graze their animals. Typically, this system causes a degradation of the pasture by overgrazing, because individual stock-owners perceive short-term economic benefits from having as many of their own livestock as possible grazing the pasture. This results in an excessive aggregate use. Each owner gets the full benefit of adding to his herd, while the dis-benefits are shared by all. One of Hardin's conclusions was that 'freedom in a commons brings ruin to all.' Such problems are avoided only if resources are managed in ways that pursue sustainability rather than growth and unbridled exploitation. It is this free-for-all which has most often led to the overexploitation of marine fish stocks in areas that are not owned or protected by any one interest group. It has also led to the overexploitation of gamebirds, waterfowl and waders on public lands, and of some seabirds on offshore islands (Chapter 17). This is sometimes true even when a 'closed season' has been imposed. A free-for-all also operates in some parts of the Mediterranean region, notably Malta and Cyprus, where hunters still kill large numbers of passing migrants.

The alternatives to an unmanaged free-for-all are of two types – what Hardin (1994) called *privatism* and *socialism*. In privatism, on his definition, the resource is subdivided into many individual properties. Each owner is responsible for his patch, and if he manages his stock sustainably, he will reap the long-term rewards. This is the way in which wild game on many private estates in Britain and Ireland has been managed for more than 150 years. In socialism, the resource is treated as common property, and is managed by some central authority for the benefit of all. This is the basis of waterfowl management in North America, where government agencies are responsible for monitoring numbers, and for setting and enforcing sustainable bag limits. The hunters themselves pay for this system by means of a charge levied on hunting permits, and care is needed to ensure that, with different interest groups harvesting the stock at successive points on a migration route, general over-harvesting does not result. Resident bird populations can be managed successfully on the basis of privatism or socialism, but for migratory populations, socialism is the only viable option in today's world, because migratory populations are inevitably shared by different interest groups as they travel from one country to another. Even though they may spend part of the year on private land where they can be protected, migrants may be exposed to hunting in other parts of their migration routes where the kill-levels have to be controlled if populations are to persist long term.

In many countries with an open season on waterfowl, sustainability in national harvest rates is generally assessed by nationwide annual monitoring of population levels, and adjusting future bag limits accordingly. In most European countries this is done by adjusting the length of the open season, or by banning hunting altogether on species at particular risk. In North America, recreational hunting is regulated by means of daily bag limits as well as by the length of an open season. In both regions, reserves or refuges exist on which birds can live free from shooting.

ARTIFICIAL REARING AND RELEASE

This practice developed from a pre-existing small scale to a very large scale in Britain and Ireland from the 1960s and 1970s when it became apparent that sizeable Grey Partridge stocks could no longer be maintained on farmland managed intensively with pesticide use. Wild game management would then entail so large a reduction in agricultural income, including subsidies, which only the exceptionally wealthy and committed were prepared to forgo. Attention therefore focused on Pheasants and Red-legged Partridges because, compared to Grey Partridges, they could be more easily reared in captivity and then released to remain locally. Initially, gamekeepers trapped remaining Pheasants in spring, and kept them in pens to produce eggs, which were then incubated under broody hens or in artificial incubators. The chicks were raised under heaters until they were large enough to be transferred to outside pens (those for Pheasants usually constructed in woodland), and eventually released in time for the shooting season beginning on 1 October. As time went by, commercial companies became increasingly involved, and now most of the eggs are produced by these companies from captive birds, and the eggs or young are sold to estates who raise the chicks themselves, initially in heated sheds and then in outside pens.

The industrial scale of the enterprise is more akin to poultry-keeping than to wild game management, and the main concern of the gamekeeper is to raise as many chicks as possible for the hunting season, feeding them well enough after release to reduce their wanderings beyond the estate boundaries. The long-term maintenance of local breeding stock is less important than in the past, because

FIG 182. The Red-legged Partridge *Alectoris rufa* is an introduced species which, through artificial rearing, has become the second most commonly hunted gamebird in lowland Britain. (Richard Chandler)

fresh birds can be bought in for each season. The numbers of Pheasants released in Britain each year have increased steadily since the 1970s. Initially, similar numbers were shot, but with progressive increase in the numbers released, the proportions shot have declined to less than a half. Figures published by the GWCT gave the recent annual releases at around 35 million, and the numbers shot at around 15 million.

The scale of this operation has other consequences. Pheasants alone are so numerous that they have come to represent more than a third of the total land-bird biomass in Britain (Dolton & Brooke 1999). Along with their feed, they support huge numbers of predators and grain-eating species, including rats. Again on GWCT figures, more than 200,000 tonnes of wheat are thought to be provided each year in feed-hoppers, with food provision continued at least until the end of January. Red-legged Partridge releases have also increased since the 1970s to their current annual level of around six million, with about 2.6 million shot.[26] These are probably the largest-scale releases of any alien animal species anywhere in the world. For the most part, they are unregulated, falling outside any legislation concerning either wildlife or domestic animals.

Other rear-and-release programmes involved Mallards, but these releases have declined in popularity, partly because of the difficulty of preventing the birds from leaving the area. Hand-reared birds also become tame, so cannot present the challenging targets provided by wild ducks. The birds prefer to fly at dusk when they are hard to see, and the difficulties of maintaining ponds for a small return at antisocial hours has contributed to the demise of captive duck rearing.

In all commonly released species, it has been found that released birds survive in the wild less well than wild-bred birds, independently of shooting, partly because they are more naive with respect to predators. If they survive long enough to breed, they reproduce less well than the wild-bred birds (Brittas *et al.* 1992, Dowell 1992). Concerns have also been expressed over the impact of released birds on the wild stock (through competition, disease transmission or interbreeding), and over their impact on other bird species, on other animal species, and on the general environment. Interbreeding with wild birds brings concerns that the wild-traits of free-ranging populations may be replaced by the less desirable traits (such as greater tameness) present in captive stocks.

One example of parasite transfer from pen-reared Pheasants to wild Grey Partridges involves the nematode gapeworm *Syngamus trachea*. These worms infect the windpipe, and their presence is revealed by behaviour called 'snicking' in which birds try and cough up the worms which restrict their breathing,

---

26 Other recent estimates put the figure for released Pheasants as high as 40 million per year, and for Red-legged Partridges as high as 7.5 million.

causing some mortality. Earthworms, slugs and snails act as intermediate hosts, but on cool damp ground with lots of faeces no intermediate host is necessary, and birds can be infected directly. Gapeworms are now found in Partridges mainly on estates that rear Pheasants, with the heaviest infections occurring among birds living around the pens. Viable cysts can last for years in the soil, acting as a source of infection long after the pens have been removed (Potts 2012). However, the use of anthelmintic drugs in penned Pheasants in recent years has greatly reduced the prevalence of gapeworms and other helminth parasites. For this reason, together with the differing availability of intermediate hosts, the parasites found to predominate on modern game farms are not the same as those that predominate in wild populations.

CONCLUDING REMARKS

The effect of hunting on bird populations clearly depends on whether the quarry species are managed as a renewable resource, with appropriate controls, or whether they are hunted on a free-for-all system with no effective restraints. Providing that habitat is suitably maintained, the former can provide sustained bags indefinitely, whereas the latter usually leads to population decline. Sustained harvesting is most readily achieved where the 'stock' is owned and managed by a single interest group, as on a large estate. It is more difficult to achieve where (as in migratory waterfowl) the stock is exploited by several competing interest groups, a situation that almost always leads to overexploitation unless universal harvest limits or protection can be firmly enforced (as in much of Europe at the present time). Moreover, where several species are hunted simultaneously (again as in many waterfowl), the more vulnerable species can be shot to rarity, while others maintain their numbers.

Shooting can cause three types of loss: shot birds killed immediately, shot birds wounded and not retrieved which die later, and healthy birds which die at some later late through ingesting spent gunshot (supposedly mistaken for grit) and succumb to lead poisoning (Chapter 19). It is important to set bag limits that allow for all three types of loss. One incidental value in exploiting wildlife on a sustained basis for recreation or profit is that it transmits an economic value to good habitat, and apart from the associated reduction in predator populations, often promotes the conservation of other species too. This is especially true where the emphasis is on wild game, but much less so where it depends on birds artificially reared and released, which may have negative effects on wild game and on other species.

CHAPTER 17

Other Bird Killing

I N BRITAIN AND IRELAND IN TIMES PAST, as in many other parts of the world, birds were killed primarily for subsistence, and populations were sometimes overexploited so that they declined and eventually disappeared from parts of their range. Earlier human communities used wild birds as food much more than we do today, eating a much wider range of species and eggs, whenever opportunities arose. How many species were overexploited is open to argument, but it is clear that, in past centuries, many culinary favourites declined and disappeared from large parts of Britain and Ireland. While most of the information in this book is based on scientific study, much of the information from the distant past given in this chapter is based on historical accounts, whose accuracy is now hard to assess (for reviews see Shrubb 2003, Lovegrove 2007). Nevertheless, the different accounts are broadly consistent in the picture they portray, and help to explain the population trends more reliably recorded during the twentieth century.

In earlier centuries, many bird populations in Britain and Ireland were clearly overexploited, especially waterfowl, waders and seabirds, while raptors were killed to protect domestic stock and game. Over the years, some species were reduced to a fraction of what their habitats could support, while others disappeared totally from Britain and Ireland at various dates between the seventeenth and twentieth centuries. Since the mid-twentieth century, many species have been killed unintentionally in other ways, as victims of collisions with road traffic, wires and buildings, while seabirds have been killed as by-catch in fishery operations. Many of these deaths were probably compensated by reductions in natural mortality, but at least in some species, they contributed to population declines (see later).

From old accounts, it is clear that the Crane* disappeared from both Britain and Ireland before the end of the seventeenth century, and the Greylag Goose

FIG 183. Cranes *Grus grus* were long ago hunted to extinction in Britain, but the species is now making a slow comeback, having colonised East Anglia naturally, and been aided in the southwest of Britain by a reintroduction programme. (Richard Chandler)

had almost gone by the end of the eighteenth century. Both species become flightless during moult, enabling them to be rounded up and killed in large numbers. Several other wetland birds that figured abundantly on mediaeval menus, including the various egrets and herons, also disappeared before the end of the seventeenth century (Bourne 1999). The Capercaillie* had been eliminated before the end of the eighteenth century, and other commonly hunted species had gone before the end of the nineteenth century, including Great Bustard*, Bittern*, Black Tern, Avocet*, Black-tailed Godwit* and Ruff, as well as some birds of prey discussed later. For some of the wetland species, land drainage played a role, but for all of them suitable habitat remained long after their disappearance. In addition, before the end of the nineteenth century, many species of waterfowl, waders and seabirds had been greatly reduced, as had most remaining raptor species that were killed to protect domestic stock or game. Species marked above with an asterisk have subsequently re-colonised Britain or have been reintroduced.

In earlier times there was no obvious conservation ethic, and no protective legislation (apart from the Mute Swan, protected on common land at least from the twelfth century as property of the Crown).[27] In addition, occasional areas were protected as hunting preserves for the aristocracy and church leaders, and some raptor nests were protected to provide birds for falconry. But some of the earliest general legislation concerning birds came in during the fifteenth century

27 Other people of standing could also own Mute Swans, and farm them for consumption, providing they owned land on which to keep them. This became a profitable business, which continued from medieval times into the 1880s, only the cygnets being fattened for consumption. The famous Swannery at Abbotsbury in Dorset was originally set up in the eleventh century by Benedictine monks to produce birds for the table.

in Scotland, and the sixteenth century in England and Wales. This legislation was concerned not with protecting birds but with killing them, mainly in the interests of food production, and at least in England and Wales was accompanied by payment of bounties. Various grain-eating species were targeted, as were fish-eaters, and raptors likely to take small lambs or young poultry (Box 6).

In the nineteenth century, the killing of wild birds probably reached its peak. This was a time when guns became more efficient and affordable, when intensive gamekeeping developed on a wide scale, and when a new national rail network opened up many previously remote areas. The railways allowed hunters to access previously unexploited populations, and provided a means for local people to convey fresh bird carcasses or eggs rapidly to city markets. These various developments led to much greater and more widespread exploitation of bird populations for food and recreation, greatly increasing the numbers of all kinds of birds that were killed. It was not until after 1869 that a legal closed season was introduced to protect birds in the breeding season. Some seabirds, wildfowl, rarer waders, raptors, owls and corvids were all seriously reduced in

---

Box 6. Early legislation on bird killing

Apart from earlier attempts to protect some raptor nesting areas, as a source of falconry birds, the first widely applied wildlife legislation for England and Wales was introduced in 1532 by King Henry VIII. But rather than protecting birds, it was aimed at encouraging the killing of nuisance birds and mammals, for which payments were made. Among birds, the emphasis was on Crows, Rooks and Jackdaws, because of their effects on the grain harvest. The list of 'pest' species was subsequently extended in 1566 under the reign of Henry's daughter, Elizabeth I, to include other species that impinged on human interests, including Magpie, Jay, Raven, Buzzard, Kite, harriers, and Osprey; Shag, Cormorant, Kingfisher; Green Woodpecker (for damaging wooden roof shingles and church timbers); together with the Bullfinch or any other species that 'devoureth the blowthe of fruit'. The onus was placed on parishes throughout England and Wales to organise the killing and to raise the money for bounty payments, for which heads were required as proof of death.

We cannot know how well or extensively this legislation was applied, but putting it in the hands of parishes meant that churchwardens were responsible for keeping records of the bounties paid. Some of these records survive today, and reveal some interesting figures, such as the 329 Red Kites, 1,775 Jays, 2,500 crows and 1,230 Bullfinches killed in the parish of Tenderden in Kent during 1679–93; the 2,838 Bullfinches and 3,052 Magpies at Bunbury in Cheshire during 1678–92; the 1,775 Ravens at Wirksworth in Derbyshire in 1707–25; the 1,245 Red Kites at Lezant in Cornwall in 1755–1809; the 184 dozen House

Sparrows at Hambledon in Buckinghamshire in 1804; and the 20,000 dozen House Sparrows at Eaton Socon in Bedfordshire in 1819–42. One rural parish in Cheshire killed over 6,600 Bullfinches in 36 years, with as many as 452 in a single year (1676), while a few years later the same parish disposed on 696 Kites in eight years (Lovegrove 2007). The lists themselves are curious, as species disappeared and re-appeared over the years, and some were well represented in the accounts from some parishes but absent from those of neighbouring parishes. The shifting pattern of records suggests that funds were limited, and that priorities changed over the years and from place to place. As populations were depleted in one place, they could be replenished by immigrants from another. But because pests were worth money, the incentive was probably to concentrate activities after the breeding season when numbers were high, and not to waste time when they were low. For people with exclusive access to private land, the temptation would be to harvest populations sustainably, so as to maintain income in future years, and not to eliminate a lucrative business. It is therefore hard to judge whether this killing had more than temporary and local effects on many species, and even before the Acts were introduced, some species, such as the White-tailed Eagle and Osprey, had gone from most of southern Britain.

The attitudes and practices initiated by this early legislation prevailed through into the twentieth century, as did the payment of bounties, latterly chiefly by fisheries boards. The involvement of churchwardens petered out in the early nineteenth century, and gradually the control of most unwanted species fell to private landowners, especially of the new sporting estates, whose main concern was with the control of meat-eating and fish-eating species that could conflict with their hunting and fishing interests. Gamekeepers on these estates greatly reduced the numbers of raptors in Britain from the late eighteenth to the mid-twentieth centuries, with respites during the two world wars of 1914–18 and 1939–45. Besides killing corvids, raptors and owls, they also shot fish-eaters such as Grey Heron, Goosander, Cormorant and even Dipper and Kingfisher, together with all carnivorous mammal species.

In Scotland, some official bird protection, which extended back to the twelfth and thirteenth centuries, was primarily concerned with Goshawks, Sparrowhawks and Peregrines, valued for falconry. The earliest statute aimed at killing wildlife dates from 1424, about a century earlier than in England and Wales, when James I passed an Act aimed specifically at Rooks. This Act was extended by his son James II in 1457 to other species, including some raptors. We have no indication of the extent to which these Acts were enforced across Scotland, and of what effect, if any, they had on the species targeted. If any records were kept, they seem not to have survived, but the persecution of eagles is known to have greatly increased after the arrival of extensive sheep ranching in Scotland in the eighteenth century (Lovegrove 2007).

numbers, together with some favoured cage birds, such as the Goldfinch. Most ornithologists writing in the eighteenth and nineteenth centuries commented on the widespread declines of many species, which they attributed primarily to hunting, coupled in some cases with drainage and other land-use change.

The first modern legislation in Britain aimed at conserving wild birds was the Seabird Preservation Act of 1869, which gave protection to 33 seabird species during the breeding season (1 April – 1 August). In 1876 and 1880 other Acts came into force, listing 82 wild bird species recommended for protection. This legislation was revised and extended in several Wild Bird Protection Acts between 1880 and 1908, and much further legislation was introduced during the twentieth century, with major Acts in 1954 and 1981. The general effect was to strengthen bird protection, and extend year-round protection to a greater range of species.

WATERFOWL

In earlier centuries, the landscapes of Britain and Ireland were generally wetter than they are now, and many thousands of waterfowl were taken each year as food. Large numbers were caught in special traps, called *decoys*, built over wetlands. They were large tunnels of netting into which birds were driven when flightless and caught by hand. But as the East Anglian Fens were progressively drained, the taking of flightless adults and unfledged young became unproductive because breeding populations were drastically reduced. The practice of catching flightless moulting birds was banned in 1710. A different type of decoy was developed by the Dutch in the sixteenth century, which made use of a trained dog to lure birds into the trap, being aimed at catching free-flying (mainly migrant) birds in autumn and winter. Duck decoys of Dutch design soon became widespread in England, especially in eastern counties, catching birds throughout the non-breeding season. About 250 decoys were known in England, but by 1918 only 28 were still in operation. Their decline was attributed to the expansion of shooting, particularly following the introduction of breech-loading guns, which many people preferred, and also to the decline in native Mallard (largely through land drainage) which made decoys uneconomic (Kear 1990).

Another method of killing wildfowl in numbers was the punt gun, effectively a giant shotgun introduced in the nineteenth century for shooting many ducks at a time while they were resting on the water surface or shorelines. Punt guns varied widely, but they could have bore diameters exceeding 50 mm and could fire about 0.45 kg of shot, killing over 50 birds at a time. Being too big to hold, with a strong recoil, they were mounted onto punts, hence their name. Lying low, hunters would manoeuvre their punts into position using small oars. To improve efficiently, hunters would often work together in fleets of around ten boats. A survey in 1995 showed that less than 50 punt guns were still in use in Britain, where they are still legal, although the barrel diameters are now limited to 44 mm.

Daniel Defoe in 1727 mentioned that waterfowl were sent to London 'twice a week in wagon loads at a time'. In 1790, a statistical survey of the capital published in the third edition of *Encyclopaedia Britannica* revealed that its million inhabitants consumed weekly '700 dozens of wildfowl of several sorts, for six months'. This adds up to over 200,000 birds in a season lasting from September to February (although many decoys operated from August to March) (Kear 1990). The bags recorded in county bird books indicate that the overall numbers taken declined through the nineteenth century, presumably because the populations themselves were declining (Shrubb 2003). For much of that century, the wildfowling season extended well into the breeding season, but the Act of 1876 reduced the open season back to 15 February. By the end of the nineteenth century, county bird books say little about waterfowl on inland wetlands, those remaining being largely confined to coasts and estuaries.

Nevertheless, several ducks were first recorded nesting in Britain and Ireland during the nineteenth century, including the Goosander (first confirmed nesting Scotland 1871, Ireland 1969), Common Scoter (Scotland 1855, Ireland 1905), Wigeon (Scotland 1834), Pintail (Scotland 1869, Ireland 1917), Pochard (England 1818, Scotland 1871, Ireland 1907), Tufted Duck (England 1849, Scotland 1872, Ireland 1877) and Gadwall (England 1850, Scotland 1909, Ireland 1933). It is uncertain how many of these species were genuine new colonists, as opposed to re-colonists after an earlier elimination. Some of them are now common, having spread in association with reduced shooting pressure and the increasing provision of man-made lakes, reservoirs and gravel-pits. Similarly, small numbers of Goldeneyes were present in Scotland in summer for many years, but the first confirmed breeding (in 1970) and subsequent range expansion accompanied the erection of suitable nest-boxes (Chapter 5).

Following the imposition of effective close seasons from the 1870s, and the subsequent legislation and creation of refuges in the twentieth century, many overexploited species started to recover, and the latter half of the twentieth century was a period of generally increasing waterfowl populations (Monval & Pirot 1989, Kirby *et al.* 1995). Within the space of 50 years, most goose populations had grown between two and ten times larger. For example, the numbers of Icelandic Pink-footed Geese wintering in Britain increased from 20,000–30,000 in the 1950s to more than 350,000 in 2008/09, while the numbers of Svalbard Barnacle Geese expanded from around 3,000–4,000 birds in the 1960s to 30,210 in winter 2008/09.

Both populations winter in Britain. Shooting had been responsible for most of the known adult mortality, and when it diminished adult survival rates improved dramatically, allowing growth in breeding numbers and increased recruitment of young birds into breeding populations (Owen et al. 1986). However, as goose numbers continued to grow, the overall rate of increase in some species declined, as did the proportion of young in winter flocks (Chapter 2). This implied the operation of some density-dependent limiting factor, slowing the rate of increase through reduced reproduction (Fig. 20; Owen & Black 1991, Trinder et al. 2009).

In the 1980s, it was estimated from surveys that around 185,000 people in Britain owned a shotgun, that 160,000 shot waterfowl as a hobby, and that they killed around a million birds per year (Owen et al. 1986). About three-quarters of these birds were Mallard, with substantial numbers of Teal and Wigeon, and smaller numbers of other species. By 2004, the number of people shooting waterfowl had declined to about 101,000 (PACEC 2006). Over this period, human hunting continued to be a substantial cause of mortality in waterfowl, and some protected species were also shot. Despite legal protection throughout their range, some 34% of 272 live Bewick's Swans x-rayed in Britain in the 1970s were found to have lead shot embedded in their body tissues, including 44% of adults, 25% of yearlings and 12% of cygnets. Repeat studies in subsequent years revealed a significant decline, with 23% of Bewick's Swans x-rayed in 2001–09 showing lead shot, with the age difference maintained (Newth et al. 2011). In contrast, lead shot was found in the tissues of a smaller proportion of Whooper Swans examined, but with no significant decline over time (14.9% in the 1980s and 13.2% in 2001–09). Although these birds had survived, illegal hunting had clearly continued, with the chance of a bird containing shot increasing with age. Bewick's Swans have a long overland migration from Britain to the Russian Arctic, passing through several countries with poor law enforcement, whereas Whooper Swans migrate only between Iceland and the British Isles. It is hard to say how much the carrying of lead pellets incapacitates birds, but among Pink-footed Geese survival rates were significantly depressed in the short term in birds that had initially survived being shot (Madsen & Noer 1996). The same was true for Mallard studied in the Camargue (Chapter 19).

WADERS

In earlier centuries, waders were highly prized as table birds, and accounts from well-to-do households show that practically every available species was eaten, including Curlew, Snipe, Woodcock, Dotterel and other plovers, Knot, godwits, stints, Ruff and others. Black-tailed Godwits were especially prized, while Ruffs were caught alive and sold to dealers who specialised in fattening them up. The nineteenth-century bird literature includes descriptions of many methods used to take these birds, and in some areas trapping formed a traditional occupation. Around the Fens and the Wash, plovers were the principal quarry, but other species were taken too. Netting was pursued mainly at migration times, September–October and March–April, when birds were abundant, fat and tasty. In spring, breeding birds were also taken, and the combination of spring trapping and land drainage was said to have exterminated native breeding populations of Ruff and Black-tailed Godwit in the early nineteenth century. Dotterel were also sharply reduced, being tame and easy to take on spring passage at traditional stopping places. Nineteenth-century authors who commented on the trapping invariably felt that it was causing or contributing to declines, despite continually shrinking inland habitats (Shrubb 2003). Large-scale shooting of waders by professional fowlers operating on shorelines continued well into the twentieth century, and the large-scale netting of plovers continued in the Lincolnshire marshes until the Lapwing received total protection in 1946. During the nineteenth century, Snipe, Woodcock and plovers were increasingly regarded as game, and trapping them was probably discouraged as game preserving increased.

In addition, the eggs of many wader species were eaten whenever opportunity arose; and by the nineteenth century the eggs of some were exploited commercially. In many eastern counties commercial egg collecting increased with an improved rail network, supplying a growing demand in cities, especially London. Today the past scale of the trade seems mind-boggling. As mentioned in a review by Shrubb (2003), one dealer in Norfolk sent 600–700 dozen Lapwing eggs (1,800–2,100 clutches) to London and other markets during the season. Some 200 dozen eggs (600 clutches) were sent from Romney Marsh in Kent in 1839, and

FIG 184. Nest of Lapwing *Vanellus vanellus*, whose eggs were once harvested on a commercial scale in Britain. (Ian Newton)

280 dozen eggs (840 clutches) were sent each year from a single estate in Norfolk. Not all 'plovers' eggs' were laid by plovers, those from Norfolk including eggs from Redshank, Ruff, Black Tern and Stone-curlew. Several contemporary authors felt that this trade was reducing Lapwing populations, which, however, recovered following enactment of the Bird Protection Acts from the 1870s. Many species of inland and coastal waders increased progressively during much of the twentieth century, which may well have represented a recovery from earlier exploitation.

Only three wader species are still legal quarry in Britain, namely Snipe, Woodcock and Golden Plover, but many other species are shot in substantial numbers on migration and wintering areas, especially in France. These include not only common species, such as Lapwing and Redshank, but rarer ones, such as Ruff and Little Ringed Plover, as is reflected, for example, in ring recoveries. Around 100,000 Golden Plovers are estimated to be shot annually in France, but these include a relatively low proportion of British breeding birds (Byrkjedal & Thompson 1998).

SEABIRDS

For centuries seabirds have been vulnerable to human exploitation because of their colonial nesting, making it possible to collect large numbers of birds or eggs. Some of these long-lived species would have been sensitive to even small increases in adult mortality. The Great Auk was driven to global extinction by the mid-nineteenth century (with the last in Britain taken in 1840, on St Kilda, and the last ever in 1844 in Iceland). Skin-collecting threatened the Great Skua during the early 1800s (Furness 1987), and the millinery trade drove tern populations throughout northern Europe to critically low levels in the late nineteenth century (along with egrets and grebes). At that time, fashionable ladies' hats were decorated with bird feathers, for which adult breeding birds were required.

In parts of western Scotland and Ireland, harvests of seabirds and eggs were integral to a subsistence economy, and on St Kilda up to an estimated 12,000 Fulmar chicks and 90,000 Puffins were taken annually during the nineteenth century (Harris & Wanless 2011). Until about a century ago, large numbers of young Gannets were killed at various colonies for human consumption and for baiting lobster and crab creels. Almost certainly, numbers were held down by this practice. The men of Ness, Isle of Lewis, are still licensed to take 2,000 nearly fledged young Gannets (known as *gugas*) from Sula Sgeir each year for salting and then sale and consumption, both locally and abroad. This figure represents about 30% of the young produced at this colony each year, but in addition other young fall from the cliffs during the disturbance. Young Gannets tend to return and breed in their local colonies, and interestingly, numbers at Sula Sgeir – while not declining – increased much more slowly during the twentieth century than expected for a colony of this size (Wanless & Harris, in Mitchell *et al.* 2004). In other parts of the world too, some seabird colonies have long been harvested by local people for food, sometimes without causing long-term declines in breeding numbers, as exemplified by Puffins on the Westmann Islands (Iceland), and by Guillemots and others on the Faeroe Islands.

Manx Shearwater colonies were for many centuries exploited as both a local food source and as a revenue earner, principally through the export of barrels of salted fledglings. Such records date back to the fourteenth century. Early eighteenth-century records from the Calf of Man indicate harvests of up to 10,000 chicks per annum. This colony now holds less than 50 pairs. On Mingulay in the Outer Hebrides, a barrel of young shearwaters reportedly also once formed part of the annual crofting rents. This colony is now extinct. However, as both these places have been colonised by Brown Rats, it is impossible to judge the role that harvesting by humans may have played.

Colossal numbers of eggs were sometimes taken from specific sites, with 44,000 Black-headed Gull eggs taken from Scoulton Mere in 1840, and 130,000 Guillemot eggs from Bempton Cliffs in 1884. The hair-raising activities of the 'eggers and climmers' on Flamborough and Bempton cliffs in Yorkshire have been well described. A team of three climbers were said to be able to collect 200–300 Guillemot eggs per day for up to five weeks each year, with up to four teams working the cliffs at a time. The Black-headed Gull was a widespread favourite, with many colonies farmed for eggs and young (called *squabs*). The first modern protective legislation passed for birds in Britain, the Seabird Act of 1869, represented an attempt to curb this onslaught. However, egg collection as a source of human food remained legal into the 1950s, and as a boy at this time I can remember buying Guillemot and gull eggs that were openly on sale on the Yorkshire coast.

Exploitation of seabirds probably reached a peak in the nineteenth century owing to increased human populations, better transport and high demand for seabird products. The shooting of seabirds at nesting colonies (as near Flamborough Head) was a popular pastime for hundreds of well-to-do people. This was largely a recreational activity, and no use was made of the majority of carcasses, other than for a short time in the millinery trade (for which Kittiwake and tern wings were favoured).

The huge increase and spread of some seabird populations that occurred over much of the latter half of the twentieth century can again be seen partly as a recovery from past human exploitation, but as explained in earlier chapters, this increase was aided by a huge upsurge in food supplies, resulting mainly from human fishing activities. By the 1970s, some gull colonies had become large and perceived as a threat to: (1) other birds, especially terns, (2) human safety, by increasing the risk of aircraft accidents and pollution of water supplies, and (3) human amenity because of disturbance by roof-nesting gulls in coastal towns and conflicts with sporting interests on grouse moors (mainly Lesser Black-backed Gulls, but only local in importance). These concerns led to control measures being undertaken at many colonies. On some nature reserves, gull eggs were systematically destroyed each year to deter the birds from nesting there, but outside nature reserves, and particularly on grouse moors, whole colonies were eradicated by killing adults, usually by placing poisoned or narcotic baits near nests. On the Isle of May, in a population of some 1,500–2,500 Herring Gulls and 500–1,500 Lesser Black-backs, the destruction of about 90% of eggs over a five-year period led to a slow decline in the numbers of nesting Herring Gulls (to the benefit of terns), but not in the smaller numbers of Lesser Black-backed Gulls, in which losses were compensated by immigration (Wanless *et al.* 1996). At the time of the *Seabird* 2000 survey, the largest cull of adult gulls had been undertaken at an inland colony on moorland in the Bowland Fells (Lancashire) where over 29,000 gulls, mostly Lesser Black-backs, were killed in 1999–2002 (Sowter 2002). Similar repeated disturbance and culling eradicated large colonies of Lesser Black-backed Gulls on Flanders Moss near Stirling, and several other sites, mostly grouse moors. Among other seabirds, Cormorants can be shot under licence to protect angling and fishery interests, Black-headed Gull eggs are still collected under licence in some parts of Britain, and the traditional harvesting of Gannet chicks on Sula Sgeir persists to the present day. In addition, illegal killing still occurs at

FIG 185. The Cormorant *Phalacrocorax carbo* is shot under licence in Britain to reduce damage to fisheries. This one, photographed on the River Nith in Dumfries, has caught a Sea Trout *Salmo t. trutta*. (Edmund Fellowes)

rates sufficient to affect population trends of some other species, such as Great Skuas. Thus, while persecution of seabirds has been greatly reduced since the nineteenth century, leading to recovery of populations, some local destruction of eggs and adults continues, some for good conservation reasons.

Further persecution of seabirds that nest around Britain and Ireland occurs abroad. Boys in west Africa trap large numbers of immature terns for sport, food and sale, which may have slowed the recovery of Roseate Terns in Britain. Other victims include Sandwich, Common and Little Terns. Catches are greatest in years when the sardines on which terns feed come close inshore during the daytime (Dunn & Mead 1982). Protective legislation and education in Ghana caused a substantial reduction of tern trapping along the coast by 1994, but it has resurged subsequently. Other seabird species which nest in Britain or Ireland are shot in their migration or wintering areas, particularly various auks.

PASSERINES

During the nineteenth and early twentieth centuries, many passerines were caught as cage birds; these were chiefly finches, but also others considered good songsters, such as Woodlarks and Nightingales. It is hard to assess the impact on populations, but the Goldfinch was often cited as being severely reduced. The numbers caught were large, especially in the south of Britain at migration times. For example, Gray & Hussey (1860) recorded 400–500 dozen Goldfinches being sent to London from the Worthing area annually, with up to 1,050 dozen in some years, and a record exists of 12 dozen being caught in a single morning on the site now occupied by Paddington Station in London. Trapping on this scale apparently occurred every autumn all along the South Downs from Worthing to Rottingdean (Shrubb 2003). The newly formed Society for the Protection of Birds (now the RSPB) made 'saving the Goldfinch' one of its first tasks. A close season to protect breeding birds was imposed at the end of the nineteenth century, and successive legislation during the twentieth century has effectively brought this practice to an end.

Some songbirds were also caught for human consumption. Skylark netting was prevalent in the eighteenth and early nineteenth centuries, and was practised commercially in several areas. According to Thomas Pennant, Dunstable was famous for its larks in the eighteenth century, up to 4,000 dozen per season being sent to market. By the late nineteenth century, Skylark trapping seems to have been restricted to land with open access, such as downland. The main victims were probably passage migrants and winter visitors, evidently present in numbers unimaginable today. In the nineteenth century, huge numbers of Wheatears and

FIG 186. Skylark
Alauda arvensis, a
declining farmland
bird once trapped
in large numbers in
southeast England and
eaten as a delicacy.
(Richard Chandler)

Skylarks were taken (in small funnel traps) mainly on the Sussex Downs and on
the Isle of Portland in Dorset. The birds were trapped for market from late July to
late September each year, during the migration season, and were considered a great
delicacy. By 1872 numbers were declining, and the trapping eventually petered out.

SKIN AND EGGSHELL COLLECTING

Collecting the skins and eggshells of birds became popular in Victorian times
and persisted well into the twentieth century. Some of these specimens went to
the new museums, but most to private collectors, who usually commissioned
gamekeepers and other country people to collect for them. Dealer–taxidermists
occurred in almost every town, and most large country houses had their
collections of local bird skins. As species declined for whatever reasons, specimens

FIG 187. Once
common in Britain
and Ireland, the
Bittern *Botaurus
stellaris* disappeared
altogether through
habitat destruction
and hunting, but
re-colonised naturally,
and is now expanding,
largely through a
programme of reedbed
creation. (Alan Martin)

became more valuable, and the collecting of skins and eggs probably accentuated the demise of several rare species, causing their extinction as breeding species in Britain during the nineteenth and early twentieth centuries. Likely examples include the White-tailed Eagle, Osprey, Black-tailed Godwit, Ruff and Bittern, while other species, such as Bearded Tit, were almost wiped out. Other rare species were similarly prevented from re-establishing themselves, Ruff and Avocet being likely examples. Even into the 1960s and 1970s, egg collecting could have affected several species in Britain, including the Red-backed Shrike.

RAPTORS

Some raptor species are still limited by human killing, despite protective legislation. In previous centuries birds of prey were killed as predators of domestic poulty, but today, when most poultry are kept indoors, this is no longer a significant problem. The main antagonism against raptors now stems from people who shoot gamebirds. Because some raptors take gamebirds that could otherwise be shot, the raptors are viewed as competitors. The two eagles also take lambs in some places – mostly dead but some alive – and this brings eagles into conflict with sheep farmers. Most killing of raptors is deliberate, but some species which eat carrion are also killed incidentally in attempts to get rid of Foxes by use of poisoned meat baits.

FIG 188. Once widespread, the White-tailed Eagle *Haliaeetus albicilla* was totally eliminated from Britain and Ireland, but has now been reintroduced to both. (Edmund Fellowes)

In attempts to protect domestic stock, the killing of large raptors was officially encouraged in Britain and parts of Europe as early as the sixteenth century by payment of bounties (Box 6; Newton 1979). These payments seem to have been sporadic, however, and to have had limited long-term effects on the populations of most species. However, to judge from old bone remains, place names and historical accounts, the White-tailed Eagle is likely once to have occurred around all the coasts of Britain and Ireland, as well as at all sizeable inland wetlands and rivers (Fig. 189). The Osprey was also widespread throughout Britain and Ireland, and was probably killed because of its habit of raiding fish ponds. Both species had been eliminated from most of both islands by the end of the seventeenth century, long before the days of intensive game preservation, remaining only in a few remote areas.

From the mid-nineteenth century, the killing of raptors in Britain and Ireland was carried out on a more systematic basis, mainly by gamekeepers who were employed partly for the express purpose of 'vermin' control. Following the rise in the management of small game at this time, persecution of raptors reached its peak, and spread to smaller species. The killing was done on the insistence of landowners, who coordinated operations and often ran private bounty schemes. The objective of total eradication was soon achieved for some raptor species over large areas. Much of the killing occurred in the breeding season, when pairs were present at traditional nesting sites. In time, five species were apparently eliminated from Britain as breeders, namely the Goshawk (last recorded nesting attempt 1893), Marsh Harrier (1898), Honey-buzzard (1911), Osprey (1916) and White-tailed Eagle (1916) (Newton 1979). Total elimination seems certainly to have been achieved for

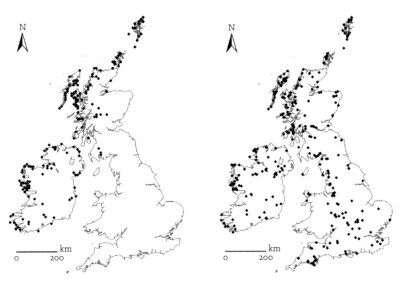

FIG 189. The past distribution of the White-tailed Eagle *Haliaeetus albicilla* in Britain and Ireland. Left: based on nineteenth-century breeding records. Right: based on place-names interpreted as indicating the former presence of this species in the last 1,500 years. Based on densities within the current range, the pre-medieval population size was estimated at 800–1,400 pairs. (From Evans *et al.* 2012)

FIG 190. The Osprey *Pandion haliaetus* is thought to have been eliminated from Britain in the early years of the twentieth century, but re-colonised naturally from the 1950s, and reached around 225 pairs in 2010. (Alan Martin)

the Goshawk and White-tailed Eagle, but we can be less certain about the other three, in which odd pairs may have hung on unknown to ornithologists. For the Osprey, Dennis (2008) listed several instances of likely breeding attempts in the period between 1916 and 1954, when conventional wisdom maintained they were no longer breeding in Britain.

In the late nineteenth century, several other previously widespread species became much restricted in range, the Buzzard remaining only in some northern and western hill districts, the Hen Harrier on the Outer Hebrides and Orkney Islands, and the Red Kite in a small area in central Wales, where game preservation did not take hold. The species least affected were the Merlin, Kestrel and Sparrowhawk, although the numbers of all three were reduced. These were all small species with relatively high breeding rates, and thus having the best ability to recover year after year from sustained killing.

Several species disappeared earlier from Ireland than from Britain, with the last known nesting dates of the Osprey, Buzzard and Red Kite in the late eighteenth century, the Goshawk in the early nineteenth century, and the Golden and White-tailed Eagles in the early twentieth century. Overall, the most marked reductions were seen in species that had low and localised populations at the start, frequently fed on carrion (which made them easy to poison), or had low breeding rates, or some combination of these features. Lesser reductions were associated with large populations living partly away from game-preserving areas, little or no carrion-feeding and relatively high breeding rates (Newton 1979).

Some have doubted that species could have been eradicated by gamekeepers when some areas remained free of intensive game management. But not every last individual had to be killed. All that was necessary was that more individuals were killed each year than could be replaced by annual breeding. Providing this level of killing was maintained over enough years (related to the longevity of the species), regional extinction would inevitably follow. Moreover, young raptors would have repeatedly wandered outside safe areas, and any individuals lingering for a time on a game-rearing estate would have been at risk. With their abundance of game and other species, game-rearing estates are likely to have always attracted raptors, a feature enhanced in recent years as land-use changes have greatly reduced the abundance of prey-species in the wider countryside. In recent years, many ringed and radio-tagged eagles, kites and others have died during their first year of life more than 100 km from where they were raised. Moreover, while most of the killing in the past (as now) was by gamekeepers, rural attitudes were different then, and many other people destroyed raptors or their nests.

On large estates, records were usually kept of the total raptors, corvids and other predators killed each year, along with the game that was shot. The sheer magnitude of the figures has since led some people to doubt them, but they were repeated in similar order in region after region, and on most estates feet, beak or carcasses – the latter displayed on gibbets – were required as proof of killing. However, the annual figures for many estates included many more raptors than could have lived there at one time, a testimony to the effects of movements or to the existence of neighbouring less disturbed populations from which new recruits continually came. For example, from a single 6,700 ha estate at Glengarry in Inverness-shire during 1837–40, the documented kills over the four years were listed as 475 Ravens, 1,431 Hooded Crows, 98 'Blue Hawks', six Gyr Falcons, 78 Merlins, 462 Kestrels, 285 Buzzards, 371 Rough-legged Buzzards, three Honey-buzzards, 15 Golden Eagles, 27 White-tailed Eagles, 18 Ospreys, 63 Goshawks, 275 Red Kites, five Marsh Harriers, 63 Hen Harriers, and nine 'Ash-coloured Hawks', together with 71 'Fern Owls', 35 'Horned Owls' and 14 'Golden Owls'. This gives a total of 1,778 diurnal birds of prey, or nearly 445 per year on average, and 120 owls, or 30 per year on average (Lovegrove 2007). The numbers may be correct, but the identifications of some of these Glengarry species should perhaps be treated with reserve. Vernacular names were more variable in the past than now, and different keepers may have used different names for the same species. If the term Rough-legged Buzzard referred to *Buteo lagopus*, the alleged number killed is hard to accept, unless the species wintered in northern Scotland in much greater numbers in the 1830s than it does now. The 98 'Blue Hawks' were presumably Sparrowhawks or Peregrines (otherwise not mentioned), Ash-coloured Hawks were probably male Hen Harriers, while Fern, Horned and Golden Owls were probably Short-eared, Long-eared and Barn Owls respectively (although in some areas 'Fern Owl' was also used for Nightjar, an unlikely target for gamekeepers). Similar or smaller totals were listed not only for other British estates but also for some central European ones in the same era (Bijleveld 1974, Newton 1979, Lovegrove 2007). Hence, the

FIG 191. The Marsh Harrier *Circus aeruginosus* was totally eliminated from both Britain and Ireland by habitat destruction and then persecution, but re-colonised eastern Britain naturally and is now expanding in numbers and distribution, reaching roughly 350 pairs in 2010. (Andy Thompson)

overall figures from Glengarry could be correct, even if some of the identifications were askew by today's standards.

Comparing the figures on many lists from the mid-nineteenth with those from the early twentieth century, the main difference is in the reduced representation of large and medium-sized species in some lists and their complete disappearance from others. That this was in some regions due to the culling itself is suggested by the large initial kills, followed by a swift decline in subsequent years. For smaller species, however, on many estates the totals showed no obvious decline over many years, suggesting that for these species the gamekeepers were merely cropping the populations concerned, and causing no long-term decline. This was also indicated in some official statistics from Austria, which show that between 1948 and 1968, premiums were paid annually on about 12,000–20,000 birds. Likewise, the cull of 6,000 Goshawks destroyed each year by Finland's 170,000 hunters was also thought to have caused no long-term decline in Goshawk breeding numbers, for most of the cull was of juveniles killed in the few months following breeding (Saurola 1976). However, this cull may still have reduced the numbers of gamebirds killed by Goshawks in autumn and early winter.

Records have recently become available from the 5,830 ha Atholl Estate in Perthshire (McMillan 2011). Over the 44-year period 1867–1910, some 14,386 'hawks' (assumed to have included all diurnal raptors), 5,495 owls and 1,921 Ravens were recorded as killed there, giving annual averages of 327, 125 and 44 respectively. There was no significant trend in these figures over the whole period, suggesting that overall numbers were maintained by continuing immigration. But because the species were not separated, it is impossible to say whether species composition changed over this period, and whether any species was lost totally. Some uncommon species may have gone before recording began. The introduction of protective legislation in the mid-twentieth century made little obvious difference to persecution levels, and similar overall numbers of raptors and owls were killed up to 1988 when recording was stopped. Gamekeepers on individual beats seemed able to decide whether they killed raptors or not, and a change of keeper on a beat often denoted a change in the numbers of raptors killed. One keeper was present on one beat from 1951 to 1976 but did not kill raptors or owls; reasonable grouse bags were maintained on his beat throughout his period.

Evidence for the impact of human predation on raptor populations has come, not only from the declines in populations that followed widespread killing, but also from the recoveries in numbers and distributions that followed its reduction. During the twentieth century, the decline in gamekeeper numbers, the change in public attitudes, the abolition of bounty schemes and the enactment of protective legislation enabled many raptor species to increase and spread, so that in Britain some species were probably more numerous by the end of the twentieth century than at any time in the previous 150 years. From the mid-twentieth century, most of the raptor species in Britain made spectacular recoveries, re-occupying parts or much of their former range (including species whose recoveries were delayed by organochlorine pesticide poisoning). The most impressive example was the Buzzard, which, from surviving remnant populations mostly in northern and western hill districts, re-colonised the whole of Britain within 50 years, and is now breeding commonly again in every county. It also began to nest again, and is steadily expanding, in Ireland, from which it had been totally eradicated. Like the Buzzard, the Raven in Britain also became restricted to northern and western districts, and is now spreading to re-occupy eastern districts from which, according to written record, it was eliminated in the eighteenth and nineteenth centuries.

On some estates where game shooting is important, continued killing of raptors is evident from the reduced densities of certain species there, the disappearance of breeding pairs during the nesting season, the finding of traps and poisoned baits, and the occasional prosecutions of gamekeepers who get caught. The main targeted species are Golden Eagle, Hen Harrier, Peregrine and Goshawk, and ongoing persecution is evidently the main factor currently limiting the overall numbers and distributions of these species in Britain. Nevertheless, there are many areas where populations of these four species are apparently at capacity level, regularly spaced and relatively stable from year to year, and where breeding is generally successful. In the lowlands, Peregrines are nesting increasingly on churches and other town buildings (Chapter 5). Despite ongoing persecution, some species are continuing to expand in Britain, in recovery from past killing, but are still not occupying their full potential range, as judged by availability of food and nest-sites. Examples include the White-tailed Eagle, Red Kite, Osprey, Goshawk and Marsh Harrier. For the first three

FIG 192. Under past persecution, the Buzzard *Buteo buteo* became restricted to western hill districts of Britain by the late nineteenth century, but under reduced persecution has expanded to re-occupy much of Britain, and has also re-colonised Ireland. (Keith Kirk)

FIG 193. The Raven *Corvus corax*, the largest corvid in Britain, much persecuted but now showing signs of recovery. (David Boyle)

of these species, recovery has been helped by well-managed reintroduction programmes, and the fourth by falconry escapes and releases. Other species, such as Buzzard and Sparrowhawk, seem to be maintaining good numbers, despite the fact that on some game-rearing estates they are killed every year. Nevertheless, the killing of raptors in Britain and Ireland is now conducted on a more limited scale than in the nineteenth and early twentieth centuries, and these birds are accordingly more widespread and numerous.

Populations of various raptors in Britain around 2010 could be estimated roughly as Honey-buzzard 50 pairs, Red Kite 1,600 pairs, White-tailed Eagle 52 pairs, Marsh Harrier 350 pairs, Hen Harrier 600 pairs, Montagu's Harrier 16 pairs, Goshawk 435 pairs, Golden Eagle 440 pairs, Osprey 225 pairs, Merlin 1,100 pairs, Hobby 2,800 pairs, Peregrine Falcon 1,500 pairs (various sources). More approximate estimates were given for the Sparrowhawk of around 33,000 pairs, Buzzard around 66,000 pairs and Kestrel around 45,000 pairs. Following its recent recovery, the Buzzard has thus become – on the basis of these figures – the commonest raptor in Britain.

In those species that are still heavily persecuted, the impact can be great. Golden Eagles and Hen Harriers are currently judged to be occupying only about half their potential breeding range in the British Isles, Red Kites less than a third and Goshawks less than a tenth. Despite the difficulties of studying an illegal activity, attempts have been made to compare the success of birds of prey nesting on land with a gamekeeper with that on land without. In a wide-ranging study of Hen Harriers in Scotland during 1988–95, annual production was 0.8 fledglings per breeding female per year on grouse moors, compared with 2.4 on other moorland, and 1.4 in young conifer plantations (Etheridge *et al* 1997). Human interference was recorded on more than half of grouse-moor estates studied, and accounted for at least 30% of breeding failures among harriers there. Failures were much less frequent elsewhere. The annual survival of female harriers breeding on grouse moors was about half that of females breeding on other moorland. In addition, the survival of females which bred unsuccessfully on grouse moors was much lower than that of females which raised at least one young there, implying that many had been killed while nesting. Survival of breeding females on other moorland was high and unrelated to breeding success. Under current levels of killing and nest destruction, it was estimated that the numbers of Hen Harriers nesting on grouse moors would decline rapidly without continuing immigration. During the study period, Hen Harriers on other moors produced a surplus of female recruits approximately sufficient to compensate for losses on grouse moors. More yearling females bred on grouse moors than elsewhere. In other words, owing to illicit killing and nest destruction, grouse moor was a sink habitat for harriers which received two-thirds of its female recruits from other habitats. Without this destruction, the Hen Harrier population of Scotland could increase by an estimated 13% per year until a new, but unknown, equilibrium level was reached.

In an earlier study, the potential numbers of Hen Harriers in Britain as a whole were estimated on the basis of the habitat available at around 1,588 females (1,660 females in the UK). This was nearly three times the population known to be there at that time (Potts 1998). Only about 70% of the total available nesting habitat (moorland and heathland) was occupied, much of it at artificially low density. These various figures indicate the extent to which the numbers and distribution of the species were continuing to be held down by gamekeeping. They exclude the possibility that, if Hen Harriers were more abundant, they might also nest in cereal fields, as they do on parts of the continent. On grouse moors, persecution of Hen Harriers and other raptors seems to have increased in recent years, and national numbers of harriers decreased by about one-fifth between 2004 and 2010 (Holling *et al.* 2012).

In the central and eastern Highlands of Scotland, where grouse-moor management predominates, the Golden Eagle population declined between 1992 and 2003 to levels where increasingly large areas became devoid of breeding pairs. In some of these areas, more than 60% of known territories had become vacant by 2003, although the old nests still remained. No evidence was found that other factors were involved, and away from grouse moors Golden Eagle populations remained stable (Whitfield *et al.* 2007). When adult Golden Eagles are killed at the nest, they are often replaced by younger birds in subadult plumage. The proportion of subadult birds at nests in Scotland was found to correlate, over 11 different regions, with the number of proven poisoning incidents in those regions. In the regions with the most such incidents, the proportions of subadults stood at more than 20% (Whitfield *et al.* 2004).

Following its near elimination in the nineteenth century, the Red Kite was reintroduced to several areas of Britain in the 1990s. Subsequent population growth varied between areas and was exceptionally low in northern Scotland. Reproduction in this area was as good as in the best of the other areas, but annual survival rates were much lower (Smart *et al.* 2010). Some 40% of 103 Red Kites found dead in this area had been killed illegally, mainly by poisoning. The annual survival rates of marked first-year, second-year and older birds were measured at 0.37, 0.22 and 0.87 respectively, but in the absence of illegal killing these rates could have become 0.54, 0.78 and 0.87. In a mathematical model, the observed demographic rates gave a population trend which matched that of the wild population, but if the additive illegal deaths were excluded, the projected population growth rate emerged as similar to that in the fastest-growing population, in southern England. It was therefore concluded that the growth of this Scottish population was being constrained by illegal killing.

FIG 194. The Red Kite *Milvus milvus* survived only in a tiny area in central Wales, but under protection and a reintroduction programme it now breeds over large parts of Britain, with a total breeding population in 2010 of around 1,600 pairs. (Tony Cross)

In a wide-ranging study of Peregrines in northern England, involving 1,081 nest histories between 1980 and 2000, productivity on grouse moors was only half that on other upland areas. Clutch and brood sizes in successful nests did not differ between habitats, and the difference was mainly due to more complete nest failures on grouse moors. Analysis of wildlife crime records for the region showed that persecution was much greater on grouse moors than elsewhere (Amar *et al.* 2012). During the study period, Peregrine breeding numbers in most of the area increased, whereas on grouse moors they declined. Population modelling confirmed that, at the prevailing levels of loss, Peregrines could not sustain themselves on grouse moors without continual immigration.

Although the original British population of Goshawks was eliminated, the species was often imported for falconry, leading to occasional escapes and releases. Sporadic breeding was said to have occurred in southwest England from the 1920s, but these birds did not persist (Meinertzhagen 1950). However, during the 1960s and 1970s, Goshawks started nesting in at least 13 widely separated regions of Britain, with five leading to established breeding populations (Marquiss & Newton 1982). They probably arose from birds imported from central Europe in the 1960s and from Finland in the 1970s. It was estimated that, during 1970–80, an average of 20 Goshawks per year escaped from captivity, and a further 30–40 were released (Kenward *et al.* 1981b). These birds probably influenced the distribution of subsequent breeding attempts, and the number of new nesting areas and the overall population trajectory increased following years with high importations (Marquiss 1981). By 1980, the overall breeding numbers in Britain were estimated at around 60 pairs, but imports were then restricted and subsequent population growth varied according to the annual productivity and deliberate killing of established birds (Marquiss *et al.* 2003). In some areas, breeding production was reduced by half due to the destruction of breeders, eggs and young (Marquiss & Newton 1982).

FIG 195. The Goshawk *Accipiter gentilis* was totally eliminated from Britain by deforestation and then persecution, but has become re-established in many areas, mainly from escapes of birds imported for falconry. It was estimated to number more than 430 pairs in 2010. (Roy Blewitt)

More than any other raptors, Goshawks are attracted to Pheasant rearing pens, where many are killed. Others are killed after entering Larsen crow traps, attracted by the decoy bird. The impact of this killing away from nesting sites was inferred from a comparison of population growth in two regions: the Scottish Borders, where Goshawks lived in large state-owned forests remote from game interests, and northeast Scotland, where many of the birds nested in privately owned woods close to Pheasant rearing sites (Marquiss *et al.* 2003). In both regions, Goshawk breeding performance was little affected by the killing, and production was similarly good at 2.45 young per nest. However, in the northeast, Goshawks were said to be a problem at Pheasant release sites, with ample evidence of Goshawks being shot and trapped. The population growth rate in the northeast was less than half of that in the Borders, and three types of evidence suggested a lack of potential recruits. Firstly, on average only 70% of known breeding sites were occupied each year in the northeast, compared with virtually complete occupancy each year in the Borders. Secondly, breeding numbers in the northeast increased or decreased from one year to the next according to the number of young produced two years earlier. Finally, the birds in the northeast bred at a younger mean age, with 13% of nesting females being in their first year, compared to none in the Border forests. Both populations started in the early 1970s, but by 1996 the northeast held 17 breeding pairs, compared with at least 87 in the Borders. In Britain as a whole, the number of breeding pairs increased slowly but steadily, reaching about 400 by the 1990s (Petty 1996), with continuing growth since then. Nevertheless, illegal killing is common and widespread, accounting for at least 42% of ring recoveries (Petty 2002).

Two main lessons emerge from the recent history of the Goshawk in Britain. Following its largely unauthorised 'reintroduction', the success of the species in re-establishing itself was almost certainly due to the presence in many regions of large state-owned forests, where pairs could nest largely free of persecution. Secondly, much of the killing occurred in late summer and autumn, away from breeding sites, and involved mainly young birds, rather than breeding adults at their nests (which are too time-consuming for gamekeepers to find in large forests). Much of the recent killing has therefore occurred at the time each year when numbers were near their seasonal peak. Calculations based on data from Swedish ringing, supplemented by radio-tracking, suggested that a loss of up to 35% of all young Goshawks might be sustained without leading to population decline (Kenward *et al.* 1991). In contrast, where breeders at nests were the main targets, such losses probably add to other mortality, and hence have greater potential impact on breeding numbers. Various studies in continental Europe show a clear relationship between the timing and intensity of killing and

Goshawk population trends, with the removal of nesting adults having much the greatest impact (Bijlsma 1991, Rutz *et al.* 2006).

One of the commonest methods used to kill birds of prey is the laying of poisoned meat baits (often rabbit carcasses) in the open. Although illegal since 1911, the practice continued, and hundreds of baits have been discovered accidentally and reported in recent decades, often in association with dead raptors. Chemical analyses identified the poisons involved (Chapter 18). Because the chance of anyone detecting these baits is considered low, it is assumed that the numbers found represent a small fraction of a very large total. Sometimes such baits kill multiple birds, one after another, as exemplified by the ten Buzzards found dead from carbofuran poisoning at a site in south Scotland in 2004, and the 28 Ravens found killed by fenthion on farmland in west Wales in 1999 (Lovegrove 2007). Recent known poisoning incidents were widely spread through Britain, but particularly common on grouse moors. This was probably not because poisoning had increased there, but because it had declined in lowland areas (Whitfield *et. al.* 2003). In an analysis of illegal bird killing, the RSPB revealed that 85% of people convicted of killing raptors since 1985 had game interests and most were gamekeepers. One gamekeeper in Scotland in 2011 was convicted of possessing 10 kg of carbofuran, allegedly enough concentrate of this highly toxic chemical to kill all the raptors in Britain.

OTHER BIRD KILLING

Under current UK legislation, modified from the Wildlife and Countryside Act of 1981, all birds are protected, but each year the government issues general licences which allow authorised persons to shoot certain 'pest species' in any numbers at any time, or game species within specified 'open seasons'. Twelve native species classed as pests include the Carrion Crow, Hooded Crow, Rook, Jackdaw, Jay and Magpie, the Great Black-backed, Lesser Black-backed and Herring Gulls, and the Feral Pigeon, Woodpigeon and Collared Dove. The House Sparrow and Starling were removed from the list in 2005, following large declines in their numbers (for reasons other than killing). Three introduced species can also be killed under special licence at any time in England, namely the Ruddy Duck, Canada Goose and Egyptian Goose. These various species can be controlled because of concerns over damage to farm crops, game stocks, other native species, or public health and well-being.

Additional species that cause severe problems for particular interest groups can be controlled in limited numbers under special licence, including other

FIG 196. The Magpie *Pica pica* is a common predator of bird eggs and chicks, much increased in recent years. (Frank Snijkers)

species that might threaten farm crops and fisheries, aircraft safety, or public health and safety. In this way, the popular tradition of killing fish-eating birds has been maintained in Britain, with Cormorants, Goosanders and Grey Herons often shot under licence, and occasionally also Eiders. Detailed studies at individual fish farms during 1985–87, together with wider survey results, suggested that around 800 Herons, 1,643 Cormorants and 1,405 Shags were killed annually at fish farms around Scotland (Carss 1994). This killing did not reduce the numbers of birds present at fish farms because removed birds were rapidly replaced. Since that time, more fish farms have become established, but non-lethal methods of damage control have come into wider use. In addition, during 1956–74, a total of no fewer than 27,000 Oystercatchers were shot under licence at the Bury Inlet and Morecambe Bay in an attempt to protect cockle stocks. This costly experiment failed to stop cockles from declining, and has not been repeated. Probably all these five species have been killed in sufficient numbers to affect their breeding populations, at least locally and temporally. In contrast, Woodpigeons are much more widespread and numerous, and the millions shot each winter, partly in attempts to protect farm crops, probably have had no significant effect on subsequent breeding numbers (Murton 1968). An estimated 3.6 million were shot in the UK in 2004, most of which went for human consumption (PACEC 2006).

All other species listed in the Tudor Acts of the sixteenth century, as given in Box 6, are now protected under current law, including the Raven, Bullfinch, Dipper, Kingfisher, Green Woodpecker and all birds of prey. Changes in agricultural procedures in the late twentieth century greatly reduced the opportunities for some species to cause damage, for example from the way in which grain is now efficiently harvested and securely stored, or the shift of poultry rearing from outside to inside.

FIG 197. A Goosander *Mergus merganser* tackling a lamprey. This is another unpopular fish-eating species that is controlled by fishery interests. (Edmund Fellowes)

Species officially classed as game can of course be shot in season, but are protected when breeding. Besides the six gallinaceous birds mentioned in the previous chapter,[28] they include nine ducks (Mallard, Gadwall, Pintail, Shoveler, Wigeon, Teal, Tufted Duck, Pochard, Goldeneye), four geese (Greylag, Pink-footed, European White-fronted and Canada Goose), three waders (Snipe, Woodcock and Golden Plover) and, somewhat surprisingly, Coot and Moorhen. Adding all these species together with the pests, at least 36 native bird species can still be legally and regularly killed in Britain without a special licence, as can at least three non-native species. When special licences are issued for other species, a limit is usually placed on the numbers to be killed, with compliance taken on trust.

FIG 198. The Greylag Goose *Anser anser* was once hunted to extinction over most of Britain and Ireland, but it survived as a breeder in remote parts of northwest Scotland and the Outer Hebrides. The species was reintroduced to many parts of Britain, and is again numerous over much of the country. The Icelandic population also winters here, and some individuals have recently established a breeding population in Shetland. (Ian Newton)

---

28 The migratory Quail is the only gallinaceous species to be fully protected by law in Britain and Ireland.

FIG 199. The Woodcock *Scolopax rusticola* is one of the three wader species still legally hunted in Britain, the others being the Snipe *Gallinago gallinago* and Golden Plover *Pluvialis apricaria*. (Laurie Campbell)

OTHER HUMAN-RELATED BIRD DEATHS

Nowadays many birds die through collisions with road traffic, buildings and other structures, and overhead wires. This is a relatively new form of mortality in the evolutionary history of birds, and has grown in importance over the past century or so, as cities, transmission towers, communication wires and transport systems have grown. A national enquiry from May 1960 to April 1961 produced details for 5,269 road casualties covering 80 species on a total of 349 miles of road (Hodson & Snow 1965). From this, it was calculated that the annual total number of bird deaths on British roads was probably about 2.5 million, the average annual rate being 15.1 birds per mile (10 per km), but varying from none to 177 per mile. House Sparrows were common victims, many dying in July–August when they were frequenting roadside cereal fields, but Blackbirds, Dunnocks, Chaffinches and Song Thrushes were also often killed. These road deaths were commonest from April to August and many involved juveniles. Since that time, more roads have been constructed, and the numbers and speeds of vehicles have increased greatly, while bird numbers have generally declined, so whatever the impact of road deaths on bird populations in the 1960s, it is presumably much greater now. Another study is needed.

As indicated by ring recoveries, collisions of one sort or another cause substantial mortality in several species, including Mute Swans (with overhead wires), Sparrowhawks (with large windows), Barn Owls (with road traffic) and Capercaillies (with fences). In the first three species, such collisions are now the main cause of death in these species reported through ring recoveries. An extreme event occurred on a foggy night of 3 December 1989, when 50 Bewick's and Whooper Swans were killed in collisions with power-lines as they flew from fields to their evening roost at Welney (Rees *et al.* 1990). The increasing amounts of glass used in city buildings is also causing concern, killing birds as they try to fly towards the sky, trees or other structures that are reflected in the mirror-like surfaces. This has become a major problem in North America, with new buildings almost entirely faced with glass, but it has been little studied here. On the other hand, the big losses of migrants which formerly occurred at lighthouses on dark misty nights have been greatly reduced by the change from continuous to flicking lights.

The effect of collision deaths in some species is not trivial. The Capercaillie has been declining in Scotland since the 1970s. This has been attributed to a reduced reproductive rate associated with climate change, and deaths of full-grown birds flying into forest fences (erected to keep deer from young trees). In the 1990s, the mean annual rate of decline for adult hens was 18% (SE 5%). Without fence deaths, it was calculated that the hen population could have increased at an annual rate of 6% (SE 10%). If recent trends persist, the bird will soon be extinct again in Scotland, but without forest fences it would probably survive (Moss 2001).

A more recent form of bird mortality results from collisions with wind turbines. As I write this chapter in 2012, some 3,400 turbines are operational in Britain, but this number is projected to increase rapidly, reaching a proposed target of 32,000 by 2050. The numbers of birds killed by these structures depends largely on their location, and for obvious reasons large birds are most vulnerable. Many large species are also long-lived, with low reproductive rates, so that even small increases in the annual losses could cause declines in populations. With such large numbers of turbines in the landscape, only tiny rates of kill per turbine can mount up to excessive mortality overall. Over a five-year period, 39 White-tailed Eagles were killed at a large wind-farm on the island of Smøla off Norway, an average of nearly eight per year (Dahl *et al.* 2012). The island holds a large and dense nesting population exceeding 50 pairs. Territories within 500 m of the turbines suffered significantly lower breeding success after turbine construction than before, and several former territories within the wind-farm area fell vacant. This extreme situation provides an example of a wind-farm inappropriately cited. Against this, some developers have modified or abandoned their construction plans for areas where ornithological impacts were likely to be great. A second effect of turbines results from disturbance, because many birds are deterred from feeding nearby, as detected in seven out of twelve land-bird species studied by Pearce-Higgins *et al.* (2009). Species showing reduced densities within 500 m of turbines included Buzzard, Hen Harrier, Golden Plover, Snipe, Curlew, Meadow Pipit and Wheatear. Among seabirds, the scarecrow effect is especially marked among divers. This disturbance is tantamount to habitat loss.

Agricultural operations

Species that nest on the ground or in low vegetation in fields are especially vulnerable to agricultural operations, whether ploughing, harrowing, rolling or harvesting. This problem is less evident today than in the past, because most affected species have largely disappeared from lowland farmland. Mechanised grass mowing is thought to have caused the loss of the Corncrake from much of lowland Britain, and probably many other species, such as Whinchat, were similarly affected. Some species that still nest on arable land survive only because of the special care taken to protect their nests, the Stone-curlew being an example from Britain, and Montagu's Harrier from the cereal fields of southern Europe. Apart from any other aspect of agricultural procedure, the physical destruction of nests by farm machinery led to the declines of several species in the past, and could still be limiting their occupation of farmland today.

Fisheries by-catch

A consequence of modern fishing methods has been the accidental capture and death of millions of seabirds worldwide. The two most lethal methods employed are drift netting and long-line fishing. Monofilament nylon drift (or gill) nets came into widespread use from the 1960s. Being inconspicuous and tough, they are a particular hazard to diving seabirds, of which more than 60 species worldwide have become major casualties. Marine mammals and turtles are also frequent victims.

In offshore waters, drift nets may be hung from lines of floating buoys, while in inshore waters they may be fixed using buoys or stakes. By the time they were banned in 1993, pelagic drift nets had killed millions of seabirds, turtles and cetaceans. Their use in the northwest Atlantic was confined to a small tuna fishing fleet, and their effects on British and Irish seabirds are likely to have been minor. However, inshore nets had bigger impacts, and the following are some published estimates of the numbers of birds killed at different places in particular years:

- 100,000 Guillemots killed in 1985 in a cod fishery off Norway (Vader *et al.* 1990).
- 215,000–350,000 birds, mainly Brünnich's Guillemots, killed annually in 1970–72 in salmon and cod fisheries off southwest Greenland and eastern Canada (Evans & Nettleship 1985).
- 17,500 birds per year in the Gulf of Gdansk, Poland, during 1972–76 and 1986–90, about 10–20% of the total birds in the area, mainly Long-tailed Ducks (8,400), Velvet Scoters (4,000), Scaup (1,300), Common Scoters (1,000) and Eiders (1,000) (Stempniewicz 1994).
- 5,000 Razorbills and Guillemots caught in salmon nets in Galway Bay in 1979

(Whilde 1979), with similar losses thought to have occurred in other years and elsewhere in western Ireland.

Bird mortalities caused by drift nets are largely hidden from the public eye, and fishermen are understandably reluctant to disclose figures. It is therefore hard to assess the impact of this mortality on populations, except in localities where colonies have been monitored. Inshore net casualties are thought to have accounted for a decline in the numbers of Brünnich's Guillemots at two sites in north Norway from 250,000 in 1965 to 12,000 in 1989 (Strann *et al.* 1991), and for big declines in this and other species in eastern Canada and western Greenland (Piatt & Reddin 1984, Evans & Nettleship 1985). Around Britain and Ireland, inshore nets were used in the 1970s and 1980s to catch salmonids, gadoids and bass. Large numbers of auks were drowned, but seemingly not enough to cause declines in breeding populations, except for some colonies in the west of Ireland (Lloyd *et al.* 1991). Since then, the use of inshore gill nets has declined, owing mainly to decline in fish stocks, so the threat to auks has receded. However, these nets are still in widespread use along the coasts of Europe, and many British-bred ringed birds have been killed there, but so far this again seems not to have caused declines in breeding numbers. Almost all diving species are caught, including Gannets, Manx Shearwaters, Cormorants and Shags, as well as auks, divers, grebes and sea-ducks (Harrison & Robins 1992). During fishing activities, nets are often lost or discarded, and continue to ensnare birds for long afterwards. Many other seabirds killed in northern waters are from species that breed in the southern hemisphere, mostly from colonies that have not been counted.

Long-line fishing for tuna developed mainly in the 1970s. A boat may tow one or two lines, each up to 100 km long and carrying up to several thousand baited hooks. It takes about five hours to set the lines, and throughout the process the last 100 m or so of line remain near the surface where the baits attract birds, some of which become hooked and drowned. This is mainly a problem in the southern hemisphere, but in the northeast Atlantic long-lining has occurred along the shelf edges of Britain and Ireland, Norway, and around Iceland and the Faeroes (Brothers *et al.* 1999). The Fulmar is the species most often hooked, but large gulls, Gannets and Great Skuas are also caught (Dunn & Steel 2001). Norwegian vessels used sets of lines with 30,000–40,000 hooks per day. A study in 1997–98 of the Norwegian offshore fleet conservatively estimated that about 20,000 Fulmars were taken each year (Dunn & Steel 2001). If these figures were extrapolated to include equivalent fleets in the Faeroes and Iceland, some 50,000–100,000 Fulmars might have been killed per year in the North Atlantic. This by-catch may have contributed to the slowing of the rate of increase in the overall Fulmar population in the North Atlantic, which had been maintained over the previous 120 years or more, with declines now recorded on Shetland. In any case, fish stocks are being reduced, and mitigation measures, such as use of streamer lines, may also reduce the future impact of long-lining on birds. Developing mitigation measures has been the subject of much research conducted jointly by fishing and ornithological interest groups.

CONCLUDING REMARKS

The main conclusions to emerge from historical accounts is that past human hunting was a major factor reducing the numbers and distributions of many bird species in Britain and Ireland, eliminating some species totally from these islands. Some of these species were also affected by declining habitat, but there seems no doubt that excessive shooting reduced their populations well below the level that remaining habitat would support. From the available literature, it is hard to avoid the conclusion that the nineteenth century was a time of massive slaughter of birds. There was little in prevailing public attitudes to curb these activities. Wild birds and their eggs had long provided a food source for country people, and large-scale recreational hunting and collecting took off as never before. The increased scale of killing was aided by more efficient and available firearms, by the rise of gamekeeping, and by improved communications and transport. Conservation was in its infancy, and there was practically no protective legislation before 1869.

Once this killing was controlled, with suitable habitat still available, most depleted bird populations recovered steadily over periods of several decades. Many of the increases in the numbers and distributions of waterfowl, waders, seabirds and raptors recorded during the twentieth century almost certainly represented recoveries from past persecution. Recoveries could be attributed primarily to a rise in the conservation movement, with resulting protective legislation, creation of nature reserves, and general public abhorrence at the scale of killing. In addition, animal welfare issues gained influence, progressively restricting the types of methods that could be legally used to kill birds and other animals. Population increases were apparent in most of the affected species through much of the twentieth century, although in the last three decades of that century some began to decline again, as a result mainly of adverse changes in land-use and fishery practices.

The birds that are now most obviously affected by direct human killing are the raptors, some species of which are still held well below the levels that their habitats and prey supplies would support. The same may be true of some legally controllable species, such as corvids in game-preserving areas, or Cormorants, Goosanders and other fish-eaters in some wetland areas.

An outsider might well wonder why conservationists have little concern over the regular killing of Crows and Magpies, but are so opposed to the killing of raptors. The reason is that the situation is totally different between the two groups. Most corvids are common and widespread, and in some areas are so numerous than many individuals are unable to obtain territories and breed, leading to a large non-breeding surplus. So when holes are knocked in their distributions every spring by gamekeepers, these holes can be re-filled before the next year by immigration of surplus birds from other areas. In effect, gamekeepers are harvesting such populations, reducing predation on bird eggs in the process, but causing no obvious overall long-term population decline. In the case of the target game species, the gamekeeper gains the advantages from repeated short-term reductions in corvid numbers, but little or no longer-lasting benefit. In contrast, the killing of raptors in the past eliminated most such species from large parts of Britain and Ireland, and some entirely from both islands. Because this happened before, it could happen again. Most species have still not recovered from this past onslaught, and ongoing illegal killing is unequivocally limiting the numbers and distributions of some species in Britain today. The breeding populations of several target species number in the hundreds or less, not in the hundreds of thousands, as is the case in some corvids. The two groups differ in abundance by three orders of magnitude. The larger raptors have low reproductive rates, and even slight increases in adult mortality rates are enough to tip their numbers into decline. Unlike corvids, they are unable to withstand heavy annual culling.

Nevertheless, there is no question that in some areas predation by raptors is enough to hold wild game populations below the level needed to provide a break-even economic enterprise for the landowner (Chapter 7). It is hard to see how to resolve this impasse, except by first ensuring that vulnerable raptor species are both widespread and numerous enough to withstand some local reductions in their numbers or breeding output. Through habitat management for game species, some other birds are also more abundant in the countryside than they might otherwise be. Not only are certain habitats, such as heather moors, woods and rough areas, preserved specifically for game, but predators are controlled, and specific cover crops are grown which provide shelter and food for many other species, notably seed-eaters. Regarding legal predator control, it was estimated that in 2004 alone some 38,000 rats, 1,000 mink and 380,000 corvids were killed in the interests of game preservation (PACEC 2006). From the experiments discussed in Chapter 7, this predator control would have benefited some other species too. Gamekeeping may have some conservation benefits as well as some unpalatable costs.

CHAPTER 18

Effects of Pesticides

O NE CONSEQUENCE OF OUR CURRENT lifestyles is that toxic chemicals are continually added to natural environments, as pesticides, as industrial and household effluents, or as combustion emissions. Some of these chemicals are wholly man-made, while others are natural substances whose concentration locally has been increased by human action. Sometimes they become important agents of declines in animal populations, influencing patterns of distribution and abundance. This chapter is concerned with the effects of pesticides on birds, and the next chapter with the effects of other pollutants. Both chapters focus on bird population declines induced by chemicals, using particular case studies to illustrate the issues involved.

For our purposes, a pollutant can be defined as any substance that occurs in the environment at least in part through human action, and that, at the levels found, has deleterious effects on living organisms. Inevitably this definition includes all pesticides. Some pesticides and pollutants act directly by causing breeding failures or deaths. They reduce breeding populations only if they add to natural losses, and are not offset by reduced losses from other causes. Birds absorb most such chemicals through their food, but some also through their skin, or by preening and inhalation. Ground-nesting and other birds may have pesticides incidentally sprayed onto their eggs, which can then be transferred to the brood-patch or plumage. Other pesticides and pollutants act indirectly on birds by reducing their food supplies, and thereby causing declines in numbers. Yet others, notably atmospheric pollutants, can alter the physical or chemical nature of habitats, making them less suitable for certain species. The most significant pollutants of this type are the 'greenhouse gases', such as carbon dioxide and methane, which cause climate warming, as discussed in Chapter 15.

SOME GENERAL POINTS ABOUT PESTICIDES

Pesticides include any chemicals that are used to kill unwanted plants and animals, whether marketed as insecticides, molluscicides, fungicides or herbicides. If such chemicals destroyed only the target pests and then quickly broke down to harmless by-products, problems from their use would be minimal. But most pesticides are non-specific and kill a wide range of organisms. Secondly, while some pesticides break down rapidly, others last for weeks, months or even years in animal bodies or in the physical environment, so can have effects well beyond their date of application. And the longer a pesticide persists in the environment, the more likely it is to be transported far from its site of application, in air or water currents or in the bodies of migrating animals. Many marine animals, including seabirds, now contain residues of pesticides applied on land. Thirdly, some pesticides accumulate in animal bodies and readily pass from prey to predator, causing secondary poisoning. They may even pass along several steps in a food-chain, affecting animals far removed in ecological position from the target pest. Depending on their chemical properties, pesticides thus differ from one another in specificity, persistence and propensity to accumulate in animal bodies. Other problems are caused by the manufacture of pesticides, which, through accidental and deliberate discharges, has led to pollution of rivers, lakes and coastal areas, with loss of aquatic life. These problems are often accentuated by many local accidents and abuses, excessive application, drift and careless disposal. Some of the same points also apply to some other chemical pollutants, but, unlike pesticides, they have not been deliberately applied to large land areas, so the problems they cause have been local or slower to appear.

In Britain and Ireland, the use of pesticides rose more than tenfold during the latter half of the twentieth century. This resulted from increase in the land area treated, the numbers of applications per year, and the variety of chemicals which became available. Over the same period, the use of pesticides also grew in Africa, where many of our summer visiting birds spend the winter. By 1990, about 300 chemicals were in use worldwide as insecticides, 290 as herbicides, and 165 as fungicides and other biocides, with a grand total of more than 3,000 formulations (Freedman 1995). In Britain and Ireland, more than 180 toxic products in various formulations are now available for use as pesticides. For all these various reasons, then, we can expect that the indirect effects of pesticides on bird populations, via depression of their food supplies, are likely to have increased progressively over the past 60 years.

The main types of pesticides applied against animal pests since the 1950s include the organochlorines, organophosphates, carbamates, pyrethroids and most recently the neonicotinoids (nicotine-like). The specificity of such chemicals has been examined in experimental trials. One of the earliest (in the 1960s) involved the application of a commonly used carbamate insecticide, carbaryl, to one of two adjacent 1 acre (0.4 ha) patches of millet (Barrett 1968). Applied in midsummer, the carbaryl remained toxic for only a few days, but in this time the numbers and biomass of arthropods on the sprayed plots declined to almost nil. Their populations took seven weeks to recover in biomass, and longer to recover in numbers and diversity. The chemical is also likely to have affected other organisms not studied, including micro-arthropods, earthworms and other soil-dwellers, as evidenced by the greater build-up of leaf-litter. There was nothing unusual in this result, as similar effects were obtained in trials with other chemicals. Several North American studies that examined the effects of aerial forest spraying with the organochlorine pesticide dichlor-diphenyl-trichlor-ethane (DDT) recorded up to 90% declines in the overall insect population following a single application, and a similar reduction of aquatic insects in forest streams (Adams et al. 1949, Hoffmann et al. 1949, Crouter & Vernon 1959). These various studies exemplified the effects of a single application of insecticide.

In small field trials, invertebrate populations usually recovered within two months of spraying, but recovery probably depended largely on immigration from surrounding areas. Immigration is much less likely now, in modern extensively farmed landscapes, where the treatment of almost every hectare leaves few refuges in which vulnerable species can survive to re-colonise sprayed areas. Recovery is likely to depend mainly on reproduction by the few individuals that remain, taking much longer than recovery by immigration. Moreover, on recovery, some pest species sometimes become more abundant than before, especially if their predators take longer to recover than they do. This usually leads to further applications of pesticides – the so-called 'pesticide treadmill' – so that many invertebrate species become depressed over even longer periods. Different species vary greatly in their susceptibility to any particular pesticide, but in general the greater the amount applied, the greater the range of organisms killed. The mode of application is also influential. Whereas spraying from the ground has limited spread beyond the crop, spraying from the air can result in considerable drift, affecting semi-natural areas interspersed among the crops and beyond. Aerial spraying is usual in the widespread control programmes of Africa aimed against locusts, tsetse flies or mosquitoes.

The effects of pesticides on land animals can also extend to aquatic ones, as water drains from farmland into nearby streams and ponds. One group of pesticides, the pyrethroids, has proved especially toxic to aquatic organisms. At extremely low concentrations of two parts per trillion of water, they proved lethal to mayflies, gadflies and other invertebrates that form the base of many aquatic food-chains, some involving birds. When they were first used as sheep dips (as alternatives to organophosphates, which had affected some users), they contaminated many upland streams, killing aquatic invertebrates, with knock-on effects on fish and birds, and extending for tens of kilometres downstream. One of the most toxic, cypermethrin, was withdrawn as a sheep dip from 2010.

Herbicides are intended to reduce weed growth, while not killing the crop. Since the 1950s, progressive increases in the numbers of herbicidal chemicals, their modes of action and formulations have gradually expanded the range of weed species that can be controlled effectively, and most species important to birds have declined strikingly in recent decades (Wilson *et al.* 1999, Firbank & Smart 2002). The same holds for their seeds in the soil, which were reduced by more than 90% during the twentieth century, with some of the biggest reductions in the ones important to finches, such as Fat-hen *Chenopodium album*, Persicaria *Polygonum persicaria*, Chickweed *Stellaria media* and Charlock *Sinapis arvensis* (Robinson & Sutherland 2002). Weeds also support insects, which form important foods for other bird species, so in several ways weed control has reduced the food supplies available to birds. The impact of herbicide use could increase further in the years ahead, as more herbicide-resistant crop varieties are developed, enabling chemical weed control to be used on an even wider range of crop types than at present.

Organochlorines

Although DDT and other organochlorine pesticides have now been banned in many parts of the world, including Britain and Ireland, they are discussed here in some detail because they have had more severe direct impacts on birds than any other pesticides. They have also been well studied and illustrate all the main issues involved. DDT was developed during the Second World War, mainly to control body lice on people, but it soon became widely used in the open countryside, as a 'miracle insecticide' against many insect pests of farmland and orchards, and elsewhere to control forest pests, locusts and mosquitoes. Its persistence in the natural environment meant that its effects were long-lasting, and it had huge effects on non-target animals, including some birds. The phenomenon of secondary poisoning by pesticides first became apparent in the USA in the late 1940s when DDT was applied twice each summer to elm trees to control the insect vectors of Dutch elm disease (Barker 1958). The insecticide was picked up from fallen leaves and soil by earthworms which were then eaten by American Robins with lethal consequences. The dead birds were found to contain 50–200 ppm (mg per kg) residues in the brain, a fatal dose obtained by eating about 100 worms. Most deaths occurred, not at the time of spraying, but

FIG 200. The Peregrine *Falco peregrinus* was a widespread victim of organochlorine pesticides; it declined and disappeared from much of Britain and Ireland in the 1950s–1960s, but recovered slowly when organochlorine use was reduced. (Edmund Fellowes)

in spring or after heavy rain, when worms were most available to birds. On one campus of Michigan State University, the Robin population was reduced within two years from 370 to a few individuals, and virtually no young were raised (Wallace *et al.* 1961). Similarly, the use of a related chemical, DDD, over several years to control midges on Lake Clear, California, resulted in the decline of Western Grebes from more than 1,000 pairs in 1949 to 30 non-breeding adults in 1960 (Hunt & Bischoff 1960). This was again associated with food-chain contamination, as confirmed by chemical analyses of midges, fish and grebes found dead. Such secondary poisoning is particularly associated with DDT and other organochlorines, but has also been recorded from some other pesticides.

Because of their high fat-solubility and persistence, organochlorines readily accumulate in animal bodies and pass up food-chains from prey to predator. Increasing concentrations at successive trophic levels were evident in many (but not all) studies in which different kinds of organisms from the same place were examined (Newton 1979). Concentrations were lowest in plants (first trophic level), higher in herbivorous animals (second trophic level), and higher still in carnivores (third trophic level) and so on up the food-chain. It is probably not the trophic level as such that is important, but the rates of intake – which, because of accumulation, tend to be higher in carnivores. In addition, rates of accumulation are often greater in aquatic than in terrestrial systems because many aquatic animals absorb organochlorines directly from the water (through their gills), as well as from their food. Fish rapidly pick up fat-soluble pollutants in this way, and have been found to have concentrations in their bodies 1,000 or 10,000 times greater than in the surrounding water (Stickel 1975).

DIRECT EFFECTS ON BIRD POPULATIONS

Organochlorine pesticides and predatory birds

Two direct effects of pesticides on bird populations can be illustrated by different types of organochlorine compounds (Fig. 201). This group of chemicals contains not only the well-known DDT but also the more toxic cyclodienes, such as aldrin, dieldrin and heptachlor. DDT was first introduced into widespread agricultural use in the late 1940s, and the cyclodienes after 1955. For a time they were widely used throughout the 'developed' world, but during the 1970s and 1980s they were banned progressively in one country after another, as their environmental effects became increasingly apparent. They continue to be used without restriction mainly in some tropical and subtropical areas.

Three groups of birds were particularly affected, namely: (1) raptors, especially bird-eating and fish-eating species such as the Peregrine, Sparrowhawk, Osprey and White-tailed Eagle; (2) various other fish-eating birds, such as cormorants and pelicans; and (3) various seed-eating species, such as doves, geese and cranes, which ate newly sown seeds of cereals and other plants that had been treated with organochlorines as protection against insect attack. In Britain and Ireland, population declines were most apparent in birds of prey in the 1950s and 1960s, when Sparrowhawks, Peregrines and Merlins disappeared altogether from many regions, and became much reduced in others. Other raptors, such as Kestrels,

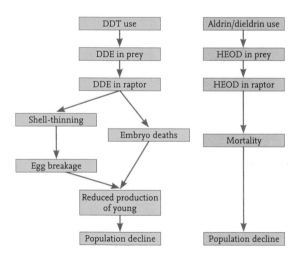

FIG 201. Modes of action of DDE (from the insecticide DDT) and HEOD (from aldrin and dieldrin) on raptor populations. (From Newton 1986)

declined sharply in the more arable parts of southeast England, where pesticide use was heaviest, but maintained their numbers elsewhere.

DDT is not especially toxic to birds, and very high exposures (as in the early forest spraying) are needed to kill birds outright. The main effects are on breeding. Once in the bird's body, most of the DDT is rapidly converted to a much more stable metabolite, DDE, which forms the bulk of the residue detected in bird eggs and carcasses. At sub-lethal level, DDE reduces the availability of calcium carbonate during eggshell formation so that the eggs are thin-shelled and break when the birds tread or sit on them. Some thin-shelled eggs survive incubation, but the embryo may die from dehydration caused by excess water loss through a thinned shell. If reduction in the average breeding rate of individuals is sufficiently marked, it leads to population decline, because reproduction is no longer sufficient to offset the usual annual mortality. The effects of DDT/DDE on eggshells were initially deduced from field studies by ornithologist Derek Ratcliffe (1970), and subsequently confirmed by experiments on captive birds (Cooke 1973, Newton 1979). All these effects were via the female, but DDT and its derivatives are also oestrogenic (mimicking the effects of the hormone oestrogen), and were found to reduce sperm production in domestic fowl (Albert 1962).

Other organochlorines, such as aldrin and dieldrin, are several hundred times more toxic to birds than is DDT or DDE (Hudson *et al.* 1984). These chemicals act mainly by killing birds outright, increasing mortality above the natural level so as to cause rapid population decline (Fig. 201). In Britain and Ireland, as in many other countries, they were used chiefly as seed-treatments, so killed seed-eaters as well as their predators. During their period of peak usage in Britain in the late 1950s and early 1960s, widespread mortalities were recorded in seed-eating finches, pigeons and gamebirds, and totals of many thousands of birds were found dead and dying around fields where grain treated with aldrin or dieldrin had been recently sown (Cramp *et al.* 1962). These poisoned birds formed easy pickings for predators and scavengers. In the same period, dieldrin was also used in a dip to kill insect parasites on the skin and wool of sheep. It transpired that the dieldrin was also absorbed through the skin into the flesh of the sheep. Golden Eagles, feeding on sheep carrion, were found to be contaminated by dieldrin, which appeared in their eggs, but it is not known to what extent it affected them (Lockie *et al.* 1969) – or the many people in Britain who ate sheep meat at the time.

The massive declines in the numbers of some bird-eating and fish-eating raptors in Europe and North America in the 1960s were thus attributed to the combined action of DDE reducing breeding rate and HEOD (from aldrin and dieldrin) increasing mortality rate. The relative importance of these mechanisms of population decline seems to have differed between regions, depending on the relative quantities of the different chemicals used. In western Europe, deaths from HEOD were probably more important, but in much of North America reproductive failure from DDE seems to have been paramount (Newton 1986).

In Britain, the numbers of Peregrines and Sparrowhawks fell by more than 50% in the north and west of Britain, but the Peregrine disappeared altogether from the south and east, and the Sparrowhawk almost so, despite its much greater numbers. This pattern of decline matched the distribution of arable land, which was greater in southern and eastern districts, leading to greater pesticide use there. But it was the speed of the declines that shocked ornithologists. Both species went from abundant to scarce within three years following the introduction of aldrin and dieldrin in the late 1950s. This could only have happened with increased mortality. Many carcasses of these and other species were found, and in some the cause of death was confirmed by chemical analysis. The main source of aldrin and dieldrin was seed dressings, as mentioned above, which passed directly to seed-eating birds and then to raptors.

Owing to their environmental impacts, and contamination of the human food-chain, the use of these chemicals was reduced progressively from the

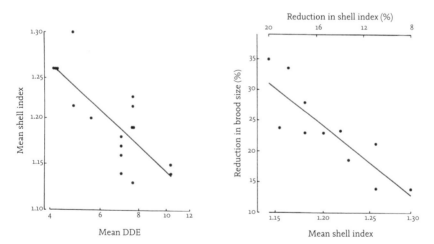

FIG 202. Shell-thickness index and breeding success of different Sparrowhawk *Accipiter nisus* populations in relation to geometric mean concentrations (μg per g) of DDE in eggs. Shell index measured as shell weight (mg)/shell length × breadth (mm) (from Newton 1986). Note that the relationship between the concentration of DDE in the egg content and the degree of shell-thinning was linear with DDE plotted on a logarithmic scale. This held for all the raptor species examined, including Peregrine *Falco peregrinus* and Merlin *Falco columbarius* (Newton 1979).

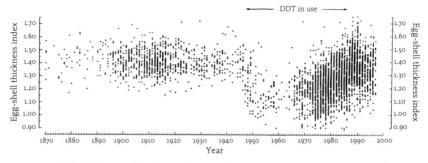

FIG 203. Shell-thickness index of British Sparrowhawks *Accipiter nisus*, 1870–1997. Shells became thin abruptly from 1947, following the widespread introduction of DDT in agriculture, and recovered from the 1970s, following progressive restrictions in the use of the chemical, which was banned altogether from 1986. Each spot represents the mean shell index of a clutch (or part-clutch), and more than 2,000 clutches are represented from all regions of Britain. Based on shells housed in museums and private collections, and formerly at Monks Wood Research Station. Shell index measured as shell weight (mg)/shell length × breadth (mm). (Extended from Newton 1986)

mid-1960s. Over the next three decades, shell thickness, breeding success, survival and population levels of affected species largely recovered, enabling them to re-colonise areas from which they had been extirpated. Peregrines and Sparrowhawks had fully re-occupied their former range by the mid-1990s (see Figs 203 & 204 for Sparrowhawk; Cade *et al.* 1988, Crick & Ratcliffe 1995 for Peregrine). All these improvements were associated with reductions in the residues of organochlorine chemicals in eggs and tissues. In Britain, the recovery of Sparrowhawk numbers in different regions followed the decline in HEOD residues in Sparrowhawk liver tissue to below 1 ppm geometric mean in wet weight (Fig. 204).

Worldwide, environmental contamination with DDT was well reflected in the patterns of shell-thinning in the Peregrine, which breeds on all continents except Antarctica (Peakall & Kiff 1988). The greatest degree of shell-thinning (average 26%) was found in the eastern United States, from which Peregrines disappeared altogether within 20 years after DDT came into wide-scale use (Cade *et al.* 1988). Marked shell-thinning also occurred in Peregrines nesting across the Arctic of Eurasia and North America (17–25% in different regions), reflecting the fact that these falcons and their prey migrated to winter further south in regions of DDT use. The smallest levels of shell-thinning occurred in falcon populations that were resident in areas with no DDT use, and where they fed on prey species that were also year-round residents. An example was the Peregrine population of

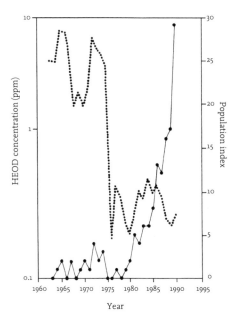

FIG 204. Trend in geometric mean HEOD levels (dotted line) in the livers of Sparrowhawks *Accipiter nisus* found dead in eastern England in relation to an index of population level in the same area (continuous line). HEOD is the chemical residue derived from the insecticides aldrin and dieldrin, and the population index is based on the number of carcasses received for analysis. (From Newton & Wyllie 1992)

the Scottish Highlands, at that time dependent mainly on Red Grouse (Ratcliffe 1980). The falcons in that region showed only 4% shell-thinning, compared with more than 19% in most of the rest of Britain (Ratcliffe 1980).

Comparing the various Peregrine populations studied across the world, mean levels of DDE residues in eggs were highest in those populations showing most shell-thinning. All populations with an average of less than 17% shell-thinning maintained their numbers, while all those with more than 17% declined, some to the point of extinction (Peakall & Kiff 1988). An average of 17% shell-thinning thus emerged as critical to population persistence, associated with an average of 15–20 ppm DDE in the wet weight of egg content. These were average figures applicable at the level of populations and did not apply rigidly to individual eggs. The same mean level of shell-thinning was also associated with population declines in other raptor species (Newton 1979). As mentioned above, in many Peregrine and other raptor populations, decline was often more rapid than expected on DDT alone, because mortality was also enhanced to varying degrees through aldrin and dieldrin poisoning.

Some kinds of birds proved more sensitive to DDT/DDE than others. For any given concentration of DDE in their eggs, raptors and pelicans showed the greatest degree of shell-thinning, and gulls and gallinaceous birds the least. Raptors and pelicans thus emerged as particularly vulnerable to DDE, partly because their position high in food-chains led them to accumulate large amounts, but also because of their high physiological sensitivity compared to other birds (Newton 1979). The greatest degree of shell-thinning recorded in any species involved Brown Pelicans in California, which were contaminated by the effluent from a DDT factory. On Anacapa Island off Los Angeles, only two chicks resulted from 1,272 nesting attempts in 1969. Virtually all the eggs collapsed on laying, and the shells were on average 50% thinner than normal (Risebrough *et al.* 1971). This species was the most sensitive to DDE of all those studied, an average of 3 ppm in the content of fresh eggs being associated with nearly total breeding failure (Blus 1982). The European populations of pelicans could be similarly sensitive, but I know of no relevant information.

Another general finding was that, among raptors, species that ate mainly birds declined more rapidly and to greater extent than those that ate mainly mammals. Years later, an explanation for this difference emerged, namely that birds are less able to metabolise and excrete organochlorines than are mammals, so birds tended to accumulate these chemicals to a greater level in their bodies. Hence, bird-eating raptors were much more likely to accumulate lethal levels from their prey than were mammal eaters, such as Kestrels, and thereby suffered greater mortality and shell-thinning. The bird-feeders also top longer food-chains than the mammal-feeders do, giving more opportunities for residues to concentrate. The relationship between vulnerability and feeding habits was shown repeatedly in many studies in different regions (Newton 1979).

The problems caused by organochlorines, as already indicated, result partly from their extreme persistence, a quality that adds to their effectiveness as

FIG 205. Eating small birds made the Sparrowhawk *Accipiter nisus* (adult male shown here) especially vulnerable to organochlorine pesticides. The species disappeared from most of eastern Britain in the years around 1960, but has since recolonised. (Keith Kirk)

pesticides. The longevity of chemicals in any medium is usually measured by their *half-life*, the period taken for the concentration to fall by half. The half-life of DDE in soils has been variously calculated at between 12 years in some cultivated soils and 57 years in some uncultivated soils (Cooke & Stringer 1982, Buck *et al.* 1983). So even after the use of DDT is stopped, soil-dwelling organisms can remain a source of residue for some bird species for years to come. HEOD is much less persistent, with an estimated half-life in soil of 2.5 years, but it is probably much longer than this in some areas (Brown 1978). In the tropics, the turnover of DDT and other organochlorines may be faster than in temperate areas, however, because higher temperatures favour faster degradation and evaporation to the atmosphere (Berg 1995).

Organochlorines can disappear from animal bodies much more rapidly than from soil, but again DDE lasts longer than HEOD. In pigeons the half-life of DDE has been measured at 240 days, compared with 47 days for HEOD (Walker 1983). These rates vary between species, and with the condition of the individual. However, the persistence of organochlorines in the body means that their effects can become manifest weeks or months after acquisition. Death is most likely to occur at times when body-fat is metabolised, releasing organochlorines into circulation and enabling them to reach lethal levels in the nervous system (Bernard 1966). Such delayed mortality occurred among female Eider Ducks nesting on the Dutch Waddensee, where nest numbers declined by 77% between 1960 and 1968, mainly through deaths of incubating females (Swennen 1972). The birds became contaminated via their food (mussels) from organochlorines discharged into the River Rhine, but died mainly during incubation. At this time female Eiders do not normally feed, but depend on their body-fat. Discharges to the river were stopped in 1965, and within three years the Eider population began to recover. Similarly in North America, wintering Snow Geese initially survived winter contamination with organochlorine pesticides, but succumbed during northward migration when fat mobilisation freed the accumulated residues. The geese were exposed in Texas but died in Missouri, more than 1,000 km to the north (Babcock & Flickinger 1977).

Among seabirds, the largest population effects of organochlorines were seen in pelicans, as noted above, and also in cormorants, but again mainly in places where factory effluent led to exceptionally high pollution. In Europe, spills of the pesticide dieldrin into the River Rhine in 1967 caused mass mortality of gulls and terns in the southern North Sea (Becker 1991). Tern populations were reduced to perilously low levels from which they took many years to recover. In Britain, analyses showed that organochlorines occurred in the bodies and eggs of many seabird species examined in the 1960s–1990s, but usually at levels too low to have effects.

Other chemicals with direct effects on birds

Other chemicals noted for their persistence and accumulation properties include industrial polychlorinated biphenyls (PCBs) and polybrominated diphenylethers (PBDEs). PCBs were used in coolants in transformers, capacitors, electric motors and other industrial products. They were linked with some forms of cancer, and although their manufacture has been banned in Europe and North America they still escape to the environment from existing products, and are commonly found in wildlife tissues. They are oestrogenic and thought by some to affect mammalian reproduction, but they have not been shown to have major effects on bird populations despite their frequent presence in bird bodies. They were associated with a massive kill of auks in the Irish Sea in 1969; these birds may have died primarily from starvation, but chemical analyses revealed that many contained high levels of PCBs (Holdgate 1971). PBDEs are used as flame retardants added to various manufactured products, including plastics, synthetic textiles and electronic products. In recent decades they have been found in increasing amounts in many aquatic and terrestrial animals (Chen & Hale 2010). Some of the highest concentrations have been found in Peregrine and Sparrowhawk eggs from Britain and other parts of western Europe (Leslie *et al.* 2011, Crosse *et al.* 2012). Effects on these wild raptors have not been confirmed, but in captive birds of other species PBDEs have affected hormone levels, organ morphology, growth, neurodevelopment and reproduction.

Alkyl-mercury pesticides were widely used as seed-dressings in the 1960s, when they killed many seed-eating birds and raptors, contributing to population declines, notably in Sweden (Borg *et al.* 1969). Like the organochlorines, they were persistent and fat-soluble. Their replacement by other pesticides led to immediate reductions of the mercury levels in affected species, especially raptors, and contributed (along with the banning of organochlorines) to population recoveries.

Some chemicals among the carbamate, organophosphate and pyrethroid pesticides are highly toxic to vertebrates and have caused large-scale mortalities. One of the most toxic is the carbamate insecticide carbofuran, which in the 1980s was thought to kill at least two million birds per year in the United States, more than any other pesticide in use at the time (Mineau 1993). It was available in granular form, so could remain on the soil surface, to be eaten directly by birds as grit or food or to contaminate earthworms and other food organisms (Flickinger *et al.* 1986). In Switzerland, it was found to contaminate earthworms, which were then consumed by Buzzards, with fatal consequences (Dietrich *et al.* 1995).

Field evidence for lethal effects of pesticides on birds has come mainly from carcasses found after spraying, with the cause of death confirmed by chemical analysis. Some studies also included counts of live birds before and after spraying, comparing them with counts in nearby untreated areas. Such studies mostly involved chemicals that were very toxic to birds, and often revealed local population reductions exceeding 70%, with total elimination of certain species from sprayed areas (Newton 1998). For example, reductions of this order were recorded in Switzerland after forest spraying with the organophosphate phosphamidon (Schneider 1966). Providing the spraying was not repeated, songbird populations usually recovered within 1–3 years, but other slower-breeding species took longer (Brown 1978). These studies were done mainly in the 1950s and 1960s, since when most of the chemicals concerned have been replaced by less toxic ones, at least in Europe and North America, so that their overall direct impact on bird populations has been reduced (apart from carbofuran). Although many modern pesticides kill birds, sometimes in large numbers, they break down more quickly than organochlorines, so do not have such lasting or far-reaching effects.

Despite these beneficial changes, poisoning of wild geese by organophosphate seed dressings occurred in Britain during the 1970s and 1980s. One such chemical, carbophenothion, killed hundreds of Greylag and Pink-footed Geese, but was later replaced by chlorphenvinphos, which posed a lower risk to geese but killed large numbers of Woodpigeons, with recorded incidents occurring throughout the 1980s. In turn chlorphenvinphos was partially replaced by fonofos, which carries a lower risk to pigeons but still resulted in some mortality (Burn 2000). In 1992, 91 Brent Geese died in Lincolnshire as a result of the misuse of the insecticide triazophos (Lovegrove 2007). One of the most lethal organophosphate compounds ever sold is monocrotophos, which has killed many thousands of birds abroad, but has never been authorised for use in Britain.

Whatever the chemical, large birds usually need bigger doses than small birds to kill them, but birds from different families also differ greatly in their sensitivity, regardless of body size (Tucker & Crabtree 1970, Hill et al. 1975, Hudson et al. 1984). Under experimental conditions, many chemicals in current use have been found to cause embryo deaths and deformities when applied directly to eggs. The chemicals most toxic to eggs include the herbicides paraquat and trifluralin (Hoffman & Albers 1984) and some organophosphate insecticides, such as parathion and diazinon (Hoffman & Eastin 1981, Hoffman 1990). Whether they affect wild bird populations through contamination of eggs is unknown. Other potential and less obvious effects of certain pesticides include immunosuppression, which can render birds and other animals more susceptible to pathogens (Chapter 13).

Rodenticides. In some countries, chemicals used to control rodents in farm crops have had major effects on local bird populations. In parts of Israel in

FIG 206. Through feeding on contaminated rodents, the Barn Owl *Tyto alba* is a frequent victim of rodenticide poisoning. (Alan Hale)

the 1950s, wintering raptors were almost obliterated in this way (Mendelssohn 1972). The main chemical used was thallium sulphate, which was administered on cereal grains. These grains were also eaten by seed-eating birds, causing their deaths. The raptors died mainly through eating dead and dying rodents. In addition, an estimated 100,000 wintering Rooks disappeared completely. Similar problems occurred in the Russian steppes in the 1950s, when zinc phosphide was used on grain baits against rodents, reducing the numbers of seed-eating birds (including Grey Partridge, Great Bustard and Demoiselle Crane) and raptors (including Steppe Eagle, Pallid Harrier and Long-legged Buzzard) (Belik & Mikalevich 1995).

In some regions, including the British Isles, rats and mice have become resistant to the anticoagulant warfarin, which has therefore been replaced by newer compounds such as difenacoum, bromadiolone, brodifacoum and flocoumafen. These *second-generation* rodenticides act in the same way as warfarin, but are more toxic and more persistent, giving rise to secondary poisoning in rodent predators (Newton & Wyllie 2002). In Britain, Barn Owls killed by these rodenticides have been found frequently since the 1980s, many showing the typical symptoms of haemorrhaging. Among 836 Barn Owl carcasses examined in Britain over the period 1983–98, rodenticide residues were found in 28% overall, but the proportion increased over the years from 5% in 1983–84 to 40% in 1997–98, as these compounds came into wider use. Only 7% of the contaminated owls (or 2% of the overall sample) were judged on postmortem symptoms and residue levels to have died of rodenticide poisoning. This mortality therefore seemed not to have caused widespread population decline, as in Barn Owls in some other parts of the world (Duckett 1984). Deaths from rodenticide poisoning have been reported from other rodent-eating species in Britain and Ireland, including other owls, Kestrels and Red Kites. The more potent of these chemicals are still restricted for use in buildings or sewers, but if they were approved for outside use in Britain, they could kill much greater numbers of Barn Owls, Red Kites and other species.

Avicides. All the above impacts on birds occurred as incidental consequences of pesticide use. Sometimes, however, pesticides have been deliberately applied against birds. One large-scale example is the use of the organophosphate compounds, fenthion or parathion, to kill seed-eating Red-billed Quelea in Africa. The chemical is usually sprayed from the air over roosts or feeding flocks, and in the 1970s and 1980s it killed hundreds of millions of birds per year through inhalation or oral ingestion (Feare 1991). Its widespread use still continues, killing many other species in the area at the same time, including wintering birds from European breeding areas. The same is true for the aerial spraying of locusts, which relies mainly on highly toxic organophosphate and pyrethroid pesticides.

Birds of prey are often killed by use of poison baits, deliberately targeted at the birds themselves or at other predators. This is a big problem in parts of Britain, where some gamekeepers use poisons illegally to kill various predators, applying the pesticide to carcasses of rabbits or other animals which are then laid out for raptors and other scavengers to find and eat (Chapter 17). Natural carrion-feeders, such as Golden Eagles, Buzzards and Red Kites, are especially vulnerable, but almost any raptor species can be killed in this way, as can corvids, gulls and other scavengers. Over the years, various poisons have been used for this purpose, including strychnine, the narcotic alpha-chloralose, the organophosphate phosdrin (or mevinphos) and various other pesticides, the current favourite being the carbamate compound carbofuran. Such illegal use of poisons is almost certainly the major factor restricting the numbers and distributions of at least Red Kites and Golden Eagles in Britain, but every year it also kills large numbers of Common Buzzards, Goshawks and others (Chapter 17). Elsewhere in Europe, several cases of population declines in raptors through use of poison baits were documented during the twentieth century, involving eagles, vultures, kites and others (Bijleveld 1974).

Veterinary products. Some veterinary products also cause problems for wildlife. Examples from Britain and Ireland include the anthelmintics which are fed to farm animals to destroy or expel parasitic worms in the gut. The most widely used is ivermectin, employed with similar products since the 1980s (Wall & Strong 1987). These persistent chemicals are excreted over a period of weeks in the faeces, and will kill most of the animals that would normally feed on the dung, together with others in the soil below. Dung flies and dung beetles are major casualties. Adverse effects of ivermectin on the decomposing fauna of cattle dung, especially diptera, lasted up to 30 days post treatment (Madsen *et al.* 1990). These insects had previously provided a food source for birds, notably wagtails and corvids, but this source is now much reduced on British farmland. One incidental consequence is that cowpats, which in the past disappeared

FIG 207. Various wagtails (White *Motacilla alba* above) formerly fed on insects at dung piles, but lost this food source when cattle began to be treated with ivermectin or similar products. (Frank Snijkers)

within weeks, now remain in the fields for months on end. Replacement compounds have similar effects.

Elsewhere, other veterinary products have had more direct effects on birds. By far the most significant is the non-steroidal anti-inflammatory drug diclophenac, which is frequently fed to sick cattle, especially in the Indian subcontinent (Pain *et al.* 2008). Being sacred animals to Hindus, cattle are not slaughtered for food but are left to die natural deaths, when they become available to vultures, which thereby acquire the drug. The large *Gyps* vultures are especially susceptible, suffering huge mortality, so that the population of the subcontinent was reduced by more than 99% within ten years from 1994. At least three species continue to be affected, and are now at perilously low levels. The drug is used in Europe but not so widely, and could potentially kill vultures in the south of the continent, but I know of no proven cases. The birds seem much less susceptible to a similar drug, meloxicam, which hopefully will gradually replace the cheaper diclophenac, and allow vultures to recover. There are several other less widely used chemicals in this group, however, and it remains to be seen which ones are toxic to vultures and which are not.

Mixed exposure

Birds are often exposed to combinations of pesticides, either because two or more have been applied together, or because the birds themselves move from one crop to another. For some chemicals the combined effect is much greater than expected from their individual toxicities. Such synergism happens where one chemical activates another or slows its detoxification. An example is provided by prochloraz fungicides, which can accentuate the effects on birds of organophosphate insecticides (Johnson *et al.* 1994). So far this aspect has been studied only in laboratory conditions, but it could presumably occur as a widespread phenomenon on farmland.

Water-bodies near industrial sites may receive cocktails of chemical pollutants, together with run-off from farmland. Animals living there are exposed to so many pollutants that it is sometimes impossible to pinpoint the causal ones for any observed effects. For many years, gulls, terns and cormorants nesting around the Great Lakes in North America showed reduced hatching success and chick deformities and, although analyses of eggs showed many different chemicals, their relative contributions to the problem remained obscure. However, organochlorines probably played a major role, especially as populations increased when organochlorine manufacture and use ceased (Gilbertson *et al.* 1976, Gilbertson & Fox 1977, Hoffman *et al.* 1987).

INDIRECT EFFECTS ON BIRD POPULATIONS

Pesticides and farmland birds

Indirect effects of pesticides on bird populations include the removal of crucial food supplies. This problem arises partly because, as described above, pesticides kill a wide range of organisms besides the target pests. Most insecticides kill many kinds of invertebrates, some fungicides kill some invertebrates as well as removing the fungal food supplies of others, while herbicides may remove the food-plants of other insects as well as the seeds eaten by granivorous birds. For example, cereal fields can hold 700–800 different insect species, only 10% of which damage the crop, yet almost all these insects are typically removed by pesticide applications (Buckwell & Armstrong-Brown 2004). In many countries, including Britain, the use of pesticides is now so ubiquitous – often with several applications per growing season – that insect populations over huge areas are held permanently at much reduced levels, not only in the crops themselves but also in hedges and other adjoining habitats to which the chemicals are carried by wind.

The best documented example of widespread population decline caused by the effects of pesticides on food organisms concerns the Grey Partridge, whose dramatic decline from the 1970s was attributed largely to poor production of young, in turn due mainly to lack of insect food for chicks (Potts 1986, Potts & Aebischer 1991). This occurred because broadleaved weed species, which form the food-plants of the relevant insects (notably sawfly larvae), are now absent from most modern cereal fields, as a result of herbicide use, and many other insects are affected directly or indirectly by fungicides or directly by insecticides. The survival of young Partridges (up to three weeks old) was found to be directly correlated with the abundance of insects in cereal fields. In experimental field trials, reduced herbicide use resulted in improved weed and insect populations, better chick survival, and greater Partridge densities (Rands 1985).

The decline in Grey Partridge numbers is not restricted to Britain, where this research was done, but is general throughout the agricultural range of the species, with an estimated decline in the world population from around 120 million in 1950 to ten million in 1990 (Potts 1991), with further reduction since then. Research findings led to the recommendation that farmers keen to conserve partridges should leave an unsprayed strip of crop around the edges of fields, so-called *conservation headlands*. This procedure enabled weeds to grow, which in turn supported the insects necessary for partridges and other birds, and led to increased local densities of partridges. Unfortunately, not enough farmers were interested in conserving Grey Partridges, and the overall population in Britain continued to decline, with a net loss of around 95% between 1970 and 2010, according to counts collated by the BTO.

In other studies, chick survival in Red-legged Partridges and Pheasants was also correlated with the abundance of preferred insects (Green 1984, Hill 1985). Were it not for the fact that Pheasants can be easily reared and released, they would almost certainly have declined over much of their range. Low insect densities, caused by pesticide use, have also been found in field experiments to

FIG 208. The Corn Bunting *Emberiza calandra*, whose catastrophic decline in Britain has been attributed to food shortage, mainly insects in summer and cereal grains gleaned from stubble fields in winter. (Alan Martin)

reduce the breeding success of Corn Buntings, Yellowhammers and other birds (Brickle *et al*. 2000, Morris *et al*. 2001, Hart *et al*. 2006). On the basis of their diets and ecology, at least 18 other bird species are likely to have been affected indirectly by pesticide use in Britain and Ireland (Campbell & Cooke 1997, Boatman *et al*. 2004).

During the past 40 years, as shown by the monitoring programmes of the BTO, most of the bird species found on British farmland have declined (Chapter 4). The same seems to have been true over much of western Europe (Tucker & Heath 1994). In the absence of more detailed studies, it is hard to say how much these declines were due to pesticide use, and how much to other agricultural changes that occurred at the same time. However, declines in many species steepened from the mid-1970s when pesticide use increased greatly.

There is no doubt that arthropod populations on farmland have declined progressively since the 1950s. Favourite food-species of birds in farmland include grasshoppers, sawflies, leaf beetles, weevils, butterflies and moths (or their caterpillars), aphids, craneflies and their larvae, but all have widely declined, again mainly through pesticide use (Wilson *et al*. 1999, Potts 2012). Many people have noticed big reductions in some species of large insects, such as butterflies and moths, grasshoppers, cockchafers and other large beetles, but the declines extend in lesser degree to smaller insects too (Campbell & Cooke 1997, Wilson *et al*. 1999). One of the best long-term datasets results from the regular sampling of cereal fields in Sussex (Potts 1991). When this study began in 1969, insecticides had already been in use for more than 20 years and herbicides for more than 15 years, yet during in the next 20 years overall arthropod numbers continued to decline by about 4% per year (equivalent to about 50% in the 20 years). Some 640 km to the north, suction-trap catches of aerial arthropods at the University of Stirling showed a similar downward trend over three decades (Benton *et al*. 2002). In southern England, nocturnal moths sampled by light-trapping declined by 67% between 1933–50 and 1960–89 in arable land, but no change occurred in nearby woodland (Woiwood 1991), while in a wider study 66% of 337 large moth species monitored across Britain during 1968–2002 declined significantly (Conrad *et al*. 2006). In Germany, some 50–80% of species of beetles and ants were lost from arable land during 1951–81 (Heydemann 1983). These various declines coincided with increases in the numbers and range of pesticide applications per year in the areas treated, but it is not possible to establish a firm causal link or to exclude other factors. However, some recovery in insect populations occurred within 1–2 years on arable land when pesticide use was experimentally curtailed, with density of weed cover increasing more than fourfold, insect numbers more than threefold, all with significant effects on the survival of young Grey and Red-legged Partridges and Pheasants (Sotherton 1991). This type of study, involving reduction of pesticide use, has been repeated many times subsequently, with similar results (Potts 2012).

Over the years, as mentioned above, herbicide use has enormously reduced the populations of various farmland weeds, on which many seed-eating birds depend. Some once-common arable weeds have now become rare in lowland Britain. Most herbicides are not themselves cumulative, but their effects are, as they lead to progressive depletion of the seed-bank in the soil. Each year, seeds turned to the surface by cultivation germinate to produce plants which are killed before they can seed. Several species of seed-eating birds, notably the Linnet, once fed extensively on weed seeds (especially *Polygonum* and *Chenopodium*) turned to the surface each time a field was cultivated (Newton 1972). The old adage 'one year's seeding means seven years weeding' is an understatement, because the seeds of many farmland weed species may remain viable for decades (Salisbury 1961). Such seeds could once be counted on the surface of newly-turned farmland soil at thousands per square metre (references in Salisbury 1961), but after more than 50 years of herbicide use, they have now almost disappeared from the soil of cereal-growing regions, replaced to some extent by wild grass seeds uncontrolled by the herbicides in commonest use. From information on the past diets of 26 species of farmland bird species, the seeds of *Polygonum*, *Stellaria*, *Chenopodium*, Brassicaceae and Compositae were all once widely eaten, and all have declined in recent decades. For many years, herbicides could not be used on fodder root crops (such as turnips) which therefore remained as a major source of weed seeds for birds into winter. This changed with the development of pre-emergent herbicides, but meanwhile fodder crops dwindled along with the decline in mixed farming, from 9% of arable land in the 1930s to less than 1% by the 1980s (Shrubb 2003). Given these changes, it is not surprising that the bird species most dependent on broadleaved arable weeds have declined too, and that their declines did not become apparent until herbicides had been in use for several years. Besides the Linnet, such species include the Twite, Lesser Redpoll, Tree Sparrow, Reed Bunting and Skylark. Other species, such as the Greenfinch and Chaffinch, also relied heavily on farmland weed seeds, but have shown no obvious long-term declines, having found alternative food sources at garden feeders, game-food hoppers and elsewhere (Chapter 4).

Widespread monitoring of bird populations, followed by appropriate research and experiment, has played a crucial role in highlighting some of the long-term consequences of pesticide use and in confirming pesticides as a major factor in reducing, not just pest numbers, but the entire spectrum of biodiversity in farmed landscapes (and beyond, in the case of organochlorines). The number of well-documented case studies is limited because declines in bird numbers have mostly been gradual, and in recent years have seldom involved conspicuous large-scale kills. Also, any effects of pesticides have proved hard to disentangle retrospectively from those of other procedural changes.

In other parts of the world, anti-locust spray programmes have greatly reduced the populations of some other bird species, including the Rose-coloured Starling on the European steppes (Belik & Mikalevich 1995). Again the main effects are indirect, through removal of food supplies. It is hard to judge how much the extensive spraying in Africa to kill locusts, tsetse flies or other pests has affected birds, including European migrants wintering there. However, after the spraying of the organophosphates fenitrothion and chlorpyrifos to control locusts in Senegal, total bird numbers decreased significantly on all treated plots. Some of the decrease was due directly to bird mortality (adults and chicks), but most was attributed to emigration following the sudden reduction in arthropod prey (Mullié & Keith 1993).

New pesticides

The latest pesticides to come into wide use are the neonicotinoids, chemically similar to nicotine, the natural insecticide found in tobacco leaves. These neurotoxins were developed during the 1990s and, while it is too soon to assess their full effects on biodiversity, the omens look bad. They are extremely toxic to a great range of insects, and are known to affect the behaviour of honey bees, although to what extent they are responsible for the collapse of bee populations across Europe and elsewhere is still uncertain. Nevertheless, they have been banned from use for a trial period in several countries, including Britain and Ireland. They are used for a range of different purposes, including seed-dressings, from which they contaminate soil that can be blown as dust onto vegetation, appearing in the pollen and nectar of flowers. The amount on any one plant is tiny, but bees and other insects visiting flower after flower can soon accumulate lethal levels. Another concern is that they are systemic, being taken into plants and killing any insects which suck the sap or eat the leaves. They are also fairly persistent, lasting more than a month in bright sunlight, but up to several years in darker situations, and can wash from soil into watercourses. They are not especially toxic to mammals, and probably not to birds, so their main impacts are again likely to result from their effects on bird food supplies.

Pesticides and behaviour

Sub-lethal effects of pesticides on bird behaviour can also occur. Various chemicals at low levels of exposure have been shown to affect the learning ability of birds, their response to stimuli, their flight coordination, their nest-building and incubation, and their general activity, making them more or less active than normal (Peakall 1985). Although such studies relate to birds in captivity, the changes in behaviour induced could influence the ability of birds in the wild to obtain food or to avoid predators and other risks. Predatory birds are more likely to take affected prey behaving abnormally than normal prey, and thus increase their own risk (Hunt *et al.* 1992). By such indirect means, therefore, pesticide or pollutant exposure could influence the survival and reproductive prospects of birds in the wild through increasing their vulnerability to other limiting factors. Clearly, this is an aspect that is difficult to study in free-living wild birds.

CONCLUDING REMARKS

Although the numbers of most bird species can recover quickly from short-term direct pesticide impacts, if usage continues year after year, as is now the case, local populations may remain permanently reduced or die out. During the past 60 years, pesticide impacts over large areas have held some bird species well below the level that contemporary landscapes could otherwise have supported. They have caused massive declines in some birds of prey through direct effects, and massive declines in many other species of farmland birds by greatly reducing their food supplies. The main problems arise because existing pesticides are not sufficiently selective in their effects, and kill a wide range of other organisms besides the target pests.

Like any other form of loss in birds, direct mortality from pesticides may be offset to greater or lesser extent by reductions in any natural losses that are density-dependent. Experience in Britain with the Sparrowhawk and Peregrine showed that production of young could be reduced to less than half its normal level without causing a decline in breeding numbers. This was presumably because, with reduced competition, the survival of remaining young was higher, and with more territories than usual falling vacant, these young could begin to breed at an earlier age than usual. However, further reproductive failure could not be fully compensated, and the populations of both species then declined, to nil in some regions. Using field experience of this type, it should be possible to calculate for other populations the degree of additive breeding failure or mortality that could occur from pesticides or pollutants without causing population decline; in other words to calculate, in the conditions prevailing, the *maximum sustainable yield*, as described in Chapter 16. The next step is to relate this level of breeding failure or mortality to some threshold level of pollutant that will cause it, as in the DDE response of the Peregrine or the HEOD response of the Sparrowhawk discussed above. If usage could then be held below this threshold, populations could persist (Newton 1988).

But the effects of pesticides on wildlife are far greater than the direct and indirect effects discussed above, for they are central to the kinds of farming now practised throughout the lowlands of Britain and Ireland (Shrubb 2003). In particular, the use of herbicides and other chemicals has enabled farmers to do away with crop rotation. The same types of crop can now be grown year after year on the same land without the risk of weeds, pests or diseases getting out of hand. Without an ability to control competitive weeds, insect pests and disease, more traditional forms of mixed farming would have had to be retained, and with them much greater diversity in the plants and animals of farmland, of which bird populations are just a part.

Pesticides were originally developed 'in good faith' to enhance crop production, and in ignorance of their subsequent environmental impacts. It is an open question whether the rapidly expanding human population could have been supported at its current level without them. Looking back, however, the organochlorine episode had a big impact on the perception of pesticides by the general public. It highlighted for the first time the potentially severe environmental consequences that could result from the widespread use of chemicals, hitherto regarded by most people as wholly beneficial. The effects of DDT were not apparent immediately, but only after several years, and could not have been predicted beforehand by the testing procedures in operation at the time. They provided the first example (after nuclear fallout) of a genuine and well-documented global pollution problem, on a scale that we now take for granted. They led to wide debate on the value of circumstantial versus experimental evidence, for at first the case against the organochlorines rested entirely on correlations, a point exploited to the full by the agricultural and agrochemical lobbies. This in turn led to the suggestion, perhaps for the first time by non-ecologists, that the precautionary principle should be applied, and that no pesticide should be widely used until its potential effects were understood. This appreciation led to overhaul in the procedures required for testing pesticides before they were cleared for general use. Lastly, the events of more recent years have confirmed that, if remedial action is taken and if remnant populations still persist, such populations can and do respond by recovery. In other words, reducing pesticide use can rapidly bring measurable conservation benefits. And, as we shall see in the next chapter, the same holds true for some other pollutants.

CHAPTER 19

Effects of Other Pollutants

S TILL ON THE THEME OF POLLUTION, this chapter discusses chemicals other than pesticides, which nevertheless reach dangerous concentrations in the environment as a result of human activity. Some of these pollutants act in the same way as pesticides, having direct or indirect effects on birds, while others act through altering the chemical composition of air or water, with adverse effects on plants and animals. Five main problems are discussed here, namely those resulting from lead poisoning, oil spillage, plastic disposal, and the acidification and nutrient enrichment of lakes and rivers.

LEAD POISONING

Lead occurs naturally in the environment but has become dangerous to some animals because of its human use. It affects most bodily systems, including the blood, muscular and nervous systems. Its toxic effects on people have been known for more than 2,000 years, and in recent decades attempts have been made to reduce exposure. During my own lifetime, lead pipes have been removed from buildings, and lead compounds banned from use in paints, gasoline and other products. The main remaining problem results from the continued use of lead in ammunition, which is affecting some bird populations, as well as the health and well-being of some people. Each shotgun cartridge contains up to 300 pieces of lead shot, almost all of which fall to the ground after being fired. The annual estimated weight of lead discharged over the surface of Britain in 1990 was 2,000 tonnes, of which 160 tonnes went specifically into wetlands, and were thus available to waterfowl. In Ireland, the equivalent figures were 153 and 46 tonnes (Pain 1992). This amount may not sound much over the whole land surface of Britain and Ireland, but lead does not degrade, and these are annual figures, building on previous amounts dating back over many years. Moreover, shooting is not evenly distributed, but tends to be concentrated in particular areas such as wetlands and game-rearing estates.

The use of lead in ammunition dates back as far as guns themselves. Apart from the direct targeted mortality it causes, two main categories of birds are affected indirectly by its use. One includes herbivorous birds, which deliberately ingest grit to assist in the breakdown of leaves and seeds in the gut. They sometimes ingest spent gunshot pellets along with grit, and in consequence have suffered from lead poisoning. This problem has affected a wide range of species from doves to gamebirds, but waterfowl are the main casualties.

Once in the gizzard, spent gunshot is gradually eroded and absorbed, but the resulting poisoning may not become evident until 2–3 weeks after ingestion. The complete absorption of 1–3 lead pellets (depending on their size) is considered sufficient to kill any waterfowl species from duck to swan. The initial symptoms are fairly obvious. The bird may be reluctant to fly when approached, and may droop its wings. Later, it is unable to lift its head, so the neck is laid along the back, giving a condition known as *limber neck*. The gut itself becomes paralysed, and peristalsis stops. The foregut may be full of food which remains there, so that the bird gradually starves to death, losing 30–50% of its body mass and producing green bile-stained droppings. The gall bladder itself is usually extended with green bile. On chemical analysis, elevated levels of lead are found in the blood, liver and kidneys, and after long exposure also in bone, where lead is relatively immobile. Lead pellets can also be detected in the gut by direct search or by use of x-ray.

Lead-poisoned waterfowl are often mistaken for hunting-season cripples. But because afflicted individuals can take several weeks to die, becoming gradually weaker, they often seek cover or are removed by predators, so that few carcasses remain as evidence (Zwank *et al.* 1985). Affected birds also tend to die a few at a time over periods of months, with no conspicuous mass mortality events that would exceed the capacity of scavengers to remove them. In the early stages, lead-poisoned birds were also found to be nearly twice as vulnerable to human hunters as were healthy birds (Bellrose 1959).

Surveys of a number of wetlands in Britain in recent decades have revealed densities of lead shot of up to about 30 per square metre of the surface layer of bottom sediment (Mateo 2009). Concentrations tend to be lower further north in Europe, and higher further south, where more birds spend the winter. Correspondingly, the highest levels of lead shot in waterfowl gizzards have been found in the dry Mediterranean region, where birds concentrate in large numbers on a limited number of wetlands which have been intensively shot over for decades. Among Mallard, the prevalence of lead shot ingestion varies from 2% to 10% of birds in the wetlands of northern Europe, up to 25–45% in some Mediterranean deltas of southern Europe. In this region, the Pintail and Pochard show the highest prevalence of lead shot ingestion, affecting up to 60–70% of birds in some river deltas (Mateo 2009). In northern Europe, lead has been found at highest frequency in Goldeneye and Tufted Duck, with a prevalence reaching 32% and 58% respectively in samples from Finland (Pain 1990, Mateo 2009).

Regardless of intake, lead does not become toxic until it is eroded and absorbed, so that waterfowl feeding on hard foods, such as cereal grains, and therefore taking in much grit, experience greater rates of absorption from a given number of pellets than those eating soft foods. In addition, species whose diets are rich in protein, calcium and phosphorus tend to absorb less lead from the gut and accumulate less in tissues than species whose diets are low in these components. Hence, species with the highest rates of intake do not necessarily suffer the greatest mortality; and as diets may change with season, poisoning cases do not necessarily peak at the time of greatest lead ingestion.

Although poisoned birds are found, it is not easy to estimate the effect of lead poisoning on overall survival rates in waterfowl. However, an attempt was made using recoveries of Mallard ringed in the Camargue in southern France during 1960–71 (Tavecchia et al. 2001). When these birds were caught, the amount and type of lead in each was determined by x-ray examination, following which they were ringed and released. The percentage of birds with lead in the gizzard remained constant at about 11% throughout, while the proportion with lead shot embedded in body tissues increased from 19% to 29% during the years of study (the latter birds having been shot but not killed). Males and females were affected similarly from both sources. The relative monthly survival of birds with more than one pellet in their gizzard or muscle tissue was about 19% lower than that of birds carrying 0–1 pellets.

Several experiments in the United States have also tested the effects of lead shot ingestion. Some of the clearest results were obtained from Mallard drakes that were ringed, dosed and released during 1949–51, then checking the proportion recovered. Comparing ring recoveries with those from undosed birds, an increase in annual mortality of 9% was recorded for birds dosed with one lead pellet, an increase of 23% for birds dosed with two pellets, 36% for birds dosed with four pellets, and 50% for those dosed with six pellets (Bellrose 1959). As expected, the amount consumed affected survival chances. However, a similar experiment with Pintail revealed no such difference between dosed and undosed birds. This result was attributed to dietary differences between the species which resulted in less erosion and absorption of lead by Pintail (Deuel 1985).

Differences in diet mean that not all waterfowl species are equally vulnerable (Bellrose 1959, Sanderson & Bellrose 1986). Further research indicated that bottom-feeding diving species, such as Tufted Ducks, are likely to have the highest rates of intake, followed by dabbling species, such as Mallards and Pintails, and then grazers, such as Wigeon. Fish-eaters, such as Goosanders, are not normally exposed to pellet intake. Other factors influencing intake rates include the amount of lead shot in the local environment, grit size and selection, and whether the bottoms of wetlands consist of hard material on which pellets can persist or soft mud in which they sink. Flight ponds, dug specially for shooting waterfowl, are often extremely heavily contaminated.

Overall, the impact of lead poisoning of waterfowl is not trivial. From its frequency in different species, and their relative vulnerabilities, lead poisoning has been estimated to kill nearly a million waterfowl per year in western Europe, some 8–9% of a total wintering population of more than 11 million birds of 17 species (Mateo 2009). The equivalent percentage is lower in North America, 2–3% of an estimated autumn population of 100 million waterfowl (Bellrose 1959, 1980). Moreover, comparing equivalent species on the two continents, the prevalence of ingested gunshot is invariably greater in the European than in the North American species (Mateo 2009).

Because most deaths from lead poisoning occur in late winter, after the shooting season, they are not necessarily offset by reduced deaths from other causes. They could therefore act to lower breeding numbers (Bellrose 1959, Sanderson & Bellrose 1986). However, effects on breeding numbers have not been clearly separated from more direct effects of shooting. Nevertheless, comparing 15 species of waterfowl from western Europe, the population trend was negatively correlated with the prevalence of ingested lead, with the most frequently contaminated species showing the greatest rates of decline (Fig. 209). This does not necessarily mean that ingested lead is causing population declines, but certainly raises this as a possibility.

Although lead poisoning of birds in Britain has been known since 1875, attempts to reduce the use of lead in ammunition have been repeatedly and vigorously opposed by the shooting lobby. In consequence, legislation intended to reduce the use of lead shot over wetlands was not introduced into England, Wales, Scotland and Northern Ireland until 1999, 2002, 2004 and 2009 respectively, the precise wording of the legislation varying from one country to another. Nevertheless, a survey of waterfowl bought from game dealers, butchers, supermarkets and game shoots in England in 2008 revealed that 70% of birds

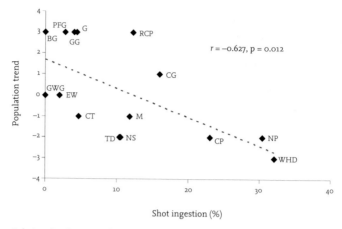

Shot ingestion (%)

FIG 209. Relationship between the prevalence of ingested lead shot in 15 waterfowl species and the recent trends of their wintering populations in Europe. Species with the greatest proportions of individuals containing ingested lead shot showed some of the greatest declines since the 1960s. PFG, Pink-footed Goose *Anser brachyrhynchus*; GWG, Greater White-fronted Goose *Anser albifrons*; GG, Greylag Goose *Anser anser*; BG, Barnacle Goose *Branta leucopsis*; EW, Eurasian Wigeon *Anas penelope*; G, Gadwall *Anas strepera*; CT, Common Teal *Anas crecca*; M, Mallard *Anas platyrhynchos*; NP, Northern Pintail *Anas acuta*; NS, Northern Shoveler *Anas clypeata*; RCP, Red-crested Pochard *Netta rufina*; CP, Common Pochard *Aythya ferina*; TD, Tufted Duck *Aythya fuligula*; CG, Common Goldeneye *Bucephala clamgula*; WHD, White-headed Duck *Oxyura leucocephala*. (From Mateo 2009)

had been shot with lead, so compliance with legislation was evidently low (Pain *et al.* 2010). The same holds for several other European countries in which the use of lead shot over wetlands has been made illegal, and the incidence of lead in waterfowl has remained relatively high. In Britain and Ireland, there is still no restriction on the use of lead on dry-land habitats, and the same holds in most European countries.

In Britain and Ireland, a related problem arose from the use of lead sinkers on fishing lines. Over the years, many such sinkers were lost or discarded by anglers, and from the 1970s became a major cause of mortality in Mute Swans, resulting in marked population declines on several major river systems, including the Thames, the Trent and the Warwickshire Avon (Birkhead & Perrins 1985, Sears 1988). On the Thames, counts during the annual swan upping fell from 1,212 in 1969 to only 153 in 1981, and on the Avon at Stratford, numbers fell from 70–80 in the early 1960s to nil in the late 1970s. Lead sinkers were found in the gizzards of dead swans, presumably again swallowed as grit. Some 3,000–3,500 birds were estimated to die

FIG 210. Until the 1980s, the Mute Swan *Cygnus olor* was a frequent victim of lead poisoning from discarded fishing weights, experiencing sufficient mortality to cause big population declines over parts of Britain and Ireland. Following a ban on the use of lead fishing weights, the species subsequently recovered. (Ian Newton)

per year from lead poisoning in England in the 1970s. Postmortem examinations of 210 full-grown Mute Swans found dead in England during 1980–81 revealed that lead poisoning had caused 50% of deaths, the commonest single cause of mortality (Sears & Hunt 1991). This was followed by flying accidents, some of which could themselves be related to lead effects. In Scotland during 1980–86, some 14% of 147 Mute Swan deaths were attributed to lead poisoning, as were 47% of 57 Whooper Swan deaths (Spray & Milne 1988). In Ireland during 1984–87, almost 70% of 101 Mute Swan deaths were attributed to lead poisoning, both from sinkers and from shot, the latter especially at Lough Neagh (O'Halloran *et al.* 1991). On the shore of this lough was a clay-pigeon centre, and along 100 m of nearby shoreline, extending up to 60 m offshore, the density of lead pellets in the upper 5 cm of bottom sediment averaged about 2,400 per square metre.

After the introduction of alternative materials to weight the lines, the proportion of lead-poisoned Mute Swans in England dropped to 40% of 429 dead birds in 1983–86, and after a legislative ban on the use of split lead shot and other sinkers from 1987, the proportion dropped to 30% of 236 dead birds in 1987–88. In the Thames valley, the number of lead-poisoned swans found dead or dying dropped by 70% within two years, and with the resulting improvement in survival, numbers began to recover, with an overall 23% increase between 1990 and 2002. A similar problem occurs from the continuing use of lead sinkers in North America, where Trumpeter Swans, Great Northern Divers (Common Loons), Sandhill Cranes and Brown Pelicans are some of the most frequent casualties (Friend & Franson 2002, Watson *et al.* 2009).

Besides waterfowl, at least 63 other species have been recorded as affected by the ingestion of lead ammunition (Pain *et al.* 2009). Many herbivorous gamebirds take in lead shot, again apparently in mistake for grit. Pheasants, Grey Partridges, Red-legged Partridges, Woodpigeons, Cranes, Moorhens, Coots and others have been found poisoned in this way, as have some waders that eat seeds in winter, such as Black-tailed Godwit and Ruff. Away from wetlands, the problem in Britain may be worsening. The proportion of shot partridges that contain ingested lead shot has increased significantly over the last 60 years, and has recently exceeded 8%, about three-quarters of which would have died from ingested lead had they not been shot (Potts 2012). This suggests a somewhat less serious problem than in wetlands, but one that is growing.

The second major impact of the use of lead in ammunition involves meat-eating animals, such as birds of prey, some of which ingest lead bullet fragments and pellets from the carcasses of shot but unretrieved waterfowl and game animals, and from the discarded grallochs (entrails) of deer. For example, postmortem examinations of 390 White-tailed Eagles found dead in Germany over a period of years revealed that about 23% had died from lead poisoning (Krone *et al.* 2009). The main source of this lead was pellets within the bodies of dead and living waterfowl (some 21% of captured wild geese were found to have lead shot in their tissues). Deaths caused by lead have also been documented in Golden Eagles, Buzzards, Red Kites, Marsh Harriers, vultures, Ravens and others, even though some of these species regurgitate in their castings some of the lead fragments they consume (Fisher *et al.* 2006). In a study in southern France, lead levels in the blood of Marsh Harriers were monitored year-round, and significantly more individuals had elevated lead levels inside the hunting season than outside it, reflecting their changing seasonal exposure to lead (Pain *et al.* 1993). In addition, a higher proportion of regurgitated pellets from Marsh Harriers contained lead shot inside the hunting season than outside it, confirming that prey carcasses were the main source. In North America, lead has been a major killer of California Condors, Bald Eagles, Golden Eagles and Ravens, while in Japan it is killing increasing numbers of wintering Steller's Sea Eagles (see various papers in Watson *et al.* 2009).

Lead ammunition also poses health risks to people. Lead bullets explode and fragment into tiny particles in shot game and can spread widely from the point of impact. Radiographs of shot deer show that numerous imperceptible dust-sized particles of lead can infect meat up to 50 cm from the bullet wound. Lead pellets sometimes also fragment in the same way. Both types of ammunition thereby cause a greater health risk than previously thought to people who consume game killed by lead-based ammunition, and especially to vulnerable groups such as children (Watson *et al.* 2009, Pain *et al.* 2010). A survey of six game species (including Mallard and Pheasant) bought from game dealers, butchers and supermarkets in Britain during 2001–08 revealed lead in the meat of at least 96% of 121 birds, and that (even after removal of detectable pellet fragments) a high proportion of these birds had lead concentrations in their meat above the European Union maximum level for domestic animal meat (no level is set for game), some by several orders of magnitude (Pain *et al.* 2010).

For most wild species, we still have no assessment of the effect of lead-based mortality on population levels. However, in current conditions in North America at least one species, the California Condor, can no longer exist as a self-sustaining population in its historic range. The mortality from lead-based ammunition obtained from game carcasses and discarded entrails well exceeds its natural reproductive rate. As long as lead-based bullets of current design are used as now in game hunting, the Condor is unlikely to survive without help anywhere in North America. It is being kept from extinction in the wild only by a programme of intensive conservation management-cum-veterinary care, involving frequent capture and chelation therapy to reduce the lead levels in the blood and tissues of individuals. Yet perfectly acceptable non-toxic alternatives to lead are now available as ammunition, with ballistic properties as good. Ignorance and resistance to change in much of the hunting community prevents their widespread take-up. Many hunters see anti-lead information as anti-hunting propaganda, and disregard it.

Lead poisoning is thus likely to occur wherever birds feed in areas where lead shot has been deposited, or where predators or scavengers feed on game species. Whilst most research has been done in Europe or North America, this is a global problem, and wherever we look we find further candidates to add to the list of lead-poisoned casualties – currently exceeding 130 species, including waterfowl. Hopefully, we will soon see lead ammunition replaced by the non-lead substitutes already freely available, but even if this happens, the large amounts of lead previously deposited in places where birds feed will ensure that cases of lead poisoning decline less rapidly than they otherwise would. In view of the impacts of ingested lead on wildlife and people, and poor compliance with previous legislation relating to wetlands, the use of lead in game hunting has now been banned totally in Denmark, Norway and the Netherlands. Such legislation is long overdue in the rest of Europe, including Britain and Ireland. For Britain it is now 30 years since the Royal Commission on Environmental Pollution (1983) recommended that lead be phased out from all ammunition, but in the interim little has changed.

While most problems of lead poisoning in birds have been due to lead ammunition or fishing weights, other mortality has resulted from industrial use. A major incident occurred on the Mersey in the winter of 1979–80, when more than 2,500 birds were found dead. Analysis of their tissues revealed high levels of organic lead. The source was not discovered with certainty, but at that time organic lead was manufactured locally for use in petrol (a use now banned). Smaller numbers of birds died the following winter, but the lead levels in their tissues were lower (Bull *et al.* 1983, Royal Commission on Environmental Pollution 1983).

OIL SPILLS AND SEABIRDS

In recent decades, millions of seabirds worldwide have died from oil pollution. After major accidents, the high-profile media coverage of dead and dying birds washed ashore ensures that this problem is well known to the general public. Because newly released oil floats on water, a relatively small volume can cover a large area, affecting mainly surface-swimming birds such as auks, sea-ducks and grebes, with aerial diving species, such as terns and Gannets, being much less vulnerable. When seabirds swim into oil their feathers become soiled and matted, allowing water to penetrate and causing loss of insulation and buoyancy. Affected birds soon lose their ability to fly, and die from hypothermia, drowning, exhaustion, dehydration or starvation, or from ingesting oil removed from feathers during preening (Clarke 1984). The toxic effects of ingested oil vary with the type of oil, but often include gastrointestinal irritation, haemorrhaging and osmoregulatory dysfunction (Friend & Franson 2002).

FIG 211. An oiled Shag *Phalacrocorax aristotelis*, a victim of a major tanker wreck. (RSPB Images)

After a time under wave action, floating oil can form an emulsion with water, known to the clean-up teams as chocolate mousse. The volatile part gradually evaporates (faster at higher temperatures), leaving a sticky asphaltic residue, and eventually 'tar-balls', which turn up on beaches but cause much less harm to birds. However, the effects of oil pollution can persist long after the visible spill is cleaned or dispersed. Oily compounds usually last less than six months in the water column, but much longer in other parts of the environment. For example, chemical from the *Exxon Valdez* spill in Alaska in 1989 was still present in molluscs ten years later, and was thus still available to birds which ate them.

Perhaps the first major oil spill in British waters was in 1907, involving the largest seven-mast schooner ever built, the *Thomas W. Lawson*, which was wrecked on the Isles of Scilly on her maiden voyage. The release of her entire cargo, consisting of 'two million gallons' of crude oil, caused a vast slaughter of local seabirds, especially Puffins (Bourne 1968). In those days, the uninhabited island of Annet is supposed to have supported about 100,000 Puffins, whereas today less than 100 pairs remain. The loss at sea of vessels carrying oil during the 1914–18 war resulted in a large increase in the numbers of oiled seabirds. This led the RSPB to publish figures in 1921 which were influential in the introduction of the *Oil in Navigable Waters Act* soon after. In the Second World War, most tankers carried petroleum spirits, and the destruction of shipping presented less hazard. But this situation soon changed as growing industrial development increased the demand for oil, resulting in a vast expansion of oil traffic at sea. For the 1940s and 1950s, RSPB staff estimated that between 50,000 and 250,000 birds per year were being killed in home waters. In subsequent years, the situation worsened, before getting better.

Major oiling incidents, resulting from the wrecking of laden tankers, often kill many thousands of birds at a time, as the examples in Box 7 from Britain and Europe show. The images of dying auks on beaches mean that the names of the ships involved have become etched on the memories of both bird-watchers and the general public.

In any incident, the numbers of birds killed depends not only on the numbers and species of birds in the area at the time, but also on the amount of oil spilled, whether it is heavy or light, how long it persists (which varies with sea temperature and clean-up operations), and where it drifts, which in turn depends on sea and weather conditions at the time. Winter storms increase the likelihood of shipping accidents, making January–March the peak season, a time of year when seabirds congregate in large numbers in wintering areas. The size of a spill alone thus tells little about its potential for damage. Moreover, it is hard to estimate the total casualties from any incident, for while some oiled birds appear

Box 7. Major oiling incidents resulting from the wrecking of laden tankers around Britain and Western Europe
Incidents are listed in date order by name of vessel, and except where otherwise stated, the information is taken from websites found under these names.

- *Torrey Canyon*, March 1967, Isles of Scilly, England, spilling 117,000 tonnes of crude oil, resulted in 10,000 birds found dead and an estimated total kill of at least 30,000 birds, mainly Razorbills and other auks (Bourne *et al.* 1967, Bourne 1970). Local colonies of Guillemots and other species in Scilly and Cornwall were considerably reduced, but the main effects were on birds nesting on the Sept Isles off Brittany, where, compared with the previous year, Guillemot pairs had fallen from 270 to 50 pairs, Razorbills from 450 to 50 pairs, and Puffins from 2,500 to 400 pairs, giving an overall reduction of nearly 85% (Bourne 1970).
- *Amoco Cadiz*, April 1978, northern France, spilling 233,000 tonnes of light crude oil, resulted in 4,600 birds found dead, and an estimated total kill of 15,000–20,000 birds, mainly Puffins and other auks (Hope Jones *et al.* 1978, Conan *et al.* 1982).
- *Christos Bitas*, October 1978, off south Wales, spilling 4,000 tonnes of heavy crude oil, resulted in 1,035 birds found dead on Skomer Island, and another 485 found alive and sent for treatment. The main victims were Guillemots and Razorbills.
- *Esso Bernicia*, December 1978, Sullom Voe Terminal, Shetland, spilling 1,200 tons of heavy fuel oil. Some 3,702 birds of 49 species were found dead, and the total kill was estimated at up to twice that number. Casualties included 146 Great Northern Divers, 683 Shags, 570 Eiders, 306 Long-tailed Ducks, 336 Guillemots and 633 Black Guillemots. Local breeding colonies of Black Guillemots were virtually eliminated, and lesser effects were apparent elsewhere in northeast Shetland (Heubeck & Richardson 1980, Heubeck 2000). In subsequent years, in the absence of further spills, populations gradually recovered.
- *Braer*, January 1993, south Shetland, Scotland, spilling at least 85,000 tonnes of light crude oil, resulted in 1,600 birds found dead, and an estimated total of 6,500 killed. Compared with counts from the previous winter, by March 1993, numbers of Great Northern Divers around south Mainland had declined by 22%, Shags by 40%, Eiders by 10%, Long-tailed Ducks by 20% and Black Guillemots by 3%. Breeding numbers of Shags were also much reduced (Heubeck 1997).
- *Sea Empress*, February 1996, Milford Haven, Wales, spilling 73,000 tonnes of crude oil, resulted in 7,000 birds found dead, including 4,700 Common Scoters and 1,100 Guillemots, and an estimated total kill of more than 17,000 birds (Edwards 1996 and others).

- *Erika*, December 1999, Brittany, France, spilling 13,000 tons of heavy fuel oil, resulted in 63,600 birds found dead, and an estimated total of 120,000–300,000 killed. More than 80% of casualties were Guillemots, including many ringed birds from Ireland and western Britain, while the rest included other auk species, Gannets, Eiders and Common Scoters.

- *Prestige*, November 2002, 200 km off Galicia, northwest Spain, spilling 77,000 tonnes of heavy fuel oil, resulted in 23,180 birds of 90 species found dead, mainly Guillemots (51%), Razorbills (17%) and Puffins (17%), including many ringed birds from western Britain and Ireland, with an estimated total kill of 115,000–250,000 individuals (Garcia *et al.* 2003). This spill was unusual in the large numbers of Puffins that died, of which more than half of those examined were adults, mainly from colonies in the north and west of Britain. Local Shag populations showed roughly 10% declines in nest numbers and 50% declines in nest success, compared to other populations in the same region. Such effects were attributed to oil-effects on the birds themselves or on their prey (Velando *et al.* 2005).

on nearby shores where they can be counted, others appear on more distant shores or sink without trace, the proportions varying with wind and other conditions (Bibby & Lloyd 1977).

It is surprisingly difficult to assess the overall impact of large-scale local kills on seabird populations. This is partly because pre-incident counts are seldom available, and in any case it is usually hard to tell from how wide a breeding area the casualties are drawn, or what proportion consist of breeders, as opposed to immature non-breeders. However, incidents in the spring near nesting colonies can greatly reduce local nesting numbers, as illustrated by the 85% reduction in auk numbers on the Sept Isles after the *Torrey Canyon* disaster (Box 7). Oiling incidents on Shetland, including the *Braer* disaster, reduced the numbers of breeding Black Guillemots, but within 1–5 years most colonies had recovered to pre-spill levels (Heubeck 2000). One detailed study examined the impact of oil spills on the survival of adult Guillemots breeding on Skomer Island, off Wales. During the 20-year study, overwinter survival of adult Guillemots was negatively affected not only by the incidence of four major oil spills in the wintering areas, but also by high values of the NAO index (North Atlantic Oscillation index: see Chapter 14). After controlling for the NAO values, winter mortality was approximately doubled by each major oil spill (Votier *et al.* 2005).

Whether in the breeding or non-breeding season, however, major oiling incidents increase the frequency of catastrophic mortalities to which many seabird populations are exposed naturally. Whether they tip populations into long-term decline will depend on their frequency relative to the recovery powers of the population. Despite the low reproductive rates shown by some species, heavy losses of seabirds could be made good within a few years by immigration from elsewhere and by non-breeders starting to nest at an earlier age than usual. Many seabird species around the British Isles increased through a large part of the twentieth century, despite the ongoing mortality from oiling incidents, food supplies having much greater impacts on their population trends (Chapter 4).

While major tanker accidents attract the headlines, they are said to account only for an estimated 10–15% of the oil that reaches the sea. Most comes from the thousands of minor incidents, accidental and deliberate, that occur each year wherever oil is stored or transported, including waste oil disposal and tank washing at sea (now banned). From one oil tanker, the *Stylis*, some 600 tonnes were deliberately discharged into the Skagerrak in 1980, killing 30,000 birds; this was a relatively small amount of material, but killed more birds than some of the wrecked tankers discussed in Box 7 (Camphuysen 2007). In addition, about 10,000 seabirds, mainly Guillemots, died as a result of oil illegally discharged off eastern Scotland in 1971, as did 8,000 in a series of oil incidents around Shetland in the winter of 1978/79 (Harris & Wanless 2007). These ongoing minor incidents provide a frequent source of seabird mortality, over and above the occasional major catastrophes. They occur chiefly around the main shipping lanes, especially in areas of heavy tanker traffic, so that oiled birds are nowadays continually found on shorelines. In addition to incidents at sea, spills on land occur from well blow-outs and pipeline ruptures. These usually affect small areas, unless they reach a watercourse.

In the past, oil seems to have been a major cause of seabird mortality, as judged from systematic searches for dead birds along shorelines (called 'beached bird surveys'). Such surveys conducted on 2,000 km of coastline in Britain and Ireland during the winters of 1971–76 revealed that some 54% of 6,821 dead auks were oiled, as were 42% of 665 sea-ducks, 69% of 197 divers, and smaller percentages of other species (Cadbury 1978). The proportion of oiled birds was greatest on the northeast, southeast and southwest coasts of England, reflecting the greater tanker traffic in the southern North Sea and English Channel at the time. Since then, the levels of background oil contamination have generally declined, as have the numbers of oiled birds found dead or dying on beaches. More recent national surveys in 2008 and 2009 gave figures of around 22% of 299 auks, 4% of 28 sea-ducks and none of five divers (Schmitt 2008–09). In addition, from a survey of dead seabirds washed up on a Northumbrian beach each week over an 11-year period (1991–2002), only about 3% of 3,748 bodies found were oiled, the most frequent victims being Guillemots (Newton & Little 2009).

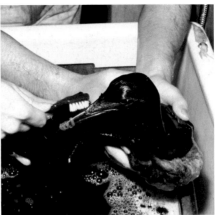

FIG 212. Left: An oiled Guillemot *Uria aalge* unable to fly. Right: Cleaning an oiled Guillemot. (RSPB Images)

So despite the occasional tanker disaster, the overall situation seems to have improved. This is probably due to tighter legislation and enforcement, and to the provision of facilities at ports where the tanks of vessels can be washed.

Much effort has been devoted to the rescue and cleaning of oiled birds, on the assumption that their subsequent survival chances are improved. Based on North American ring recoveries, the median survival time of oiled Guillemots after cleaning, ringing and release was just six days (range 0–919 days), compared with 216 (1–9,259) days for unoiled birds after ringing. Equivalent figures for Western Grebes were 11 (1–763) days for cleaned oiled birds and 624 (19–658) days for unoiled ones, and for Velvet Scoters the figures were seven (1–16) days for cleaned oiled birds and 466 (8–4,939) days for unoiled ones (Sharp 1996). With such low post-release survival, the cleaning of oiled birds seemed pointless, a common experience elsewhere (Clarke 1984). On the other hand, off southern Africa, some 37–84% of Jackass Penguins were seen on their breeding colonies after cleaning, so had evidently survived the process, but how long they survived was not recorded (Morant *et al.* 1981). Much could depend on how the birds were cleaned, on how much oil they had consumed while preening, and on the extent of intestinal damage. Generally speaking, however, severely oiled seabirds, whether cleaned or not, are most realistically regarded as lost to the population.

Birds that are exposed to small amounts of oil and other hydrocarbons while breeding can also transfer lethal amounts to their eggs, only 5–20 microlitres on the shell surface being enough to kill the embryo within. This has been shown in various aquatic species when microlitre amounts of crude or refined oils were applied experimentally to the surface of fertile eggs, either in laboratory or field conditions (Clarke 1984). The resulting mortality depended on both the dose and the stage of embryo development, with malformation occurring when oil was applied during the first few days of incubation (Eastin & Hoffman 1979). To my knowledge, this type of contamination has not yet resulted in massive breeding failure in any wild population, but it remains a threat.

It is not just the oil-induced direct mortality of birds which affects their populations, but the impacts of oil on their food organisms. In several localities after a major spill, shellfish and crustaceans were found to take up to several years to recover their numbers, depending on the severity of the spill and the dispersants used in the clean-up. Petroleum compounds administered experimentally to food organisms affected their reproduction, reducing egg and sperm production, fertility and hatchability, and impaired body functions.

To summarise, oil contamination results in high mortality of seabirds, which is sometimes reflected in declines of local breeding colonies. It may in the past have eliminated some seabird populations from parts of their former range, as possibly exemplified by auks in the English Channel – one of the busiest waterways in the world. Despite increasing tanker traffic, accidental and deliberate discharges around the British Isles have become less frequent in recent decades, as reflected in the reduced incidence of oiled birds on beaches.

PLASTICS AND SEABIRDS

Plastics have been manufactured in increasing quantities since the 1950s, and since then have been found in ever greater amounts floating on the sea and piled on shorelines. Two types are distinguished: user-plastics, consisting of fragments of items such as polystyrene cups, plastic toys or synthetic netting; and plastic pellets which derive from user-products but look like the raw material from which such products are made. Mixtures of both types have been found at up to several thousand particles per km^2 of sea surface, and in all the world's oceans (Colton et al. 1974, Morris 1980, Azzarello & van Vleet 1987). Concentrations vary depending on geographical patterns of usage, air and water currents. Seabirds frequently become entangled in discarded fishing nets and lines, and eventually starve or drown, but the small particles are often ingested by many species, accumulating in their stomachs.

Plastic materials are not biodegradable, but may break down very slowly in response to ultraviolet radiation. They eventually erode to the small pellets mentioned above which float on the sea surface. Seabirds swallow such particles apparently in mistake for food. They are indigestible but can be eroded slowly in the gizzard, where they may release other contaminants, such as PCBs. Their main effects are to reduce the effective gizzard volume, theoretically to the point when the bird can no longer feed (Connors & Smith 1982). Surface-feeding species are most vulnerable. Gulls, terns and skuas, which habitually regurgitate pellets of hard materials, can get rid of plastic particles, but shearwaters and petrels apparently cannot, and large quantities have been found in their stomachs (Furness 1985). Larger species take larger particles, and most species seem to prefer darker over lighter ones. They have been found in Fulmars, Manx Shearwaters, Leach's Petrels and others around Britain, and also in some southern hemisphere species, such as Great Shearwater and Wilson's Petrel, which spend the austral winter (northern summer) in the North Atlantic. During 2003–07, 95% of 1,295 Fulmars washed up on beaches around the North Sea contained plastic (on average 35 pieces weighing 0.31 g), with regional variations ranging from 48% to 78% (van Franeker et al. 2011). Data from the Netherlands since the 1980s show a decrease of pelleted plastics in the stomachs of Fulmars, but an increase of user plastics, with shipping and fisheries as the main sources. Synthetic materials were also found in 81% of 185 stomachs of Cory's Shearwaters found dead during the northern winter on the shores of southern Brazil (Petry et al. 2009). Their effects on seabird populations are unknown, but as more and more plastic is used and discarded, increasing quantities are likely to be encountered and consumed by seabirds.

ACIDIFICATION OF HABITATS

Some other pollutants, in the amounts released, have little or no direct impact on living organisms, but can alter the physical and chemical environment so as to affect population levels. Combustion of coal and other industrial activities over the last 200 years has greatly increased the amounts of sulphur and other pollutants in the atmosphere. Such pollutants can be blown long distances, reaching areas up to several hundred kilometres from their source. One major consequence is the acidifying effect of sulphur dioxide and nitrogen oxides on rain. Analyses of stored rainwater samples extending back to the nineteenth century indicated progressive acidification at least until the 1980s. The impact of 'acid rain' on well-buffered soils is probably negligible, but on granitic or other poorly buffered soils, the pH of soils, streams and lakes can be lowered from 6–7 to 4–5 or less.[29] Normal precipitation has a pH range of 6.5–7.0, but pH values of less than 4.0 have been recorded from rainfall in parts of northwest Britain, and of less that 3.0 in parts of Scandinavia. Acidification has in turn affected the mobility of toxic metals (notably aluminium, mercury, cadmium and lead), which move from soils to waters and become generally more available to plants and animals, while calcium and magnesium become less available. The resulting impacts on invertebrate and fish populations have led in turn to declines in the bird populations that depend on them. Other identified effects on birds result from metal toxicity and reduced dietary calcium.

Acidification is particularly severe in parts of northwest Europe, eastern North America and southwest China, and is gradually spreading. In southern Norway, for example, which has high rainfall and a geologically vulnerable substrate, lakes in an area of more than 13,000 km^2 became practically devoid of fish, and in another 19,000 km^2 held much reduced fish stocks (Elsworth 1984). This represented a massive loss of habitat and food supply for inland fish-eating birds, including divers. In the absence of relevant studies, it is hard to say how many lakes on Scotland's acidic bedrock have been similarly affected, although fishermen claim that many western lakes are poorer in animal life than they used to be, and practically devoid of fish. First appearances are often deceptive, for acidified lakes typically have unusually clear water, caused by the settling of decaying organic matter. It seems strange that such clean-looking lakes should support so little life.

In any one region, the effects of acidification on the aquatic fauna are progressive, and involve threshold responses as the pH falls below about pH 6.5 (Schindler et al. 1989). In general, when the water reaches around pH 6.0, crustaceans and molluscs with mineralised shells find it hard to survive. Such creatures form an important source of calcium for many birds. At pH 5.5, many insects favoured by birds disappear, including mayflies, caddisflies and damselflies, though others remain. Among fish, salmonids and Roach start to go as the pH falls below 6.0, whitefish and Grayling at pH 5.5, followed by Perch and Pike at pH 5.0, and eels at pH 4.5. The loss of species occurs sequentially with increasing acidification because species differ in their physiology and susceptibility to toxic metals, as well as in their diets. As acidification continues, the end result is a sterile ecosystem capable of supporting only a limited range of species, and very few birds.

---

29 Nowadays *acid deposition* is a blanket term used to embrace several phenomena, including acid rain (pH less than 5.65), occult precipitation (weak solutions of sulphuric and nitric acid in mist and dew), dry deposition on plants and ground, and even heavy metals, released into the atmosphere from industrial and road traffic emissions.

FIG 213. The Dipper *Cinclus cinclus* lives at greater densities on streams with neutral or alkaline waters, holding abundant invertebrate prey, than on streams with acidic waters holding fewer prey items. As many streams have turned more acid over recent decades, Dipper numbers have declined. (Edmund Fellowes)

The main effects on aquatic birds result from changed food supplies (Blancher & McAuley 1987, Graveland 1990). As pH declines and fish disappear, some arthropods may become temporarily very abundant. This benefits some ducks, such as Goldeneye as well as dabbling ducks, including Mallard (Blancher & McAuley 1987, Parker *et al.* 1992). However, as pH falls more and invertebrates decline further, so do the ducks and other birds that depend on them. In southwest Sweden, a long-term decline in Osprey breeding success was halted in the 1980s following the liming of acidified lakes and the restoration of fish populations (Eriksson & Walter 1994), a process that must be continued if the fish are to stay, unless acidification ceases.

In Britain, high rainfall in western hill districts has multiplied sulphur and nitrogen deposition onto base-poor rocks and soils to affect extensive areas (Reynolds *et al.* 1999). In Wales, sections of half of the 24,000 km stream network became acidified to values less than pH 4–5.7 either chronically or intermittently (Edwards *et al.* 1990). Some land uses exacerbated this effect, especially conifer plantations at high altitudes (Fowler *et al.* 1989, Ormerod *et al.* 1989). Among Dippers in Wales, numbers counted along streams were positively correlated with the pH of the water, as were clutch sizes and breeding success (Ormerod *et al.* 1985, 1991). On one river system, recorded as becoming more acid over a 30-year period,

Dipper numbers declined in association with reduced food supplies. Among favoured food-items, the crustacean *Gammarus* was absent from acidified streams, while caddisfly and mayfly nymphs were present in much reduced numbers (Ormerod *et al.* 1985, 1991). Similar relationships between Dipper densities and stream acidity were described in southwest Scotland (Vickery 1991).

Acidification and calcium shortage

Other effects of acidification, affecting land-birds as well as aquatic ones, result from the reduced availability of calcium (through the disappearance of calcium-rich food sources) and increased exposure to toxic metals. Some passerine species which breed in acidified forest areas have failed to lay (instead incubating empty nests) or have shown shell-thinning, which leads to the breakage or desiccation of eggs (Carlsson *et al.* 1991, Graveland *et al.* 1994). In one area of the Netherlands, the proportion of Great Tit females that produced defective eggs rose from 10% in 1983–84 to 40% in 1987–88 (Graveland *et al.* 1994). This was associated with the leaching of calcium from acidified soils, reduction in vegetation, and consequent loss of snails, whose shells form a major source of calcium for laying songbirds. In one experiment, the provision of broken snail shells and chicken eggshells resulted in an improvement in the eggshells and breeding success of local tits (Graveland *et al.* 1994).

Similar calcium-related problems have been identified in various other insectivorous birds that nest beside acidified lakes, such as the Pied Flycatcher in northern Europe (Nyholm 1981). All affected species feed largely on insects that emerge from aquatic larvae, including aerial midges. Their diets are low in calcium and also often high in aluminium (released from acidified soils) which may disrupt calcium metabolism, enhancing the deficiency. Some aquatic bird species also have high mercury contents, a result of the conversion under acid conditions of inorganic mercury to the more readily absorbed methyl mercury.

Signs of recovery

Interest in acid rain peaked in the 1970s and 1980s, following which, in both Europe and North America, attempts were made to reduce sulphur and nitrogen oxide emissions. Throughout the 1990s, the rate of acidification on both continents slowed, and in some areas invertebrate and fish populations began to recover (Stoddard *et al.* 1999). In other areas on less favourable geological substrates, it may take many further years before lakes can be re-stocked with appropriate fish. Sulphur dioxide emissions in Britain have now declined to less than 15% of their peak in the 1970s and 1980s, with sulphur deposition falling in many locations by at least 50%.

The last full survey of Dippers on acid-sensitive sites in Wales was in 1995, and at this time it appeared that populations were still declining despite the first hints of chemical recovery, the latter being too weak or sustained to allow major ecological change (Buckton et al. 1998). Around Llyn Brianne in Wales, modest recovery of pH and slight reduction in aluminium had occurred by 2005 in streams flowing through grassy sheepwalk, but streams through catchments with conifer plantations showed no change in these respects. Recovering streams had gained four species of invertebrates out of a possible 30 (Ormerod & Durance 2009). In general, many streams in the British uplands are still too acidified, either continuously or episodically (during rainstorms) to achieve any more than partial or patchy recovery (Kowalik et al. 2007). Not surprisingly, Dippers are still thinly spread across the acid-sensitive uplands.

In general, it is hard to assess impacts of acid rain in Britain because of lack of historical information, but by analogy with other better-studied regions, we can assume that invertebrate, fish and bird populations of acidic lakes in northwest Britain are much reduced from what they once were. Owing to measures aimed at reducing sulphur pollution, the situation may be improving, and this is implied in the few measures available. The potentially much bigger problem resulting from the acidification of sea water was mentioned in Chapter 15.

Forest dieback

Air pollution is held responsible for forest dieback in several parts of the world, including montane areas in central Europe. These are again all areas with heavy rainfall on base-poor soils. The problem became evident in the 1970s, and has increased subsequently. Whether the trees die from exposure to air pollutants as such, from exposure to acidification or to aluminium and other toxic metals, or from shortages of calcium and other essential nutrients probably varies between areas, but the net result is loss of forest habitat, together with the acidification of streams, as discussed above.

In forests, as in aquatic habitats, the effects are progressive, depending on the initial base status of the soils and the rates of acid deposition. Some tree species appear more sensitive than others, and die at an earlier stage in the acidification process, with Silver Fir, Norway Spruce and Beech seeming particularly vulnerable in central Europe. The geographical scale of the problem is continually changing, but in 1986 in Europe, more than 190,000 km^2, or 14% of the total forest area, was classed as damaged (Nilsson & Duinker 1987). This damage was at various levels, but included some areas where whole forests had died, mainly near point sources of pollution, as in Silesia (Poland), Bohemia (Czech Republic) and some montane areas of Germany and Switzerland.

Whereas the trees are affected directly, the animal inhabitants are affected indirectly, through destruction of their habitat and food supplies. Most bird studies have involved comparisons of breeding numbers in plots showing different amounts of tree damage. On a gradient from completely healthy to completely dead, overall bird numbers declined, in studies in both Europe and North America (Desgranges *et al.* 1987, Oelke 1989, Graveland 1990). Species dependent on insects from foliage declined the most, while those dependent on insects from dead wood (such as woodpeckers) may have benefited temporarily, as may seed-eaters (because trees respond to adversity by seed production), but the net result in all studies was an overall decline in the numbers of species and individuals. In some studies, declines of up to 50% in overall bird densities on particular areas occurred within a five-year period (Flousek 1989), and over a longer period a high-density forest community was replaced by a sparse open-land one. To my knowledge, forest dieback from this cause has not been identified as a major problem in any part of Britain.

EUTROPHICATION

Not all pollutant effects are entirely negative. Over a certain range, some pollutants may cause environmental changes that favour some species at the expense of others. In recent decades, the widespread eutrophication of lowland and coastal waters, mainly by nitrates and phosphates (derived from fertilisers, sewage, animal wastes and domestic effluent) has led to changes in plant, invertebrate and fish populations, with resulting effects on birds. Impacts vary with the initial nutrient status of the water, because lakes and rivers vary naturally on a gradient from poor (*oligotrophic*) to rich (*eutrophic*). As nitrates and phosphates leach into nutrient-poor waters, underwater plants may grow, providing new substrates for invertebrates, more food and cover for fish, and a greatly increased food supply for both herbivorous and carnivorous birds. Salmonid and coregonid fish give way to coarse fish, initially percids and then cyprinids (such as Roach and Bream). These species mature early, and have high reproductive rates, so can perhaps support larger numbers of fish-eating birds. They also occur in shoals, so are easier than salmonids for most fish-eating birds to catch, despite the murky water in which they often live. Such fish populations can sometimes achieve a biomass exceeding 1,000 kg per hectare.

If nutrients continue to increase, however, algae multiply and cloud the water, reducing light penetration and causing losses of all the organisms that had previously benefited, from water-weeds to invertebrates and fish. Some algae and other microorganisms produce toxins that poison fish and the birds that eat them. As a result, massive bird mortalities have been recorded in both inland and coastal waters, from which affected species can take several years to recover (Chapter 9). In deep lakes, the dense algal populations may sink and their decomposition may de-oxygenate the water. Under extreme circumstances, the water may become almost lifeless.

The addition of organic matter to lakes and rivers, and its decomposition to support new life, is a natural process, but the addition of too much human sewage and other organic waste can result in problems because the bacteria that cause decomposition need oxygen to survive. Within limits, a river naturally re-aerates itself, but under heavy organic input the water can become devoid of oxygen, resulting in the deaths of fish and other animals. The bacteria that cause decay are sometimes replaced by anaerobic bacteria, which can trigger other processes inimical to most organisms. The problems are increased if river flow is reduced by the extraction of water for irrigation and other purposes. Most of the waters in lowland agricultural Britain now show some level of eutrophication, and not surprisingly, its effects have also become increasingly apparent in shallow coastal areas. On the other hand, the pollution of rivers by industrial effluent and sewage has been progressively reduced, and many inland waters have been restored to a level at which they again support a wide range of plants and animals. Agricultural chemicals remain as the principal problem pollutants.

Over the past 150 years the fresh and coastal waters around the British Isles have been subjected to a barrage of pollutants, many of which have acted to reduce plant and animal life. Besides pesticides, the continuing input of sewage has brought with it pharmaceuticals such as antibiotics and hormone-disrupting chemicals. These 'medical pollutants' are now attracting increasing attention, as they are likely to grow in importance as the years go by, not least because of their presence in drinking water.

CONCLUDING REMARKS

The chemical impacts described in this and the preceding chapter show that the effects of some pollutants may be indirect, delayed, unexpected and widespread. Pesticides have wide-scale effects because they are applied to large areas of land, and some other chemicals because they are dispersed widely from point sources by wind or water. They may then affect organisms hundreds or thousands of kilometres from places of production or use. Other pollutant effects may remain undetected, because they are not obvious, because they occur in remote areas, or because certain familiar phenomena are not recognised as resulting from pollution. Almost all the impacts discussed above are products of the last 150 years, and those of pesticides mainly of the last 60 years. They are therefore new forces in the population ecology of all organisms. One might reasonably ask, then, why pollution has been allowed to become so serious in so short a time.

One reason is that, traditionally, the polluter has not been required to pay the cost of his actions. The owners of factories that pollute the atmosphere have not paid for the deaths of remote forests, for the loss of fish from rivers or for the harm to human health. Nor has the farmer paid for the side-effects of his pesticides: the loss of wildlife, the pollution of drinking water and the human health effects. This is partly because such costs have been considered acceptable in the development of the modern industrial state, and partly because they are often intangible, difficult to pin down and to value in cash terms. Moreover, many problems, such as acidification, involve threshold effects that did not become apparent until the polluting activity had continued for many years. We may reasonably wonder how many other ecological time bombs lie in the offing.

Another reason for the problems is the application of restricted economics. The value of pesticide use, for example, is judged primarily on whether the extra crop yield that year exceeds the cost of the chemical used. It takes no account of any longer-term effects on soil productivity, future crops, water quality, loss of wildlife and human medical expenses. The costs of all these, where they can be expressed in cash terms, are borne by society at large, and at some later date, sometimes by future generations. Few other modern problems offer politicians more excuse for inaction. The evidence is often circumstantial and equivocal, remedies are always too uncertain, too difficult, too expensive or too long-term, and powerful corporate industries are often prepared to legally defend their activities to maintain the status quo. Obvious disasters to human health and well-being are usually needed before action is taken.

Having said all this, the situation with the most obvious of industrial pollutants in Britain has greatly improved since the 1950s when the first Clean Air Acts came into being. We now have cleaner air to breathe, industrial 'smogs' being a thing of the past, and many of our rivers are now clean enough for fish and other wildlife to thrive again. Yet again, the lesson is that it is worth tackling pollution problems: wildlife can respond in an improved environment, providing there are enough individuals left to sustain a recovery. The political response is slow, however: we may have cleaner air and cleaner water, but we have many other threats. In theory, one current problem easily solved would be that resulting from the continued use of lead in ammunition, ignorance and intransigence being the only apparent obstacles.

CHAPTER 20

Reflections

M Y AIM IN THIS FINAL CHAPTER is to highlight some of the principal findings on bird population limitation which have emerged over the past century or so, since detailed studies began. Over this period, we have moved from a time when many (perhaps most) bird species in Britain and Ireland were limited by human killing to a time when most are limited by more 'natural' factors (such as food, predation and parasitism), and only a small number by direct human killing. Developing technology has also provided other forms of bird mortality that were more localised or non-existent in the past, including effects of pesticides and pollutants, drowning by fishing gear, or collisions with buildings, wires and road traffic. At the same time, continuing atmospheric pollution is changing habitats in several ways that impact on bird and other animal populations.

One of the main findings to emerge from previous chapters is that all the natural factors that might constrain bird numbers – whether resources (notably food and nest-sites) or natural enemies (predators, parasites, pathogens and competitors) – have been shown unequivocally to do so, limiting bird breeding numbers at particular times and places. It also seems that particular groups of birds have in recent decades been more often limited by certain factors than by others: seabirds by food supply, raptors (where not killed by gamekeepers) by food supply and nest-sites, gamebirds and waders by predation, and some waterfowl and other birds by parasitic diseases. It is the species that depend on specialised nest-sites, such as tree-cavities, cliff-ledges or caves, whose breeding numbers are most often limited by shortages of nest-sites. However, the same bird species may be limited by different factors at different times or in different places.

It is also important, in considering limiting factors, to separate those that influence the general level of a population, or cause its progressive long-term change, from those that cause annual fluctuations. Long-term and short-term factors are often the same, but they can also differ. The general level of many bird populations might be determined by food supply, for example, while the annual fluctuations about this level might be influenced mainly by other factors, such as weather or disease outbreaks.

Weather influences bird populations mainly through its effects on habitat and food supply, acting over prolonged periods as during droughts and hard winters, or as short-lived storms or other events that can cause sudden catastrophic nest losses or adult deaths. Of all potential limiting factors, however, food supply seems to be of widest importance, and even in species whose adult populations are limited by some other agent, chick production is often affected by food availability (such as insects for Grey Partridge chicks). In some species, of course, human killing can override any natural limiting factor, and reduce numbers well below the level that would otherwise occur, with examples in the past from waterfowl, waders, seabirds, raptors and others. Among some raptors and fish-eaters, human killing is still acting to limit numbers and distributions in parts of Britain and Ireland.

Because different species of birds and other animals share some of the same resources, they sometimes compete, and the numbers of one can thereby influence the numbers of another. Experiments have confirmed that many birds can compete over both food and nest-sites. However, a largely unexplored problem concerns the competition that could occur between individuals from different populations of the same species which are found together in winter. It is hard to imagine that the huge numbers of ducks that visit the British Isles in winter have no effect on the local breeding populations with which they interact. In most species, the winter visitors far outnumber the local breeders. For example, only about 500 pairs of Wigeon breed in Britain and Ireland, compared with 500,000 that winter here, and less than 100 pairs of Pintail breed here, compared with 30,000 that winter. The breeders are so scarce that they seem to occupy only part of the nesting habitat available, but competition for winter food from visiting immigrants may be one of the factors involved, assuming that the two populations utilise the same resources. This has wide implications, because it could mean that the individuals in many bird breeding populations could be limited in numbers in this way. It is a potential consequence of any bird migration system which leads different breeding populations to share the same wintering area. It is a hitherto largely neglected issue in bird population ecology.

CORRELATIVE EVIDENCE

Much of what we know about population limitation in birds derives from correlations between bird numbers (N) and some limiting agent (L): when N varies in parallel with L, the relationship may be positive or negative. Numbers may increase along with growth in a food supply, or may decrease along with rising predator numbers. The problem with correlations, affecting most aspects of ecological science, is that they do not necessarily indicate cause and effect. N may be correlated with L because N influences L, or because L influences N, or because some third factor, T, influences both N and L independently. Alternatively, N and L may be correlated because they are totally unrelated but happen to change at the same time as one another under the influence of quite different factors. As an example, some bird species, such as the Woodpigeon and Buzzard, have increased greatly in recent decades as climate has warmed. However, on the basis of research, the increase in Woodpigeons can be attributed to the expanded cultivation of oilseed rape, an important winter food, and the increase in Buzzards to recovery from past persecution. Neither species has been affected by the other or in any obvious way by climate change, the correlations being entirely coincidental.

These examples also illustrate the problem that arises when two or more potential limiting factors change at the same time, making it hard to discern their separate effects on bird numbers. For example, in the late twentieth century, many species of farmland birds declined in Britain and Ireland, at a time when their food supplies were collapsing because of agricultural changes, but over the same period predator numbers were increasing and climate was changing. Use of statistical procedures, analysing all relevant variables together, has sometimes helped with bird data, by estimating the closeness of correlations between bird numbers and each independent variable after allowing for the effects of the others. But the most reliable testing procedures have involved experiments, where one variable was manipulated at a time, independently of the others, and the effect on the population monitored. Regarding the question of farmland birds, from both types of approach decline in food supply emerged as the major factor, at least in most declining species, but in some species predation may have had additional influence, or even played the major role (as perhaps in urban House Sparrows).

An example of a farmland species affected by more than one factor is the Grey Partridge, whose population collapse was brought about by three main changes on British farmland: first, the removal of hedgerows and other field boundaries (and hence nesting cover), which reduced the carrying capacity of the landscape for breeding pairs; second, reduced predator control, which increased the rate of nest failure; and third, the introduction of herbicides and insecticides, which greatly reduced the insect food supply for chicks (Potts 2012). Each of these factors contributed to the decline, but the last was probably most important because it resulted in populations becoming unsustainable at any density, whatever the other conditions. In recent years, the recovery in raptor numbers may have made it difficult for Partridges at low population densities in modern farmland to stage a recovery even if the summer food shortage is rectified. Other changes are needed, such as the provision of more cover.

EXPERIMENTAL EVIDENCE

Potential problems of assessing cause and effect from correlations are evident in many aspects of bird population work. Occasionally, the observer can make use of 'natural experiments' where some unpredicted change occurs, providing an opportunity to study its effects independently of other changes (such as the removal of raptors from large areas by organochlorine pesticides in the 1950s). But to reiterate, the most satisfactory way of addressing the question of cause and effect is by use of well-designed field experiments, manipulating one variable at a time and measuring its impact on local bird numbers, against an appropriate control in which the variable of interest is not altered.

Despite their costs, field experiments have been increasingly used in studies of bird populations. They have confirmed that all the potential factors that could limit bird numbers actually do so in specific circumstances. Most of the published experiments, discussed in earlier chapters, involved the manipulation of only one limiting factor at a time, such as food, nest-sites or predation. The provision of food or removal of predators led in extreme cases to a doubling of breeding densities, compared to control areas, but provision of nest-sites sometimes led to much bigger increases – up to 20-fold in the most pronounced examples.

The fact that most of the experimental results described in previous chapters confirmed the hypothesis being tested should not surprise us, because the experiments were usually done only after observational evidence had indicated what the main limiting factor might be. If species had been chosen at random for each type of manipulation, rather than on the basis of prior knowledge, fewer positive results might have emerged. The findings cannot therefore be expected to reflect the relative importance of different limiting factors in nature. Also, not all bird species lend themselves to small-scale field experiments, and those that do may not be typical of all bird species.

While it is clear that particular limiting factors have an overriding influence on certain species, it is also obvious that different mortality agents can interact with one another, and with weather and habitat structure, to limit numbers, and that the effects of different limiting factors may not always be additive. Food supplies can influence the vulnerability of birds to predators and parasitic diseases, while predators and parasites can in turn influence the extent to which birds can exploit their potential food supplies. Well-fed birds can afford to feed in less dangerous places, even if food is scarcer there than elsewhere, and can spend more time on vigilance, looking around for approaching predators. They can also afford to mount more vigorous immune responses against parasitic diseases, lessening their impacts. In contrast, birds weakened by food shortage can afford neither of these luxuries, and are therefore predisposed to the effects of predation and parasitism. Thus, even in populations that are clearly limited by food, the removal of predators or parasites might often be expected to lead to an increase in numbers because it enables existing food supplies to be more efficiently exploited.

In other cases, two mortality agents acting together might result in fewer deaths than one acting alone. For example, by continually removing diseased individuals from a population, predators might restrict the spread of the pathogen and thus prevent a large-scale lethal epidemic (Chapter 13). The population could thus be maintained at a higher level than would occur if predators were absent and the disease took hold. Similarly, many bird species have a non-renewing stock of food to last the winter, so that the removal of a proportion of individuals by predators or parasites before winter set in might reduce the rate at which food was depleted, and enable more birds to survive the winter than might otherwise have done so. Although both of these possibilities have emerged from field studies, neither can be considered as proven for birds, and further study of the combined effects of different limiting factors is needed. Nevertheless, the implication is that, just because a particular factor kills individuals and reduces numbers in the short term, paradoxically – through interactions with other factors – that same factor may actually increase numbers in the longer term. These and other examples show that different limiting factors may interact in various ways.

Birds come up against different constraints at different times of year, depending on whether they are breeding, moulting, migrating or simply surviving. Changes from one state to another alter the balance of risks, and the probability of dying from particular causes. In some bird species, the act of breeding, which normally occurs when food is plentiful, seems to increase the risks to the adults from predators and pathogens. Parents become vulnerable to predation because of the greater foraging and other activity that breeding entails, and the fact that they are tied to nesting places for long periods. Females of ground-nesting species, especially ducks and gamebirds, are often taken from their nests when incubating (Chapter 6). Adults are more vulnerable to parasitic diseases while breeding, because breeding is a time of stress when immune responses may be weakened, and because some parasites accumulate in nest-sites (Chapter 13).

Because mortality agents change in relative importance during the course of a year, this can influence our assessment of which factors are most important. Throughout this book the focus has been on spring breeding numbers, and in many species winter food supply emerges as the most influential limiting factor. But if we were concerned with late-summer post-breeding numbers, then weather, predation or parasitism would emerge as of overriding importance in some of these same species.

DENSITY-DEPENDENCE

This concept came initially from a simple observation. If a species is introduced to a new and favourable area, it at first increases rapidly, but is soon checked, and thereafter its numbers normally fluctuate between limits that are extremely restricted compared to what is theoretically possible (Lack 1954). It follows that natural populations are in some way regulated, in that the controlling factors act more severely when numbers are high than when they are low. The importance of such density-dependence in population regulation has long been recognised, but it is only in the last few decades that it has been measured. In this time, almost any demographic parameter, whether clutch size, nest success, survival of young or adults, has been found to vary in a density-dependent manner in one bird species or another, affecting increasing proportions of individuals as their numbers rise, and thereby serving to regulate numbers rather than merely limit them.

Such regulation occurs mainly through competition for food or other resources, or through the action of predators or parasites, all of which can affect an increasing proportion of individuals as their numbers grow. However, perhaps the most widespread regulating mechanism in birds is territorial behaviour, which, by constraining the numbers that can breed in limited habitat, can lead to the creation of a non-breeding 'surplus' of individuals – birds that are physiologically capable of breeding but are unable to do so through lack of a suitable territory or nest-site. Territorial behaviour can thus result in a progressive decline in the overall reproductive rate (the ratio of young to adults) as the total population of breeders and non-breeders rises. Finer adjustments occur through variations in habitat quality, when some birds are pushed into increasingly poorer habitats (defined by the poor survival or breeding of their occupants), as the total numbers in an area rise.

Not all factors that influence bird numbers act in a density-dependent manner. Some act independently of density, while others act in an inversely density-dependent manner, affecting a decreasing proportion of individuals as their numbers grow, and thereby accentuating fluctuations in numbers. Yet others act in a delayed density-dependent manner, acting to promote cyclic fluctuations in numbers (Chapter 2). Bird numbers fluctuate because of all the factors that act on them, however they relate to density, but it is those that act in a direct density-dependent manner that serve to keep numbers within limits, acting to resist boundless increase or extinction.

Compensatory mortality

One consequence of density-dependence is that a reduction in reproduction or survival rates brought about by one factor does not necessarily result in reduced breeding numbers. This is because increased losses from one cause may be offset by reduced losses from another. Such compensation is especially evident in species that suffer much predation and parasitism but are ultimately limited by winter food supplies. With the overall losses density-dependent, the numbers that starve to death are reduced if some individuals have already died from predation or parasitism. Much depends on the proportions and timing of deaths from different causes. Predation or parasitism may still be limiting if they kill more birds than would otherwise starve, or if they kill substantial numbers in late winter or spring, after deaths from starvation have already occurred and ended. Even then, their effects on the numbers of breeders may not be apparent by spring if the population still contains more individuals than could occupy all the available nesting territories or nest-sites. In these circumstances, predation and parasitism can kill many individuals, but without limiting breeding numbers. The same can hold for human killing, which forms the basis of sustainable hunting.

The impact of predators (or human hunters) thus depends partly on the proportion of individuals that they kill each year and partly on when these losses occur. Only when predators or hunters kill enough individuals to remove the non-breeding surplus do they also begin to reduce the numbers of breeders. This is not to say that individual breeding birds are protected from predation in the presence of non-breeders, only that when breeders are killed, they can be quickly replaced from the non-breeding surplus while ever it exists, so that up to a point breeder numbers can be maintained.

WITHSTANDING MORTALITY

Birds and other animals have such high annual death rates that their average age in the wild is far lower than the age to which they are capable of surviving. The high death rate is linked with high fecundity, for in a stable population the death rate balances the birth rate. People are often surprised at the level of mortality that some bird populations can withstand without it causing long-term decline in breeding numbers. This is especially true for short-lived species with high reproductive rates.

Take the Blue Tit, for example, in which, given a secure nest-site and a good food supply, each pair can produce an average of ten chicks per year, so that for every two birds at the start of the season there are twelve at the end. This implies that, if the breeding population is to remain stable from year to year, ten out of every twelve Blue Tits must die between the end of one breeding season and the start of the next, from whatever mortality causes operate locally. Of course, not all Blue Tit pairs can raise ten or more young, but this example makes the point that many small birds can die each year without reducing breeding numbers in the long term.

Even longer-lived species, with low reproductive rates, can also withstand substantial annual losses, again given secure nest-sites and good food supplies. The Guillemot, which produces at most one egg per year, is an interesting example, because it is hard to imagine a more disaster-prone species. In addition to much ongoing mortality from entanglement in fishing nets, and human hunting in parts of its winter range, it suffers occasional catastrophic losses from oil spillage and winter wrecks, some killing many thousands of birds in a short time. Despite these ongoing losses, breeding numbers in Britain and Ireland continued to increase through most of the twentieth century, rising by 32% between surveys in 1985–88 and 1998–2002. The species maintained its position as our commonest seabird, with an estimated 1.5 million pairs in Britain and Ireland by the end of the twentieth century.

Several factors contribute to this resilience. Despite the one-egg clutch, breeding success is generally high; and while Guillemots do not normally breed until they are about six years old, they can breed at a younger age if existing breeders suffer heavy losses, creating vacancies at breeding sites. In addition, during their early years of life, the young disperse widely, so no one mass mortality incident is likely to kill an entire cohort. Most of the recorded mass mortality events have involved chiefly immatures, many of which might in any case die before reaching breeding age. However, this resilience is possible only under an abundant food supply, as emphasised in Chapter 4.

MORTALITY AND EVOLUTION

Although mortality agents that kill individuals do not necessarily reduce breeding numbers, they can have major effects on the course of evolution, by influencing which individuals die and which survive to reproduce. It is through such selective mortality that all anti-predator and anti-parasite behaviour is likely to have evolved. Other things being equal, any individuals that possess inherent qualities that protect them against predators or parasites will survive in greater numbers than those lacking those features, and thus come to form increasing proportions of future generations. Similarly, competition could be a major force in affecting the morphology or behaviour of species, by selecting for inherent attributes that reduce the impacts of competition. Such natural selection might, for example, influence the bill structure of a species if this led to individuals of that species dealing more efficiently with foods also taken by competing species. In other words, such selection can promote and maintain ecological segregation between species. These evolutionary processes occur through the impact of mortality agents on individuals, regardless of whether or not these agents influence breeding densities or population trends.

TERRITORIAL BEHAVIOUR

Three questions have been repeatedly asked about territorial behaviour in birds and its role in population regulation. The first concerns the benefits to the individual. In many birds, territorialism in the breeding season provides a nest-site and a place to mate with minimal interference from other individuals, and in some species it also provides a feeding area from which other birds are excluded or at least restricted in access. A bird cannot breed without a nesting territory, even though in some species this territory may represent only a small area within a colony. There is thus no doubt about the value of a territory to the individual and little wonder that territories are strongly contested. The second question is whether, in dispersed species, territorial behaviour restricts breeding density, or merely spaces out individuals already limited in some other way. That territorial behaviour can restrict breeding density is clearly shown in many species by the proven existence of 'surplus' adults, which can breed only when a gap is made available through the death or removal of a territory owner. The third question is whether territorial spacing is related to local food resources. In raptors and others, the correlation between nest spacing and food supply in areas where nest-sites are not limiting strongly implies that this is so, as does the change in spacing observed in populations subject to change in food supply, whether this occurs naturally or as a result of experiments (Newton 1998). Since individuals hold larger territories in areas where food is scarce, this automatically sets breeding density at a lower level than where food is plentiful. Some observers have tended to confuse the consequences of territoriality for the individual with its consequences for the population, supposing that it served primarily to regulate population density. On present understanding, the most rational view is that territoriality serves to ensure that the individual obtains certain needs, including a restriction on other individuals in the vicinity. But with all birds behaving territorially for their own sakes, a limit to breeding density is also achieved.

Any bird that cannot obtain a territory must normally live as a non-territorial non-breeder, waiting until a vacancy becomes available. However, in limiting the numbers of breeders in a population, territorial behaviour must also indirectly limit the numbers of non-breeders too. This is because, once all available breeding places are occupied, with no room for further settlers, a ceiling is set both on the numbers of breeders and on the annual output of young. The maximum possible number of non-breeders would then be set at whatever level the annual inputs to the non-breeder contingent (mainly from reproduction) matched the annual losses (mainly from mortality and entry to the breeding sector). The numbers of non-breeders would then stabilise at that level, unless other factors were acting to reduce them (Newton 1992). On this basis, in some bird populations, non-breeders could outnumber breeders, as found in some long-lived species such as the Oystercatcher and Mute Swan (Ens *et al.* 1995, Meek 1993, Spray 1991).

* * * *

No birds in Britain and Ireland can now live in wholly natural environments (in the sense of being unperturbed by human activity). Human impacts – whether habitat destruction and degradation, pollution, direct killing, or control or introduction of predators – may have changed the relative importance of different limiting factors compared with long ago. But it is in this human-dominated environment in which the birds of Britain and Ireland now live, and in which conservation bodies seek to preserve viable populations for the benefit of future generations of people. With continuing human population growth, further demands on land and sea, and a changing climate, we can expect that bird populations will continue to change, and that further studies will be needed if we are to understand these changes, and take appropriate conservation measures in response to new situations. In an environmentally conscious society, therefore, the study of wild bird populations is likely to remain a scientific necessity for long into the future, and also a continuing source of fascination and pleasure for ornithologists.

References

Abrams, R. W. (1985). Pelagic seabird community structure in the southern Benguela region: changes in response to man's activities? *Biol. Conserv.* **32**, 33–49.

Adams, L., Hanavan, M. G., Hosley, N. W. & Johnston, D. W. (1949). The effects on fish, birds and mammals of DDT issued in the control of forest insects in Idaho and Wyoming. *J. Wildl. Manage.* **13**, 245–254.

Adcock, M. (1993). Essex storm. *BTO News* **185**, 20.

Aebischer, N. J. (1986). Retrospective investigation of an ecological disaster in the Shag, *Phalacrocorax aristotelis:* a general method based on long-term marking. *J. Anim. Ecol.* **55**, 613–29.

Aebischer, N. J. & Ewald, J. A. (2004). Managing the UK Grey Partridge recovery: population change, reproduction, habitat and shooting. *Ibis* **146** (S2), 181–91.

Aebischer, N. J. & Ewald, J. A. (2010). Grey Partridge *Perdix perdix* in the UK: recovery status, set-aside and shooting. *Ibis* **152**, 530–42.

Aebischer, N. J., Coulson, N. C. & Colebrook, J. M. (1990). Parallel long term trends across four marine tropic levels and weather. *Nature* **347**, 753–5.

Aho, T., Kuitunen, M., Suhonen, J., Jantti, A. & Hakkari, T. (1997). Behavioural responses of Eurasian Treecreepers, *Certhia familiaris*, to competition with ants. *Anim. Behav.* **54**, 1283–90.

Aho, T., Kuitunen, M., Suhonen, J., Jantti, A. & Hakkari, T. (1999). Reproductive success of Eurasian Treecreepers, *Certhia familiaris*, lower in territories with wood ants. *Ecology* **80**, 998–1007.

Alatalo, R. V. & Moreno, J. (1987). Body size, interspecific interactions, and use of foraging sites in tits (Paridae). *Ecology* **68**, 1773–7.

Alatalo, R. V., Gustafsson, L., Linden, M. & Lundberg, A. (1985). Interspecific competition and niche shifts in tits and the Goldcrest: an experiment. *J. Anim. Ecol.* **54**, 977–84.

Alatalo, R. V., Eriksson, D., Gustafsson, L. & Larsson, K. (1987). Exploitation competition influences the use of foraging sites by tits: experimental evidence. *Ecology* **68**, 284–90.

Albert, T. F. (1962). The effect of DDT on the sperm production of the domestic fowl. *Auk* **79**, 104–7.

Allen, D. L. (1954). *Our Wildlife Legacy.* Funk & Wagnalls, New York.

Allin, C. C., Chasko, G. G. & Husband, T. P. (1987). Mute Swans in the Atlantic Flyway: a review of the history, population growth and management needs. *Trans. Northeast Sect. Wildl. Soc.* **44**, 32–47.

Allison, A., Newton, I. & Campbell, C. R. G. (1974). *Loch Leven National Nature Reserve: a Study of Waterfowl Biology.* Wildfowlers Association of Great Britain and Ireland, Chester.

Amar, A. & Redpath, S. (2005). Habitat use by Hen Harriers *Circus cyaneus* on Orkney: implications of land use change for this declining population. *Ibis* **147**, 37–47.

Amar, A., Court, I. R., Davison, M. et al. (2012). Linking nest histories, remotely sensed land use data and wildlife crime records to explore the impact of grouse moor management on Peregrine Falcon populations. *Biol. Conserv.* **145**, 86–94.

Anderson, N. C., Grahn, R. A., van Hoosear, K. & Bondurant, R. H. (2009). Studies of trichonomonad protozoa in free ranging songbirds: prevalence of *Trichomonas gallinae* in House Finches (*Carpodacus mexicanus*) and corvids and a novel trichomonad in Mockingbirds (*Mimus polyglottos*). *Vet. Parasitol.* **161**, 178–86.

Anderson, R. M. & May, R. M. (1978). Regulation and stability of host–parasite population interactions: 1. Regulatory processes. *J. Anim. Ecol.* **47**, 219–49.

Anderson, R. M. & May, R. M. (1979). Population biology of infectious diseases. Part 1. *Nature* **280**, 361–7.

Anderson, T. R. (1990). Excess females in a breeding population of House Sparrow *Passer domesticus* (L.). In: *Proceedings, General Meetings of the Working Group on Granivorous Birds, INTECOL, 1986* (ed. J. Pinowski & J. D. Summers-Smith). Polish Scientific Publishers, Warsaw, pp. 87–93.

Andersson, M. & Wiklund, C. (1978). Clumping versus spacing out: experiments on nest predation in Fieldfares (*Turdus pilaris*). *Anim. Behav.* **26**, 1207–12.

Andrén, H. (1990). Despotic distribution, unequal reproductive success, and population regulation in the Jay *Garrulus glandarius* L. *Ecology* **71**, 1796–803.

Angelstam, P. (1983). Population dynamics of tetraonids, especially the Black Grouse *Tetrao tetrix* L. in boreal forests. PhD thesis, Uppsala University.

Angelstam, P. (1984). Sexual and seasonal differences in mortality of the Black Grouse *Tetrao tetrix* in boreal Sweden. *Ornis Scand.* **15**, 123–4.

Angelstam, P., Lindström, E. C. & Widén, P. (1984). Role of predation in short-term population fluctuations of some birds and mammals in Fennoscandia. *Oecologia* **62**, 199–208.

Angelstam, P., Lindström, E. & Widén, P. (1985). Synchronous short-term population fluctuations of some birds and mammals in Fennoscandia: occurrence and distribution. *Holarctic Ecology* **8**, 285–98.

Anker-Nilssen, T. (1987). The breeding performance of Puffins *Fratercula arctica* on Røst, northern Norway in 1979–85. *Fauna Norv. Ser C, Cinclus* **10**, 21–38.

Anker-Nilssen, T. & Aarvak, T. (2003). The population ecology of Puffins at Røst. Status after the breeding season 2002. *NINA Oppdragsmelding 784*.

Apanius, V. (1998). Stress and immune response. In: *Stress and Behavior* (ed. A. P. Møller, M. Milinski & P. J. B. Slater). Academic Press, New York. pp. 133–54.

Arcese, P. & Smith, J. N. M. (1988). Effects of population density and supplemental food on reproduction in Song Sparrows. *J. Anim. Ecol.* **57**, 119–36.

Arcese, P., Smith, J. N. M., Hochachka, W. M. & Ludwig, G. (1992). Stability, regulation and determination of abundance in an insular Song Sparrow population. *Ecology* **73**, 805–22.

Arendt, W. J. (1985). *Philornis* ectoparasitism of Pearly-eyed Thrashers, II. Effects on adults and reproduction. *Auk* **102**, 281–92.

Arlettaz, R., Schaad, M., Reichlin, T. S. & Schaub, M. (2010). Impact of weather and climate variation on Hoopoe reproductive ecology and population growth. *J. Ornithol.* **151**, 889–99.

Armstrong, I. H., Coulson, J. C., Hawkey, P. & Hudson, K. J. (1978). Further mass seabird deaths from paralytic shellfish poisoning. *Brit. Birds* **71**, 58–68.

Arnott, S. A. & Ruxton, G. D. (2002). Sandeel recruitment in the North Sea: demographic, climatic and trophic effects. *Marine Ecol. Prog. Ser.* **238**, 199–210.

Ashbrook, K., Wanless, S., Harris, M. P. & Hamer, K. C. (2008). Hitting the buffers: conspecific aggression undermines benefits of colonial breeding under adverse conditions. *Biol. Lett.* **4**, 630–3.

Ashford, R. W., Wyllie, I. & Newton, I. (1990). *Leucocytozoon toddi* in British Sparrowhawks *Accipiter nisus*: observations on the dynamics of infection. *J. Nat. Hist.* **24**, 1101–7.

Ashmole, N. P. (1963). The regulation of numbers of tropical oceanic birds. *Ibis* **103**, 458–73.

Askenmo, C. (1979). Reproductive effort and return rate of male Pied Flycatchers. *Amer. Nat.* **114**, 748–53.

Atkinson, P. W., Clark, N. A., Bell, M. C., Dare, P. J. & Ireland, P. L. (2003). Changes in commercially fished shellfish stocks and shorebird populations in the Wash, England. *Biol. Conserv.* **114**, 127–41.

Atkinson, P. W., Clark, N. A., Dodd, S. G. & Moss, D. (2005). Changes in fisheries practices and Oystercatcher survival, recruitment and body mass in a marginal cockle fishery. *Ardea* **93**, 199–212.

Avery, M. I., Suddaby, D., Ellis, P. M. & Sim, I. M. W. (1992). Exceptionally low body weights of Arctic terns *Sterna paradisaea* on Shetland. *Ibis* **134**, 87.

Avery, M. L., Pavelka, M. A., Bergman, D. L. *et al.* (1995). Aversive conditioning to reduce Raven predation on California Least Tern eggs. *Colonial Waterbirds* **18**, 131–8.

Axell, H. E. (1966). Eruptions of Bearded Tits during 1959–65. *Brit. Birds* **559**, 513–43.

Azzarello, M. Y. & van Vleet, E. S. (1987). Marine birds and plastic pollution. *Mar. Ecol. Prog. Ser.* **37**, 295–303.

Babcock, K. M. & Flickinger, E. L. (1977). Dieldrin mortality of Lesser Snow Geese in Missouri. *J. Wildl. Manage.* **41**, 100–103.

Bacon, P. J. & Andersen-Harild, P. (1989). Mute Swan. In: *Lifetime Reproduction in Birds* (ed. I. Newton). Academic Press, London, pp. 363–86.

Bagyura, J., Szitta, T., Haraszthy, L. *et al.* (2004). Population trend of the Saker Falcon in Hungary between 1980 and 2002. In: *Raptors Worldwide* (ed. R. D. Chancellor & B.-U. Meyburg). WWGBPO & MME/ Birdlife Hungary. Budapest, pp. 663–72.

Bailey, E. (1993). *Introduction of Foxes to Alaskan Islands: History, Effects on Avifauna and Eradication*. Resource Publication 193. US Fish & Wildlife Service, Washington DC.

Baillie, S. R. (1990). Integrated population monitoring of breeding birds in Britain and Ireland. *Ibis* **132**, 151–66.

Baillie, S. R. & Peach, W. J. (1992). Population limitation in Palaearctic–African migrant passerines. *Ibis* **134** (S1), 120–32.

Baillie, S. R., Clark, N. A. & Ogilvie, M. A. (1986). *Cold Weather Movements of Waterfowl and Waders: an Analysis of Ringing Recoveries*. British Trust for Ornithology Research Report 19. BTO, Tring.

Baines, D. (1990). The roles of predation, food

and agricultural practice in determining the feeding success of the Lapwing *Vanellus vanellus* on upland grasslands. *J. Anim. Ecol.* **59**, 915–29.

Baines, D. (1996). The implications of grazing and predator management on the habitats and breeding success of Black Grouse *Tetrao tetrix. J. Appl. Ecol.* **33**, 54–62.

Baines, D., Sage, R. B. & Baines, M. M. (1994). The implications of Red Deer grazing to ground vegetation and the invertebrate communities of Scottish native pinewoods. *J. Appl. Ecol.* **31**, 776–83.

Baines, D., Baines, M. M. & Sage, R. B. (1995). The importance of large herbivore management to woodland grouse and their habitats. In: *Proceedings of the International Symposium on Grouse, Vol. 6.* World Pheasant Association, Reading, pp. 93–100.

Baines, D., Redpath, S., Richardson, M. & Thirgood, S. (2008). The direct and indirect effects of predation by Hen Harriers *Circus cyaneus* on trends in breeding birds on a Scottish grouse moor. *Ibis* **150** (Suppl. 1), s27–36.

Bairlein, F. (1996). Long-term ecological studies on birds. *Verh. Dtsch. Zool. Ges.* **89**, 165–79.

Baker, P. J., Molony, S. E., Stone, E., Cuthill, I. C. & Harris, S. (2008). Cats about town: is predation by free-ranging pet cats *Felis catus* likely to affect urban bird populations? *Ibis* **150** (S1), 86–99.

Balfour, E. (1955). Kestrels nesting on the ground in Orkney. *Bird Notes* **26**, 245–53.

Ball, K. E. (1950). Breeding behaviour of the Ring-necked Pheasant on Pelee Island, Ontario. *Can. Field Nat.* **64**, 201–7.

Bang, J., Jensen, B. & Sunde, P. (2005). Woodpigeons *Columba palumbus* breeding in open land associate with Kestrel *Falco tinnunculus* nests. *Bird Study* **52**, 93–5.

Barker, R. J. (1958). Notes on some ecological effects of DDT sprayed on elms. *J. Wildl. Manage.* **22**, 269–74.

Barnard, C. J. (1979). Interactions between House Sparrows and Sparrowhawks. *Brit. Birds* **72**, 569–73.

Barnard, C. J. (1980). Flock feeding and time budgets in the House Sparrow (*Passer domesticus*). *Anim. Behav.* **28**, 295–309.

Barrett, G. W. (1968). The effects of an acute insecticide stress on a semi-enclosed grassland ecosystem. *Ecology* **49**, 1019–35.

Barrett, R. T. & Vader, W. (1984). The status and conservation of seabirds breeding in Norway. In: *Status and Conservation of the World's Seabirds* (ed. J. P. Croxall, P. G. H. Evans & R. W. Schreiber). International Council for Bird Preservation, Cambridge.

Barry, T. W. (1962). Effects of late seasons on Atlantic Brant reproduction. *J. Wildl. Manage.* **26**, 19–26.

Bartholomew, G. A., Howell, T. R. & Cade, T. J. (1957). Torpidity in the White-throated Swift, Anna Hummingbird and Poorwill. *Condor* **59**, 145–55.

Batten, L. A. (1973). Population dynamics of suburban Blackbirds. *Bird Study* **20**, 251–8.

Baudvin, H. (1975). Biologie de reproduction de la Chouette effraie (*Tyto alba*) en Cote d'Or: premiers resultants. *Jean-de-Blair* **14**, 1–51.

Bauer, Z., Trnka, M., Baurova, J. *et al.* (2010). Changing climate and phonological response of Great Tit and Collared Flycatcher populations in floodplain forest ecosystems in Central Europe. *Int. J. Biometeorol.* **54**, 99–111.

Bayliss, M. (1988). Cuckoo X breaks records. *BTO News* **159**, 7.

Beale, C. & Monaghan, P. (2004). Behavioural responses to human disturbance: a matter of choice. *Anim. Behav.* **68**, 1065–9.

Beale, C. M., Burfield, I. J., Sim, I. M. W. *et al.* (2006). Climate change may account for the decline in British Ring Ouzels *Turdus torquatus*. *J. Anim. Ecol.* **75**, 826–35.

Bearhop, S., Hilton, G. M., Votier, S. C. & Waldron, S. (2004). Stable isotope ratios indicate that body condition in migrating passerines is influenced by winter habitat. *Proc. R. Soc. Lond. B* **271** (Suppl. 4), s215–18.

Becker, P. H. (1991). Population and contamination studies in coastal birds: the Common Tern *Sterna hirundo*. In: *Bird Population Studies: Relevance to Conservation and Management* (ed. C. M. Perrins, J.-D. Lebreton & G. J. M. Hirons). Oxford University Press, Oxford, pp. 433–60.

Beebe, F. L. (1960). The marine Peregrines of the northwest Pacific coast. *Condor* **62**, 145–89.

Beintema, A. J. & Muskens, G. J. D. M. (1987). Nesting success of birds breeding in Dutch agricultural grasslands. *J. Appl. Ecol.* **24**, 743–58.

Belik, V. & Mikalevich, I. (1995). The pesticides use in the European steppes and its effects on birds. Research Notes on Avian Biology: selected contributions from the 21st International Ornithological Congress. *J. Ornithol.* **135**, 233.

Bell, C. P., Baker, S. W., Parkes, N. G., Brooke, M. de L. & Chamberlain, D. E. (2010). The role of the Eurasian Sparrowhawk *Accipiter nisus* in the decline of the House Sparrow *Passer domesticus* in Britain. *Auk* **127**, 411–20.

Bellrose, F. C. (1959). Lead poisoning as a mortality factor in waterfowl populations. *Bull. Illinois Nat. Hist. Surv.* **27**, 235–88.

Bellrose, F. C. (1980). *Ducks, Geese and Swans of North America.* Stackpole Books, Harrisburg, Pennyslvania.

Bellrose, F. C., Scott, T. G., Hawkins, A. S. & Low, J. B. (1961). Sex ratios and age ratios in North American ducks. *Bull. Illinois Nat. Hist. Surv.* **27**, 391–474.

Bellrose, F. C., Johnstone, K. L. & Meyers, T. C. (1964). Relative value of natural cavities and nesting houses for Wood Ducks. *J. Wildl. Manage.* **28**, 661–76.

Bengston, S. A. (1963). On the influence of snow upon the nesting success in Iceland 1961. *Vår Fågelvärld* **22**, 77–122.

Benkman, C. W. (1997). Feeding behaviour, flock-size dynamics, and variation in sexual selection in Crossbills. *Auk* **114**, 163–78.

Bennett, G. F., Caines, J. R. & Bishop, M. A. (1988). Influence of blood parasites on the body mass of passeriform birds. *J. Wildl. Dis.* **24**, 339–43.

Bennett, G. F., Peirce, M. A. & Ashford, R. W. (1993). Avian hematozoa: mortality and pathogenicity. *J. Nat. Hist.* **27**, 993–1001.

Benton, T. G., Bryant, D. M., Cole, L. & Crick, H. Q. P. (2002). Linking agricultural practice to insect and bird populations: a historical study over three decades. *J. Appl. Ecol.* **39**, 673–87.

Berg, H. (1995). Modelling of DDT dynamics in Lake Kariba, a tropical man-made lake, and its implications for the control of tsetse flies. *Ann. Zool. Fenn.* **32**, 331–53.

Bergerud, A. T., Mossop, D. H. & Myrberget, S. (1985). A critique of the mechanics of annual changes in Ptarmigan numbers. *Can. J. Zool.* **63**, 2240–8.

Bernard, R. F. (1966). DDT residues in avian tissues. *J. Appl. Ecol.* **3** (Suppl. 1), s193–8.

Berthold, P. (2001). *Bird Migration: a General Survey*, 2nd edition. Oxford University Press, Oxford.

Bevanger, K. (1995). Estimates and population consequences of tetraonid mortality caused by collisions with high tension power lines in Norway. *J. Appl. Ecol.* **32**, 745–53.

Bibby, C. J. & Lloyd, C. S. (1977). Experiments to determine the fate of dead birds at sea. *Biol. Conserv.* **12**, 295–309.

Biebach, H. (1996). Energetics of winter and migratory fattening. In: *Avian Energetics and Nutritional Ecology* (ed. C. Carey). Chapman & Hall, London, pp. 280–323.

Bierman, J. M., Fairbairn, J. P., Petty, S. J. et al. (2006). Changes over time in the spatiotemporal dynamics of cyclic populations of Field Voles (*Microtus agrestis* L.). *Amer. Nat.* **167**, 583–90.

Bijleveld, M. (1974). *Birds of Prey in Europe*. Macmillan, London.

Bijlsma, R. (1984). [On the breeding association between Woodpigeons *Columba palumbus* and Hobbies *Falco subbuteo*.] *Limosa* **57**, 133–9.

Bijlsma, R. G. (1990). Predation by large falcons on wintering waders on the Banc d'Arguin, Mauritania. *Ardea* **78**, 75–82.

Bijlsma, R. G. (1991). Trends in European Goshawks *Accipiter gentilis*: an overview. *Bird Census News* **4**, 3–47.

Birkhead, M. (1982). Causes of mortality in the Mute Swan on the River Thames. *J. Zool. Lond.* **198**, 15–25.

Birkhead, M. & Perrins, C. M. (1985). The breeding biology of the Mute Swan *Cygnus olor* on the River Thames with special reference to lead poisoning. *Biol. Conserv.* **32**, 1–11.

Birkhead, T. R. (1977). The effect of habitat and density on breeding success in Common Guillemot (*Uria aalge*). *J. Anim. Ecol.* **46**, 751–64.

Birkhead, T. R. & Furness, R. W. (1985). Regulation of seabird populations. In:

Behavioural Ecology (ed. R. M. Sibly & R. H. Smith), Blackwell, Oxford, pp. 145–67.

Birkhead, T. R. & Nettleship, D. (1995). Arctic Fox influence on a seabird community in Labrador: a natural experiment. *Wilson Bull.* **107**, 397–412.

Birkhead, T. R., Eden, S. F., Clarkson, K., Goodburn, S. F. & Pellatt, J. (1986). Social organisation of a population of Magpies *Pica pica*. *Ardea* **74**, 59–68.

Birt, V. L., Birt, T. P., Goulet, D., Cairns, D. K. & Montevecchi, N. A. (1987). Ashmole's halo: direct evidence for prey-depletion by a seabird. *Mar. Ecol. Prog. Ser.* **40**, 205–8.

Bize, P., Roulin, A., Bersier, L. F., Pfluger, D. & Richner, H. (2003). Parastism and developmental plasticity in Alpine Swift nestlings. *J. Anim. Ecol.* **72**, 633–9.

Bize, P., Roulin, A., Tella, J., Bersier, L. F. & Richner, H. (2004). Additive effects of ectoparasites over reproductive attempts in the long-lived Alpine Swift. *J. Anim. Ecol.* **73**, 1080–8.

Bize, P., Klopfenstein, A., Jeanneret, C. & Roulin, A. (2007). Intra-individual variation in body temperature and pectoral muscle size in nestling Alpine Swifts *Apus melba* in response to an episode of inclement weather. *J. Ornithol.* **148**, 387–93.

Blancher, P. J. & McAuley, D. G. (1987). Influence of wetland acidity on avian breeding success. *Trans. N. A. Wildl. Nat Res. Conf.* **52**, 628–35.

Blancher, P. J. & Robertson, R. J. (1985). Predation in relation to spacing of Kingbird nests. *Auk* **102**, 654–8.

Blem, C. R. (1990). Avian energy storage. *Curr. Ornithol.* **7**, 59–113.

Block, B. (2009). Long-term trends in population densities and reproductive success of Long-eared Owl *Asio otus* in Brandenburg, Germany. *Ardea* **97**, 439–43.

Blondel, J., Pradel, R. & Lebreton, J.-D. (1992). Low fecundity insular Blue Tits do not survive better as adults than high fecundity mainland ones. *J. Anim. Ecol.* **61**, 205–13.

Blount, J. D., Houston, D. C., Møller, A. P. & Wright, J. (2003). Do individual branches of immune defence correlate? A comparative case study of scavenging and non-scavenging birds. *Oikos* **102**, 340–50.

Blus, L. J. (1982). Further interpretation of the relation of organochlorine residues in Brown Pelican eggs to reproductive success. *Environ. Pollut.* **28**, 15–33.

Boatman, N., Brickle, N., Hart, J. D. et al. (2004). Evidence for the indirect effects of pesticides on farmland birds. *Ibis* **146** (S2), 131–43.

Boddington, D. (1960). Unusual mortality of young Puffins on St Kilda, 1959. *Scott. Birds* **1**, 218–20.

Bolton, M. (1996). Energy expenditure, body-weight and foraging performance of Storm Petrels *Hydrobates pelagicus* breeding in artificial nest chambers. *Ibis* **138**, 405–9.

Bolton, M., Medeiros, R., Hothersall, B. & Campos, A. (2004). The use of artificial breeding chambers as a conservation measure for cavity-nesting procellariiform seabirds: a case study of the Madeiran Storm Petrel (*Oceanodroma castro*). *Biol. Conserv.* **116**, 73–80.

Bolton, M., Tyler, G., Smith, K. & Bamford, R. (2007). The impact of predator control on Lapwing *Vanellus vanellus* breeding success on wet grassland nature reserves. *J. Appl. Ecol.* **44**, 534–44.

Booth, D. T., Clayton, D. H. & Block, B. A. (1993). Experimental demonstration of the energetic cost of parasitism in wild hosts. *Proc. R. Soc. Lond. B* **253**, 125–9.

Booth, V. & Morrison, P. (2010). Effectiveness of disturbance methods and egg removal to deter large gulls *Larus* spp. from competing with nesting tern *Sterna* spp. on Coquet Island RSPB reserve, Northumberland, England. *Conserv. Evid.* **7**, 39–43.

Borg, K., Wanntorp, H., Erne, K. & Hanko, E. (1969). Alkyl mercury poisoning in terrestrial Swedish wildlife. *Viltrevy* **6**, 301–79.

Borralho, R., Rito, A., Rego, F., Simões, H. & Pinto, P. V. (1998). Summer distribution of Red-legged Partridges *Alectoris rufa* in relation to water availability on Mediterranean farmland. *Ibis* **140**, 620–5.

Both, C. (1998). Experimental evidence for density dependence of reproduction in Great Tits. *J. Anim. Ecol.* **67**, 667–74.

Both, C. & Visser, M. E. (2001). Adjustment to climatic change is constrained by arrival date in a long-distance migratory bird. *Nature* **411**, 296–8.

Both, C., Artemyev, A. V., Blaauw, B. et al. (2004). Large-scale geographical variation confirms that climate change causes birds to lay earlier. *Proc R. Soc. Lond. B.* **271**, 1657–62.

Both, C., Bouwhuis, S., Lessells, C. M. & Visser, M. E. (2006). Climate change and population declines in a long-distance migratory bird. *Nature* **441**, 81–83.

Both, C., van Turnhout, C. A. M., Bijlsma, R. G. et al. (2010). Avian population consequences of climate change are most severe for long-distance migrants in seasonal habitats. *Proc. R. Soc. B.* **277**, 1259–66.

Botzler, R. G. (1991). Epizootiology of avian cholera in wildfowl. *J. Wildl. Dis.* **27**, 367–95.

Boulinier, T. & Danchin, E. (1996). Population trends in Kittiwake *Rissa tridactyla* colonies in relation to tick infestation. *Ibis* **138**, 326–34.

Bourne, W. R. P. (1968). Oil pollution and bird populations. *Field Studies* **2** (Suppl), 200–18.

Bourne, W. R. P. (1970). Special review: after the 'Torrey Canyon' disaster. *Ibis* **112**, 120–5.

Bourne, W. R. P. (1999). The past status of the herons in Britain. *Bull. B. O. C.* **119**, 192–6.

Bourne, W. R. P., Parrack, J. D. & Potts, G. R. (1967). Birds killed in the Torrey Canyon disaster. *Nature* **215**, 1123–5.

Boyce, D. G., Lewis, M. R. & Worm, B. (2010). Global phytoplankton decline over the past century. *Nature* **466**, 591–6.

Boyd, H. (1954). The 'wreck' of Leach's Petrels in the autumn of 1954. *Brit. Birds* **47**, 137–63.

Bradley, M., Johnstone, R., Court, G. & Duncan, T. (1997). Influence of weather on breeding success of Peregrine Falcons in the Arctic. *Auk* **114**, 786–91.

Brand, C. J. (1984). Avian cholera in the Central and Mississippi flyways during 1979–1980. *J. Wildlife Manage.* **48**, 399–406.

Bregnballe, T., Madsen, J. & Rasmussen, P. A. F. (2004). Effects of temporal and spatial hunting control on waterbird reserves. *Biol. Conserv.* **19**, 93–104.

Brickle, N. W. & Harper, D. G. (2002). Agricultural intensification and the timing of breeding of Corn Buntings *Miliaria calandra*. *Bird Study* **49**, 219–28.

Brickle, N. W., Harper, D. G. C., Aebischer, N. J. & Cockayne, S. H. (2000). Effects of agricultural intensification on the breeding success of Corn Buntings *Emberiza calandra*. *J. Appl. Ecol.* **37**, 742–55.

Brindley, E., Mudge, G., Dymond, M. *et al.* (1999). The status of Arctic Terns at Shetland and Orkney in 1994. *Atlantic Seabirds* **1**, 135–43.

Brinkhof, M. W. G. & Cavé, A. S. (1997). Food supply and seasonal variation in fledging success: an experiment in the European Coot. *Proc. R. Soc. Lond. B* **264**, 291–6.

Brittas, R., Marcström, V., Kenward, R. E. & Karlbom, M. (1992). Survival and breeding success of reared and wild Ring-necked Pheasants in Sweden. *J. Wildl. Manage.* **56**, 368–76.

Brittingham, M. C. & Temple, S. A. (1988). Impacts of supplemental feeding on survival rates of Black-capped Chickadees. *Ecology* **69**, 581–9.

Bro, E., Reitz, F., Clobert, J., Migot, P. & Massot, M. (2001). Diagnosing the environmental causes of the decline in Grey Partridge *Perdix perdix* in France. *Ibis* **143**, 120–32.

Broggi, J. & Brotons, L. (2001). Coal Tit fat-storing patterns during the non-breeding season: the role of residence status. *J. Avian Biol.* **32**, 333–7.

Broggi, J., Langset, M., Ronning, B., Welcker, J. & Bech, C. (2010). Parent Kittiwakes experience a decrease in cell-mediated immunity as they breed. *J. Ornithol.* **151**, 723–7.

Brockman, H. J. & Barnard, C. J. (1979). Kleptoparasitism in birds. *Anim. Behav.* **27**, 487–514.

Brommer, J. E. (2004). The range margins of northern birds shift northwards. *Ann. Zool. Fennici* **41**, 391–7.

Bromssen, A. V. & Jansson, C. (1980). Effects of food addition to Willow Tit *Parus montanus* and Crested Tit *P. cristatus* at the time of breeding. *Ornis Scand.* **11**, 173–8.

Brooke, M. de L. (1979). Differences in the quality of territories held by Wheatears (*Oenanthe oenanthe*). *J. Anim. Ecol.* **48**, 21–32.

Brooke, M. de L. (1992). *The Manx Shearwater*. Poyser, Calton.

Brooke, M. de L., Douse, A., Haysom, S., Jones, F. C. & Nicolson, A. (2002). The Atlantic Puffin population of the Shiant Islands, 2000. *Scott. Birds* **23**, 22–6.

Brothers, N. P., Cooper, J. & Løkkeborg, S. (1999). The incidental catch of seabirds by longline fisheries: worldwide review and technical guidelines for mitigation. *FAO Fisheries Circular* **937**.

Brown, A. (1978). *Ecology of Pesticides*. Wiley, New York.

Brown, A., Price, D., Slader, P. *et al.* (2011). Seabirds on Lundy: their current status, recent history and prospects for the restoration of a once-important bird area. *Brit. Birds* **104**, 139–58.

Brown, A., Gilbert, G. & Wotton, S. (2012). Bitterns and Bittern conservation in the UK. *Brit. Birds* **105**, 58–87.

Brown, C. R. & Brown, M. B. (1986). Ectoparasitism as a cost of coloniality in Cliff Swallows (*Hirundo pyrrhonata*). *Ecology* **67**, 1206–18.

Brown, C. R. & Brown, M. B. (2000). Weather-mediated natural selection on arrival time in Cliff Swallows (*Petrochelidon pyrrhonata*). *Behav. Ecol. Sociobiol.* **47**, 339–45.

Browne, S. J. & Aebischer, N. J. (2001). *The Role of Agricultural Intensification in the Decline of the Turtle Dove* Streptopelia turtur. English Nature Research Report 421. English Nature, Peterborough.

Browne, S. J. & Aebischer, N. J. (2003). Temporal changes in the migration phenology of Turtle Doves *Streptopelia turtur* in Britain, based on sightings from coastal bird observatories. *J. Avian Biol.* **34**, 66–71.

Bryant, D. M. (1975). Breeding biology of the House Martin *Delichon urbica*, in relation to aerial insect abundance. *Ibis* **117**, 180–215.

Bryant, D. M. & Jones, G. (1995). Morphological changes in a population of Sand Martins *Riparia riparia* associated with fluctuations in population size. *Bird Study* **42**, 57–65.

Bucher, E. H. (1988). Do birds use biological control against nest parasites? *Parasitol. Today* **4**, 1–3.

Buck, N. A., Estesen, B. J. & Ware, G. W. (1983). DDT moratorium in Arizona: residues in soil and alfalfa after 12 years. *Bull. Environ. Contam. Toxicol.* **31**, 66–72.

Buckton, S. T., Brewin, P. A., Lewis, A., Stevens, P. & Ormerod, S. J. (1998). The distribution of Dippers, *Cinclus cinclus* (L.), in the acid-sensitive region of Wales, 1984–95. *Freshwater Biol.* **39**, 387–96.

Buckwell, A. & Armstrong-Brown, S. (2004). Changes in farming and future prospects: technology and policy. *Ibis* **146** (S2), 14–21.

Buenestado, F. J., Rerreras, P., Blanco-Aguiar, J. A., Tortosa, F. S. & Villafuerte, R. (2009). Survival and causes of mortality among wild Red-legged Partridges *Alectoris rufa* in southern Spain: implications for conservation. *Ibis* **151**, 720–30.

Bull, K. R., Every, W. J., Freestone, P. et al. (1983). Alkyl lead pollution and bird mortalities on the Mersey Estuary, U.K. 1979–81. *Environ. Pollut. A* **31**, 239–59.

Bumpus, H. (1899). The elimination of the unfit as illustrated by the introduced sparrow, *Passer domesticus*. *Mar. Biol. Lab., Biol. Lect. (Woods Hole, 1898)* 209–28.

Burgess, E. C., Ossa, J. & Yuill, T. M. (1979). Duck plague: a carrier state in waterfowl. *Avian Dis.* **24**, 940–9.

Burn, A. (2000). Pesticides and their effects on lowland farmland birds. In: *Ecology and Conservation of Lowland Farmland Birds* (ed. N. J. Aebischer, A. D. Evans, P. V. Grice & J. A. Vickery). British Ornithologists' Union, Tring, pp. 89–104.

Burton, J. F. (1995). *Birds and Climate Change*. Christopher Helm, London.

Busche, G., Raddatz, H.-J. & Kostrzewa, A. (2005). Nistplatz-Koncurrenz und Prädation zwichen Uho (*Bubo bubo*) und Habicht (*Accipiter gentilis*): erste Ergebnisse aus Norddeutschland. *Die Vogelwarte* **42**, 169–77.

Bustnes, J. O., Anker-Nilssen, T. & Lorentsen, S.-H. (2010). Local and large-scale climatic variables as predictors of the breeding numbers of endangered Lesser Black-backed Gulls on the Norwegian coast. *J. Ornithol.* **151**, 19–26.

Buxton, N. E. (2007). Common Goldeneye. In: *The Birds of Scotland* (ed. R. Forrester & I. J. Andrews). Scottish Ornithologists' Club, Aberlady, pp. 271–4.

Byrkjedal, I. & Thompson, D. (1998). *Tundra Plovers: the Eurasian, Pacific and American Golden Plovers and Grey Plover*. Poyser, London.

Cabot, D. & West, B. (1973). Population dynamics of Barnacle Geese *Branta leucopsis* wintering on the Inishkea Islands, Co. Mayo. 1. Population dynamics 1961–1983. *Irish Birds* **2**, 318–36.

Cadbury, C. J. (1978). The Beached Bird Survey and other seabird surveillance. *Ibis* **120**, 119–20.

Cade, T. J., Enderson, J. H., Thelander, C. G. & White, C. M. (1988). *Peregrine Falcon Populations: Their Management and Recovery*. The Peregrine Fund, Boise, Idaho.

Cadiou, B., Bioret, F. & Chesseneau, D. (2010). Response of breeding European Storm Petrels *Hydrobates pelagicus* to habitat change. *J. Ornithol.* **151**, 317–27.

Cain, A. P. & Hillgarth, N. (1974). Nesting relationships between *Columba palumbus* and *Milvus migrans*. *Doñana Acta Vert.* **1**, 97–102.

Caldow, R. W. G. & Furness, R. W. (2000). The effect of food availability on Great Skuas *Catharacta skua* and Arctic Skuas *Stercorarius parasiticus*. *J. Avian Biol.* **31**, 367–75.

Calladine, J., Baines, D. & Warren, P. (2002). Effects of reduced grazing on population density and breeding success of Black Grouse in northern England. *J. Appl. Ecol.* **39**, 772–780.

Campbell, L., Cayford, J. & Pearson, D. (1996). Bearded Tits in Britain and Ireland. *Brit. Birds* **89**, 335–46.

Campbell, L. H. (1984). The impact of changes in sewage treatment on seaducks wintering in the Firth of Forth, Scotland. *Biol. Conserv.* **28**, 173–80.

Campbell, L. H. & Cooke, A. S. (eds). (1997). *The Indirect Effects of Pesticides on Birds*. Joint Nature Conservation Committee, Peterborough.

Camphuysen, C. J. (2007). *Chronic Oil Pollution in Europe: a Status Report*. Royal Netherlands Institute for Sea Research and International Fund for Animal Welfare.

Camphuysen, C. J., Ens, B. T., Heg, D. et al. (1996). Oystercatcher *Haematopus ostralegus* winter mortality in the Netherlands: the effect of severe weather and food supply. *Ardea* **84A**, 469–92.

Camphuysen, C. J., Wright, P. J., Leopold, M., Hüppop, O. & Reid, J. B. (1999). A review of the causes, and consequences at the population level, of mass mortalities of seabirds. In: *Diets of seabirds and* consequences of changes in food supply (ed. R. W. Furness & M. L. Tasker). ICES Cooperative Research Report 232.

Camphuysen, C. J., Berrevoets, C. M., Cremers, H. J. W. M. et al. (2002). Mass mortality of Common Eiders (Somateria mollissima) in the Dutch Wadden Sea, winter 1999/2000: starvation in a commercially exploited wetland of international importance. Biol. Conserv. 106, 303–17.

Caraco, T., Martindale, S. & Pulliam, H. R. (1980). Avian time budgets and distance to cover. Auk 97, 872–5.

Carillo, J. & Gonzales-Davila, E. (2010). Impact of weather on breeding success of the Eurasian Kestrel Falco tinnunculus in a semi-arid island habitat. Ardea 98, 51–8.

Carlsson, H., Carlsson, L., Wallin, C. & Wallin, N.-E. (1991). Great Tits incubating empty nest cups. Ornis Svec. 1, 51–2.

Carroll, M. J., Dennis, P., Pearce-Higgins, J. W. & Thomas, C. D. (2011). Maintaining northern peatland ecosystems in a changing climate: effects of soil moisture, drainage and drain blocking on craneflies. Global Change Biol. 17, 2991–3001.

Carss, D. N. (1994). Killing of piscivorous birds at Scottish finfish farms, 1984–1987. Biol. Conserv. 68, 181–8.

Carss, D. N. & Elkins, G. R. (2002). Futher European integration: mixed subspecies colonies of Great Cormorants in Britain – colony establishment, diet, and implications for fisheries management. Ardea 90, 23–41.

Casey, S., Moore, N., Ryan, L. et al. (1995). The Roseate Tern Conservation Project on Rockabill, Co. Dublin: a six year review 1989–1994. Irish Birds 5, 251–64.

Catry, I., Franco, A. M. A. & Sutherland, W. J. (2011). Adapting conservation efforts to face climate change: modifying nest site provisioning for Lesser Kestrels. Biol. Conserv. 144, 1111–19.

Cavé, A. J. (1968). The breeding of the Kestrel, Falco tinnunculus L., in the reclaimed area Oostelijk Flevoland. Netherlands J. Zool. 18, 313–407.

Cavé, A. J. (1983). Purple Heron survival and drought in tropical West Africa. Ardea 71, 217–24.

Cavé, A. J. & Visser, J. (1985). Winter severity

and breeding bird numbers in a Coot population. Ardea 73, 129–38.

Cawthorne, R. A. & Marchant, J. H. (1980). The effects of the 1978/79 winter on British bird populations. Bird Study 27, 163–72.

Chamberlain, D. E. & Wilson, J. D. (2000). The contribution of hedgerow structure to the value of organic farms to birds. In: Ecology and Conservation of Lowland Farmland Birds (ed. N. J. Aebischer, A. D. Evans, P. V. Grice & J. A. Vickery). British Ornithologists' Union, Tring, pp. 57–68

Chamberlain, D. E., Wilson, J. D. & Fuller, R. J. (1999). A comparison of bird populations on organic and conventional farmland in southern Britain. Biol. Conserv. 88, 307–20.

Chamberlain, D. E., Gosler, A. G. & Glue, D. E. (2007). Effects of the winter beechmast crop on bird occurrence in British gardens. Bird Study 54, 120–6.

Chandler, R. J. (1981). Influxes into Britain and Ireland of Red-necked Grebes and other water birds during winter 1978/79. Brit. Birds 74, 55–81.

Charles, J. K. (1972). Territorial behaviour and the limitation of population size in Crows, Corvus corone and Corvus cornix. PhD thesis, University of Aberdeen.

Charmantier, A., McCleery, R. H., Cole, L. R. et al. (2008). Adaptive phenotypic plasticity in response to climate change in a wild bird population. Science 320, 800–3.

Charter, M., Meyrom, K., Leshem, Y. et al. (2010). Does nest box location and orientation affect occupation rate and breeding success of Barn Owls Tyto alba in a semi-arid environment? Acta Ornithol. 45, 115–19.

Chen, D. & Hale, R. C. (2010). A global review of polybrominated diphenyl ether flame retardant contamination in birds. Environment International 36, 800–11.

Cheylan, G. (1973). Notes sur la compétition entré l'Aigle royal Aquila chrysaetos et l'Aigle de Bonelli Hieraaétus fasciatus. Alauda 41, 303–12.

Christe, P., Richner, H. & Oppliger, A. (1993). Begging, food provision and nestling competition in Great Tit broods infected with ectoparasites. Behav. Ecol. 7, 127–31.

Christe, P., Oppliger, A. & Richner, H. (1994). Ectoparasites affect choice and use of roost sites in the Great Tit *Parus major*. *Anim. Behav.* **47**, 895–8.

Christensen, K. D., Jacobsen, E. M. & Nøhr, H. (1996). A comparative study of bird faunas in conventionally and organically farmed areas. *Dansk. Orn. Foren. Tidsskr.* **90**, 21–8.

Christensen, T. K. (2008). Factors affecting population size of Baltic Common Eiders *Somateria mollissima*. Dissertation, Department of Ecology and Biodiversity. Aarhus University: National Environment Research Institute.

Christensen, T. K., Bregnballe, T., Anderson, T. H. & Duz, H. H. (1997), Outbreak of pasteurellosis among wintering and breeding Common Eiders *Somateria mollissima* in Denmark. *Wildl. Biol.* **3**, 125–8.

Churcher, P. B. & Lawton, J. H. (1987). Predation by domestic cats in an English village. *J. Zool. Lond.* **212**, 439–55.

Cichón, M., Olejniczak, P. & Gustafsson, L. (1998). The effect of body condition on the cost of reproduction in female Collared Flycatchers *Ficedula albicollis*. *Ibis* **140**, 128–30.

Clark, J. A. (2009). Selective mortality of waders during severe weather. *Bird Study* **56**, 96–102.

Clark, J. A., Baillie, S. R., Clark, N. A. & Langston, R. H. W. (1993). *Estuary Wader Capacity Following Severe Weather Mortality*. British Trust for Ornithology Research Report 103. BTO, Thetford.

Clark, L. & Mason, J. R. (1985). Use of nest material as insecticidal and antipathogenic agents by the European Starling. *Oecologia* **67**, 169–76.

Clark, R. G., Meger, D. E. & Ignatiuk, J. B. (1995). Removing American Crows and duck nest success. *Can. J. Zool.* **73**, 518–22.

Clarke, R. B. (1984). Impact of oil pollution on seabirds. *Environ. Poll.* **33**, 1–22.

Clayton, D. H. (1990). Mate choice in experimentally parasitised Rock Doves: lousy males lose. *Amer. Zool.* **30**, 251–62.

Clayton, D. H. (1991). Coevolution of avian grooming and ectoparasite avoidance. In: *Bird–Parasite Interactions* (ed. J. E. Loye & M. Zuk). Oxford University Press, Oxford, pp. 258–89.

Clayton, D. H. & Wolfe, N. D. (1993). The adaptive significance of self medication. *Trends Ecol. Evol.* **8**, 60–3.

Colton, J. B., Knapp, F. D. & Burns, B. R. (1974). Plastic particles in surface waters of the northwestern Atlantic. *Science* **185**, 491–7.

Colvile, K. M., Lawson, B., Pocknell, A. M. *et al.* (2012). Chlamydiosis in British songbirds. *Vet. Rec.* **171**, 177.

Committee of Inquiry on Grouse Disease (1911). *The Grouse in Health and in Disease*. Smith, Elder & Co, London.

Conan, G., Dunnet, G. M. & Crisp, D. J. (1982). The long-term effects of the *Amoco Cadiz* oil spill. *Phil. Trans. R. Soc. Lond. B* **297**, 323–3.

Connell, J. H. (1983). On the prevalence and relative importance of interspecific competition: evidence from field experiments. *Amer. Nat.* **122**, 611–96.

Connors, P. G. & Smith, K. G. (1982). Oceanic plastic particle pollution: suspected effect on fat deposition in Red Phalaropes. *Mar. Poll. Bull.* **13**, 18–20.

Conrad, K. F., Warren, M. F., Fox, R., Parsons, M. S. & Woiwood, I. P. (2006). Rapid declines of common, widespread British moths provide evidence of an insect biodiversity crisis. *Biol. Conserv.* **132**, 279–91.

Cooke, A. S. (1973). Shell-thinning in avian eggs by environmental pollutants. *Environ. Poll.* **4**, 85–152.

Cooke, A. S. (1975). The effects of fishing on waterfowl on Grafham Water. *Cambridge Bird Club* **48**, 40–6.

Cooke, B. K. & Stringer, A. (1982). Distribution and breakdown of DDT in orchard soil. *Pestic. Sci.* **13**, 545–51.

Coombes, C. (1996). Parasites, biodiversity and ecosystem stability. *Biodiv. Conserv.* **5**, 953–62.

Cooper, J. E. & Petty, S. J. (1988). Trichomoniasis in free-living Goshawks (*Accipiter gentilis gentilis*) from Great Britain. *J. Wildl. Dis.* **24**, 80–7.

Coulson, J. C. (1983). The changing status of the Kittiwake *Rissa tridactyla* in the British Isles 1969–1979. *Bird Study* **30**, 9–16.

Coulson, J. C. (1984). The population dynamics of the Eider Duck *Somateria mollissima* and evidence of extensive non-breeding by adult ducks. *Ibis* **126**, 525–43.

Coulson, J. C. (1991). The population dynamics of culling Herring Gulls and Lesser Black-backed Gulls. In: *Bird Population Studies: Relevance to Conservation and Management* (ed. C. M. Perrins, J.-D. Lebreton & G. J. M. Hirons). Oxford University Press, Oxford, pp. 479–7.

Coulson. J. C. (2010). A long-term study of the population dynamics of Common Eiders *Somateria mollissima*: why do several parameters fluctuate markedly? *Bird Study* **57**, 1–18.

Coulson, J. C. (2011). *The Kittiwake*. Poyser, London.

Coulson, J. C. & Strowger, J. (1999). The annual mortality rate of Black-legged Kittiwakes in NE England from 1954 to 1968 and a recent exceptionally high mortality. *Waterbirds* **22**, 3–13.

Coulson, J. C. & Thomas, C. S. (1985). Changes in the biology of the Kittiwake *Rissa tridactyla*: a 31-year study of a breeding colony. *J. Anim. Ecol.* **54**, 9–26.

Coulson, J. C. & Wooller, R. D. (1976). Differential survival rates among breeding Kittiwake Gulls *Risa tridactyla* (L). *J. Anim. Ecol.* **45**, 205–13.

Coulson, J. C., Potts, G. R., Deans, I. R. & Fraser, S. M. (1968). Exceptional mortality of Shags and other seabirds caused by paralytic shellfish poison. *Brit. Birds* **61**, 381–404.

Coulson, J. C., Duncan, N. & Thomas, C. (1982). Changes in the breeding biology of the Herring Gull (*Larus argentatus*) induced by reduction in the size and density of the colony. *J. Anim. Ecol.* **51**, 739–56.

Cowardin, L. M., Shaffer, T. L. & Kraft, K. M. (1995). How much habitat management is needed to meet Mallard production objectives. *Wildl. Soc. Bull.* **23**, 48–55.

Cowie, R. J. & Simons, J. R. (1991). Factors affecting the use of feeders by garden birds: 1. The positioning of feeders with respect to cover and housing. *Bird Study* **38**, 145–50.

Cowley, E. & Siriwardena, G. M. (2005). Long-term variation in survival rates of Sand Martins *Riparia riparia*: dependence on breeding and wintering ground weather, age and sex, and their population consequences. *Bird Study* **52**, 237–51.

Craik, J. C. A. (1995). Effects of North American Mink on the breeding success of terns and smaller gulls in west Scotland. *Seabird* **17**, 3–11.

Craik, J. C. A. (1997). Long term effects of North American Mink *Mustela vison* on seabirds in western Scotland. *Bird Study* **44**, 303–9.

Craik, J. C. A. (1998). Recent mink-related declines of gulls and terns in western Scotland and the beneficial effects of Mink control. *Argyll Bird Report* **14**, 98–110.

Craik, J. C. A. (1999). Breeding success of Common Gulls *Larus canus* in west Scotland: I. Observations at a single colony. *Atlantic Seabirds* **1**, 169–81.

Cramp, S., Condor, P. J. & Ash, J. (1962). *Deaths of Birds and Mammals from Toxic Chemicals.* Second Report of the Joint Committee of the British Trust for Ornithology, the Royal Society for the Protection of Birds and the Game Research Association.

Cresswell, W. (1994). Age-dependent choice of Redshank (*Tringa totanus*) feeding location: profitability or risk. *J. Anim. Ecol.* **63**, 589–600.

Cresswell, W. (2008). Non-lethal effects of predation risk in birds. *Ibis* **150**, 3–17.

Cresswell, W. & McCleery, R. (2003). How Great Tits maintain synchronization of their hatch date with food supply in response to long-term variability in temperature. *J. Anim. Ecol.* **72**, 356–66.

Cresswell, W. & Whitfield, D. P. (1994). The effects of raptor predation on wintering wader populations at the Tyninghame Estuary, southeast Scotland. *Ibis* **136**, 223–32.

Cresswell, W. & Whitfield, D. P. (2008). How starvation risk in Redshanks *Tringa totanus* results in predation mortality from Sparrowhawks *Accipiter nisus*. *Ibis* **150** (S1), 209–18.

Cresswell, W., Lind, J. & Quinn, J. L. (2010). Predator hunting success and prey vulnerability: quantifying the spatial scale over which lethal and non-lethal effects of predation occur. *J. Anim. Ecol.* **79**, 556–62.

Crick, H. Q. P. (2004). The impact of climate change on birds. *Ibis* **146** (S1), 48–56.

Crick, H. Q. P. & Ratcliffe, D. A. (1995). The Peregrine, *Falco peregrinus* breeding population of the United Kingdom in 1991. *Bird Study* **42**, 1–19.

Crick, H. Q. P. & Sparks, T. H. (1999). Climate related to egg-laying trends. *Nature* **399**, 423–4.

Crick, H. Q. P., Dudley, C., Glue, D. E. & Thomson, D. L. (1997). UK birds are laying eggs earlier. *Nature* **388**, 526.

Cross, D. E. (2010). Effects of feeding stations on population density and breeding success of the Red Kite in mid Wales. *Boda Wennol* **25**, 26–7.

Crosse, J. D., Shore, R. F., Wadsworth, R. A., Jones, K. C. & Pereira, M. G. (2012). Long-term trends in PBDEs in Sparrowhawk (*Accipiter nisus*): eggs indicate sustained contamination of UK terrestrial ecosystems. *Environ. Sci. Technol.* **46**, 13504–11.

Crossner, K. A. (1977). Natural selection and clutch size in the European Starling. *Ecology* **58**, 885–92.

Crouter, R. A. & Vernon, E. H. (1959). Effects of Black-headed Budworm control on salmon and trout in British Columbia. *Can. Fish. Cult.* **24**, 23–40.

Dahl, E. L., Bevanger, K., Nygard, T., Røskaft, E., Stokke, B. G. (2012). Reduced breeding success in White-tailed Eagles at Smøla windfarm, western Norway, is caused by mortality and displacement. *Biol. Conserv.* **145**, 79–85.

Dallinga, J. H. & Schoenmakers, S. (1989). Population changes of the White Stork *Ciconia ciconia* since the 1850s in relation to food resources. In: *White Stork: Status and Conservation* (ed. G. Rheinwald, J. Ogden & H. Schulz). Dachverband Deutscher Avifaunisten, International Council for Bird Preservation, Bonn, pp. 231–62.

Danchin, E. (1992). The incidence of the tick parasite *Ixodes uriae* in Kittiwake colonies in relation to the age of the colony, and a mechanism of infecting new colonies. *Ibis* **134**, 134–41.

Danchin, E., Boulinger, T. & Massot, M. (1998). Conspecific reproductive success and breeding habitat selection: implications for the study of coloniality. *Ecology* **79**, 2415–28.

Dane, D. S. (1948). A disease of Manx Shearwaters (*Puffinus puffinus*). *J. Anim. Ecol.* **17**, 158–64.

Dare, P. (1961). Ecological observations on a breeding population of the Common Buzzard *Buteo buteo*. PhD thesis, Exeter University.

Davenport, D. L. (1982). Influxes into Britain of Hen Harriers, Long-eared Owls and Short-eared Owls in winter 1978/79. *Brit. Birds* **75**, 309–16.

Davey, C. M., Chamberlain, D. E., Newson, S. E., Noble, D. G. & Johnston, A. (2011). Rise of the generalists: evidence for climate driven homogenization in avian communities. *Global Ecol. Biogeog.* **21**, 568–78.

Davidson, N. C. & Evans, P. R. (1982). Mortality of Redshanks and Oystercatchers from starvation during severe weather. *Bird Study* **29**, 183–8.

Davies, J. C. & Cooke, F. (1983). Annual nesting production in Snow Geese: prairie droughts and arctic springs. *J. Wildl. Manage.* **47**, 291–6.

Davies, Z. G., Fuller, R. A., Loram, A. *et al.* (2009). A national scale inventory of resource provision for biodiversity within domestic gardens. *Biol. Conserv.* **142**, 761–71.

Davis, M. B. (1981). Quaternary history and the stability of forest communities. In: *Forest Succession: Concepts and Application* (ed. D. C. West, H. H. Shugart & D. B. Botkin). Springer, New York, pp. 132–53.

Davis, P. E. & Newton, I. (1981). Population and breeding of Red Kites in Wales over a 30-year period. *J. Anim. Ecol.* **50**, 759–72.

Davis, S. E., Nager, R. G. & Furness, R. W. (2005). Food availability affects adult survival as well as breeding success of Parasitic Jaegers. *Ecology* **86**, 1047–56.

Dawson, A. & Visser, M. E. (2010). The effects of temperature on photoperiodic repsonses: implications for climate change. *BOU Proceedings: Climate Change and Birds*. http://www.bou.org.uk/bouproc-net/ccb/dawson&visser.pdf.

Debout, G., Rov, N. & Sellars, R. M. (1995). Status and population development of Cormorants *Phalacrocorax carbo carbo* breeding on the Atlantic coast of Europe. *Ardea* **83**, 47–59.

Deerenberg, C., Arpanius, V., Daan, S. & Bos, N. (1997). Reproductive effort decreases antibody responsiveness. *Proc. R. Soc. Lond. B* **264**, 1021–9.

De Leon, A., Minguez, E., Harvey, P. *et al.* (2006). Factors affecting breeding distribution of Storm-petrels *Hydrobates pelagicus* in Orkney and Shetland. *Bird Study* **53**, 64–72.

Delius, J. D. (1965). A population study of Skylarks *Alauda arvensis. Ibis* **167**, 466–92.

de Lope, F. & Møller, A. P. (1993). Effects of ectoparasites on reproduction of their Swallow hosts: a cost of being multi-brooded. *Oikos* **67**, 557–62.

de Lope, F., Gonzalez, G., Perez, J. J. & Møller, A. P. (1993). Increased detrimental effects of ectoparasites on their bird hosts during adverse environmental conditions. *Oecologia* **95**, 234–40.

de Lope, F., Møller, A. P. & de la Cruz, C. (1998). Parasitism, immune response and reproductive success in the House Martin *Delichon urbica. Oecologia* **114**, 188–93.

de Neve, L., Soler, J. J., Ruiz-Rodríguez, M. *et al.* (2007). Habitat-specific effects of a food supplementation experiment on immunocompetence in Eurasian Magpie *Pica pica* nestlings. *Ibis* **149**, 763–73.

den Held, J. D. (1981). Population changes of the Purple Heron in relation to drought in the wintering area. *Ardea* **69**, 185–91.

Dennis, R. (2008). *A Life of Ospreys*. Whittles, Dunbeath.

Desgranges, J. L., Manuffette, Y. & Gagnon, G. (1987). Sugar maple forest decline and implications for forest insects and birds. *Trans. N. A. Wildl. Nat. Res. Conf.* **52**, 677–89.

Desholm, M., Christensen, T. K., Scheiffarth, G. *et al.* (2002). Status of the Baltic/Wadden Sea population of the Common Eider *Somateria m. mollissima. Wildfowl* **53**, 167–203.

Desrochers, A., Hannon, S. J. & Nordin, K. E. (1988). Winter survival and territory acquisition in a northern population of Black-capped Chickadees. *Auk* **105**, 727–36.

Deuel, B. (1985). Experimental lead dosing of Northern Pintails in California. *California Fish & Game* **71**, 125–8.

Devictor, V., Julliard, R., Couvet, D. & Jiguet, F. (2008). Birds are tracking climate change but not fast enough. *Proc. R. Soc. B* **275**, 2743–8.

Dhondt, A. A. (1989). Ecological and evolutionary effects of interspecific competition in tits. *Wilson Bulletin* **101**, 198–216.

Dhondt, A. A. (2012). *Interspecific Competition in Birds*. Oxford University Press, Oxford.

Dhondt, A. A. & Adriaensen, F. (1999). Experiments on competition between Great and Blue Tit: effects on Blue Tit reproductive success and population processes. *Ostrich* **70**, 39–48.

Dhondt, A. A. & Eyckerman, R. (1980). Competition between the Great Tit and the Blue Tit outside the breeding season in field experiments. *Ecology* **61**, 1291–6.

Dhondt, A. A., Kempenaers, B. & Clobert, J. (1998). Sparrowhawk *Accipiter nisus* predation and Blue Tit *Parus caeruleus* adult annual survival rate. *Ibis* **140**, 580–4.

Dierschke, V. (2003). Predation hazard during migratory stopover: are light or heavy birds under risk? *J. Avian Biol.* **34**, 24–9.

Dietrich, D. R., Schmid, P., Zweifel, U. *et al.* (1995). Mortality of birds of prey following field application of granular carbofuran: a case study. *Arch. Environ. Contam. Toxicol.* **29**, 140–45.

Dietz, M. W. & Piersma, T. (2007). Red Knots give up flight capacity and defend food processing capacity during winter starvation. *Functional Ecol.* **21**, 899–904.

Dijkstra, C., Vuursteen, L., Daan, S. & Masman, D. (1982). Clutch-size and laying date in the Kestrel *Falco tinnunculus*: effects of supplementary food. *Ibis* **124**, 210–13.

Dijkstra, C., Bult, A., Bijlsma, S. *et al.* (1990). Brood size manipulations in the Kestrel (*Falco tinnunculus*): effects on offspring and parent survival. *J. Anim. Ecol.* **59**, 269–85.

Dixon, A., Richards, C., Lawrence, A. & Thomas, M. (2003). Peregrine (*Falco peregrinus*) predation on racing pigeons (*Columba livia*) in Wales. In: *Birds of Prey in a Changing Environment* (ed. D. B. A. Thompson, S. M. Redpath, A. H. Fielding, M. Marquiss & C. A. Galbraith). The Sationery Office, Edinburgh, pp. 255–61.

Dobinson, H. M. & Richards, A. J. (1964). The effects of the severe winter of 1962/63 on birds in Britain. *Brit. Birds* **59**, 373–434.

Dobson, A. P. & Hudson, P. J. (1992). Regulation and stability of a free-living host–parasite system: *Trichostrongylus tenuis* in Red Grouse. II. Population models. *J. Anim. Ecol.* **61**, 487–98.

Dobson, A. P. & May, R. M. (1991). Parasites, cuckoos and avian population dynamics. In: *Bird Population Studies: Relevance to Conservation and Management* (ed. C. M. Perrins, J.-D. Lebreton & G. J. M. Hirons). Oxford University Press, Oxford, pp. 391–412.

Dolton, C. S. & Brooke, M. de L. (1999). Changes in the biomass of birds breeding in Great Britain, 1968–88. *Bird Study* **46**, 274–8.

Donald, P. F. & Evans, A. D. (1994). Habitat selection by Corn Buntings in winter. *Bird Study* **41**, 199–210.

Donald, P. F., Evans, A. D., Muirhead, L. B. *et al.* (2002). Survival rates, causes of failure and productivity of Skylark *Alauda arvensis* nests on lowland farmland. *Ibis* **144**, 652–64.

Doswald, N., Willis, S. G., Collingham, Y. C. *et al.* (2009). Potential impacts of climate change on the breeding and non-breeding ranges and migration distance of European *Sylvia* warblers. *J. Biogeog.* **36**, 1194–208.

Dowell, S. D. (1992). Problems and pitfalls of gamebird reintroduction and restocking: an overview. *Gibier Faune Sauvage* **9**, 773–80.

Doxa, A., Theodorou, K., Hatzilhacou, D., Crivelli, A. & Robert, A. (2010). Joint effects of inverse density-dependence and extreme environmental variation on the viability of a social bird species. *Ecoscience* **17**, 203–15.

Draycott, R. A. H., Hoodless, A. N., Woodburn, M. I. A. & Sage, R. B. (2008). Nest predation of Common Pheasants *Phasianus colchicus*. *Ibis* **150** (S1), 37–44.

Duckett, J. E. (1984). Barn Owls (*Tyto alba*) and the second generation rat-baits utilised in oil palm plantations in Peninsular Malaysia. *Planter, Kuala Lumpur* **60**, 3–11.

Duebbert, H. F. & Kantrud, H. A. (1974). Upland duck nesting related to land use and predator reduction. *J. Wildl. Manage.* **38**, 257–65.

Duebbert, H. F. & Lokemoen, J. T. (1980). High duck nesting success in a predator-reduced environment. *J. Wildl. Manage.* **44**, 428–37.

Du Feu, C. R. (1992). How tits avoid flea infestation at nest-sites. *Ringing & Migration* **13**, 120–1.

Duffy, D. C. (1983). Competition for nesting space among Peruvian guano birds. *Auk* **100**, 680–8.

Dugan, P. J., Evans, P. R., Goodyer, L. R. & Davidson, N. C. (1981). Winter fat reserves in shorebirds: disturbance of regulated levels by severe weather conditions. *Ibis* **123**, 359–63.

Duncan, J. S., Reid, H. W., Moss, R., Philips, J. D. P. & Watson, A. (1979). Ticks, louping ill and Red Grouse on moors in Speyside, Scotland. *J. Wildl. Manage.* **42**, 500–5.

Duncan, N. (1978). Effects of culling Herring Gulls (*Larus argentatus*) on recruitment and population dynamics. *J. Appl. Ecol.* **15**, 697–713.

Dunlop, C. L., Blokpoel, H. & Jarvie, S. (1991). Nesting rafts as a management tool for a declining Common Tern (*Sterna hirundo*) colony. *Colonial Waterbirds* **14**, 116–20.

Dunn, E. K. (1977). Predation by Weasels (*Mustela nivalis*) on breeding tits (*Parus* spp.) in relation to the density of tits and rodents. *J. Anim. Ecol.* **46**, 633–52.

Dunn, E. K. & Mead, C. J. (1982). Relationships between sardine fisheries and recovery rates of ringed terns in West Africa. *Seabird* **6**, 98–104.

Dunn, E. K. & Steel, C. (2001). *The Impact of Longline Fishing on Seabirds in the North-east Atlantic: Recommendations for Reducing Mortality*. RSPB, Sandy.

Dunn, P. O. (2004). Breeding dates and reproductive performance. In: *Birds and Climate Change* (ed. A. P. Møller, W. Fiedler & P. Berthold). *Adv. Ecol. Res.* **35**, 69–87.

Dunnet, G. M. & Patterson, I. J. (1968). The Rook problem in north-east Scotland. In: *The Problems of Birds as Pests* (ed. R. K. Murton & E. N. Wright). Academic Press, London, pp. 119–39.

Durell, S. E. A. le V. Dit, Goss-Custard, J. D., Clarke, R. T. & McGrorty, S. (2000). Density-dependent mortality in Oystercatchers *Haematopus ostralegus*. *Ibis* **142**, 132–8.

East, M. L. & Perrins, C. M. (1988). The effect

of nestboxes on breeding populations of birds in broadleaved temperate woodlands. *Ibis* **130**, 393–401.

Eastin, W. C. & Hoffman, D. J. (1979). Biological effects of petroleum on aquatic birds. In: *Proceedings of the Conference on Assessment of Ecological Impacts of Oil Spills* (ed. C. C. Bates). American Institute of Biological Sciences, Arlington, Virginia, pp. 561–82.

Ebbinge, B. S. & Spaans, B. N. (1995). The importance of body reserves accumulated in spring staging areas in the temperate zone for breeding in Dark-bellied Brent Geese *Branta b. bernicla* in the High Arctic. *J. Avian Biol.* **26**, 105–13.

Eccles, M. A. (1939). Le rôle des oiseaux dans la propagation de la fièvre aphteuse. *Bull. Int. Office Epizootics* **18**, 118.

Edington, J. M. & Edington, M. A. (1972). Spatial patterns and habitat partitioning in the breeding birds of an upland wood. *J. Anim. Ecol.* **41**, 331–57.

Edwards, M. & Richardson, A. J. (2004). Impact of climate change on marine pelagic phenology and trophic mismatch. *Nature* **430**, 881–4.

Edwards, R. (1996). *Sea Empress Environmental Evaluation Committee Initial Report.* Sea Empress Environmental Evaluation Committee, Cardiff.

Edwards, R. W., Stoner, J. H. & Gee, A. S. (1990). *Acid Waters in Wales.* Kluwer, Dordrecht.

Eglington, S. M. & Pearce-Higgins, J. W. (2012). Disentangling the relative importance of changes in climate and land-use intensity in driving recent bird population trends. *PLoS One* **7** (3), e30407.

Eglington, S. M., Gill, J. A., Smart, M. A. et al. (2009). Habitat management and patterns of predation of Northern Lapwings on wet grasslands: the influence of linear habitat structures at different spatial scales. *Biol. Conserv.* **142**, 314–24.

Ekman, J., Cederholm, G. & Askenmo, C. (1981). Spacing and survival in winter groups of Willow Tit *Parus montanus* and Crested Tit *Parus cristatus*: a removal study. *J. Anim. Ecol.* **50**, 1–9.

Elgar, M. A. (1989). Predator vigilance and group size in mammals and birds: a

critical review of the empirical evidence. *Biol. Rev.* **64**, 13–33.

Elkins, N. (2004). *Weather and Bird Behaviour*, 3rd edition. Poyser, London.

Elkins, N. & Yésou, P. (1998). Sabine's Gulls in western France and southern Britain. *Brit. Birds* **91**, 386–97.

Ellenberg, H. & Dreifke, R. (1993). 'Abrition': Der Kolkrabe als Schutzschild vor dem Habicht. *Corax* **15**, 2–10.

Ellenberg, H., Gast, F. & Dietrich, J. (1984). Elster, Krähe und Habicht: ein Beziehungsgefuge aus Territorialitat, Konkurrenz und Prädation. *Verhandlungen der Gesellschaft für Ökologie* **12**, 319–30.

Ellison, L. N., Léonard, P. & Ménoni, E. (1988). Effect of shooting on a Black Grouse population in France. *Supplemento Ricerchi Biol. Selvaggina* **14**, 117–28.

Elsworth, S. (1984). *Acid Rain.* Pluto Press, London.

Elton, C. S. (1942). *Voles, Mice and Lemmings.* Oxford University Press, Oxford.

Elwes, H. J. (1869). The bird stations of the Outer Hebrides. *Ibis* **5**, 20–37.

Enemar, A. B. & Sjöstrand, B. (1972). Effects of the introduction of Pied Flycatchers *Ficedula hypoleuca* on the composition of a passerine bird community. *Ornis Scand.* **3**, 79–87.

Enoksson, B. (1990). Autumn territories and population regulation in the Nuthatch *Sitta europaea*: an experimental study. *J. Anim. Ecol.* **59**, 1047–62.

Ens, B. J., Weissing, F. J. & Drent, R. H. (1995). The despotic distribution and deferred maturity: two sides of the same coin. *Amer. Nat.* **146**, 625–50.

Ens, B. J., Smaal, A. C. & de Vlas, J. (2004). *The Effects of a Shellfish Fishery on the Ecosystem of the Dutch Wadden Sea and Oosterschleide.* Alterra-rapport 1011, RIVO-rapport C056/04, RIKZ-rapport RKz/2004.031. Alterra, Wageningen.

Eraud, C., Duriez, O., Chastel, O. & Faivre, B. (2005). The energetic cost of humoral immunity in the Collared Dove *Streptopelia decaocto*: is the magnitude sufficient to force energy-based trade-offs? *Funct. Ecol.* **19**, 110–18.

Eraud, C., Boutin, J.-M., Riviere, M. et al. (2009). Survival of Turtle Doves *Streptopelia* *turtur* in relation to western African environmental conditions. *Ibis* **151**, 186–90.

Eriksson, M. O. G. (1979). Competition between freshwater fish and Goldeneye *Bucephala clangula* L. for common prey. *Oecologia* **41**, 99–107.

Eriksson, M. O. G. (1982). Differences between old and newly established Goldeneye (*Bucephala clangula*) populations. *Ornis Scand.* **59**, 13–19.

Eriksson, M. O. G. & Götmark, G. (1982). Habitat selection: do passerines nest in association with Lapwings *Vanellus vanellus* as defence against predators? *Ornis Scand.* **13**, 189–92.

Eriksson, M. O. G. & Walter, K. (1994). Survival and breeding success of the Osprey *Pandion haliaetus* in Sweden. *Bird. Conserv. Int.* **4**, 263–77.

Erikstäd, K. E., Blom, R. & Myrberget, S. (1982). Territorial Hooded Crows as predators on Willow Ptarmigan nests. *J. Wildl. Manage.* **46**, 109–14.

Erlinge, S., Göransson, G., Hansson, L. *et al.* (1983). Predation as a regulating factor on small rodent populations in southern Sweden. *Oikos* **40**, 36–52.

Erlinge, S., Göransson, G., Högstedt, G. *et al.* (1984). Can vertebrate predators regulate their prey? *Amer. Nat.* **123**, 125–33.

Errington, P. L. (1946). Predation and vertebrate populations. *Quart. Rev. Biol.* **21**, 145–77, 221–45.

Esler, D. & Grand, J. B. (1993). Factors influencing depredation of artificial duck nests. *J. Wildl. Manage.* **57**, 244–8.

Estes, J. A., Terborgh, J., Brashares, J. S. *et al.* (2011). Trophic downgrading of planet earth. *Science* **333**, 301–6.

Etheridge, B., Summers, R. W. & Green, R. E. (1997). The effects of illegal killing and destruction of nests by humans on the population dynamics of the Hen Harrier in Scotland. *J. Appl. Ecol.* **34**, 1081–105.

Evans, D. M. & Day, K. R. (2001). Does shooting disturbance affect diving ducks wintering on large shallow lakes? A case study on Lough Neagh, Northern Ireland. *Biol. Conserv.* **99**, 315–23.

Evans, P. G. H. & Nettleship, D. N. (1985). Conservation of the Atlantic Alcidae. In: *The Atlantic Alcidae* (ed. D. N. Nettleship &

T. R. Birkhead). Academic Press, London, pp. 427–88.

Evans, P. R. (1969). Winter fat deposition and overnight survival of Yellow Buntings (*Emberiza citrinella*). *J. Anim. Ecol.* **38**, 415–23.

Evans, R. J., O'Toole, L. & Whitfield, D. P. (2012). The history of eagles in Britain and Ireland: an ecological review of placename and documentary evidence from the last 1500 years. *Bird Study* **59**, 335–49.

Exo, K. M. (1992). Population ecology of Little Owls *Athene noctua* in Central Europe: a review. In: *The Ecology and Conservation of European Owls* (ed. C. A. Galbraith, I. R. Taylor & S. Percival). Joint Nature Conservation Committee, Peterborough, pp. 64–75.

Fargallo, J. A., Blanco, G., Potti, J. & Vinuela, J. (2001). Nestbox provisioning in a rural population of Eurasian Kestrels: breeding performance, nest predation and parasitism. *Bird Study* **48**, 236–44.

Feare, C. J. (1972). The seasonal pattern of feeding in the Rook (*Corvus frugilegus*) in northwest Scotland. *Proc. Int. Ornithol. Congr.* **15**, 643.

Feare, C. J. (1976). Desertion and abnormal development in a colony of Sooty Terns *Sterna fuscata* infested by virus-infected ticks. *Ibis* **118**, 112–15.

Feare, C. J. (1991). Control of pest bird populations. In: *Bird Population Studies: Relevance to Conservation and Management* (ed. C. M. Perrins, J.-D. Lebreton & G. J. M. Hirons). Oxford University Press, Oxford, pp. 63–78.

Feare, C. J., Dunnet, M. & Patterson, I. J. (1974). Ecological studies of the Rook (*Corvus frugilegus* L.) in north-east Scotland: food intake and feeding behaviour. *J. Appl. Ecol.* **11**, 867–96.

Ferrer, M. & Donazar, J. A. (1996). Density dependent fecundity by habitat hetero-geneity in an increasing population of Spanish Imperial Eagles. *Ecology* **77**, 69–74.

Fiedler, W. (2003). Recent changes in migratory behaviour of birds: a compilation of field observations and ringing data. In: *Avian Migration* (ed. P. Berthold, E. Gwinner & E. Sonnenschein). Springer, Berlin, pp. 21–38.

Fielding, A. H., Haworth, P. F., Morgan, D. H., Thompson, D. B. A. & Whitfield, D. P.

(2003). The impact of Golden Eagles on a diverse bird-of-prey assemblage. In: *Birds of Prey in a Changing Environment* (ed. D. B. A. Thompson, S. M. Redpath, A. H. Fielding, M. Marquiss & C. A. Galbraith). The Sationery Office, Edinburgh, pp. 221–32.

Firbank, L. G. & Smart, S. (2002). The changing status of arable plants that are important food items for birds. *Aspects Appl. Biol.* **67**, 165–70.

Fisher, I. J., Pain, D. J. & Reynolds, V. G. (2006). A review of lead poisoning from ammunition sources in terrestrial birds. *Biol. Conserv.* **131**, 421–32.

Fisher, J. (1966). The Fulmar population of Britain and Ireland, 1959. *Bird Study* **13**, 5–76.

Fleskes, J. P. & Klaas, E. E. (1991). Dabbling duck recruitment in relation to habitat and predators at Union Slough National Wildlife Refuge, Iowa. *US Dept. Interior Fish Wildl. Tech. Rep.* **32**, 1–19.

Fletcher, K., Aebischer, N. J., Baines, D., Foster, R. & Hoodless, A. N. (2010). Changes in breeding success and abundance of ground-nesting moorland birds in relation to the experimental deployment of legal predator control. *J. Appl. Ecol.* **47**, 263–72.

Flickinger, E. L., Mitchell, C. A., White, D. H. & Kolbe, E. J. (1986). Bird poisoning from misuse of the carbamate Furadan in a Texas rice field. *Wildl. Soc. Bull.* **14**, 59–62

Flousek, J. (1989). Impact of industrial emissions on bird populations breeding in mountain spruce forests in central Europe. *Ann. Zool. Fenn.* **26**, 255–63.

Follestad, A. (1994). Innspill til en forvaltningsplanfor gjens in Norge. *Norsk Institut for Naturforskning, NINA Utredriung* **65**, 1–78.

Forsman, J. T. & Mönkkönen, M. (2001). The complex coexistence of the Sparrowhawk and its prey. *Suomen Riista* **47**, 7–17.

Forsman, J. T., Mönkkönen, M., Helle, P. & Inkeröinen, J. (1998). Heterospecific attraction and food resources in migrants' patch selection in the northern boreal forest. *Oecologia* **115**, 278–86.

Forsman, J. T., Seppanen, J. T. & Mönkkönen, M. (2002). Positive fitness consequences of interspecific interaction with a potential competitor. *Proc. R. Soc. Lond. B* **269**, 1619–23.

Forster, J. A. (1975). Electric fencing to protect Sandwich Terns against foxes. *Biol. Conserv.* **7**, 85.

Foster, W. A. (1968). Total brood mortality in late-nesting Cliff Swallows. *Condor* **70**, 275.

Fowler, D., Cape, J. N. & Unsworth, M. H. (1989). Deposition of atmospheric pollutant on forests. *Phil. Trans. R. Soc. Lond. B*, **324**, 247–65.

Fox, A. D. & Kahlert, J. (2000). Do moulting Greylag Geese *Anser anser* forage in close proximity to water in response to food availability and/or quality? *Bird Study* **47**, 266–74.

Fox, A. D. & Madsen, J. (1997). Behavioural and distributional effects of hunting disturbance on waterbirds in Europe: implications for refuge design. *J. Appl. Ecol.* **34**, 1–17.

Fox, A. D., Gitay, H., Owen, M., Salmon, D. G. & Ogilvie, M. A. (1989). Population dynamics of Icelandic-nesting geese, 1960–1987. *Ornis Scand.* **20**, 289–97.

Frederiksen, M. & Bregnballe, T. (2000). Evidence for density-dependent survival of adult Cormorants from a combined analysis of recoveries and resightings. *J. Anim. Ecol.* **69**, 737–52.

Frederiksen, M., Harris, M. P., Daunt, F., Rothery, P. & Wanless, S. (2004a). Scale-dependent climate signals drive breeding phenology of three seabird species. *Global Change Biol.* **10**, 1214–21.

Frederiksen, M., Wanless, S., Harris, M. P., Rothery, P. R. & Wilson, L. J. (2004b). The role of industrial fisheries and oceanographic change in the decline of North Sea Black-legged Kittiwakes. *J. Appl. Ecol.* **41**, 1129–39.

Frederiksen, M., Edwards, M., Richardson, A. J., Halliday, N. C. & Wanless, S. (2006). From plankton to top predators: bottom-up control of a marine food-web across four trophic levels. *J. Anim. Ecol.* **75**, 1259–68.

Frederiksen, M., Edwards, M., Mavor, R. A. & Wanless, S. (2007). Regional and annual variation in Black-legged Kittiwake breeding productivity is related to sea surface temperature. *Mar. Ecol. Prog. Ser.* **350**, 137–43.

Frederiksen, M., Daunt, F., Harris, M. P. & Wanless, S. (2008). The demographic impact of extreme events: stochastic weather drives survival and population dynamics in a long-lived seabird. *J. Anim. Ecol.* **77**, 1020–9.

Fredga, S. & Dow, H. (1984). Factors affecting the size of a local population of Goldeneye *Bucephala clangula* (L.) breeding in Sweden. *Viltrevy* **13**, 225–55.

Freedman, B. (1995). *Environmental Ecology.* Academic Press, London.

Fretwell, S. D. (1972). *Populations in a Seasonal Environment.* Princeton University Press, Princeton, New Jersey.

Friend, M. (1992). Environmental influences on major waterfowl diseases. *Trans. N. Am. Wildl. Nat. Res. Conf.* **57**, 517–25.

Friend, M. (2006). *Disease Emergence and Resurgence: the Wildlife–Human Connection.* US Geological Survey, Circular 1285. USGS, Reston, Virginia.

Friend, M. & Franson, J. C. (2002). *Field Manual of Wildlife Diseases.* US Geological Survey, Biological Resources Division, National Wildlife Health Center, Madison, Wisconsin.

Friend, M. & Pearson, G. L. (1973). Duck plague: the present situation. *Western Proc. Ann. Conf. Western Assoc. State Game and Fish Commissioners* **53**, 315–25.

Friend, M. & Trainer, D. O. (1970). Polychlorinated byphenyl: interaction with DHV. *Science* **170**, 1314–16.

Furness, R. W. (1982). Competition between fisheries and seabird communities. *Adv. Mar. Biol.* **20**, 225–307.

Furness, R. W. (1985). Plastic particle pollution: accummulation by procellariiform seabirds at Scottish colonies. *Mar. Poll. Bull.* **16**, 103–6.

Furness, R. W. (1987). *The Skuas.* Poyser, Calton.

Furness, R. W. (2003). Impacts of fisheries on seabird communities. *Scientia Marina* **67**, doi:10.3989/scimar.2003.67s233.

Furness, R. W. & Barrett, R. T. (1991). Ecological responses of seabirds to reductions in fish stocks in North Norway and Shetland. *Proc. Int. Ornithol. Congr.* **20**, 2241–5.

Furness, R. W. & Birkhead, T. R. (1984). Seabird colony distributions suggest competition for food supplies during the breeding season. *Nature* **311**, 655–6.

Furness, R. W. & Greenwood, J. J. D. (1993). *Birds as Monitors of Environmental Change.* Chapman & Hall, London.

Furness, R. W., Galbraith, H., Gibson, I. P. & Metcalfe, N. B. (1986). Recent changes in the numbers of waders on the Clyde Estuary and their significance for conservation. *Proc. R. Soc. Edinburgh* **90B**, 171–84.

Furness, R. W., Ensor, K. & Hudson, A. V. (1992). The use of fishery waste by gull populations around the British Isles. *Ardea* **89**, 105–13.

Garamszegi, L. Z. (2011). Climate change increases the risk of malaria in birds. *Global Change Biol.* **17**, 1751–9.

Garcia, E. F. J. (1983). An experimental test of competition for space between Blackcaps *Sylvia atricapilla* and Garden Warblers *Sylvia borin* in the breeding season. *J. Anim. Ecol.* **52**, 795–805.

Garcia, L., Viada, C., Moreno-Oro, R. et al. (2003). *Impact of Prestige oil slick on seabirds.* SEO/Birdlife, Madrid.

Gardarsson, A. & Einarsson, A. (1994). Responses of breeding duck populations to changes in food supply. *Hydrobiologia* **279–280**, 15–27.

Gardarsson, A. & Einarsson, A. (1997). Numbers and production of Eurasian Wigeon in relation to conditions in a breeding area, Lake Myvatn, Iceland. *J. Anim. Ecol.* **66**, 439–51.

Garden, B. S., Rayski, C. & Thom, V. M. (1964). A parasitic disease in Eider Ducks. *Bird Study* **11**, 280–7.

Gasparini, J., Boulinier, T., Gill, V. A. et al. (2007). Food availability affects the maternal transfer of androgens and antibodies into eggs of a colonial seabird. *J. Evol. Biol.* **20**, 874–80.

Gaston, A. J. (1985). Development of the young in the Atlantic Alcidae. In: *The Atlantic Alcidae* (ed. D. N. Nettleship & T. R. Birkhead). Academic Press, London, pp. 319–54.

Gaston, A. J., Hipfner, J. M. & Campbell, D. (2002). Heat and mosquitoes cause breeding failures and adult mortality in an Arctic-nesting seabird. *Ibis* **144**, 185–91.

Gauthier-Clerc, M., Lebarbenchon, C. & Thomas, F. (2007). Recent expansion of highly pathogenic avian influenza H5N1: a critical review. *Ibis* **149**, 202–14.

Geer, T. A. (1978). Effects of nesting Sparrow-hawks on nesting tits. *Condor* **80**, 419–22.

Gentle, L. K. & Gosler, A. G. (2001). Fat reserves and perceived predation risk in the Great Tit, *Parus major. Proc. R. Soc. Lond. B* **268**, 487–91.

Gibb, J. (1960). Populations of tits and Goldcrests and their food supply in pine plantations. *Ibis* **102**, 163–208.

Gibbons, D. W., Reid, J. B. & Chapman, R. A. (1993). *The New Atlas of Breeding Birds in Britain and Ireland: 1988–1991.* Poyser, London.

Gibbons, D. W., A. Amar, G. Q. A. Anderson *et al.* (2007). *The Predation of Wild Birds in the UK. A Review of its Conservation Impact and Management.* RSPB Research Report 23. RSPB, Sandy.

Gilbertson, M. & Fox, G. A. (1977). Pollutant-associated embryonic mortality of Great Lakes Herring Gulls. *Environ. Poll.* **12**, 211–16.

Gilbertson, M., Morris, R. D. & Hunter, R. A. (1976). Abnormal chicks and PCB residue levels in eggs of colonial birds on the lower Great Lakes (1971–1973). *Auk* **93**, 434–42.

Giles, N. (1992). *Wildlife After Gravel.* Game Conservancy, Fordingbridge.

Gilg, O., Sittler, B. & Hanski, I. (2009). Climate change and cyclic predator–prey dynamics in the High Arctic. *Global Change Biol.* **115**, 2634–52.

Gill, J. A., Sutherland, W. J. & Watkinson, A. R. (1996). A method to quantify the effects of human disturbance on animal populations. *J. Appl. Ecol.* **33**, 786–92.

Gill, J. A., Norris, K. & Sutherland, W. J. (2001). The effects of disturbance on habitat use by Black-tailed Godwits *Limosa limosa. J. Appl. Ecol.* **38**, 846–56.

Glas, P. (1960). Factors governing density in the Chaffinch (*Fringilla coelebs*) in different types of wood. *Arch. Néere. Zool.* **13**, 466–72.

Glick, B. (1983). Bursa of Fabricius. In: *Avian Biology, Vol. 7* (ed. D. S. Farner & J. R. King). Academic Press, London, pp. 443–500.

Glick, B. (1994). The bursa of Fabricius: the evolution of a discovery. *Poult. Sci.* **73**, 979–83.

Glück, E. (1986). Flock size and habitat dependent food and energy intake of foraging Goldfinches. *Oecologia* **71**, 149–55.

Golet, G. H. & Irons, D. B. (1999). Raising young reduces body condition and fat stores in Black-legged Kittiwakes. *Oecologia* **120**, 530–8.

Golet, G. H., Irons, D. B. & Estes, J. A. (1998). Survival costs of chick rearing in Black-legged Kittiwakes. *J. Anim. Ecol.* **67**, 827–41.

González, G., Sorci, G., Møller, A. P. *et al.* (1999). Immunocompetence and condition-dependent sexual advertisement in male House Sparrows (*Passer domesticus*). *J. Anim. Ecol.* **68**, 1225–34.

González, L. M., Margalida, A., Sanchez, R. & Oria, J. (2006). Supplementary feeding as an effective tool for improving breeding success in the Spanish Imperial Eagle *Aquila adalberti. Biol. Conserv.* **129**, 477–86.

Göransson, G., Karlsson, J., Nilsson, S. G. & Ulfstrand, S. (1975). Predation on birds' nests in relation to antipredator aggression and nest density: an experimental study. *Oikos* **26**, 117–20.

Gosler, A. G. (1996). Environmental and social determinants of winter fat storage in the Great Tit *Parus major. J. Anim. Ecol.* **65**, 1–17.

Gosler, A. G. & Carruthers, T. D. (1994). Bill size and niche breadth in the Irish Coal Tit *Parus ater hibernicus. J. Avian Biol.* **25**, 171–7.

Gosler, A. G., Greenwood, J. J. D. & Perrins, C. M. (1995). Predation risk and the cost of being fat. *Nature* **377**, 621–3.

Götmark, F. (1992). The effects of investigator disturbance on nesting birds. *Curr. Ornithol.* **9**, 63–104.

Grant, M. C., Orsman, C., Easton, J. *et al.* (1999). Breeding success and causes of breeding failure of Curlew *Numenius arquata* in Northern Ireland. *J. Appl. Ecol.* **36**, 59–74.

Graveland, J. (1990). Effects of acid precipitation on reproduction in birds. *Experientia* **46**, 962–70.

Graveland, J., van Derwal, R., van Balen, H. & van Noordwijk, A. (1994). Poor reproduction in forest passerines from decline in snail abundance. *Nature* **368**, 446–8.

Gray, R. & Hussey, A. (1860). The trade in Goldfinches. *Zoologist* **18**, 711–14.

Green, G. H., Greenwood, J. J. D. & Lloyd, L. S. (1977). The influence of snow conditions on the date of breeding of wading birds in north-east Greenland. *J. Zool. Lond.* **183**, 311–28.

Green, R. E. (1984). The feeding ecology and survival of Partridge chicks *Alectoris rufa* and *Perdix perdix* on arable farmland in East Anglia. *J. Appl. Ecol.* **21**, 817–30.

Green, R. E. (1988a). Stone Curlew conservation. *RSPB Conservation Review* **2**, 30–3.

Green, R. E. (1988b). Effects of environmental factors on the timing and success of breeding of Common Snipe *Gallinago gallinago* (Aves, Scolopacidae). *J. Appl. Ecol.* **25**, 79–93.

Greenwood, J. J. D. & Baillie, S. R. (1991). Effects of density-dependence and weather on population changes of English passerines using a non-experimental paradigm. *Ibis* **133**, 121–33.

Greenwood, J. J. D., Baillie, S. R. & Crick, H. Q . P. (1994). Long-term studies and monitoring of bird populations. In: *Long-term Experiments in Agricultural and Ecological Sciences* (ed. R. A. Leigh & A. E. Johnston). CAB International, Oxford, pp. 343–64.

Greenwood, R. J., Sargeant, A. B., Johnson, D. H., Cowardin, L. M. & Shaffer, T. L. (1987). Mallard nest success and recruitment in prairie Canada. *Trans. N. A. Wildl. Nat. Res. Conf.* **52**, 298–309.

Greenwood, R. J., Sargeant, A. B., Johnson, D. H., Cowardin, L. M. & Shaffer, T. L. (1995). Factors associated with duck nest success in the prairie pothole region of Canada. *Wildl. Monogr.* **128**, 1–57.

Gregory, R. D., Keymer, A. E. & Harvey, P. H. (1991). Life history, ecology and parasite community structure in Soviet birds. *Biol. J. Linn. Soc.* **43**, 249–62.

Gregory, R. D., Noble, D. G. & Custance, J. (2004). The state of play of farmland birds: population trends and conservation status of lowland farmland birds in the United Kingdom. *Ibis* **146** (S2), 1–13.

Grenquist, P. (1951). On the recent fluctuations in numbers of waterfowl in the Finnish archipelago. *Proc. Int. Ornithol. Congr.* **10**, 494–6.

Grenquist, P., Henriksson, K. & Raites, T. (1972). On intestinal occlusion in male Eider ducks. *Suomen Riista* **24**, 91–6.

Grosbois, V. & Thompson, P. M. (2006). North Atlantic climate variation influences survival in adult Fulmars. *Oikos* **109**, 273–90.

Gruar, D., Peach, W. J. & Taylor, R. (2003). Summer diet and body condition of Song Thrushes in stable and declining farmland populations. *Ibis* **145**, 637–49.

Gulickx, M. & Kemp, J. B. (2007). Provision of nest cages to reduce Little Ringed Plover *Charadrius dubius* nest predation at Welney, Norfolk, England. *Conserv. Evid.* **4**, 30–32.

Gunnarsson, T. G., Gill, J. A., Newton, J., Potts, P. M. & Sutherland, W. J. (2005). Seasonal matching of habitat quality and fitness in a migratory bird. *Proc. R. Soc. B* **272**, 2319–23.

Gustafsson, L. (1987). Interspecific competition lowers fitness in Collared Flycatchers *Ficedula albicollis*, an experimental demonstration. *Ecology* **68**, 291–6.

Gustafsson, L. (1988). Inter- and intraspecific competition for nest-holes in a population of the Collared Flycatcher *Ficedula albicollis*. *Ibis* **130**, 11–15.

Gwinner, H. & Berger, S. (2005). European Starlings: nestling condition, parasites and green nest material during the breeding season. *J. Ornithol.* **146**, 365–71.

Haapanen, A. (1965). Bird fauna of Finnish forests in relation to forest succession. *Ann. Zool. Fenn.* **2**, 153–96.

Haas, K., Köhler, U., Diehl, S. *et al.* (2007). Influence of fish on habitat choice of water birds: a whole system experiment. *Ecology* **88**, 2915–25.

Haemig, P. D. (1992). Competition between ants and birds in a Swedish Forest. *Oikos* **65**, 479–83.

Haemig, P. D. (1994). Effects of ants on the foraging of birds in spruce trees. *Oecologia* **97**, 35–40.

Haemig, P. D. (1996). Interference from ants alters foraging ecology of Great Tits. *Behav. Ecol. Sociobiol.* **38**, 25–9.

Haemig, P. D. (1999). Predation risk alters

interactions among species: competition and facilitation between ants and nesting birds in a boreal forest. *Ecol. Lett.* **2**, 178–84.

Hagen, Y. (1969). Norwegian studies on the reproduction of birds of prey and owls in relation to micro-rodent population fluctuations. *Fauna* **22**, 73–126.

Hakkarainen, H. & Korpimäki, E. (1996). Competitive and predatory interactions among raptors: an observational and experimental study. *Ecology* **77**, 1134–42.

Hakkarainen, H., Ilmonen, P., Koivunen, V. & Korpimaki, E. (1998). Blood parasites and nest defence behaviour of Tengmalm's Owls. *Oecologia* **114**, 574–7.

Halupka, L., Dyrch, A. & Boroweic, M. (2008). Climate change affects breeding of Reed Warblers *Acrocephalus scirpaceus*. *J. Avian Biol.* **39**, 95–100.

Hamer, K. C. (2010). The search for winners and losers in a sea of climate change. *Ibis* **152**, 3–5.

Hamer, K. C., Furness, R. W. & Caldow, R. W. G. (1991). The effects of changes in food availability on the breeding ecology of Great Skuas *Catharacta skua* in Shetland. *J. Zool. Lond.* **223**, 175–88.

Hamer, K. C., Monaghan, P., Uttley, J. D., Walton, P. & Burns, M. D. (1993). The influence of food supply on the breeding ecology of Kittiwakes *Rissa tridactyla* in Shetland. *Ibis* **135**, 255–63.

Hancock, M. (2000). Artificial floating islands for nesting Black-throated Divers *Gavia arctica* in Scotland: construction, use and effect on breeding success. *Bird Study* **47**, 165–75.

Hancock, M. & Wilson, J. D. (2003). Winter habitat associations of seed-eating passerines on Scottish farmland. *Bird Study* **50**, 116–30.

Hansen, A. J. (1987). Regulation of Bald Eagle reproductive rates in southeast Alaska. *Ecology* **68**, 1387–92.

Hanski, I., Hansson, L. & Henttonen, H. (1991). Specialist predators, generalist predators, and the microtine rodent cycle. *J. Anim. Ecol.* **60**, 353–67.

Hanssen, S. A., Folstad, I. & Erikstad, K. E. (2003a). Reduced immunocompetence and cost of reproduction in Common Eiders. *Oecologia* **136**, 457–64.

Hanssen, S. A., Folstad, I., Erikstad, K. E. & Oksanen, A. (2003b). Costs of parasites in Common Eiders: effects of anti-parasite treatment. *Oikos* **100**, 105–11.

Hanssen, S. A., Hasselquist, D., Folstad, I. & Erikstad, K. E. (2004). Costs of immunity: immune responsiveness reduces survival in a vertebrate. *Proc. R. Soc. Lond. B* **271**, 925–30.

Hanssen, S. A., Hasselquist, D., Folstad, I. & Erikstad, K. E. (2005). Cost of reproduction in a long-lived bird: incubation effort reduces immune function and future reproduction. *Proc. R. SocLond. B* **272**, 1039–46.

Hardin, G. (1968). The tragedy of the commons. *Science* **162**, 1245–8.

Hardin, G. (1994). The tragedy of the unmanaged commons. *Trends Ecol. Evol.* **9**, 199.

Hario, M., Rintala, J. & Nordenswan, G. (2009). Dynamics of wintering Long-tailed Ducks in the Baltic Sea: the connection with lemming cycles, oil disasters and hunting. *Suomen Riista* **55**, 83–96.

Harris, M. P. (1962). Weights from five hundred birds found dead on Skomer Island in January 1962. *Brit. Birds* **55**, 97–103.

Harris, M. P. (1965). Puffinosis on Skokholm. *Brit. Birds* **58**, 426–33.

Harris, M. P. (1970). Territory limiting the size of the breeding population of the Oystercatcher (*Haematopus ostralegus*): a removal experiment. *J. Anim. Ecol.* **39**, 707–13.

Harris, M. P. & Wanless, S. (1991). Population studies and conservation of Puffins *Fratercula arctica*. In: *Bird Population Studies: Relevance to Conservation and Management* (ed. C. M. Perrins, J.-D. Lebreton & G. J. M. Hirons). Oxford University Press, Oxford, pp. 230–48.

Harris, M. P. & Wanless, S. (1996). Differential responses of Guillemot *Uria aalge* and Shag *Phalacrocorax aristotelis* to a late winter wreck. *Bird Study* **43**, 220–30.

Harris, M. P. & Wanless, S. (2007). Northern Guillemot. In: *The Birds of Scotland* (ed. R. Forrester & I. J. Andrews). Aberlady: Scottish Ornithologists' Club, Aberlady, pp. 846–8.

Harris, M. P. & Wanless, S. (2011). *The Puffin*. Poyser, London.

Harris, M. P., Buckland, S. T., Russell, S. M. & Wanless, S. (1994). Year- and age-related variation in the survival of adult European Shags over a 24-year period. *Condor* **96**, 600–5.

Harris, M. P., Anker-Nilssen, T., McCleery, R. H. *et al.* (2005). Effect of wintering area and climate on the survival of adult Atlantic Puffins *Fratercula atlantica* in the eastern Atlantic. *Marine. Ecol. Prog. Ser.* **297**, 283–96.

Harris, M. P., Daunt, F., Newell, M., Phillips, R. A. & Wanless, S. (2010). Wintering areas of adult Atlantic Puffins *Fratercula arctica* from a North Sea colony as revealed by geolocation technology. *Mar. Biol.* **157**, 827–36.

Harris, S. W. & Marshall, W. H. (1957). Some effects of a severe windstorm on Coot nests. *J. Wildl. Manage.* **21**, 471–3.

Harrison, A., Newey, S., Gilbert, L., Haydon, D. T. & Thirgood, S. (2010). Killing wildlife hosts to control disease: Mountain Hares, Red Grouse and louping ill. *J. Appl. Ecol.* **47**, 926–30.

Harrison, J. & Hudson, M. (1964). Some effects of severe weather on wildfowl in Kent in 1962–63. *Wildfowl Trust Ann. Rep.* **15**, 26–32.

Harrison, N. & Robins, M. (1992). The threat from nets to seabirds. *RSPB Conservation Review* **6**, 51–6.

Hart, J. D., Milsom, T. P., Baxter, A., Kelly, P. F. & Parkin, W. K. (2002). The impact of livestock on Lapwing Vanellus vanellus breeding densities and performance on coastal grazing marsh. *Bird Study* **49**, 67–78.

Hart, J. D., Milsom, T. P., Fisher, G. *et al.* (2006). The relationship between Yellowhammer breeding performance, arthropod abundance and insecticide applications on arable farmland. *J. Appl. Ecol.* **43**, 81–91.

Hasselquist, D., Östman, Ö., Waldenström, J. & Bensch, S. (2007). Temporal patterns of occurrence and transmission of the blood parasite *Haemoproteus payevskyi* in the Great Reed Warbler *Acrocephalus arundinaceus*. *J. Ornithol.* **148**, 401–9.

Hatchwell, B. J., Chamberlain, D. E. & Perrins, C. M. (1996). The reproductive success of Blackbirds *Turdus merula* in relation to habitat structure and choice of nest site. *Ibis* **138**, 256–62.

Haukioja, E. & Hakala, T. (1975). Herbivore cycles and periodic outbreaks. Formulation of a general hypothesis. *Rep. Kevo Subarctic Res. Stn.* **12**, 1–19.

Heaney, V., Ratcliffe, N., Brown, A., Robinson, P. J. & Lock, L. (2002). The status and distribution of European Storm Petrels *Hydrobates pelagicus* and Manx Shearwaters *Puffinus puffinus* on the Isles of Scilly. *Atlantic Seabirds* **4**, 1–16.

Henderson, I. G., Cooper, J., Fuller, R. J. & Vickery, J. A. (2000). The relative abundance of birds on set-aside and neighbouring fields in summer. *J. Appl. Ecol.* **37**, 335–47.

Hengeveld, R. (1988). Mechanisms of biological invasions. *J. Biogeog.* **15**, 819–28.

Heubeck, M. (1989). Breeding success of Shetland seabirds: Arctic Skua, Kittiwake, Guillemot, Razorbill and Puffin. In: *Seabirds and Sandeels: Proceedings of a Seminar Held in Lerwick, Shetland, 15–16 October 1988*. Shetland Bird Club, Lerwick.

Heubeck, M. (1997). The direct effect of the *Braer* oil spill on seabird populations, and an assessment of the role of the wildlife response centre. In: *The Impact of an Oil Spill in Turbulent Waters: the Braer* (ed. J. M. Davies & G. Topping). Stationery Office, Edinburgh, pp. 73–90.

Heubeck, M. (2000). Population trends of Kittiwake *Rissa tridactyla*, Black Guillemot *Cepphus grylle* and Common Guillemot *Uria aalge* in Shetland, 1978–98. *Atlantic Seabirds* **2**, 227–44.

Heubeck, M. & Richardson, M. G. (1980). Bird mortality following the *Esso Bernicia* oil spill, Shetland, December 1978. *Scott. Birds* **11**, 97–108.

Heubeck, M., Mellor, R. M. & Harvey, P. V. (1997). Changes in the breeding distribution and numbers of Kittiwakes *Rissa tridactyla* around Unst, Shetland, and the presumed role of predation by Great Skuas *Catharacta skua*. *Seabird* **19**, 12–21.

Heubeck, M., Mellor, R. M., Harvey, P. V., Mainwood, A. R. & Riddington, R. (1999). Estimating the population size and rate of decline of Kittiwakes *Rissa tridactyla* breeding in Shetland, 1981–97. *Bird Study* **46**, 48–61.

Heusmann, H. W. & Bellville, R. (1978). Effects of nest removal on Starling populations. *Wilson Bull.* **90**, 287–90.

Heydemann, B. (1983). Die Beurteilung von Zeikonflikten zwischen Landwirtschaft, Landschaftspflege und Naturschutz aus Sicht der Landschaftspflege und des Naturschutzes. *Schriftenreihe für ländliche Sozialfragen* **88**, 51–78.

Hickling, R., Roy, D. B., Hill, J. K., Fox, R. & Thomas, C. D. (2006). The distributions of a wide range of taxonomic groups are expanding polewards. *Global Change Biol.* **12**, 450–5.

Hill, D. (1983). Compensatory mortality in the Mallard. *Game Conservancy Ann. Rev.* **14**, 87–92.

Hill, D. A. (1984). Population regulation in the Mallard. *J. Anim. Ecol.* **53**, 191–202.

Hill, D. A. (1985). The feeding ecology and survival of Pheasant chicks on arable farmland. *J. Appl. Ecol.* **22**, 645–54.

Hill, D. A. (1988). Population dynamics of Avocets (*Recurvirostra avosetta* L.) breeding in Britain. *J. Anim. Ecol.* **57**, 669–83.

Hill, E. F., Heath, R. G., Spann, J. W. & Williams, J. D. (1975). *Lethal Dietary Toxicities of Environmental Pollutants to Birds.* US Fish & Wildlife Service, Washington, DC.

Hilton, G. M., Ruxton, G. D. & Cresswell, W. (1999). Choice of foraging area with respect to predation risk in Redshanks: the effects of weather and predator activity. *Oikos* **87**, 295–302.

Hindman, L. J. & Ferrigno, F. (1990). Atlantic flyway goose populations, status and management. *Trans. N. A. Wildl. Nat. Res. Conf.* **55**, 292–311.

Hinsley, S. A., Bellamy, P. & Moss, D. (1995). Sparrowhawk *Accipiter nisus* predation and feeding site selection by tits. *Ibis* **137**, 418–19.

Hinsley, S. A., Redhead, J. W., Bellamy, P. E. *et al.* (2010). Testing agri-environment delivery for farmland birds at the farm scale: the Hillesden experiment. *Ibis* **152**, 500–14.

Hipkiss, T. Gustafsson, J., Eklund, U. & Hörnfeldt, B. (2013). Is the long-term decline of Boreal Owls in Sweden caused by avoidance of old boxes? *J. Raptor Res.* **47**, 15–20.

Hirons, G. J. M., Hardy, A. R. & Stanley, P. I. (1979). Starvation in young Tawny Owls. *Bird Study* **26**, 59–63.

Hjernquist, B. & Hjernquist, M. B. (2010). The effects of quantity and quality of prey on population fluctuations of three seabird species. *Bird Study* **57**, 19–25.

Hochachka, W. M. & Dhondt, A. A. (2000). Density dependent decline of host abundance resulting from a new infectious disease. *Proc. Nat. Acad. Sci.* **97**, 5303–6.

Hodson, N. L. & Snow, D. W. (1965). The road deaths enquiry, 1960–61. *Bird Study* **12**, 90–9.

Hoffman, D. J. (1990). Embryotoxicity and teratogenicity of environmental contaminants to bird eggs. *Rev. Environ. Contam. Toxicol.* **115**, 40–89.

Hoffman, D. J. & Albers, P. H. (1984). Evaluation of embryotoxicity and teratogenicity of 42 herbicides, insecticides, and petroleum contaminants to Mallard eggs. *Arch. Environ. Contam. Toxicol.* **13**, 15–27.

Hoffman, D. J. & Eastin, W. C. (1981). Effects of malathion, diaxinon and parathion on Mallard embryo development and cholinesterase activity. *Environ. Res.* **26**, 472–85.

Hoffman, D. J., Rattner, B. A., Sileo, L., Docherty, D. & Kubiak, T. J. (1987). Embryotoxicity, teratogenicity, and aryl hydrocarbon hydroxylase activity in Forster's Terns on Green Bay, Lake Michigan. *Environ. Res.* **42**, 176–84.

Hoffmann, C. H., Townes, H. K., Swift, H. H. & Sailer, R. I. (1949). Field studies on the effects of airplane applications of DDT on forest invertebrates. *Ecol. Monogr.* **19**, 1–46.

Hogstad, O. (1975). Quantitative relations between hole-nesting and open-nesting species within a passerine breeding community. *Norw. J. Zool.* **23**, 261–7.

Hogstad, O. (1988). Social rank and antipredator behaviour of Willow Tits *Parus montanus* in winter flocks. *Ibis* **130**, 45–56.

Hogstad, O. (1993). Structure and dynamics of a passerine bird community in a spruce-dominated boreal forest: a 12-year study. *Ann. Zool. Fenn.* **30**, 43–54.

Hogstad, O. (2005). Numerical and functional responses of breeding passerine species to mass occurrence of geometrid caterpillars in a subalpine birch forest: a 30-year study. *Ibis* **147**, 77–91.

Högstedt, G. (1980). Prediction and test of the effects of interspecific competition. *Nature* **283**, 64–6.

Högstedt, G. (1981). Effect of additional food on reproductive success in the Magpie (*Pica pica*). *J. Anim. Ecol.* **50**, 219–29.

Holdgate, M. W. (1971). *The Sea Bird Wreck in the Irish Sea Autumn 1969*. Natural Environment Research Council, London.

Holgersen, H. (1958). Pinkfeet in Europe: the effect of the cold weather of February 1956 on the distribution of Pink-Footed Geese in Northwest Europe. *Wildfowl Trust Ann. Rep.* **9**, 1956–7.

Hollands, P. K. & Yalden, D. W. (1991). Population dynamics of Common Sandpipers *Actitis hypoleucos* breeding along an upland river system. *Bird Study* **38**, 151–9.

Holling, M. and the Rare Birds Breeding Panel. (2012). Rare breeding birds in the United Kingdom in 2010. *Brit. Birds* **105**, 352–416.

Hollmén, T., Franson, J. C., Kilpi, M. *et al.* (2002). Isolation and charcterisation of a teovirus from Common Eiders (*Somateria mollissima*) from Finland. *Avian Diseases* **46**, 478–84.

Holm, T. E. & Haugaard, L. (2013). Effects of a Danish action plan on reducing shotgun wounding of Common Eider *Somateria mollissima. Bird Study* **60**, 131–4.

Holm, T. E. & Laursen, K. (2009). Experimental disturbance by walkers affects behaviour and territory density of nesting Black-tailed Godwit *Limosa limosa. Ibis* **151**, 77–87.

Holmstad, P. R., Hudson, P. J. & Skorping, A. (2005). The influence of a parasite community on the dynamics of a host population: a longitudinal study on Willow Ptarmigan and their parasites. *Oikos* **111**, 377–91.

Holmstad, P. R., Jensen, K. H. & Skorping, A. (2008). Ectoparasite intensities are correlated with endoparasite infection loads in Willow Ptarmigan. *Oikos* **117**, 515–20.

Hoogland, J. L. & Sherman, P. W. (1976). Advantages and disadvantages of Bank Swallow (*Riparia riparia*) coloniality. *Ecol. Monogr.* **46**, 33–58.

Hope Jones, P. (1962). Mortality and weights of Fieldfares in Anglesey in January 1962. *Brit. Birds* **55**, 178–81.

Hope Jones, P., Monnat, J.-Y., Cadbury, C. J. & Stowe, T. J. (1978). Birds oiled during the *Amoco Cadiz* incident: an interim report. *Mar. Poll. Bull.* **9**, 307–11.

Hörnfeldt, B. (1978). Synchronous population fluctuations in voles, small game, owls and tularemia in northern Sweden. *Oecologia* **32**, 141–52.

Hörnfeldt, B. (2004). Long-term declines in numbers of cyclic voles in boreal Sweden: analysis and presentation of hypotheses. *Oikos* **107**, 376–92.

Hörnfeldt, B., Löfgren, O. & Carlson, B.-G. (1986). Cycles in voles and small game in relation to variations in plant production indices in northern Sweden. *Oecologia* **68**, 496–502.

Hötker, H. & Segebade, A. (2000). Effects of predation and weather on the breeding success of Avocets *Recurvirostra avosetta. Bird Study* **47**, 91–101.

Houghton, J. T., Ding, Y., Griggs, D. J. *et al.* (2001). *Climate Change 2001*. Cambridge University Press, Cambridge.

Hromada, M., Tryjanowski, P. & Antczak, M. (2002). Presence of the Great Grey Shrike *Lanius excubitor* affects breeding passerine assemblage. *Ann. Zool. Fenn.* **39**, 125–30.

Hudson, P. J. (1986). The effect of a parasitic nematode on the breeding production of Red Grouse. *J. Anim. Ecol.* **55**, 85–92.

Hudson, P. J. (1992). *Grouse in Space and Time: the Population Biology of a Managed Gamebird*. Game Conservancy Trust, Fordingbridge.

Hudson, P. J. & Dobson, A. P. (1991). The direct and indirect effects of the caecal nematode *Trichostrongylus tenuis* on Red Grouse. In: *Bird–Parasite Interactions* (ed. J. E. Loye & M. Zuk). Oxford University Press, Oxford, pp. 49–68.

Hudson, P. J., Dobson, A. & Newborn, D. (1992a). Do parasites make prey vulnerable to predation? Red Grouse and parasites. *J. Anim. Ecol.* **61**, 681–92.

Hudson, P. J., Newborn, D. & Dobson, A. P. (1992b). Regulation and stability of a free-living host-parasite sytem, *Trichostrongylus tenuis* in Red Grouse. 1: Monitoring and parasite reduction experiments. *J. Anim. Ecol.* **61**, 477–86.

Hudson, R. (1972). Collared Doves in Britain and Ireland during 1965–1970. *Brit. Birds* **65**, 139–55.

Hudson, R. H., Tucker, R. K. & Haegele, M. A. (1984). *Handbook of Toxicity of Pesticides to Wildlife*, 2nd edition. US Fish & Wildlife Service, Washington, DC.

Hughes, S. L., Holliday, N. P., Kennedy, J. *et al.* (2010). Temperature (air and sea) in MCCIP *Annual Report Card 2010–11*. MCCIP Science Review. www.mccip.org.uk/arc.

Hulme, M., Jenkins, G. J., Lu, X. *et al.* (2002). *Climate Change Scenarios for the United Kingdom: The UKCIP02 Scientific Report.* Tyndall Centre for Climate Change Research, University of East Anglia, Norwich.

Hulscher, J. B. (1982). The Oystercatcher as a predator of the bivalve, *Macoma balthica*, in the Dutch Wadden Sea. *Ardea* **70**, 89–152.

Hunt, E. C. & Bischoff, A. I. (1960). Inimical effects on wildlife of periodic DDD applications to Clear Lake. *Calif. Fish Game* **46**, 91–106.

Hunt, G. L. (1972). Influence of food distribution and human distribution on the reproductive success of Herring Gulls. *Ecology* **53**, 1057–61.

Hunt, G. L., Eppley, Z. A. & Schneider, D. C. (1986). Reproductive performance of seabirds: the importance of population and colony size. *Auk* **103**, 306–17.

Hunt, K. A., Bird, D. M., Mineau, P. & Schutt, L. (1992). Selective predation of organophosphate-exposed prey by American Kestrels. *Anim. Behav.* **43**, 971–6.

Hunter, M. L., Withan, J. W. & Dow, H. (1984). Effects of a carbaryl-induced depression in invertebrate abundance on the growth and behaviour of American Black Duck and Mallard ducklings. *Can. J. Zool.* **62**, 452–6.

Huntley, B. (1991). How plants respond to climate change: migration rates, individualism and the consequences for plant communities. *Ann. Botany* **67** (Suppl. 1), s15–22.

Huntley, B. & Green, R. (2011). The utility of bioclimatic models for projecting future changes in the distribution of birds in response to climate change. In: *Gyrfalcons and Ptarmigan in a Changing World, Vol. 2* (ed. R. T. Watson, T. J. Cade, M. Fuller, G. Hunt & E. Potapov). The Peregrine Fund, Boise, Idaho, pp. 117–23.

Huntley, B., Green, R. E., Collingham, Y. C. & Willis, S. G. (2007). *A Climatic Atlas of European Breeding Birds.* Lynx Edicions, Barcelona.

Hurrell, J. W., Kushnir, Y., Ottersen, G. & Visbeck, N. (eds.) (2003). *The North Atlantic Oscillation: Climate Significance and Environmental Impact.* Geophysical Monograph Ser. 134. American Geophysical Union, Washington, DC.

Hurtrez-Boussès, S., Perret, P., Renaud, F. & Blondel, J. (1997). High blowfly parasite loads affect breeding success in a Mediterranean population of Blue tits. *Oecologia* **112**, 514–17.

Hušek, J. & Adamik, P. (2008). Long-term trends in the timing of breeding and brood size in the Red-backed Shrike *Lanius collurio* in the Czech Republic, 1964–2004. *J. Ornithol.* **149**, 97–103.

Iason, G. R., O'Reilly-Wapstra, J. M., Brewer, M. J., Summers, R. W. & Moore, B. D. (2011). Do multiple herbivores maintain chemical diversity of Scots Pine monoterpines? *Phil. Trans. R. Soc. B* **366**, 1337–45.

Ibáñez-Álamo, J. D., Sanllorente, O. & Soler, M. (2012). The impact of researcher disturbance on nest predation rates: a meta-analysis. *Ibis* **154**, 5–14.

Ilmonen, P., Hakkarainen, H., Koivunen, V. *et al.* (1999). Parental efforts and blood parasitism in Tengmalm's Owl: effects of natural and experimental variation in food abundance. *Oikos* **86**, 79–86.

Ilmonen, P., Taarna, T. & Hasselquist, D. (2000). Experimentally activated immune defence in female Pied Flycatchers results in reduced breeding success. *Proc. R. Soc. Lond. B* **267**, 665–70.

Ims, R. A. & Fuglei, E. (2005). Trophic interaction cycles in tundra ecosystems and the impact of climate change. *BioScience* 35, 311–22.

Ims, R. A., Henden, J. A. & Killengreen, S. T. (2008). Collapsing population cycles. *Trends Ecol. Evol.* 23, 79–86.

Inglis, I. R., Isaacson, A. J., Thearle, R. J. P. & Westwood, N. J. (1990). The effects of changing agricultural practice upon Woodpigeon *Columba palumbus* numbers. *Ibis* 132, 262–72.

IPCC (Intergovernmental Panel on Climate Change) (2007). *IPCC Fourth Assessment Report: Climate Change 2007 (AR4).* IPCC, Geneva.

Isaacson, A. J., Inglis, I. R. & Hayes, P. J. (2002). A long-term study of the Woodpigeon in relation to changes in agricultural practice. *Aspects Appl. Biol.* 67, 51–8.

Isaksson, D., Lallander, J. & Larsson, M. (2007). Managing predation on ground nesting birds: the effectiveness of nest exclosures. *Biol. Conserv.* 136, 136–42.

Jackson, D. B. (2001). Experimental removal of introduced Hedgehogs improves wader nest success in the Western Isles, Scotland. *J. Appl. Ecol.* 38, 802–12.

Jackson, D. B. & Green, R. E. (2000). The importance of the introduced Hedgehog (*Erinaceus europaeus*) as a predator of the eggs of waders (Charadrii) on machair in South Uist, Scotland. *Biol. Conserv.* 93, 333–48.

Jackson, D. B., Fuller, R. J., Campbell, S. T. (2004). Long-term changes among breeding shorebirds in the Outer Hebrides, Scotland, in relation to introduced Hedgehogs (*Erinaceus europaeus*). *Biol. Conserv.* 117, 155–66.

Jacobsen, K.-O., Erikstad, K. E. & Saether, B. E. (1995). An experimental study of the costs of reproduction in the Kittiwake *Rissa tridactyla. Ecology* 76, 1636–42.

Jansson, C., Ekman, J. & von Brömssen, A. (1981). Winter mortality and food supply in tits (*Parus* spp.). *Oikos* 37, 313–22.

Jantti, A., Aho, T., Hakkarainen, H., Kuitunen, M. and Suhonen, J. (2001). Prey depletion by the foraging of the Eurasian Treecreeper, *Certhia familiaris*, on tree-trunk arthropods. *Oecologia* 128, 488–91.

Jantti, A., Suorsa, P., Hakkarainen, H. *et al.* (2007). Within territory abundance of Red

Wood Ants *Formica rufa* is associated with the body condition of nestlings in the Eurasian Treecreeper *Certhia familiaris. J. Avian Biol.* 38, 619–24.

Järvinen, O. (1985). Predation causing extended low densities in microtine cycle: implications from predation on hole-nesting passerines. *Oikos* 45, 157–8.

Järvinen, O. (1990). Changes in the abundance of birds in relation to small rodent density and predation rate in Finnish Lapland. *Bird Study* 37, 36–9.

Jenkins, D. (1961). Population control in protected Partridges (*Perdix perdix*). *J. Anim. Ecol.* 30, 235–58.

Jenkins, D. & Sparks, T. H. (2010). The changing phenology of Mid Deeside, Scotland 1974–2006. *Bird Study* 57, 407–14.

Jenkins, D., Watson, A. & Miller, G. R. (1963). Population studies on Red Grouse *Lagopus lagopus scoticus* (Lath.) in north-east Scotland. *J. Anim. Ecol.* 32, 317–76.

Jenkins, D., Watson, A. & Miller, G. R. (1964). Predation and Red Grouse populations. *J. Appl. Ecol.* 1, 183–95.

Jenkins, D., Murray, M. G. & Hall, P. (1975). Structure and regulation of a Shelduck (*Tadorna tadorna* (L.)) population. *J. Anim. Ecol.* 44, 201–31.

Jenkins, D., Newton, I. & Brown, C. (1976). Structure and dynamics of a Mute Swan population. *Wildfowl* 27, 77–82.

Jenni, L. & Kéri, M. (2003). Timing of autumn bird migration under climate change: advances in long distance migrants, delays in short distance migrants. *Proc R. Soc Lond. B* 270, 1467–72.

Jennings, A. R., Soulsby, E. J. L. & Wainwright, C. B. (1961). An outbreak of disease in Mute Swans at an Essex reservoir. *Bird Study* 8, 19–24.

Jiguet, F., Gadot, A.-S., Julliard, R., Newson, S. E. & Couvet, D. (2007). Climate envelope, life history traits and the resilience of birds facing global change. *Global Change Biol.* 13, 1672–84.

Jiguet, F., Gregory, R. D., Devictor, V. *et al.* (2010). Population trends of European common birds are predicted by characteristics of their climatic niche. *Global Change Biol.* 16, 497–505.

Joensen, A. (1977). Oil pollution and seabirds in

Denmark, 1971–1976. *Dan. Rev. Game Biol.* **10**, 1–31.

John, A. W. G. & Roskell, J. (1985). Jay movements in autumn 1983. *Brit. Birds* **78**, 611–37.

Johnson, G., Walker, C. H. & Dawson, A. (1994). Interactive effects of prochloraz and malathion in Pigeon, Starling and hybrid Red-legged Partridge. *Environ. Toxicol. Chem.* **13**, 115–20.

Jones, H. P., Tershy, B., Zavaleta, E. S. *et al.* (2008). Severity of the effects of invasive rats on seabirds: a global review. *Conserv. Biol.* **22**, 116–26.

Jourdain, F. C. R. & Witherby, H. F. (1918). The effect of the winter of 1916–1917 on our resident birds. *Brit. Birds* **11**, 266–71; **12**, 26–35.

Kalela, O. (1952). Changes in the geographic distribution of Finnish birds and mammals in relation to recent changes in climate. *Fennia* **75**, 38–57.

Källander, H. (1981). The effects of provision of food in winter on a population of the Great Tit *Parus major* and the Blue Tit *P. caeruleus*. *Ornis Scand.* **12**, 244–8.

Källander, H. & Smith, H. G. (1990). Food storage in birds: an evolutionary perspective. *Curr. Ornithol.* **7**, 147–207.

Kalmbach, E. R. & Gunderson, M. F. (1934). Western duck sickness, a form of botulism. *US Dept. Agr. Tech. Bull.* **411**, 1–81.

Kanyamibwa, S., Schierer, A., Pradel, R. & Lebreton, J. D. (1990). Changes in adult survival rates in a western European population of the White Stork *Ciconia ciconia*. *Ibis* **132**, 27–35.

Kanyamibwa, S., Bairlein, F. & Schierer, A. (1993). Comparison of survival rates between populations of the White Stork *Ciconia ciconia* in central Europe. *Ornis Scand.* **24**, 297–302.

Karlsson, J. & Källander, H. (1977). Fluctuations and density of suburban populations of the Blackbird *Turdus merula*. *Ornis Scand.* **8**, 139–44.

Kautz, E. J. & Malecki, R. A. (1990). Effects of harvest on feral Rock Dove survival, nest success and population size. *U.S. Dept. Interior Fish Wildl. Tech. Rep.* **31**, 1–16.

Kear, J. (1990). *Man and Wildfowl.* Poyser, London.

Keith, L. B. (1963). *Wildlife's Ten-Year Cycle.* Wisconsin University Press, Madison, Wisconsin.

Keith, L. B. & Rusch, D. H. (1988). Predation's role in the cyclic fluctuations of Ruffed Grouse. *Proc. Int. Orn. Congr.* **19**, 699–732.

Kenward, R. E. (1977). Predation on released Pheasants (*Phasianus colchicus*) by Goshawks (*Accipiter gentilis*) in central Sweden. *Swedish Game Res.* **10**, 79–112.

Kenward, R. E. (1978). Hawks and doves: factors affecting success and selection in Goshawk attacks on Woodpigeons. *J. Anim. Ecol.* **47**, 449–60.

Kenward, R. E. (1985). Problems of Goshawk predation on pigeons and other game. *Proc. Int. Ornithol. Congr.* **18**, 666–78.

Kenward, R. E. (2006). *The Goshawk.* Poyser, London.

Kenward, R. E., Marcström, V. & Karlbom, M. (1981a). Goshawk winter ecology in Swedish Pheasant habitats. *J. Wildl. Manage.* **45**, 397–408.

Kenward, R. E., Marquiss, M. & Newton, I. (1981b). What happens to Goshawks trained for falconry? *J. Wildl. Manage.* **45**, 803–6.

Kenward, R. E., Marcström, V. & Karlbom, M. (1991). The Goshawk (*Accipiter gentilis*) as predator and renewable resource. *Gibier Faune Sauvage* **8**, 367–78.

Kenward, R. E., Marcström, V. & Karlbom, M. (1993). Causes of death in radio-tagged northern Goshawks. In: *Raptor Biomedicine* (ed. P. T. Redig, J. E. Cooper, J. D. Remple & D. B. Hunter). Minnesota University Press, Minneapolis, Minnesota, pp. 57–61.

Kerbes, R. H., Kotanen, P. M. & Jefferies, R. L. (1990). Destruction of wetland habitats by Lesser Snow Geese: a keystone species on the west coast of Hudson Bay. *J. Appl. Ecol.* **27**, 242–58.

Kilpi, M. & Öst, M. (1998). Reduced availability of refuse and breeding output in a Herring Gull (*Larus argentatus*) colony. *Ann. Zool. Fenn.* **35**, 37–42.

Kilpi, M. & Öst, M. (2002). The effect of White-tailed Sea Eagle predation on breeding Eider females off Tvärminne, Western Gulf of Finland. *Suomen Riista* **48**, 27–33.

King, G. A. & Herstrom, A. A. (1997). Holocene tree migration rates objectively determined from fossil pollen data. In: *Past and Future Rapid Environmental Changes: the Spatial and Evolutionary Responses of Terrestrial Biota* (ed. B. Huntley, W. Cramer, A. V. Morgan, H. C. Prentice & J. R. M. Allen). Springer, London, pp. 91–107.

Kirby, J. S., Salmon, D. G., Atkinson-Willes, G. L. & Cranswick, P. A. (1995). Index numbers for waterfowl populations. III. Long-term trends in the abundance of wintering wildfowl in Great Britain, 1966/67 to 1991/92. *J. Appl. Ecol.* **32**, 536–51.

Kirkwood, J. K. & MacGregor, S. K. (1998). Salmonellosis in provisioned free-living Greenfinches (*Carduelis chloris*) and other garden birds. In: *European Association of Zoo and Wildlife Veterinarians and BVZS 2nd Scientific Meeting* (ed. P. Zwart). Bunnik, Netherlands, pp. 229–34.

Klein, M. L., Humphrey, S. R. & Percival, H. F. (1995). Effects of ecotourism on distribution of waterbirds in a wildlife refuge. *Conserv. Biol.* **9**, 1454–65.

Klomp, N. I. & Furness, R. W. (1992). Non-breeders as a buffer against environmental stress: declines in numbers of Great Skuas on Foula, Shetland, and prediction of future recruitment. *J. Appl. Ecol.* **29**, 341–8.

Kluijver, H. N. (1951). The population ecology of the Great Tit, *Parus m. major* (L.). *Ardea* **39**, 1–135.

Kluijver, H. N. (1966). Regulation of a bird population. *Ostrich (Suppl.)* **6**, 389.

Kluijver, H. N. & Tinbergen, L. (1953). Territory and the regulation of density in titmice. *Arch. Néerl. Zool.* **10**, 265–89.

Koning, F. J., Koning, H. J. & Baeyens, G. (2009). Long-term study on interactions between Tawny Owls *Strix aluca*, Jackdaws *Corvus monedula* and Northern Goshawks *Accipiter gentilis*. *Ardea* **97**, 453–6.

Korpimäki, E. (1985). Clutch size and breeding success in relation to nest boxes in Tengmalm's Owl *Aegolius funereus*. *Holarctic Ecol.* **8**, 175–80.

Korpimäki, E. (1988). Effects of territory quality on occupancy, breeding performance and breeding dispersal in Tengmalm's Owl. *J. Anim. Ecol.* **57**, 97–108.

Korpimäki, E. (1989). Breeding performance of Tengmalm's Owl *Aegolius funereus*: effects of supplementary feeding in a peak vole year. *Ibis* **131**, 51–6.

Korpimäki, E. & Norrdahl, K. (1989). Predation of Tengmalm's Owls: numerical responses, functional responses and dampening impact on population fluctuations of voles. *Oikos* **54**, 154–64.

Korpimäki, E. & Norrdahl, K. (1991). Numerical and functional responses of Kestrels, Short-eared Owls and Long-eared Owls to vole densities. *Ecology* **72**, 814–26.

Korpimäki, E., Hakkarainen, H. & Bennett, G. F. (1993). Blood parasites and reproductive success of Tengmalm's Owls: detrimental effects on females but not males. *Funct. Ecol.* **7**, 420–6.

Koskimies, J. (1950). The life of the Swift *Micropus apus* (L.) in relation to the weather. *Suom. Tied. Toim. Ann. Acad. Sci. Fenn.* **15**, 1–151.

Kostrzewa, A. & Kostrzewa, R. (1989). The relationship of spring and summer weather with density and breeding performance of the Buzzard *Buteo buteo*, Goshawk *Accipiter gentilis* and Kestrel *Falco tinnunculus*. *Ibis* **132**, 550–9.

Kostrzewa, R. & Kostrzewa, A. (1991). Winter weather, spring and summer density and subsequent breeding success of Eurasian Kestrels, Common Buzzards, and Northern Goshawks. *Auk* **108**, 342–7.

Kowalik, R. A., Cooper, D. M., Evans, C. D. & Ormerod, S. J. (2007). Acidic episodes retard the biological recovery of upland British streams from chronic acidification. *Global Change Biol.* **13**, 2439–52.

Kraan, C., van Gils, J. A., Spaans, B. *et al.* (2009). Landscape-scale experiment demonstrates that Wadden Sea intertidal flats are used to capacity by molluscivore migrant shorebirds. *J. Anim. Ecol.* **78**, 1259–68.

Krebs, J. R. (1970). Regulation of numbers of the Great Tit (Aves: Passeriformes). *J. Zool. Lond.* **162**, 317–33.

Krebs, J. R. (1971). Territory and breeding density in the Great Tit *Parus major* L. *Ecology* **52**, 2–22.

Krebs, J. R., Clayton, N. S., Healy, S. *et al.* (1996). The ecology of the avian brain: food-storing memory and the hippocampus. *Ibis* **138**, 34–46.

Kress, S. W. (1983). The use of decoys,

sound recordings, and gull control for re-establishing a tern colony in Maine. *Colonial Waterbirds* **6**, 185–96.

Krone, O., Kenntner, N., Trinogga, A. *et al.* (2009). Lead poisoning in White-tailed Eagles: causes and approaches to solutions in Germany. In: *Ingestion of Lead from Spent Ammunition: Implications for Wildlife and Humans* (ed. R. T. Watson, M. Fuller, M. Pokras & G. Hunt). The Peregrine Fund, Boise, Idaho, pp. 289–301.

Kruger, O. & Lindström, J. (2008). Habitat heterogeneity affects population growth in Goshawk *Accipiter gentilis*. *J. Anim. Ecol.* **70**, 173–81.

Kruger, O., Chakarov, N., Nielsen, J. T. *et al.* (2012). Population regulation by habitat heterogeneity or individual adjustment? *J. Anim. Ecol.* **81**, 330–40.

Kruuk, H. (1964). Predators and anti-predator behaviour of the Black-headed Gull (*Larus ridibundus* L.). *Behaviour (Suppl.)* **11**, s1–130.

Kübler, S., Kupko, S., Zeller, U. (2005). The Kestrel (*Falco tinnunculus* L.) in Berlin: investigation of breeding biology and feeding ecology. *J. Ornithol.* **146**, 271–8.

Kullberg, C., Fransson, T. & Jacobsson, S. (1996). Impaired predator evasion in fat Blackcaps (*Sylvia atricapilla*). *Proc. R. Soc. Lond. B* **263**, 1671–5.

Kullberg, C., Jakobsson, S. & Fransson, T. (2000). High migratory fuel loads impair predator evasion in Sedge Warblers. *Auk* **117**, 1034–8.

Kvitek, R. G. (1991). Sequestered paralytic shellfish poisoning toxins mediate Glaucous-winged Gull predation on bivalve prey. *Auk* **108**, 381–92.

Lachish, S., Bonsall, M. B., Lawson, B., Cunningham, A. A. & Sheldon, B. C. (2012a). Individual and population-level impacts of an emerging poxvirus disease in a wild population of Great Tits. *PLoS One* **7** (11), e48545.

Lachish, S., Lawson, B., Cunningham, A. A. & Sheldon, B. C. (2012b). Epidemiology of the emergent disease Paridae pox in an intensively studied wild bird population. *PLoS One* **7** (11), e38316.

Lack, D. (1954). *The Natural Regulation of Animal Numbers.* Oxford University Press, Oxford.

Lack, D. (1966). *Population Studies of Birds.*

Oxford University Press, Oxford.

Lack, D. (1971). *Ecological Isolation in Birds.* Blackwell, Oxford.

Lambrechts, M. M., Wiebe, K. L., Sunde, P. *et al.* (2012). Nest box design for the study of diurnal raptors and owls is still an overlooked point in ecological, evolutionary and conservation studies: a review. *J. Ornithol.* **153**, 23–34.

Lampio, T. (1946). Game diseases in Finland 1924–43. *Suomen Riista* **1**, 93–142.

Lanner, R. M. (1996). *Made for Each Other: a Symbiosis of Birds and Pines.* Oxford University Press, Oxford.

La Sorte, F. A. & Thompson, F. R. (2007). Poleward shifts in winter ranges of North American birds. *Ecology* **88**, 1803–12.

Lawson, B., Howard, T., Kirkwood, J. K. *et al.* (2010). Epidemiology of salmonellosis in garden birds in England and Wales, 1993 to 2003. *Ecohealth* **7**, 294–306.

Lawson, B., Hughes, L. A., Peters, T. *et al.* (2011). Pulsed gel electrophoresis supports the presence of host-adapted *Salmonella enterica* subsp. *enterica* serovar Typhimurium strains in the British garden bird population. *Appl. Environ. Microbiol.* **77**, 8139–44.

Lawson, B., Lachish, S., Colvile, K. M. *et al.* (2012a). Emergence of a novel avian pox disease in British tit species. *PLoS One* **7** (11), e40176. doi:10.1371/journal. pone.0040176

Lawson, B., Robinson, R. A., Colvile, K. M. *et al.* (2012b). The emergence and spread of finch trichomonosis in the British Isles. *Phil. Trans. R. Soc. B* **367**: 2852–63.

Lebreton, J.-D. & Isenmann, P. (1976). Dynamique de la population camarguaise de Mouettes Rieuses *Larus ridibundus* L.: un modèle mathématique. *Terre et Vie* **30**, 529–49.

Lehikoinen, E. & Sparks, T. (2010). Changes in migration. In: *Effects of Climate Change on Birds* (ed. A. P. Møller, W. Fiedler & P. Berthold). Oxford University Press, Oxford, pp. 89–112.

Lehikoinen, E. Sparks, T. H. & Zalakevicius, M. (2004). Arrival and departure dates. In: *Birds and Climate Change* (ed. A. P. Møller, W. Fiedler & P. Berthold). *Adv. Ecol. Res.* **35**, 1–28.

Lehikoinen, A., Kilpi, M. & Ost, M. (2006). Winter climate affects subsequent breeding success of Common Eider. *Global Change Biol.* **12**, 1355–65.

Lens, L. & Dhondt, A. A. (1992). The effect of a severe storm on a population of Crested Tits *Parus cristatus* in Belgium. *Bird Study* **39**, 31–3.

Leslie, H. A., Leonards, P. E. G., Shore, R. F. *et al.* (2011). Decabromodiphenylether and hexabromocyclodecane in wild birds from the United Kingdom, Sweden and the Netherlands. *Chemosphere* **82**, 88–95.

Lewis, S., Sherratt, T. N., Hamer, K. C. & Wanless, S. (2001). Evidence of intraspecific competition for food in a pelagic seabird. *Nature* **412**, 816–19.

Lid, G. (1981). Reproduction of the Puffin on Røst in the Lofoten Islands in 1964–80. *Cinclus* **4**, 30–9.

Liley, D. & Clarke, R. T. (2003). The impact of urban development and human disturbance on the numbers of Nightjar *Caprimulgus europaeus* on heathlands in Dorset, England. *Biol. Conserv.* **114**, 219–30.

Liley, D. & Sutherland, W. J. (2007). Predicting the population consequences of human disturbance for Ringed Plovers *Charadrius hiaticula*: a game theory approach. *Ibis* **149** (S1), 82–94.

Lima, S. L. (1986). Predation risk and unpredictable feeding conditions: determinants of body mass in birds. *Ecology* **67**, 377–85.

Lima, S. L. (2002). Putting predators back into behavioural predator–prey interactions. *Trends Ecol. Evol.* **17**, 70–5.

Lind, J., Fransson, T., Jacobsson, S. & Kullberg, C. (1999). Reduced take-off ability in Robins due to migratory fuel load. *Behav. Ecol. Sociobiol.* **46**, 65–70.

Lindén, H. (1988). Latitudinal gradients in predator-prey interactions, cyclicity and synchronism in voles and small game populations in Finland. *Oikos* **52**, 341–9.

Lindén, H. & Wikman, M. (1983). Goshawk predation on tetraonids: availability of prey and diet of the predator in the breeding season. *J. Anim. Ecol.* **52**, 953–68.

Lindström, Å., Enemar, A., Andersson, G., von Proschwitz, T. & Nyholm, N. E. I. (2005). Density-dependent reproductive output in relation to a drastically varying food supply: getting the density measure right. *Oikos* **110**, 155–63.

Lindström, E., Angelstam, P., Widén, P. & Andrén, H. (1987). Do predators synchronize vole and grouse fluctuations? An experiment. *Oikos* **48**, 121–4.

Lindström, E., Andrén, H., Angelstam, P. *et al.* (1994). Disease reveals the predator; sarcoptic mange, Red Fox predation, and prey populations. *Ecology* **75**, 1042–9.

Lloyd, C. S., Thomas, G. J., MacDonald, J. W. *et al.* (1976). Wild bird mortality caused by botulism in Britain, 1975. *Biol. Conserv.* **10**, 119–29.

Lloyd, C. S., Tasker, M. L. & Partridge, K. (1991). *The Status of Seabirds in Britain and Ireland*. Poyser, Calton.

Lochmiller, R. L. & Deerenberg, C. (2000). Trade-offs in evolutionary immunology: just what is the cost of immunity? *Oikos* **88**, 87–98.

Lockie, J. D., Ratcliffe, D. A. & Balharry, D. R. (1969). Breeding success and dieldrin contamination of Golden Eagles in west Scotland. *J. Appl. Ecol.* **6**, 381–9.

Löhrl, H. (1957). Populationsökologische Untersuchungen beim Halsbandschnapper (*Ficedula albicollis*). *Bonn. Zool. Beiträge* **8**, 130–77.

Löhrl, H. (1970). Unterschleidliche Brutholenanspruche von Meisenarten und Kleibern als Beitrag zum Nischenproblem. *Verh. Dtsch. Zool. Ges.* **64**, 314–17.

Löhrl, H. (1977). Nistökologische und ethologische Anpassungserscheinungen bei Höhlenbrütern. *Die Vogelwarte* **29**, 92–101.

Loison, A., Saether, B.-E., Jerstad, K. & Rostad, O. W. (2002). Disentangling the sources of variation in the survival of the European Dipper. *J. Appl. Stat.* **29**, 289–304.

Lokemoen, J. T., Doty, H. A., Sharp, D. E. & Neaville, J. E. (1982). Electric fences to reduce mammalian predation on waterfowl nests. *Wildl. Soc. Bull.* **10**, 318–23.

Looft, V. & Biesterfeld, G. (1981). Habicht – *Accipiter gentilis*. In: *Vogelwelt Schleswig-Holsteins, Band 2: Greifvogel* (ed. V. Looft & G. Busche). Karl Wachholtz Verlag, Neumünster, pp. 101–115.

Lovegrove, R. (2007). *Silent Fields: the Long*

Decline of a Nation's Wildlife. Oxford University Press, Oxford.

Loxton, R. G. & Silcocks, A. (1997). The rise and fall of Bardsey Blackbirds. *Rep. Bardsey Bird Fld. Obs.* **40**, 76–99.

Ludescher, F.-B. (1973). Sumpfmeise (*Parus p. palustris* L.) und Weidenmeise (*P. montanus salicarius* Br.) als sympatrische Zwillingarten. *J. Ornithol.* **114**, 3–56.

Ludwig, G. (2009). Impact of climate and environmental change on Finnish grouse populations. *Suomen Riista* **55**, 7–18.

Lundberg, A., Alatalo, R. V., Carlson, A. & Ulfstrand, S. (1981). Biometry, habitat distribution and breeding success in the Pied Flycatcher *Ficedula hypoleuca*. *Ornis Scand.* **12**, 68–79.

MacArthur, R. H. (1972). *Geographical Ecology: Patterns in the Distribution of Species*. Harper & Row, New York.

Macdonald, J. W., McMartin, D. D., Walker, K. G., Cairns, M. & Dennis, R. H. (1967). Puffinosis in Fulmars in Orkney and Shetland. *Brit. Birds* **60**, 356–360.

Macdonald, J. W. & Standring, K. T. (1978). An outbreak of botulism in gulls on the Firth of Forth, Scotland. *Biol. Conserv.* **14**, 149–155.

MacDonald, M. A. & Bolton, M. (2008). Predation on wader nests in Europe. *Ibis* **150** (S1), 54–73.

MacLean, I. M., Austin, G. E., Rehfisch, M. M. *et al.* (2008). Climate change causes rapid changes in the distribution and site abundance of birds in winter. *Global Change Biol.* **14**, 2489–500.

MacLeod, R. & Gosler, A. G. (2006). Capture and mass change: perceived predation risk or interrupted foraging. *Anim. Behav.* **71**, 1081–7.

Macleod, R., Barnett, P., Clark, J. A. & Cresswell, W. (2005a). Body mass change strategies in Blackbirds *Turdus merula*: the starvation-predation risk trade-off. *J. Anim. Ecol.* **74**, 292–302.

MacLeod, R., Gosler, A. G. & Cresswell, W. (2005b). Diurnal mass gain strategies and perceived predation risk in the Great Tit *Parus major*. *J. Anim. Ecol.* **74**, 956–64.

MacLeod, R., Barnett, P. Clark, J. A. & Cresswell, W. (2006). Mass-dependent predation risk as a mechanism for House Sparrow declines? *Biol. Lett.* **2**, 43–6.

MacLeod, R., Clark, J. A. & Cresswell, W. (2008). The starvation–predation risk trade-off, body mass and population status in the Common Starling *Sturnus vulgaris*. *Ibis* **150** (S1), 199–208.

Madsen, J. (1995). Impacts of disturbance on migratory waterfowl. *Ibis* **137** (S1), 67–74.

Madsen, J. & Jepsen, P. U. (1992). Passing the buck: need for a flyway management plan for the Svalbard Pink-footed Goose. In: *Waterfowl and Agriculture: Review and Future Perspective of the Crop Damage Conflict in Europe* (ed. M. van Roomen & J. Madsen). IWRB Special Publication 21. International Waterfowl & Wetlands Research Bureau, Slimbridge, pp. 109–10.

Madsen, J. & Noer, H. (1996). Decreased survival of Pink-footed Geese *Anser brachyrhynchus* carrying shotgun pellets. *Wildl. Biol.* **2**, 75–82.

Madsen, J., Bregnballe, T. & Hehlum, F. (1989). Study of the breeding ecology and behaviour of Svalbard population of Light-bellied Brent Goose *Branta bernicla hrota*. *Polar Res.* **7**, 1–21.

Madsen, J., Cracknell, G. & Fox, T. (1999). *Goose Populations of the Western Palearctic. A Review of Status and Distribution*. Wetlands International/Natural Environmental Research Institute, Wageningen, Netherlands/Ronde, Denmark.

Madsen, M., Nielsen, B. O., Holter, P. *et al.* (1990). Treating cattle with Ivermectin and effects on the fauna and decomposition of dung pats. *J. Appl. Ecol.* **27**, 1–15.

Maggini, R., Shroder, B., Zimmermann, N. E. *et al.* (2010). Modelling range shifts for Swiss breeding birds. *BOU Proceedings: Climate Change and Birds*. http://www.bou.org.uk/bouproc-net/ccb/maggini-etal.pdf.

Mallord, J. W., Dolman, P. M., Brown, A. F. & Sutherland, W. J. (2007). Linking recreational disturbance to population size in a ground-nesting passerine. *J. Appl. Ecol.* **44**, 185–95.

Malpas, L. R., Kennerley. R. J., Hirons, G. J. M. *et al.* (2012). The use of predator fences as a management tool to improve the breeding success of waders on lowland wet grassland. *J. Nat. Conserv.* http://dx.doi.org/10.1016/j.jnc.2012.09.002.

Mänd, R., Leivits, A., Leivits, M. & Rodenhouse, N. L. (2009). Provision of nest boxes raises the breeding density of Great Tits *Parus major* equally in coniferous and deciduous woodland. *Ibis* **151**, 487–92.

Mannan, R. W., Meslow, E. C. & Wight, H. M. (1980). Use of snags by birds in Douglas fir forests. *J. Wildl. Manage.* **44**, 787–97.

Marchant, J. H., Hudson, R., Carter, S. P. & Whittington, P. (1990). *Population Trends in British Breeding Birds*. British Trust for Ornithology, Tring.

Marcström, V. & Mascher, J. W. (1979). Weights and fat in Lapwings *Vanellus vanellus* and Oystercatchers *Haematopus ostralegus* starved to death during a cold spell in spring. *Ornis Scand.* **10**, 235–40.

Marcström, V., Kenward, R. E. & Engren, E. (1988). The impact of predation on boreal tetraonids during vole cycles: an experimental study. *J. Anim. Ecol.* **57**, 859–72.

Marjakangas, A. (1987). Does the provision of extra food in winter affect the abundance of Finnish Black Grouse? In: *Proceedings of the 4th International Grouse Symposium* (ed. T. Lovel & P. J. Hudson). Lam, Germany, pp. 133–8.

Marjakangas, A. & Puhto, J. (1999). Effect of supplemental winter feeding on the breeding success of female Black Grouse. *Suomen Riista* **45**, 7–15.

Marquiss, M. (1981). The Goshawk in Britain: its provenance and current status. In: *Understanding the Goshawk* (ed. R. E. Kenward & I. M. Lindsay). International Association for Falconry and Conservation of Birds of Prey, Oxford, pp. 43–57.

Marquiss, M. (2007). Seasonal pattern in hawk predation on Common Bullfinches *Pyrrhula pyrrhula*; evidence of an interaction with habitat affecting food availability. *Bird Study* **54**, 1–11.

Marquiss, M. & Newton, I. (1982). The Goshawk in Britain. *Brit. Birds* **75**, 243–60.

Marquiss, M., Petty, S. J., Anderson, D. I. K. & Legge, G. (2003). Contrasting population trends of the Northern Goshawk (*Accipiter gentilis*) in the Scottish/English Borders and north-east Scotland. In: *Birds of Prey in a Changing Environment* (ed. D. B. A. Thompson, S. M. Redpath, A. H. Fielding,

M. Marquiss & C. A. Galbraith). Sationery Office, Edinburgh, pp. 143–8.

Martin, T. E. (1987). Food as a limit on breeding birds: a life history perspective. *Ann. Rev. Ecol. Syst.* **18**, 453–87.

Marzal, A., de Lope, F., Navarro, C. & Møller, A. P. (2005). Malarial parasites decrease reproductive success: an experimental study in a passerine bird. *Oecologia* **142**, 541–5.

Marzal, A., Reviriego, M., de Lope, F. & Møller, A. P. (2007). Fitness costs of an immune response in the House Martin *Delichon urbica*. *Behav. Ecol. Sociobiol.* **61**, 1573–80.

Massemin-Challet, S., Gendner, J.-P., Samtmann, S. *et al.* (2006). The effect of migration strategy and food availability on White Stork *Ciconia ciconia* breeding success. *Ibis* **148**, 503–8.

Mateo, R. (2009). Lead poisoning in wild birds in Europe and the regulations adopted by different countries. In: *Ingestion of Lead from Spent Ammunition: Implications for Wildlife and Humans* (ed. R. T. Watson, M. Fuller, M. Pokras & W. G. Hunt). The Peregrine Fund, Boise, Idaho, pp. 71–98.

Matthysen, E. (1989). Territorial and nonterritorial settling in juvenile Eurasian Nuthatches (*Sitta europaea* L.) in summer. *Auk* **106**, 560–7.

Matthysen, E. (1990). Behavioural and ecological correlates of territory quality in the Eurasian Nuthatch (*Sitta europaea*). *Auk* **107**, 86–95.

May, R. M. & Anderson, R. M. (1978). Regulation and stability of host-parasite interactions. II. Destabilising processes. *J. Anim. Ecol.* **47**, 249–67.

Mayhew, P. & Houston, D. (1999). Effects of winter and early spring grazing by Wigeon *Anas penelope* on their food supply. *Ibis* **141**, 80–4.

Mayot, P., Patillaud, J.-P. & Stahl, P. (1993). Influence de la predation sur la survie des Faisans (*Phasianus colchicus*) de repeuplement. In: *Actes du Colloque Predation et Gestion des Predateurs* (ed. P. Migot & P. Stahl). ONC – UNFDC, Paris, pp. 51–7.

McCleery, R. H. & Perrins, C. M. (1991). Effects of predation on the numbers of Great Tits *Parus major*. In: *Bird Population Studies:*

Relevance to Conservation and Management (ed. C. M. Perrins, J.-D. Lebreton & G. J. M. Hirons). Oxford University Press, Oxford, pp. 129–47.

McCleery, R. H., Clobert, J., Julliard, R. & Perrins, C. M. (1996). Nest predation and delayed cost of reproduction in the Great Tit. *J. Anim. Ecol.* **65**, 96–104.

McDonald, M. E. (1969). *Catalogue of Helminths of Waterfowl (Anatidae)*. US Bureau of Sport Fisheries and Wildlife, Washingotn, DC.

McGowan, A., Cresswell, W. & Ruxton, G. D. (2002). The effects of daily weather variation on foraging and responsiveness to disturbance in overwintering Red Knot (*Calidris canutus*). *Ardea* **90**, 229–37.

McGowan, J. D. (1975). Effects of autumn and spring hunting on Ptarmigan population trends. *J. Wildl. Manage.* **39**, 491–5.

McIlhenny, F. A. (1934). *Bird City*. Christopher Publishing House, Boston, Massachusetts.

McKechnie, A. E. & Wolf, B. O. (2010). Climate change increases the likelihood of catastrophic avian mortality events during extreme heat waves. *Biol. Lett.* **6**, 253–6.

McKenzie, A. J., Petty, S. J., Toms, M. P. & Furness, R. W. (2007). Importance of Sitka Spruce *Picea sitchensis* seed and garden bird-feeders for Siskins *Carduelis spinus* and Coal Tits *Periparus ater*. *Bird Study* **54**, 236–47.

McMillan, R. L. (2011). Raptor persecution on a large Perthshire estate: a historical study. *Scott. Birds* **31**, 195–205.

McNamara, J. M. & Houston, A. I. (1990). The value of fat reserves and the tradeoff between starvation and predation. *Acta Biotheor.* **38**, 37–61.

Mearns, R. & Newton, I. (1988). Factors affecting breeding success of Peregrines in south Scotland. *J. Anim. Ecol.* **57**, 903–16.

Meek, E. (1993). Population fluctuations and mortality of Mute Swans on an Orkney loch system in relation to a Canadian pondweed growth cycle. *Scott. Birds* **17**, 85–92.

Meese, R. J. & Fuller, M. R. (1989). Distribution and behaviour of passerines around Peregrine *Falco peregrinus* eyries in western Greenland. *Ibis* **131**, 27–32.

Meinertzhagen, R. (1950). The Goshawk in Great Britain. *Bull. BOC* **70**, 46–9.

Mendelssohn, H. (1972). The impact of pesticides on bird life in Israel. *ICBP Bull.* **11**, 75–104.

Menzel, A., Sparks, T. H., Esrella, N. et al. (2006). European phenological response to climate changes matches the warming pattern. *Global Change Biol.* **12**, 1969–76.

Meriggi, A., Brangi, A., Cuccus, P. & Mazzoni delia Stella, P. (2002). High mortality rate in a reintroduced Grey Partridge population in central Italy. *Ital. J. Zool.* **69**, 19–24.

Merilä, J. & Allander, K. (1995). Do Great Tits (*Parus major*) prefer ectoparasite-free roost sites? An experiment. *Ethology* **99**, 53–60.

Merilä, J. & Wiggins, D. A. (1995). Interspecific competition for nest holes causes adult mortality in the Collared Flycatcher. *Condor* **97**, 445–50.

Merino, S. & Potti, J. (1995). Mites and blowflies decrease growth and survival of nestling Pied Flycatchers. *Oikos* **73**, 95–103.

Merino, S. & Potti, J. (1998). Growth, nutrition and blow fly parasitism in nestling Pied Flycatchers. *Can. J. Zool.* **76**, 936–41.

Merino, S. & Potti, J. (2006). Weather-dependent effect of nest ectoparasites on their bird hosts. *Ecography* **19**, 107–13.

Merino, S., Møller, A. P. & de Lope, F. (2000). Seasonal changes in cell-mediated immunocompetence and mass gain in nestling Barn Swallows: a parasite mediated effect. *Oikos* **90**, 327–32.

Merricks, P. (2010). Lapwings, farming and environmental stewardship. *British Wildlife*, October 2010, 10–13.

Metcalfe, N. B. (1984). The effects of habitat on the vigilance of shorebirds: is visibility important? *Anim. Behav.* **32**, 981–5.

Metcalfe, N. B. & Ure, S. E. (1995). Diurnal variation in flight performance and hence potential predation risk in small birds. *Proc. R. Soc. Lond. B* **261**, 395–400.

Meyrom, K., Motro, Y., Leshem, Y. et al. (2009). Nest box use by the Barn Owl *Tyto alba* in a biological pest control program in the Bei She'an valley, Israel. *Ardea* **97**, 463–7.

Mihoub, J.-B., Gimenez, O., Pilard, P. & Sarrazin, F. (2010). Challenging conservation of migratory species: Sahelian rainfall drives first-year survival of the vulnerable Lesser Kestrel *Falco naumanni*. *Biol. Conserv.* **143**, 839–47.

Mikola, J., Miettinen, M., Lehikoinen, E. & Lehtila, K. (1994). The effects of disturbance caused by boating on survival and behaviour of Velvet Scoter *Melanitta fusca* ducklings. *Biol. Conserv.* **67**, 119–24.

Miller, G. R., Jenkins, D. & Watson, A. (1966). Heather performance and Red Grouse populations. 1. Visual estimates of heather performance. *J. Appl. Ecol.* **3**, 313–26.

Miller, G. R., Watson, A. & Jenkins, D. (1970). Responses of Red Grouse populations to experimental improvement in their food. In: *Animal Populations in Relation to Their Food Resources* (ed. A. Watson). Blackwell, Oxford, pp. 323–35.

Milonoff, M. (1994). An overlooked connection between Goshawks and tetraonids: corvids! *Suomen Riista* **40**, 91–7.

Milwright, R. D. P. (1998). Breeding biology of the Golden Oriole *Oriolus oriolus* in the fenland basin of eastern Britian. *Bird Study* **45**, 320–30.

Minderman, J., Lind, J. & Cresswell, W. (2006). Behaviourally mediated indirect effects: interference competition increases predation mortality in foraging Redshanks. *J. Anim. Ecol.* **75**, 713–23.

Mineau, P. (1993). *The Hazard of Carbofuron to Birds and Other Vertebrate Wildlife.* Environment Canada, Canadian Wildlife Service, Wildlife Toxicology Section, Ottawa. Tech. Rep. No. 177.

Minot, E. O. (1981). Effects of interspecific competition for food in breeding Blue and Great Tits. *J. Anim. Ecol.* **50**, 375–85.

Minot, E. O. & Perrins, C. M. (1986). Interspecific interference competition – nest sites for Blue and Great Tits. *J. Anim. Ecol.* **55**, 331–50.

Mitchell, C., Fox, A. D., Harradine, J. & Clausager, I. (2008). Measures of annual breeding success amongst Eurasian Wigeon *Anas penelope*. *Bird Study* **55**, 43–51.

Mitchell, I., Ratcliffe, N., Newton, S. & Dunn, T. E. (2004). *Seabird Populations of Britain and Ireland: Results of the 'Seabird 2000' Census 1999–2002*. Poyser, London.

Mitrus, C., Walankiewicz, W. & Czeszczewik, D. (2007). Frequency of nest-hole occupation and breeding success of Collared Flycatchers *Ficedula albicollis*. *Ibis* **149**, 414–18.

Moleon, M., Almaraz, P. & Sanchez-Zapata, J. A. (2008). An emerging infectious disease triggering large-scale hyperpredation. *PLoS One* **4** (3), e2307.

Møller, A. P. (1982). Characteristics of Magpie *Pica pica* territories of varying duration. *Ornis Scand.* **13**, 94–100.

Møller, A. P. (1989a). Parasites, predators and nest boxes: facts and artefacts in nest box studies of birds? *Oikos* **56**, 421–3.

Møller, A. P. (1989b). Population dynamics of a declining Swallow *Hirundo rustica* population. *J. Anim. Ecol.* **58**, 1051–63.

Møller, A. P. (1990). Effects of parasitism by the haematophagous mite on reproduction in the Barn Swallow. *Ecology* **71**, 2345–57.

Møller, A. P. (1993). Ectoparasites increase the cost of reproduction in their hosts. *J. Anim. Ecol.* **62**, 309–22.

Møller, A. P. (1994). Parasites as an environmental component of reproduction in birds as exemplified by the Swallow *Hirundo rustica*. *Ardea* **82**, 161–72.

Møller, A. P. (2002a). North Atlantic Oscillation (NAO) effects of climate on the relative importance of first and second clutches in a migratory passerine bird. *J. Anim. Ecol.* **71**, 201–10.

Møller, A. P. (2002b). Temporal change in mite abundance and its effect on Barn Swallow reproduction and sexual selection. *J. Evol. Biol.* **15**, 495–504.

Møller, A. P. (2010). Host–parasite interactions and vectors in the Barn Swallow in relation to climate change. *Global Change Biol.* **16**, 1158–70.

Møller, A. P. & Erritzøe, J. (2000). Predation against birds with low immunocompetence. *Oecologia* **122**, 500–4.

Møller, A. P. & Erritzøe, J. (2002). Coevolution of host immune defence and parasite-induced mortality: relative spleen size and mortality in altricial birds. *Oikos* **99**, 95–100.

Møller, A. P. & Hobson, K. A. (2004). Heterogeneity in stable isotope profiles predicts coexistence of populations of Barn Swallows *Hirundo rustica* differing in morphology and reproductive performance. *Proc. R. Soc. Lond. B* **271**, 1355–62.

Møller, A. P. & Merilä, J. (2004). Analysis and interpretation of long-term studies investigating responses to climate change. In: *Birds and Climate Change* (ed. A. P. Møller, W. Fiedler & P. Berthold). *Adv. Ecol. Res.* **35**, 111–30.

Møller, A. P. & Nielsen, J. T. (2007). Malaria and risk of predation: a comparative study of birds. *Ecology* **88**, 871–81.

Møller, A. P. & Saino, N. (2004). Immune response and survival. *Oikos* **104**, 299–304.

Møller, A. P., Christe, Ph., Erritzøe, J. & Mavarez, J. (1998). Condition, disease and immune defense. *Oikos* **83**, 301–6.

Møller, A. P., Merino, S., Brown, C. R. & Robertson, R. J. (2001). Immune defence and host sociality: a comparative study of swallows and martins. *Amer. Nat.* **158**, 136–45.

Møller, A. P., Erritzøe, J. & Saino, N. (2003). Seasonal changes in immune response and parasite impact on hosts. *Amer. Nat.* **161**, 657–71.

Møller, A. P., de Lope, F. & Saino, N. (2004). Parasitism, immunity and arrival date in a migratory bird, the Barn Swallow. *Ecology* **85**, 206–19.

Møller, A. P., Rubolini, D. & Lehikoinen, E. (2008). Populations of migratory bird species that do not show a phenological response to climate change are declining. *Proc. Nat. Acad. Sci.* **105**, 16195–200.

Møller, A. P., Saino, N, Adamik, P. *et al.* (2011). Rapid change in host use of the Common Cuckoo *Cuculus canorus* linked to climate change. *Proc. R. Soc. B* **278**, 733–8.

Mols, C. M. M. & Visser, M. E. (2002). Great Tits can reduce caterpillar damage in apple orchards. *J. Appl. Ecol.* **39**, 888–99.

Monaghan, P. (1979). Aspects of the breeding biology of Herring Gulls *Larus argentatus* in urban colonies. *Ibis* **121**, 475–81.

Monaghan, P. (1992). Seabirds and sandeels: the conflict between exploitation and conservation in the northern North Sea. *Biodiver. Conserv.* **1**, 98–111.

Monaghan, P., Uttley, J. F. D., Burns, M. D., Thaine, C. & Blackwood, J. (1989a). The relationship between food supply, reproduction effort and breeding success in Arctic Terns *Sterna paradisea*. *J. Anim. Ecol.* **58**, 261–74.

Monaghan, P., Uttley, J. D. & Okill, J. D. (1989b). Terns and sandeels: seabirds as indicators of marine fish populations. *J. Fish Biol. (suppl. A)* **35**, S339–40.

Monaghan, P., Uttley, J. F. D. & Burns, M. D. (1992). Effects of changes in food availability on reproductive effort in Arctic Terns. *Ardea* **80**, 71–81.

Mönkkönen, L. & Forsman, J. (2002). Heterospecific attraction among forest birds: a review. *Ornithological Science* **1**, 41–51.

Mönkkönen, M., Helle, P. and Soppela, K. (1990). Numerical and behavioural responses of migrant passerines to experimental manipulation of resident tits (*Parus spp*): heterospecific attraction in northern breeding bird communities. *Oecologia* **85**, 218–25.

Mönkkönen, M., Tornberg, R. & Vaisanen, P. (2000). Goshawks may reduce predation rates on birds' nests. *Suomen Riista* **46**, 27–36.

Montier, D. (1968). A survey of the breeding distribution of the Kestrel, Barn Owl and Tawny Owl in the London area in 1967. *Lond. Bird Rep.* **32**, 81–92.

Monval, J.-Y. & Pirot, J.-Y. (1989). *Results of the IWRB International Waterfowl Census 1967–86.* IWRB Special Publication 8. International Waterfowl & Wetlands Research Bureau, Slimbridge.

Moorcroft, D., Whittingham, M., Bradbury, R. B. & Wilson, J. D. (2002). The selection of stubble fields by wintering granivorous birds reflects vegetation cover and food abundance. *J. Appl. Ecol.* **39**, 535–47.

Morant, P. D., Cooper, J. & Randall, R. M. (1981). The rehabilitation of oiled Jackass Penguins *Spheniscus demersus*, 1970–1980. In: *Proceeding of a Symposium on Birds of the Sea and Shore* (ed. J. Cooper). African Seabird Group, Capetown, pp. 267–85.

Moreno-Rueda, G. & Rivas, J. M. (2007). Recent changes in allometric relationships among morphological traits in the dipper (*Cinclus cinclus*). *J. Ornithol.* **148**, 489–94.

Morgan, G. (2012). The bird populations of Ramsey and Grassholm. *Brit. Birds* **105**, 716–32.

Morosinotto, C., Thomson, R. L. & Korpimäki, E. (2010). Habitat selection as an antipredator behaviour in a multi-predator landscape: all enemies are not equal. *J. Anim. Ecol.* **79**, 327–33.

Morris, A. J. & Gilroy, J. J. (2008). Close to the edge: predation risks for two declining farmland passerines. *Ibis* **150** (S1), 168–77.

Morris, A. J., Whittingham, M. J., Bradbury, R. B. *et al.* (2001). Foraging habitat selection by Yellowhammers (*Emberiza citrinella*) in agriculturally contrasting regions of lowland England. *Biol. Conserv.* **98**, 197–210.

Morris, R. D., Blokpoel, H. & Tessier, G. D. (1992). Management efforts for the conservation of Common Tern *Sterna hirundo* colonies in the Great Lakes: 2 case histories. *Biol. Conserv.* **60**, 7–14.

Morris, R. J. (1980). Floating plastic debris in the Mediterranean. *Mar. Poll. Bull.* **11**, 125.

Morse, S. S. (1991). The orgins of new viral diseases. Environmental carcinogenesis and ecotoxicology reviews – Part C. *J. Environ. Sci. Health* **9**, 207–28.

Moss, D. (1978). Song-bird populations in forestry plantations. *Quart. J. For.* **72**, 5–14.

Moss, R. (1969). A comparison of Red Grouse (*Lagopus l. scoticus*) stocks with the production and nutritive value of heather (*Calluna vulgaris*). *J. Anim. Ecol.* **38**, 103–22.

Moss, R. (1986). Rain, breeding success and distribution of Capercaillie *Tetrao urogallus* and Black Grouse *Tetrao tetrix* in Scotland. *Ibis* **128**, 65–72.

Moss, R. (2001). Second extinction of the Capercaillie (*Tetrao urogallus*) in Scotland? *Biol. Conserv.* **101**, 255–7.

Moss, R. Oswald, J. & Baines, D. (2001). Climate change and breeding success: decline of the Capercaillie in Scotland. *J. Anim. Ecol.* **70**, 47–61.

Moss, W. W. & Camin, J. H. (1970). Nest parasitism, productivity and clutch size in Purple Martins. *Science* **168**, 1000–3.

Mudge, G. P. (1978). The gull increase, as illustrated by studies in the Bristol Channel. *Ibis* **120**, 115–16.

Mullié, W. C. & Keith, J. O. (1993). The effects of aerially applied fenitrothion and chlorpyrifos on birds in the savannah of northern Senegal. *J. Appl. Ecol.* **30**, 536–50.

Murray, S. (2002). Birds of St Kilda. *Scott. Birds* **23** (Suppl.), s1–64.

Murray, S. & Wanless, S. (1997). The status of the Gannet in Scotland in 1994–95. *Scott. Birds* **19**, 10–27.

Murton, R. K. (1964). Do birds transmit foot and mouth disease? *Ibis* **106**, 289–98.

Murton, R. K. (1965). *The Woodpigeon.* Collins, London.

Murton, R. K. (1968). Some predator relationships in bird damage and population control. In: *The Problems of Birds as Pests* (ed. R. K. Murton & E. N. Wright). Academic Press, London, pp. 157–69.

Murton, R. K. & Westwood, N. J. (1977). *Avian Breeding Cycles.* Clarendon Press, Oxford.

Murton, R. K., Westwood, N. J. & Isaacson, A. J. (1964). A preliminary investigation of the factors regulating population size in the Woodpigeon. *Ibis* **106**, 482–507.

Murton, R. K., Isaacson, A. J. & Westwood, N. J. (1966). The relationships between Woodpigeons and their clover food supply and the mechanism of population control. *J. Appl. Ecol.* **3**, 55–96.

Myrberget, S. (1972). Fluctuations in a North Norwegian population of Willow Grouse. *Proc. Int. Ornithol. Congr.* **15**, 107–20.

Myrberget, S. (1984). Population dynamics of Willow Grouse *Lagopus lagopus* on an island in north Norway. *Fauna Norv. Ser. C. Cinclus* **7**, 95–105.

Navarro, C., de Lope, F., Marzal, A. & Møller, A. P. (2004). Predation risk, host immune response, and parasitism. *Behav. Ecol.* **15**, 629–35.

Nelson, J. B. (1978). *The Gannet.* Poyser, Berkhamsted.

Nelson, R. W. & Myres, M. T. (1975). Changes in the Peregrine population and its sea bird prey at Langara Island, British Columbia. In: *Population Status of Raptors* (ed. J. R. Murphy, C. M. White & B. E. Harrell). Raptor Research Foundation, Fort Collins, Colorado, pp. 13–31.

Nelson, T. H. (1907). *The Birds of Yorkshire, Vol. 1.* A. Brown & Sons, London.

Nettleship, D. N. (1975). Effects of *Larus* gulls on breeding performance, nest distribution and winter fattening in Atlantic Puffins. In: *Proceedings of Gull Seminar, Sackville, New Brunswick.* Canadian Wildlife Service, Sackville, New Brunswick, pp. 47–69.

New, L. F., Matthiopoulos, J., Redpath, S. & Buckland, S. T. (2009). Fitting models of multiple hypotheses to partial population data: investigating the causes of cycles in Red Grouse. *Amer. Nat.* **174**, 399–412.

Newson, S. E. (2000). Colonisation and range expansion of inland breeding Great Cormorants *Phalacrocorax carbo* in England. PhD thesis, University of Bristol.

Newson, S. E., Rexstad, E. A., Baillie, S. R., Buckland, S. T. & Aebischer, N. J. (2010). Population change of avian predators and Grey Squirrels in England: is there evidence for an impact on avian prey populations? *J. Appl. Ecol.* **47**, 244–52.

Newth, J. L., Brown, M. J. & Rees, E. (2011). Incidence of embedded shotgun pellets in Bewick's Swans *Cygnus columbianus bewickii* and Whooper Swans *Cygnus cygnus* wintering in the UK. *Biol. Conserv.* **144**, 1630–7.

Newton, I. (1967). The feeding ecology of the Bullfinch (*Pyrrhula pyrrhula*) in southern England. *J. Anim. Ecol.* **36**, 721–44.

Newton, I. (1969). Winter fattening in the Bullfinch. *Physiol. Zool.* **42**, 96–107.

Newton, I. (1972). *Finches.* New Naturalist 55. Collins, London.

Newton, I. (1977). Timing and success of breeding in tundra-nesting geese. In: *Evolutionary Ecology* (ed. B. Stonehouse & C. M. Perrins). Macmillan, London, pp. 113–26.

Newton, I. (1979). *Population Ecology of Raptors.* Poyser, Berkhamsted.

Newton, I. (1986). *The Sparrowhawk.* Poyser, Calton.

Newton, I. (1988). Determination of critical pollutant levels in wild populations, with examples from organochlorine pesticides in birds of prey. *Environ. Pollut.* **55**, 229–40.

Newton, I. (1991). The role of recruitment in population regulation. *Proc. Int. Ornithol. Congr.* **20**, 1689–99.

Newton, I. (1992). Experiments on the limitation of bird numbers by territorial behaviour. *Biol. Rev.* **67**, 129–73.

Newton, I. (1993). Predation and limitation of bird numbers. *Curr. Ornithol.* **11**, 143–98.

Newton, I. (1998). *Population Limitation in Birds.* Academic Press, London.

Newton, I. (2002). Population limitation in Holarctic owls. In: *Ecology and Conservation of Owls* (ed. I. Newton, R. Kavanagh, J. Olsen & I. Taylor). CSIRO Publishing, Collingwood, Australia, pp. 3–29.

Newton, I. (2004). The recent declines of farmland bird populations in Britain: an appraisal of causal factors and conservation actions. *Ibis* **146**, 579–600.

Newton, I. (2008). *The Migration Ecology of Birds.* Academic Press, London.

Newton, I. (2010). *Bird Migration.* New Naturalist 113. Collins, London.

Newton, I. & Campbell, C. R. G. (1975). Breeding of ducks at Loch Leven, Kinross. *Wildfowl* **26**, 83–103.

Newton, I. & Little, B. (2009). Assessment of wind-farm and other bird casualties from carcasses found on a Northumbrian beach over an 11-year period. *Bird Study* **56**, 158–67.

Newton, I. & Marquiss, M. (1981). Effect of additional food on laying dates and clutch sizes of Sparrowhawks. *Ornis Scand.* **12**, 224–9.

Newton, I. & Perrins, C. M. (1997). Sparrowhawks and song birds. *Birds* **16**, 65–8.

Newton, I. & Rothery, P. (2001). Estimation and limitation of numbers of floaters in a Eurasian Sparrowhawk population. *Ibis* **143**, 442–9.

Newton, I. & Wyllie, I. (1992). Recovery of a Sparrowhawk population in relation to declining pesticide contamination. *J. Appl. Ecol.* **20**, 476–84.

Newton, I. & Wyllie, I. (2002). Rodenticides in British Barn Owls. In: *Ecology and Conservation of Owls* (ed. I. Newton, R. Kavanagh, J. Olsen & I. Taylor). CSIRO Publishing, Collingwood, Australia, pp. 286–95.

Newton, I., Thom, V. & Brotherston, W. (1973). Behaviour and distribution of wild geese in southeast Scotland. *Wildfowl* **24**, 111–21.

Newton, I., Bell, A. A. & Wyllie, I. (1982). Mortality of Sparrowhawks and Kestrels. *Brit. Birds* **75**, 195–204.

Newton, I., Wyllie, I. & Mearns, R. M. (1986). Spacing of Sparrowhawks in relation to food supply. *J. Anim. Ecol.* **55**, 361–70.

Newton, I., Wyllie, I. & Rothery, P. (1993).

Annual survival of Sparrowhawks *Accipiter nisus* breeding in three areas of Britain. *Ibis* **135**, 49–60.

Newton, I., Dale, L. & Rothery, P. (1997a). Apparent lack of impact of Sparrowhawks on the breeding densities of some woodland songbirds. *Bird Study* **44**, 129–35.

Newton, I., Wyllie, I. & Dale, L. (1997b). Mortality causes in British Barn Owls (*Tyto alba*) based on 1,101 carcasses examined during 1963–1996. In: *Biology and Conservation of Owls of the Northern Hemisphere. Second International Symposium, February 5–9, 1997, Winnipeg, Manitoba, Canada* (ed. J. R. Duncan, D. H. Johnson & T. H. Nicholls). United States Department of Agriculture, pp. 299–307.

Newton, I., Rothery, P. & Dale, L. C. (1998). Density-dependence in the bird populations of an oak wood over 22 years. *Ibis* **140**, 131–6.

Nichols, J. D. (1991). Extensive monitoring programs viewed as long-term population studies: the case of North American waterfowl. *Ibis* **133** (S1), 89–98.

Nichols, J. D., Conroy, M. J., Anderson, D. R. & Burnham, K. P. (1984). Compensatory mortality in waterfowl populations: a review of the evidence and implications for research and management. *Trans. N. A. Wildl. Nat. Res. Conf.* **49**, 535–54.

Nielsen, O. K. (1999). Gyrfalcon predation on Ptarmigan: numerical and functional response. *J. Anim. Ecol.* **68**, 1034–50.

Nielsen, O. K. (2011). Gyrfalcon population and reproduction in relation to Rock Ptarmigan numbers in Iceland. In: *Gyrfalcons and Ptarmigan in a Changing World, Vol. 2* (ed. R. T. Watson, T. J. Cade, M. Fuller, G. Hunt & E. Potapov). The Peregrine Fund, Boise, Idaho, pp. 21–47.

Nieman, D. J., Hochbaum, G. S., Caswell, F. D. & Turner, B. C. (1987). Monitoring hunter performance in prairie Canada. *Trans. N. A. Wildl. Nat. Res. Conf.* **52**, 233–45.

Nilsson, L. (1979). Variation in the production of young of swans wintering in Sweden. *Wildfowl* **30**, 129–34.

Nilsson, S. & Duinker, P. (1987). The extent of forest decline in Europe. *Environment* **29**, 4–31.

Nilsson, S. G. (1982). Seasonal variation in the survival rate of adult Nuthatches *Sitta europaea* in Sweden. *Ibis* **124**, 96–100.

Nilsson, S. G. (1984). The evolution of nest-site selection among hole-nesting birds: the importance of nest predation and competition. *Ornis Scand.* **15**, 167–75.

Nilsson, S. G. (1987). Limitation and regulation of population density in the Nuthatch *Sitta europaea* (Aves) breeding in natural cavities. *J. Anim. Ecol.* **56**, 921–37.

Nilsson, S. G. & Nilsson, I. N. (1978). Breeding bird community densities and species richness in lakes. *Oikos* **31**, 214–21.

Nilsson, S. G., Johnson, K. & Tjernberg, M. (1991). Is avoidance by Black Woodpeckers of old holes due to predators? *Anim. Behav.* **41**, 439–41.

Nordberg, O. (1936). Biologisch-ökologische Untersuchungen über die Vogelnidicolen. *Acta Zool. Fenn.* **21**, 1–168.

Nordling, D., Andersson, M., Zohari, S. & Gustafsson, L. (1998). Reproductive effort reduces specific immune response and parasite resistance. *Proc. R. Soc. Lond. B* **265**, 1291–8.

Norris, D. R., Marra, P. P., Kyser, T. K., Sherry, T. W. & Ratcliffe, I. M. (2004). Tropical winter habitat limits reproductive success on the temperate breeding grounds in a migratory bird. *Proc. R. Soc. Lond. B* **271**, 59–64.

Norris, K., Anwar, M. & Read, A. F. J. (1994). Reproductive effort influences the prevalence of haematozoan parasites in Great Tits. *J. Anim. Ecol.* **63**, 601–10.

Norte, A. C., Ramos, J. A., Sousa, J. P. & Sheldon, B. C. (2009). Variation of adult body condition and blood parameters in relation to sex, age, year and season. *J. Ornithol.* **150**, 651–60.

Nur, N. (1988). The consequences of brood size for breeding Blue Tits. III. Measuring the cost of reproduction: survival, future fecundity, and differential dispersal. *Evolution* **42**, 351–62.

Nussey, D. H., Postma, E., Giennapp, P. & Visser, M. E. (2005). Selection on heritable phenotypic plasticity in a wild bird population. *Science* **310**, 304–6.

Nuttall, P. A., Perrins, C. M. & Harrap, K. A.

(1982). Further studies on puffinosis, a disease of the Manx Shearwater (*Puffinus puffinus*). *Can. J. Zool.* **60**, 3462–5.

Nyholm, N. E. (1981). Evidence of involvement of aluminium in causation of defective formation of eggshells and of impaired breeding of wild passerine birds. *Environ. Res.* **26**, 363–71.

Nyström, J., Ekenstedt, J., Engström, J. & Angerbjörn, A. (2005). Gyr Falcons, ptarmigan and microtine rodents in northern Sweden. *Ibis* **147**, 587–97.

O'Brien, S. J. & Evermann, J. F. (1988). Interactive influence of infectious disease and genetic diversity in natural populations. *Trends Ecol. Evol.* **3**, 253–9.

O'Connor, R. J. (1980). Pattern and process in Great Tit (*Parus major*) populations in Britain. *Ardea* **68**, 165–83.

O'Halloran, J., Myers, A. A. & Duggan, P. F. (1991). Lead poisoning in Mute Swans *Cygnus olor* in Ireland: a review. *Wildfowl* Suppl. 1, s389–95.

Oelke, H. (1989). Effect of acid rain syndrome on bird populations (Hartz Mountains, Lower Saxony, FR Germany). *Beitr. Naturk. Nieders.* **42**, 109–28.

Ojanen, M. (1979). Effect of a cold spell on birds in northern Finland in May 1968. *Ornis Fenn.* **56**, 148–55.

Olea, P. P. & Baglione, V. (2008). Population trends of Rooks *Corvus frugilegus* in Spain and the importance of refuse tips. *Ibis* **150**, 98–109.

Olsen, B., Munster, V. J., Wallensten, J. *et al.* (2006). Global patterns of influenza A virus in wild birds. *Science* **312**, 384–8.

Oosterhuis, R. & van Dijk, K. (2002). Effect of food shortage on the reproductive output of Common Eiders *Somateria mollissima* breeding at Griend (Wadden Sea). *Atlantic Seabirds* **4**, 229–38.

Opdam, P. (1978). Feeding ecology of a Sparrowhawk population (*Accipiter nisus*). *Ardea* **66**, 137–55.

Oppliger, A., Richner, M. & Christe, D. (1994). Effect of an ectoparasite on lay date, nest site choice, desertion and hatching success in the Great Tit (*Parus major*). *Behav. Ecol.* **5**, 130–4.

Orell, M. (1989). Population fluctuations and survival of Great Tits *Parus major*

dependent on food supplied by man in winter. *Ibis* **131**, 113–27.

Orians, G. H. & Willson, M. F. (1964). Interspecific territories of birds. *Ecology* **45**, 736–45.

Ormerod, S. J. & Durance, I. (2009). Restoration and recovery from acidification in upland Welsh streams over 25 years. *J. Appl. Ecol.* **46**, 164–74.

Ormerod, S. J., Tyler, S. J. & Lewis, J. M. S. (1985). Is the breeding distribution of Dippers influenced by stream acidity? *Bird Study* **32**, 32–9.

Ormerod, S. J., Donald, A. P. & Brown, S. J. (1989). The influence of plantation forestry on the pH and aluminium concentrations of upland Welsh waters: a re-examination. *Environ. Pollut.* **62**, 47–62.

Ormerod, S. J., O'Halloran, J., Griffin, D. D. & Tyler, S. J. (1991). The ecology of Dippers (*Cinclus cinclus* (L.)) in relation to stream acidity in upland Wales: breeding performance, calcium physiology and nestling growth. *J. Appl. Ecol.* **28**, 419–33.

Oro, D. & Furness, R. W. (2002). Influences of food availability and predation on survival rates of Kittiwakes. *Ecology* **83**, 2516–28.

Oro, D., Jover, L. & Ruiz, X. (1995). The effect of a trawl moratorium on some breeding parameters of Audouin's Gull *Larus audouinii* in the Ebro Delta, NE Spain. In: *Threats to Seabirds: Proceedings of the 5th International Seabird Group Conference* (ed. M. L. Tasker). Seabird Group, Sandy, pp. 36–7.

Orr, J. C., Fabry, V. J., Aumont, O. *et al.* (2005). Anthropogenic ocean acidification over the twenty-first century and its impact on calcifying organisms. *Nature* **437**, 681–6.

Ortego, J. & Espada, F. (2007). Ecological factors influencing disease risk in Eagle Owls *Bubo bubo*. *Ibis* **149**, 386–95.

Ortego, J., Cordero, P. J., Aparicio, J. M. & Calabuig, G. (2008). Consequences of chronic infections with three different avian malaria lineages on reproductive performance of Lesser Kestrels (*Falco naumanni*). *J. Ornithol.* **149**, 337–43.

Österblom, H., Van Der Jeugd, H. P. & Olsson, O. (2004). Adult survival and avian cholera in Common Guillemots *Uria aalge* in the Baltic Sea. *Ibis* **146**, 531–4.

Oswald, S. A., Bearhop, S., Furness, R. W., Huntley, B. & Hamer, K. C. (2008). Heat-stress in a high-latitude seabird: effects of temperature and food supply on bathing and nest attendance of Great Skuas *Catharacta skua. J. Avian Biol.* **39**, 163–9.

Ots, I., Kerimov, A. B., Ivankina, E. V., Ilyina, T. A., Hõrak, P. (2001). Immune challenge affects basal metabolic activity in wintering Great Tits. *Proc. R. Soc. Lond. B* **268**, 1175–81.

Owen, M. & Black, J. M. (1991). The importance of migration mortality in non-passerine birds. In: *Bird Population Studies: Relevance to Conservation and Management* (ed. C. M. Perrins, J.-D. Lebreton & G. J. M. Hirons). Oxford University Press, Oxford, pp. 360–72.

Owen, M., Atkinson-Willes, G. L. & Salmon, D. G. (1986). *Wildfowl in Great Britain*, 2nd edition. Cambridge University Press, Cambridge.

PACEC (Public & Corporate Economic Consultants) (2006). *Shooting Sports*. BPG Ltd, Stamford.

Pain, D. J. (1990). Lead poisoning of waterfowl: a review. In: *Managing Waterfowl Populations* (ed. G. V. T. Matthews). International Waterfowl & Wetlands Research Bureau. Slimbridge, pp. 172–81.

Pain, D. J. (1992). Lead poisoning in waterfowl: a summary of national reports. In: *Lead Poisoning in Waterfowl* (ed. D. J. Pain). IWRB Special Publication 16. International Waterfowl & Wetlands Research Bureau, Slimbridge, pp. 86–94.

Pain, D. J., Amiart-Triquet, C., Baboux, C. *et al.* (1993). Lead poisoning in wild populations of Marsh Harrier (*Circus aeruginosus*) from Charente-Maritime, France: relationship with the hunting season. *Biol. Conserv.* **81**, 1–7.

Pain, D. J., Bowden, C. G. R., Cunningham, A. A. *et al.* (2008). The race to prevent the extinction of South Asian vultures. *Biol. Conserv. Internat.* **18**, s30–48.

Pain, D. J., Fisher, I. J. & Thomas, V. G. (2009). A global update of lead poisoning in terrestrial birds from ammunition sources. In: *Ingestion of Lead from Spent Ammunition: Implications for Wildlife and Humans* (ed. R. T. Watson, M. Fuller, M.

Pokras & W. G. Hunt). The Peregrine Fund, Boise, Idaho, pp. 99–118.

Pain, D. J., Cromie, R. L., Newth, J. *et al.* (2010). Potential hazard to human health from exposure to fragments of lead bullets and shot in the tissues of game animals. *PLoS One* **5** (4), e10315.

Palmgren, P. (1930). Quantitative Untersuchungen über die Vogelfauna in den Wäldern Sudfinnlands. *Acta Zool. Fenn.* **7**, 1–218.

Panek, M. (1997). Density-dependent brood production in the Grey Partridge *Perdix perdix*, in relation to habitat quality. *Bird Study* **44**, 235–8.

Panek, M. (2002). Space use, nesting sites and breeding success of Grey Partridge (*Perdix perdix*) in two agricultural management systems in western Poland. *Game Wildl. Sci.* **19**, 313–26.

Pap, P. L., Tokolyi, J. & Szép, T. (2005). Frequency and consequences of feather holes in Barn Swallows *Hirundo rustica. Ibis* **147**, 169–75.

Pap, P. L., Vágáni, C. I., Tokolyi, J., Czirják, G. Á. & Barta, Z. (2010). Variation in haematological indices and immune function during the annual cycle in the Great Tit *Parus major. Ardea* **98**, 105–12.

Paracuellos, M. & Nevado, J. C. (2010). Culling Yellow-legged Gulls *Larus michahellis* benefits Audouin's Gulls *Larus audouinii* at a small and remote colony. *Bird Study* **57**, 26–30.

Parish, D. M. B. & Sotherton, N. W. (2008). Landscape-dependent use of a seed-rich habitat by farmland passerines: relative importance of game cover crops in a grassland versus arable region of Scotland. *Bird Study* **55**, 118–23.

Park, K. J., Graham, K. E., Calladine, J. & Wernham, C. W. (2008). Impacts of birds of prey on gamebirds in the UK: a review. *Ibis* **150** (S1), 9–26.

Parker, G. L., Petrie, M. J. & Sears, D. T. (1992). Waterfowl distribution relative to wetland acidity. *J. Wildl. Manage.* **56**, 268–74.

Parker, H. (1984). Effect of corvid removal on reproduction of Willow Ptarmigan and Black Grouse. *J. Wildl. Manage.* **48**, 1197–205.

Parker, H. & Holm, H. (1990). Patterns of nutrient and energy-expenditure in female

Common Eiders nesting in the high arctic. *Auk* **107**, 660–8.

Parmesan, C. & Yohe, G. (2003). A globally coherent fingerprint of climate change impacts across natural systems. *Nature* **421**, 37–42.

Parr, R. (1993). Nest predation and numbers of Golden Plovers *Pluvialis apricaria* and other moorland waders. *Bird Study* **40**, 223–31.

Parrott, D., Henderson, I., Deppe, C. & Whitfield, P. (2008). Scottish racing pigeons killed by Peregrine Falcons *Falco peregrinus*: estimation of numbers from ring recoveries and Peregrine daily food intake. *Bird Study* **55**, 32–42.

Parsons, J. (1976). Nesting density and breeding success in the Herring Gull *Larus argentatus*. *Ibis* **118**, 537–47

Pashby, B. S. & Cudworth, J. (1969). The Fulmar 'wreck' of 1962. *Brit. Birds* **62**, 97–109.

Patterson, I. J. (1977). The control of Fox movement by electric fencing. *Biol. Conserv.* **11**, 267–78.

Patterson, I. J., Makepeace, M. & Williams, M. (1983). Limitation of local population size in the Shelduck. *Ardea* **71**, 105–16.

Pauliny, A., Larsson, M. & Bloqvist, D. (2008). Nest predation management: effects on reproductive success in endangered shorebirds. *J. Wildl. Manage.* **72**, 1579–83.

Payne, R. B. (1997). Avian brood parasitism. In: *Host–Parasite Evolution* (ed. D. H. Clayton & J. Moore). Oxford University Press, Oxford, pp. 338–69.

Peach, W. J., Baillie, S. R. & Underhill, L. (1991). Survival of British Sedge Warblers *Acrocephalus schoenobaenus* in relation to West Africa rainfall. *Ibis* **133**, 300–5.

Peach, W. J., Thompson, P. S. & Coulson, J. C. (1994). Annual and long-term variation in the survival rates of British Lapwings *Vanellus vanellus*. *J. Anim. Ecol.* **63**, 60–70.

Peach, W. J., du Feu, C. & McMeeking, J. (1995). Site tenacity and survival rates of Wrens *Troglodytes troglodytes* and Treecreepers *Certhia familiaris* in a Nottinghamshire wood. *Ibis* **137**, 497–507.

Peach, W. J., Siriwardena, G. M. & Gregory, R. D. (1999). Long-term changes in overwinter survival rates explain the decline of Reed Buntings *Emberiza*

schoeniclus in Britain. *J. Appl. Ecol.* **36**, 798–811.

Peakall, D. B. (1985). Behavioural responses of birds to pesticides and other contaminants. *Residue Rev.* **96**, 45–77.

Peakall, D. B. & Kiff, L. F. (1988). DDE contamination in Peregrines and American Kestrels and its effects on reproduction. In: *Peregrine Falcon Populations: Their Management and Recovery* (ed. T. J. Cade, J. H. Enderson, C. G. Thelander & C. M. White). The Peregrine Fund, Boise, Idaho, pp. 337–50.

Pearce-Higgins, J. W. & Yalden, D. W. (2004). Habitat selection, diet, arthropod availability and growth of a moorland wader: the ecology of European Golden Plover *Pluvialis apricaria* chicks. *Ibis* **146**, 335–46.

Pearce-Higgins, J. W., Yalden, D. W. & Whittingham, M. J. (2005). Warmer springs advance the breeding phenology of Golden Plovers *Pluvialis apricaria* and their prey (Tipulidae). *Oecologia* **143**, 470–6.

Pearce-Higgins, J. W., Stephen, L., Langston, R. H. W., Bainbridge, I. P. & Bullman, R. (2009). The distribution of breeding birds around upland wind farms. *J. Appl. Ecol.* **46**, 1323–31.

Pearce-Higgins, J. W., Dennis, P., Whittingham, M. J. & Yalden, D. W. (2010). Impacts of climate on prey abundance account for fluctuations in a population of a northern wader at the southern edge of its range. *Global Change Biol.* **16**, 12–23.

Pehrson, O. (1976). Duckling production of Long-tailed Duck in relation to spring weather and small rodent fluctuations. PhD thesis, University of Gothenburg.

Peiponen, V. A. (1962). Über Brütbiologie Nahrung und geographische Verbreitung des Birkenzeisigs (*Carduelis flammea*). *Ornis Fenn.* **39**, 37–60.

Perkins, A. J., Hancock, M. H., Butcher, N. & Summers, R. W. (2005). Use of time-lapse video cameras to determine causes of nest failure of Slavonian Grebes *Podiceps auritus*. *Bird Study* **52**, 159–65.

Péron, G., Lebreton, J.-D. & Crochet, P.-A. (2010). Costs and benefits of colony size vary during the breeding cycle in Black-headed gulls *Chroicocephalus ridibundus*. *J. Ornithol.* **151**, 881–8.

Perrins, C. M. (1979). *British Tits.* New Naturalist 62. Collins, London.

Perrins, C. M. & Geer, T. A. (1980). The effect of Sparrowhawks on tit populations. *Ardea* 68, 133–42.

Perrins, C. M. & Smith, S. B. (2000). The breeding *Larus* gulls on Skomer Island National Nature Reserve, Pembrokeshire. *Atlantic Seabirds* 2, 195–210.

Persson, L., Borg, K. & Falt, H. (1974). On the occurrence of endoparasites in Eider Ducks in Sweden. *Swed. Wildl. Viltrevy* 9, 1.

Petrides, G. A. & Bryant, C. R. (1951). An analysis of the 1949–50 fowl cholera epizootic in Texas Panhandle waterfowl. *Trans. N. A. Wildl. Nat. Res. Conf.* 16, 193–216.

Petry, M. J., Kruger, L., Fonseca, V. S. da S., Brummelhaus, J. & Piuco, R. da C. (2009). Diet and ingestion of synthetics by Cory's Shearwater *Calonectris diomedia* off southern Brazil. *J. Ornithol.* 150, 601–6.

Petty, S. J. (1989). Productivity and density of Tawny Owls *Strix aluco* in relation to the structure of a Spruce forest in Britain. *Ann. Zool. Fenn.* 26, 227–33.

Petty, S. J. (1992). Ecology of the Tawny Owl *Strix aluco* in the spruce forests of Northumberland and Argyll. PhD thesis, Open University.

Petty, S. J. (1996). History of the Northern Goshawk *Accipiter gentilis* in Britain. In: *The Introduction and Naturalisation of Birds* (ed. J. S. Holmes & J. R. Simons). HMSO, London, pp. 95–102.

Petty, S. J. (2002). Northern Goshawk. In: *The Migration Atlas: Movements of the Birds of Britain and Ireland* (ed. C. V. Wernham, M. P. Toms, J. H. Marchant *et al.*). Poyser, London, pp. 232–34.

Petty, S. J., Shaw, G. & Anderson, D. I. K. (1994). Value of nest boxes for population studies and conservation of owls in coniferous forests in Britain. *J. Raptor Res.* 28, 134–42.

Petty, S. J., Patterson, I. J., Anderson, D. I. K., Little, B. & Davison, M. (1995). Numbers, breeding performance, and diet of the Sparrowhawk *Accipiter nisus* and Merlin *Falco columbarius* in relation to cone crops and seed-eating finches. *For. Ecol. Manage.* 79, 133–46.

Petty, S. J., Anderson, D. I. K., Davison, M. et al. (2003). The decline of Common Kestrels *Falco tinnunculus* in a forest area of northern England: the role of predation by Northern Goshawks *Accipiter gentilis*. *Ibis* 145, 472–83.

Phillips, R. A., Caldow, R. W. G. & Furness, R. W. (1996). The influence of food availability on the breeding effort and reproductive success of Arctic Skuas *Stercorarius parasiticus*. *Ibis* 138, 410–19.

Phillips, R. A., Furness, R. W. & Stewart, F. M. (1998). The influence of territory density on the vulnerability of Arctic Skuas *Stercorarius parasiticus* to predation. *Biol. Conserv.* 86, 21–31.

Phillips, R. A., Bearhop, S., Thompson, D. R. & Hamer, K. C. (1999a). Rapid population growth of Great Skuas at St. Kilda: implications for management and conservation. *Bird Study* 46, 174–83.

Phillips, R. A., Thompson, D. R. & Hamer, K. C. (1999b). The impact of Great Skua predation on seabird populations at St. Kilda: a bioenergetic model. *J. Appl. Ecol.* 36, 218–32.

Phillips, V. E. (1992). Variation in winter wildfowl numbers on gravel pit lakes at Great Linford, Buckinghamshire, 1974–79 and 1984–91, with particular reference to the effects of fish removal. *Bird Study* 39, 177–85.

Piatt, J. F. & Reddin, D. G. (1984). Recent trends in the west Greenland salmon fishery and implications for Thick-billed Murres. In: *Marine Birds: Their Feeding Ecology and Commercial Fisheries Relationships* (ed. D. N. Nettleship, G. A. Sanger & P. F. Springer). Canadian Wildlife Service, Ottawa, pp. 208–10.

Piersma, T. (1997). Do global patterns of habitat use and migration strategies co-evolve with relative investments in immunocompetence due to spatial variation in parasite pressure? *Oikos* 80, 623–31.

Piersma, T. & van Gils, J. A. (2011). *The Flexible Phenotype.* Oxford University Press, Oxford.

Piersma, T., Koolhaas, A. & Jukema, J. (2003). Seasonal body mass changes in Eurasian Golden Plovers *Pluvialis apricaria* staging in the Netherlands: decline in late autumn mass peak correlates with increase in raptor numbers. *Ibis* **145**, 565–71.

Pons, J. M. (1992). Effects of changes in the availability of human refuse on breeding parameters in a Herring Gull *Larus argentatus* population in Brittany, France. *Ardea* **80**, 143–50.

Pons, J. M. & Migot, P. (1995). Life history strategy of the Herring Gull: changes in survival and fecundity in a population subjected to various feeding conditions. *J. Anim. Ecol.* **64**, 592–9.

Popy, S., Bordignon, L. & Prodon, R. (2010). A weak upward elevational shift in the distributions of breeding birds in the Italian Alps. *J. Biogeog.* **37**, 57–67.

Potts, G. R. (1980). The effects of modern agriculture, nest predation and game management on the population ecology of Partridges *Perdix perdix* and *Alectoris rufa*. *Adv. Ecol. Res.* **11**, 2–79.

Potts, G. R. (1986). *The Partridge: Pesticides, Predation and Conservation*. Collins, London.

Potts, G. R. (1991). The environmental and ecological importance of cereal fields. In: *The Ecology of Temperate Cereal Fields* (ed. L. G. Firbank, N. Carter, J. F. Darbyshire & G. R. Potts). Blackwell, Oxford, pp. 3–21.

Potts, G. R. (1998). Global dispersion of nesting Hen Harriers *Circus cyaneus*: implications for grouse moors. *Ibis* **140**, 76–88.

Potts, G. R. (2012). *Partridges: Countryside Barometer*. New Naturalist 121. Collins, London.

Potts, G. R. & Aebischer, N. J. (1991). Modelling the population dynamics of the Grey Partridge: conservation and management. In: *Bird Population Studies: Relevance to Conservation and Management* (ed. C. M. Perrins, J.-D. Lebreton & G. J. M. Hirons). Oxford University Press, Oxford, pp. 373–90.

Potts, G. R., Coulson, J. C. & Deans, I. R. (1980). Population dynamics and breeding success of the Shag, *Phalacrocorax aristotelis* on the Farne Islands, Northumberland. *J. Anim. Ecol.* **49**, 465–84.

Potts, G. R., Tapper, S. C. & Hudson, P. J. (1984). Population fluctuations in Red Grouse: analysis of bag records and a simulation model. *J. Anim. Ecol.* **53**, 21–36.

Pöysä, H. & Pöysä, S. (2002). Nest site limitation and density dependence of reproductive output in the Common Goldeneye *Bucephala clangula*: implications for the management of cavity nesting birds. *J. Appl. Ecol.* **39**, 502–10.

Prater, A. J. (1981). *Estuary Birds of Britain and Ireland*. Poyser, Calton.

Price, P. W. (1980). *Evolutionary Biology of Parasites*. Princeton University Press, Princeton, New Jersey.

Prop, J. (2004). Food finding: on the trail to successful reproduction in migrating geese. PhD thesis, University of Groningen.

Prop, J., van Eerden, M. & Drent, R. H. (1984). Reproductive success of the Barnacle Goose in relation to food exploitation on the breeding grounds, western Spitsbergen. *Norsk Polarinst. Skrift.* **181**, 87–117.

Przybylo, R., Sheldon, B. C. & Merilä, J. (2000). Climate effects on breeding and morphology: evidence for phenotypic plasticity. *J. Anim. Ecol.* **7**, 395–403.

Pulido, F. & Berthold, P. (2004). Microevolutionary response to climate change. In: *Birds and Climate Change* (ed. A. P. Møller, W. Fiedler & P. Berthold). *Adv. Ecol. Res.* **35**, 151–83.

Pulliainen, E. (1978). Influence of heavy snowfall in June 1977 on the life of birds in NE Finnish Forest, Lapland. *Aquila. Ser. Zool.* **18**, 1–14.

Quinn, J. L. & Cresswell, W. (2004). Predator hunting behaviour and prey vulnerability. *J. Anim. Ecol.* **73**, 143–54.

Quinn, J. L. & Cresswell, W. (2006). Testing for domains of danger in the selfish herd: Sparrowhawks target widely spaced Redshanks in flocks. *Proc. R. Soc. B* **273**, 2521–6.

Quinn, J. L. & Kokorev, Y. (2002). Trading off risks from predators and from aggressive hosts. *Behav. Ecol. Sociobiol.* **51**, 455–460.

Råberg, L., Nilsson, J.-A., Ilmonen, P., Stjernman, M. & Hasselquist, D. (2000). The cost of an immune response: vaccination reduces parental effort. *Ecol. Lett.* **3**, 382–6.

Ramos, J. A., Monteiro, L. R., Sola, E. & Moniz, Z. (1997). Characteristics and competition for nest cavities in burrowing Procellariiformes. *Condor* **99**, 634–41.

Ramos, J. A., Bowler, J., Davis, L. *et al.* (2001). Activity patterns and effects of ticks on growth and survival of tropical Roseate Tern nestlings. *Auk* **118**, 709–18.

Rands, M. R. W. (1985). Pesticide use on cereals and the survival of Partridge chicks: a field experiment. *J. Appl. Ecol.* **22**, 49–54.

Rands, M. R. W. (1986). The survival of gamebird (Galliformes) chicks in relation to pesticide use on cereals. *Ibis* **128**, 57–64.

Ranta, E., Lindstrom, J. & Lindén, H. (1995). Synchrony in tetraonid population dynamics. *J. Anim. Ecol.* **64**, 767–76.

Raphael, M. G. & White, M. (1984). Use of snags by cavity-nesting birds in the Sierra Nevada. *Wildl. Monogr.* **86**, 1–66.

Rappole, J. H., Derrickson, S. R. & Hubálek, Z. (2000). Migratory birds and spread of West Nile virus in the Western Hemisphere. *Emerg. Infect. Dis.* **6**, 319–28.

Ratcliffe, D. A. (1969). Population trends of the Peregrine Falcon in Great Britain. In: *Peregrine Falcon Populations* (ed. J. J. Hickey). University of Wisconsin Press, Madison, Wisconsin, pp. 239–69.

Ratcliffe, D. A. (1970). Changes attributable to pesticides in egg breakage frequency and eggshell thickness in some British birds. *J. Appl. Ecol.* **7**, 67–107.

Ratcliffe, D. A. (1980). *The Peregrine Falcon.* Poyser, Calton.

Ratcliffe, N. (2003). Little Terns in Britain and Ireland: estimation and diagnosis of population trends. Cited in Mitchell *et al.* (2004).

Ratcliffe, N. (2004). Causes of seabird population change. In: *Seabird populations of Britain and Ireland* (ed. P. I. Mitchell, S. Newton, N. Ratcliffe & E. Dunn). Poyser, London, pp. 407–37.

Ratcliffe, N., Pickerell, G. & Brindley, E. (2000). Population trends of Little and Sandwich Terns *Sterna albifrons* and *S. sandvicensis* in Britain and Ireland from 1969 to 1998. *Atlantic Seabirds* **2**, 211–26.

Ratcliffe, N., Catry, P., Hamer, K. C., Klomp, N. I. & Furness, R. W. (2002). The effect of age and year on the survival of breeding adult Great Skuas *Catharacta skua* in Shetland. *Ibis* **144**, 384–92.

Ratcliffe, N., Mitchell, I., Varnham, K., Verboven, N. & Higson, P. (2009). How to prioritize rat management for the benefit of petrels: a case study of the UK, Channel Islands and Isle of Man. *Ibis* **151**, 699–708.

Raven, S. J. & Coulson, J. C. (1997). The distribution and abundance of large gulls nesting in buildings in Britain and Ireland. *Bird Study* **44**, 13–34.

Raven, S. J. & Coulson, J. C. (2001). Effects of cleaning a tidal river of sewage on gull numbers: a before-and-after study of the River Tyne, northeast England. *Bird Study* **48**, 48–58.

Rayner, N. A., Brohan, P., Parker, D. E. *et al.* (2006). Improved analyses of changes and uncertainties in sea surface temperature measured in situ since the mid-nineteenth century: the HadSST2 dataset. *J. Clim.* **19**, 446–69.

Real, J., Mañosa, S. & Muñoz, E. (2000). Trichomoniasis in a Bonelli's Eagle population in Spain. *J. Wildl. Dis.* **36**, 65–70.

Redondo, T. & Castro, F. (1992). The increase in risk of predation with begging activity in broods of Magpies *Pica pica*. *Ibis* **134**, 180–7.

Redpath, S. M. & Thirgood, S. J. (1997). *Birds of Prey and Red Grouse.* Stationery Office, London.

Redpath, S. M. & Thirgood, S. J. (1999). Numerical and functional responses in generalist predators: Hen Harriers and Peregrines on Scottish grouse moors. *J. Anim. Ecol.* **68**, 879–92.

Redpath, S. M., Thirgood, S. J., Rothery, P. & Aebischer, N. J. (2000). Raptor predation and population limitation in Red Grouse. *J. Anim. Ecol.* **69**, 504–16.

Redpath, S. M., Thirgood, S. & Leckie, F. M. (2001). Does supplementary feeding reduce predation of Red Grouse by Hen Harriers? *J. Appl. Ecol.* **38**, 1157–68.

Redpath, S. M., Mougeot, F., Leckie, F. M., Elston, D. A. & Hudson, P. J. (2006). Testing the role of parasites in driving the cyclic population dynamics of a gamebird. *Ecol. Lett.* **9**, 410–18.

Reed, T. M. (1982). Interspecific territoriality in the Chaffinch and Great Tit on islands and the mainland of Scotland: playback and removal experiments. *Anim. Behav.* **30**, 171–81.

Rees, E. C., Bowler, J. M. & Butler, L. (1990). Bewick's and Whooper Swans: the 1989-90 season. *Wildfowl* **41**, 176–81.

Reeves, S. A. & Furness, R. W. (2002). Net loss – seabirds gain? Implications of fisheries management for seabirds scavenging discards in the northern North Sea. RSPB, Sandy.

Reid, H. W. (1975). Experimental infection of Red Grouse with louping-ill virus (flavivirus group). I. The viraemia and antibody response. *J. Comp. Pathol.* **85**, 223–9.

Reid, H. W. & Moss, R. (1980). The response of four species of birds to louping-ill virus. In: *Arboviruses in the Mediterranean Countries* (ed. J. Vesenjak-Hirjan & J. S. Porterfield). Gustav Fischer, Stuttgart, pp. 219–23.

Reid, J. M., Bignal, E. M., Bignal, S., McCracken, D. I. & Monaghan, P. (2003). Environmental variability, life history covariation and cohort effects in the Red-billed Chough *Pyrrhocorax pyrrhocorax*. *J. Anim. Ecol.* **72**, 36–46.

Reijnen, R., Foppen, R. & Meeuwsen, H. (1996). The effects of traffic on the density of breeding birds in Dutch agricultural grasslands. *Biol. Conserv.* **75**, 255–60.

Reinikainen, A. (1937). The irregular migrations of the Crossbill, *Loxia c. curvirostra*, and their relation to the cone-crop of the conifers. *Ornis Fenn.* **14**, 55–64.

Renwick, A. R., Massinimo, D., Newson, S. E. *et al.* (2012). Modelling changes in species abundance in response to projected climate change. *Divers. Distrib.* **18**, 121–32.

Reynolds, B., Lowe, J. A. H., Smith, R. I. *et al.* (1999). Acid deposition in Wales: the results of the 1995 Welsh Acid Waters Survey. *Environ. Pollut.* **105**, 251–66.

Reynolds, T. J., Harris, M. P., King, R. *et al.* (2011). Among-colony synchrony in the survival of Common Guillemots *Uria aalge* reflects shared wintering areas. *Ibis* **153**, 818–31.

Ribaut, J. (1964). Dynamique d'une population des Merles noirs *Turdus merula* L. *Revue Suisse Zool.* **71**, 815–902.

Richner, H. (1992). The effect of extra food on fitness in breeding Carrion Crows. *Ecology* **73**, 330–5.

Richner, H. & Triplet, F. (1999). Ectoparasitism

and the trade-off between current and future reproduction. *Oikos* **86**, 535–8.

Richner, H., Oppliger, A. & Christe, P. (1993). Effect of an ectoparasite on the reproduction in Great Tits. *J. Anim. Ecol.* **62**, 703–10.

Richner, H., Oppliger, A. & Christe, P. (1993). Effect of an ectoparasite on reproduction in Great Tits. *J. Anim. Ecol.* **62**, 703–10.

Richner, H., Christe, P. & Oppliger, A. (1995). Parental investment affects prevalence of malaria. *Proc. Natl. Acad. Sci.* **92**, 1192–4.

Ricklefs, R. E. (1969). An analysis of nestling mortality in birds. *Smithson. Contr. Zool.* **9**, 1–48.

Rindorf, A., Wanless, S. & Harris, M. P. (2000). Effects of changes in sandeel availability on reproductive output of seabirds. *Mar. Ecol. Prog. Ser.* **202**, 241–52.

Risebrough, R. W., Sibley, F. C. & Kirven, M. N. (1971). Reproductive failure of the Brown Pelican on Anacapa Island in 1969. *Amer. Birds* **25**, 8–9.

Robertson, P. A. & Rosenberg, A. A. (1988). Harvesting gamebirds. In: *Ecology and Management of Gamebirds* (ed. P. J. Hudson & M. R. W. Rands). BSP Professional Books, London, pp. 177–201.

Robinson, R. A. & Sutherland, W. J. (1999). The winter distribution of seed-eating birds: habitat structure, seed density and seasonal depletion. *Ecography* **22**, 447–54.

Robinson, R. A. & Sutherland, W. J. (2002). Post-war changes in arable farming and biodiversity: Great Britain. *J. Appl. Ecol.* **39**, 157–76.

Robinson, R. A., Green, R. E., Baillie, S. R., Peach, W. J. & Thomson, D. L. (2004). Demographic mechanisms of the population decline of the Song Thrush *Turdus philomelos* in Britain. *J. Anim. Ecol.* **73**, 670–82.

Robinson, R. A., Baillie, S. & Crick, H. Q. P. (2007). Weather-dependent survival: implications of climate change for passerine population processes. *Ibis* **149**, 357–64.

Robinson, R. A., Lawson, B., Toms, M. P. *et al.* (2010). Emerging infectious disease leads to rapid population declines of common British Birds. *PLoS One* **5** (8), e12215.

Rock, P. (2003). Birds of a feather flock together. *Environ. Health J.* May 2003, 132–5.

Rockwell, R. F., Gormezano, L. J. & Koons, D. N. (2011). Trophic matches and mismatches: can Polar Bears reduce the abundance of nesting Snow Geese in western Hudson Bay? *Oikos* **120**, 696–709.

Rodenhouse, N. L. & Holmes, R. T. (1992). Results of experiments and natural food reductions for breeding Black-throated Blue Warblers. *Ecology* **73**, 357–72.

Rodriguez, C. & Bustamente, J. (2003). The effect of weather on Lesser Kestrel breeding success: can climate change explain historical population declines? *J. Anim. Ecol.* **72**, 793–810.

Roodbergen, M., van der Werf, B. & Hötker, H. (2012). Revealing the contributions of reproduction and survival to the Europe-wide decline in meadow birds: a review and meta-analysis. *J. Ornithol.* **153**, 53–74.

Roos, S. & Pärt, T. (2004). Nest predators affect spatial dynamics of breeding Red-backed Shrikes *Lanius collurio. J. Anim. Ecol.* **73**, 117–27.

Root, T. L., Price, J. T., Hall, K. R. *et al.* (2003). Fingerprints of global warming on wild animals and plants. *Nature* **421**, 57–60.

Rose, M. E. (1981). Lymphatic system. In: *Form and Function in Birds, Vol.* 2 (ed. A. S. King & J. McLelland). Academic Press, London, pp. 341–84.

Roselaar, C. S. (1979). Fluctuaties in aantallen Krombek Strandlopers *Calidris ferruginea. Watervogels* **4**, 202–10.

Roskaft, E. (1985). The effect of enlarged brood size on the future reproductive potential of the Rook. *J. Anim. Ecol.* **54**, 255–60.

Rothschild, M. & Clay, T. (1952). *Fleas, Flukes and Cuckoos.* Collins, London.

Rowan, W. (1921–22). Observations on the breeding habits of the Merlin. *Brit. Birds* **15**, 122–9, 194–202, 222–31, 246–53.

Royal Commission on Environmental Pollution (1983). *Ninth Report: Lead in the Environment.* Department for Environmental, Food and Rural Affairs, London.

RSPB (Royal Society for the Protection of Birds) (2012). *Hope Farm: Farming for Food, Profit and Wildlife.* RSPB, Sandy.

Rutz, C., Bijlsma, R. G., Marquiss, M. & Kenward, R. E. (2006). Population limitation in the Northern Goshawk in Europe: a review of case studies. *Stud. Avian Biol.* **31**, 158–97.

Rytkönen, S., Lehtonen, R. & Orell, M. (1998). Breeding Great Tits *Parus major* avoid nest boxes infected with fleas. *Ibis* **140**, 687–90.

Saether, B.-E. (1983). Mechanism of interspecific spacing out in a territorial system of the Chiffchaff *Phylloscopus collybita* and the Willow Warbler *Phlloscopus trochilus. Ornis Scand.* **14**, 154–60.

Saether, B.-E. & Engen, S. (2010). Population consequences of climate change. In: *Effects of Climate Change in Birds* (ed. A. P. Møller, W. Fiedler & P. Berthold). Oxford University Press, Oxford, pp. 191–211.

Saether, B.-E., Tufto, J., Engen, S. *et al.* (2000). Population dynamical consequences of climate change for a small temperate landbird. *Science* **287**, 854–6.

Saether, B.-E., Engen, S., Møller, A. P. *et al.* (2003). Climate variation and regional gradients in population dynamics of two hole-nesting passerines. *Proc. R. Soc. Lond. B* **270**, 2397–404.

Saether, B.-E., Sutherland, W. J & Engen, S. (2004). Climate influences on avian population dynamics. *Adv. Ecol. Res.* **35**, 185–209.

Safina, C., Burger, J. Gochfield, M. & Wagner, R. H. (1988). Evidence for prey limitation of Common and Roseate Tern reproduction. *Condor* **40**, 852–9.

Saino, N., Møller, A. P. & Bolzern, A. M. (1995). Testosterone effects on the immune system and parasite infestations in the Barn Swallow (*Hirundo rustica*): an experimental test of the immunocompetence hypothesis. *Behav. Ecol.* **6**, 397–404.

Saino, N., Calza, S. & Møller A. P. (1997). Immunocompetence of nestling Barn Swallows (*Hirundo rustica*) in relation to brood size and parental effort. *J. Anim. Ecol.* **66**, 827–36.

Saino, N., Calza, J. & Møller, A. P. (1998). Effects of a dipteran ectoparasite on immune response and growth trade-offs in Barn Swallow *Hirundo rustica* nestlings. *Oikos* **81**, 217–28.

Saino, N., Ferrari, R., Romano, M., Ambrosini, R. & Møller, A. P. (2002a). Ectoparasites and reproductive trade-offs in the Barn

Swallow (*Hirundo rustica*). *Oecologia* **133**, 139–45.

Saino, N., Ferrari, R., Martinelli, R. *et al.* (2002b). Early maternal effects mediated by immunity depend on sexual ornamentation of the male partner. *Proc. R. Soc. Lond. B* **269**, 1005–9.

Saino, N., Szép, T., Ambrosini, R., Romano, M. & Møller, A. P. (2004a). Ecological conditions during winter affect sexual selection and breeding in a migratory bird. *Proc. R. Soc Lond. B* **271**, 681–6.

Saino, N., Szép, T., Romano, M. *et al.* (2004b). Ecological conditions during winter predict arrival date at the breeding quarters in a trans-Saharan migratory bird. *Ecol. Lett.* **7**, 215.

Salisbury, E. (1961). *Weeds and Aliens.* New Naturalist 43. Collins, London.

Sanderson, F. J., Donald, P. F., Pain, D. J., Burfield, I. J. & van Bommel, F. P. J. (2006). Long-term population declines in Afro-Palearctic migrant birds. *Biol. Conserv.* **131**, 93–105.

Sanderson, G. C. & Bellrose, F. C. (1986). *A Review of the Problem of Lead Poisoning in Waterfowl.* Illinois Natural History Survey, Champaign, Illinois. Special Publication 4.

Sanderson, R. F. (2001). Autumn bird counts in Kensington Gardens, 1925–2000. *Lond. Bird Rep.* **65**, 206–14.

Sandvik, H., Erikstad, K. E., Barrett, R. & Yoccoz, G. (2005). The effect of climate on adult survival in five species of North Atlantic seabirds. *J. Anim. Ecol.* **74**, 817–31.

Sandvik, H., Coulson, T. & Saether, B.-E. (2008). A latitudinal gradient in climatic effects on seabird demography: results from interspecific analyses. *Global Change Biol.* **14**, 1–11.

Sanz, J. J., Potti, J., Moreno, J., Merino, S. & Frías, O. (2003). Climate change and fitness components of a migratory bird breeding in the Mediterranean region. *Global Change Biol.* **9**, 461–72.

Saurola, P. (1976). Mortality of Finnish Goshawks. *Suomen Luonto* **6**, 310–14.

Saurola, P. (1989). Ural Owl. In: *Lifetime Reproduction in Birds* (ed. I. Newton). Academic Press, London, pp. 327–45.

Saurola, P. (1992). Population studies of the Ural Owl *Strix uralensis* in Finland. In: *The Ecology and Conservation of European Owls* (ed. I. R. Taylor & S. Percival). Joint Nature Conservation Committee, Edinburgh, pp. 28–31.

Saurola, P. (1997). Monitoring Finnish owls 1982–1999: methods and results. In: *Biology and Conservation of Owls of the Northern Hemisphere. Second International Symposium, February 5–9, 1997, Winnipeg, Manitoba, Canada* (ed. J. R. Duncan, D. H. Johnson & T. H. Nicholls). United States Department of Agriculture, pp. 363–80.

Saurola, P. (2009). Bad news and good news: population changes in Finnish owls during 1982–2007. *Ardea* **97**, 469–82.

Schaefer, T. (2004). Video monitoring of shrub nests reveals nest predators. *Bird Study* **51**, 170–7.

Schekkerman, H., Teunissen, W. & Oosterveld, E. (2009). Mortality of Black-tailed Godwit *Limosa limosa* and Northern Lapwing *Vanellus vanellus* chicks in wet grasslands: influence of predation and agriculture. *J. Ornithol.* **150**, 133–45.

Schifferli, L. (1979). Waterfowl counts and duck wing analysis in Switzerland. In: *Proceedings of the 2nd Technical Meeting on Western Palaearctic Migratory Bird Management.* International Waterfowl Research Bureau, Slimbridge, pp. 129–36.

Schindler, D. W., Kaspian, S. E. M. & Hessiene, R. H. (1989). Biological impoverishment in lakes of the midwestern and northeastern United States from acid rain. *Environ. Sci. Technol.* **23**, 573–80.

Schipper, W. J. A. (1979). A comparison of breeding ecology in European harriers (*Circus*). *Ardea* **66**, 77–102.

Schmaljohann, H. & Dierschke, V. (2005). Optimal bird migration and predation risk: a field experiment with Northern Wheatears *Oenanthe oenanthe*. *J. Anim. Ecol.* **74**, 131–8.

Schmitt, S. (2008–09). *The National Beached Bird Survey, 2008, 2009.* RSPB reports. RSPB, Sandy.

Schneider, F. (1966). Some pesticide–wildlife problems in Switzerland. *J. Appl. Ecol.* **3** (Suppl.), 15–20.

Schoener, T. W. (1983). Field experiments on interspecific competition. *Amer. Nat.* **122**, 240–85.

Schultz, A. M. (1964). The nutrient recovery
hypotheses for arctic microtine cycles. II.
Ecosystem variables in relation to arctic
microtine cycles. *Symp. Br. Ecol. Soc.* **4**,
57–68.

Sciple, G. W. (1953). Avian botulism:
information on earlier research. *U.S. Dept.
Interior Spec. Sci. Rep. Wildlife* **23**.

Scott, V. E. (1979). Bird responses to snag
removal in Ponderosa Pine. *J. For.* **77**, 26–8.

Sears, J. (1988). Regional and seasonal
variations in lead poisoning in the
Mute Swan *Cygnus olor* in relation to the
distribution of lead and lead weights in
the Thames area, England. *Biol. Conserv.*
46, 115–34.

Sears, J. & Hunt, A. (1991). Lead poisoning in
Mute Swans in England. *Wildfowl* Suppl.
1, S383–8.

Seiskari, P. (1962). On the winter ecology of the
Capercaillie, *Tetrao urogallus*, and the Black
Grouse, *Lyrurus tetrix*, in Finland. *Pap.
Game Res.* **22**, 1–119.

Selås, V. & Kålås, J. A. (2007). Territory
occupancy rate of Goshawk and Gyrfalcon:
no evidence of delayed numerical
response to grouse numbers. *Oecologia* **153**,
555–61.

Sergio, F. & Hiraldo, F. (2008). Intraguild
predation in raptor assemblages: a review.
Ibis **150** (S1), 132–45.

Sergio, F. & Newton, I. (2003). Occupancy as a
measure of territory quality. *J. Anim. Ecol.*
72, 857–65.

Sergio, F., Marchesi, L. & Pedrini, P. (2003).
Spatial refugia and the coexistence of
a diurnal raptor with its intraguild owl
predator. *J. Anim. Ecol.* **72**, 232–45.

Sergio, F., Marchesi, L., Pedrini, P. &
Penteriani, V. (2007). Coexistence of a
generalist owl with its intraguild predator:
distance-sensitive or habitat-mediated
avoidance? *Anim. Behav.* **74**, 1607–16.

Serrano, D., Forero, M. G., Donazur, J. A. &
Tella, J. L. (2004). Dispersal and social
attraction affect colony selection and
dynamics of Lesser Kestrels. *Ecology* **85**,
3438–47.

Seymour, A. S., Harris, S., Ralston, C. & White,
P. C. L. (2003). Factors influencing the
nesting success of Lapwings *Vanellus
vanellus* and behaviour of Red Fox *Vulpes*

vulpes in Lapwing nesting sites. *Bird Study*
50, 339–46.

Sharp, B. E. (1996). Post-release survival of
oiled, cleaned seabirds in North America.
Ibis **138**, 222–8.

Shaw, J. (1988). Arrested development of
Trichostrongylus tenuis as third stage larvae
in Red Grouse. *Res. Vet. Sci.* **45**, 256–8.

Shawyer, C. R., Clarke, R. & Dixon. N. (2003).
Causes of racing pigeon (*Columba livia*)
losses, including predation by raptors,
in the United Kingdom. In: *Birds of Prey
in a Changing Environment* (ed. D. B. A.
Thompson, S. M. Redpath, A. H. Fielding,
M. Marquiss & C. A. Galbraith). The
Sationery Office, Edinburgh, pp. 263–7.

Sheldon, R. D., Chaney, K. & Tyler, G. A.
(2007). Factors affecting nest survival of
Northern Lapwings *Vanellus vanellus* in
arable farmland: an agri-environment
scheme prescription can enhance nest
survival. *Bird Study* **54**, 168–75.

Sherman, K., Jones, C., Sullivan, L. *et al.* (1981).
Congruent shifts in sandeel abundance
in western and eastern North Atlantic
ecosystems. *Nature* **291**, 486–9.

Shields, W. M. & Crook, J. R. (1987). Barn
Swallow coloniality: a net cost for group
breeding in the Adirondacks. *Ecology* **68**,
1373–86.

Shrubb, M. (2003). *Birds, Scythes and Combines:
a History of Birds and Agricultural Change.*
Cambridge University Press, Cambridge.

Sih, A., Crowley, P., McPeek, M., Petranka,
J. & Stohmeier, K. (1985). Predation,
competition, and prey communities: a
review of field experiments. *Ann. Rev. Ecol.
Syst.* **16**, 269–311.

Siikamäki, P. (1996). Nestling growth and
mortality of Pied Flycatchers *Ficedula
hypoleuca* in relation to weather and
breeding effort. *Ibis* **138**, 471–8.

Sirén, M. (1951). Increasing the Goldeneye
population with nest-boxes. *Suomen Riista*
6, 189–90.

Siriwardena, G. M., Baillie, S. R. & Wilson,
J. D. (1999). Temporal variation in the
annual survival rates of six granivorous
birds with contrasting population trends.
Ibis **141**, 621–36.

Siriwardena, G. M., Baillie, S. R., Crick,
H. Q. P., Wilson, J. D. & Gates, S. (2000).

The demography of lowland farmland birds. In: *Ecology and Conservation of Lowland Farmland Birds* (ed. N. J. Aebischer, A. D. Evans, P. V. Grice & J. A. Vickery). British Ornithologists' Union, Tring, pp. 117–33.

Siriwardena, G. M., Stevens, D. K., Anderson, G. Q. A. et al. (2007). The effect of supplementary seed food on breeding populations of farmland birds: evidence from two large-scale experiments. *J. Appl. Ecol.* 44, 920–32.

Siriwardena, G. M., Calbrade, N. E. & Vickery, J. A. (2008). Farmland birds and late winter food: does seed supply fail to meet demand? *Ibis* 150, 585–95.

Skórka, P., Wójcik, J. D. & Martyka, R. (2005). Colonisation and population growth of Yellow-legged Gull *Larus cachinnans* in southeastern Poland: causes and influence on native species. *Ibis* 147, 471–82.

Slagsvold, T. (1975). Critical period for regulation of Great Tit (*Parus major*) and Blue Tit (*Parus caeruleus*) populations. *Norw. J. Zool.* 23, 67–88.

Slagsvold, T. (1979). Competition between Great Tit *Parus major* and Pied Flycatcher *Ficedula hypoleuca* – an experiment. *Ornis Scand.* 9, 46–50.

Small, R. J., Marcström, V. & Willebrandt, T. (1993). Synchronous and nonsynchronous population fluctuations of some predators and their prey in central Sweden. *Ecography* 16, 360–4.

Smart, J. (2004). Managing colonies for Little Terns *Sterna albifrons*. Pp. 19-28 in *Proceedings of a Symposium on Little Terns* (ed. R. Allcorn). RSPB Research Report 8. RSPB, Sandy, pp. 19–28.

Smart, J., Amar, A., Sim, I. M. W. et al. (2010). Illegal killing slows population recovery of a re-introduced raptor of high conservation concern: the Red Kite *Milvus milvus*. *Biol. Conserv.* 143, 1278–86.

Smith, J. N. M., Montgomerie, R. D., Taitt, M. J. & Yom-Tov, Y. (1980). A winter feeding experiment on an island Song Sparrow population. *Oecologia* 47, 164–70.

Smith, K. W. (2005). Has the reduction in nest-site competition from Starlings *Sturnus vulgaris* been a factor in the recent increase of Great Spotted Woodpecker *Dendrocopos*

major numbers in Britain? *Bird Study* 52, 307–13.

Smith, K. W. (2007). The utilization of dead wood resources by woodpeckers in Britain. *Ibis* 149 (S2), 183–92.

Smith, P. A., Elliott, K. H., Gaston, A. J. & Gilchrist, H. G. (2010). Has early ice clearance increased predation on breeding birds by Polar Bears? *Polar Biol.* 33, 1149–53.

Smith, R. K., Pullin, A. S., Stewart, G. B. & Sutherland, W. J. (2010). Effectiveness of predator removal for enhancing bird populations. *Conserv. Biol.* 24, 820–9.

Snow, B. & Snow, D. (1988). *Birds and Berries.* Poyser, Calton.

Snow, D. W. (2008). *Birds in Our Life.* William Sessions, York.

Sodhi, N. S., Didiuk, A. & Oliphant, L. W. (1990). Differences in bird abundance in relation to proximity of Merlin nests. *Can. J. Zool.* 68, 852–4.

Sokolov, L. V. (2006). Influence of the global warming on the timing of migration and breeding of passerines in the 20th century. *Zoologichesky Zhurnal* 85, 317–42.

Soler, J. J., De Neve, L., Perez-Contreras, T., Soler, M. & Sorci, G. (2003). Trade-off between immunocompetence and growth in Magpies: an experimental study. *Proc. R. Soc. Lond. B* 270, 241–8.

Soler, M. (1990). Relationships between the Great Spotted Cuckoo *Clamator glandarius* and its corvid hosts in a recently colonized area. *Ornis Scand.* 21, 212–23.

Soler, M. & Soler, J. J. (1996). Effects of experimental food provisioning on reproduction in the Jackdaw *Corvus monedula*, a semi-colonial species. *Ibis* 138, 379–83.

Solonen, T. (1997). Effect of Sparrowhawk predation on forest birds in southern Finland. *Ornis Fenn.* 74, 1–14.

Sonerud, G. (1993). Reduced predation by nest box relocation: differential effect in Tengmalm's Owl nests and artificial nests. *Ornis Scand.* 24, 249–53.

Sotherton, N. W. (1991). Conservation headlands: a practical combination of intensive cereal farming and conservation. In: *The Ecology of Temperate Cereal Fields* (ed. L. G. Firbank, N. Carter, J. F. Darbyshire & G. R. Potts). Blackwell, Oxford, pp. 373–97.

Souliere, G. J. (1988). Density of suitable Wood Duck nest cavities in a northern hardwood forest. *J. Wildl. Manage.* **52**, 86–9.

Southern, H. N. (1970). The natural control of a population of Tawny Owls (*Strix aluco*). *J. Zool. Lond.* **162**, 27–35.

Sowter, D. J. (2002). The Tarnbrook Fell gullery: 2002 report. Unpublished report cited in Mitchell *et al.* (2004).

Spaans, A. L. & Swennen, C. (1968). De Vogels van Vlieland Wetenschappelijke. *Mededelinge* **75**, 1–104.

Spaans, A. L., De Wit, A. A. N. & van Vlaardingen, M. A. (1987). Effects of increased population size in Herring Gulls on breeding success and other parameters. *Stud. Avian Biol.* **10**, 57–65.

Sparks, T. H., Huber, K., Bland, R. L. *et al.* (2007). How consistent are trends in arrival (and departure) dates of migrant birds in the UK? *J. Ornithol.* **148**, 503–11.

Spray, C. J. (1991). Population dynamics of Mute Swans *Cygnus olor* in the Outer Hebrides, Scotland. *Wildfowl* Suppl. **1**, s143.

Spray, C. J. & Milne, H. (1988). The incidence of lead poisoning among Whooper and Mute Swans *Cygnus cygnus* and *C. olor* in Scotland. *Biol. Conserv.* **44**, 265–81.

Stempniewicz, L. (1994). Marine birds drowning in fishing nets in the Gulf of Gdansk (southern Baltic): numbers, species composition, age and sex structure. *Ornis Svecica* **4**, 123–32.

Stevens, D. K., Anderson, G. Q. A., Grice, P. V., Norris, K. & Butcher, N. (2008). Predators of Spotted Flycatcher *Muscicapa striata* nests in southern England as determined by digital nest cameras. *Bird Study* **55**, 179–89.

Stickel, L. F. (1975). The costs and effects of chronic exposure to low-level pollutants in the environment. In: *Hearings Before the Sub-committee on the Environment and the Atmosphere* (Committee on Science and Technology). US House of Representatives, Washington, DC, pp 716–28.

Stillman, R. & Goss-Custard, J. G. (2002). Seasonal changes in the response of Oystercatchers *Haematopus ostralegus* to human disturbance. *J. Avian Biol.* **33**, 358–65.

Stoate, C. & Szczur, J. (2001). Could game management have a role in the conservation of farmland passerines? A

case study from a Leicestershire farm. *Bird Study* **48**, 279–92.

Stoate, C. & Szczur, J. (2006). Potential influence of habitat and predation on local breeding success and population in Spotted Flycatchers *Muscicapa striata*. *Bird Study* **53**, 328–30.

Stoate, C., Szczur, J. & Aebischer, N. J. (2003). Winter use of bird cover crops by passerines on farmland in northeast England. *Bird Study* **50**, 15–21.

Stoddard, J. L., Jeffries, D. S., Lükewille, A. *et al.* (1999). Regional trends in aquatic recovery from acidification in North America and Europe. *Nature* **401**, 575–8.

Stokke, B. G., Møller, A. P., Saether, B. E., Goetz, R. & Gutscher, H. (2005). Weather in the breeding area and during migration affects the demography of a small long-distance passerine migrant. *Auk* **122**, 637–47.

Storaas, T., Wegge, P. & Sonerud, G. (1982). Déstruction des nids de Grand Tétras et cycle des petits rongeurs dans l'est de la Norvège. In: *Actes du Colloque International sur le Grand Tétras* (Tetrao urogallus major) (ed. C. Kempf). Union Nationale des Associations Ornithologiques, Colmar, France, pp. 166–72.

Strann, K. B., Vader, W. & Barrett, R. T. (1991). Auk mortality in fishing nets in north Norway. *Seabird* **13**, 22–9.

Suddaby, D. & Ratcliffe, N. (1997). The effects of fluctuating food availability on breeding Arctic Terns *Sterna paradisaea*. *Auk* **114**, 524–30.

Suhonen, J., Alatalo, R. V., Carlson, A. & Höglund, J. (1992). Food resource distribution and the organisation of the *Parus* guild in a spruce forest. *Ornis Scand.* **23**, 467–74.

Suhonen, J., Norrdahl, K. & Korpimäki, E. (1994). Avian predation risk modifies breeding bird community on a farmland area. *Ecology* **75**, 1626–34.

Summers, R. W. (2004). Use of pine snags by birds in different stand types of Scots Pine *Pinus sylvestris*. *Bird Study* **51**, 212–21.

Summers, R. W. & Underhill, L. G. (1987). Factors related to breeding production of Brent Geese *Branta b. bernicla* and waders (Charadrii). *Bird Study* **37**, 161–71.

Summers, R. W. & Underhill, L. G. (1991). The growth of the population of Dark-bellied Brent Geese *Branta b. bernicla* between 1955–1988. *J. Appl. Ecol.* **28**, 574–85.

Summers, R. W., Green, R. E., Proctor, R. *et al.* (2004). An experimental study of the effects of predation on the breeding productivity of Capercaillie and Black Grouse. *J. Appl. Ecol.* **41**, 513–25.

Summers, R. W., Dugan, D. & Proctor, R. (2010). Numbers and breeding success of Capercaillies *Tetrao urogallus* and Black Grouse *T. tetrix* at Abernethy Forest, Scotland. *Bird Study* **57**, 437–46.

Summers-Smith, J. D. (1988). *The Sparrows.* Poyser, Calton.

Summers-Smith, J. D. (1996). *The Tree Sparrow.* J. D. Summers-Smith, Guisborough, Cleveland.

Sundell, J., Huitu, O., Henttonen, H. *et al.* (2004). Large scale spatial dynamics of vole populations in Finland revealed by the breeding success of vole-eating avian predators. *J. Anim. Ecol.* **73**, 167–78.

Sutcliffe, S. J. (1997). Populations of breeding *Larus* gulls on Welsh islands. In *Welsh Islands: Ecology, Conservation and Land-Use* (ed. P. M. Rhind, T. H. Blackstock & S. J. Parr). Countryside Commission for Wales, Bangor.

Suter, W. & van Eerden, M. R. (1992). Simultaneous mass starvation of wintering diving ducks in Switzerland and the Netherlands: a wrong decision in the right strategy. *Ardea* **80**, 229–42.

Svärdson, G. (1957). The 'invasion' type of bird migration. *Brit. Birds* **48**, 425–8.

Svensson, E., Råberg, L., Koch, C., Hasselquist, D. (1998). Energetic stress, immunosuppression and the costs of an antibody response. *Funct. Ecol.* **12**, 912–19.

Swann, B. (2003). What is happening to Canna seabirds? *Scott. Bird News* **67**, 14–15.

Swennen, C. (1972). Chlorinated hydrocarbons attacked the Eider population in The Netherlands. *TNO nieuws* **27**, 556–60.

Swennen, C. (1989). Gull predation upon Eider *Somateria mollissima* ducklings: destruction or elimination of the unfit? *Ardea* **77**, 21–45.

Swennen, C. & Duiven, P. (1983). Characteristics of Oystercatchers killed by

cold-stress in the Dutch Wadden Sea area. *Ardea* **71**, 155–9.

Swennen, C. & Smit, T. (1991). Pasteurellosis among breeding Eiders *Somateria mollissima* in the Netherlands. *Wildfowl* **42**, 94–7.

Sylven, M. (1979). Interspecific relations between sympatrically wintering Common Buzzards *Buteo buteo* and Rough-legged Buzzards *Buteo lagopus*. *Ornis. Scand.* **9**, 197–206.

Szép, T. & Møller, A. P. (1999). Cost of parasites and host immune defence in the Sand Martin *Riparia riparia*: a role for parent–offspring conflict. *Oecologia* **119**, 9–15.

Szép, T. & Møller, A. P. (2000). Exposure to ectoparasites increases within-brood variability in size and body mass in the Sand Martin. *Oecologia* **125**, 201–7.

Szostek, K. L. & Becker, P. H. (2012). Terns in trouble: demographic consequences of low breeding success and recruitment on a Common Tern population in the German Wadden Sea. *J. Ornithol.* **153**, 313–26.

Tamisier, A., Bechet, A., Jarry, G., Lefeuvre, J. C. & Le Mayo, Y. (2003). Effects of hunting disturbance on waterbirds. A review of literature. *La Terre et La Vie* **58**, 435–49.

Tapper, S. (1992). *Game Heritage: an Ecological View from Shooting and Gamekeeper Records.* Game Conservancy Trust, Fordingbridge.

Tapper, S. (ed.) (1999). *A Question of Balance.* Game Conservancy Trust, Fordingbridge.

Tapper, S. C., Potts, G. R. & Brockless, M. H. (1996). The effect of an experimental reduction in predation pressure on the breeding success and population density of Grey Partridges *Perdix perdix*. *J. Appl. Ecol.* **33**, 965–78.

Tate, J. L. (1972). The changing seasons. *Amer. Birds* **26**, 828–31.

Tavecchia, G., Pradel, R., Lebreton, J.-D., Johnson, A. R. & Mondain-Monval, J.-Y. (2001). The effect of lead exposure on survival of adult Mallards in the Camargue, southern France. *J. Appl. Ecol.* **38**, 1197–207.

Taylor, I. (1994). *Barn Owls: Predator–Prey Relationships and Conservation.* Cambridge University Press, Cambridge.

Tella, J. L., Forest, M. G., Gajón, A., Hiraldo, F. & Donázar, J. A. (1996). Absence of blood parasitisation effects on Lesser Kestrel fitness. *Auk* **113**, 253–6.

te Marvelde, L., Meninger, P. L., Flamant, R. & Dingemanse, N. J. (2009). Age-specific density-dependent survival in Mediterranean Gulls *Larus melanocephalus*. *Ardea* **97**, 305–12.

Temple, S. A. (1987). Do predators always capture substandard individuals disproportionately from prey populations? *Ecology* **68**, 669–74.

Teunissen, W., Schekkerman, H., Willems, F. & Majoor, F. (2008). Identifying predators of eggs and chicks of Lapwing *Vanellus vanellus* and Black-tailed Godwit *Limosa limosa* in the Netherlands and the importance of predation on wader reproductive output. *Ibis* **150** (S1), 74–85.

Thackeray, S. J., Sparks, T. H., Frederiksen, M. *et al.* (2010). Trophic level asynchrony in rates of phenological change for marine, freshwater and terrestrial environments. *Global Change Biol.* **16**, 3304–13.

Tharme, A. P., Green, R. E., Baines, D., Bainbridge, I. P. & O'Brien, M. (2001). The effect of management for Red Grouse shooting on the population density of breeding birds on heather-dominated moorland. *J. Appl. Ecol.* **38**, 439–57.

Thaxter, C. B., Joys, A. C., Gregory, R. D., Baillie, S. R. & Noble, D. (2010). Hypotheses to explain patterns of population change among breeding birds in England. *Biol. Conserv.* **143**, 2006–19.

Thiollay, J.-M. (1988). Comparative predation pressure on solitary and colonial breeding passerines. *Proc. Int. Ornithol. Congr.* **19**, 660–73.

Thirgood, S., Redpath, S., Haydn, D. T. *et al.* (2000). Habitat loss and raptor predation: disentangling long- and short-term causes of Red Grouse declines. *Proc. R. Soc. Lond. B* **267**, 651–6.

Thompson, D. B. A. & Barnard, C. J. (1983). Anti-predator associations in mixed species responses of Lapwings, Golden Plovers and gulls. *Anim. Behav.* **31**, 585–93.

Thompson, D. B. A. & Thompson, M. L. P. (1985). Early warning and mixed species association: the 'Plover's Page' revisited. *Ibis* **127**, 559–62.

Thompson, D. B. A. & Whitfield, D. P. (1993).

Research on mountain birds and their habitats. *Scott. Birds* **17**, 1–8.

Thompson, P. M. & Ollason, J. C. (2001). Lagged effects of ocean climate change on Fulmar population dynamics. *Nature* **413**, 417–20.

Thomson, D. L., Green, R. E., Gregory, R. D. & Baillie, S. R. (1998). The widespread declines in songbirds in rural Britain do not correlate with the spread of their avian predators. *Proc. R. Soc. Lond. B* **265**, 2057–62.

Threlfall, W., Eveleigh, E. & Maunder, J. E. (1974). Seabird mortality in a storm. *Auk* **91**, 846–9.

Ticehurst, N. F. & Hartley, P. H. T. (1948). Report on the effect of the severe winter of 1946–1947 on bird-life. *Brit. Birds* **41**, 322–34.

Tinbergen, L. (1946). De sperver als roofvijand van zangvogels. *Ardea* **34**, 1–123.

Tinbergen, N., Impekoven, M. & Franck, D. (1967). An experiment on spacing out as a defence against predation. *Behaviour* **28**, 307–21.

Toivanen, P. & Toivanen, A. (eds). 1987. *Avian Immunology.* CRC Press, Boca Raton, Florida.

Tompkins, D. M., Jones, T. & Clayton, D. H. (1996). Effect of vertically transmitted ectoparasites on the reproductive success of Swifts (*Apus apus*). *Funct. Ecol.* **10**, 733–40.

Tornberg, R. (2001). Pattern of Goshawk predation on four forest grouse species in northern Finland. *Wildl. Biol.* **7**, 245–56.

Tornberg, R., Korpimäki, E., Reif, V., Jungell, S. & Mykra, S. (2005). Delayed numerical response of Goshawks to population fluctuations in forest grouse. *Oikos* **111**, 408–15.

Tornberg, R., Korpimäki, E. & Byholm, P. (2006). Ecology of the Northern Goshawk in Fennoscandia. *Stud. Avian Biol.* **31**, 141–57.

Török, J. (1987). Competition for food between Great Tit *Parus major* and Blue Tit *P. caeruleus* during the breeding season. *Acta. Reg. Soc. Sci. Litt. Gothoburgensis. Zoologica* **14**, 149–52.

Trinder, M. N., Hassell, D. & Votier, S. (2009). Reproductive performance in arctic-nesting geese is influenced by environmental conditions during the wintering, breeding and migration seasons. *Oikos* **118**, 1093–101.

Triplet, F. & Richner, H. (1997). Host responses to ectoparasites: food compensation by parent Blue Tits. *Oikos* **78**, 557–61.

Triplet, F., Glaser, M. & Richner, H. (2002). Behavioural responses of ectoparasites: time budget adjustments and what matters to Blue Tits *Parus caeruleus* infected by fleas. *Ibis* **144**, 461–9.

Tryjanowski, P. (2001). Proximity of Raven (*Corvus corax*) nests modifies breeding bird community on intensively used farmland. *Ann. Zool. Fenn.* **38**, 131–8.

Tucker, G. & Heath, M. (1994). *Birds in Europe: their Conservation Status.* Birdlife International, Cambridge.

Tucker, R. K. & Crabtree, D. G. (1970). *Handbook of Toxicity of Pesticides to Wildlife.* Resource Publication 84. US Fish & Wildlife Service, Washington DC.

Tuomenpuro, J. (1991). Effect of nest site on nest survival in the Dunnock *Prunella modularis. Ornis Fenn.* **68**, 49–56.

Underhill, L. G., Waltner, M. & Summers, R. W. (1989). Three-year cycles in breeding productivity of Knots *Calidris canutus* wintering in southern Africa suggest Taimyr Peninsula provenance. *Bird Study* **36**, 83–7.

Underwood, L. A. & Stowe, T. J. (1984). Massive wreck of seabirds in eastern Britain, 1983. *Bird Study* **31**, 79–88.

Uttley, J., Monaghan, P. & White, S. (1989). Differential effects of reduced sandeel availability on two sympatrically breeding species of tern. *Ornis Scand.* **20**, 273–7.

Väänänen, V.-M. (2000). Predation risk associated with nesting in gull colonies by two **Aythya** species: observation and experimental test. *J. Avian Biol.* **31**, 31–5.

Väänänen, V.-M. (2001). Hunting disturbance and the timing of autumn migration in *Anas* species. *Wildl. Biol.* **7**, 3–9.

Vader, W., Barrett, R. T., Erikstad, K. E. & Strann, K.-B. (1990). Differential response of Common and Thick-billed Murres to a crash in the capelin stock in the southern Barents Sea. *Stud. Avian Biol.* **14**, 175–80.

van Balen, J. H. (1980). Population fluctuations of the Great Tit and feeding conditions in winter. *Ardea* **68**, 143–64.

van Balen, J. H., Booy, C. J. H., van Franeker, J. A. & Osieck, E. R. (1982). Studies on hole nesting birds in natural nest sites, 1. Availability and occupation of natural nest sites. *Ardea* **70**, 1–24.

van den Hout, P. J., Piersma, T., Dekinga, S. A., Lubbe, S. K. & Visser, G. H. (2006). Ruddy Turnstones rapidly build pectoral muscle after a raptor scare. *J. Avian Biol.* **37**, 425–30.

van den Hout, P. J., Spaans, B. & Piersma, T. (2008). Differential mortality of wintering shorebirds on the Banc d'Arguin, Mauritania, due to predation by large falcons. *Ibis* **150** (S1), 219–30.

van den Hout, P. J., Mathot, K. J., Maas, L. R. M. & Piersma, T. (2010). Predator escape tactics in birds, linking ecology and aerodynamics. *Behav. Ecol.* **21**, 16–25.

van der Veen, I. T. (2000). Daily routines and predator encounters in Yellowhammers *Emberiza citrinella* in the field during winter. *Ibis* **142**, 413–20.

van der Vliet, R. E., Schuller, E. & Wassen, M. J. (2008). Avian predators in a meadow landscape: consequences of their occurrence for breeding open-area birds. *J. Avian Biol.* **39**, 523–9.

van der Winden, J. & van Horssen, P. W. (2008). A population model for the Black Tern *Chlidonias niger* in West Europe. *J. Ornithol.* **149**, 487–94.

van Dobben, W. H. (1952). The food of the Cormorants in the Netherlands. *Ardea* **40**, 1–63.

van Franeker, J. A., Blaize, C., Danielsen, J. et al. (2011). Monitoring plastic ingestion by the Northern Fulmar *Fulmarus glacialis* in the North Sea. *Environ. Pollut.* **159**, 2609–15.

van Gils, J. A., Munster, V. J., Radersma, R. et al. (2007). Hampered foraging and migratory performance in swans infected with low-pathogenic avian influenza A virus. *PLoS One* **2** (1), e184.

van Haaff, G. (2001). Postduifringen als indicator voor vroegere nestbezetting door *Acipiter gentilis.* Over de archeologie van treekse havikhorsten. *De Takkeling* **9**, 137–49.

Van Impe, J. (1996). Long term reproductive performance in White-fronted Geese *Anser a. albifrons* and Tundra Bean Geese *A. fabalis rossicus* wintering in Zeeland (The Netherlands). *Bird Study* **40**, 280–9.

Velando, A., Álvarez, D., Mouriñ, J., Arcos, F. & Barros, Á. (2005). Population trends and reproductive success of the European Shag *Phalacrocorax aristotelis* on the Iberian peninsular following the *Prestige* oil spill. *J. Ornithol.* **146**, 116–20.

Verhulst, S., Oosterbeek, K., Rutten, A. I. & Ens, B. J. (2004). Shellfish fishery severely reduces condition and survival of Oystercatchers despite creation of large marine protected area. *Ecol. Society* **9**, 17 (online).

Vespäläinen, K. (1968). The effect of the cold spring 1966 upon the Lapwing *Vanellus vanellus* in Finland. *Ornis Fenn.* **45**, 33–47.

Vickery, J. (1991). Breeding density of Dippers *Cinclus cinclus*, Grey Wagtails *Motacilla cinerea* and Common Sandpipers *Actitis hypoleucos* in relation to the acidity of streams in south-west Scotland. *Ibis* **133**, 178–87.

Vickery, J. A. & Ormerod, S. J. (1991). Dippers as indicators of stream acidity. *Proc. Int. Ornithol. Congr.* **20**, 2494–502.

Village, A. (1990). *The Kestrel.* Poyser, Calton.

Villanúa, D., Höfle, U., Pérez-Rodríguez, L. & Gortázar, C. (2006). *Trichomonas gallinae* in wintering Common Wood Pigeons *Columba palumbus* in Spain. *Ibis* **148**, 641–8.

Virolainen, M. (1984). Breeding biology of the Pied Flycatcher *Ficedula hypoleuca* in relation to population density. *Ann. Zool. Fenn.* **21**, 187–97.

Visser, M. E. & Both, C. (2005). Shifts in phenology due to climate change. *Proc. R. Soc. B* **272**, 2561–9.

Visser, M. E. & Lessells, C. M. (2001). The costs of egg production and incubation in Great Tits (*Parus major*). *Proc. R. Soc. Lond. B* **268**, 1271–7.

Visser, M. E., van Noordwijk, A. J., Tinbergen, J. M. & Lessells, C. M. (1998). Warmer springs lead to mistimed reproduction in Great Tits (*Parus major*). *Proc. R. Soc. Lond. B* **265**, 1867–70.

Visser, M. E., Adriaensen, F., van Balen, J. H. *et al.* (2003). Variable responses to large-scale climate change in European Parus populations. *Proc. R. Soc. Lond. B* **270**, 367–72.

Visser, M. E., Perdeck, A. C., van Balen, J. H. & Both, C. (2009). Climate change leads to decreasing bird migration distances. *Global Change Biol.* **15**, 1859–65.

Vlugt, D. (2002). De postduif *Columba livia* als pooi van de Havik *Accipiter gentilis* in de duinen van Noord-Holland. *De Takkeling* **10**, 135–49.

von Haartman, L. (1957). Adaptation in hole-nesting birds. *Evolution* **11**, 339–47.

von Haartman, L. (1971). Population dynamics. In: *Avian Biology, Vol. 1* (ed. D. S. Farner & J. R. King). Academic Press, London, pp. 391–459.

von Haartman, L. (1973). Talgmespopulationen Lemsjöholm. *Lintumies* **8**, 7–9.

Votier, S. C., Bearhop, S., Ratcliffe, N. R, Phillips, R. A. & Furness, R. W. (2004a). Predation by Great Skuas at a large Shetland seabird colony. *J. Appl. Ecol.* **41**, 1117–28.

Votier, S. C., Furness, R. W., Bearhop, S. *et al.* (2004b). Changes in fisheries discard rates and seabird communities. *Nature* **427**, 727–30.

Votier, S. C., Hatchwell, B. J., Beckerman, A. *et al.* (2005). Oil pollution and climate have wide-scale impacts on seabird demographies. *Ecol. Lett.* **8**, 1157–64.

Votier, S. C, Bearhop, S., Fyfe, R. & Furness, R. W. (2008). Linking temporal and spatial variation in the diet of a marine top predator with commercial fisheries. *Marine Ecol. Prog. Ser.* **367**, 223–32.

Votier, S. C., Hatchwell, B. J., Mears, M. & Birkhead, T. R. (2009). Changes in the timing of egg-laying of a colonial seabird in relation to population size and environmental conditions. *Marine Biology Progress Series* **393**, 225–33.

Vrezec, A. & Tome, D. (2004). Altitudinal segregation between Ural Owl *Strix uralensis* and Tawny Owl *Strix aluco*: evidence for competitive exclusion in raptorial birds. *Bird Study* **51**, 264–9.

Walker, C. H. (1983). Pesticides and birds: mechanisms of selective toxicity. *Agric. Ecosys. Environ.* **9**, 211–26.

Walker, M. D. & Rotherham, I. D. (2010). The breeding success of Common Swifts *Apus apus* is not correlated with the abundance of their Louse Fly *Crataerina pallida* parasites. *Bird Study* **57**, 504–8.

Wall, R. & Strong, L. (1987). Environmental

consequences of treating cattle with the anti-parasitic drug ivermectin. *Nature* **327**, 418–21.

Wallace, G. J., Nickell, W. P. & Bernard, R. F. (1961). Bird mortality in the Dutch Elm Disease program in Michigan. *Cranbrook Inst. Sci. Bull.* **41**, 1–44.

Wanless, S. (2007). Climate change and northeast Atlantic seabirds. *J. Ornithol.* **147** (Suppl. 1), s155–9.

Wanless, S., Harris, M. P., Calladine, J. & Rothery, P. (1996). Modelling responses of Herring Gull and Lesser Black-backed Gull populations to reduction of reproductive output: implications for control measures. *J. Appl. Ecol.* **33**, 1420–32.

Wanless, S., Wright, P. J., Harris, M. P. & Elston, D. A. (2004). Evidence for a decrease in size of Lesser Sandeels *Ammodytes marinus* in a North Sea aggregation over a 30-year period. *Marine Ecol. Prog. Ser.* **2279**, 237–46.

Warner, R. E. (1968). The role of introduced diseases in the extinction of the endemic Hawaiian avifauna. *Condor* **70**, 101–20.

Warner, R. E. (1984). Declining survival of Ring-necked Pheasant chicks in Illinois agricultural ecosystems. *J. Wildl. Manage.* **48**, 82–8.

Waters, J. R., Noon, B. R. & Verner, J. (1990). Lack of nest site limitation in a cavity-nesting bird community. *J. Wildl. Manage.* **54**, 239–45.

Watson, A. (1985). Social class, socially-induced loss, recruitment and breeding of Red Grouse. *Oecologia* **67**, 493–8.

Watson, A. & Jenkins, D. (1968). Experiments on population control by territorial behaviour in Red Grouse. *J. Anim. Ecol.* **37**, 595–614.

Watson, A. & Moss, R. (1979). Population cycles in the Tetraonidae. *Ornis Fenn.* **56**, 87–109.

Watson, A. & Moss, R. (2008). *Grouse: the Natural History of British and Irish species.* New Naturalist 107. Collins, London.

Watson, A. & Rae, R. (1997). Some effects of set-aside on breeding birds in northeast Scotland. *Bird Study* **44**, 245–51.

Watson, A., Moss, R. & Parr, R. (1984). Effects of food enrichment on numbers and spacing of Red Grouse. *J. Anim. Ecol.* **53**, 663–78.

Watson, A. & O'Hare, P. J. (1979). Red grouse populations on experimentally treated and untreated Irish bog. *J. Appl. Ecol.* **16**, 433–52.

Watson, A., Moss, R. & Rothery, P. (2000). Weather and synchrony in 10-year population cycles of Rock Ptarmigan and Red Grouse in Scotland. *Ecology* **81**, 2126–36.

Watson, J. (2010). *The Golden Eagle*, 2nd edition. Poyser, London.

Watson, M., Aebishcher, N. J. & Cresswell, W. (2007a). Vigilance and fitness in Grey Partridges *Perdix perdix*: the effects of group size and foraging-vigilance trade-offs on predation mortality. *J. Anim. Ecol.* **76**, 211–21.

Watson, M., Aebisher, N. J., Potts, G. R. & Ewald, J. A. (2007b). The relative effects of raptor predation and shooting on overwinter mortality of Grey Partridges in the UK. *J. Appl. Ecol.* **44**, 972–82.

Watson, R. T., Fuller, M., Pokras, M. & Hunt, G. (2009). *Ingestion of Lead from Spent Ammunition: Implications for Wildlife and Humans.* The Peregrine Fund, Boise, Idaho.

Weatherhead, P. J. & Bennett, G. F. (1991). Ecology of Red-winged Blackbird parasitism by haematozoa. *Can. J. Zool.* **69**, 2352–9.

Weatherhead, P. J. & Bennett, G. F. (1992). Ecology of parasitism of Brown-headed Cowbirds by haematozoa. *Can. J. Zool.* **70**, 1–7.

Weeden, R. B. & Theberge, J. B. (1972). The dynamics of a fluctuating population of Rock Ptarmigan in Alaska. *Proc. Int. Orn. Congr.* **15**, 90–106.

Weidinger, K. (2009). Nest-predators of woodland open-nesting songbirds in central Europe. *Ibis* **151**, 352–60.

Wellenstein, G. (1968). Weitere Ergebnisse über die Auswirkungen einer planmässigen Ansiedlung von Waldameisen und höhlenbrütenden Vögel im Lehr- und Versuchsrevier Schwetzingen. *Angewandte Ornithologie* **3**, 40–53.

Wernham, C. V. & Bryant, D. M. (2002). An experimental study of reduced parental effort and future reproductive success in the Puffin *Fratercula arctica*. *J. Anim. Ecol.* **67**, 25–40.

Wernham, C. V., Toms, M. P., Marchant, J. H. et al. (2002). *The Migration Atlas: Movements of the Birds of Britain and Ireland.* Poyser, London.

Whilde, A. (1979). Auks trapped in salmon drift-nets. *Irish Birds* **1**, 370–6.

Whiteley, P. L. & Yuill, T. M. (1991). Interactions of environmental contaminants and infectious disease in avian species. *Proc. Int. Orn. Congr.* **20**, 2338–42.

Whitfield, D. P. (2003a). Density-dependent mortality of wintering Dunlins *Calidris alpina* through predation by Eurasian Sparrowhawks *Accipiter nisus*. *Ibis* **145**, 432–8.

Whitfield, D. P. (2003b). Predation by Eurasian Sparrowhawks produces density-dependent mortality of wintering Redshanks. *J. Anim. Ecol.* **72**, 27–35.

Whitfield, D. P. (2003c). Redshank *Tringa totanus* flocking behaviour, distance from cover and vulnerability to Sparrowhawk *Accipiter nisus* predation. *J. Avian Biol.* **34**, 163–9.

Whitfield, D. P., McLeod, D. R. A., Watson, J., Fielding, A. H. & Haworth, P. F. (2003). The association of grouse moor in Scotland with the illegal use of poisons to control predators. *Biol. Conserv.* **114**, 157–63.

Whitfield, D. P., Fielding, A. H., McLeod, D. R. A. & Haworth, P. F. (2004). Modelling the effects of persecution on the population dynamics of Golden Eagles in Scotland. *Biol. Conserv.* **119**, 319–33.

Whitfield, D. P., Fielding, A. H., McLeod, D. R. A. et al. (2007). Factors constraining the distribution of Golden Eagles in Scotland. *Bird Study* **54**, 199–211.

Whittingham, M., Butler, S. K., Quinn, J. L. & Cresswell, W. (2004). The effect of limited visibility on vigilance behaviour and speed of predator detection implications for the conservation of granivorous passerines. *Oikos* **106**, 377–85.

Widén, P. (1987). Goshawk predation during winter, spring and summer in a boreal forest area of Sweden. *Holarctic Ecology* **10**, 104–9.

Widén, P. (1994). Habitat quality for raptors: a field experiment. *J. Avian Biol.* **25**, 219–23.

Wiehn, J. & Korpimäki, E. (1997). Food limitation on brood size: experimental evidence in the Eurasian Kestrel. *Ecology* **78**, 2043–50.

Wiens, J. A. (1989). *The Ecology of Bird Communities. Vol. 2, Processes and Variations.* Cambridge University Press, Cambridge.

Wiklund, C. G. (1982). Fieldfare (*Turdus pilaris*) breeding success in relation to colony size, nest position and association with Merlins (*Falco columbarius*). *Behav. Ecol. Sociobiol.* **11**, 165–72.

Willebrand, T. (1988). Demography and ecology of a Black Grouse (*Tetrao tetrix* L.) population. PhD thesis, Uppsala University.

Williams, T. D., Christians, J. K., Aiken, J. J. & Evanson, M. (1999). Enhanced immune function does not depress reproductive output. *Proc. R. Soc. Lond. B.* **266**, 753–7.

Wilson, J. & Peach, W. (2006). Impact of an exceptional winter flood on the population dynamics of Bearded Tits (*Panurus biarmicus*). *Anim. Conserv.* **9**, 463–73.

Wilson, J. D., Taylor, I. & Muirhead, L. B. (1996). Field use by farmland birds in winter: an analysis of field type preferences using resampling methods. *Bird Study* **43**, 320–32.

Wilson, J. D., Evans, A. D., Browne, S. J. & King, J. R. (1997). Territory distribution and breeding success of Skylarks *Alauda arvensis* on organic and intensive farmland in southern England. *J. Appl. Ecol.* **34**, 1462–78.

Wilson, J. D., Morris, A. J., Arroyo, B. E., Clark, S. C. & Bradbury, R. B. (1999). A review of the abundance and diversity of invertebrate and plant foods of granivorous birds in northern Europe in relation to agricultural change. *Agric. Ecosys. Environ.* **75**, 13–30.

Winfield, D. K. & Winfield, I. J. (1994). Possible competitive interactions between overwintering Tufted Duck *Aythya fuligula* (L) and fish populations of Lough Neagh, Northern Ireland: evidence from diet studies. *Hydrobiologia* **280**, 377–86.

Winfield, I. J., Winfield, D. K. & Tobin, C. M. (1992). Interactions between the Roach, *Rutilus rutilus*, and waterfowl populations of Lough Neagh, Northern Ireland. *Environ. Biol. Fishes* **33**, 207–14.

Wingfield, J. C., Hunt, K., Breuner, C. et al. (1998). Environmental stress, field endocrinology, and conservation biology.

In: *Behavioral Approaches to Conservation in the Wild* (ed. J. R. Clemmons & R. Buchholz). Cambridge University Press, Cambridge, pp. 95–131.

Winstanley, D. R., Spencer, R. & Williamson, K. (1974). Where have all the Whitethroats gone? *Bird Study* **21**, 1–14.

Witter, M. S., Cuthill, I. C. & Bonser, R. (1994). Experimental investigations of mass-dependent predation risk in the European Starling *Sturnus vulgaris*. *Anim. Behav.* **48**, 201–22.

Wobeser, G. A. (1981). *Diseases of Wild Waterfowl*. Plenum Press, New York.

Woiwood, I. P. (1991). The ecological importance of long-term synoptic monitoring. In: *The Ecology of Temperate Cereal Fields* (ed. L. G. Firbank, N. Carter, J. F. Darbyshire & G. R. Potts). Blackwell, Oxford, pp. 275–304.

Woodburn, M. (1995). Do parasites alter Pheasant breeding success? *Game Conservancy Rev.* **26**, 96–7.

Woods, M., McDonald, R. A. & Harris, S. (2003). Predation of wildlife by domestic cats *Felis catus* in Great Britain. *Mammal Rev.* **33**, 174–88.

Wotton, S. R., Langston, R. H. W., Gibbons, D. W. & Pierce, A. J. (2000). The status of the Cirl Bunting in the UK and the Channel Islands in 1998. *Bird Study* **47**, 138–46.

Wotton, S. R., Conway, G., Eaton, M., Henderson, I. & Grice, P. (2009). The status of the Dartford Warbler in the UK and the Channel Islands in 2006. *Brit. Birds* **102**, 230–46.

Wrånes, E. (1988). Massedød av aerfugl på Sørlandet vinteren 1981/82. *Vår Fuglefauna* **11**, 71–4.

Wright, L. J., Hoblyn, R. A., Green, R. E. *et al.* (2009). Importance of climatic and environmental change in the demography of a multi-brooded passerine, the Woodlark *Lullula arborea*. *J. Anim. Ecol.* **78**, 1191–202.

Wright, R. M. & Phillips, V. E. (1990). Mallard response to increased food-supply in the wildfowl reserve. *Game Conservancy Ann. Rev.* **1**, 105–8.

Wyllie, I. (1981). *The Cuckoo*. Batsford, London.

Wyllie, I. & Newton, I. (1991). Demography of an increasing population of Sparrowhawks. *J. Anim. Ecol.* **60**, 749–66.

Wyllie, I., Dale, L. & Newton, I. (1996). Unequal sex-ratio, mortality causes and pollutant residues in Long-eared Owls in Britain. *Brit. Birds* **89**, 429–36.

Yalden, D. W. & Pearce-Higgins, J. W. (1997). Density dependence and winter weather as factors affecting the size of a population of Golden Plovers *Pluvialis apricaria*. *Bird Study* **44**, 227–34.

Yasué, M. (2005). The effects of human presence, flock size and prey density on shorebird foraging rates. *J. Ethol.* **23**, 199–204.

Yates, M. G., Goss-Custard, J. D., McGrorty, S. *et al.* (1993). Sediment characteristics, invertebrate densities and shorebird densities on the inner banks of the Wash. *J. Appl. Ecol.* **30**, 599–614.

Yom-Tov, Y. (1974). The effect of food and predation on breeding density and success, clutch size and laying date of the Crow (*Corvus corone* L.). *J. Anim. Ecol.* **43**, 479–98.

Yom-Tov, Y & Geffen, E. (2011). Recent temporal and spatial changes in body size of terrestrial vertebrates: probable causes and pitfalls. *Biol. Rev.* **86**, 531–41.

Yom-Tov, Y. & Yom-Tov, S. (2006). Decrease in body size of Danish Goshawks during the twentieth century. *J. Ornithol.* **147**, 644–7.

Yom-Tov, Y., Yom-Tov, S., Wright, J., Thorne, C. J. R. & Du Feu, R. (2006). Recent changes in body weight and wing length among some British passerine birds. *Oikos* **112**, 91–101.

Zonfrillo, B. (2002). Puffins return to Ailsa Craig. *Scott. Bird News*, **66**, 1–2.

Zonfrillo, B. & Nogales, M. (2002). First breeding records of Shelduck and Black Guillemot on Ailsa Craig. *Glasgow Nat.* **22**, 197–8.

Zwank, P. J., Wright, V. L., Shealy, P. M. & Newsom, J. D. (1985). Lead toxicosis in waterfowl on two major wintering areas in Louisiana. *Wildl. Soc. Bull.* **13**, 17–26.

Indexes

SPECIES INDEX

Pochard, *Aythya farina* 260, 288, 319, 436, 457, 490, 492
Pochard, Red-crested, *Netta rufina* 492
Podiceps auritus – see Grebe, Slavonian
Podiceps grisegena – see Grebe, Red-necked
Podiceps nigricollis – see Grebe, Black-necked
Poecile cinctus – see Tit, Siberian
Poecile montanus – see Tit, Willow
Poecile palustris – see Tit, Marsh
Pollachius virens – see Saithe
Polygonum persicaria – see Persicaria
Polymorphus boschadis 235–6
Poorwill, Common, *Phalaenoptilus nuttallii* 54
Procyon lotor – see Raccoon
Profilicollis botulus – see Worm, Thorny-headed
Protocalliphora – see blowfly
Prunella modularis – see Dunnock
Psittacula krameri – see Parakeet, Ring-necked
Ptarmigan (Rock Ptarmigan), *Lagopus muta* 10, 46, 75, 77, 141, 180–1, 183, 184, 228–9, 357, 412, 421
Ptarmigan, Willow, *Lagopus lagopus* 141, 152, 182, 183, 228–9, 240, 425
Puffin, *Fratercula arctica* 23, 36, 48, 58, 59, 60, 66, 70, 84, 85, 135, 136, 141, 186, 189, 190, 267, 281, 287, 371, 397, 439, 440, 497, 498, 499
Puffinus baroli – see Shearwater, Macaronesian
Puffinus gravis – see Shearwater, Great
Puffinus griseus – see Shearwater, Sooty
Puffinus puffinus – see Shearwater, Manx
Pyrrhula pyrrhula – see Bullfinch

Quail, *Coturnix coturnix* 169, 283, 457
Quail, Bobwhite, *Colinus virginianus* 160, 168
Quelea quelea – see Quelea, Red-billed
Quelea, Red-billed, *Quelea quelea* 479
Quercus – see oak

Rabbit, *Oryctolagus cuniculus* 57, 78, 135, 141, 147, 188, 195, 204, 228, 267, 308, 341, 419, 455, 479
Raccoon, *Procyon lotor* 137
Rat, Black, *Rattus rattus* 188, 190
Rat, Brown, *Rattus norvegicus* 89, 136, 140, 188–90, 198, 199, 309, 429, 440, 463, 478
Rattus norvegicus – see Rat, Brown
Rattus rattus – see Rat, Black
Raven, *Corvus corax* 180, 290, 433, 447, 448, 449, 450, 455, 456, 494
Razorbill, *Alca torda* 58, 81, 84, 131, 135, 189, 191, 371, 396, 419, 460, 498, 499
Recurvirostra avosetta – see Avocet
Redpoll, Common, *Carduelis flammea* 91, 92, 98
Redpoll, Lesser, *Carduelis cabaret* 96, 484
Redshank, *Tringa tetanus* 40, 71, 152, 177, 179, 193, 197, 297–8, 354, 355, 356, 439

Redstart, *Phoenicurus phoenicurus* 71, 116, 117, 119, 123, 221, 290, 309
Redstart, Black, *Phoenicurus ochrurus* 399
Redwing, *Turdus iliacus* 271, 351, 401
Regulus ignicapilla – see Firecrest
Regulus regulus – see Goldcrest
Riparia riparia – see Martin, Sand
Rissa tridactyla – see Kittiwake
Roach, *Rutilus rutilus* 504, 508
Robin, *Erithacus rubecula* 155, 246, 353, 355, 312, 316
Robin, American, *Turdus migratorius* 467–8
Rook, *Corvus frugilegus* 6, 13, 69, 88, 112
Ruff, *Philomachus pugnax* 432, 438, 439, 444, 494
Rutilus rutilus – see Roach

Saithe, *Pollachius virens* 59, 83, 85
Salmo salar – see Salmon
Salmon, *Salmo salar* 88, 460
Salmonella 241
Sandeel, Lesser, *Ammodytes marinus* 58, 59–60, 70, 80, 81, 82–4, 85, 113, 286–7, 290–1, 311, 374, 396–7
Sanderling, *Calidris alba* 185
Sandpiper, Common, *Actitis hypoleucos* 102, 350, 369
Sandpiper, Curlew, *Calidris ferruginea* 185
Sandpiper, Purple, *Calidris maritime* 2, 401
Sandpiper, Wood, *Tringa glareola* 401
Saxicola rubetra – see Whinchat
Saxicola torquatus – see Stonechat
Scaup, *Aythya marila* 86, 87, 98, 319, 460
Sciurus carolinensis – see Squirrel, Grey
Sciurus vulgaris – see Squirrel, Red
Scomber scombrus – see Mackerel
Scoter, Common, *Melanitta nigra* 86, 98, 401, 436, 460, 498, 499
Scoter, Velvet, *Melanitta fusca* 323, 460, 501
Scolopax rusticola – see Woodcock
Serin, *Serinus serinus* 400
Serinus serinus – see Serin
Setophaga caerulescens – see Warbler, Black-throated Blue
Shag, *Phalacrocorax aristotelis* 9, 48, 58, 80, 81, 85, 131, 189, 190, 218, 238–9, 268, 280, 281, 371–2, 377, 396, 397, 433, 456, 461, 496, 498, 499
Shearwater, Cory's, *Calonectris diomedea* 266, 503
Shearwater, Great, *Puffinus gravis* 22, 503
Shearwater, Little – see Shearwater, Macaronesian
Shearwater, Macaronesian, *Puffinus baroli* 266
Shearwater, Manx, *Puffinus puffinus* 135, 145, 189, 190, 218, 219, 267, 280, 440, 461, 503
Shelduck, *Tadorna tadorna* 7, 45, 46, 71, 190, 354, 375
Shoveler, *Anas clypeata* 71, 260, 457, 492
Shrike, Great Grey, *Lanius excubitor* 307
Shrike, Red-backed, *Lanius collurio* 2, 308, 358, 444
Sinapis arvensis – see Charlock
Siskin, *Carduelis spinus* 14, 89, 91, 96, 97, 251

GENERAL INDEX